Business Marketing Management: B2B

9e

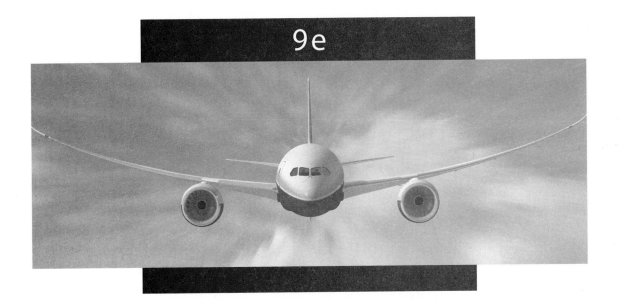

MICHAEL D. HUTT
Arizona State University

•

THOMAS W. SPEH
Miami University

SOUTH-WESTERN

Australia · Brazil · Canada · Mexico · Singapore · Spain · United Kingdom · United States

THOMSON

SOUTH-WESTERN

Business Marketing Management: B2B, Ninth Edition
Michael D. Hutt, Thomas W. Speh

Vice President/Editorial Director:
Jack W. Calhoun

Publisher:
Neil Marquardt

Senior Developmental Editor:
Trish Taylor

Marketing Manager:
Nicole C. Moore

Senior Marketing Communications Manager:
Terron Sanders

Content Project Manager:
Amy Hackett

Manager of Technology, Editorial:
Vicky True

Technology Project Editor:
Pam Wallace

Senior Manufacturing Coordinator:
Diane Lohman

Production House:
Graphic World Inc.

Compositor:
International Typesetting and Composition

Printer:
Thomson/West

Art Director:
Stacy Jenkins Shirley

Internal Designer:
Joseph Pagliaro Graphic Design

Cover Designer:
Joseph Pagliaro Graphic Design

Cover Image:
All Images are ALL RIGHTS RESERVED. Copyright © Boeing Management Company. The Image(s) are protected under U.S. and international copyright laws.

Photography Manager:
John Hill

Photo Researcher:
Karyn Morrison

Library of Congress Control Number: 2006924824

For more information about our products, contact us at:
Thomson Learning Academic Resource Center
1-800-423-0563

Thomson Higher Education
5191 Natorp Boulevard
Mason, OH 45040
USA

To Rita and to Sara, and in memory of Michele

PREFACE

Special challenges and opportunities confront the marketer who intends to serve the needs of organizations rather than households. Business-to-business customers represent a lucrative and complex market worthy of separate analysis. A growing number of collegiate schools of business in the United States, Canada, and Europe have added industrial or business marketing to their curricula. In addition, a large and growing network of scholars in the United States and Europe is actively engaged in research to advance theory and practice in the business marketing field. Both the breadth and quality of this research has increased markedly during the past decade.

The rising importance of the field can be demonstrated by several factors. First, because more than half of all business school graduates enter firms that compete in business markets, a comprehensive treatment of business marketing management appears to be particularly appropriate. The business marketing course provides an ideal platform to deepen a student's knowledge of the competitive realities of the global marketplace, customer relationship management, cross-functional decision-making processes, supply chain management, e-commerce, and related areas. Such core content areas strike a responsive chord with corporate recruiters and squarely address key educational priorities established by the American Assembly of Collegiate Schools of Business (AACSB).

Second, the business marketing course provides a perfect vehicle for examining the special features of high-technology markets and for isolating the unique challenges that confront the marketing strategist in this arena. High-tech markets represent a rapidly growing and dynamic sector of the world economy and a fiercely competitive global battleground, but often receive only modest attention in the traditional marketing curriculum. Electronic (e) commerce also falls squarely into the domain of the business market. In fact, the market opportunity for e-commerce in the business-to-business market is estimated to be ten times larger than the opportunity that exists in the business-to-consumer market.

Third, the Institute for the Study of Business Markets (ISBM) at Pennsylvania State University has provided important impetus to research in the area. ISBM has become a major information resource for researchers and practitioners and has assumed an active role in stimulating and supporting research on substantive business marketing issues. In turn, the number of research studies centered on the business-to-business domain have significantly expanded in recent years, and specialized journals in the area attract a steady stream of submissions. The hard work, multiyear commitments, and leadership of the editors of these journals are worthy of note: *Journal of Business-to-Business Marketing*, J. David Lichtenthal, Baruch College; *Journal of Business & Industrial Marketing*, Wesley J. Johnston, Georgia State University; and *Industrial Marketing Management*, Peter LaPlaca, University of Connecticut.

Three objectives guided the development of this edition:

1. *To highlight the similarities between consumer goods and business-to-business marketing and to explore in depth the points of departure.* Particular attention is given to market analysis, organizational buying behavior, customer relationship management,

---

Cover photo of the Boeing 787, powered by jet engines from General Electric—two leading B2B companies.

supply chain management, and the ensuing adjustments required in the marketing strategy elements used to reach organizational customers.

2. *To present a managerial rather than a descriptive treatment of business marketing.* Whereas some descriptive material is required to convey the dynamic nature of the business marketing environment, the relevance of the material is linked to marketing strategy decision making.

3. *To integrate the growing body of literature into a strategic treatment of business marketing.* In this text, relevant work is drawn from organizational buying behavior, procurement, organizational behavior, supply chain management, strategic management, and the behavioral sciences, as well as from specialized studies of business marketing strategy components.

The book is structured to provide a complete and timely treatment of business marketing while minimizing the degree of overlap with other courses in the marketing curriculum. A basic marketing principles course (or relevant managerial experience) provides the needed background for this text.

New to This Edition

Although the basic objectives, approach, and style of earlier editions have been maintained, several changes and additions have been made that reflect both the growing body of literature and the emerging trends in business marketing practice. Specifically, the following themes and distinctive features are incorporated into the ninth edition:

- **Customer Profitability Analysis and Relationship Management:** new and expanded coverage of customer profitability analysis and strategies for building a relational advantage.

- **Integrated Strategic Perspective Using the Balanced Scorecard and Strategy Mapping Tools:** a timely and richly illustrated discussion of alternative customer strategies, internal business processes, and critical performance metrics.

- **Rapidly Developing Economies:** the challenges that rapidly developing economies like China and India present to business marketing firms, along with the opportunities to seize significant cost, market access, and capability advantages.

- **Disruptive Innovation Strategies:** new coverage of strategies for managing products across the technology life cycle and reaching underserved customers.

- **A Customer Solutions Perspective:** a timely description of how leading firms use products as the platform for the delivery of services, yielding more durable competitive advantages.

- **Account Management Success:** coverage of the characteristics of high-performing account managers and the strategies that they follow across the sales process.

- **B2B Top Performers:** a new boxed feature that highlights the people, practices, or firms that demonstrate superior performance in business marketing.

Organization of the Ninth Edition

The needs and interests of the reader provided the focus in the development of this volume. The authors' goal is to present a clear, timely, and interesting examination of business marketing management. To this end, each chapter provides an overview, highlights key concepts, and includes several carefully chosen examples of contemporary business marketing practice, as well as a cogent summary and a set of provocative discussion questions. Contemporary business marketing strategies and challenges are illustrated with three types of vignettes: "B2B Top Performers," "Inside Business Marketing," and "Ethical Business Marketing."

The book is divided into six parts with a total of 18 chapters. Part I introduces the distinguishing features of the business marketing environment. Careful examination is given to each of the major types of customers, the nature of the procurement function, and key trends that are reshaping buyer-seller relationships. Relationship management establishes the theme of Part II, in which chapter-length attention is given to organizational buying behavior and customer relationship management. By thoroughly updating and illustrating the core content, this section provides a timely and comprehensive treatment of customer profitability analysis and relationship management strategies for business markets. After this important background is established, Part III centers on the techniques that can be applied in assessing market opportunities: market segmentation and demand analysis, including sales forecasting.

Part IV centers on the planning process and on designing marketing strategy for business markets. Recent work drawn from the strategic management and strategic marketing areas provides the foundation for this section. This edition provides an expanded and integrated treatment of marketing strategy development using the balanced scorecard, enriched by strategy mapping. Special emphasis is given to defining characteristics of successful business-to-business firms and to interfacing of marketing with other key functional areas such as manufacturing, research and development, and customer service. This functionally integrated planning perspective serves as a focal point in the analysis of the strategy development process. Here at the core of the volume, a separate chapter provides an integrated treatment of strategy formulation for the global market arena, giving particular attention to the new forms of competitive advantage that rapidly developing economies present (for example, China). Next, each component of the marketing mix is examined from a business marketing perspective. Adding further depth to this core section are the chapters on managing product innovation and managing services for business markets. In turn, special attention is given to e-commerce and supply chain strategies for business markets.

Part V examines techniques for evaluating business marketing strategy and performance. It provides a compact treatment of marketing control systems and uses the balanced scorecard as an organizing framework for marketing profitability analysis. Special attention is given to the critical area of strategy implementation in the business marketing firm. Part VI includes a collection of cases tailored to the business marketing environment.

Cases

Part VI includes 15 cases, 7 of which are new to this edition. These cases, of varying lengths, isolate one or more business marketing problems. Included among the selections for this edition are cases that raise provocative issues and illustrate the challenges and opportunities that small firms confront and the best practices of leading-edge firms such as Deere & Company and Pfizer. Other cases new to this edition provide students with a variety of business marketing strategy applications. A *Case Planning Guide*, which keys the cases to relevant text chapters, provides an organizing structure for Part VI. In addition, a short case, isolating core concepts, is included with each chapter. Two-thirds of the end-of-chapter cases are new to this edition.

Ancillary Package

We are most indebted to Chris Moberg of Ohio University, Athens, for his fine work in bringing together all of the elements of the ancillary package so that all supplements work together seamlessly. The Ancillary Package includes:

Instructor's Resource CD (IRCD)

The Instructor's Resource CD delivers all the traditional instructor support materials in one handy place: a CD. Electronic files are included on the CD for the complete Instructor's Manual, Test Bank, computerized Test Bank and computerized Test Bank software (ExamView), and chapter-by-chapter PowerPoint presentation files that can be used to enhance in-class lectures.

Instructor's Manual   The Instructor's Manual for the ninth edition of *Business Marketing Management: B2B* provides a variety of creative suggestions designed to help the instructor incorporate all the materials available to him/her and create a dynamic learning environment. A few of the key features available in the Instructor's Manual for this edition include

- course design suggestions
- chapter outlines and supporting chapter materials
- suggested readings listed by chapter
- case analysis suggestions
- cooperative learning exercises
- ideas for effectively integrating the video package into the classroom discussion

The Instructor's Manual files are located on the IRCD in Microsoft Word 2000 format and are also available for download at the text support site, **www.thomsonedu. com/marketing/hutt.**

Test Bank   The revised and updated Test Bank includes over 1,500 multiple choice and true/false questions, emphasizing the important concepts presented in each chapter, along with an average of five essay questions per chapter. The Test Bank questions vary in levels of difficulty so that each instructor can tailor his/her testing to meet his/her specific needs. The Test Bank files are located on the IRCD in Microsoft Word 2000 format.

ExamView (Computerized) Test Bank   The Test Bank is also available on the IRCD in computerized format (ExamView), allowing instructors to select problems at random by level of difficulty or type, customize or add test questions, and scramble questions to create up to 99 versions of the same test. This software is available in DOS, Mac, or Windows formats.

PowerPoint Presentation Slides   Edited to fit within class periods more effectively, these PowerPoint presentation slides bring classroom lectures and discussions to life with the Microsoft PowerPoint 2000 presentation tool. The presentations are organized by chapter, helping to create an easy-to-follow lecture, and are extremely professor friendly and easy to read. The PowerPoint presentation slides are available on the IRCD in Microsoft 2000 format and as downloadable files on the text support site, **www.thomsonedu.com/marketing/hutt.**

Web Site

Visit the text web site at **www.thomsonedu.com/marketing/hutt** to find instructor's support materials, as well as study resources that will help students practice and apply the concepts they have learned in class.

Videos

A new video package has been prepared to provide a relevant and interesting visual teaching tool for the classroom. Each video segment applies text materials to the real-world, demonstrating how everyday companies effectively deal with business marketing management issues.

Student Resources

- Online quizzes for each chapter are available on the Web site for those students who would like additional study materials. After each quiz is submitted, automatic feedback tells the students how they scored and what the correct answers are to the questions they missed. Students are then able to email their results directly to their instructor if desired.

- Crossword quizzing of key terms and definitions arranged by chapter is also available to the student.

Acknowledgments

The development of a textbook draws upon the contributions of many individuals. First, we would like to thank our students and former students at Arizona State University, Miami University, the University of Alabama, and the University of Vermont. They provided important input and feedback when selected concepts or chapters were originally class-tested. We would also like to thank our colleagues at each of these institutions for their assistance and support.

Second, we express our gratitude to several distinguished colleagues who carefully reviewed the volume and provided incisive comments and valuable suggestions that improved the ninth edition. They include: Jonathan Hibbard, *Boston University*; Lee Hibbert, *Freed-Hardeman University*; Joe H. Kim, *Rider University*; Kenneth M. Lampert, *Metropolitan State University, Minnesota*; K.C. Pang, *University of Alabama at Birmingham*; and Ugut Yucelt, *Pennsylvania State University at Harrisburg*. We would also like to express our continuing appreciation to others who provided important suggestions that helped shape earlier editions: Kenneth Anselmi, *East Carolina University*; Joseph A. Bellizzi, *Arizona State University–West Campus*; Paul D. Boughton, *Saint Louis University*; Michael R. Czinkota, *Georgetown University*; S. Altan Erdem, *University of Houston–Clear Lake*; Troy Festervand, *Middle Tennessee State University*; Srinath Gopalakrishna, *University of Missouri, Columbia*; Paris A. Gunther, *University of Cincinnati*; Jon M. Hawes, *University of Akron*; Jonathan Hibbard, *Boston University*; George John, *University of Minnesota*; Jay L. Laughlin, *Kansas State University*; J. David Lichtenthal, *Baruch College*; Gary L. Lilien, *Pennsylvania State University*; Lindsay N. Meredith, *Simon Fraser University*; Richard E. Plank, *Western Michigan University*; Constantine Polytechroniou, *University of Cincinnati*; Bernard A. Rausch, *Illinois Institute of Technology*; David A. Reid, *The University of Toledo*; Paul A. Roobol, *Western Michigan University*; Beth A. Walker, *Arizona State University*; Elizabeth Wilson, *Suffolk University*; James F. Wolter, *Grand Valley State University*; and John M. Zerio, *American Graduate School of International Management*.

We are especially indebted to three members of the Board of Advisors for Arizona State University's Center for Services Leadership. Each served as a senior executive sponsor for a funded research study, provided access to the organizations, and contributed valuable insights to the research. Collectively, these studies sharpened the strategy content of the volume. Included here are Michael Wiley, *IBM*; Greg Reid, *YRC Worldwide Inc.*; and Merrill Tutton, *AT&T*. We would like to thank Jim Ryan, Group President, *W. W. Grainger*, and Stephen Kohler, Senior Director, Services Marketing, *Siemens Building Technologies, Inc.*, for their insights and contributions to this edition. We would also like to thank Mohan Kuruvilla, Adjunct Professor, *Indian Institute of Management Kozhikode*, for his keen insights and recommendations for the ninth edition. We also extend our special thanks to Dr. Joseph Belonax, *Western Michigan University*, for contributing a Marketing Plan module to the teaching package. Examine this new Marketing Plan feature in our Instructor's Manual. Instructors will find this class-tested framework to be a valuable tool for creating course projects and highlighting key strategy concepts.

The talented staff of South-Western displayed a high level of enthusiasm and deserves special praise for their contributions in shaping this edition. In particular, Neil Marquardt provided valuable advice and direction for this edition. In turn, we were indeed fortunate to have Trish Taylor, our development editor, on our team. Her spirit, enthusiasm, and superb coordinating skills advanced the project. Alison Trulock and her team contributed excellent copyediting skills and Amy Hackett, our Project Manager, provided a confident style and a steady hand during the production process. We express our gratitude to Diane A. Davis, Arizona State University, for lending her superb administrative skills to the project and for delivering under pressure.

Finally, but most importantly, our overriding debt is to our wives, Rita and Sara, whose encouragement, understanding, and direct support were vital to the completion of this edition. Their involvement and dedication are deeply appreciated.

Michael D. Hutt
Thomas W. Speh

Michael D. Hutt (PhD, Michigan State University), is the Ford Motor Company Distinguished Professor of Marketing at the W. P. Carey School of Business, Arizona State University. He has also held faculty positions at Miami University (Ohio) and the University of Vermont.

Dr. Hutt's teaching and research interests are concentrated in the areas of business-to-business marketing and strategic marketing. His current research centers on the cross-functional role that marketing managers assume in the formation of strategy. Dr. Hutt's research has been published in the *Journal of Marketing, Journal of Marketing Research, MIT Sloan Management Review, Journal of Retailing, Journal of the Academy of Marketing Science*, and other scholarly journals. He is also the co-author of *Macro Marketing* (John Wiley & Sons) and contributing author of *Marketing: Best Practices* (South-Western).

Assuming a variety of leadership roles for American Marketing Association programs, he recently co-chaired the Faculty Consortium on Strategic Marketing Management. He is a member of the editorial review boards of the *Journal of Business-to-Business Marketing, Journal of Business & Industrial Marketing, Journal of Strategic Marketing*, and the *Journal of Business Research*. For his 2000 contribution to *MIT Sloan Management Review*, he received the Richard Beckhard Prize. Dr. Hutt has consulted on marketing strategy issues for firms such as IBM, Motorola, Lucent Technologies, AT&T, Arvin Industries, ADT, and Black-Clawson, and for the food industry's Public Policy Subcommittee on the Universal Product Code.

Thomas W. Speh, PhD, is the James Evans Rees Distinguished Professor of Marketing at the Richard T. Farmer School of Business, Miami University (Ohio). Dr. Speh earned his PhD from Michigan State University. Prior to his tenure at Miami, Dr. Speh taught at the University of Alabama.

Dr. Speh has been a regular participant in professional marketing and logistics meetings and has published articles in a number of academic and professional journals, including the *Journal of Marketing, Harvard Business Review, Journal of the Academy of Marketing Sciences, Journal of Business Logistics, Journal of Retailing, Journal of Purchasing and Materials Management*, and *Industrial Marketing Management*. He was the recipient of the Beta Gamma Sigma Distinguished Faculty award for excellence in teaching at Miami University's School of Business and of the Miami University Alumni Association's Effective Educator award.

Dr. Speh has been active in both the Warehousing Education and Research Council (WERC) and the Council of Logistics Management (CLM). He has served as president of WERC and as president of the CLM. Dr. Speh has been a consultant on strategy issues to such organizations as Xerox, Procter & Gamble, Burlington Northern Railroad, Sara Lee, J. M. Smucker Co., and Millenium Petrochemicals, Inc.

CASE CONTRIBUTORS

Erin Anderson, *INSEAD*
Jan Willem Bol, *Miami University (Ohio)*
Bradley W. Brooks, *Queens University of Charlotte*
Nancy A. Campbell, *Sonoma State University*
Theresa T. Coates, *Rensselaer Polytechnic Institute*
Bruno Dyck, *University of Manitoba*
John H. Friar, *Northeastern University*
John B. Gifford, *Miami University (Ohio)*
Armand Gilinsky, Jr., *Sonoma State University*
Kenneth G. Hardy, *University of Western Ontario*
Jon M. Hawes, *University of Akron*
John Haywood-Farmer, *University of Western Ontario*
P. Fraser Johnson, *University of Western Ontario*
Robert Klassen, *University of Western Ontario*
Steve Marley, *University of Western Ontario*
Michael K. Mauws, *University of Alberta*
Marc H. Meyer, *Northeastern University*
Gary A. Mischke, *University of Alberta*
Jakki Mohr, *University of Montana*
Deborah L. Owens, *University of Akron*
David V. Rudd, *Queens University of Charlotte*
Frederick Starke, *University of Manitoba*
Alan J. Stenger, *Pennsylvania State University*
Sara Streeter, *University of Montana*
Marilyn L. Taylor, *University of Missouri-Kansas City*
Joe Thomas, *Middle Tennessee State University*
Ralph Williams, *Middle Tennessee State University*

CONTENTS IN BRIEF

CONTENTS

Chapter 12 Managing Business Marketing Channels

PART V EVALUATING BUSINESS MARKETING STRATEGY AND PERFORMANCE — 439

Chapter 18 Controlling Business Marketing Strategies — 441

PART
I

THE ENVIRONMENT
OF BUSINESS MARKETING

A Business Marketing Perspective

The business market poses special challenges and significant opportunities for the marketing manager. This chapter introduces the complex forces that are unique to the business marketing environment. After reading this chapter, you will understand:

1. the dynamic nature of the business marketing environment and the basic similarities and differences between consumer-goods and business marketing.

2. the underlying factors that influence the demand for industrial goods.

3. the nature of buyer-seller relationships in a product's supply chain.

4. the types of customers in this important market.

5. the basic characteristics of industrial products and services.

Business Marketing

Business marketers serve the largest market of all: The dollar volume of transactions in the industrial or business market significantly exceeds that of the ultimate consumer market. In the business market, a single customer can account for an enormous level of purchasing activity. For example, the General Motors (GM) purchasing department spends more than $125 billion annually on industrial products and services—more than the gross domestic products of Ireland, Portugal, Turkey, or Greece.[1] The 1,350 professional buyers at GM each spend more than $50 million annually.[2] Others, such as General Electric (GE), DuPont, and International Business Machines (IBM), spend more than $60 million per day on purchases to support their operations.[3] Indeed, all formal organizations—large or small, public or private, profit or not-for-profit—participate in the exchange of industrial products and services, thus constituting the business market.

Business markets are "markets for products and services, local to international, bought by businesses, government bodies, and institutions (such as hospitals) for incorporation (for example, ingredient materials or components), for consumption (for example, process materials, office supplies, consulting services), for use (for example, installations or equipment), or for resale. . . . The only markets not of direct interest are those dealing with products or services which are principally directed at personal use or consumption such as packaged grocery products, home appliances, or consumer banking."[4] The factors that distinguish business marketing from consumer marketing are the nature of the customer and how that customer uses the product. In business marketing, the customers are organizations (businesses, governments, institutions).

Business firms buy industrial goods to form or facilitate the production process or use as components for other goods and services. Government agencies and private institutions buy industrial goods to maintain and deliver services to their own market: the public. Industrial or business marketing (the terms can be used interchangeably) accounts for more than half the economic activity in the United States, Canada, and most other nations. More than 50 percent of all business school graduates join firms that compete directly in the business market. The heightened interest in high-technology markets—and the sheer size of the business market—has spawned increased emphasis on business marketing management in universities and corporate executive training programs.[5]

This book explores the business market's special opportunities and challenges and identifies the new requirements for managing the marketing function in this vital sector of the global economy. The following questions establish the theme of this first chapter: What are the similarities and differences between consumer-goods marketing and business marketing? What customers constitute the business market? How can the

---

[1] Anne Millen Porter, "The Top 250: Tough Measures for Tough Times," *Purchasing* 132 (November 7, 2002): pp. 31–35.

[2] Gregory L. White, "How GM, Ford Think Web Can Make Splash on the Factory Floor," *The Wall Street Journal*, December 3, 1999, p. A1.

[3] Anne Millen Porter, "Big Spenders: The Top 250," *Purchasing*, 127 (November 6, 1997): pp. 40–51.

[4] Prospectus for the Institute for the Study of Business Markets, College of Business Administration, the Pennsylvania State University.

[5] J. David Lichtenthal, "Business-to-Business Marketing in the 21st Century," *Journal of Business-to-Business Marketing* 12 (1,2 1998): pp. 1–5 and Michael D. Hutt and Thomas W. Speh, "Business Marketing Education: A Distinctive Role in the Undergraduate Curriculum," *Journal of Business-to-Business Marketing* 12 (1, 2 1998): pp. 103–126.

FIGURE 1.1 | **POWERFUL B2B BRANDS**

multitude of industrial goods be classified into manageable categories? What forces influence the behavior of business market demand?

Business Marketing Management

Many large firms that produce goods such as steel, production equipment, or computer-memory chips cater exclusively to business market customers and never directly interact with their ultimate consumers. Other firms participate in both the consumer-goods and the business markets. The introduction of laser printers and personal computers brought Hewlett-Packard, historically a business-to-business marketer, into the consumer market. Conversely, lagging consumer markets prompted Sony Corporation to expand to the business market by introducing office automation products. Both companies had to reorient their marketing strategies dramatically because of significant differences in the buying behavior of consumer versus business markets.

Products like cell phones, office furniture, personal computers, and software are purchased in both the consumer and the business markets. What distinguishes business marketing from consumer-goods marketing is the *intended use of the product* and the *intended consumer*. Sometimes the products are identical, but a fundamentally different marketing approach is needed to reach the organizational buyer. Interestingly, some of the most valuable brands in the world belong to business marketers: Cisco, Caterpillar, IBM, FedEx, GE, DuPont, Intel, Hewlett-Packard, and 3M[6] (Figure 1.1).

---

[6] Frederick E. Webster, Jr. and Kevin Lane Keller, "A Roadmap for Branding in Industrial Markets," *Journal of Brand Management* 11 (May 2004): pp. 388–402.

FIGURE 1.2 | **THE CONSUMER MARKET (B2C) AND THE BUSINESS MARKET (B2B) AT DELL**

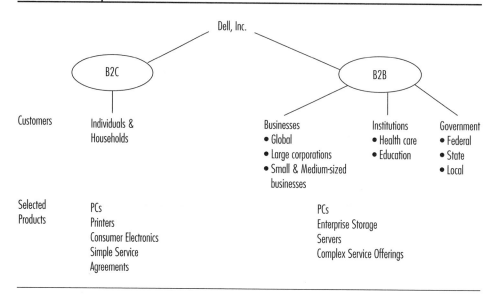

Business Market Customers

Business market customers can be broadly classified into three categories: (1) commercial enterprises—that is, businesses; (2) institutions—for example, universities; and (3) government. Consider Dell, Inc.: The firm serves both the business market (B2B) and the consumer market (B2C) (Figure 1.2). Importantly, however, more than 80 percent of its sales come from B2B customers!

Dell serves each sector of the business market.[7] First, the firm has developed close relationships with large global enterprises, like Boeing, and large corporate customers. These customers purchase thousands of personal computers (PCs) and now turn to Dell for a full range of information technology (IT) products and services. The volume of business coming from a single business customer can be huge: One customer bought 20,000 laptop computers for its global sales organization, and some enterprises have an installed base of more than 100,000 Dell computers. Second, small and medium-sized businesses (SMB) represent a substantial market, and Dell demonstrates special skills in understanding and reaching these customers. SMB firms now represent more than 1 million of Dell's customers in the United States, and this base is growing rapidly around the world. Third, the firm serves the government market at all levels as well as institutional customers like universities and health-care organizations. To compensate for the maturing PC business, Dell has expanded the scope of its product offerings to include a broader array of IT products, including servers and data storage for the business market, and a growing list of consumer electronics products, such as flat-screen TVs and MP3 players, for the consumer market.

---

[7]V. Kasturi Rangan and Marie Bell, "Dell—New Horizons," Harvard Business School Case #9-502-022, October 10, 2002 (Boston, MA: Harvard Business School Publishing).

Business Markets versus Consumer-Goods Markets

The basic task of management cuts across both consumer-goods and business marketing. Marketers serving both sectors can benefit by rooting their organizational plan in a *market orientation*, which requires superior proficiency in understanding and satisfying customers.[8] Such market-driven firms demonstrate

- a set of values and beliefs that places the customers' interests first[9];
- the ability to generate, disseminate, and productively use superior information about customers and competitors[10];
- the coordinated use of interfunctional resources (for example, research and development, manufacturing).[11]

Distinctive Capabilities   A close examination of a market-driven firm reveals two particularly important capabilities: market sensing and customer linking.[12] First, the **market-sensing capability** concerns how well the organization is equipped to continuously sense changes in its market and anticipate customer responses to marketing programs. Market-driven firms spot market changes and react well in advance of their competitors (for example, Coca-Cola in the consumer-goods market and 3M in the business market). Second, the **customer-linking capability** comprises the particular skills, abilities, and processes an organization has developed to create and manage close customer relationships.

Consumer-goods firms, such as Procter and Gamble (P&G), demonstrate these capabilities in working with powerful retailers like Wal-Mart. Here, multifunctional teams in both organizations work together by sharing delivery and product-movement information and by jointly planning promotional activity and product changes. Although evident in manufacturer-reseller relations in the consumer-goods market, strong customer-linking capabilities are crucial in the business market, where close buyer-seller relationships prevail.

Managing Customers as Assets   Marketing expenditures that were once viewed as short-term expenses are now being considered as customer assets that deliver value for the firm and its shareholders.[13] As global competition intensifies, marketing managers are under increasing pressure to demonstrate the return on investment from marketing spending, deliver strong financial performance, and be more accountable to shareholders.[14] To meet these performance standards, firms must

---

[8] George S. Day, "The Capabilities of Market-Driven Organizations," *Journal of Marketing* 58 (October 1994): pp. 37–52.

[9] Rohit Deshpande, John U. Farley, and Frederick E. Webster Jr., "Corporate Culture, Customer Orientation, and Innovativeness in Japanese Firms: A Quadrad Analysis," *Journal of Marketing* 57 (January 1993): pp. 23–37.

[10] Ajay K. Kohli and Bernard J. Jaworski, "Market Orientation: The Construct, Research Propositions, and Managerial Implications," *Journal of Marketing* 54 (April 1990): pp. 1–18.

[11] John C. Narver and Stanley F. Slater, "The Effect of a Market Orientation on Business Profitability," *Journal of Marketing* 54 (October 1990): pp. 20–35.

[12] Day, "Capabilities of Market-Driven Organizations," pp. 37–52.

[13] John E. Hogan, Katherine N. Lemon, and Roland T. Rust, "Customer Equity Management: Charting New Directions for the Future," *Journal of Service Research* 5 (August 2002): pp. 4–12. See also, Roland T. Rust, Katherine N. Lemon, and Das Narayandas, *Customer Equity Management* (Upper Saddle River, NJ: Prentice-Hall, 2005).

[14] Frederick E. Webster, Jr., Alan J. Malter, and Shankar Ganesan, "The Decline and Dispersion of Marketing Competence," *MIT Sloan Management Review* 46 (summer 2005): pp. 35–43.

B2B TOP PERFORMERS

Career Path for B2B CEOs: For Many, It Began in Marketing!

Executives with a strong background in sales and marketing are taking the top position at leading business marketing firms. Why? Companies now place increased importance on customer relationships. "They've changed their sales strategies to emphasize building long-term partnerships with customers. And they're building profitable businesses on the notion that it's far cheaper to sell to current customers than it is to acquire new ones." Sales and marketing executives understand customers, know the competitive landscape, and have keen insights concerning how to add value to the firm's offerings and to the customer's organization. That is why many firms are tapping sales and marketing executives for the CEO position. Here are two examples:

- Xerox Corporation—Ann Mulcahy spent the majority of her 25 years at the firm in sales positions before being appointed president and CEO.
- GE—In a 20-year career, Jeffrey Immelt held a variety of GE sales and marketing

positions before being named to succeed Jack Welch as CEO.

Both of these CEOs have taken steps to make their respective organization more customer centered. For example, Jeffrey Immelt's priorities for GE reflect his background in B2B marketing. These are "making sure all the processes work correctly, for example, so deliveries are always on time; ensuring that whatever GE's proposition to the customer is, it will make that customer more money; and increasing the effectiveness of GE's sales force."[1] Looking ahead, he seeks new leaders for growth at GE—people who are passionate about customers and innovation, people who really know markets and products.[2]

[1] Eilene Zimmerman, "So You Wanna Be a CEO," *Sales & Marketing Management* (January 2002): pp. 31–35.
[2] Patricia O'Connell, "Bringing Innovations to the Home of Six Sigma," *BusinessWeek Online*, August 1, 2005, accessed at http://www.businessweek.com.

develop and nurture **customer relationship management capabilities,** which include all the skills required to identify, initiate, develop, and maintain profitable customer relationships.

Marketing Tasks: What Managers Do   To bring the job of business marketing professionals to life, let's examine some of the day-to-day assignments they perform. In customer relationship management, some critical marketing tasks include "identifying and categorizing customer segments; determining a customer's current and potential needs; visiting customers to learn about the uses and applications of individual products; developing and executing the individual components of sales, advertising, promotion, and services programs; assessing price sensitivities; and determining customer response to rivals' current and potential offerings."[15] Research clearly demonstrates that the customer relationship management process has an important impact on a firm's financial performance.[16]

[15] Rajendra K. Srivastava, Tasadduq A. Shervauie, and Liam Fahey, "Marketing, Business Processes, and Shareholder Value: An Organizationally Embedded View of Marketing Activities and the Discipline of Marketing," *Journal of Marketing* 63 (Special Issue, 1999): pp. 168–179.
[16] Sridhar N. Ramaswami, Mukesh Bhargava, and Rajandra Srivastava, "Market-Based Assets and Capabilities, Business Processes, and Financial Performance," *MSI Report No. 04-102* (Boston, MA: Marketing Science Institute, 2004).

INSIDE BUSINESS MARKETING

Google: B2C or B2B?

It's a B2B marketer! Google operates the world's leading Internet search engine, and the company generates revenue by delivering targeted advertising messages. With more than 100,000 business customers, namely advertisers, and more than 200 million searches a day by Internet users, Google represents one of the largest aggregators of buyers and sellers in the business-to-business market. Google's performance-based keyword advertising program enables businesses to reach customers across all stages of the buying cycle, from awareness through retention. Eric Gates, a strategist at the Dow Chemical Company, describes the benefits: "Google enables Dow to effectively target

messages to the right people at the right time. With click-through rates ranging from two and one-half to seven percent, the Google advertising program continues to be a key component of our overall marketing efforts." Google also provides tools that advertisers like Dow can use to track the effectiveness of advertising on its sites and measure the return on advertising spending (that is, ROI).

SOURCE: "Google Names Top 5 Business-to-Business Media Property," May 2003 press release accessed at http://www.google.com; and Matthew B. Albrecht, "Google, Inc.," *Value Line Investment Survey*, May 27, 2005.

Partnering for Increased Value   A business marketer becomes a preferred supplier to major customers such as Citigroup, Texas Instruments, or Motorola by working closely as a partner, developing an intimate knowledge of the customer's operations, and contributing unique value to that customer's business. Business marketing programs increasingly involve a customized blend of tangible products, service support, and ongoing information services both before and after the sale. Market-driven firms place a high priority on customer-linking capabilities and closely align product decisions—as well as delivery, handling, service, and other supply chain activities—with the customer's operations. For firms like Intel or Boeing to deliver maximum value to their customers, each must receive maximum value from its suppliers. For instance, Intel could not have achieved its commanding global market share without the cost, quality, technology, and other advances its suppliers contribute.[17]

Creating the Value Proposition[18]   Business marketing strategy must be based on an assessment of the company, the competitor, and the customer. A successful strategy focuses on identifying those opportunities in which the firm can deliver superior value to customers based on its distinctive competencies. From this perspective, marketing can be best understood as the process of defining, developing, and delivering value.

Market-driven firms attempt to match their resources, skills, and capabilities with particular customer needs that are not being adequately served. By understanding customer needs, marketing managers can define value from the customer's perspective and convert that information into requirements for creating satisfied customers. In turn, a firm's capabilities and skills determine the degree to which the company can meet these requirements and provide greater value than its competitors.

---

[17] Gina Roos, "Intel Corporation: It Takes Quality to Be Preferred by World's Biggest Chipmaker," *Purchasing* 131 (November 15, 2001): pp. 21–22.

[18] Frederick E. Webster Jr., *Market-Driven Management: Using the New Marketing Concept to Create a Customer-Oriented Company* (New York: John Wiley & Sons, 1994), p. 60.

Given many strategic paths, the value proposition signals the chosen direction by specifying how the organization proposes to deliver superior value to customers. The **value proposition** is the program of products, services, ideas, and solutions that a business marketer offers to advance the performance goals of the customer organization. The value proposition is an important organizing force in the firm because it directs all employees to focus on customer requirements, and it provides the means for the firm to position its offerings in the minds of customers.

Designing Customer Solutions

Instead of centering on products or services, a uniquely powerful value proposition can emerge by providing **customer solutions**—offerings that integrate goods and services to provide customized outcomes for specific customers.[19] Rather than beginning with the product, a true customer focus defines a customer problem and works toward creating a solution that solves this problem. Consider this novel solution:

> A business-to-business firm that supplied paint to automobile producers "transformed itself into an integrated provider of painted cars. The supplier's expertise allowed it to take over its customers' paint shop operations, one of the most expensive elements in automotive assembly. In doing so, the supplier changed the value metric from the traditional, product-oriented dollars per gallon of paint to the customer-oriented dollars per painted car. The firm became the leading supplier to automakers worldwide, gaining 70 percent of the market."[20]

To design such winning solutions, business marketing managers require a deep understanding of customer needs. Beyond the goal of merely selling products, a market-driven customer-relationship management process views customer relationships as a means to learn more about customer needs and how best to create solutions that satisfy them.

Marketing's Cross-Functional Relationships

Rather than operating in isolation from other functional areas, the successful business marketing manager is an integrator—one who understands manufacturing, research and development (R&D), and customer service and who applies these strengths in developing marketing strategies that respond to customer needs.[21] Close and tightly integrated cross-functional relationships underlie the strategy success stories of firms such as Hewlett-Packard and 3M. As firms adopt leaner and more agile structures and emphasize cross-functional teams, the business marketing manager assumes an important and challenging role in strategy formation.

Working Relationships   A day in the life of a business marketing manager centers on building relationships with customers *and* in forging one-to-one relationships with

---

[19] Mohanbir Sawhney, "Going Beyond the Product: Defining, Designing, and Delivering Customer Solutions," Working Paper, Kellogg School of Management, Northwestern University, December 2004.

[20] Chandra Krishnamurthy, Juliet Johansson, and Hank Schlissberg, "Solution Selling: Is the Pain Worth the Gain?" *McKinsey Marketing Solutions* (April 2003): pp. 1–12.

[21] Michael D. Hutt, "Cross-Functional Working Relationships in Marketing," *Journal of the Academy of Marketing Science* 23 (fall 1995): pp. 351–357.

FIGURE 1.3 | **BUSINESS MARKETING PLANNING: A FUNCTIONALLY INTEGRATED PERSPECTIVE**

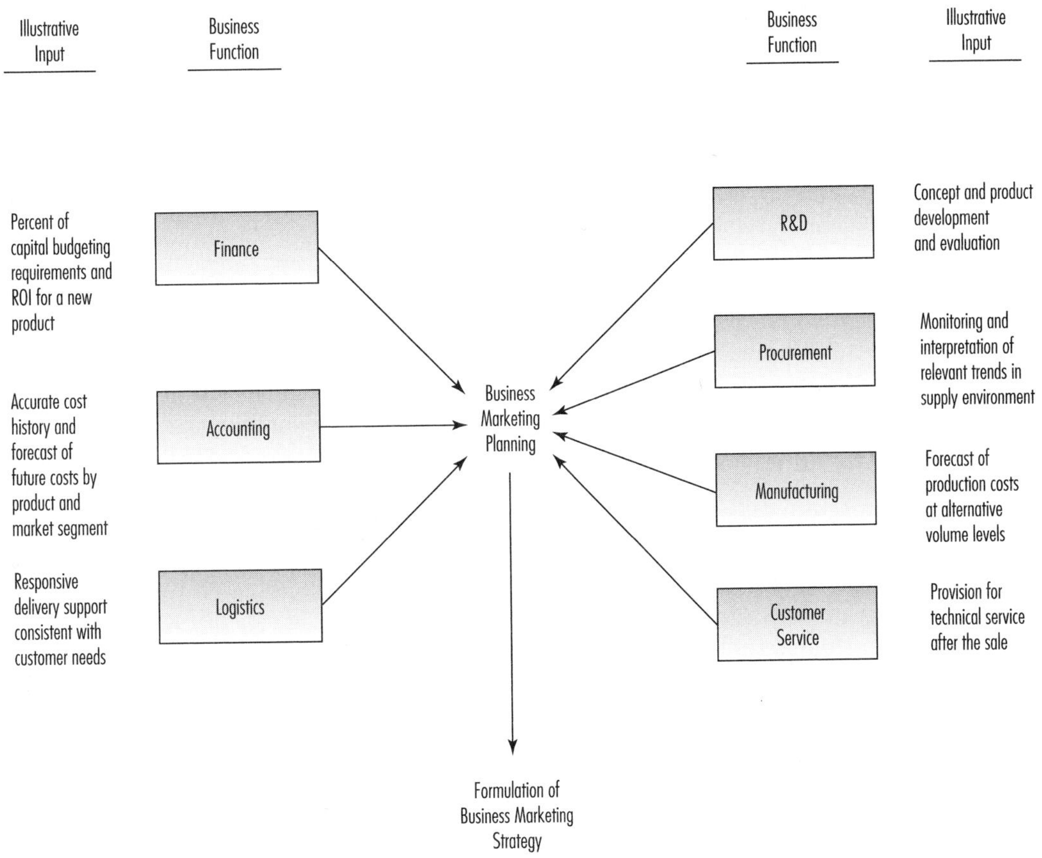

Illustrative Input — Business Function — Business Function — Illustrative Input

Percent of capital budgeting requirements and ROI for a new product → Finance

Accurate cost history and forecast of future costs by product and market segment → Accounting

Responsive delivery support consistent with customer needs → Logistics

→ Business Marketing Planning ←

R&D ← Concept and product development and evaluation

Procurement ← Monitoring and interpretation of relevant trends in supply environment

Manufacturing ← Forecast of production costs at alternative volume levels

Customer Service ← Provision for technical service after the sale

Formulation of Business Marketing Strategy

managers in the firm's other functional areas. By building effective cross-functional connections, the marketer is ideally equipped to respond to customers' changing needs.

Business marketing success depends to a large degree on such functional areas in the firm as engineering, R&D, manufacturing, and technical service. Planning in the industrial setting thus requires more functional interdependence and a closer relationship to total corporate strategy than planning in the consumer-goods sector. B. Charles Ames points out that "changes in marketing strategy are more likely to involve capital commitments for new equipment, shifts in development activities, or departures from traditional engineering and manufacturing approaches, any one of which would have companywide implications."[22] All business marketing decisions—product, price, promotion, and distribution—are affected, directly or indirectly, by other functional areas. In turn, marketing considerations influence business decisions in R&D and in manufacturing and procurement, as well as adjustments in the overall corporate strategy. Business marketing planning must be coordinated and synchronized with corresponding planning efforts in R&D, procurement, finance, production, and other areas (Figure 1.3).

---

[22] B. Charles Ames, "Trappings vs. Substance in Industrial Marketing," *Harvard Business Review* 48 (July–August 1976): pp. 95–96.

Characteristics of Business Markets

Business marketing and consumer-goods marketing are different. A common body of knowledge, principles, and theory applies to both consumer and business marketing, but because their buyers and markets function quite differently, they merit separate attention. Consumer and business marketing differ in the nature of markets, market demand, buyer behavior, buyer-seller relationships, environmental influences (economic, political, legal), and market strategy. Yet, the potential payoffs are high for the firm that can successfully penetrate the business market. The nature of the demand for industrial products poses unique challenges—and opportunities—for the marketing manager.

Derived Demand   **Derived demand** refers to the direct link between the demand for an industrial product and the demand for consumer products: *The demand for industrial products is derived from the ultimate demand for consumer products.* Consider the materials and components used in a Harley-Davidson motorcycle. Harley-Davidson manufactures some of the components, but the finished product reflects the efforts of more than 200 suppliers or business marketers who deal directly with the firm. In purchasing a Harley-Davidson motorcycle, the customer is stimulating the demand for a diverse array of products manufactured by business marketing firms—such as tires, electrical components, coil springs, aluminum castings, and other items.

Fluctuating Demand   Because demand is derived, the business marketer must carefully monitor demand patterns and changing buying preferences in the household consumer market, often on a worldwide basis. For example, a decline in mortgage rates can spark an increase in new home construction and a corresponding increase in appliance sales. Retailers generally respond by increasing their stock of inventory. As appliance producers like Maytag increase the rate of production to meet the demand, business marketers that supply these manufacturers with items such as motors, timers, or paint experience a surge in sales. A downturn in the economy creates the opposite result. This explains why the demand for many industrial products tends to *fluctuate* more than the demand for consumer products.

Stimulating Demand   Some business marketers must not only monitor final consumer markets but also develop a marketing program that reaches the ultimate consumer directly. Aluminum producers use television and magazine ads to point out the convenience and recycling opportunities that aluminum containers offer to the consumer—the ultimate consumer influences aluminum demand by purchasing soft drinks in aluminum, rather than plastic, containers. More than 4 billion pounds of aluminum are used annually in the production of beverage containers. Similarly, Boeing promotes the convenience of air travel in a media campaign targeted to the consumer market to create a favorable environment for longer-term demand for its planes; DuPont advertises to ultimate consumers to stimulate the sales of carpeting, which incorporates their product.

Price Sensitivity   **Demand elasticity** refers to the responsiveness of the quantity demanded to a change in price. Demand is elastic when a given percentage change in price brings about an even larger percentage change in the quantity demanded. Inelasticity results when demand is insensitive to price—that is, when the percentage change in demand is less than the percentage change in price. Consider the demand for electronic components that is stimulated by companies making digital cameras. As long as final consumers continue to purchase these cameras and are generally insensitive to price, manufacturers of the equipment are relatively insensitive to the price of electronic components. At the opposite end of the spectrum, if consumers are price sensitive when purchasing soup and other canned grocery products, manufacturers of soup will be price sensitive when purchasing metal cans. Thus, the derived demand indicates that the demand for metal cans is price elastic.

Final consumer demand has a pervasive impact on the demand for products in the business market. By being sensitive to trends in the consumer market, the business marketer can often identify both impending problems and opportunities for growth and diversification.

A Global Market Perspective   A complete picture of the business market must include a horizon that stretches beyond the boundaries of the United States. The demand for many industrial goods and services is growing more rapidly in many foreign countries than in the United States. Countries like Germany, Japan, Korea, and Brazil offer large and growing markets for many business marketers. In turn, China and India represent economies with exploding levels of growth. Countless small firms and many large ones—such as GE, 3M, Intel, Boeing, Dow Chemical, Caterpillar, and Motorola—derive a significant portion of their sales and profits from international markets. For example, China plans to invest more than $300 billion over the next few years in the country's infrastructure, representing an enormous market opportunity for all of GE's industrial businesses, including power generation, health care, and infrastructure (for example, water purification). For cell phone makers such as Motorola, China already represents a fiercely competitive market and features the world's largest base of subscribers—350 million—and this will grow to 600 million customers by 2009.[23]

Business and Consumer Marketing: A Contrast

Many consumer-goods companies with a strong reputation in the consumer market decide to capitalize on opportunities they perceive in the business market. The move is often prompted by a maturing product line, a desire to diversify operations, or the strategic opportunity to profitably apply R&D or production strength in a rapidly growing business market. P&G, departing from its packaged consumer-goods tradition, is using its expertise in oils, fats, and pulps to diversify into fast-growing industries.

The J. M. Smucker Company operates successfully in both the consumer and the business markets. Smucker, drawing on its consumer product base (jellies and preserves), produces filling mixes used by manufacturers of yogurt and dessert items. Marketing strawberry preserves to ultimate consumers differs significantly from marketing

[23] Pete Engardio, "A New World Economy," *Business Week*, August 22/29, 2005, pp. 52–58.

a strawberry filling to a yogurt manufacturer. Key differences are highlighted in the following illustration.

Smucker: A Consumer and Business Marketer

Smucker reaches the consumer market with a line of products sold through retail outlets. New products are carefully developed, tested, targeted, priced, and promoted for particular market segments. To secure distribution, the firm employs food brokers who call on both wholesale- and retail-buying units. The company's own sales force reaches selected larger accounts. Achieving a desired degree of market exposure and shelf space in key retail food outlets is essential to any marketer of consumer food products. Promotional plans for the line include media advertising, coupons, special offers, and incentives for retailers. Pricing decisions must reflect the nature of demand, costs, and the behavior of competitors. In sum, the marketer must manage each component of the marketing mix: product, price, promotion, and distribution.

The marketing mix takes on a different form in the business market. Attention centers on manufacturers that potentially could use Smucker products to produce other goods; the Smucker product will lose its identity as it is blended into yogurt, cakes, or cookies. Once Smucker has listed all the potential users of its product (for example, large food processors, bakeries, yogurt producers), the business marketing manager attempts to identify meaningful market segments that Smucker can profitably serve. A specific marketing strategy is developed for each market segment.

When a potential organizational consumer is identified, the company's sales force calls directly on the account. The salesperson may begin by contacting a company president but, at first, generally spends a great deal of time with the R&D director or the product-development group leader. The salesperson is thus challenged to identify the **key buying influentials**—those who have power in the buying process. Senior-level Smucker executives may also assist in the selling process.

Armed with product specifications (for example, desired taste, color, calories), the salesperson returns to the Smucker R&D department to develop samples. Several months may pass before a mixture is finally approved. Next, attention turns to price, and the salesperson's contact point shifts to the purchasing department. Because large quantities (truckloads or drums rather than jars) are involved, a few cents per pound can be significant to both parties. Quality and service are also vitally important.

Once a transaction is culminated, the product is shipped directly from the Smucker warehouse to the manufacturer's plant. The salesperson follows up frequently with the purchasing agent, the plant manager, and other executives. Product movement and delivery information is openly shared, and close working relationships develop between managers at Smucker and key decision makers in the buying organization. How much business can Smucker expect from this account? The performance of the new consumer product in the marketplace determines this: The demand for industrial goods is, as noted, derived from ultimate consumer demand. Note also the importance of (1) developing a close and continuing working relationship with business market customers, and (2) understanding the requirements of the total range of buying influentials in the target company.

Distinguishing Characteristics

The Smucker illustration spotlights some of the features that differentiate business marketing strategy from consumer-goods marketing strategy. The business marketer emphasizes personal selling rather than advertising (TV, newspaper) to reach potential buyers. Only a small portion of the business marketer's promotional budget is likely to be invested in advertising, most commonly through trade journals or direct mail. This advertising, however, often establishes the foundation for a successful sales call. The industrial salesperson must understand the technical aspects of the organization's requirements and how those requirements can be satisfied, as well as knowing who influences the buying decision and why.

The business marketer's product also includes an important service component. The organizational consumer evaluates the quality of the physical product and the quality of the attached services. Attention centers on the total package of benefits the consumer receives. Price negotiation is frequently an important part of the industrial buying/selling process. Products made to particular quality or design specifications must be individually priced. Business marketers generally find that direct distribution to larger customers strengthens relationships between buyer and seller. Smaller accounts can be profitably served through intermediaries—manufacturers' representatives or industrial distributors.

As the Smucker example illustrates, business marketing strategies differ from consumer-goods marketing strategies in the relative emphasis given to certain elements of the marketing mix. It is important to note that the example also highlights fundamental differences between the buyers in each market. In an organization, a variety of individuals influence the purchase decision. Several major questions confront Smucker's business marketing manager: Who are key participants in the purchasing process? What is their relative importance? What criteria does each apply to the decision? Thus, the business marketer must understand the *process* an organization follows in purchasing a product and identify which organizational members have roles in this process. Depending on the complexity of the purchase, this process may span many weeks or months and may involve the participation of several organization members. The business marketer who becomes involved in the purchase process early may have the greatest chance for success.

A Relationship Emphasis

Relationships in the business market are often close and enduring. Rather than constituting the end result, a sale signals the beginning of a relationship. By convincing a large food processor such as General Foods to use its product, Smucker initiates a potential long-term business relationship. More than ringing up a sale, Smucker creates a customer! To maintain that relationship, the business marketer must develop an intimate knowledge of the customer's operations and contribute unique value to its business. **Relationship marketing** centers on all marketing activities directed toward establishing, developing, and maintaining successful exchanges with customers.[24] Building one-to-one relationships with customers is the heart of business marketing. Figure 1.4 provides a recap of key characteristics of business market customers.

---

[24]Robert M. Morgan and Shelby D. Hunt, "The Commitment-Trust Theory of Relationship Marketing," *Journal of Marketing* 58 (July 1994): pp. 20–38.

FIGURE 1.4 | CHARACTERISTICS OF BUSINESS MARKET CUSTOMERS

Characteristic	Example
• Business market customers are composed of commercial enterprises, institutions, and governments.	• Among Dell's customers are Boeing, Arizona State University, and numerous state and local government units.
• A single purchase by a business customer is far larger than that of an individual consumer.	• An individual may buy one unit of a software package upgrade from Microsoft while Citigroup purchases 10,000.
• The demand for industrial products is derived from the ultimate demand for consumer products.	• New home purchases stimulate the demand for carpeting, appliances, cabinets, lumber, and a wealth of other products.
• Relationships between business marketers tend to be close and enduring.	• IBM's relationship with some key customers spans decades.
• Buying decisions by business customers often involve multiple buying influences, rather than a single decision maker.	• A cross-functional team at Procter & Gamble (P&G) evaluates alternative laptop personal computers and selects IBM.
• While serving different types of customers, business marketers and consumer-goods marketers share the same job titles.	• Job titles include marketing manager, product manager, sales manager, account manager.

The Supply Chain

Figure 1.5 further illuminates the importance of a relationship perspective in business marketing by considering the chain of suppliers involved in the creation of an automobile. Consider Honda and Ford. At its Marysville, Ohio, auto assembly plant, Honda spends more than $5 billion annually for materials and components from some 300 North American suppliers.[25] These expenditures by Honda's 300-member purchasing staff represent 80 percent of the firm's annual sales. Similarly, Ford relies on a vast supplier network, including firms such as TRW and Johnson Controls, to contribute half of the more than 10,000 parts of a typical Ford car.

The relationships between these auto producers and their suppliers fall squarely into the business marketing domain. Similarly, business marketers such as TRW rely on a whole host of others farther back on the supply chain for raw materials, components, and other support. Each organization in this chain is involved in the creation of a product, marketing processes (including delivery), and support and service after the sale. In performing these value-creating activities, each also affects the quality level of the Honda or Ford product. Michael Porter and Victor Millar observe that "to gain competitive advantage over its rivals, a company must either perform these activities at a lower cost or perform them in a way that leads to differentiation and a premium price (more value)."[26]

---

[25] Kevin R. Fitzgerald, "For Superb Supplier Development: Honda Wins!" *Purchasing*, 125 (September 21, 1995): pp. 32–40.

[26] Michael E. Porter and Victor E. Millar, "How Information Gives You Competitive Advantage," *Harvard Business Review* 63 (July–August 1985): pp. 149–160; see also Michael E. Porter, *Competitive Advantage* (New York: The Free Press, 1985).

FIGURE 1.5 | THE SUPPLY CHAIN

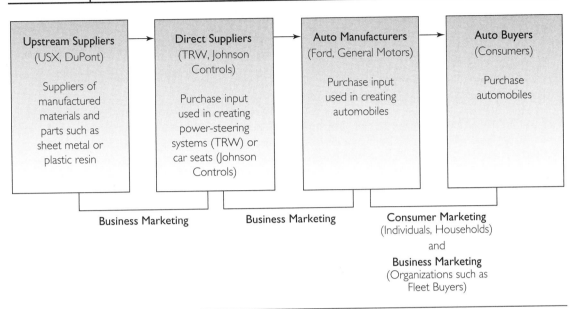

Supply Chain Management

Supply chain management is a technique for linking a manufacturer's operations with those of all of its strategic suppliers and its key intermediaries and customers to enhance efficiency and effectiveness. The Internet allows members of the supply chain all over the world to exchange timely information, exchange engineering drawings during new product development, and synchronize production and delivery schedules. The goal of supply chain strategy is to improve the speed, precision, and efficiency of manufacturing through strong supplier relationships. This goal is achieved through information sharing, joint planning, shared technology, and shared benefits. If the business marketer can become a valued partner in a customer's supply chain, the rewards are substantial: The focus shifts from price to value and from products to solutions.[27] To achieve these results, the business marketing firm must demonstrate the ability to meet the customer's precise quality, delivery, service, and information requirements.

Managing Relationships in the Supply Chain

Customers in the business market place a premium on the business marketer's supply chain management capabilities. IBM spends 85 percent of its purchasing dollars with 50 suppliers.[28] Of particular importance to IBM is the quality of engineering support it receives from suppliers. IBM actively seeks supplier partners that will contribute fresh ideas, responsive service, and leading-edge technology to attract buyers of future IBM products.

---

[27] Marc Bourde, Charlie Hawker, and Theo Theocharides, "Taking Center Stage: The 2005 Chief Procurement Officer Survey," (Sommers, N.Y.: IBM Global Services, 2005), pp. 1–13, accessed at http://www.ibm.com on July 15, 2005.

[28] James Carbone, "Reinventing Purchasing Wins Medal for Big Blue," *Purchasing* 129 (September 16, 1999): pp. 45–46.

INSIDE BUSINESS MARKETING

Career Profile: Delivering Service Solutions to IBM Customers

After receiving a BS in business management from the University of Maryland, John R. Roope III began his career at IBM, working in field engineering. He then served in several management positions that included national account customer executive, branch manager, and director of customer satisfaction. Following this leadership track, John is now vice president of IBM Global Services—Integrated Technology Services (ITS) for the Midwestern Region. John is responsible for sales, service delivery, and customer satisfaction for the diverse business market customers that make up this region.

John observes that "successful customer relationships are forged by connecting real technical solutions to the needs and requirements of a particular customer's business." To that end, John's team is organized around five industry sectors: distribution, financial, industrial, public/government, and small-medium businesses. "A sector leader and a set of account principals give dedicated attention to each segment and pursue this mission: build customer relationships, consult, continue to sell the entire ITS portfolio, and increase customer satisfaction with those delivered services."

IBM is embracing industry specialization to secure a deeper understanding of the customer's business. For example, supply chain solutions for an industrial customer differ from those for a retailer. Deep industry and customer knowledge coupled with a rich understanding of IBM's services portfolio allow account managers to craft tailored customer solutions and build long-term relationships. John asserts that by building this base of knowledge and a deep skill set, "we become a strategy partner by using our technical solutions to directly advance the mission and goals of our customer. In delivering these service solutions, we are working not only with Information Technology specialists on the customer side, but also with the key strategists who are shaping the future of the customer organization."

Many business school students feel that you need a technical degree to succeed at IBM. "That's a myth," according to John. His successful career at IBM speaks for itself and proves his point.

SOURCE: Interview with John R. Roope III by Michael Hutt, February 18, 2002, in Michael Czinkota et al., *Marketing Best Practices*, 2nd ed. (Mason, Ohio: South-Western Publishing, 2003), Chapter 6.

To effectively initiate and sustain a profitable relationship with a customer like IBM, Honda, or Procter & Gamble, the marketing manager must carefully coordinate the multiple linkages that define the relationship. Given these new marketing requirements, Frank V. Cespedes emphasizes the importance of "concurrent marketing" among the groups that are most central to customer contact efforts: product, sales, and service units.[29] In his view, recent market developments place more emphasis on the firm's ability to

- generate timely market knowledge by segment and by individual account;
- customize product service packages for diverse customer groups; and
- capitalize on local field knowledge from sales and service units to inform product strategy in real time.

Developing and nurturing close, long-term relationships is an important goal for the business marketer. Built on trust and demonstrated performance, such strategic

---

[29] Frank V. Cespedes, *Concurrent Marketing: Integrating Products, Sales, and Service* (Boston: Harvard Business School Press, 1995), chap. 2.

partnerships require open lines of communication between multiple layers of the buying and selling organizations. Given the rising importance of long-term, strategic relationships with both customers and suppliers, organizations are increasingly emphasizing relationship management skills. Because these skills reside in people rather than in organizational structures, roles, or tasks, marketing personnel with these skills become valuable assets to the organization.[30]

Commercial Enterprises as Consumers

Business market customers, as noted at the outset of the chapter, can be broadly classified into three categories: (1) commercial enterprises, (2) governmental organizations, and (3) institutions. Each is be explored in Chapter 2. However, the supply chain concept provides a solid foundation for describing the commercial customers that constitute the business market. Commercial enterprises can be divided into three categories: (1) users, (2) original equipment manufacturers (OEMs), and (3) dealers and distributors.

Users   Users purchase industrial products or services to produce other goods or services that are, in turn, sold in the business or consumer markets. User customers purchase goods—such as computers, photocopiers, or automated manufacturing systems—to set up or support the manufacturing process. When purchasing machine tools from GE, an auto manufacturer is a user. These machine tools do not become part of the automobile but instead help to produce it.

Original Equipment Manufacturers (OEMs)   The OEM purchases industrial goods to incorporate into other products it sells in the business or ultimate consumer market. For example, Intel Corporation produces the microprocessors that constitute the heart of Dell's personal computer. In purchasing these microprocessors, Dell is an OEM.

Dealers and Distributors   Dealers and distributors include commercial enterprises that purchase industrial goods for resale (in basically the same form) to users and OEMs. The distributor accumulates, stores, and sells a large assortment of goods to industrial users, assuming title of the goods it purchases. Handling billions of dollars worth of transactions each year, industrial distributors are growing in size and sophistication. The strategic role assumed by distributors in the business market is examined in detail in Chapter 14.

Overlap of Categories   The three categories of commercial enterprises are not mutually exclusive. Their classification is based on the intended purpose the product serves for the customer. Ford is a user when purchasing a machine tool for the manufacturing process, but the same company is an OEM when purchasing radios to be installed in the ultimate consumer product.

A marketer must have a good understanding of the diverse organizational consumers that make up the business market. Properly classifying commercial customers as users, OEMs, or dealers or distributors is an important first step to a sharpened understanding of the buying criteria that a particular commercial customer uses in evaluating an industrial product.

---

[30] Frederick E. Webster Jr., "The Changing Role of Marketing in the Corporation," *Journal of Marketing*, 56 (October 1992): p. 14. See also, Joseph P. Cannon and William D. Perreault Jr., "Buyer-Seller Relationships in Business Markets," *Journal of Marketing Research* 36 (November 1999): pp. 439–460.

Understanding Buying Motivations   Consider the different types of commercial customers that purchase a particular industrial product such as electrical timing mechanisms. Each class of customer views the product differently because each purchases the product for a different reason.

A food-processing firm such as Pillsbury buys electrical timers for use in a high-speed canning system. For this customer, quality, reliability, and prompt and predictable delivery are critical. Whirlpool, an OEM that incorporates the industrial product directly into consumer appliances, is concerned with the effect of the timers on the quality and dependability of the final consumer product. Because the timers are needed in large quantities, the appliance manufacturer is also concerned about the producer's production capacity and delivery reliability. Finally, an industrial distributor is most interested in matching the capability of the timing mechanisms to the needs of customers (users and OEMs) in a specific geographical market.

Classifying Goods for the Business Market[31]

Having classified business market customers, we must now ask what type of goods they require, and how each type is marketed. One useful method of classifying industrial goods is to ask the following questions: How does the industrial good or service enter the production process, and how does it enter the cost structure of the firm? The answer enables the marketer to identify those who are influential in the organizational buying process and to understand how to design an effective business marketing strategy. In general, industrial goods can be divided into three broad categories: entering goods, foundation goods, and facilitating goods (Figure 1.6).

Entering Goods

Entering goods become part of the finished product. This category of goods consists of raw materials and manufactured materials and parts. Their cost is an expense item assigned to the manufacturing process.

Raw Materials   Observe in Figure 1.6 that **raw materials** include both farm products and natural products. Raw materials are processed only to the level required for economical handling and transport; they basically enter the buying organization's production process in their natural state. Fueled by the massive growth in the Chinese economy, Phelps Dodge, the copper producer, has seen demand surge. McDonald's uses more than 700 million pounds of potatoes each year and dictates the fortunes of many farmers in that agricultural segment. In fact, when attempting to introduce a raspberry sorbet, McDonald's found, to its surprise, that not enough raspberries were being grown![32]

Manufactured Materials and Parts   In contrast to raw materials, **manufactured materials and parts** undergo more initial processing. Component materials such as

---

[31] Data on the dollar purchases of particular products by selected customers are drawn from Anne Millen Porter and Elena Epatko Murphy, "Hey Big Spender . . . The 100 Largest Industrial Buyers," *Purchasing* (November 9, 1995): pp. 31–42.

[32] James Brian Quinn, *Intelligent Enterprise: A Knowledge and Service Based Paradigm for Industry* (New York: The Free Press, 1992), p. 20.

FIGURE 1.6 | CLASSIFYING GOODS FOR THE BUSINESS MARKET

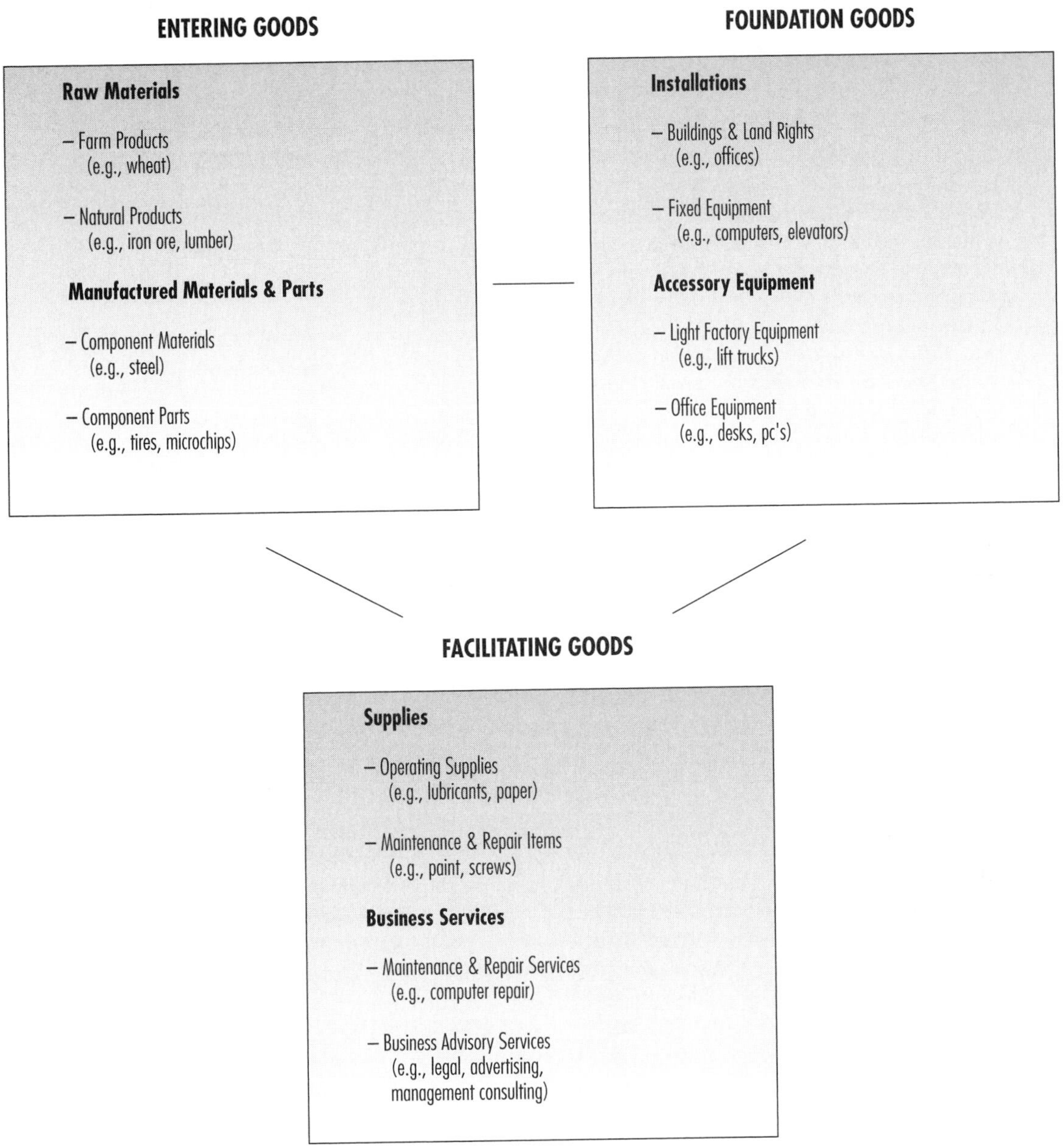

ENTERING GOODS

FOUNDATION GOODS

Raw Materials

– Farm Products
  (e.g., wheat)

– Natural Products
  (e.g., iron ore, lumber)

Manufactured Materials & Parts

– Component Materials
  (e.g., steel)

– Component Parts
  (e.g., tires, microchips)

Installations

– Buildings & Land Rights
  (e.g., offices)

– Fixed Equipment
  (e.g., computers, elevators)

Accessory Equipment

– Light Factory Equipment
  (e.g., lift trucks)

– Office Equipment
  (e.g., desks, pc's)

FACILITATING GOODS

Supplies

– Operating Supplies
  (e.g., lubricants, paper)

– Maintenance & Repair Items
  (e.g., paint, screws)

Business Services

– Maintenance & Repair Services
  (e.g., computer repair)

– Business Advisory Services
  (e.g., legal, advertising,
  management consulting)

SOURCE: Adapted from Philip Kotler, *Marketing Management: Analysis, Planning, and Control*, 4th ed. (Englewood Cliffs, N.J.: Prentice-Hall, 1980), p. 172, with permission of Prentice-Hall, Inc.

textiles or sheet steel have been processed before reaching a clothing manufacturer or automaker but must be processed further before becoming part of the finished consumer product. Both Ford and GE spend more than $900 million annually on steel. Component parts, on the other hand, include small motors, motorcycle tires, and automobile batteries; they can be installed directly into another product with little or

B2B TOP PERFORMERS

Jim Ryan, Group President, W.W. Grainger, Inc.

W.W. Grainger, Inc. (NYSE: GWW), with sales of $5.5 billion, is the leading broad line supplier of facilities maintenance products serving businesses and institutions throughout North America. Through its network of nearly 600 branches, 18 distribution centers, and multiple Web sites, Grainger helps customers save time and money by providing them with the right products to keep their facilities running.

Jim Ryan was elected to group president of Grainger in April 2004. He has profit and loss responsibility for the company's businesses operating under the Grainger brand in the United States. Ryan's career at Grainger is testimony to his philosophy that "you prepare to be a leader by deliberately taking on unfamiliar and difficult assignments—those that many shy away from. Challenging assignments are the training ground that provide the highest level of learning, preparing you for leadership at the top levels of large companies." Jim's rise through the ranks of Grainger includes senior assignments in IT, Grainger Parts, Marketing, Sales & Service, and the company's eBusiness. While in IT, Ryan oversaw the implementation of the SAP system and achieved corporate Y2K compliance. Both of these accomplishments reflect Ryan's focus on seeking out challenging undertakings.

Grainger's success is focused on helping its customers reduce the overall acquisition costs for maintenance, repair, and operating (MRO) items. Grainger encourages customers to eliminate their inventories of MRO items and rely on Grainger's responsive distribution systems and expertise to provide these items just when they are needed,

reducing the acquisition costs of these indirect materials. Grainger's philosophy is to be "customer intimate," where a customer's and a supplier's (Grainger) processes are fully integrated so that the customer becomes more efficient. Essentially, Grainger seeks to reduce the customer's total costs of acquiring MRO products.

Ryan believes that students preparing to be future leaders of B2B companies can best prepare for that role by developing four skills during their college education: (1) discipline and a strong work ethic; (2) cultivating "people skills"; (3) building analytical skills; and (4) organizational skills. He advises young people to focus on the strong work ethic early in their careers and to accept tough jobs other managers are not interested in tackling. Echoing his own tactics, Ryan advises students that "you learn the critical management skills when you take on those assignments that are unfamiliar and complicated." His accomplishments as a leader of a successful company are testimony to the wisdom of his approach.

SOURCE: Reprinted by permission of Grainger.

no additional processing. For example, Black & Decker spends $100 million each year on plastic parts, and Sun Microsystems spends more than $200 million on displays and monitors.

Foundation Goods

The distinguishing characteristic of foundation goods is that they are capital items. As capital goods are used up or worn out, a portion of their original cost is assigned to the production process as a depreciation expense. Foundation goods include installations and accessory equipment.

Installations   **Installations** include the major long-term investment items that underlie the manufacturing process, such as buildings, land rights, and fixed equipment. Large computers and machine tools are examples of fixed equipment. The demand for installations is shaped by the economic climate (for example, favorable interest rates) but is driven by the market outlook for a firm's products. In the face of strong worldwide demand for its microprocessors, Intel is building new plants, expanding existing ones, and making significant investments in capital equipment. A typical semiconductor chip plant costs at least $3 billion to build; equipment accounting for $600 million of the cost, and the land and building account for the rest.[33]

Accessory Equipment   **Accessory equipment** is generally less expensive and short-lived compared with installations, and it is not considered part of the fixed plant. This equipment can be found in the plant as well as in the office. Portable drills, personal computers, and fax machines illustrate this category.

Facilitating Goods

Facilitating goods are the supplies and services (see Figure 1.6) that support organizational operations. Because these goods do not enter the production process or become part of the finished product, their costs are handled as expense items.

Supplies   Virtually every organization requires operating supplies, such as printer cartridges, paper, or business forms, and maintenance and repair items, such as paint and cleaning materials. These items generally reach a broad cross-section of industrial users. In fact, they are very similar to the kinds of supplies that consumers might purchase at a hardware or discount store.

Services   Says analyst James Brian Quinn, "As the service sector has grown to embrace 80 percent of all U.S. employment, specialized service firms have become very large and sophisticated relative to the scale and expertise that individual staff and service groups have within integrated companies."[34] To capture the skills of these specialists and to direct attention to what they do best, many firms are shifting or "outsourcing" selected service functions to outside suppliers. This opens up opportunities for firms that provide such services as computer support, payroll processing, logistics, food operations, and equipment maintenance. These specialists possess a level of expertise or efficiency that organizations can profitably tap. For example, Cisco Systems turned to FedEx to coordinate the movement of parts through its supply chain and on to the customer. By merging the parts shipments in transit for a single customer, the desired product can be assembled at the customer's location, never spending a moment in a Cisco warehouse.[35] Business services include **maintenance and repair support** (for example, machine repair) and **advisory support** (for example, management consulting or information management). Like supplies, services are considered expense items.

---

[33] Dean Takahashi, "Makers of Chip Equipment Beginning to Share the Pain," *The Wall Street Journal*, August 14, 1996, p. B6.

[34] James Brian Quinn, "Strategic Outsourcing: Leveraging Knowledge Capabilities," *Sloan Management Review* 40 (summer 1999): p. 9. See also, Mark Gottfredson, Rudy Puryear, and Stephen Phillips, "Strategic Sourcing: From Periphery to Core," *Harvard Business Review* 83 (February 2005): pp. 132–139.

[35] Douglas A. Blackman, "Overnight, Everything Changed for FedEx: Can It Reinvent Itself?" *The Wall Street Journal*, November 4, 1999, pp. A1, A16.

Moreover, the explosive growth of the Internet has increased the demand for a range of electronic commerce services, from Web site design to the complete hosting of an e-commerce site. The Internet also provides a powerful new channel for delivering technical support, customer training, and management development programs. In turn, the Internet provides the opportunity to manage a particular activity or function from a remote, or even offshore, location. To illustrate, IBM manages the procurement functions for United Technologies Corporation via the Web.[36]

Business Marketing Strategy

Marketing pattern differences reveal the significance of a goods classification system. A marketing strategy appropriate for one category of goods may be entirely unsuitable for another. Often, entirely different promotional, pricing, and distribution strategies are required. The physical nature of the industrial good and its intended use by the organizational customer dictate to an important degree the marketing program's requirements. Some strategy highlights follow.

Illustration: Manufactured Materials and Parts

Recall that manufactured materials and parts enter the buying organization's own product. Whether a part is standardized or customized often dictates the nature of marketing strategy. For custom-made parts, personal selling and customer relationship–management activities assume an important role in marketing strategy. The value proposition centers on providing a product that advances the customer's competitive position. The business marketer must also demonstrate strong supply chain capabilities. Standardized parts are typically purchased in larger quantities on a contractual basis, and the marketing strategy centers on providing a competitive price, reliable delivery, and supporting services. Frequently, industrial distributors are used to provide responsive delivery service to smaller accounts.

For manufactured materials and parts, the marketer's challenge is to locate and accurately define the unique needs of diverse customers, uncover key buying influentials, and create solutions to serve these customers profitably.

Illustration: Installations

Installations such as fixed equipment were classified earlier as foundation goods because they are capital assets that affect the buyer's scale of operations. Here the product or technology itself, along with the service capabilities of the firm, are the central factors in marketing strategy, and direct manufacturer-to-user channels of distribution are the norm. Less costly, more standardized installations such as a drill press may be sold through marketing intermediaries.

Once again, personal selling or account management is the dominant promotional tool. The salesperson or account team works closely with prospective organizational buyers. Negotiations can span several months and involve the top executives in the buying organization, especially for buildings or custom-made equipment. Customer

---

[36] Ira Sager, "Inside IBM: Internet Business Machines," *Business Week E.Biz*, December 13, 1999, pp. ED21–23.

buying motives center on economic factors (such as the projected performance of the capital asset) and emotional factors (such as industry leadership). A buyer may be quite willing to select a higher-priced installation if the projected return on investment supports the decision. The focal points for the marketing of installations include a strong customer relationship–management effort, effective engineering and product design support, and the ability to offer a product or technology solution that provides a higher return on investment than its competition. Initial price, distribution, and advertising play lesser roles.

Illustration: Supplies

The final illustration centers on a facilitating good: supplies. Again we find different marketing patterns. Most supply items reach a broad market of organizational customers from many different industries. Although some large users are serviced directly, a wide variety of marketing intermediaries are required to cover this broad and diverse market adequately.

The goal of the business marketer is to secure a place on the purchasing function's list of preferred or preapproved suppliers. Importantly, many firms are adopting e-procurement systems to dramatically streamline the process employees follow in buying supplies and other operating resources.[37] From the desktop, an employee simply logs on to the system, selects the needed items from an electronic catalog of suppliers the purchasing function has preapproved, and sends the order directly to the supplier.

For supplies, the marketer's promotional mix includes catalog listings, advertising, and, to a lesser extent, personal selling. Advertising is directed to resellers (industrial distributors) and final users. Personal selling is less important for supplies than it is for other categories of goods with a high unit value, such as installations. Thus, personal selling efforts may be confined to resellers and large users of supplies. Price may be critical in the marketing strategy because many supply items are undifferentiated. However, customized service strategies might be designed to differentiate a firm's offerings from those of competitors. By providing the right product assortment, timely and reliable delivery, and customized services, the business marketer may be able to provide distinctive value to the customer and develop a long-term, profitable relationship.

A Look Ahead

Figure 1.7 shows the chief components of the business marketing management process. Business marketing strategy is formulated within the boundaries established by the corporate mission and objectives. A corporation determining its mission must define its business and purpose, assess environmental trends, and evaluate its strengths and weaknesses. Building e-commerce capabilities and transforming these capabilities into offerings that provide superior customer value constitute vital corporate objectives at leading organizations like GE. Corporate objectives provide guidelines for forming specific marketing objectives. Business marketing planning must be coordinated and synchronized with corresponding planning efforts in R&D, procurement, finance, production, customer service, and other areas. Clearly, strategic plans emerge out of a bargaining process among

---

[37] Ravi Kalkota and Marcia Robinson, *e-Business: Road Map for Success* (Reading, Mass: Addison-Wesley, 1999), pp. 237–251.

FIGURE 1.7 | A FRAMEWORK FOR BUSINESS MARKETING MANAGEMENT

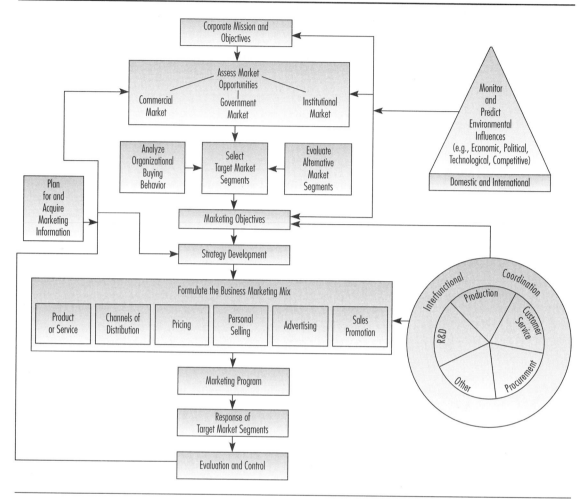

functional areas. Managing conflict, promoting cooperation, and developing coordinated strategies are all fundamental to the business marketer's interdisciplinary role.

The business marketing management framework (see Figure 1.7) provides an overview of the five major parts of the volume. This chapter introduced some of the features that distinguish industrial from consumer-goods marketing, whereas the next chapter explores the major types of customers that make up the business market: commercial enterprises, governmental units, and institutions. Each sector represents a sizable market opportunity, presents special characteristics and needs, and requires a unique marketing strategy response.

Part II examines the organizational buying process and the myriad forces that affect the organizational decision maker. Occupying a central position in Part II is customer relationship management—a managerial process that leading firms in business-to-business marketing have mastered. Here special attention is given to the specific strategies that business marketers can follow in developing profitable relationships with customers. Part III turns to the selection of target segments and specific techniques for measuring the response of these segments. Part IV centers on designing market-driven strategies. Each component of the marketing mix is treated from the business marketing perspective. Special attention is given to creating and managing offerings and managing connections, including treatment of e-commerce and supply chain strategies. Particular emphasis is also given to defining value from the customer's perspective and developing responsive pricing, advertising, and personal selling strategies to deliver that value proposition to target segments.

The processes of implementing, monitoring, and controlling the marketing program are analyzed in Part V. A central theme is how business-marketing managers can enhance profitability by maximizing the return on marketing strategy expenditures.

Summary

The business market offers significant opportunities and special challenges for the marketing manager. Market-driven firms in the business market demonstrate superior skills in understanding and satisfying customers. They also possess strong market-sensing and customer-linking capabilities. To deliver strong financial performance, business-to-business firms must also demonstrate customer relationship management skills, which include all the skills required to identify, initiate, develop, and monitor profitable customer relationships. Although a common body of knowledge and theory spans all of marketing, important differences exist between consumer and business marketing, among them the nature of markets, demand patterns, buyer behavior, and buyer-seller relationships.

The dramatic rise in competition on a worldwide basis requires a global perspective of markets. To secure a competitive advantage in this challenging environment, business market customers are developing closer, more collaborative ties with fewer suppliers than they have used in the past. They are using the Internet to promote efficiency and real-time communication across the supply chain, and demanding quality and speed from their suppliers to an unprecedented degree. These important trends in procurement place a premium on the supply chain management capabilities of the business marketer. Business marketing programs increasingly involve a customized blend of tangible products, service support, and ongoing information services both before and after the sale. Customer relationship management constitutes the heart of business marketing.

The diverse organizations that make up the business market can be broadly divided into (1) commercial enterprises, (2) governmental organizations, and (3) institutions. Because purchases these organizational consumers make are linked to goods and services they generate in turn, derived demand is an important and often volatile force in the business market. Industrial goods can be classified into three categories, based on how the product enters the buying organization's cost structure and the production process: (1) entering goods, (2) foundation goods, and (3) facilitating goods. Specific categories of goods may require unique marketing programs.

Discussion Questions

1. Home Depot is quite busy each morning because local contractors, home remodelers, and other small business customers are buying the products they require for the day's projects. Such small-business customers represent a huge market opportunity for Home Depot or Lowe's. Describe particular strategies these retailers could follow to target and serve these customers.

2. DuPont, one of the largest industrial producers of chemicals and synthetic fibers, spends millions of dollars annually on advertising its products to final consumers. For example, DuPont invested more than $1 million in a TV advertising blitz that emphasized the comfort of jeans made of DuPont's stretch polyester-cotton blend. DuPont does not produce jeans or market them to final consumers, so why are large expenditures made on consumer advertising?

3. What are the chief differences between consumer-goods marketing and business marketing? Use the following matrix as a guide in organizing your response:

	Consumer-Goods Marketing	Business Marketing
Customers		
Buying Behavior		
Buyer–Seller Relationship		
Product		
Price		
Promotion		
Channels		

4. Explain how a company such as GE might be classified by some business marketers as a user customer but by others as an OEM customer.

5. Spending a day in the life of a marketing manager would demonstrate the critical importance of relationship-management skills as that manager interacts with employees of other functional areas and, indeed, with representatives from both customer and supplier organizations. Explore the strategic significance of such relationships.

6. Auto executives are enamored with the success that Dell Computer has achieved with its "build to order" model. Dell builds a computer to the customer's precise specifications *after* the order is received. Is the approach feasible for Ford or GM? To succeed, what changes would be required in how automakers manage the supply chain?

7. Consumer products are frequently classified as convenience, shopping, or specialty goods. This classification system is based on how consumers shop for particular products. Would this classification scheme apply equally well in the business-marketing environment?

8. Evaluate this statement: "The ways that leading companies manage time in the supply chain—in new product development, in production, in sales and distribution—are the most powerful new sources of competitive advantage."

9. Evaluate this statement: "The demand for major equipment (a foundation good) is likely to be less responsive to shifts in price than that for materials, supplies, and components." Do you agree or disagree? Support your position.

10. Many firms are shifting selected service functions to outside suppliers. For example, Lucent Technologies recently outsourced its information management

function to IBM. What factors would prompt such a decision, and what criteria would a customer like Lucent Technologies emphasize in choosing a supplier?

Internet Exercises

1. Many firms, large and small, have outsourced key functions, like payroll processing to ADP. Go to adp.com and (1) identify the range of services that ADP offers; (2) describe the types of customers the firm serves.

2. BASF "doesn't make the products you buy, but makes them better." Go to http://www.basf.com and (1) outline the markets that BASF serves and (2) the products it sells.

CASE

Wireless E-mail: A Challenger to BlackBerry?

Research in Motion, Ltd., or RIM, is the innovative Canadian firm that created and now dominates the wireless e-mail market with its BlackBerry device. Since its introduction, BlackBerry's legion of devoted business users has grown to more than 3 million. The surge in popularity of wireless e-mail has attracted a host of new competitors for BlackBerry, including PalmOne Inc.'s Treo, and a number of other upstarts in recent years have emerged to provide wireless e-mail software for handsets such as Good Technology, Inc. But now Motorola has its sights on the mobile e-mail market.[38] The decision to challenge BlackBerry represents one of several initiatives that Edward Zander has launched since he was appointed CEO at Motorola in January 2004.

Mr. Zander revamped the company's once "old fashioned" image with a slew of cool devices and ads featuring Motorola's "batwings" logo.[39] Its ultraslim Razr cellphone has been wildly popular and has become the must-have handset since it was introduced in late 2004. Zander says that what the Razr did "was get Motorola in the minds of a lot of people around the world for being cool again. I also think that it did a lot for employees, because if you start getting employees believing again, you win."

To compete against RIM's BlackBerry, Motorola is introducing a handset called Q with a specialized keyboard and designed with the style of the company's ultraslim Razr cellphone. In addition to e-mail, the handset has Internet-surfing capabilities and a 1.3-megapixel camera.

Discussion Questions

1. Think about the wireless e-mail market and describe the characteristics of potential customers who now use the product or are likely to adopt it. In developing a customer profile, you might consider factors such as age, education, occupation, or job function, industry sector, tech aptitude, and so on.

2. Since the BlackBerry created the wireless e-mail market and represents a strong and appealing brand, what marketing strategies should Motorola pursue in challenging RIM with its Q product?

---

[38] Roger O. Crockett, Cliff Edwards, and Spencer E. Ante, "Motorola: Getting Its Groove Back," *BusinessWeek online*, July 28, 2005, pp. 1–4, accessed at http://www.businessweek.com.

[39] Christopher Rhoads, "Motorola's Modernizer," *The Wall Street Journal*, June 23, 2005, p. B1.

CHAPTER

2

The Business Market: Perspectives on the Organizational Buyer

The business marketer must understand the needs of a diverse mix of organizational buyers drawn from three broad sectors of the business market—commercial enterprises, government (all levels), and institutions—as well as from an expanding array of international buyers. After reading this chapter, you will understand:

1. the nature and central characteristics of each of these market sectors.

2. how the purchasing function is organized in each of these components of the business market.

3. the dramatic role that online purchasing assumes in the business market.

4. the need to design a unique marketing program for each sector of the business market.

Cisco Systems, Inc., provides the networking solutions that are the foundation of the Internet and of most corporate, education, and government networks on a global scale. Today, the Internet and computer networking are a fundamental part of business, education, personal communications, and entertainment. Virtually all messages or transactions passing over the Internet are carried efficiently and securely through Cisco equipment. Cisco provides the hardware and software solutions for transporting data, voice, and video within buildings, across campuses, or around the world.

Rather than serving individuals or household consumers, Cisco is a leading-edge business-to-business firm that markets its products and services to organizations: commercial enterprises (for example, corporations and telecommunications firms), governmental units, and institutions (for example, universities and health-care organizations). Marketing managers at Cisco give special attention to transforming complex technology products and services into concrete solutions to meet customer requirements. For example, when Outback Steakhouse, Inc., wanted to upgrade its information systems so that the executive team at headquarters and managers at each of its restaurants—spread across 50 U.S. states and 21 countries—could access timely data, anytime, Cisco provided the solution.[1] Likewise, when Procter & Gamble (P&G) wanted to launch a major Internet initiative to meet its aggressive growth targets, the firm turned to Cisco.[2] The sales team from Cisco described how an efficient Internet strategy could improve the way companies interact with employees, suppliers, and customers. Working with Cisco, P&G implemented several initiatives, including an online system called "Web Order Management" that enables retail customers, like Target, to connect to P&G anytime to place and manage orders on the Web. In working with Cisco, P&G Chief Information Officer (CIO) Steve David commented: "We like to hook our wagon to people who are the best so they can help us be the best at creating that all-important competitive advantage."[3]

Each of the three business market sectors—commercial firms, institutions, and governments—has identifiable and unique characteristics that business marketers must understand if marketers wish to grow their client bases. A significant first step in creating successful marketing strategy is to isolate the unique dimensions of each major business market sector. How much market potential does each sector represent? Who makes the purchasing decisions? The answers provide a foundation on which managers can formulate marketing programs that respond to the specific needs and characteristics of each business market sector.

Commercial Enterprises: Unique Characteristics

Commercial enterprises include manufacturers, construction companies, service firms (for example, hotels), transportation companies, selected professional groups (for example, dentists), and resellers (wholesalers and retailers purchasing equipment and supplies to use in their operations). Manufacturers are the most important commercial customers: The 250 largest ones purchase more than $1.2 trillion of goods and services annually.[4]

---

[1] Cisco Success Story: "Outback Steakhouse Likes Its Network . . . Well Done," http://www.cisco.com, accessed June 14, 2005, pp. 1–3.

[2] "Cisco Customer Profile: Procter & Gamble," http://www.cisco.com, accessed July 23, 2002, pp. 1–3.

[3] Ibid., p. 3.

[4] Anne Millen Porter, "Big Companies Struggle to Act Their Size," *Purchasing* 130 (November 1, 2001): pp. 25–32.

Distribution by Size

A startling fact about the study of manufacturers is that so few of them remain. Available evidence suggests that there are approximately 350,000 manufacturing firms in the United States.[5] And although only 36,000 manufacturing firms (10 percent) employ more than 100 workers each, this handful of firms ships more than 75 percent of all U.S. manufactured products. Because manufacturing operations are so concentrated in the United States, the business marketer normally serves *far fewer but far larger* customers than does a consumer-product marketer. For example, Intel sells microprocessors to a few large manufacturers, like Dell and Hewlett-Packard, who, in turn, target millions of potential computer buyers. Clearly, large buyers are generally vitally important to business marketers. Because each large firm has such vast buying power, business marketers often tailor particular marketing strategies for each customer.

Smaller manufacturing firms also constitute an important business market segment. In fact, almost two-thirds of all U.S. manufacturers employ fewer than 20 people.[6] In addition to small manufacturers, more than 5 million small businesses in the United States employ fewer than six people each. Based on sheer numbers, small businesses represent a dominant category of business-market customers—but a market that is often difficult to serve.[7] Because the organizational buyer in smaller firms has different needs—and often a very different orientation—astute marketers adjust their marketing programs to this market segment's particular needs. To illustrate, FedEx wanted to increase its share of the small shipper market but recognized that picking up packages at many small businesses is more expensive than picking them up at one larger location.[8] To cost-effectively reach these customers, FedEx encourages small shippers to bring their packages to conveniently located FedEx drop-off points. The strategy has been successful.

Geographical Concentration

Size is not the only concentration factor important to the business marketer: Manufacturers are also concentrated geographically. More than half of all U.S. manufacturers appear in only eight states: California, New York, Ohio, Illinois, Michigan, Texas, Pennsylvania, and New Jersey. Most large metropolitan areas are lucrative business markets. Geographical concentration of industry, however, means only that a large potential volume exists in a given area; each buyer's requirements may still vary significantly.

Geographic concentration has important implications for formulating marketing strategy. First, firms can concentrate their marketing efforts in high market potential areas, making effective use of full-time personal sales forces in these markets. Second, distribution centers in large-volume areas can ensure rapid delivery to a large proportion

[5] U.S. Department of Commerce, Bureau of the Census, *Annual Survey of Manufacturers: Statistics for Industry Groups: 2003* (Washington, D.C., 2005), p. 1.

[6] U.S. Department of Commerce, Bureau of the Census, *2000 County Business Patterns,* accessed at www.censtats.gov, June 15, 2005.

[7] Arun Sharma, R. Krishnan, and Dhruv Grewal, "Value Creation in Business Markets," *Industrial Marketing Management* 30 (June 2001): pp. 391–402.

[8] Thomas H. Davenport, Jeanne G. Harris, and Ajay K. Kohli, "How Do They Know Their Customers So Well?" *MIT Sloan Management Review* 42 (winter 2001): p. 65.

of customers. Finally, firms may not be able to tie their salespeople to specific geographic areas because many large buying organizations entrust the responsibility for purchasing certain products and materials for the entire company to a single individual. For example, Wendy's International, Inc., operates a centralized purchasing system from its Dublin, Ohio, headquarters that supports the entire Wendy's network—all corporate and franchise restaurants on a global basis. The centralized staff purchases all direct materials for all of the restaurants—food, packaging, and supplies. Judith Hollis, Vice President of supply chain management at Wendy's, notes:

> We view our job as developing supplier partnerships that are going to assist Wendy's with maintaining our competitive advantage. We look to . . . companies that are involved in technological innovation in quality, food, safety, and preparation efficiency.[9]

By understanding how a potential buyer's purchasing organization is structured, business marketers are better equipped to identify buying influentials and to develop responsive strategy.

Classifying Commercial Enterprises

Marketers can gain valuable strategy insights by identifying the needs and requirements of different types of commercial enterprises or business customers. The **North American Industrial Classification System (NAICS)** organizes business activity into meaningful economic sectors and identifies groups of business firms that use similar production processes.[10] The NAICS results from the North American Free Trade Agreement (NAFTA); it provides for standard economic data reporting among Canada, Mexico, and the United States. Every plant or business establishment receives a code that reflects the primary product produced at that location. The new system, which includes traditional industries while incorporating new and emerging-technology industries, replaces the Standard Industrial Classification (SIC) system that was used for decades.

Figure 2.1 illustrates the building blocks of the system. Observe that the first two digits identify the economic sector and that as more digits are added, the classification becomes finer. For example, all business establishments that create, disseminate, or provide the means to distribute information are included in the Information sector: NAICS Code 51. Nineteen other economic sectors are included in the system. More specifically, U.S. establishments that produce paging equipment are assigned an NAICS Code of 513321. Individual countries customize the six-digit codes for industry subdivisions, but at the five-digit level they are standardized across the three countries.

Using the NAICS   If marketing managers understand the needs and requirements of a few firms within a classification category, they can project requirements for other firms that share that category. Each group should be relatively homogeneous in terms of raw materials required, component parts used, and manufacturing processes

---

[9]Michael Fredette, "An Interview with Judith Hollis," *Journal of Supply Chain Management* 37 (summer 2001): p. 3.

[10]www.naics.com, "History of SIC/NAICS," accessed June 15, 2005.

FIGURE 2.1 | NORTH AMERICAN INDUSTRIAL CLASSIFICATION SYSTEM

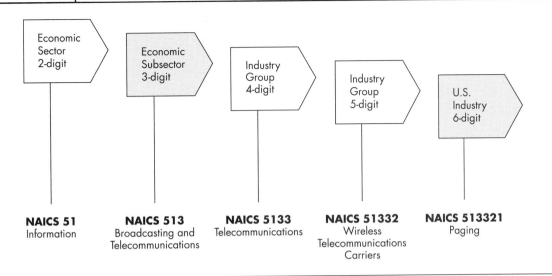

SOURCE: Reprinted from K. Douglas Hoffman, et al., *Marketing: Best Practices* (Mason, Ohio: South-Western/Thomson Learning, 2003), p. 171.

employed. The NAICS provides a valuable tool for identifying new customers and for targeting profitable segments of business buyers.

The Purchasing Organization

Regardless of its organizational characteristics, every firm must procure the materials, supplies, equipment, and services it needs to operate the business successfully. On average, firms spend more than half of every dollar earned from sales of manufactured products on the materials, supplies, services, and equipment needed to produce the goods.[11] For example, Ford spends nearly $80 billion annually in the business market. When a customer buys a $28,000 sports utility vehicle from Ford, the automaker has already spent more than $14,000 to buy steel, paint, glass, fabric, aluminum, and electrical components to build it. How goods and services are purchased depends on such factors as the nature of the business, the size of the firm, and the volume, variety, and technical complexity of items purchased. Rarely do individual departments in a corporation do their own buying. An individual whose title is manager of purchasing, purchasing agent, director of purchasing, or director of procurement usually administers procurement for all departments.

The day-to-day purchasing function is carried out by buyers, each of whom is responsible for a specific group of products. Organizing the purchasing function in this way permits buyers to acquire a high level of technical expertise about a limited number of items. As products and materials become more sophisticated, buyers must become

---

[11] Anne Millen Porter, "The Top 250: Tough Measures for Tough Times," *Purchasing* 131 (November 7, 2002): pp. 31–35.

TABLE 2.1 | **THE GOALS OF PURCHASING**

Goals	Description
Uninterrupted Flow of Materials	Provide an uninterrupted flow of the materials, supplies, and services required to operate the organization.
Manage Inventory	Minimize the investment in inventory.
Improve Quality	Maintain and improve quality by carefully evaluating and choosing products and services.
Developing and Managing Supplier Relationships	Find competent suppliers and forge productive relationships with supply chain.
Achieve Lowest Total Cost	Purchase required products and services at lowest total cost.
Reduce Administrative Costs	Accomplish the purchasing objectives at the lowest possible level of administrative costs.
Advance Firm's Competitive Position	Improve the firm's competitive position by reducing supply chain costs or capitalizing on the capabilities of suppliers.

SOURCE: Adapted with modifications from Michael R. Leenders, Harold E. Fearon, Anna E. Flynn, and P. Fraser Johnson, *Purchasing and Supply Management*, 12th ed. (Chicago: Irwin, 2002), pp. 40–43, and David Hannon, "Supplier Relationships Key to Future Success," *Purchasing* 134 (June 2, 2005): pp. 21–24.

more knowledgeable about material characteristics, manufacturing processes, and design specifications. Frequently, a sizable group is employed to conduct research, evaluate materials, and perform cost studies.

Goals of the Purchasing Function

To address the needs of business customers of all types, the marketer has to understand the purchasing manager's goals and how the purchasing function contributes to the organization's objectives (Table 2.1). The purchasing decision maker must juggle a number of different objectives that often clash. For example, the lowest-priced component part is unacceptable if it does not meet quality standards or is delivered two weeks late. In addition to protecting the cost structure of the firm, improving quality, and keeping inventory investment to a minimum, purchasing assumes a central role in managing relationships with suppliers. Here purchasing assumes a central role in supply chain management.

Supply chain management is a technique for linking a manufacturer's operations with those of all of its strategic suppliers, key intermediaries, and customers. The approach seeks to integrate the relationships and operations of both immediate, first-tier suppliers and those several tiers back in the supply chain, in order to help second-, third-, and fourth-tier suppliers meet requirements like quality, delivery, and the timely exchange of information. Firms that embrace supply chain management also solicit ideas from key suppliers and involve them directly in the new-product-development process. By managing supply chain costs and linking supplier capabilities to new product development, the purchasing function is advancing corporate performance in many organizations.

INSIDE BUSINESS MARKETING

The Supply Chain for McNuggets

Purchasing managers at McDonald's Corporation have worked closely with suppliers to develop a sophisticated model to reduce the cost of chicken. The model isolates how various feed mixes affect weight gain in chickens, and suppliers are able to optimize chicken weight gain in response to changing food prices.

McDonald's also closely manages and tightly coordinates its supply chain from hatchery to processor and into the restaurants. "McDonald's explicitly orders hatcheries to place eggs in anticipation of the sales forecast for chicken products. Product movement through the supply base is so well orchestrated that a supplier can confidently place the eggs in the hatcheries seventy-five days before McDonald's expects to sell the chicken as McNuggets."

SOURCE: Timothy M. Laseter, *Balanced Sourcing: Cooperation and Competition in Supplier Relationships* (San Francisco: Jossey-Bass, 1998), p. 14.

Strategic Procurement[12]

Leading-edge organizations like Dell Computer, GE, and Honda demonstrate the critical role that purchasing can assume in creating profit opportunities in their industries. To illustrate, Honda, long recognized for purchasing excellence and its ability to sustain customer loyalty, was able to reduce by 20 percent the costs of external purchases that are embodied in the current Accord. A senior purchasing executive at Honda described how it was done:

> The first thing we did was compile a big list of every possible way we could remove costs from the Accord; most of them, in fact, came from suppliers' work with purchasing and engineering. We studied each idea, prioritized them according to their likelihood of success, and then just started focusing our work on developing them.[13]

Understanding the Total Cost To unlock savings and growth opportunities, the purchasing function must develop a keen understanding of the total cost and value of a good or service to the firm. Such an approach requires purchasing managers to consider not only the purchase price but also an array of other considerations:

- The factors that drive the cost of the product or service in the supply chain, such as transportation.

- The costs of acquiring and managing products or services.

- Quality, reliability, and other attributes of a product or service over its complete life cycle.

- The value of a product or service to a firm and its customers.

Fundamental to this total system cost perspective is the concept of total cost of ownership. "**Total cost of ownership** considers both supplier and buyer activities, and

---

[12] This section is based on Matthew G. Anderson and Paul B. Katz, "Strategic Sourcing," *International Journal of Logistics Management* 9, no. 1 (1998): pp. 1–13.

[13] Timothy M. Laseter, *Balanced Sourcing: Cooperation and Competition in Supplier Relationships* (San Francisco: Jossey-Bass, 1998), p. 224.

costs over a product's or service's complete life cycle."[14] For example, a firm can justify buying a higher-quality product and paying a premium price because the initial purchase cost will be offset by fewer manufacturing defects, lower inventory requirements, and lower administrative costs. The total cost of ownership means understanding a range of cost-value relationships associated with individual purchases.

Levels of Procurement Development   In capturing cost savings through improved procurement, Matthew Anderson and Paul Katz of Mercer Management Consulting suggest that firms operate at different levels of development and emphasize different pathways to cost reduction and revenue enhancement (Figure 2.2). Ranging from the least to the most developed, these approaches include (1) Buy for Less; (2) Buy Better; (3) Consume Better; and (4) Sell Better. Note that the most developed strategy—Sell Better—ties purchasing activities directly to strategy. Here procurement builds supplier relationships that ultimately enhance the growth and the market strength of the organization.

Level 1—Leveraged Buy (Buy for Less)   Many firms demonstrate Level 1 procurement practices and achieve cost savings by centralizing decision-making authority, which permits the consolidation of volume and by selecting suppliers that provide the best prices and terms.

Level 2—Linked Buy (Buy Better)   The next level of procurement development is triggered when the procurement organization takes an external view of the supply chain and develops mutually beneficial relationships with suppliers. It achieves cost savings by streamlining the bidding process, optimizing delivery and information flows, and making stable commitments to enable efficient production by suppliers. Incremental cost savings of 5 to 25 percent result from moving from Level 1 to Level 2.

Level 3—Value Buy (Consume Better)   The goal of Level 3 is to advance the performance of the procurement function by optimizing the life cycle costs and value of products and services. Value analysis, complexity management, and early supplier involvement in product design allow buyers and suppliers to uncover added value.

- **Value analysis** is a method of weighing the comparative value of materials, components, and manufacturing processes from the standpoint of their purpose, relative merit, and cost in order to uncover ways of improving products, lowering costs, or both. For example, Ferro Corporation developed a new coating process that allows Maytag to paint a refrigerator cabinet in 10 minutes compared with the old process, which took 3 hours.[15] The new process provided significant cost savings for Maytag.

- **Complexity management** seeks cost reductions by simplifying the design of products or by using standardized component parts in products and across product lines. For example, several years ago, Motorola used 140 different batteries for its cell phones. The company realized significant cost savings by reducing that number to 30.[16] Complexity management can also involve the outsourcing of production or assembly tasks to supply chain partners. Rather

[14] Anderson and Katz, "Strategic Sourcing," p. 3. See also, James Carbone, "Using TCO to Rate Suppliers," *Purchasing* 133 (February 19, 2004): pp. 30–34.

[15] Elizabeth Baatz, "How Purchasing Handles Intense Cost Pressure," *Purchasing* 127 (October 8, 1999): pp. 61–66.

[16] James Carbone, "Motorola Leverages Its Way to Lower Cost," *Purchasing* 133 (September 16, 2004): pp. 31–38.

FIGURE 2.2 | LEVELS OF PROCUREMENT DEVELOPMENT AND PATHWAYS TO SAVINGS/REVENUE ENHANCEMENT

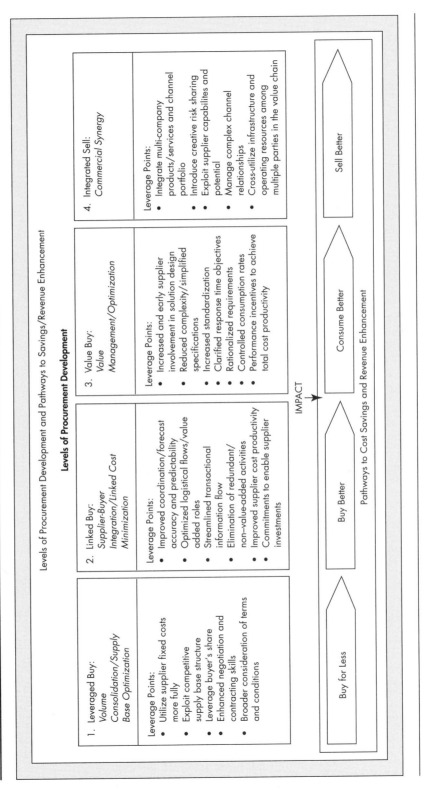

Levels of Procurement Development and Pathways to Savings/Revenue Enhancement

Levels of Procurement Development

1. Leveraged Buy:
   Volume Consolidation/Supply Base Optimization

   Leverage Points:
   • Utilize supplier fixed costs more fully
   • Exploit competitive supply base structure
   • Leverage buyer's share
   • Enhanced negotiation and contracting skills
   • Broader consideration of terms and conditions

2. Linked Buy:
   Supplier-Buyer Integration/Linked Cost Minimization

   Leverage Points:
   • Improved coordination/forecast accuracy and predictability
   • Optimized logistical flows/value added roles
   • Streamlined transactional information flow
   • Elimination of redundant/non-value-added activities
   • Improved supplier cost productivity
   • Commitments to enable supplier investments

3. Value Buy:
   Value Management/Optimization

   Leverage Points:
   • Increased and early supplier involvement in solution design
   • Reduced complexity/simplified specifications
   • Increased standardization
   • Clarified response time objectives
   • Rationalized requirements
   • Controlled consumption rates
   • Performance incentives to achieve total cost productivity

4. Integrated Sell:
   Commercial Synergy

   Leverage Points:
   • Integrate multi-company products/services and channel portfolio
   • Introduce creative risk sharing
   • Exploit supplier capabilites and potential
   • Manage complex channel relationships
   • Cross-utilize infrastructure and operating resources among multiple parties in the value chain

Buy for Less   Buy Better   Consume Better   Sell Better

IMPACT

Pathways to Cost Savings and Revenue Enhancement

SOURCE: Reprinted with permission from Matthew G. Anderson and Paul B. Katz, "Strategic Sourcing," *International Journal of Logistics Management* 9, no. 1 (1998), p. 4, Figure 3. Website at http://www.ijlm.org.

FIGURE 2.3 | **Segmenting the Buy**

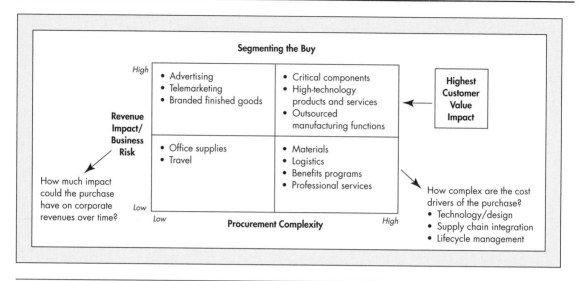

SOURCE: Reprinted with permission from Matthew G. Anderson and Paul B. Katz, "Strategic Sourcing," *International Journal of Logistics Management* 9, no. 1 (1998), p. 7, Figure 8. Website at http://www.ijlm.org.

than supplying a single item like a muffler, Ford might ask a supply chain partner to provide a complete exhaust system.

- To capture fresh ideas, technologies, and cost savings, leading purchasing organizations emphasize **early supplier involvement in new product development.** At firms like Boeing, Harley-Davidson, Maytag, and Honda, key suppliers actively contribute to the new-product-development process from the design stage to the product's introduction, often spending months onsite collaborating with the development team.

By using these methods, Level 3 savings opportunities can be substantial but vary with the nature of the product, capabilities of the suppliers, and the strength of buyer-seller relationships.

Level 4—Integrated Sell (Sell Better)   Level 4 development applies when specific product and service choices the purchasing organization makes have a significant effect on revenue and also involve a high degree of business risk. For example, the investments of a telecommunications firm such as AT&T in technology products that form its infrastructure have a major effect on the future of the firm. Under such conditions, choosing the right technologies and sharing the risks with important suppliers are crucial to the success of AT&T's corporate strategy. Highly skilled and knowledgeable purchasing professionals are required to achieve this advanced level of procurement development, which unites purchasing decisions with corporate growth strategies.

Segmenting Purchase Categories   Each firm purchases a unique portfolio of products and services. Leaders in procurement are giving increased attention to segmenting total purchases into distinct categories and sharpening their focus on those purchases that have the greatest effect on revenue generation or present the greatest risk to corporate performance. From Figure 2.3, observe that various

INSIDE BUSINESS MARKETING

Harley-Davidson's World-Class Purchasing Organization

Like Honda of America, IBM, and a select group of others, Harley-Davidson is widely recognized as an organization that possesses a world-class purchasing organization. Here are some achievements that set it apart:

- Cost reduction—the firm implemented a five-year cost improvement program with suppliers that reduced the costs of purchased goods and services from $86 million to $57 million annually.

- Inventory strategy—Harley-Davidson handles its inventory on a just-in-time schedule.

- Supplier relationships—the purchasing staff cut the number of suppliers with which it transacts business and now concentrates 80 percent of its purchases with a critical group of suppliers that can meet the firm's new objectives of cost reduction, quality improvement, and reduced new-product-development time.

- Supplier involvement—on-site suppliers assume a central role in the new-product-development process.

- Quality targets—Harley-Davidson is aggressively pursuing a quality goal of 48 parts per million (ppm) or better. Highly trained specialists are assigned to suppliers that are having quality problems.

Jeff Bluestein, chairman and CEO of Harley-Davidson, attributes the firm's success to adopting beneficial relationships with suppliers and taking a strategic approach to purchasing. "That means we are trying to have real close affiliations, close relationships with each of these suppliers. It starts with the understanding that we want long-term relationships."

SOURCE: Brian Milligan, "Medal of Excellence: Harley-Davidson Wins by Getting Suppliers on Board," *Purchasing* 129 (September 21, 2000), pp. 52–65. See also, Dave Nelson, Patricia E. Moody, and Jonathan Stegner, *The Purchasing Machine* (New York: The Free Press, 2001), pp. 83–100.

categories of purchases are segmented on the basis of procurement complexity and the nature of the effect on corporate performance (that is, revenue impact/business risk).

Which Purchases Affect Performance? Procurement complexity considers factors such as the technical complexity, the scope of supply chain coordination required, and the degree to which life cycle costs are relevant. The revenue impact/business risk dimension considers the degree to which a purchase category can influence customers' perceptions of value. For example, purchasing managers at Ford decided that some components are important to brand identity, such as steering wheels, road wheels, and other highly visual parts.

Purchasing managers can use a segmentation approach to isolate those purchase categories that have the greatest effect on corporate revenues. For example, advertising services could have tremendous risk implications relative to customer perceptions of value, whereas office supplies remain a cost issue. Or, in the high-tech arena, the procurement of a new generation of semiconductor technology may essentially be a bet on the company's future.[17]

Business marketers should assess where their offerings are positioned in the portfolio of purchases a particular organization makes. This varies by firm and by industry. The

---

[17] Anderson and Katz, "Strategic Sourcing," p. 7.

revenue and profit potential for the business marketer is greatest in those purchasing organizations that view the purchase as strategic—high revenue impact and high customer value impact. Here the marketer can contribute offerings directly tied to the customer organization's strategy. If the business marketer can become a central component of the customer's supply chain, the effect is significant: an attractive, long-term relationship in which the customer views the supplier as an extension of its organization. For categories of goods that purchasing organizations view as less strategic (for example, office supplies), the appropriate marketing strategy centers on providing a complete product assortment, competitive pricing, timely service support, and simplified ordering. By understanding how customers segment their purchases, business marketers are better equipped to target profitable customer groups and develop customized strategies.

E-Procurement[18]

Like consumers who are shopping at Amazon (http://www.amazon.com), purchasing managers use the Internet to find new suppliers, communicate with current suppliers, or place an order. While providing a rich base of information, purchasing over the Internet is also very efficient: It is estimated that purchase orders processed over the Internet cost only $5, compared with the current average purchase order cost of $100. For example, IBM has moved all of its purchasing to the Web and has created a "private exchange" that links its suppliers. A **private exchange** allows a company like IBM to automate its purchases and collaborate in real time with a specially invited group of suppliers.[19] By handling nearly all its invoices electronically (some 400,000 e-invoices a month), IBM saves nearly $400 million per year using its more efficient Web purchasing strategy.

Everyone Is Getting Wired

Less than a decade ago, pioneering enterprises like IBM, GE, and United Technologies began testing Internet-based negotiations as part of their strategic purchasing programs. Today, more than 80 percent of *Fortune* 1000 enterprises have adopted e-procurement software, and new low-cost, hosted options are driving the adoption of e-procurement solutions among medium-sized enterprises. Leading suppliers of e-procurement software include Ariba, Inc. (http://www.ariba.com), Emptoris (http://www.emptoris.com), and Oracle Corporation (http://www.oracle.com). To compete effectively in this information-rich environment, business marketing managers must develop a firm understanding of the e-procurement tools that customers are embracing.

Enhancing the Buyer's Capabilities

Rather than a strategy, e-procurement is a technology platform that enables information to be exchanged efficiently and processes to be automated. E-procurement is "the use of Web-based applications, decision support tools, and associated services to streamline

---

[18]Tim A. Minahan, "Best Practices in E-Sourcing: Optimizing and Sustaining Supply Savings," September 2004, research report by Aberdeen Group, Inc., Boston, Massachusetts; accessed at http://www.ariba.com, June 15, 2005.

[19]Nicole Harris, "'Private Exchanges' May Allow B-to-B Commerce to Thrive After All," *The Wall Street Journal*, March 16, 2001, p. B4.

and enhance strategic sourcing processes and knowledge management."[20] Included among the distinguishing components of e-procurement solutions are the following capabilities:

- *Online negotiations* that enable the buyer to query suppliers with a request-for-proposal (RFP), request-for-quote (RFQ), or request-for-information (RFI), and to conduct reverse auctions (discussed below).

- *Collaboration tools* that enable the purchasing manager to (1) collaborate with internal stakeholders (for example, departments) to develop detailed specifications and priorities for goods or services to be purchased and (2) provide a detailed description of requirements to suppliers through an RFP.

- *Knowledge management* capabilities that provide the procurement function and senior management with a central repository of valuable data and information on supplier performance, material and component costs, process flows, and best practices.

- *Analytical tools* that support detailed analysis and modeling of purchasing costs and total spending by category across the enterprise.

Delivering Measurable Results

Why are purchasing organizations embracing online purchasing technologies? Because they "deliver measurable benefits in the form of material cost savings, process efficiencies, and performance enhancements" according to Tim Minahan, a supply chain consultant at the Aberdeen Group.[21] Studying procurement processes at 60 companies, including American Express, Motorola, and Alcoa, Aberdeen found that e-procurement cut purchasing cycle time in half, reduced material costs by 14 percent and purchasing administrative costs by 60 percent, and enhanced the ability of procurement units to identify new suppliers on a global scale.

Buying Direct and Indirect Goods

In the United States alone, organizations spend more than $1.4 trillion annually on *indirect* goods or operating resources—items that organizations of all types need to run day-to-day operations. Examples encompass everything from personal computers and spare parts for factory equipment to office furniture and employee travel, including airline tickets, hotel rooms, and car rental services.[22] During the Internet-boom years, companies invested heavily in e-procurement systems but used them primarily to buy indirect goods. As adopters reaped huge cost savings and began to trust Internet-based purchasing systems, many firms began to use e-procurement to buy *direct* materials or entering goods—the raw materials or component parts that are core to a firm's manufacturing process. As e-procurement systems become more affordable, some experts predict that small and medium-sized firms will soon adopt the purchasing practices of the industry leaders. To illustrate best practices in e-procurement, let's examine how employees purchase indirect goods, such as software or a photocopier, at leading firms like Cisco Systems or Motorola.

---

[20] Minahan, "Best Practices in E-Sourcing," p. 3.

[21] Ibid., p. 3.

[22] Mark Vigoroso, "Buyers Prepare for Brave New World of e-Commerce," *Purchasing* 127 (April 22, 1999): pp. S4–S12.

FIGURE 2.4 | THE BUY-SIDE REQUISITIONING PROCESS

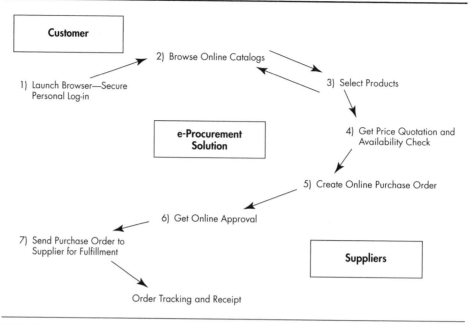

SOURCE: Adapted from Ravi Kalkota and Marcia Robinson, *e-Business: Roadmap for Success* (Reading, Mass.: Addison-Wesley, 1999), p. 248.

The Electronic (e) Requisitioning Process[23]   **E-procurement software** enables individual employees to buy online while the company retains control of the purchasing process. By tying the corporate intranet to suppliers' Web-based commerce sites, buy-side software routes employee purchase requests internally before turning them into firm orders. This e-procurement solution allows a company to channel purchases to preferred suppliers, reduce administrative overhead, capture favorable quantity discounts, and significantly reduce operating resource costs.

Here's how the requisitioning process works (see Figure 2.4).

- *Secure Personal Log-in:* Each employee is given a secure personal log-in code that contains a user profile (for example, job title, expenditure limits). These profiles are used to customize the presentation so employees can order those catalog items they are authorized to purchase.

- *Browse Authorized Supplier Catalogs and Select Products:* Employees use search and browse capabilities to review multiple supplier catalogs. Only contracted products and prices are shown. Purchasing administrators can add details to steer employees to preferred products or to identify products that require approval before purchase.

---

[23] This section draws on Ravi Kalkota and Marcia Robinson, *e-Business: Roadmap for Success* (Reading, Mass.: Addison-Wesley, 1999), pp. 237–238.

- *Requisition/Order Creation:* Requisitions are created online and can include products from one or more suppliers.

- *Approval Routing:* Internal purchase controls ensure that employees cannot purchase restricted items or place orders beyond certain limits (for example, dollar amount per order). Once submitted, a requisition is routed for approval based on an organization's purchasing policies.

- *Order Submission/Fulfillment:* If more than one supplier is involved, the requisition is broken down into one purchase order per supplier and is automatically routed to each supplier.

- *Order Tracking and Receipt:* Employees are notified via e-mail of internal approval status, order acknowledgment from the supplier, shipment status, and delivery date.

Powered by software from Ariba, Motorola has used its global e-requisitioning system to reduce procurement costs and control indirect purchasing, yielding more than $300 million of cost savings in a recent year.[24]

Reverse Auctions

One online procurement tool that sparks debate in the business market is the reverse auction. Rather than one seller and many buyers, a **reverse auction** involves one buyer who invites bids from several prequalified suppliers who face off in a dynamic, real-time competitive bidding process. Reverse auctions are most widely used in the automobile, electronics, aerospace, and pharmaceutical industries. Proponents claim that reverse auctions can lower the cost of procuring products and services by 20 percent or more. A case in point: Cable television equipment manufacturer Scientific Atlanta saved 30 percent on the commodities it purchased through reverse auctions.[25] Critics counter that reverse auctions can inflict real damage on supplier relationships and that the realized savings are often overstated.[26] For example, during the recent economic downturn, many firms used reverse auctions as a tactical weapon to drive supplier prices down but often found that the winning bidder delivered less value—lower quality and poorer service than existing suppliers.

Reverse auctions are best suited for commodity-type items like purchasing materials, diesel fuel, metal parts, chemicals, and many raw materials. On the other hand, reverse auctions are generally *not* appropriate for strategic relationships, where suppliers have specialized capabilities and few suppliers can meet quality and performance standards. Rob Harlan, senior director of e-procurement for Motorola, aptly states: "We pride ourselves on strong supplier relationships. We are not going to jeopardize these for short-term gains with online auctions. You need to ensure the integrity of the bidding environment, educate suppliers on how best to compete, and clearly communicate your intentions and requirements."[27]

---

[24]James Carbone, "Motorola Leverages Its Way to Lower Cost," *Purchasing* 133 (September 16, 2004): pp. 31–38.

[25]James Carbone, "Reverse Auctions: Not Just a Cost-Reduction Tool," *Purchasing* 134 (February 17, 2005): pp. 43–44.

[26]Mohanbir Sawhney, "Forward Thinking About Reverse Auctions," June 1, 2003, Issue of *CIO Magazine*, accessed at http://www.cio.com, June 20, 2005, pp. 1–6.

[27]Tim A. Minahan, "Best Practices in E-Sourcing," p. 52.

ETHICAL BUSINESS MARKETING

Gift Giving: "Buy Me These Boots and You'll Get My Business"

Greg Davies, director of sales for Action Printing in Fond du Lac, Wisconsin, encountered this awkward situation. Leaving a restaurant after taking a potential customer to lunch, the prospective client stopped to examine the window display of a country-and-western store located nearby. That's when Davies's prospect turned to him and said very slowly: "I have always wanted a pair of boots like this." "There was no mistaking it: He expected me to buy him the boots," recalls Davies, who simply smiled and began walking again. He declined because company policy, as well as his personal value system, forbids the exchange of expensive personal gifts

for business. As you would imagine, from that day forward, Greg felt awkward around the prospect.

Sales experts suggest that Greg made the right business decision, as well as the right moral decision. He stood behind a well-conceived company policy. In turn, Jacques Werth, a sales consultant, agreed with the decision to walk away. "If your relationship is based on extravagant gifts, entertainment, and other perks, you're likely to lose the business when a bigger bribe comes along, anyway."

SOURCE: Melinda Ligos, "Gimme, Gimme, Gimme!" *Sales & Marketing Management* (March 2002), pp. 33–40.

How Organizational Buyers Evaluate Potential Suppliers

E-procurement systems provide purchasing managers with a rich information environment and a sophisticated set of analytical tools they can use to evaluate the performance of suppliers. Many criteria may be factored into a buyer's ultimate decision: quality, price, delivery reliability, company image, and capability. Buyer perceptions are critical. When products are perceived as highly standardized or commodity-like, price assumes special importance in the purchasing decision and the business marketer faces the intense competitive pressure that reverse auctions impose. On the other hand, when the value offerings of the business marketer are perceived as unique, other criteria dominate and the opportunity exists to develop a strategic relationship with the customer. At a fundamental level, customers in the business market are interested in the total capabilities of a supplier and how those capabilities can assist them in advancing their competitive position—now and in the future.

To this point, the discussion has centered on one sector of the business market—commercial enterprises—and the role the purchasing function assumes. Attention now turns to the government market.

Governments: Unique Characteristics

Federal (1), state (50), and local (87,000) **government units** generate the greatest volume of purchases of any customer category in the United States. Collectively, these units spend more than $1.7 trillion on goods and services each year—the federal government accounts for $590 billion, and states and local government account for the rest.[28]

---

[28] U.S. Department of Commerce, Bureau of the Census, *Statistical Abstract of the United States: 2001* (Washington, D.C., 2001), p. 260.

Governmental units purchase from virtually every category of goods and services—office supplies, personal computers, furniture, food, health care, and military equipment. Business marketing firms, large and small, serve the government market. In fact, 25 percent of the purchase contracts at the federal level are with small firms.[29]

E-Government

Across all levels of government, public officials are embracing the Internet as the best means of delivering services to constituents. E-government, then, involves transferring traditional government operations to an integrated Internet environment to improve public-sector accessibility, efficiency, and customer service. For example, www.govbenefits.com now provides users with access to information about 200 special government benefit programs, and www.recreation.gov provides a description of all publicly managed recreation sites in the United States. Many states, such as Texas, Arizona, Michigan, and Illinois, are launching creative e-government initiatives to deliver service to citizens. For business-marketing firms like IBM and Hewlett-Packard that sell information technology products and services, e-government initiatives are sparking a large market opportunity.

Influences on Government Buying

Another level of complexity is added to the governmental purchasing process by the array of influences on this process. In federal, state, and large city procurement, buyers report to and are influenced by dozens of interested parties who specify, legislate, evaluate, and use the goods and services. Clearly, the range of outside influences extends far beyond the originating agency.

Understanding Government Contracts

Government purchasing is also affected by goals and programs that have broad social overtones, including compliance, set-asides, and minority subcontracting. The **compliance program** requires government contractors to maintain affirmative action programs for minorities, women, and the handicapped. Firms failing to do so are barred from holding government contracts. In the **set-aside program,** a certain percentage of a given government contract is "set aside" for small or minority businesses; no others can participate in that proportion of the contract. The **minority subcontracting program** may require that major contractors subcontract a certain percentage of the total contract to minority firms. For example, Ohio law requires that 7 percent of all subcontractors on state construction projects be minorities. The potential government contractor must understand these programs and how they apply to the firm.

Most government procurement, at any level, is based on laws that establish contractual guidelines.[30] The federal government has set forth certain general contract provisions as part of the federal procurement regulations. These provisions include stipulations regarding product inspection, payment methods, actions as a result of default, and disputes, among many others.

---

[29] Stephanie N. Mehta, "Small Firms Are Getting More Government Contracts," *The Wall Street Journal*, April 27, 1995, p. B2.

[30] Michael R. Leenders and Harold E. Fearon, *Purchasing and Supply Management*, 11th ed. (Chicago: Irwin, 1997), pp. 537–566.

Without a clear comprehension of the procurement laws, the vendor is in an unfavorable position during the negotiation phase. The vendor particularly needs to explore the advantages and disadvantages of the two basic types of contracts:

1. **Fixed-price contracts.** A firm price is agreed to before the contract is awarded, and full payment is made when the product or service is delivered as agreed.

2. **Cost-reimbursement contracts.** The vendor is reimbursed for allowable costs incurred in performance of the contract and is sometimes allowed a certain number of dollars above cost as profit.

Each type of contract has built-in incentives to control costs or to cover future contingencies.

Generally, the fixed-price contract provides the greatest profit potential, but it also poses greater risks if unforeseen expenses are incurred, if inflation increases dramatically, or if conditions change. However, if the seller can reduce costs significantly during the contract, profits may exceed those estimated when the contract was negotiated. The government carefully administers cost-reimbursement contracts because of the minimal incentives for contractor efficiency. Contracts of this type are usually employed for government projects involving considerable developmental work for which it is difficult to estimate efforts and expenses.

To overcome the inefficiencies of both the cost-reimbursement contract (which often leads to cost overruns) and the fixed-price contract (which can discourage firms from bidding because project costs are uncertain), the government often employs incentive contracts. The incentive contract rewards firms when their actual costs on a project are below target costs, and it imposes a penalty when they exceed target costs.

Telling Vendors How to Sell: Useful Publications

Unlike most customers, governments often go to great lengths to explain to potential vendors exactly how to do business with them. For example, the federal government makes available such publications as *Doing Business with the General Services Administration*, *Selling to the Military*, and *Selling to the U.S. Air Force*. Government agencies also hold periodic seminars to orient businesses to the buying procedures the agency uses. The objective is to encourage firms to seek government business.

Purchasing Organizations and Procedures: Government

Government and commercial purchasing are organized similarly. However, governments tend to emphasize clerical functions because of the detailed procedures the law requires. Although the federal government is the largest single industrial purchaser, it does not operate like a single company but like a combination of several large companies with overlapping responsibilities and thousands of small independent units.[31] The federal government has more than 15,000 purchasing authorities (departments, agencies, and so on). Every government agency possesses some degree of buying influence or authority. Federal government procurement is divided into two categories: defense and nondefense.

[31] Ibid., pp. 552–559.

Defense Procurement   The Department of Defense (DOD) spends a large proportion of the federal government's total procurement budget. The DOD's procurement operation is said to be the largest business enterprise in the world. The era of declining budgets for the DOD was quickly reversed with the terrorist attacks on the United States in September 2001. Defense and homeland security became funding priorities in the federal budget.

Each DOD military division—Army, Navy, and Air Force—is responsible for its own major purchases. However, the Defense Logistics Agency (DLA) procures billions of dollars worth of supplies used in common by all branches. The DLA's budget for procurement exceeds $10 billion annually.[32] The purposes of the DLA are to obtain favorable prices through volume purchasing and to reduce duplication of purchasing within the military. Defense-related items may also be procured by other government agencies, such as the General Services Administration (GSA). In fact, the DOD is the GSA's largest customer. Under current agreements between the GSA and the DOD, the military purchases through the GSA many items such as cars, desks, office machines, and hand tools.[33] Also, many supplies for military-base operations are procured locally.

Nondefense Procurement   Nondefense procurement is administered by a wide variety of agencies, including cabinet departments (for example, Health and Human Services, Commerce), commissions (for example, the Federal Trade Commission), the executive branch (for example, the Bureau of the Budget), federal agencies (for example, the Federal Aviation Agency), and federal administrations (for example, the GSA). The Department of Commerce centralizes the procurement of supplies and equipment for its Washington office and all local offices. The Department of the Interior, on the other hand, instructs each area and district office of the Mining Enforcement and Safety Administration to purchase mine-safety equipment and clothing locally.

Like the DLA, the GSA centralizes the procurement of many general-use items (for example, office furniture, pens, lightbulbs) for all civilian government agencies. The Federal Supply Service of the GSA is like the purchasing department of a large diversified corporation because it provides a consolidated purchasing, storing, and distribution network for the federal government. The Federal Supply Service purchases many items commonly used by other government agencies, including office supplies, small tools, paint, paper, furniture, maintenance supplies, and duplicating equipment. In some cases, the GSA operates retail-like stores, where any federal buyer can go to purchase equipment and supplies. The GSA has enormous purchasing power, buying more than $18 billion of products and services annually.[34]

Under the Federal Supply Schedule Program, departments within the government may purchase specified items from an approved supplier at an agreed-on price. This program provides federal agencies with the sources of products such as furniture, appliances, office equipment, laboratory equipment, and the like. Once a supplier has bid and been approved, the schedule may involve an indefinite-quantity contract for a term of one to three years. The schedule permits agencies to place orders directly with suppliers. Like corporate purchasing units, the GSA is using the Internet to streamline purchasing processes and to facilitate communication with suppliers (see http://www.gsa.gov).

---

[32] Leslie Kaufman, "The Top Government Purchasers: Defense Logistics Agency—Supply Budget Bucks Downward Trend," *Government Executive* 26 (August 1994): p. 113.

[33] U.S. General Services Administration, "Doing Business with the GSA" (Washington, D.C., 1996).

[34] U.S. General Services Administration, "GSA FY 2003 Congressional Justification," http://www.gsa.gov, accessed July 24, 2002.

Federal Buying

The president may set the procurement process in motion when he signs a congressional appropriation bill, or an accountant in the General Accounting Office may initiate the process by requesting a new desktop computer. Business marketers can identify the current needs of government buyers by consulting *FedBizOpps (FBO)* at http://www.fbodaily.com. The *FBO*, published by the Department of Commerce, lists all government procurement proposals, subcontracting leads, contract awards, and sales of surplus property. A potential supplier has at least 30 days to respond before bid opening. By law, all intended procurement actions of $10,000 or more, both civilian and military, are published in the *FBO*. Copies of the *FBO* are available at various government field offices, as well as local public libraries.

Once a procurement need is documented and publicly announced, the government follows one of two general procurement strategies: formal advertising (also known as open bid) or negotiated contract.

Formal Advertising   **Formal advertising** means the government solicits bids from appropriate suppliers; usually, the lowest bidder is awarded the contract. This strategy is followed when the product is standardized and the specifications straightforward. The interested supplier must gain a place on a bidder's list (or monitor the *FBO* on a daily basis—which suggests that a more effective approach is to get on the bidder's list by filing forms available from the GSA Business Service Centers). Then, each time the government requests bids for a particular product, the supplier receives an invitation to bid. The invitation to bid specifies the item and the quantity to be purchased, provides detailed technical specifications, and stipulates delivery schedules, warranties required, packing requirements, and other purchasing details. The bidding firm bases its bid on its own cost structure and on the bids it believes its competitors might make.

Procurement personnel review each bid for conformance to specifications. Contracts are generally awarded to the lowest bidder; however, the government agency may select the next-to-lowest bidder if it can document that the lowest bidder would not responsibly fulfill the contract. For example, the Internal Revenue Service (IRS) held a reverse auction for 11,000 desktop PCs and 16,000 notebook PCs. The prebid pricing started at $130 million; when the auction closed, the price was down to $63.4 million.[35]

Negotiated Contract Buying   A negotiated contract is used to purchase products and services that cannot be differentiated on the basis of price alone (such as complex scientific equipment or R&D projects) or when there are few suppliers. There may be some competition because the contracting office can conduct negotiations with several suppliers simultaneously.

Obviously, negotiation is a much more flexible procurement procedure; the government buyers may exercise considerable personal judgment. Procurement is based on the more subjective factors of performance and quality, as well as on price. The procurement decision for the government is much like that of the large corporation: Which is the best possible product at the lowest price, and will the product meet performance standards?

---

[35] Richard Walker and Kevin McCaney, "Reverse Auctions Win Bid of Acceptance," *Buyers.Gov* (December 2001): p. 1.

FIGURE 2.5 | **THE JOINT STRIKE FIGHTER: LOCKHEED MARTIN'S WINNING DESIGN SELECTED BY THE DEPARTMENT OF DEFENSE**

SOURCE: Reprinted by permission of Lockheed Martin Corporation.

For example, Lockheed Martin Corporation emerged as the winner in a five-year battle with Boeing Company to manufacture the Joint Strike Fighter, an agile radar-evading aircraft intended to serve as the workhorse for the Army, Navy, and Marines. The competition included a fly-off where both firms demonstrated the performance of its plane. After this contest, the Pentagon conducted a thorough analysis of cost and performance data before picking Lockheed as the prime contractor for this lucrative contract—a project expected to total more than $200 billion and involve the production of 3,000 fighters over the next four decades[36] (Figure 2.5).

A Different Strategy Required

A marketer positioned to sell to the government has a much different marketing strategy focus than does a firm that concentrates on the commercial sector. The government seller emphasizes (1) understanding the complex rules and standards that must

---

[36]Laura M. Holson, "Pushing Limits; Finding None," *New York Times*, November 1, 2001, pp. C1, C6. See also, Leslie Wayne, "A New Workhorse's Heavy Load," *New York Times*, April 27, 2005, pp. C1, C3.

be met; (2) developing a system to keep informed of each agency's procurement plans; (3) generating a strategy for product development and R&D that facilitates the firm's response to government product needs; (4) developing a communications strategy that focuses on how technology meets agency objectives; and (5) generating a negotiation strategy to secure favorable terms regarding payment, contract completion, and cost overruns due to changes in product specifications.

The Institutional Market: Unique Characteristics

Institutional customers comprise the third sector of the business market. Institutional buyers make up a sizable market—total expenditures on public elementary and secondary schools alone exceed $640 billion, and national health expenditures exceed $1.3 trillion.[37] Schools and health-care organizations make up a sizable component of the institutional market, which also includes colleges and universities, libraries, foundations, art galleries, and clinics. On one hand, institutional purchasers are similar to governments in that the purchasing process is often constrained by political considerations and dictated by law. In fact, many institutions are administered by government units—schools, for example. On the other hand, other institutions are privately operated and managed like corporations; they may even have a broader range of purchase requirements than their large corporate counterparts. Like the commercial enterprise, institutions are ever cognizant of the value of efficient purchasing.

Institutional Buyers: Purchasing Procedures

Diversity is the key element in the institutional market. For example, the institutional marketing manager must first be ready to respond to a school purchasing agent who buys in great quantity for an entire city's school system through a formal bidding procedure, and then respond to a former pharmacist who has been elevated to purchasing agent for a small rural hospital.

Health-care institutions provide a good example of the diversity of this market. Some small hospitals delegate responsibility for food purchasing to the chief dietitian. Although many of these hospitals have purchasing agents, the agent cannot place an order unless the dietitian approves it. In larger hospitals, decisions may be made by committees composed of a business manager, purchasing agent, dietitian, and cook. In still other cases, hospitals may belong to buying groups consisting of many local hospitals or meal preparation may be contracted out. In an effort to contain costs, purchasing executives at large hospitals are adopting a supply chain focus and using sophisticated supplier evaluation methods, including e-procurement tools, like their counterparts in the commercial sector. Because of these varied purchasing environments, successful marketers usually maintain a separate marketing manager, staff, and sales force to tailor marketing efforts to each situation.

For many institutions, once a department's budget has been established, the department attempts to spend up to that budget limit. Thus, institutions may buy

---

[37] U.S. Department of Commerce, Bureau of the Census, *Statistical Abstract of the United States: 2001* (Washington, D.C., 2001), pp. 91, 133.

simply because there are unused funds in the budget. A business marketer should carefully evaluate the budgetary status of potential customers in the institutional segment of the market.

Because many institutions face strong budgetary pressures, they often outsource segments of their operations to specialists to enhance efficiency and effectiveness. School districts may look to third-party contractors to purchase food and supplies and to manage their meal service operations. For example, in Los Angeles, Marriott Corporation manages food service operations at the city's charter schools, and in Chicago, three different contract companies each operate 10 food-preparation departments.[38] Many universities have turned over operation of their bookstores, beverage contracts, and management of their student unions to outside contractors. Business marketers must carefully analyze and understand the operational strategy of their institutional customers. Frequently, extensive sales and marketing attention must center on the third-party contract operators.

Targeted Strategy   The institutional market offers some unique applications for the concept of multiple buying influences (discussed in Chapter 1). Many institutions are staffed with professionals—doctors, professors, researchers, and others. In most cases, depending on size, the institution employs a purchasing agent and, in large institutions, a sizable and skilled purchasing department or materials management department. There is great potential for conflict between those responsible for purchasing and the professional staff for whom the purchasing department is buying. Often, the salesperson must carefully cultivate the professional staff in terms of product benefits and service while developing a delivery timetable, maintenance contract, and price schedule to satisfy the purchasing department. Leading business marketers also use the Internet to provide added value to their customers. For example, General Electric Medical Systems has embraced e-commerce as the centerpiece of its marketing strategy and provides an online catalog, daily Internet specials, and a host of services for its customers—purchasing managers at hospitals and health-care facilities worldwide (Figure 2.6).

Group Purchasing   An important factor in institutional purchasing is group purchasing. Hospitals, schools, and universities may join cooperative purchasing associations to obtain quantity discounts. Universities affiliated with the Education and Institutional Purchasing Cooperative enjoy favorable contracts established by the cooperative and can purchase a wide array of products directly from vendors at the low negotiated prices. The cooperative spends more than $100 million on goods annually. Cooperative buying allows institutions to enjoy lower prices, improved quality (through improved testing and vendor selection), reduced administrative cost, standardization, better records, and greater competition.

Hospital group purchasing represents a significant market exceeding $10 billion. Group purchasing has become widely accepted: More than one-third of public-sector hospitals in the United States are members of some type of affiliated group. Most hospital group purchasing is done at the regional level through hospital associations. However, for-profit hospital chains, which are a growing factor in the health-care field, also engage in group buying. For example, a multihospital system with a $1 billion operating budget spends $300 to $500 million a year on medical supplies and

---

[38] Susie Stephenson, "Schools," *Restaurants and Institutions* 106 (August 1, 1996): pp. 60–64.

FIGURE 2.6 | **GE MEDICAL SYSTEMS USES THE INTERNET TO MANAGE RELATIONSHIPS WITH ITS CUSTOMERS**

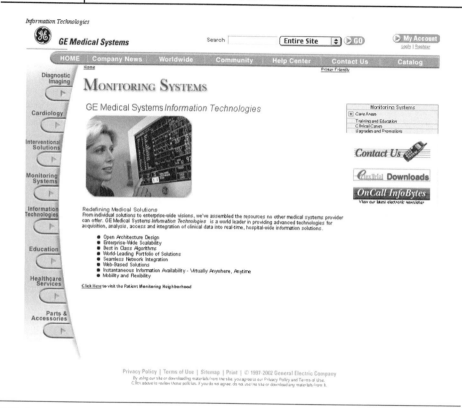

SOURCE: Reprinted by permission of General Electric.

purchased services. By channeling purchases through group purchasing organizations, these large buyers are reaping significant savings.[39]

Group purchasing poses special challenges for the business marketer. The marketer must develop not only strategies for dealing with individual institutions but also unique strategies for the special requirements of cooperative purchasing groups and large hospital chains. The buying centers—individual institution versus cooperative purchasing group—may vary considerably in composition, criteria, and level of expertise. For the purchasing groups, discount pricing assumes special importance. Suppliers who sell through purchasing groups must also have distribution systems that effectively deliver products to individual group members. And even though vendors have a contract with a large cooperative association, they must still be prepared to respond individually to each institution that places an order against the contract.

Institutional Purchasing Practices   In many respects the purchasing practices of large institutions are similar to those of large commercial firms, but there are some important differences. The policies regarding cooperative buying, preference to local vendors, and the delegation of purchasing responsibility for food, pharmaceuticals, and

---

[39]Timothy L. Chapman, Ajay Gupta, and Paul O. Mange, "Group Purchasing Is Not a Panacea for U.S. Hospitals," *McKinsey Quarterly*, no. 1 (1998): p. 160.

FIGURE 2.7 | **A MARKET-CENTERED ORGANIZATION**

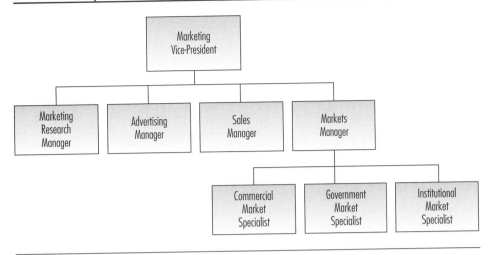

many other items are of particular importance. The business marketer must understand these characteristics to carefully develop effective strategies for these institutional customers.

Dealing with Diversity: A Market-Centered Organization

Because each sector of the business market is unique, many firms have built market specialization into the marketing organization. To illustrate, the industrial products area of the J. M. Smucker Company is organized around market sectors. The institutional, military, and business markets are each managed by different individuals, each thoroughly knowledgeable about one particular market.

Figure 2.7 illustrates one form of a market-centered organizational scheme. Observe that a market manager supervises and coordinates the activities of three market specialists. Each market specialist examines the buying processes, the product preferences, and the similarities and differences between customers in one sector of the business market. Such an analysis enables the market specialist to further categorize customers in a particular sector into meaningful market segments and to design specialized marketing programs for each. A market-centered organization provides the business marketer with a structure for dealing effectively with diversity in the business market.

Summary

In business-to-business marketing, the customers are organizations. The business market can be divided into three major sectors: commercial enterprises, governments (federal, state, and local), and institutions. Many business marketers—for example, Intel, Boeing, and IBM—generate a significant proportion of their sales and profit by serving international customers. Indeed, the demand for many industrial products is growing more rapidly in many foreign countries than in the United States.

Commercial enterprises include manufacturers, construction companies, service firms, transportation companies, selected professional groups, and resellers. Of these, manufacturers account for the largest dollar volume of purchases. Furthermore, although the majority of manufacturing firms are small, buying power is concentrated in the hands of relatively few manufacturers, which are also concentrated geographically.

Commercial enterprises, such as service establishments and transportation or utility companies, are more widely dispersed. A purchasing manager or purchasing agent administers the procurement process. In large firms, the purchasing function has been quite specialized. In addition to protecting the cost structure of the firm, improving quality, and keeping inventory investment to a minimum, purchasing assumes a central role in managing relationships with suppliers. In turn, leading-edge organizations like Dell Computer demonstrate the critical role that purchasing and supply chain management can assume in creating profit opportunities. Rather than devoting exclusive attention to "buying for less," leading organizations tie purchasing activities directly to corporate strategy and use a range of sophisticated e-procurement tools.

Governmental units also make substantial purchases of products. Government buyers use two general purchasing strategies: the formal advertising approach for standardized products and negotiated contracts for those with unique requirements. Institutional customers, such as health-care organizations and universities, comprise the third sector of the business market. Depending on size, the institution employs a purchasing agent and, in large institutions, a sizable purchasing department. Across business market sectors, purchasing managers are using the Internet to identify potential suppliers, conduct online reverse auctions, and communicate with suppliers.

Diversity is the characteristic that typifies the institutional market. The characteristics, orientations, and purchasing processes of institutional buyers are somewhere between commercial enterprises and government buyers. Cooperative purchasing—a unique aspect of this segment—necessitates a special strategic response by potential suppliers. Many business marketers have found that a market-centered organization provides the specialization required to meet the needs of each market sector.

Discussion Questions

1. A small manufacturer developed a new high-speed packaging system that could be appealing to food-processing firms like Pillsbury and General Mills. This new packaging system is far more efficient but must be priced 15 percent higher than competitors' products. Because purchasing managers evaluate the "total cost of ownership" of major purchases, what selling points should the business marketer emphasize to demonstrate the superiority of this new product?

2. Honda of America relies on 400 suppliers in North America to provide more than 60 percent of the parts and materials for the Accord. What strategies could a business marketer follow in becoming a new supplier to Honda? What criteria would Honda consider in evaluating suppliers?

3. Describe the total-cost-of-ownership orientation that purchasing managers use and illustrate how you could apply it to your next automobile purchase decision.

4. Segmentation is a tool that marketers use to identify target markets. Increasingly, purchasing managers are using the segmentation approach to determine which suppliers are most critical to the goals of the organization. Explain.

5. Compare and contrast the two general procurement strategies employed by the federal government: (1) formal advertising and (2) negotiated contract.

6. Institutional buyers fall somewhere between commercial enterprises and government buyers in terms of their characteristics, orientation, and purchasing process. Explain.

7. Explain how the decision-making process that a university might employ in selecting a new computer would differ from that of a commercial enterprise. Who would be the key participants in the process in each setting?

8. Fearing red tape and mounds of paperwork, Tom Bronson, president of B&E Electric, has always avoided the government market. A recent discussion with a colleague, however, has rekindled Tom's interest in this sector. What steps should B&E Electric take to learn more about this market?

9. General Electric (GE) has embraced e-purchasing and has saved more than $500 million per year by conducting online reverse auctions in buying a range of goods including office, computer, and maintenance supplies. What new challenges and opportunities does this auctioning process present for business marketers who serve GE?

10. One purchasing executive observed, "Online auctioning is an appropriate way to buy some categories of products and services but it's entirely inappropriate for others." Agree or disagree? Provide support for your position.

Internet Exercises

1. GE Medical Systems has developed an e-commerce initiative to support its marketing strategy, which targets health-care organizations on a worldwide basis. Go to http://www.gemedicalsystems.com and
   a. identify the products and services that the GE unit offers, and
   b. provide a critique of the Web site and consider the degree to which it provides access to the information that a potential buyer might want.

2. Ariba, Inc., is a leading provider of e-procurement software solutions. Go to http://www.ariba.com and
   a. describe the key products and services that the firm offers to its customers, and
   b. review a case history that describes a particular customer and how they have applied one of Ariba's procurement solutions.

CASE

Managing Supplier Relationships: Does Detroit Need a New Driver?[40]

The rising prices of materials from steel to plastics, the difficulty of protecting intellectual property, and intense global competition are all causing friction between buyers and suppliers in the auto industry around the world. However, a recent study suggests that purchasing–supplier tensions are particularly acute at the Big Three automakers: General Motors, Ford, and DaimlerChrysler.

Planning Perspectives, Inc., a Michigan-based automotive consulting firm, annually surveys the top 200 suppliers to the automobile industry and asks them to rate the automakers on 17 criteria related to their ability to develop relationships (for example, assistance they provide to suppliers, their willingness to collaborate in growth opportunities). Based on these ratings, an automaker–supplier working relation index score is calculated for each firm: a score of 500 is very good; zero is very poor. The results are quite revealing. The automakers rated the highest were Toyota and Honda with scores of 399 and 384, respectively, in 2004. By contrast, the scores of Daimler-Chrysler, Ford, and GM were all well below 200—at 183, 160, and 144, respectively.

John W. Henke Jr., president of Planning Perspectives, observes that the study shows that the U.S. automakers' primary orientation is toward cost reductions and that they generally treat suppliers as adversaries rather than as trusted partners. By contrast, "buyers at Honda and Toyota expect a supplier to be around for life and they don't hammer for price reductions . . . but rather expect a 2–2.5 percent savings from productivity improvements. The Big Three's constant hammering suggests that they are not selecting the right suppliers or they are using the wrong criteria for selecting suppliers."

Discussion Questions

1. What are the short-term and long-term benefits or consequences of the purchasing strategies of the Big Three versus their Japanese rivals?

2. In your view, what criteria should Ford or GM use in selecting suppliers, and what steps should they take to strengthen their relationship with their suppliers and with their present and potential customers?

---

[40] Mike Verespej, "Supplier Relations: Detroit Needs a New Driver," *Purchasing* 134 (April 7, 2005): pp. 38–42.

PART

II

MANAGING RELATIONSHIPS IN BUSINESS MARKETING

Organizational Buying Behavior

A wide array of forces inside and outside the organization influence the organizational buyer. Knowledge of these forces provides the marketer with a foundation for responsive business marketing strategies. After reading this chapter, you will understand:

1. the decision process organizational buyers apply as they confront differing buying situations and the resulting strategy implications for the business marketer.

2. the individual, group, organizational, and environmental variables that influence organizational buying decisions.

3. a model of organizational buying behavior that integrates these important influences.

4. how a knowledge of organizational buying characteristics enables the marketer to make more informed decisions about product design, pricing, and promotion.

FIGURE 3.1   **JOHNSON CONTROLS RESEARCHES THE PREFERENCES OF AUTO BUYERS—THE CUSTOMER'S CUSTOMER!**

SOURCE: Reprinted by permission of Johnson Controls.

Market-driven business firms continuously sense and act on trends in their markets. Consider Johnson Controls, Inc., a diverse, multi-industry company that is a leading supplier of auto interiors (including seats, electronics, headliners, and instrument panels) to manufacturers.[1] The striking success of the firm rests on the close relationships that its sales reps and marketing managers have formed with design engineers and purchasing executives in the auto industry. To illustrate, some of Johnson Controls' salespersons work onsite with design teams at Ford, GM, or Honda. To provide added value to the new-product-design process, the firm also invests annually in market research on the needs and preferences of auto buyers—the customer's customer! For example, based on extensive research about how families spend their time in cars, Johnson Controls developed the AutoVision rear seat entertainment system that allows passengers to play video games, watch DVDs, or listen to CDs through wireless headphones or the vehicle's speaker system (Figure 3.1). By staying close to the needs of auto buyers, Johnson Controls became the preferred supplier to design engineers who are continually seeking innovative ways to make auto interiors more distinctive and inviting.

Understanding the dynamics of organizational buying behavior is crucial for identifying profitable market segments, locating buying influences within these segments, and

---

[1] "AutoVision Family Grade Entertainment Systems," http://www.johnsoncontrols.com, accessed June 28, 2005.

FIGURE 3.2 | MAJOR STAGES OF THE ORGANIZATIONAL BUYING PROCESS

Stage	Description
1. Problem Recognition	Managers at P&G need new high-speed packaging equipment to support a new product launch.
2. General Description of Need	Production managers work with a purchasing manager to determine the characteristics needed in the new packaging system.
3. Product Specifications	An experienced production manager assists a purchasing manager in developing a detailed and precise description of the needed equipment.
4. Supplier Search	After conferring with production managers, a purchasing manager identifies a set of alternative suppliers that could satisfy P&G's requirements.
5. Acquisition and Analysis of Proposals	Alternative proposals are evaluated by a purchasing manager and a number of members of the production department.
6. Supplier Selection	Negotiations with the two finalists are conducted, and a supplier is chosen.
7. Selection of Order Routine	A delivery date is established for the production equipment.
8. Performance Review	After equipment is installed, purchasing and production managers evaluate the performance of the equipment and the service support provided by the supplier.

reaching organizational buyers efficiently and effectively with an offering that responds to their needs. Each decision the business marketer makes is based on organizational buyers' probable response. This chapter explores the key stages of the organizational buying process and isolates the salient characteristics of different purchasing situations. Next, attention turns to the myriad forces that influence organizational buying behavior. Knowledge of how organizational buying decisions are made provides the business marketer with a solid foundation for building responsive marketing strategies.

The Organizational Buying Process

Organizational buying behavior is a process, not an isolated act or event. Tracing the history of a procurement decision uncovers critical decision points and evolving information requirements. In fact, organizational buying involves several stages, each of which yields a decision. Figure 3.2 lists the major stages in the organizational buying process.[2]

---

[2] The discussion in this section is based on Patrick J. Robinson, Charles W. Faris, and Yoram Wind, *Industrial Buying and Creative Marketing* (Boston: Allyn and Bacon, 1967), pp. 12–18; see also Frederick E. Webster Jr. and Kevin Lane Keller, "A Roadmap for Branding in Industrial Markets," *Journal of Brand Management* 11 (May 2004): pp. 388–402; and Morry Ghingold and David T. Wilson, "Buying Center Research and Business Marketing Practice: Meeting the Challenge of Dynamic Marketing," *Journal of Business & Industrial Marketing*, 13, no. 2 (1998): pp. 96–108.

The purchasing process begins when someone in the organization recognizes a problem that can be solved or an opportunity that can be captured by acquiring a specific product. Problem recognition can be triggered by internal or external forces. Internally, a firm like P&G may need new high-speed production equipment to support a new product launch. Or a purchasing manager may be unhappy with the price or service of an equipment supplier. Externally, a salesperson can precipitate the need for a product by demonstrating opportunities for improving the organization's performance. Likewise, business marketers also use advertising to alert customers to problems and demonstrate how a particular product may solve them.

During the organizational buying process, many small or incremental decisions are made that ultimately translate into the final choice of a supplier. To illustrate, a production manager might unknowingly establish specifications for a new production system that only one supplier can meet (Stages 2 and 3). This type of decision early in the buying process dramatically influences the favorable evaluation and ultimate selection of that supplier.

The Search Process

Once the organization has defined the product that meets its requirements, attention turns to this question: Which of the many possible suppliers are promising candidates? The organization invests more time and energy in the supplier search when the proposed product has a strong bearing on organizational performance. When the information needs of the buying organization are low, Stages 4 and 5 occur simultaneously, especially for standardized items. In this case, a purchasing manager may merely check a catalog or secure an updated price from the Internet. Stage 5 emerges as a distinct category only when the information needs of the organization are high. Here, the process of acquiring and analyzing proposals may involve purchasing managers, engineers, users, and other organizational members.

Supplier Selection and Performance Review   After being selected as a chosen supplier (Stage 6) and agreeing to purchasing guidelines (Stage 7), such as required quantities and expected time of delivery, a marketer faces further tests. A performance review is the final stage in the purchasing process. The performance review may lead the purchasing manager to continue, modify, or cancel the agreement. A review critical of the chosen supplier and supportive of rejected alternatives can lead members of the decision-making unit to reexamine their position. If the product fails to meet the needs of the using department, decision makers may give further consideration to vendors screened earlier in the procurement process. To keep a new customer, the marketer must ensure that the buying organization's needs have been completely satisfied. Failure to follow through at this critical stage leaves the marketer vulnerable.

The stages in this model of the procurement process may not progress sequentially, and may vary with the complexity of the purchasing situation. For example, some of the stages are compressed or bypassed when organizations make routine buying decisions. However, the model provides important insights into the organizational buying process. Certain stages may be completed concurrently; the process may be discontinued by a change in the external environment or in upper-management thinking. The organizational buying process is shaped by a host of internal and external forces such as changes in economic or competitive conditions or a basic shift in organizational priorities.

Organizations with significant experience in purchasing a particular product approach the decision quite differently than first-time buyers. Therefore, attention must center on buying situations rather than on products. Three types of buying situations have been delineated: (1) new task, (2) modified rebuy, and (3) straight rebuy.[3]

New Task

In the **new-task buying situation,** organization decisions makers perceive the problem or need as totally different from previous experiences; therefore, they need a significant amount of information to explore alternative ways of solving the problem and search for alternative suppliers.

When confronting a new-task buying situation, organizational buyers operate in a stage of decision making referred to as **extensive problem solving.**[4] The buying influentials and decision makers lack well-defined criteria for comparing alternative products and suppliers, but they also lack strong predispositions toward a particular solution. In the consumer market, this is the same type of problem solving an individual or household might follow when buying a first home.

Buying Decision Approaches[5]   Two distinct buying decision approaches are used: judgmental new task and strategic new task. The greatest level of uncertainty confronts firms in **judgmental new task situations** because the product may be technically complex, evaluating alternatives is difficult, and dealing with a new suppliers has unpredictable aspects. Consider purchasers of a special type of production equipment who are uncertain about the model or brand to choose, the suitable level of quality, and the appropriate price to pay. For such purchases, buying activities include a moderate amount of information search and a moderate use of formal tools in evaluating key aspects of the buying decision.

Even more effort is invested in **strategic new task decisions.** These purchasing decisions are of extreme importance to the firm strategically and financially. If the buyer perceives that a rapid pace of technological change surrounds the decision, search effort is increased but concentrated in a shorter time period.[6] Long-range planning drives the decision process. To illustrate, a large health insurance company placed a $600,000 order for workstation furniture. The long-term effect on the work environment shaped the six-month decision process and involved the active participation of personnel from several departments.

---

[3] Robinson, Faris, and Wind, *Industrial Buying and Creative Marketing*, chap. 1; see also Erin Anderson, Wujin Chu, and Barton Weitz, "Industrial Purchasing: An Empirical Exploration of the Buyclass Framework," *Journal of Marketing* 51 (July 1987): pp. 71–86; and Morry Ghingold, "Testing the 'Buygrid' Buying Process Model," *Journal of Purchasing and Materials Management* 22 (winter 1986): pp. 30–36.

[4] The levels of decision making discussed in this section are drawn from John A. Howard and Jagdish N. Sheth, *The Theory of Buyer Behavior* (New York: John Wiley and Sons, 1969), chap. 2.

[5] The discussion of buying decision approaches in this section is drawn from Michele D. Bunn, "Taxonomy of Buying Decision Approaches," *Journal of Marketing* 57 (January 1993): pp. 38–56; see also, Michele D. Bunn, Gul T. Butaney, and Nicole P. Huffman, "An Empirical Model of Professional Buyers' Search Effort," *Journal of Business-to-Business Marketing* 8, no. 4 (2001): pp. 55–81.

[6] Allen M. Weiss and Jan B. Heide, "The Nature of Organizational Search in High Technology Markets," *Journal of Marketing Research* 30 (May 1993): pp. 230–233. See also, Christian Homburg and Sabine Kuester, "Towards an Improved Understanding of Industrial Buying Behavior: Determinants of the Number of Suppliers," *Journal of Business-to-Business Marketing* 8, no. 2 (2001): pp. 5–29.

Strategy Guidelines   The business marketer confronting a new-task buying situation can gain a differential advantage by participating actively in the initial stages of the procurement process. The marketer should gather information on the problems facing the buying organization, isolate specific requirements, and offer proposals to meet the requirements. Ideas that lead to new products often originate not with the marketer but with the customer.

Marketers who are presently supplying other items to the organization ("in" suppliers) have an edge over other firms: They can see problems unfolding and are familiar with the "personality" and behavior patterns of the organization. The successful business marketer carefully monitors the changing needs of organizations and is prepared to assist new-task buyers.

Straight Rebuy

When there is a continuing or recurring requirement, buyers have substantial experience in dealing with the need and require little or no new information. Evaluation of new alternative solutions is unnecessary and unlikely to yield appreciable improvements. Thus, a **straight rebuy** approach is appropriate.

Routine problem solving is the decision process organizational buyers employ in the straight rebuy. Organizational buyers apply well-developed choice criteria to the purchase decision. The criteria have been refined over time as the buyers have developed predispositions toward the offerings of one or a few carefully screened suppliers. In the consumer market, this is the same type of problem solving that a shopper might use in selecting 30 items in 20 minutes during a weekly trip to the supermarket. Indeed, many organizational buying decisions made each day are routine. For example, organizations of all types are continually buying **operating resources**—the goods and services needed to run the business, such as computer and office supplies, maintenance and repair items, and travel services. Procter & Gamble alone spends more than $5 billion annually on operating resources.[7]

Buying Decision Approaches   Research suggests that organizational buyers employ two buying decision approaches: causal and routine low priority. **Causal purchases** involve no information search or analysis and the product or service is of minor importance. The focus is simply in transmitting the order. In contrast, **routine low priority** decisions are somewhat more important to the firm and involve a moderate amount of analysis. Describing the purchase of $5,000 worth of cable to be used as component material, a buyer aptly describes this decision process approach:

> On repeat buys, we may look at other sources or alternate methods of manufacturing, etc. to make sure no new technical advancements are available in the marketplace. But, generally, a repeat buy is repurchased from the supplier originally selected, especially for low dollar items.

Strategy Guidelines   The purchasing department handles straight rebuy situations by routinely selecting a supplier from a list of approved vendors and then placing an order. As organizations shift to e-procurement systems, purchasing managers retain

---

[7] Doug Smock, "Strategic Sourcing: P&G Boosts Leverage," *Purchasing* 133 (November 4, 2004): pp. 40–43.

control of the process for these routine purchases while allowing individual employees to directly buy online from approved suppliers.[8] Employees use a simple point-and-click interface to navigate through a customized catalog detailing the offerings of approved suppliers, and then order required items. Individual employees like the self-service convenience, and purchasing managers can direct attention to more critical strategic issues. Marketing communications should be designed to reach not only purchasing managers but also individual employees who are now empowered to exercise their product preferences.

The marketing task appropriate for the straight rebuy situation depends on whether the marketer is an "in" supplier (on the list) or an "out" supplier (not among the chosen few). An "in" supplier must reinforce the buyer-seller relationship, meet the buying organization's expectations, and be alert and responsive to the changing needs of the organization.

The "out" supplier faces a number of obstacles and must convince the organization that it can derive significant benefits from breaking the routine. This can be difficult because organizational buyers perceive risk in shifting from the known to the unknown. The organizational spotlight shines directly on them if an untested supplier falters. Buyers may view testing, evaluations, and approvals as costly, time-consuming, and unnecessary.

The marketing effort of the "out" supplier rests on an understanding of the basic buying needs of the organization: Information gathering is essential. The marketer must convince organizational buyers that their purchasing requirements have changed or that the requirements should be interpreted differently. The objective is to persuade decision makers to reexamine alternative solutions and revise the preferred list to include the new supplier.

Modified Rebuy

In the **modified rebuy** situation, organizational decision makers feel they can derive significant benefits by reevaluating alternatives. The buyers have experience in satisfying the continuing or recurring requirement, but they believe it worthwhile to seek additional information, and perhaps to consider alternative solutions.

Several factors may trigger such a reassessment. Internal forces include the search for quality improvements or cost reductions. A marketer offering cost, quality, or service improvements can be an external precipitating force. The modified rebuy situation is most likely to occur when the firm is displeased with the performance of present suppliers (for example, poor delivery service).

Limited problem solving best describes the decision-making process for the modified rebuy. Decision makers have well-defined criteria but are uncertain about which suppliers can best fit their needs. In the consumer market, college students buying their *second* computer might follow a limited problem-solving approach.

Buying Decision Approaches   Two buying-decision approaches typify this buying-class category. Both strongly emphasize the firm's strategic objectives and long-term needs. The **simple modified rebuy** involves a narrow set of choice alternatives

---

[8]Talai Osmonbekov, Daniel C. Bello, and David I Gillilard, "Adoption of Electronic Commerce Tools in Business Procurement: Enhanced Buying Center Structure and Processes," *Journal of Business & Industrial Marketing* 17, no. 2/3 (2002): pp. 151–166.

and a moderate amount of both information search and analysis. Buyers concentrate on the long-term relationship potential of suppliers.

The **complex modified rebuy** involves a large set of choice alternatives and poses little uncertainty. The range of choice enhances the buyer's negotiating strength. The importance of the decision motivates buyers to actively search for information, apply sophisticated analysis techniques, and carefully consider long-term needs. This decision situation is particularly well suited to a competitive bidding process. For example, some firms are turning to online reverse auctions (one buyer, many sellers), where the buying organization allows multiple suppliers to bid on a contract, exerting downward price pressure throughout the process. To participate, suppliers must be prepared to meet defined product characteristics, as well as quality and service standards. "And while price will always be an issue, more buyers today use reverse auctions to determine the best value."[9] Rather than for specialized products or services where a close working relationship with the supplier is needed, auctions tend to be used for commodities and standardized parts.

Strategy Guidelines   In a modified rebuy, the direction of the marketing effort depends on whether the marketer is an "in" or an "out" supplier. An "in" supplier should make every effort to understand and satisfy the procurement need and to move decision makers into a straight rebuy. The buying organization perceives potential payoffs by reexamining alternatives. The "in" supplier should ask why and act immediately to remedy any customer problems. The marketer may be out of touch with the buying organization's requirements.

The goal of the "out" supplier should be to hold the organization in modified rebuy status long enough for the buyer to evaluate an alternative offering. Knowing the factors that led decision makers to reexamine alternatives could be pivotal. A particularly effective strategy for an "out" supplier is to offer performance guarantees as part of the proposal.[10] To illustrate, the following guarantee prompted International Circuit Technology, a manufacturer of printed circuit boards, to change to a new supplier for plating chemicals: "Your plating costs will be no more than x cents per square foot or we will make up the difference."[11] Given the nature of the production process, plating costs can be easily monitored by comparing the square footage of circuit boards moving down the plating line with the cost of plating chemicals for the period. Pleased with the performance, International Circuit Technology now routinely reorders from this new supplier.

Strategy Implications   Although past research provides some useful guidelines, marketers must exercise great care in forecasting the likely composition of the buying center for a particular purchasing situation.[12] The business marketer should attempt to identify purchasing patterns that apply to the firm. For example, the classes of industrial goods introduced in Chapter 1 (such as foundation goods versus facilitating goods) involve varying degrees of technical complexity and financial risk for the buying organization.

The business marketer must therefore view the procurement problem or need from the buying organization's perspective. How far has the organization progressed with the

---

[9] James Carbone, "Not Just a Cost Reduction Tool," *Purchasing* 134 (February 17, 2005): p. 43.

[10] Mary Siegfried Dozbaba, "Critical Supplier Relationships: Converting Higher Performance," *Purchasing Today* (February 1999): pp. 22–29.

[11] Somerby Dowst, "CEO Report: Wanted: Suppliers Adept at Turning Corners," *Purchasing* 101 (January 29, 1987): pp. 71–72.

[12] Donald W. Jackson Jr., Janet E. Keith, and Richard K. Burdick, "Purchasing Agents' Perceptions of Industrial Buying Center Influence," *Journal of Marketing* 48 (fall 1984): pp. 75–83.

FIGURE 3.3 | FORCES INFLUENCING ORGANIZATIONAL BUYING BEHAVIOR

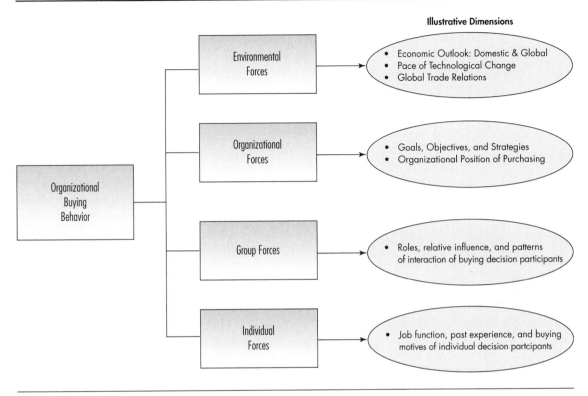

specific purchasing problem? How does the organization define the task at hand? How important is the purchase? The answers direct and form the business marketer's response and also provide insight into the composition of the decision-making unit.

Forces Shaping Organizational Buying Behavior

The eight-stage model of the organizational buying process provides the foundation for exploring the myriad forces that influence a buying decision by an organization. Observe in Figure 3.3 how organizational buying behavior is influenced by environmental forces (for example, the growth rate of the economy); organizational forces (for example, the size of the buying organization); group forces (for example, patterns of influence in buying decisions); and individual forces (for example, personal preferences).

Environmental Forces

A projected change in business conditions, a technological development, or a new piece of legislation can drastically alter organizational buying plans. Among the environmental forces that shape organizational buying behavior are economic, political, legal, and technological influences. Collectively, such environmental influences define the boundaries within which buyer-seller relationships develop. Particular attention is given to selected economic and technological forces that influence buying decisions.

Economic Influences   Because of the derived nature of industrial demand, the marketer must be sensitive to the strength of demand in the ultimate consumer market. The demand for many industrial products fluctuates more widely than the general economy. Firms that operate on a global scale must be sensitive to the economic conditions that prevail across regions. For example, as the U.S. economy moves out of a recession, the European or Asian economy may continue to sputter. A wealth of political and economic forces dictate the vitality and growth of an economy. A recent study found that the number of North American companies purchasing goods and services from China, eastern Europe, and India has increased sharply in recent years and will continue to rise. For example, by 2009, more than 70 percent of companies plan to source from China.[13]

The economic environment influences an organization's ability and, to a degree, its willingness to buy. However, shifts in general economic conditions do not affect all sectors of the market evenly. For example, a rise in interest rates may damage the housing industry (including lumber, cement, and insulation) but may have minimal effects on industries such as paper, hospital supplies, office products, and soft drinks. Marketers that serve broad sectors of the organizational market must be particularly sensitive to the differential effect of selective economic shifts on buying behavior.

Technological Influences   Rapidly changing technology can restructure an industry and dramatically alter organizational buying plans. Notably, the World Wide Web "has forever changed the way companies and customers (whether they be consumers or other businesses) buy and sell to each other, learn about each other, and communicate."[14]

The rate of technological change in an industry influences the composition of the decision-making unit in the buying organization. As the pace of technological change increases, the importance of the purchasing manager in the buying process declines. Technical and engineering personnel tend to be more important when the rate of technological change is great. Recent research also suggests that buyers who perceive the pace of technological change to be more rapid (1) conduct more intense search efforts and (2) spend less time on their overall search processes.[15] Allen Weiss and Jan Heide suggest that "in cost-benefit terms, a fast pace of change implies that distinct benefits are associated with search effort, yet costs are associated with prolonging the process" because the acquired information is "time sensitive."[16]

The marketer must also actively monitor signs of technological change and be prepared to adapt marketing strategy to deal with new technological environments. For example, Hewlett-Packard has embraced the Internet in its products, services, practices, and marketing. With search engines, spam filters, iPods, and other technologies, customers now have more control of the information they receive than ever before, notes Scott Anderson, director of enterprise brand communication at Hewlett-Packard. In

---

[13]"Global Procurement Study Finds Companies Unprepared to Manage Increased Sourcing from China and India Effectively," http://www.atkearney.com, accessed May 18, 2005.

[14]Stewart Alsop, "e or Be Eaten," *Fortune*, November 8, 1999, p. 87.

[15]Weiss and Heide, "The Nature of Organizational Search," pp. 220–233; see also Jan B. Heide and Allen M. Weiss, "Vendor Consideration and Switching Behavior for Buyers in High-Technology Markets," *Journal of Marketing* 59 (July 1995): pp. 30–43.

[16]Weiss and Heide, "The Nature of Organizational Search," p. 221.

INSIDE BUSINESS MARKETING

Pressuring Suppliers to Outsource

Facing intense competition, U.S. automakers are pressuring their North American suppliers to match the best prices for component parts that can be found anywhere in the world. Often, suppliers in low-cost countries, like China or India, offer cost savings of 20 to 40 percent on selected items. For example, Ford and General Motors use Chinese auto-parts suppliers as the benchmark for prices on certain components such as radios, speakers, small motors, and aluminum wheels. The prices reflect China's average hourly wage cost of 90 cents versus $22.50 in the United States.

Consider the case of Superior Industries International, Inc., a manufacturer of aluminum wheels, that does 85 percent of its business with GM and Ford. Both automakers said separately: Match the prices we can get from Chinese wheel suppliers or we'll go directly to the Chinese source or turn to a North American supplier that will meet our price expectations. "The message is: Close the gap no matter how," said Steve Borick, the president at Superior. In the end, for Superior that meant cutting its profit margins and finally building a joint-venture plant near Shanghai with a Chinese wheel producer.

Constrained by job-protection restrictions in their labor agreements with the United Auto Workers, Ford and GM find it hard to shift jobs overseas to take advantage of the low cost of manufacturing in China. But they "have hit upon an unusual strategy: Push their suppliers to do the outsourcing for them."

SOURCE: Norihiko Shirouzu, "Big Three's Outsourcing Plan: Make Parts Suppliers Do It," *The Wall Street Journal*, June 10, 2004, p. A1.

---

this dynamic environment, "our strategy is to engage our customers with online interactions and content," he says, pointing to the Web, e-mail, broadband, and blogs as just some of the many electronic tools H-P uses.[17] Because the most recent wave of technological change is as dramatic as any in history, the implications for marketing strategists are profound. They involve changing definitions of industries, new sources of competition, changing product life cycles, and the increased globalization of markets.[18]

Organizational Forces

An understanding of the buying organization is based on its strategic priorities, the role of purchasing in the executive hierarchy, and the firm's competitive challenges.

Growing Influence of Purchasing   As a rule, the influence of the procurement function is growing. Why? Globalization is upsetting traditional patterns of competition, and companies are feeling the squeeze from rising material costs and stiff customer resistance to price increases. Meanwhile, to enhance efficiency and effectiveness, many firms are outsourcing some functions that were traditionally performed within the organization. As a result, at companies around the world, CEOs are counting on the procurement function to keep their businesses strongly positioned in today's intensively competitive marketplace.[19]

---

[17] Kate Maddox, Sean Callahan, and Carol Krol, "Top Trends: B-to-B Marketers Have Proven Remarkably Adaptable in the Last Five Years," *B to B*, June 13, 2005, p. 3, http://www.BtoBonline.com, accessed on July 7, 2005.

[18] Rashi Glazer, "Winning in Smart Markets," *Sloan Management Review* 40 (summer 1999): pp. 56–69.

[19] Marc Bourde, Charlie Hawker, and Theo Theocharides, "Taking Center Stage: The 2005 Chief Procurement Officer Survey" (Somers, N.Y.: IBM Global Services, May 2005), pp. 1–14, http://www.ibm.com/bcs, accessed on July 1, 2005.

TABLE 3.1 | STRATEGIC PRIORITIES IN PURCHASING

Becoming Business Partners, *Not Just Buyers*	Shift from an administrative role to a value-creating function that serves internal stakeholders and provides a competitive edge in the market.
Exploring New Value Frontiers: *It's Not Just about Price*	Focus on the capabilities of suppliers emphasizing business outcomes, total cost of ownership, and the potential for long-term value creation.
Putting Suppliers Inside: *The Best Value Chain Wins*	Develop fewer and deeper relationships with strategic suppliers and involve them in decision-making processes, ranging from new product development to cost-reduction initiatives.
Pursuing Low-Cost Sources: *A World Worth Exploring*	Overcome hurdles imposed by geographical differences and seek out cost-effective suppliers around the globe.

SOURCE: Adapted from Marc Bourde, Charlie Hawker, and Theo Theocharides, "Taking Center Stage: The 2005 Chief Procurement Officer Survey," (Somers, N.Y.: IBM Global Services, May 2005), pp. 1–14. Accessed at http://www.ibm.com/bcs, on July 1, 2005.

Strategic Priorities in Purchasing

As the influence of purchasing grows, chief procurement officers feel the heat of the spotlight, so they are pursuing an ambitious set of strategic priorities (Table 3.1). They seek cost savings but realize that such savings are only part of what procurement can contribute to the bottom line. More importantly, however, procurement executives are turning to a more strategic question: How can procurement become a stronger competitive weapon? Here attention centers on corporate goals and how procurement can help their internal customers (that is, other business functions) achieve these goals. As a direct participant in the strategy process, procurement managers are giving increased emphasis to suppliers' *capabilities*, exploring new areas where a strategic supplier can add value to the firm's product or service offerings. Robert K. Harlan, director of e-procurement at Motorola, captures the idea: For new product development, "we bring many suppliers in early to design, simplify, and implement new technologies."[20]

Leading-edge purchasing organizations have also learned that the "best value chain wins," so they are building closer relationships with a carefully chosen set of strategic suppliers and aligning the activities of the supply chain with customers' needs.[21] For example, Honda of America reduced the cost of the Accord's purchased content by setting cost targets for each component—engine, chassis, and so on.[22] Then, purchasing managers worked with global suppliers to understand the cost structure of each component, observe how it is manufactured, and identify ways to reduce costs, add value, or do both.

---

[20] Jason Seigel, "Professional Profile: Robert K. Harlan," *Purchasing* 13 (October 7, 2004): p. 32.

[21] Mark Gottfredson, Rudy Puryear, and Stephen Phillips, "Strategic Sourcing: From Periphery to the Core," *Harvard Business Review* 83 (February 2005): pp. 132–139.

[22] Timothy M. Laseter, *Balanced Sourcing: Cooperation and Competition in Supplier Relationships* (San Francisco: Jossey-Bass, 1998), pp. 5–18.

Offer Strategic Solutions   As purchasing assumes a more strategic role, the business marketer must understand the competitive realities of the customer's business and develop a value proposition—products, services, ideas—that advance its performance goals. For example, IBM centers attention on customer solutions—how its information technology and assorted services can improve the efficiency of a retailer's operations or advance the customer service levels of a hotel chain. Alternatively, a supplier to Hewlett-Packard will strike a responsive chord with executives by offering a new component that will increase the performance or lower the cost of its inkjet printers. To provide such customer solutions, the business marketer needs an intimate understanding of the opportunities and threats that the customer confronts.

Organizational Positioning of Purchasing

As purchasing moves from a transaction-based support role and assumes a more prominent strategic spot at the executive level, many leading firms are centralizing the procurement function. An organization that centralizes procurement decisions approaches purchasing differently than a company in which purchasing decisions are made at individual user locations. When purchasing is centralized, a separate organizational unit has authority for purchases at a regional, divisional, or headquarters level. For example, by centralizing procurement, American Express realized nearly $600 million in purchasing savings the first three years.[23] IBM, Sara Lee, 3M, Hewlett-Packard, Wendy's International, and Citicorp are among other corporations that emphasize centralized procurement. A marketer who is sensitive to organizational influences can more accurately map the decision-making process, isolate buying influentials, identify salient buying criteria, and target marketing strategy for both centralized, as well as decentralized, organizations.[24]

Centralization of Procurement: Contributing Factors   Several factors contribute to the trend toward centralizing purchasing. First, centralization can better integrate purchasing strategy with corporate strategy, and e-procurement software tools now enable managers to monitor and analyze corporate spending data in minute detail.[25] Importantly, e-procurement software from firms such as Ariba, Inc. (http://www.ariba.com) now provides buyers with a rich set of new tools to track and manage spending across the entire enterprise. For example, the corporate procurement group at Walt Disney Company manages spending on all items common to the entertainment firm's four business units: media networks, parks and resorts, studio entertainment, and consumer products. These items include such categories as information technology, telecommunications, construction services, and insurance.[26]

Second, an organization with multiple plant or office locations can often cut costs by pooling common requirements. Before Motorola centralized its procurement function, it had 65 different software agreements globally with one supplier for the

[23] Susan Avery, "American Express Changes Ahead," *Purchasing* 133 (November 4, 2004): pp. 34–38.

[24] E. Raymond Corey, *The Organizational Context of Industrial Buyer Behavior* (Cambridge, Mass.: Marketing Science Institute, 1978), pp. 99–112.

[25] Tim A. Minahan, "Best Practices in E-Sourcing: Optimizing and Sustaining Supply Savings," September 2004, research report by Aberdeen Group, Inc., Boston, Massachusetts; http://www.ariba.com, accessed on June 15, 2005.

[26] Anne Millen Porter, "Spend a Little, Save a Lot," *Purchasing* 130 (April 4, 2002), pp. 23–34.

same software license.[27] By negotiating a global agreement that covers all Motorola operations around the world, the centralized procurement staff saved more than $40 million, or about 50 percent of what the firm had been paying for the 65 different agreements.

Third, the nature of the supply environment also can determine whether purchasing is centralized. If a few large sellers dominate the supply environment, centralized buying may be particularly useful in securing favorable terms and proper service. If the supply industry consists of many small firms, each covering limited geographical areas, decentralized purchasing may achieve better support.

Finally, the location of purchasing in the organization often hinges on the location of key buying influences. If engineering plays an active role in the process, the purchasing function must be in close organizational and physical proximity.

Centralization versus Decentralization   Centralized and decentralized procurement differ substantially.[28] Centralization leads to specialization. Purchasing specialists for selected items develop comprehensive knowledge of supply and demand conditions, vendor options, supplier cost factors, and other relevant information. This knowledge, and the significant volume of business that specialists control, enhances their buying strength and supplier options.

The priority given to selected buying criteria is also influenced by centralization or decentralization. By identifying the buyer's organizational domain, the marketer can generally identify the purchasing manager's objectives. **Centralized purchasing** units place more weight on strategic considerations such as long-term supply availability and the development of a healthy supplier complex. Decentralized buyers may emphasize more tactical concerns such as short-term cost efficiency and profit considerations. Organizational buying behavior is greatly influenced by the monitoring system that measures the performance of the unit.

Personal selling skills and the brand preferences of users influence purchasing decisions more at user locations than at centralized buying locations. At user locations, E. Raymond Corey points out that "engineers and other technical personnel, in particular, are prone to be specific in their preferences, while nonspecialized, nontechnical buyers have neither the technical expertise nor the status to challenge them,"[29] as can purchasing specialists at central locations. Differing priorities between central buyers and local users often lead to conflict. In stimulating demand at the user level, the marketer should assess the potential for conflict and attempt to develop a strategy to resolve any differences between the two organizational units.

The organization of the marketer's selling strategy should parallel the organization of the purchasing function of key accounts. To avoid disjointed selling activities and internal conflict in the sales organization, and to serve the special needs of important customers, many business marketers have developed key account management programs to establish a close working relationship that, according to Benson Shapiro and Rowland Moriarty, "cuts across multiple levels, functions, and

---

[27] James Carbone, "Motorola Leverages Its Way to Lower Cost," *Purchasing* 133 (September 16, 2004): p. 32.

[28] Joseph A. Bellizzi and Joseph J. Belonax, "Centralized and Decentralized Buying Influences," *Industrial Marketing Management* 11 (April 1982): pp. 111–115; Arch G. Woodside and David M. Samuel, "Observation of Centralized Corporate Procurement," *Industrial Marketing Management* 10 (July 1981): pp. 191–205; and E. Raymond Corey, *The Organizational Context of Industrial Buying Behavior*, pp. 6–12.

[29] Corey, *The Organizational Context*, p. 13.

INSIDE BUSINESS MARKETING

Go Digital to Target Buying Influentials

Which firms are gaining an advantage in the customer-empowered, competitive markets that are being reshaped by the Internet? Those who already excel at managing customer relationships are best equipped to capitalize on the opportunities of the Internet. Those relationship leaders are able to anticipate earlier how to use the Internet to connect with their customers, exploit it faster, and implement strategy initiatives better. Best-of-breed relationship builders, like Dell, FedEx, GE Medical, and Singapore Airlines, relish the new possibilities the Internet presents.

Consider the effective and low-cost strategy that GE Medical uses in selling expensive, mission-critical software through the digital channel. Radiologists using GE's diagnostic imaging machines can go to the Internet and try out new GE software that increases the efficiency of spinal examinations. If they like what they see, they can order the $65,000 software. About 65 percent of the time, radiologists elect to make the purchase, without ever talking to a salesperson.

SOURCE: George S. Day and Katrina J. Hubbard, "Customer Relationships Go Digital," *Business Strategy Review* 14, Issue 1 (2003): pp. 17–26.

operating units in both the buying and selling organizations."[30] For example, IBM assigns a dedicated account executive to work with large customers, like Boeing or State Farm Insurance. Thus, the trend toward the centralization of procurement by buyers has been matched by the development of key account management programs by sellers.

Group Forces

Multiple buying influences and group forces are critical in organizational buying decisions. The organizational buying process typically involves a complex set of smaller decisions made or influenced by several individuals. The degree of involvement of group members varies from routine rebuys, in which the purchasing agent simply takes into account the preferences of others, to complex new-task buying situations, in which a group plays an active role.

The industrial salesperson must address three questions.

- Which organizational members take part in the buying process?

- What is each member's relative influence in the decision?

- What criteria are important to each member in evaluating prospective suppliers?

The salesperson who can correctly answer these questions is ideally prepared to meet the needs of a buying organization and has a high probability of becoming the chosen supplier.

---

[30]Benson P. Shapiro and Rowland T. Moriarty, *National Account Management: Emerging Insights* (Cambridge, Mass.: Marketing Science Institute, 1982), p. 8; see also James Boles, Wesley Johnston, and Alston Gardner, "The Selection and Organization of National Accounts: A North American Perspective," *Journal of Business & Industrial Marketing* 14, no. 4 (1999): pp. 264–275.

The Buying Center   The concept of the buying center provides rich insights into the role of group forces in organizational buying behavior.[31] The **buying center** consists of individuals who participate in the purchasing decision and share the goals and risks arising from the decision. The size of the buying center varies, but an average buying center includes more than 4 persons per purchase; the number of people involved in all stages of one purchase may be as many as 20.[32]

The composition of the buying center may change from one purchasing situation to another and is not prescribed by the organizational chart. A buying group evolves during the purchasing process in response to the information requirements of the specific situation. Because organizational buying is a *process* rather than an isolated act, different individuals are important to the process at different times.[33] A design engineer may exert significant influence early in the process when product specifications are being established; others may assume a more dominant role in later phases. A salesperson must define the buying situation and the information requirements from the organization's perspective in order to anticipate the size and composition of the buying center. Again, the composition of the buying center evolves during the purchasing process, varies from firm to firm, and varies from one purchasing situation to another.

Isolating the Buying Situation   Defining the buying situation and determining whether the firm is in the early or later stages of the procurement decision-making process are important first steps in defining the buying center. The buying center for a new-task buying situation in the not-for-profit market is presented in Table 3.2. The product, intensive-care monitoring systems, is complex and costly. Buying center members are drawn from five functional areas, each participating to varying degrees in the process. A marketer who concentrated exclusively on the purchasing function would be overlooking key buying influentials.

Erin Anderson and her colleagues queried a large sample of sales managers about the patterns of organizational buying behavior their salespeople confront daily. Sales forces that frequently encounter new-task buying situations generally observe that:

> The buying center is large, slow to decide, uncertain about its needs and the appropriateness of the possible solutions, more concerned about finding a good solution than getting a low price or assured supply, more willing to entertain proposals from "out" suppliers and less willing to favor "in" suppliers, more influenced by technical personnel, [and] less influenced by purchasing agents.[34]

By contrast, Anderson and her colleagues found that sales forces facing more routine purchase situations (that is, straight and modified rebuys) frequently observe

---

[31] For a comprehensive review of buying center research, see Wesley J. Johnston and Jeffrey E. Lewin, "Organizational Buying Behavior: Toward an Integrative Framework," *Journal of Business Research* 35 (January 1996): pp. 1–15; and J. David Lichtenthal, "Group Decision Making in Organizational Buying: A Role Structure Approach," in *Advances in Business Marketing*, vol. 3, ed. Arch G. Woodside (Greenwich, Conn.: JAI Press, 1988), pp. 119–157.

[32] For example, see Robert D. McWilliams, Earl Naumann, and Stan Scott, "Determining Buying Center Size," *Industrial Marketing Management* 21 (February 1992): pp. 43–49.

[33] Ghingold and Wilson, "Buying Center Research and Business Marketing Practice," pp. 96–108; see also Gary L. Lilien and M. Anthony Wong, "Exploratory Investigation of the Structure of the Buying Center in the Metalworking Industry," *Journal of Marketing Research* 21 (February 1984): pp. 1–11.

[34] Anderson, Chu, and Weitz, "Industrial Purchasing," p. 82.

TABLE 3.2	THE INVOLVEMENT OF BUYING CENTER PARTICIPANTS AT DIFFERENT STAGES OF THE PROCUREMENT PROCESS

Buying Center Participants	Stages of Procurement Process for a Medical Supplier			
	Identification of Need	Establishment of Objectives	Identification and Evaluation of Buying Alternatives	Selection of Suppliers
Physicians	High	High	High	High
Nursing	Low	High	High	Low
Administration	Moderate	Moderate	Moderate	High
Engineering	Low	Moderate	Moderate	Low
Purchasing	Low	Low	Low	Moderate

SOURCE: Adapted by permission of the publisher from Gene R. Laczniak, "An Empirical Study of Hospital Buying," *Industrial Marketing Management* 8 (January 1979): p. 61. Copyright © 1979 by Elsevier Science.

buying centers that are "small, quick to decide, confident in their appraisals of the problem and possible solutions, concerned about price and supply, satisfied with 'in' suppliers, and more influenced by purchasing agents."[35]

Predicting Composition   A marketer can also predict the composition of the buying center by projecting the effect of the industrial product on various functional areas in the organization. If the procurement decision will affect the marketability of a firm's product (for example, product design, price), the marketing department will be active in the process. Engineering will be influential in decisions about new capital equipment, materials, and components; setting specifications; defining product performance requirements; and qualifying potential vendors. Manufacturing executives will be included for procurement decisions that affect the production mechanism (for example, materials or parts used in production). When procurement decisions involve a substantial economic commitment or impinge on strategic or policy matters, top management will have considerable influence.

Buying Center Influence   Members of the buying center assume different roles throughout the procurement process. Frederick Webster Jr. and Yoram Wind have given the following labels to each of these roles: users, influencers, buyers, deciders, and gatekeepers.[36]

As the role name implies, **users** are the personnel who use the product in question. Users may have anywhere from inconsequential to extremely important influence on the purchase decision. In some cases, the users initiate the purchase action by requesting the product. They may even develop the product specifications.

---

[35]Ibid.

[36]Frederick E. Webster Jr. and Yoram Wind, *Organizational Buying Behavior* (Englewood Cliffs, N.J.: Prentice-Hall, 1972), p. 77. For a review of buying role research, see J. David Lichtenthal, "Group Decision Making in Organizational Buying," pp. 119–157.

INSIDE BUSINESS MARKETING

Innovate and Win with BMW

Leading procurement organizations expect their suppliers to innovate, and they reward them when they do. At firms such as P&G, Coca-Cola, and BMW, purchasing executives use "potential to innovate" as a key criterion for selecting suppliers and evaluate contributions to innovation as part of the supplier development process.

Business marketers who contribute innovative ideas to the new-product-development process at such firms win the support of purchasing managers, marketing executives, design engineers, and other members of the buying center. For example, a salesperson for a top supplier to BMW proposed adding optic-fiber-enabled light rings to headlights to add a distinguishing feature to the brand. "Drivers on the German autobahn or elsewhere would see the distinctive lights of a high-performance BMW approaching from behind and know to move aside and let it pass. BMW and the supplier jointly developed the idea—and the contract ensures exclusive rights for the automaker." As a result of this collaboration, BMW gained access to new technology that adds value to its brand and the supplier won a lucrative, long-term contract.

SOURCE: "Creating Value through Strategic Supply Management: 2004 Assessment of Excellence in Procurement," (A. T. Kearney, February 2005). Accessed at http://www.atkearney.com, June 25, 2005.

Gatekeepers control information to be reviewed by other members of the buying center. They may do so by disseminating printed information, such as advertisements, or by controlling which salesperson speaks to which individuals in the buying center. To illustrate, the purchasing agent might perform this screening role by opening the gate to the buying center for some sales personnel and closing it to others.

Influencers affect the purchasing decision by supplying information for the evaluation of alternatives or by setting buying specifications. Typically, those in technical departments, such as engineering, quality control, and R&D, are significant influences on the purchase decision. Sometimes, outside individuals can assume this role. For high-tech purchases, technical consultants often assume an influential role in the decision process and broaden the set of alternatives being considered.[37]

Deciders actually make the buying decision, whether or not they have the formal authority to do so. The identity of the decider is the most difficult role to determine: *Buyers* may have formal authority to buy, but the president of the firm may actually make the decision. A decider could be a design engineer who develops a set of specifications that only one vendor can meet.

The **buyer** has formal authority to select a supplier and implement all procedures connected with securing the product. More powerful members of the organization often usurp the power of the buyer. The buyer's role is often assumed by the purchasing agent, who executes the administrative functions associated with a purchase order.

One person could assume all roles, or separate individuals could assume different buying roles. To illustrate, as users, personnel from marketing, accounting, purchasing, and production may all have a stake in which information technology system is selected. Thus, the buying center can be a very complex organizational phenomenon.

---

[37] Paul G. Patterson and Phillip L. Dawes, "The Determinants of Choice Set Structure in High-Technology Markets," *Industrial Marketing Management* 28 (July 1999): pp. 395–411.

TABLE 3.3 | CLUES FOR IDENTIFYING POWERFUL BUYING CENTER MEMBERS

- *Isolate the personal stakeholders.* Those individuals who have an important personal stake in the decision will exert more influence than other members of the buying center. For example, the selection of production equipment for a new plant will spawn the active involvement of manufacturing executives.

- *Follow the information flow.* Influential members of the buying center are central to the information flow that surrounds the buying decision. Other organizational members will direct information to them.

- *Identify the experts.* Expert power is an important determinant of influence in the buying center. Those buying center members who possess the most knowledge—and ask the most probing questions to the salesperson—are often influential.

- *Trace the connections to the top.* Powerful buying center members often have direct access to the top-management team. This direct link to valuable information and resources enhances the status and influence of the buying center members.

- *Understand purchasing's role.* Purchasing is dominant in repetitive buying situations by virtue of technical expertise, knowledge of the dynamics of the supplying industry, and close working relationships with individual suppliers.

SOURCE: Adapted from John R. Ronchetto, Michael D. Hutt, and Peter H. Reingen, "Embedded Influence Patterns in Organizational Buying Systems," *Journal of Marketing* 53 (October 1989): pp. 51–62.

Identifying Patterns of Influence   Key influencers are frequently located outside the purchasing department. To illustrate, the typical capital equipment purchase involves an average of four departments, three levels of the management hierarchy (for example, manager, regional manager, vice president), and seven different individuals.[38] In purchasing component parts, personnel from production and engineering are often most influential in the decision. It is interesting to note that a comparative study of organizational buying behavior found striking similarities across four countries (the United States, the United Kingdom, Australia, and Canada) in the involvement of various departments in the procurement process.[39]

Past research provides some valuable clues for identifying powerful buying center members (Table 3.3).[40] To illustrate, individuals who have an important personal stake in the decision possess, expert knowledge concerning the choice, and/or are central to the flow of decision-related information tend to assume an active and influential role in the buying center. Purchasing managers assume a dominant role in repetitive buying situations.

---

[38] Wesley J. Johnston and Thomas V. Bonoma, "The Buying Center: Structure and Interaction Patterns," *Journal of Marketing* 45 (summer 1981): pp. 143–156; see also Gary L. Lilien and M. Anthony Wong, "An Exploratory Investigation of the Structure of the Buying Center in the Metalworking Industry," *Journal of Marketing Research* 21 (February 1984): pp. 1–11 and Arch G. Woodside, Timo Liakko, and Risto Vuori, "Organizational Buying of Capital Equipment Involving Persons across Several Authority Levels," *Journal of Business & Industrial Marketing* 14, no. 1 (1999): pp. 30–48.

[39] Peter Banting, David Ford, Andrew Gross, and George Holmes, "Similarities in Industrial Procurement across Four Countries," *Industrial Marketing Management* 14 (May 1985): pp. 133–144.

[40] John R. Ronchetto, Michael D. Hutt, and Peter H. Reingen, "Embedded Influence Patterns in Organizational Buying Systems," *Journal of Marketing* 53 (October 1989): pp. 51–62; see also Ajay Kohli, "Determinants of Influence in Organizational Buying: A Contingency Approach," *Journal of Marketing* 53 (July 1989): pp. 50–65; Daniel H. McQuiston and Peter R. Dickson, "The Effect of Perceived Personal Consequences on Participation and Influence in Organizational Buying," *Journal of Business Research* 23 (September 1991): pp. 159–177 and Jerome M. Katrichis, "Exploring Departmental Level Interaction Patterns in Organizational Purchasing Decisions," *Industrial Marketing Management*, 27 (March 1998): pp. 135–146.

Based on their buying center research, Donald W. Jackson Jr. and his colleagues provide these strategy recommendations:

> Marketing efforts will depend upon which individuals of the buying center are more influential for a given decision. Because engineering and manufacturing are more influential in product selection decisions, they may have to be sold on product characteristics. On the other hand, because purchasing is most influential in supplier selection decisions, they may have to be sold on company characteristics.[41]

Individual Forces

Individuals, not organizations, make buying decisions. Each member of the buying center has a unique personality, a particular set of learned experiences, a specified organizational function, and a perception of how best to achieve both personal and organizational goals. Importantly, research confirms that organizational members who perceive that they have an important personal stake in the buying decision participate more forcefully in the decision process than their colleagues.[42] To understand the organizational buyer, the marketer should be aware of individual perceptions of the buying situation.

Differing Evaluative Criteria   **Evaluative criteria** are specifications that organizational buyers use to compare alternative industrial products and services; however, these may conflict. Industrial product users generally value prompt delivery and efficient servicing; engineering values product quality, standardization, and testing; and purchasing assigns the most importance to maximum price advantage and economy in shipping and forwarding.[43]

Product perceptions and evaluative criteria differ among organizational decision makers as a result of differences in their educational backgrounds, their exposure to different types of information from different sources, the way they interpret and retain relevant information (perceptual distortion), and their level of satisfaction with past purchases.[44] Engineers have an educational background different from that of plant managers or purchasing agents: They are exposed to different journals, attend different conferences, and possess different professional goals and values. A sales presentation that is effective with purchasing may be entirely off the mark with engineering.

Responsive Marketing Strategy   A marketer who is sensitive to differences in the product perceptions and evaluative criteria of individual buying center members is well equipped to prepare a responsive marketing strategy. To illustrate, a research study examined the industrial adoption of solar air-conditioning systems and identified

---

[41] Jackson, Keith, and Burdick, "Purchasing Agents' Perceptions of Industrial Buying Center Influence," pp. 75–83.

[42] McQuiston and Dickson, "The Effect of Perceived Personal Consequences on Participation and Influence in Organizational Buying," pp. 159–177.

[43] Jagdish N. Sheth, "A Model of Industrial Buyer Behavior," *Journal of Marketing* 37 (October 1973): p. 51; see also Sheth, "Organizational Buying Behavior: Past Performance and Future Expectations," *Journal of Business & Industrial Marketing* 11, no. 3/4 (1996): pp. 7–24.

[44] Sheth, "A Model of Industrial Buyer Behavior," pp. 52–54.

the criteria important to key decision makers.[45] Buying center participants for this purchase typically include production engineers, heating and air-conditioning (HVAC) consultants, and top managers. The study revealed that marketing communications directed at production engineers should center on operating costs and energy savings; HVAC consultants should be addressed concerning noise level and initial cost of the system; and top managers are most interested in whether the technology is state-of-the-art. Knowing the criteria of key buying center participants has significant operational value to the marketer when designing new products and when developing and targeting advertising and personal selling presentations.

Information Processing   Volumes of information flow into every organization through direct-mail advertising, the Internet, journal advertising, trade news, word of mouth, and personal sales presentations. What an individual organizational buyer chooses to pay attention to, comprehend, and retain has an important bearing on procurement decisions.

Selective Processes   Information processing is generally encompassed in the broader term **cognition**, which U. Neisser defines as "all the processes by which the sensory input is transformed, reduced, elaborated, stored, recovered, and used."[46] Important to an individual's cognitive structure are the processes of selective exposure, attention, perception, and retention.

1. *Selective exposure.*   Individuals tend to accept communication messages consistent with their existing attitudes and beliefs. For this reason, a purchasing agent chooses to talk to some salespersons and not to others.

2. *Selective attention.*   Individuals filter or screen incoming stimuli to admit only certain ones to cognition. Thus, an organizational buyer is more likely to notice a trade advertisement that is consistent with his or her needs and values.

3. *Selective perception.*   Individuals tend to interpret stimuli in terms of their existing attitudes and beliefs. This explains why organizational buyers may modify or distort a salesperson's message in order to make it more consistent with their predispositions toward the company.

4. *Selective retention.*   Individuals tend to recall only information pertinent to their own needs and dispositions. An organizational buyer may retain information concerning a particular brand because it matches his or her criteria.

Each of these selective processes influences the way an individual decision maker responds to marketing stimuli. Because the procurement process often spans several months and because the marketer's contact with the buying organization is infrequent, marketing communications must be carefully designed and targeted.[47] Key decision

---

[45] Jean-Marie Choffray and Gary L. Lilien, "Assessing Response to Industrial Marketing Strategy," *Journal of Marketing* 42 (April 1978): pp. 20–31. For related research, see R. Venkatesh, Ajay K. Kohli, and Gerald Zaltman, "Influence Strategies in Buying Centers," *Journal of Marketing* 59 (October 1995): pp. 71–82; and Mark A. Farrell and Bill Schroder, "Influence Strategies in Organizational Buying Decisions," *Industrial Marketing Management* 25 (July 1996): pp. 293–303.

[46] U. Neisser, *Cognitive Psychology* (New York: Appleton, 1966), p. 4.

[47] See, for example, Brent M. Wren and James T. Simpson, "A Dyadic Model of Relationships in Organizational Buying: A Synthesis of Research Results," *Journal of Business & Industrial Marketing* 11, no. 3/4 (1996): pp. 68–79.

B2B TOP PERFORMERS

Delivering Customer Solutions

If you review the performance of salespersons at most business marketing firms, large or small, you will observe some who consistently perform at a level that sets them apart from their peers. A recent study explores how exceptional performers acquire and use information to manage customer relationships. In depth interviews were conducted with 60 salespersons at a *Fortune* 500 firm: 20 high-performing, 20 average-performing, and 20 low-performing salespersons.

Sharp differences emerged when the salespersons were asked to categorize their customers into groups based on characteristics they found most useful in managing customer relationships. Here high performers emphasize customer goals, whereas low performers emphasize customer demographics

(for example, large versus small firms). In turn, the study reveals that high performers develop a more extensive network of relationships within the customer organization compared with their colleagues. Importantly, high performers are better able to establish and maintain profitable customer relationships because they align their organization's special capabilities to the customer's primary goals. In other words, top-performing sales specialists provide a solution that advances the performance of the customer organization.

SOURCE: Gabriel R. Gonzalez, Beth A. Walker, Dimitrios Kapelianis, and Michael D. Hutt, "The Role of Information Acquisition and Knowledge Use in Managing Customer Relationships," working paper, Arizona State University, Tempe, Ariz., 2005.

makers "tune out" or immediately forget poorly conceived messages. They retain messages they deem important to achieving goals.

Risk-Reduction Strategies   Individuals are motivated by a strong desire to reduce risk in purchase decisions. Perceived risk includes two components: (1) uncertainty about the outcome of a decision and (2) the magnitude of consequences from making the wrong choice. Research highlights the importance of perceived risk and the purchase type in shaping the structure of the decision-making unit.[48] Individual decision making is likely to occur in organizational buying for straight rebuys and for modified rebuys when the perceived risk is low. In these situations, the purchasing agent may initiate action.[49] Modified rebuys of higher risk and new tasks seem to spawn a group structure.

In confronting "risky" purchase decisions, how do organizational buyers behave? As the risk associated with an organizational purchase decision increases, the following occur[50]:

- The buying center becomes larger and comprises members with high levels of organizational status and authority.

- The information search is active and a wide variety of information sources are consulted. As the decision process unfolds, personal information sources (for

---

[48]Elizabeth J. Wilson, Gary L. Lilien, and David T. Wilson, "Developing and Testing a Contingency Paradigm of Group Choice in Organizational Buying," *Journal of Marketing Research* 28 (November 1991): pp. 452–466.

[49]Sheth, "A Model of Industrial Buyer Behavior," p. 54; see also W. E. Patton III, Charles P. Puto, and Ronald H. King, "Which Buying Decisions Are Made by Individuals and Not by Groups?" *Industrial Marketing Management* 15 (May 1986): pp. 129–138.

[50]Johnston and Lewin, "Organizational Buying Behavior: Toward an Integrative Framework," pp. 8–10. See also Puto, Patton, and King, "Risk Handling Strategies in Industrial Vendor Selection Decisions," pp. 89–95.

example, discussions with managers at other organizations that have made similar purchases) become more important.

- Buying center participants invest greater effort and deliberate more carefully throughout the purchase process.

- Sellers who have a proven track record with the firm are favored—the choice of a familiar supplier helps reduce perceived risk.

Rather than price, product quality and after-sale service are typically most important to organizational buyers when they confront risky decisions. When introducing new products, entering new markets, or approaching new customers, the marketing strategist should evaluate the effect of alternative strategies on perceived risk.

The Organizational Buying Process: Major Elements

The behavior of organizational buyers is influenced by environmental, organizational, group, and individual factors. Each of these spheres of influence has been discussed in an organizational buying context, with particular attention to how the industrial marketer should interpret these forces and, more important, factor them directly into marketing strategy planning. A model of the organizational buying process is presented in Figure 3.4, which serves to reinforce and integrate the key areas discussed so far in this chapter.[51]

This framework focuses on the relationship between an organization's buying center and the three major stages in the individual purchase decision process:

1. The screening of alternatives that do not meet organizational requirements.

2. The formation of decision participants' preferences.

3. The formation of organizational preferences.

Observe that individual members of the buying center use various evaluative criteria and are exposed to various sources of information, which influence the industrial brands included in the buyer's **evoked set of alternatives**—the alternative brands a buyer calls to mind when a need arises and represent only a few of the many brands available.[52]

Environmental constraints and organizational requirements influence the procurement process by limiting the number of product alternatives that satisfy organizational needs. For example, capital equipment alternatives that exceed a particular cost (initial or operating) may be eliminated from further consideration. The remaining brands become the **feasible set of alternatives** for the organization, from which individual

---

[51] Choffray and Lilien, "Assessing the Response to Industrial Marketing Strategy," pp. 20–31. Other models of organizational buying behavior include Webster and Wind, *Organizational Buying Behavior*, pp. 28–37; and Sheth, "A Model of Industrial Buyer Behavior," pp. 50–56. For a comprehensive review, see Sheth, "Organizational Buying Behavior," pp. 7–24; and Johnston and Lewin, "Organizational Buying Behavior," pp. 1–15.

[52] Howard and Sheth, *The Theory of Buyer Behavior*, p. 26; see also Ronald P. LeBlanc, "Environmental Impact on Purchase Decision Structure," *Journal of Purchasing and Materials Management* 17 (spring 1981): pp. 30–36; and Lowell E. Crow, Richard W. Olshavsky, and John O. Summers, "Industrial Buyers' Choice Strategies: A Protocol Analysis," *Journal of Marketing Research* 17 (February 1980): pp. 34–44.

FIGURE 3.4 | **MAJOR ELEMENTS OF ORGANIZATIONAL BUYING BEHAVIOR**

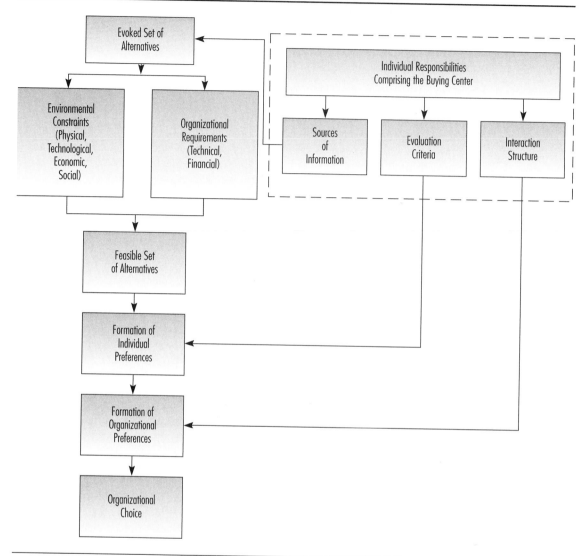

SOURCE: Jean-Marie Choffray and Gary L. Lilien, "Assessing Response to Industrial Marketing Strategy," *Journal of Marketing* 42 (April 1978): p. 22. Reprinted by permission of the American Marketing Association.

preferences are defined. The **interaction structure** of the members of the buying center, who have differing criteria and responsibilities, leads to the formation of organizational preferences and ultimately to organizational choice.

Understanding the organizational buying process enables the marketer to play an active rather than a passive role in stimulating market response. The marketer who identifies organizational screening requirements and the salient evaluative criteria of individual buying center members can make more informed product design, pricing, and promotional decisions.

Summary

Knowledge of the process that organizational buyers follow in making purchasing decisions is fundamental to responsive marketing strategy. As a buying organization moves from the problem-recognition phase, in which a procurement need is defined, to later phases, in which suppliers are screened and ultimately chosen, the marketer can play an active role. In fact, the astute marketer often triggers initial awareness of the problem and helps the organization effectively solve that problem. Incremental decisions made throughout the buying process narrow the field of acceptable suppliers and dramatically influence the ultimate outcome.

The nature of the buying process depends on the organization's level of experience with similar procurement problems. It is thus crucial to know how the organization defines the buying situation: as a new task, a modified rebuy, or a straight rebuy. Each buying situation requires a unique problem-solving approach, involves unique buying influentials, and demands a unique marketing response.

Myriad forces—environmental, organizational, group, and individual—influence organizational buying behavior. First, environmental forces define the boundaries within which industrial buyers and sellers interact, such as general business conditions or the rate of technological change. Second, organizational forces dictate the link between buying activities and the strategic priorities of the firm and the position that the purchasing function occupies in the organizational structure. Third, the relevant unit of analysis for the marketing strategist is the buying center. The composition of this group evolves during the buying process, varies from firm to firm, and changes from one purchasing situation to another. Fourth, the marketer must ultimately concentrate attention on individual members of the buying center. Each brings a particular set of experiences and a unique personal and organizational frame of reference to the buying decision. The marketer who is sensitive to individual differences is best equipped to develop responsive marketing communications that the organizational buyer will remember.

Unraveling the complex forces that encircle the organizational buying process is indeed difficult. This chapter offers a framework that enables the marketing manager to begin this task by asking the right questions. The answers provide the basis for effective and efficient business marketing strategy.

Discussion Questions

1. Ford revamped the way it purchases operating resources such as office, computer, and maintenance supplies. Instead of having employees fill out purchase orders that must be cleared by the boss days later, employees simply log on to an Internet system. They browse through the electronics catalogs of manufacturers, order from a preapproved group of suppliers, and get purchase approval in minutes. What new challenges and opportunities does the e-procurement system present for business marketers who serve Ford?

2. Jim Jackson, an industrial salesperson for Pittsburgh Machine Tool, will call on two accounts this afternoon. The first will be a buying organization Jim has been servicing for the past three years. The second call, however, poses more of a challenge. This buying organization has been dealing with a prime competitor of

Pittsburgh Machine Tool for five years. Jim, who has good rapport with the purchasing and engineering departments, feels that the time may be right to penetrate this account. Recently, Jim learned that the purchasing manager was extremely unhappy with the existing supplier's poor delivery service. Define the buying situations confronting Jim and outline the appropriate strategy he should follow in each case.

3. Karen Weber, the purchasing agent for Smith Manufacturing, views the purchase of widgets as a routine buying decision. What factors might lead her to alter this position? More important, what factors determine whether Karen considers a particular supplier, such as Albany Widget?

4. Harley-Davidson, the U.S. motorcycle producer, recently purchased some sophisticated manufacturing equipment to enhance its position in a very competitive market. First, what environmental forces might have been important in spawning this capital investment? Second, which functional units were likely to have been represented in the buying center?

5. Brunswick Corporation centralizes its procurement decisions at the headquarters level. Discuss how it would approach purchasing differently than a competitor that decentralizes purchasing across various plant locations.

6. The Kraus Toy Company recently decided to develop a new electronic game. Can an electrical parts supplier predict the likely composition of the buying center at Kraus Toy? What steps could an industrial salesperson take to influence the composition of the buying center?

7. Explain how the composition of the buying center evolves during the purchasing process and how it varies from one firm to another, as well as from one purchasing situation to another. What steps can a salesperson take to identify the influential members of the buying center?

8. Carol Brooks, purchasing manager for Apex Manufacturing Co., read *The Wall Street Journal* this morning and carefully studied, clipped, and saved a full-page ad by the Allen-Bradley Company. Ralph Thornton, the production manager at Apex, read several articles from the same paper but could not recall seeing this particular ad or, for that matter, any ads. How could this occur?

9. Organizations purchase millions of notebook computers each year. Identify several evaluative criteria that purchasing managers might use in choosing a particular brand. In your view, which criteria would be most decisive in the buying decision?

10. The levels of risk associated with organizational purchases range from low to high. Discuss how the buying process for a risky purchase differs from the process for a routine purchase.

Internet Exercise

Dell, Inc., has been wildly successful in selling its products over the Internet to customers of all types, including every category of customers in the business market: commercial enterprises, institutions, and government. Assume your university library is planning to purchase 25 new desktop computers. Go to http://www.dell.com and to the Dell Online Store for Higher Education and:

1. identify the price and product dimensions of two desktop systems that might meet your university's needs, and

2. provide a critique of the Web site and consider how well it provided access to the information that a potential buyer might want.

CASE

Dell, Inc.[53]

Started famously in Austin in a University of Texas dorm room, Dell has annual sales that exceed $50 billion, ranking the firm in the *Fortune* 500 list, ahead of familiar names like Walt Disney, Johnson & Johnson, and DuPont.

Experts suggest that Dell's success rests on the firm's superb execution of its direct sales model. Here are the basic tenets of the model. Dell works closely with its suppliers, holds minimal inventory, and keeps a tight grasp on costs. Triggered by a phone or Internet order, Dell machines are made to order and delivered directly to the customer. No retailer or distributor intervenes. The customer gets the exact computer desired and normally pays a lower price than what competitors would charge. Dell gets paid by the customer when the order is processed—weeks before it pays suppliers. Such efficiencies give Dell cost advantages over rivals such as Hewlett-Packard and Lenovo Group, Inc., China's top PC producer that purchased IBM's PC division. Lenovo relies on a large network of distributors and retailers in China.[54]

Dell's customers include large corporate, government, health-care, and educational accounts as well as small-to-medium businesses and individual customers. Roughly 70 percent of Dell's U.S. revenue comes from the business market, with the remainder accounted for by sales to individuals and households.

Looking ahead, CEO Kevin Rollins has set the ambitious goal of reaching $80 billion in revenue by 2009 or before. To achieve this goal, Dell will continue to add new product categories and make a concerted effort to strengthen its presence in the international market.

Discussion Questions

1. Dell has demonstrated its ability to use its direct model in selling PCs, printers, servers, workstations, and storage systems to small business and corporate customers. The product line has now been expanded to include MP3 players, plasma and LCD televisions, and mobile devices. Describe how the marketing strategy that might be appropriate for reaching final consumers or households (that is, the consumer market) would differ from the strategy that would fit corporate buyers? Do some product categories fit the direct sales model better than others? Explain.

2. Experts project that 80 percent of total PC unit sales from 2006 to 2010 will come from developing markets like China and India. Because many potential customers in these markets lack Web access, know little about computers, and turn to local stores for advice, should Dell modify its direct model and establish a retail presence in these developing markets?

---

[53] Olga Kharif, "Dell: Time for a New Model?" http://www.businessweek.com, accessed April 6, 2005.

[54] Evan Ramstad and Gary McWilliams, "For Dell, Success in China Tells Tale of Maturing Market," *The Wall Street Journal*, July 5, 2005, pp. A1, A8.

Customer Relationship Management Strategies for Business Markets

A well-developed ability to create and sustain successful working relationships with customers gives business marketing firms a significant competitive advantage. After reading this chapter, you will understand:

1. the patterns of buyer-seller relationships in the business market.

2. the factors that influence the profitability of individual customers.

3. a procedure for designing effective customer relationship management strategies.

4. the distinctive capabilities of firms that excel at customer relationship management.

Every night, John Chambers, CEO of Cisco Systems, receives a personal update on 15 to 20 major customers via voice-mail. "E-mail would be more efficient but I want to hear the emotion, I want to hear the frustration; I want to hear the caller's level of comfort with the strategy we're employing," says Chambers. "I can't get that through e-mail."[1]

Leading business marketing firms like Cisco succeed by providing superior value to customers, by satisfying the special needs of even the most demanding customers, and by understanding the factors that influence individual customer profitability. Compared with the consumer packaged-goods sector, customer profitability is particularly important in business markets because marketing managers allocate a greater proportion of their marketing resources at the individual customer level.[2] The ability of an organization to create and maintain profitable relationships with these most valuable customers is a durable basis of competitive advantage.[3]

A business marketer who wishes to find a place on Cisco's preferred supplier list must be prepared to help the firm provide more value to its demanding customers. To this end, the marketer must provide exceptional performance in quality, delivery, and, over time, cost competitiveness. The supplier must also understand how Cisco measures value and how its product and service offering can meet or surpass these value expectations. Building and maintaining lasting customer relationships requires careful attention to detail, meeting promises, and swiftly responding to new requirements.

The new era of business marketing is built upon effective relationship management. Many business marketing firms create what might be called a **collaborative advantage** by demonstrating special skills in managing relationships with key customers or by jointly developing innovative strategies with alliance partners.[4] These firms have learned how to be good partners, and these superior relationship skills are a valuable asset. This chapter explores the types of relationships that characterize the business market. What market and situational factors are associated with different types of buyer-seller relationships? What factors influence customer profitability? What strategies can business marketers employ to build profitable relationships with customers? What are the distinctive capabilities of firms that excel at customer relationship management?

Relationship Marketing[5]

Relationship marketing centers on all activities directed toward establishing, developing, and maintaining successful exchanges with customers and other constituents.[6] Nurturing and managing customer relationships have emerged as an important strategic priority in most firms. Why? First, loyal customers are far more profitable than customers who are price sensitive and perceive few differences among alternative offerings. Second, a firm that is successful in developing strong relationships with customers secures important and durable advantages that are hard for competitors to understand, copy, or displace.

---

[1] Frederick E. Reichheld, "Lead for Loyalty," *Harvard Business Review* 79 (July–August 2001): p. 82.

[2] Douglas Bowman and Das Narayandas, "Linking Customer Management Effort to Customer Profitability in Business Markets," *Journal of Marketing Research* 41 (November 2004): pp. 433–447.

[3] George S. Day, "Managing Market Relationships," *Journal of the Academy of Marketing Science* 28 (winter 2000): p. 24.

[4] Rosabeth Moss Kanter, "Collaborative Advantage," *Harvard Business Review* 72 (July–August 1994): pp. 96–108.

[5] This section is based on George S. Day, "Managing Market Relationships," pp. 24–30, except when others are cited.

[6] Robert M. Morgan and Shelby D. Hunt, "The Commitment-Trust Theory of Relationship Marketing," *Journal of Marketing* 58 (July 1994): pp. 20–38.

FIGURE 4.1 | **THE RELATIONSHIP SPECTRUM**

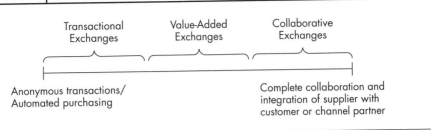

SOURCE: Figure from "Managing Market Relationships" by George S. Day from JOURNAL OF ACADEMY OF MARKETING SCIENCE 28 (Winter 2000), p. 25. Copyright © 2000. Reprinted by permission of Sage Publications, Inc.

Types of Relationships

A business marketer may begin a relationship with GE as a supplier (one of many), move to a preferred supplier status (one of a few), and ultimately enter a collaborative relationship with GE (sole source for particular items). Observe in Figure 4.1 that buyer-seller relationships are positioned on a continuum, with transactional exchange and collaborative exchange serving as the end points. Central to every relationship is an exchange process where each side gives something in return for a payoff of greater value. **Transactional exchange** centers on the timely exchange of basic products for highly competitive market prices. George Day notes that such exchanges

> include the kind of autonomous encounters a visitor to a city has with the taxi or bus from the airport, as well as series of ongoing transactions in a business-to-business market where the customer and supplier focus only on the timely exchange of standard products at competitive prices.[7]

Moving across the continuum, relationships become closer or more collaborative. The open exchange of information is a characteristic of collaborative (close) versus transactional (distant) exchange. Likewise, **operational linkages** reflect how much the systems, procedures, and routines of the buying and selling firms have been connected to facilitate operations.[8] These relationship connectors are a feature of a collaborative relationship. For example, such linkages provide the basis for order replenishment or just-in-time deliveries that Honda receives each day from suppliers at its Marysville, Ohio, production facility. **Collaborative exchange** features very close information, social, and operational linkages as well as mutual commitments made in expectation of long-run benefits. According to James Anderson and James Narus, collaborative exchange involves

> a process where a customer and supplier firm form strong and extensive social, economic, service, and technical ties over time, with the intent of lowering total costs and/or increasing value, thereby achieving mutual benefit.[9]

---

[7] Day, "Managing Market Relationships," p. 25.

[8] Joseph P. Cannon and William D. Perreault, Jr., "Buyer-Seller Relationships in Business Markets," *Journal of Marketing Research* 36 (November 1999): pp. 439–460.

[9] James C. Anderson and James A Narus, "Partnering as a Focused Market Strategy," *California Management Review* 33 (spring 1991): p. 96. See also Ven Srivam, Robert Krapfel, and Robert Spekman, "Antecedents to Buyer-Seller Collaboration: An Analysis from the Buyer's Perspective," *Journal of Business Research* (December 1992): pp. 303–320.

Value-Adding Exchanges

Between the two extremes on the relationship continuum are value-adding exchanges, where the focus of the selling firm shifts from attracting customers to keeping customers. The marketer pursues this objective by developing a comprehensive understanding of a customer's needs and changing requirements, tailoring the firm's offerings to those needs, and providing continuing incentives for customers to concentrate most of their purchases with them. To illustrate, Dell Computer provides a customized Web page for each of its premier corporate customers that individual employees in the customer organization can access for an array of information and technical support services.

Nature of Relationships

Transactional exchange involves items like packaging materials or cleaning services where competitive bidding is often employed to secure the best terms. Such exchanges are purely contractual arrangements that involve little or no emotional commitment to sustaining the relationship in the future. By contrast, customized, high-technology products—like semiconductor test equipment—fit the collaborative exchange category. Whereas transactional exchange centers on negotiations and an arm's-length relationship, collaborative exchange emphasizes joint problem solving and multiple linkages that integrate the processes of the two parties. Trust and commitment provide the foundation for collaborative exchange.[10] **Relationship commitment** involves a partner's belief that an ongoing relationship is so important that it deserves maximum efforts to maintain it. In turn, **trust** exists when one party has confidence in a partner's reliability and integrity. Recent research highlights the powerful role that contact personnel (for example, salespersons) assume in forging a long-term relationship. "Individuals who build trust in each other will transfer this bond to the firm level."[11]

Strategic Choices

Business marketers have some latitude in choosing where to participate along the relationship continuum. However, limits are imposed by the characteristics of the market and by the significance of the purchase to the buyer. A central challenge for the marketer is to overcome the gravitational pull toward the transaction end of the exchange spectrum. According to Day,

> Rivals are continually working to attract the best accounts away; customer requirements, expectations, and preferences keep changing, and the possibility of friction-free exploration of options in real time on the Web conspire to raise the rate of customer defections.[12]

---

[10] Morgan and Hunt, "The Commitment-Trust Theory," pp. 20–38. See also Patricia M. Doney and Joseph P. Cannon, "An Examination of the Nature of Trust in Buyer-Seller Relationships," *Journal of Marketing* 61 (April 1997): pp. 35–51.

[11] Das Narayandas and V. Kasturi Rangan, "Building and Sustaining Buyer-Seller Relationships in Mature Industrial Markets," *Journal of Marketing* 68 (July 2004): p. 74.

[12] Day, "Managing Market Relationships," p. 25.

B2B TOP PERFORMERS

Understanding the Customer's Business—the Key to Success

To forge a collaborative relationship with a customer, the business marketer requires a deep understanding of the customer's business, its key competitors, and its goals and strategies. In turn, a wealth of communication links are required across the partnering organizations at all levels of management. Salespersons not only work with the purchasing staff but also have close ties to senior executives. For example, for some of IBM's *Fortune* 500 customers, account executives are direct participants in the customer firm's strategy planning

sessions. Here IBM adds value to the relationship by providing specific recommendations concerning how its products and services can be used to advance the firm's competitive advantage. As a relationship with a large account grows and flourishes, a full-time sales team is often created to serve the needs of that customer. The team comprises sales, service, and technical specialists who have extensive knowledge of the customer's industry. Some team members have worked exclusively with a single customer organization for years.

Managing Buyer-Seller Relationships

Buyers and sellers craft different types of relationships in response to market conditions and the characteristics of the purchase situation. To develop specific relationship-marketing strategies for a particular customer, the business marketer must understand that some customers elect a collaborative relationship, whereas others prefer a more distant or transactional relationship. Figure 4.2 highlights the typical characteristics of relationships at the end points of the buyer-seller relationship spectrum.

FIGURE 4.2 | THE SPECTRUM OF BUYER-SELLER RELATIONSHIPS

	Transactional Exchange ←→	Collaborative Exchange
Availability of Alternatives	Many Alternatives	Few Alternatives
Supply Market Dynamism	Stable	Volatile
Importance of Purchase	Low	High
Complexity of Purchase	Low	High
Information Exchange	Low	High
Operational Linkages	Limited	Extensive

SOURCE: Adapted from Joseph P. Cannon and William D. Perreault Jr., "Buyer-Seller Relationships in Business Markets," *Journal of Marketing Research* 36 (November 1999): pp. 439–460.

Transactional Exchange

Customers are more likely to prefer a **transactional relationship** when a competitive supply market features many alternatives, the purchase decision is not complex, and the supply market is stable. This profile fits some buyers of office supplies, commodity chemicals, and shipping services. In turn, customers emphasize a transactional orientation when they view the purchase as less important to the organization's objectives. Such relationships are characterized by lower levels of information exchange and are less likely to involve operational linkages between the buying and selling firms.

Collaborative Exchange

Buying firms prefer a more **collaborative relationship** when alternatives are few, the market is dynamic (for example, rapidly changing technology), and the complexity of the purchase is high. In particular, buyers seek close relationships with suppliers when they deem the purchase important and strategically significant. This behavior fits some purchasers of manufacturing equipment, enterprise software, or critical component parts. Indeed, say Cannon and Perreault,

> the closest partnerships . . . arise both when the purchase is important and when there is a need—from the customer's perspective—to overcome procurement obstacles that result from fewer supply alternatives and more purchase uncertainty.[13]

Moreover, the relationships that arise for important purchases are more likely to involve operational linkages and high levels of information exchange. Switching costs are especially important to collaborative customers.

Switching Costs

In considering possible changes from one selling firm to another, organizational buyers consider two **switching costs:** investments and risk of exposure. First, organizational buyers invest in their relationships with suppliers in many ways. As Barbara Bund Jackson states:

> They invest *money;* they invest in *people,* as in training employees to run new equipment; they invest in *lasting assets,* such as equipment itself; and they invest in changing basic business *procedures* like inventory handling.[14]

Because of these past investments, buyers may hesitate to incur the disruptions and switching costs that result when they select new suppliers.

Risk of exposure provides a second major category of switching costs. Attention centers on the risks to buyers of making the wrong choice. Customers perceive more

---

[13] Cannon and Perreault, "Buyer-Seller Relationships," p. 453.

[14] Barbara Bund Jackson, "Build Customer Relationships That Last," *Harvard Business Review* 63 (November–December 1985): p. 125.

risk when they purchase products important to their operations, when they buy from less established suppliers, and when they buy technically complex products.

Strategy Guidelines

The business marketer manages a portfolio of relationships with customers—some of these customers view the purchase as important and desire a close, tightly connected buyer-seller relationship; other customers assign a lower level of importance to the purchase and prefer a looser relationship. Given the differing needs and orientations of customers, the business marketer's first step is to determine which type of relationship matches the purchasing situation and supply-market conditions for a particular customer. Second, a strategy must be designed that is appropriate for each strategy type.

Collaborative Customers   Relationship-building strategies, targeted on strong and lasting commitments, are especially appropriate for these customers. Business marketers can sensibly invest resources to secure commitments and directly assist customers with planning. Here sales and service personnel work not only with purchasing managers but also with a wide array of managers on strategy and coordination issues. Regular visits to the customer by executives and technical personnel can strengthen the relationship. Operational linkages and information-sharing mechanisms should be designed into the relationship to keep product and service offerings aligned with customer needs. Given the long time horizon and switching costs, customers are concerned both with the marketers' long-term capabilities and with their immediate performance. Because the customers perceive significant risk, they demand competence and commitment from sellers and are easily frightened by even a hint of supplier inadequacy.

Transaction Customers   These customers display less loyalty or commitment to a particular supplier and can easily switch part or all of the purchases from one vendor to another. A business marketer who offers an immediate, attractive combination of product, price, technical support, and other benefits has a chance of winning business from a transactional customer. The salesperson centers primary attention on the purchasing staff and seldom has important ties to senior executives in the buying organization. M. Bensaou argues that it is unwise for marketers to make specialized investments in transactional relationships:

> Firms that invest in building trust through frequent visits, guest engineers, and cross-company teams when the product and market context calls for simple, impersonal control and data exchange mechanisms are overdesigning the relationship. This path is not only costly but also risky, given the specialized investments involved, in particular, the intangible ones (for example, people, information, or knowledge).[15]

Rather than adopting the approach of "one design fits all," the astute marketer matches the strategy to the product and market conditions that surround a particular customer relationship and understands the factors that influence profitability.

---

[15] M. Bensaou, "Portfolio of Buyer-Seller Relationships," *Sloan Management Review* 40 (summer 1999): p. 43.

Measuring Customer Profitability[16]

To improve customer satisfaction and loyalty, many business-to-business firms have developed customized products and increased the specialized services they offer. Although customers embrace such actions, they often lead to declining profits, especially when the enhanced offerings are not accompanied by increases in prices or order volumes. For a differentiation strategy to succeed, "the value created by the differentiation—measured by higher margins and higher sales volumes—has to exceed the cost of creating and delivering customized features and services."[17] By understanding the drivers of customer profitability, the business marketing manager can more effectively allocate marketing resources and take action to convert unprofitable relationships into profitable ones.

Activity-Based Costing

Most studies of customer profitability yield a remarkable insight: "Only a minority of a typical company's customers is truly profitable."[18] Why? Many firms fail to examine how the costs of specialized products and services vary among individual customers. In other words, they focus on profitability at an aggregate level (for example, product or territory), fail to assign operating expenses to customers, and misjudge the profitability of individual customers. To capture customer-specific costs, many firms have adopted activity-based costing.

Activity-based costing (ABC) illuminates exactly what activities are associated with serving a particular customer and how these activities are linked to revenues and the consumption of resources.[19] The ABC system and associated software link customer transaction data from customer relationship management (CRM) systems with financial information. The ABC system provides marketing managers with a clear and accurate picture of the gross margins and cost-to-serve components that yield individual customer profitability.

Unlocking Customer Profitability

By accurately tracing costs to individual customers, managers are better equipped to diagnose problems and take appropriate action. For example, Kanthal, a heating wire manufacturer, learned to its surprise that one of its largest and most coveted accounts—General Electric's Appliance Division—was also one of its most unprofitable customers.[20] A customer order that normally would cost Kanthal $150 to process cost more than $600 from GE because of frequent order changes, expedited deliveries, and scheduling adjustments. A senior manager at Kanthal suggested to GE that the numerous change orders were costly not only to Kanthal but also to GE. After a quick internal

[16] This section, unless otherwise noted, draws on Robert S. Kaplan and V. G. Narayanan, "Measuring and Managing Customer Profitability," *Journal of Cost Management* 15, no. 5 (September–October 2001): pp. 5–15.

[17] Robert S. Kaplan, "Add a Customer Profitability Metric to Your Balanced Scorecard," *Balanced Scorecard Report*, July–August 2005 (Boston: Harvard Business School Publishing Corporation), p. 3.

[18] Kaplan and Narayanan, "Measuring and Managing Customer Profitability," p. 5.

[19] Ibid., p. 7. See also, Robert S. Kaplan and Steven R. Anderson, "Time-Driven Activity-Based Costing," *Harvard Business Review* 82 (November 2004): pp. 131–138.

[20] Kaplan and Narayanan, p. 11.

FIGURE 4.3 | THE WHALE CURVE OF CUMULATIVE PROFITABILITY

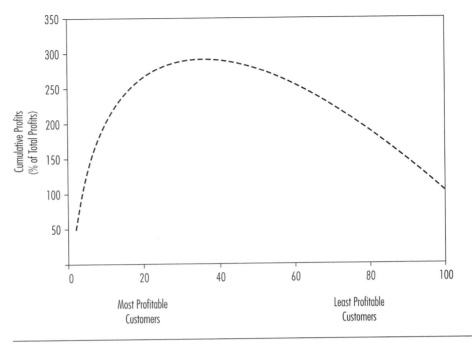

SOURCE: From "Measuring and Managing Customer Profitability" by Robert S. Kaplan from JOURNAL OF COST MANAGEMENT, September 2001. Copyright © 2001. Reprinted by permission of Warren, Gorham, Lamont via Copyright Clearance Center.

review, GE managers agreed, corrected internal inefficiencies, and then awarded Kanthal with the largest contract in the firm's history. The contract incorporated a surcharge for any change GE made to an existing order and established a minimum order size. By isolating the true cost of serving GE, Kanthal converted an unprofitable relationship to a profitable one and provided further value by helping a key customer reduce costs.

The Profitable Few

Once a firm implements an ABC approach and plots cumulative profitability against customers, a striking portrait emerges that is often referred to as the *whale curve* (Figure 4.3). Robert S. Kaplan, who is codeveloper of activity-based costing, and his colleague, V. G. Narayanan, describe the pattern that many companies find:

> Whereas cumulative sales usually follow the typical 20/80 rule (that is, 20 percent of the customers provide 80 percent of the sales), the whale curve for cumulative profitability usually reveals that the most profitable 20 percent of customers generate between 150 percent and 300 percent of total profits. The middle 70 percent of customers break even and the least profitable 10 percent of customers lose from 50 to 200 percent of total profits, leaving the company with its 100 percent of total profits.[21]

---

[21] Ibid., p. 7.

TABLE 4.1	THE CHARACTERISTICS OF HIGH- VERSUS LOW-COST-TO-SERVE CUSTOMERS

High-Cost-to-Serve Customers	Low-Cost-to-Serve Customers
Order custom products	Order standard products
Order small quantities	Order large quantities
Unpredictable order arrivals	Predictable order arrivals
Customized delivery	Standard delivery
Frequent changes in delivery requirements	No changes in delivery requirements
Manual processing	Electronic processing (EDI) (i.e., zero defects)
Large amounts of presales support (i.e., marketing, technical, and sales resources)	Little to no presales support (i.e., standard pricing and ordering)
Large amounts of postsales support (i.e., installation, training, warranty, field service)	No postsales support
Require company to hold inventory	Replenish as produced
Pay slowly (i.e., high accounts receivable)	Pay on time

SOURCE: From "Measuring and Managing Customer Profitability" by Robert S. Kaplan from JOURNAL OF COST MANAGEMENT, September 2001. Copyright © 2001. Reprinted by permission of Warren, Gorham, Lamont via Copyright Clearance Center.

As a rule, large customers tend to be included among the most profitable (see left side of Figure 4.3) or the least profitable (see right side of Figure 4.3)—they are seldom in the middle. Interestingly, some of the firm's largest customers often turn out to be among the most unprofitable. A firm does not generate enough sales volume with a small customer to incur large absolute losses. Only large buyers can be large-loss customers. In Figure 4.3, low-cost-to-serve customers appear on the profitable side of the whale curve and high-cost-to-serve customers end up on the unprofitable side unless they pay a premium price for the specialized support they require.

Managing High- and Low-Cost-to-Serve Customers

What causes some customers to be more expensive than others? Note from Table 4.1 that high-cost-to-serve customers, for example, desire customized products, frequently change orders, and require a significant amount of presales and postsales support. By contrast, low-cost-to-serve customers purchase standard products, place orders and schedule deliveries on a predictable cycle, and require little or no presales or postsales support.

Look Inside First   After reviewing the profitability of individual customers, the business marketer can consider possible strategies to retain the most valuable customers and to transform unprofitable customers into profitable ones. However, managers should first examine their company's own internal processes to ensure that it can accommodate customer preferences for reduced order sizes or special services at

FIGURE 4.4 | **CUSTOMER PROFITABILITY**

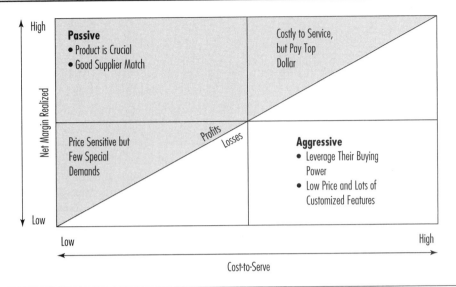

the lowest cost. For example, a large publisher of business directories reduced the cost of serving its customer base by assigning key account managers to its largest customers (that is, the 4 percent of customers who accounted for 45 percent of its sales) and serving the smallest customers over the Internet and by a telephone sales force.[22] These actions not only cut costs dramatically but also gave each group of customers what they had wanted all along: Large customers wanted a central point of contact where they could secure services customized to their needs; small customers preferred minimal contact with a direct salesperson but wanted the assurance that they could receive advice and support if required.

A Sharper Profit Lens   Business marketing managers can view their customers through the lens of a simple 2×2 diagram (Figure 4.4). The vertical axis shows the net margin earned from sales to a particular customer. The **net margin** equals the net price, after all discounts, minus manufacturing costs. The horizontal axis shows the **costs of serving the customer,** including order-related costs plus the customer-specific marketing, technical, and administrative expenses.

Identifying Profitable Customers   Observe from Figure 4.4 that profitable customers can take different forms. To illustrate, a customer like Honda of America would be at the lower left corner of the diagram: demanding low prices, so net margins are low, but also working with its suppliers to streamline activities so that the cost-to-serve is also low. High-cost-to-serve customers who occupy the upper right corner of

---

[22] George S. Day, "Creating a Superior Customer-Relating Capability," *MIT Sloan Management Review* 44 (spring 2003): pp. 77–82.

Figure 4.4 can also be profitable if the net margins earned on sales to them more than compensate the company for the cost of the resources used in serving them.

A company is indeed fortunate if several of its customers occupy the upper left-hand quadrant of the diagram: high margins *and* low cost-to-serve. Because these customers represent a valuable asset, marketing managers should forge close relationships with them, anticipate their changing needs, and have protective measures (for example, special services) in place in case competitors attempt to win them away.

Managing Unprofitable Customers[23]

The most challenging set of customers for marketing managers is found in the lower right-hand corner of Figure 4.4: low margins and high cost-to-serve. First, the marketing manager should explore possible ways to reduce the cost of activities associated with serving these customers. For example, perhaps postsales support could be shifted to the Internet. Second, the manager should direct attention to the customer actions that contribute to higher selling costs. To illustrate, the high cost-to-serve may be caused by the customer's unpredictable ordering patterns or by the large demands it places on technical and sales personnel. By detailing the costs of these activities and openly sharing this information with the customer, the business marketing manager can encourage the customer to work with the company more efficiently. From the earlier example, recall that Kanthal used this approach not only to restore profitability but also to help one of its largest customers, General Electric's Appliance Division, refine its internal processes and reduce its costs.

Firing Customers

By improving processes and refining pricing strategies, business marketing managers can transform many, but not all, customers from unprofitable to profitable. What should we do with those unprofitable customers that remain in the high-cost-to-serve quadrant of Figure 4.4? To answer this question, we have to dig deeper into the customer relationship and assess the other benefits that certain customers may provide. Some customers are new and the initial investment to attract them will ultimately be repaid in higher sales volume and profitability. Other customers provide an opportunity for learning. For example, some firms that serve Toyota or Honda incurred initial losses in serving these demanding customers but secured insights into management processes and technology they could effectively apply to all their customers.

Suppose, however, that a customer is unprofitable, not new, and offers little or no opportunity for learning. Furthermore, suppose that the customer resists all attempts to convert the unprofitable relationship into a profitable one. Under these conditions, Robert S. Kaplan and Robin Cooper observe that we might consider firing them, but a more subtle approach will do: "We can, perhaps, let the customer fire itself by refusing to grant discounts and reducing or eliminating marketing and technical support."[24]

---

[23] This section is based on Robert S. Kaplan and Robin Cooper, *Cost and Effect: Using Integrated Cost Systems to Drive Profitability and Performance* (Boston: Harvard Business School Press, 1998), pp. 193–201.

[24] Kaplan and Cooper, *Cost and Effect,* p. 200.

Customer Relationship Management

Customer retention has always been crucial to success in the business market, and it now provides the centerpiece of strategy discussions as firms embrace customer relationship management. **Customer relationship management** (CRM) is a cross-functional process for achieving

- a continuing dialogue with customers
- across all their contact and access points, with
- personalized treatment of the most valuable customers,
- to ensure customer retention and the effectiveness of marketing initiatives.[25]

To meet these challenging requirements, business marketing firms, large and small, are making substantial investments in CRM systems—enterprise software applications that integrate sales, marketing, and customer service information. To improve service and retain customers, CRM systems synthesize information from all of a company's contact points or "touch points"—including e-mail, call centers, sales and service representatives—to support later customer interactions and to inform market forecasts, product design, and supply chain management.[26] Salespersons, call center personnel, Web managers, resellers, and customer service representatives all have the same real-time information on each customer.

For an investment in CRM software to yield positive returns, a firm needs a customer strategy. Strategy experts contend that many CRM initiatives fail because executives mistake CRM software for a marketing strategy. Darrell Rigby and his colleagues contend: "It isn't. CRM is the bundling of customer strategy and processes, supported by relevant software, for the purpose of improving customer loyalty and, eventually, corporate profitability."[27] CRM software can help, but only after a customer strategy has been designed and executed. To develop responsive and profitable customer strategies, special attention must be given to five areas: (1) acquiring the right customers, (2) crafting the right value proposition, (3) instituting the best processes, (4) motivating employees, and (5) learning to retain customers (Table 4.2). Observe how CRM technology from leading producers such as Oracle Corporation and Siebel Systems can be used to capture critical customer data, transform it into valuable information, and distribute it throughout the organization to support the strategy process from customer acquisition to customer retention. Thus, a well-designed and executed customer strategy, supported by a CRM system, provides the financial payoff.

Acquiring the Right Customers

Customer relationship management directs attention to two critical assets of the business-to-business firm: its stock of current and potential customer relationships and its

---

[25] George S. Day, "Capabilities for Forging Customer Relationships," Working Paper, Report No. 00-118, Marketing Science Institute, Cambridge, Mass., 2000, p. 4

[26] Larry Yu, "Successful Customer-Relationship Management," *MIT Sloan Management Review* 42 (summer 2001): p. 18.

[27] Darrell K. Rigby, Frederick F. Reichheld, and Phil Schefter, "Avoid the Four Perils of CRM," *Harvard Business Review* 80 (January–February 2002): p. 102.

TABLE 4.2 | CREATING A CUSTOMER RELATIONSHIP MANAGEMENT STRATEGY

CRM Priorities				
Acquiring the Right Customers	**Crafting the Right Value Proposition**	**Instituting the Best Processes**	**Motivating Employees**	**Learning to Retain Customers**
Critical Tasks				
• Identify your most valuable customers. • Calculate your share of their purchases (wallet) for your goods and services.	• Determine the products or services your customers need today and will need tomorrow. • Assess the products or services that your competitors offer today and tomorrow. • Identify new products or services that you should be offering.	• Research the best way to deliver your products or services to customers. • Determine the service capabilities that must be developed and the technology investments that are required to implement customer strategy.	• Identify the tools your employees need to foster customer relationships. • Earn employee loyalty by investing in training and development and constructing appropriate career paths for employees.	• Understand why customers defect and how to win them back. • Identify the strategies your competitors are using to win your high-value customers.
CRM Technology Can Help				
• Analyze customer revenue and cost data to identify current and future high-value customers. • Target marketing communications to high-value customers.	• Capture relevant product and service behavior data from customer transactions. • Create new distribution channels. • Develop new pricing models.	• Process transactions faster. • Provide better information to customer contact employees. • Manage logistics and the supply chain more efficiently.	• Align employee incentives and performance measures. • Distribute customer knowledge to employees throughout the organization.	• Track customer-defection and retention levels. • Track customer-service satisfaction levels.

SOURCE: Adapted from Darrell K. Rigby, Frederick F. Reichheld, and Phil Schefter, "Avoid the Four Perils of CRM," *Harvard Business Review* 80 (January–February 2002): p. 106.

collective knowledge of how to select, initiate, develop, and maintain profitable relationships with these customers.[28] Customer portfolio management, then, is the process of creating value across a firm's customer relationships—from transactional to collaborative—with an emphasis on balancing the customer's desired level of relationship against the profitability of doing so.[29]

Account selection requires a clear understanding of customer needs, a tight grasp on the costs of serving different groups of customers, and an accurate forecast of

[28] John E. Hogan, Katherine N. Lemon, and Roland T. Rust, "Customer Equity Management: Charting New Directions for the Future of Marketing," *Journal of Services Research* 5 (August 2002): pp. 4–12.

[29] Michael D. Johnson and Fred Selnes, "Diversifying Your Customer Portfolio," *MIT Sloan Management Review* 46 (spring 2005): pp. 11–14.

INSIDE BUSINESS MARKETING

Diversify a Customer Portfolio Too!

For an investor, modern portfolio theory demonstrates that optimal performance, for a given level of risk, can best be achieved by building a diversified mix of investment assets that includes the stocks of both large and small firms, representing both U.S. and foreign companies. In building a customer portfolio, similar benefits can be realized by viewing customers as assets and diversifying across categories of customers. For example, after the technology bubble, many information technology (IT) companies, like IBM and Microsoft, were surprised to observe that small and medium-sized businesses (SMB) fueled the recovery in IT spending. Why? Most of the SMB customers did not overindulge in massive hardware

and software upgrades to the same extreme extent during the bubble as their large-enterprise counterparts did. So, SMB customers were the first to return and aggressively buy IT products and services. Because Dell, Microsoft, and IBM each have a customer portfolio that includes a strong representation of SMB customers, these firms enjoyed an edge over rivals such as Hewlett-Packard and Sun Microsystems that were less focused on this customer group (that is, asset category) and were "caught waiting" for large enterprise customers to return.

SOURCE: Mark Veverka, "Little Guys Lead IT Spending Recovery," *Barron's*, October 20, 2003, p. 73.

potential profit opportunities. The choice of potential accounts to target is facilitated by an understanding of how different customers define value. **Value,** as defined by James Anderson and James Narus, refers to "the economic, technical, service, and social benefits received by a customer firm in exchange for the price paid for a product offering."[30] By gauging the value of their offerings to different groups of customers, business marketers are better equipped to target accounts and to determine how to provide enhanced value to particular customers.

The account selection process should also consider profit potential. Because the product is critical to their operations, some customers place a high value on supporting services (for example, technical advice and training) and are willing to pay a premium price for them. Other customers are most costly to serve, do not value service support, and are extremely price sensitive. Because customers have different needs and represent different levels of current and potential opportunities, a marketer should divide its customers into groups. The marketer wishes to develop a broader and deeper relationship with the most profitable ones and assign a low priority to the least profitable ones.[31] Frank Cespedes asserts that

> account selection, therefore, must be explicit about which demands the seller can meet and leverage in dealings with other customers. Otherwise, the seller risks overserving unprofitable accounts and wasting resources that might be allocated to other customer groups.[32]

---

[30] Anderson and Narus, p. 98. See also, Ajay Menon, Christian Homburg, and Nikolas Beutin, "Understanding Customer Value in Business-to-Business Relationships," *Journal of Business-to-Business Marketing* 12, no. 2 (2005): pp. 1–33; and Wolfgang Ulaga and Samir Chacour, "Measuring Perceived Customer Value in Business Markets: A Prerequisite for Marketing Strategy Development and Implementation," *Industrial Marketing Management* 30 (June 2001): pp. 525–540.

[31] Frederick F. Reichheld, "Lead for Loyalty," *Harvard Business Review* 79 (July–August 2001), pp. 76–84.

[32] Frank V. Cespedes, *Concurrent Marketing: Integrating Product, Sales, and Service* (Boston: Harvard Business School Press, 1995), p. 193. See also Don Peppers, Martha Rogers, and Bob Dorf, "Is Your Company Ready for One-to-One Marketing?" *Harvard Business Review* 77 (January–February 1999): pp. 151–160.

FIGURE 4.5 | **TRANSACTIONAL AND COLLABORATIVE WORKING RELATIONSHIPS**

(a) Industry Relationship Bandwidths

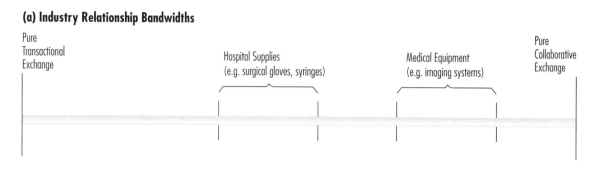

(b) "Flaring Out" from the Industry Bandwidth

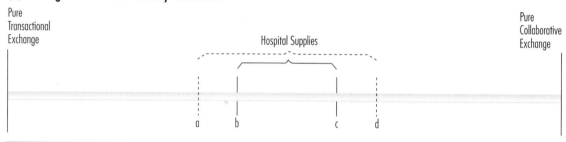

SOURCE: Adapted from James C. Anderson and James A. Narus, "Partnering as a Focused Marketing Strategy," *California Management Review* 33 (spring 1991): p. 97.

Crafting the Right Value Proposition

A **value proposition** represents the products, services, ideas, and solutions that a business marketer offers to advance the performance goals of the customer organization. To develop customer-specific product offerings, the business marketer should next examine the nature of buyer-seller relationships in the industry. The strategies competing firms in an industry pursue fall into a range referred to as the **industry bandwidth** of working relationships.[33] Business marketers either attempt to span the bandwidth with a portfolio of relationship-marketing strategies or concentrate on a single strategy, thereby having a narrower range of relationships than the industry bandwidth.

Observe in Figure 4.5 how two different industries (medical equipment and hospital supplies) are positioned on the relationship continuum. Because the underlying technology is complex and dynamic, collaborative relations characterize the medical equipment industry. Here, a range of services—technical support, installation, professional training, and maintenance agreements—can augment the core product. By contrast, collaborative relations in the hospital supply industry tend to be more focused and center on helping health-care organizations meet their operational needs (for example, efficient ordering processes and timely delivery).

---

[33] This discussion draws on Anderson and Narus, "Partnering as a Focused Market Strategy," pp. 95–113.

By diagnosing the spectrum of relationship strategies competitors in an industry follow, a business marketer can tailor strategies that more closely respond both to customers who desire a collaborative emphasis and to those who seek a transaction emphasis. The strategy involves *flaring out* from the industry bandwidth in the collaborative as well as in the transactional direction (see Figure 4.5b).

Flaring Out by Unbundling   An unbundling strategy can reach customers who desire a greater transaction emphasis. Here, related services are unbundled to yield the core product (**a** in Figure 4.5b), which meets a customer's basic price, quality, and availability requirements. For each service that is unbundled, the price is lowered. Augmented services, such as technical assistance, consulting, and just-in-time delivery, are each offered, but in a menu fashion, on an incremental price basis. Importantly, the price increments for the entire set of unbundled services should be greater than the price premium sought for the collaborative offering. This reflects the efficiencies of providing the complete bundle of services to a collaborative account. This pricing policy is market oriented in that it allows customer firms to choose the product and relationship offering that *they perceive* to provide the greatest value.

Flaring Out with Augmentation   At the other extreme, the collaborative offering (**d** in Figure 4.5b) becomes the augmented product enriched with features the customer values. Augmented features might include coordinated cost-reduction programs, technical assistance, delivery schedule guarantees, and cooperative advertising. Because collaborative efforts are designed to add value or reduce the costs of exchange between partnering firms, a price premium should be received for the collaborative offering.

Allegiance Healthcare Corporation has developed ways to improve hospital supply ordering, delivery, and billing that provide enhanced value to the customer.[34] Instead of miscellaneous supplies arriving in boxes sorted at the convenience of Alliance's needs, they arrive on "client-friendly" pallets customized to meet the distribution needs of the individual hospital. Moreover, hospitals can secure a structural connection to Allegiance through its ValueLink ordering system for added value and convenience.

Creating Flexible Service Offerings   Business marketers can gain a competitive edge by creating a portfolio of service offerings and then drawing on this portfolio to provide customized solutions for groups of customers or even individual customers.[35] First, an offering should be created that includes the bare-bones-minimum number of services valued by all customers in a particular market segment. Microsoft refers to these offerings as "naked solutions." Second, optional services are created that add value by reducing costs or improving the performance of a customer's operations. To meet the needs of particular customers, optional services can then be "custom wrapped" with the core offering to create added value.

---

[34] Valarie A. Zeithaml, Roland T. Rust, and Katherine N. Lemon, "The Customer Pyramid: Creating and Serving Profitable Customers," *California Management Review* 43 (summer 2001): p. 134.

[35] James C. Anderson and James A. Narus, "Capturing the Value of Supplementary Services," *Harvard Business Review* 73 (January–February 1995): pp. 75–83. See also James C. Anderson and James A. Narus, "Business Marketing: Understand What Customers Value," *Harvard Business Review* 76 (November–December 1998): pp. 53–67.

TABLE 4.3 | ROLE-BASED STRATEGY EXECUTION AT IBM: MEASURED ACTIONS AND RESULTS

Role	Strategy Goal	Measured Actions	Measured Results (Customer)
Relationship Owner	Improve Customer Relationships	Meet with customer twice per year to identify customer's expectations and set action plan	IBM Customer Satisfaction Survey Results
Project Owner	Exceed Customer Expectations for Each Transaction	Collect conditions of satisfaction, get customer feedback	IBM Transaction Survey Results
Problem Resolution	Fix Customer Problems	Solve in seven days or meet action plan	Customer Satisfaction with Problem Resolution

SOURCE: Adapted from Larry Schiff, "How Customer Satisfaction Improvement Works to Fuel Business Recovery at IBM," *Journal of Organizational Excellence* (spring 2001): pp. 12–14.

Instituting the Best Processes

The sales force assumes a central relationship-management role in the business market. Technical service and customer service personnel also assume implementation roles that are important and visible in buying organizations. Successful relationship strategies are shaped by an effective organization and deployment of the personal selling effort and close coordination with supporting units, such as logistics and technical service. Some firms divide the sales organization into units that each serve a distinct relationship category such as transactional accounts or partnership accounts. Through a careful screening process, promising transaction accounts are periodically upgraded to partnerships.

Best Practices at IBM[36]   In serving a particular customer, a number of IBM employees come into contact with the customer organization. To ensure consistent strategy execution, IBM identifies three customer-contact roles for each of its accounts, specifies desired measurable actions for each role, and monitors the customer's degree of satisfaction with each role (Table 4.3). The IBM client representative assigned to the customer is the *relationship owner,* but the account team may include other specialists who complete a project for the customer *(project owner)* or solve a particular customer problem *(problem resolution owner).* Any IBM employee who works on the account can secure timely information from the CRM system to identify recent actions or issues to be addressed. Moreover, for each role, there is an in-process measure and a customer feedback measure.

Consider an IBM technical manager assigned responsibility for installing CRM software for a large bank. As a project owner, this manager's goal is to determine the customer's conditions of satisfaction and then exceed those expectations. When the work is completed, members of the customer organization are queried concerning their satisfaction and the project owner acts on the feedback to ensure that all promises have been kept. Clearly, a sound complaint management process is essential.

---

[36] This discussion is based on Larry Schiff, "How Customer Satisfaction Improvement Works to Fuel Full Business Recovery at IBM," *Journal of Organizational Excellence* 20 (spring 2001): pp. 3–18.

Recent research found that if a complaint is ineffectively handled, the firm faces a high risk of losing *even* those customers who had previously been very satisfied.[37]

Research suggests that the performance attributes that influence the customer satisfaction of business buyers include:

- the responsiveness of the supplier in meeting the firm's needs
- product quality
- a broad product line
- delivery reliability
- knowledgeable sales and service personnel.[38]

Motivating Employees

Dedicated employees are the cornerstone of a successful customer relationship strategy. Frederick F. Reichheld notes,

> Leaders who are dedicated to treating people right drive themselves to deliver superior value, which allows them to attract and retain the best employees. That's partly because higher profits result from customer retention, but more important, it's because providing excellent service and value generates pride and a sense of purpose among employees.[39]

Employee loyalty is earned by investing heavily in training and development, providing challenging career paths to facilitate professional development, and aligning employee incentives to performance measures.[40] For example, Square D, an Illinois-based producer of electrical and industrial equipment, altered its performance-measurement and incentive systems to fit the firm's new customer strategy. Consistent with the goal of attracting high-value customers, salesperson incentives are no longer based on the number of units sold but on the number of customers acquired and on profit margins.

Learning to Retain Customers

Business marketers track customer loyalty and retention because the cost of serving a long-standing customer is often far less than the cost of acquiring a new customer.[41] Why? Established customers often buy more products and services from a trusted supplier and, as they do, the cost of serving them declines. The firm learns how to serve them more efficiently and also spots opportunities for expanding the relationship. Thus, the profit from that customer tends to increase over the life of the relationship. To that end, a goal for IBM is to gain an increasing share of a customer's total information technology expenditures (that is, share of wallet). Rather than merely attempting to improve

---

[37] Christian Homburg and Andreas Fürst, "How Organizational Complaint Handling Drives Customer Loyalty: An Analysis of the Mechanistic and the Organic Approach," *Journal of Marketing* 69 (July 2005): pp. 95–114.

[38] Bowman and Narayandas, "Linking Customer Management Effort," pp. 433–447.

[39] Reichheld, "Lead for Loyalty," p. 78.

[40] Rigby, Reichheld, and Schefter, "Avoid the Perils of CRM," p. 104.

[41] Reichheld, "Lead for Loyalty," pp. 76–84.

satisfaction ratings, IBM seeks to be recognized as providing superior value to its customers. Larry Schiff, an IBM strategist, notes: "If you delight your customers and are perceived to provide the best value in your market, you'll gain loyalty and market/wallet share."[42] Although loyal customers are likely to be satisfied, all satisfied customers do not remain loyal. Business marketers earn customer loyalty by providing superior value that ensures high satisfaction and by nurturing trust and mutual commitments.[43]

Pursuing Growth from Existing Customers   Business marketers should identify a well-defined set of existing customers who demonstrate growth potential and selectively pursue a greater share of their business. Based on the cost-to-serve and projected profit margins, the question becomes: Which of our existing customers represent the best growth prospects? In targeting individual customers, particular attention should be given to: (1) estimating the current share of wallet the firm has attained; (2) pursuing opportunities to increase that share; and (3) carefully projecting the enhanced customer profitability that will result.[44]

Evaluating Relationships   Some relationship-building efforts fail because the expectations of the parties do not mesh—for example, when the business marketer follows a relationship approach and the customer responds in a transaction mode.[45] By isolating customer needs and the costs of augmented service features, the marketer is better equipped to profitably match product offerings to the particular customer's needs.

The goal of a relationship is to enable the buyer and seller to maximize joint value. This points to the need for a formal evaluation of relationship outcomes. For example, Motorola sales executives work closely with their partnership accounts to establish mutually defined goals. After an appropriate period, partnerships that do not meet these goals are downgraded and shifted from the strategic market sales force to the geographic sales force.

Business marketers should also continually update the value of their product and relationship offering. Attention here should center on particular new services that might be incorporated as well as on existing services that might be unbundled or curtailed. Working relationships with customer firms are among the most important marketing assets of the firm. They deserve delicate care and continual nurturing!

Gaining a Customer Relationship Advantage[46]

George Day argues that now that CRM has become fashionable and there is broad acceptance of the need to forge close ties with customers, many firms fail to gain a competitive advantage from their CRM initiatives. Why? As software manufacturers and

[42] Schiff, "How Customer Satisfaction Improvement Works to Fuel Full Business Recovery at IBM," p. 8.

[43] Day, "Capabilities for Forging Customer Relationships," p. 11.

[44] James C. Anderson and James A. Narus, "Selectively Pursuing More of Your Customer's Business," *MIT Sloan Management Review* 44 (spring 2003): pp. 42–49.

[45] Frederick E. Webster Jr., *Market-Driven Management: Using the New Marketing Concept to Create a Customer-Oriented Company* (New York: John Wiley & Sons, 1994), pp. 166–171.

[46] This section is based on George S. Day, "Capabilities for Forging Customer Relationships," pp. 3–33. See also George S. Day, "Creating a Superior Customer-Relating Capability," pp. 77–82.

INSIDE BUSINESS MARKETING

Do Interpersonal Relationships Matter to Corporate Buyers?

Recent research by Kenneth H. Wathne, Harald Biong, and Jan B. Heide reveals new insights into the role of interpersonal relationships on a corporate buyer's decision to switch suppliers. Using a survey of 39 key account managers at a commercial bank and 114 of the bank's corporate customers, the researchers examined how three factors influence the buyer's decision to switch to another supplier: (1) interpersonal relationships between the account manager and the buyer; (2) the existence of special processes, custom software, or other switching costs on the buying side; and (3) the marketing program: product/price.

The results indicate that although interpersonal ties matter, price and switching costs are more important. Because switching costs create a buffer to competition, business marketers could create customized products, bundled services, or special training programs to connect the customer more closely to the firm's offerings. Such strategies give the buyer a greater stake in the firm's offerings, thereby making them reluctant to switch to another supplier.

SOURCE: Kenneth H. Wathne, Harald Biong, and Jan B. Heide, "Choice of Supplier in Embedded Markets: Relationship and Marketing Program Effect," *Journal of Marketing* 65 (April 2001), pp. 54–66.

consulting organizations diffuse best practices, and the relevant software becomes widely available and economical to use, all competitors are equally equipped. This raises important questions for business marketers. What are the distinctive capabilities of firms that excel at customer relationship management? Compared with rivals, why are some firms rewarded by customers with higher rates of loyalty and lower rates of defection?

Customer-Relating Capability

A customer-relating capability is best nurtured in a market-driven organization and is exercised through a complex process of knowledge acquisition, sharing, and application. Research suggests that this capability includes three tightly connected components (Figure 4.6).

1. **Orientation toward Relationships**   A relationship orientation is embedded within the culture of the firm and reveals the standards members of the organization use to set priorities and make decisions about customer retention. A firm with a superior orientation would display these characteristics:

   • Customer retention is a shared goal throughout the organization.

   • Organizational members demonstrate a commitment and act quickly on information received from customers such as complaints, requests, or changes in requirements.

   • All employees understand and appreciate the lifetime value of a customer.

   • Employees have considerable latitude when taking action to satisfy customers.

2. **Information about Relationships**   This component of a firm's customer-relating capability hinges on the availability, quality, and depth of relevant customer

FIGURE 4.6 | ACHIEVING A RELATIONSHIP ADVANTAGE

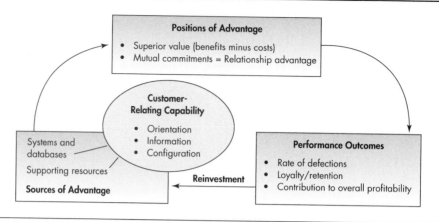

SOURCE: George S. Day, "Capabilities for Forging Customer Relationships," Working Paper, Report No. 00-118, Marketing Science Institute, Cambridge, Mass., 2000, p. 10. Copyright 2000 by Marketing Science Institute and George S. Day, Boisi Professor, The Wharton School, University of Pennsylvania.

information and, more importantly, on how that information is used to change how the organization collectively responds to customers. Clearly, some firms are better equipped than others to gather timely customer information, share the information throughout the organization, and then convert that information into knowledge that can be used to develop offerings that more precisely fit customer needs. In short, competitive advantage means outperforming rivals during all stages of the market-learning process.

3. **Configuration**   This element of customer-relating capability includes the structure, systems, and processes that enable information to be applied within the organization. Noteworthy characteristics include the organizational design, incentive systems, and activities and processes that enable personalized solutions for customers. Firms that demonstrate a superior configuration of a customer-relating capability fit the following profile:

- Organizational members support the goal and means of achieving a relationship advantage.

- The organization is designed around customers rather than partitioned by products or functions.

- Performance measures and incentive systems emphasize customer retention.

- A compelling value proposition is offered to customers "that recognizes customer differences and puts customer retention at the center of strategy."[47]

- The firm's supporting resource base features processes that enable the organization to personalize or mass-customize marketing communications, products, and services.

---

[47] Day, "Capabilities for Forging Customer Relationships," p. 15.

Leading firms with strong customer-relating capabilities, like GE Capital and Square D, emphasize a customer-centric culture and are organized around customer segments rather than product groups.[48]

Gaining a Position of Advantage

Whether a firm gains a relational advantage ultimately depends on the customer's judgment that a close relationship with a supplier provides superior value (that is, benefits that exceed costs). Such benefits, for example, might include technical assistance, superior responsiveness to service requests, or a customized solution precisely tailored to the customer's needs. Experts suggest that the strongest positional advantages are secured when customers are willing to make mutual commitments.[49] These mutual commitments might range from open information exchanges or the creation of operational linkages to the cross-firm coordination of new-product-development activities. To illustrate, key suppliers to Harley-Davidson work on-site during new product development projects, wear company badges, and have access to internal information systems.[50] However, relationship-building strategies yield more productive results in some market environments than in others.

Gauging the Payoff   The contribution of a customer-relating capability to a firm's competitive position depends on the profit potential that customized strategies may provide in the industry and the edge the firm enjoys over rivals in implementing this strategy. To justify the cost of personalization and offer the potential for positive results, the product or service must represent a continuing requirement (that is, not a one-time purchase) and the value of individual transactions must be large enough to warrant a personalized strategy. Alternatively, customized relationship-building strategies are not productive if customer needs are homogeneous, the product has a low frequency of purchase, and the value of a transaction is low. The highest payoff comes when the customer base includes a small proportion of customers who represent high levels of long-term profit potential, whereas the rest offer far less opportunity.

Achieving Performance Rewards

The contribution of a firm's customer-relating capability to the firm's position of advantage depends on (1) the degree to which the market offers an attractive opportunity for a strategy that highlights customer-relationship building and (2) the edge the firm enjoys over its competitors in pursuing this strategy. If the appropriate market conditions are present, the firm's relationship advantage will be rewarded with lower rates of customer defection, greater customer loyalty and retention, and higher profit margins than its competitors.

---

[48] Thomas H. Davenport, Jeanne G. Harris, and Ajay K. Kohli, "How Do They Know Their Customers So Well?" *MIT Sloan Management Review* 42 (winter 2001): pp. 63–72.

[49] Holm Blankenburg, D. K. Eriksson, and J. Johansson, "Creating Value through Mutual Commitments to Business Network Relationships," *Strategic Management Journal* 20 (May 1999): pp. 467–486.

[50] Dave Nelson, Patricia E. Moody, and Jonathan Stegner, *The Purchasing Machine* (New York: The Free Press, 2001), pp. 89–90.

Summary

Relationships, rather than simple transactions, provide the central focus in business marketing. By demonstrating superior skills in managing relationships with key customers as well as with alliance partners, business marketing firms can create a collaborative advantage.

To develop profitable relationships with customers, business marketers must first understand the different forms that exchange relationships can take. Transactional exchange centers on the timely exchange of basic products and services for highly competitive market prices. By contrast, collaborative exchange involves very close personal, informational, and operational connections the parties develop to achieve long-term mutual goals. Across the relationship spectrum, different types of relationships feature different relationship connectors. For example, collaborative relationships for important purchases emphasize operational linkages that integrate the operations of the buying and selling organization and involve high levels of information exchange.

Activity-based costing provides a solid foundation for measuring and managing the profitability of individual customers. When the full costs of serving customers are known, many companies find that 15 to 20 percent of the customers generate 100 percent (or much more) of the profits, a large group of customers break even, and 5 to 10 percent of the customers generate sizable losses. By measuring the cost-to-serve and the net profit from individual customers, business marketing managers can take actions to transform unprofitable relationships into profitable ones through process improvements, menu-based pricing, or relationship management.

Customer relationship management involves aligning customer strategy and business processes for the purpose of improving customer loyalty and, eventually, corporate profitability. To that end, a customer strategy encompasses (1) acquiring the right customers; (2) crafting the right value proposition; (3) instituting the best processes; (4) motivating employees; and (5) learning to retain customers. To excel at customer-relationship management, a firm requires a customer-relating capability. This capability, best nurtured in a market-driven organization, includes a strong relationship orientation among employees, a rich and widely used information base, and systems, processes, and incentives that enable personalized solutions for customers.

Discussion Questions

1. A marketing research company found that 6 percent of its clients generated 30 percent of sales and nearly all of its profits. At the other end of the continuum, 70 percent of its clients provided annual billings (revenue) that were below break-even levels, because these customers required an extensive amount of service from research employees. The company took immediate action to terminate relationships with clients who would not give them a higher share of their marketing research expenditures. Evaluate this decision and suggest a set of criteria that the firm might use to screen new clients.

2. Describe how a firm might use menu-based pricing to restore profitability to a high-cost-to-serve customer who demands extensive service and customized support.

3. Evaluate this statement: Large customers tend to be either the most or least profitable in the customer base of a business-to-business firm.

4. Ford develops "collaborative relationships" with some suppliers and "transactional relationships" with other suppliers. What criteria would purchasing executives use in segmenting suppliers into these two categories? Describe the steps a business marketer might take to move the relationship with Ford from a transaction relationship to a more collaborative one.

5. Some consulting organizations persuasively argue that by properly incorporating suppliers into their product development process, firms can cut their bills for purchased parts and materials by as much as 30 percent. Explore how a buyer-seller partnership might create these cost savings.

6. Concerning buyer-seller relationships, compare and contrast the features of a collaborative relationship versus a transactional relationship in the business market. Describe how the operational linkages might differ by relationship type.

7. Why is the cost of serving a long-standing customer far less than the cost of acquiring a new customer?

8. Discuss the switching costs that Southwest Airlines would incur if it began to phase out its fleet of Boeing airliners with replacements from Airbus Industrie. What steps could Airbus take to reduce these switching costs? How might Boeing counter to strengthen its relationship with Southwest?

9. Describe how an office supply firm may have a core offering of products and services for a small manufacturer and an augmented offering for a university.

10. Evaluate this statement: Once all firms in an industry have adopted CRM software, it will be nearly impossible for one firm to secure a competitive advantage on the basis of its customer strategy.

Internet Exercise

Oracle Corporation provides customer relationship management software solutions to all sectors of the business market. Go to http://oracle.com and review "success stories" and

1. identify a particular Oracle customer from the government sector, and

2. describe the benefits that this government customer received from the software solution.

CASE

Siebel Systems[51]

Rather than merely creating a superb company, Tom Siebel, of Siebel Systems, is identified by some as the founder of a new business area: customer relationship management (CRM). CRM software applications allow organizations to create a single source of customer information that sales, service, and marketing professionals can use to tailor product and service offerings to the needs of their customers. Although computer technology has been successfully applied to other business activities—like manufacturing and accounting—"the problems of sales and customer service had been largely untouched," Siebel notes. "It seemed highly likely that one could use computer technology to establish and maintain customer relationships. It seemed to me there would be an opportunity to build a pretty nice business here."[52]

He was right! However, the success of Siebel and the large market opportunity have attracted a field of strong competitors, including Oracle and SAP AG, the resource-planning software leader, which has launched a massive CRM initiative.

The guiding principle that drives the strategy at Siebel is the belief that, to succeed, companies must apply sophisticated information technology to identify, acquire, and retain the most valuable customers while ensuring the highest levels of customer satisfaction. Included among Siebel customers are Lockheed Martin, Whirlpool Corporation, Charles Schwab, and Chase Manhattan Bank. Based on this prized customer list, Oracle paid nearly $6 billion to acquire Siebel Systems in 2006. Despite the fast start and enormous potential, some critics charge that CRM is losing its luster because the concept was "overhyped" from the start. Research by Gartner Group found that more than half of all CRM projects fail to meet customer expectations. In addition, the cost of a CRM solution can range from $60 million to $130 million, according to Forrester Research, and it takes at least 24 months to implement CRM within an organization.[53] But experts counter that many of these shortcomings are due to "companies rushing to install the software without having a sharply-defined customer strategy in the first place."[54]

Discussion Questions

1. When evaluating alternative CRM software solutions (for example, Siebel versus SAP), the buying center includes members of top management, often including the CEO and the CIO (chief information officer), as well as senior marketing and sales executives, among others. What purchase criteria might these different members of the buying center emphasize? Would marketing executives reflect different priorities than their information technology colleagues?

2. How could a CRM system be used to improve the efficiency and effectiveness of marketing strategy?

3. Once the CRM system has been fully implemented, how could a firm gauge the financial returns that it is receiving on its investment?

---

[51] This discussion is drawn from Doug Bartholomew, "The King of Customer," *IndustryWeek.com* (February 2002): pp. 1–3.

[52] Ibid., p. 2.

[53] Darrell K. Rigby, Frederick F. Reichheld, and Phil Schefter, "Avoid the Four Perils of CRM," *Harvard Business Review* 80 (January–February 2002): p. 102.

[54] Bartholomew, "The King of Customer," p. 3.

PART

III

ASSESSING MARKET OPPORTUNITIES

Segmenting the Business Market

The business marketing manager serves a market comprising many different types of organizational customers with varying needs. Only when this aggregate market is broken down into meaningful categories can the business marketing strategist readily and profitably respond to unique needs. After reading this chapter, you will understand:

1. the benefits of and requirements for segmenting the business market.

2. the potential bases for segmenting the business market.

3. a procedure for evaluating and selecting market segments.

4. the role of market segmentation in the development of business marketing strategy.

A strategist at Hewlett-Packard notes:

> Knowing customers' needs is not enough. . . . We need to know what new products, features, and services will surprise and delight them. We need to understand their world so well that we can bring new technology to problems that customers may not yet truly realize they have.[1]

High-growth companies, large and small, succeed by

- selecting a well-defined group of potentially profitable customers.
- developing a distinctive value proposition (product and/or service offering) that meets these customers' needs better than their competitors.
- focusing marketing resources on acquiring, developing, and retaining profitable customers.[2]

The business market consists of three broad sectors—commercial enterprises, institutions, and government. Whether marketers elect to operate in one or all of these sectors, they encounter diverse organizations, purchasing structures, and decision-making styles. Each sector has many segments; each segment may have unique needs and require a unique marketing strategy. For example, some customers demonstrate attractive profit potential and are receptive to a relationship strategy, whereas others adopt a short-term, transaction focus, suggesting the need for a more streamlined strategy response.[3] The business marketer who recognizes the needs of the various market segments is best equipped to isolate profitable market opportunities and respond with an effective marketing program.

The goal of this chapter is to demonstrate how the manager can select and evaluate segments of the business market. First, the chapter delineates the benefits of and the requirements for successful market segmentation. Second, it explores and evaluates specific bases for segmenting the business market. This section demonstrates the application of key buyer behavior concepts and secondary information sources to market segmentation decisions. Third, the chapter provides a framework for evaluating and selecting market segments. Procedures for assessing the costs and benefits of entering alternative market segments and for implementing a segmentation strategy are emphasized.

Business Market Segmentation Requirements and Benefits

Yoram Wind and Richard N. Cardozo define a **market segment** as "a group of present or potential customers with some common characteristic which is relevant in explaining (and predicting) their response to a supplier's marketing

---

[1] David E. Schnedler, "Use Strategic Market Models to Predict Customer Behavior," *Sloan Management Review* 37 (spring 1996): p. 92; see also, Eric von Hippel, Stefan Thomke, and Mary Sonnack, "Creating Breakthroughs at 3M," *Harvard Business Review* 77 (September–October 1999): pp. 47–57.

[2] Dwight L. Gertz and João P. A. Baptista, *Grow to Be Great: Breaking the Downsizing Cycle* (New York: The Free Press, 1995), p. 54.

[3] Per Vagn Freytog and Ann Højbjerg Clarke, "Business to Business Market Segmentation," *Industrial Marketing Management* 30 (August 2001): pp. 473–486.

stimuli."[4] In the business market, a select group of customers often accounts for a disproportionate share of a firm's sales and profit. An extensive survey of business-to-business firms found that the top 20 percent of customers contributed a median 75 percent of sales volume to these firms and that 50 percent of a typical firm's sales came from just 10 percent of its customers.[5] What about profit? When the costs of serving particular customers are isolated, many firms are surprised to learn that a large portion of their current customer base contributes little to profitability. Often, 15 to 20 percent of the customers generate 100 percent (or more) of the profits.[6] Such patterns demonstrate the importance of choosing market segments wisely.

Requirements

A business marketer has five criteria for evaluating the desirability of potential market segments:

1. *Measurability*—The degree to which information on the particular buyer characteristics exists or can be obtained.

2. *Accessibility*—The degree to which the firm can effectively focus its marketing efforts on chosen segments.

3. *Substantiality*—The degree to which the segments are large or profitable enough to be worth considering for separate marketing cultivation.

4. *Compatibility*—The degree to which the firm's marketing and business strengths match the present and expected competitive and technological state of the market.

5. *Responsiveness*—The degree to which segments respond differently to different marketing mix elements, such as pricing or product features.

Thus, the art of market segmentation involves identifying groups of consumers that are large and unique enough to justify a separate marketing strategy. The competitive environment of the market segment is a factor that must be analyzed.

Evaluating the Competitive Environment

In selecting a market segment, the business marketer is also choosing a competitive environment. Richard A. D'Aveni emphasizes that, in extremely dynamic industries, such as the computer or telecommunications industries, "market stability is threatened by short product life cycles, short product design cycles, new technologies, frequent entry by unexpected outsiders, repositioning by incumbents, and radical redefinitions

[4]Yoram Wind and Richard N. Cardozo, "Industrial Market Segmentation," *Industrial Marketing Management* 3 (March 1974): p. 155; see also Vincent-Wayne Mitchell and Dominic F. Wilson, "Balancing Theory and Practice: A Reappraisal of Business-to-Business Segmentation," *Industrial Marketing Management* 27 (September 1998): pp. 429–455.

[5]Frank V. Cespedes, *Concurrent Marketing: Integrating Product, Sales, and Service* (Boston: Harvard Business School Press, 1995), pp. 186–188; and William A. O'Connel and William Keenan Jr., "The Shape of Things to Come," *Sales & Marketing Management* 148 (January 1996): pp. 37–45.

[6]Robert S. Kaplan, "Add a Customer Profitability Metric to Your Balanced Scorecard," *Balanced Scorecard Report*, July/August 2005 (Cambridge, Mass.: Harvard Business School Publishing Corporation).

of market boundaries as diverse industries emerge."[7] Through **competitive analysis** a firm attempts to define its industry boundaries, identify competitors, and determine the strengths and weaknesses of its rivals—while anticipating their actions. Fundamental to this process is a focus on the strategic intent of current and potential competitors. Here attention is directed to competitors' core competencies and how they can be leveraged in the pursuit of new applications, especially in divergent industries. **Core competencies** are the sets of skills, systems, and technologies a company uses to create uniquely high value for customers.[8] For example, Canon has leveraged its core competencies in fine optics and microelectronics into an impressive range of products: electronic cameras, jet printers, laser fax machines, and color copiers.[9] Examining core competencies provides a clearer portrait of Canon's strategic intent across diverse market sectors.

Spotting New Competitors   In considering the core competencies of competitors, marketers should also examine scenarios of industry change and competitor entry and exit. Which firms (current and potential) find this segment attractive? How do we match up with each? When, where, and how will they enter? Put yourself in the shoes of a potential entrant to think creatively about new competition. How could you best attack your own market position? What strategies could be developed now to preempt entrants? This line of inquiry requires challenging assumptions about the industry boundaries by probing suppliers' and customers' perceptions of substitutes and industry newcomers.

Business marketing strategists can secure additional insights by examining the actions (moves and countermoves) of competitors and evaluating what they did versus what they could have done. The particular response chosen may reveal how a competitor sees its strengths. In turn, a rapid, visible, and forceful move signals that a competitor is strongly committed to a particular market segment.[10]

Evaluating the Technological Environment

The business marketing strategist must also carefully assess the technological environment in which the firm elects to compete. Three features of this environment are especially relevant: (1) *product technology*—the set of ideas embodied in the product or service; (2) *process technology*—the set of ideas or steps involved in the production of a product or service; and (3) *management technology*—the management procedures associated with selling the product or service and with administering the business.[11] Changes in any of these areas can lead to less market-segment stability, shifts in traditional product market boundaries, and new sources of competition. To illustrate, technological change is blurring traditional boundaries in the computer,

---

[7]Richard A. D'Aveni with Robert Gunther, *Hypercompetitive Rivalries: Competing in Highly Dynamic Environments* (New York: The Free Press, 1995), p. 2.

[8]James Brian Quinn, "Strategic Outsourcing: Leveraging Knowledge Capabilities," *Sloan Management Review* 40 (summer 1999): pp. 9–21.

[9]C. K. Prahalad and Gary Hamel, "The Core Competence of the Corporation," *Harvard Business Review* 69 (May–June 1990): pp. 79–91.

[10]Liam Fahey, "Competitor Scenarios," *Strategy & Leadership* 31 (January 2003): pp. 32–44. See also Beth A. Walker, Dimitri Kapelianis, and Michael D. Hutt, "Competitive Cognition," *MIT Sloan Management Review* 46 (summer 2005): pp. 10–12.

[11]Noel Capon and Rashi Glazer, "Marketing and Technology: A Strategic Coalignment," *Journal of Marketing* 51 (July 1987): pp. 1–14.

INSIDE BUSINESS MARKETING

How to See What's Next

Strategists falter when they invest too much attention to "what is" and too little to "what could be." For example, by maintaining a strict focus on existing market segments and ignoring new ones, the business marketer may miss important signals of change that customers are sending.

To break this pattern and spot new market opportunities, business marketing strategists should examine three customer groups and the market signals they are sending:

Undershot customers—the existing solutions fail to fully satisfy their needs. They eagerly buy new product versions at steady or increasing prices.

Overshot customers—the existing solutions are too good (for example, exceed the technical performance required). These customers are reluctant to purchase new product versions.

Nonconsuming customers—those who lack the skills, resources, or ability to benefit from existing solutions. These customers are forced to turn to others with greater skills or training for service.

Although most strategists center exclusive attention on undershot customers, "watching for innovations that have the potential to drive industry change actually requires paying careful attention to the least demanding, most overshot customers and nonconsumers seemingly on the fringe of the market." For example, computing jobs that were processed by specialists in the corporate mainframe computer center are now routinely completed by millions of individuals, and corporate photocopying centers were disbanded as low-cost, self-service copiers became a common fixture in offices across organizations.

SOURCE: Clayton M. Christensen and Scott D. Anthony, "Are You Reading the Right Signals?" *Strategy & Innovation* Newsletter (Cambridge, Mass.: Harvard Business School Publishing Corporation, September/October 2004), p. 5.

---

telecommunications, and financial services industries. Kathleen Eisenhardt and Shona Brown observe:

> In turbulent markets, businesses and opportunities are constantly falling out of alignment. New technologies, novel products, and services create fresh opportunities. . . . As a result, the clear-cut partitioning of businesses into neat, equidistant rectangles on an organizational chart becomes out of date as opportunities come and go, collide and separate, grow and shrink.[12]

Especially in volatile markets, strategists must continually realign the organization to meet changing customer needs and capture promising market opportunities. For example, Hewlett-Packard's printer business was launched on a small scale in 1984, exploded into a major revenue producer for the company, and now extends into digital photography, wireless information distribution, and e-commerce imaging.[13] Such agility has also been a key factor in the success of high-performing companies like 3M, Johnson & Johnson, and Dell.

---

[12] Kathleen M. Eisenhardt and Shona L. Brown, "Patching: Restitching Business Portfolios in Dynamic Markets," *Harvard Business Review* 77 (May–June 1999): p. 82.

[13] Ibid., pp. 72–82.

Benefits

If the requirements for effective segmentation are met, several benefits accrue to the firm. First, the mere attempt to segment the business market forces the marketer to become more attuned to the unique needs of customer segments. Second, knowing the needs of particular market segments helps the business marketer focus product development efforts, develop profitable pricing strategies, select appropriate channels of distribution, develop and target advertising messages, and train and deploy the sales force. Thus, market segmentation provides the foundation for efficient and effective business marketing strategies.

Third, market segmentation provides the business marketer with valuable guidelines for allocating marketing resources. Business-to-business firms often serve multiple market segments and must continually monitor their relative attractiveness and performance. Research by Mercer Management Consulting indicates that, for many companies, nearly one-third of their market segments generate no profit and that 30 to 50 percent of marketing and customer service costs are wasted on efforts to acquire and retain customers in these segments.[14] Ultimately, costs, revenues, and profits must be evaluated segment by segment—and even account by account. As market or competitive conditions change, corresponding adjustments may be required in the firm's market segmentation strategy. Thus, market segmentation provides a basic unit of analysis for marketing planning and control.

Bases for Segmenting Business Markets

Whereas the consumer-goods marketer is interested in securing meaningful profiles of individuals (demographics, lifestyle, benefits sought), the business marketer profiles organizations (size, end use) and organizational buyers (decision style, criteria). Thus, the business or organizational market can be segmented on several bases, broadly classified into two major categories: macrosegmentation and microsegmentation.

Macrosegmentation centers on the characteristics of the buying organization and the buying situation and thus divides the market by such organizational characteristics as size, geographic location, SIC or North American Industrial Classification System (NAICS) category, and organizational structure. For example, more than 350,000 shoppers visit Dell's online store each week, and a creative segmentation approach simplifies the buying experience. At Dell's Web site (http://www.dell.com), customers are segmented into large businesses and small businesses; government accounts are split into federal, state, and local; other nonprofits are divided into segments such as education and health care. As a result, marketing strategists at Dell can stay tightly focused on serving the special needs of each segment.

In turn, Dell develops a one-to-one relationship with buying organizations through customized and secure Web sites that essentially become customer-specific stores. To illustrate, the service provides employees at Boeing with special price quotes that reflect the organization's volume of purchases. More than 100,000 business and institutional customers worldwide use a customized Web page to do business with Dell online.

---

[14]Gertz and Baptista, *Grow to Be Great*, p. 55.

Such innovative practices have been successful: Dell now accounts for nearly 25 percent of personal computer sales in the United States.[15]

In contrast, **microsegmentation** requires a higher degree of market knowledge, focusing on the characteristics of decision-making units within each macrosegment—including buying decision criteria, perceived importance of the purchase, and attitudes toward vendors. Yoram Wind and Richard Cardozo recommend a two-stage approach to business market segmentation: (1) identify meaningful macrosegments, and then (2) divide the macrosegments into microsegments.[16]

In evaluating alternative bases for segmentation, the marketer is attempting to identify good predictors of differences in buyer behavior. Once such differences are recognized, the marketer can approach target segments with an appropriate marketing strategy. Secondary sources of information, coupled with data in a firm's information system, can be used to divide the market into macrolevel segments. The concentration of the business market allows some marketers to monitor the purchasing patterns of each customer. For example, a firm that sells industrial products to paper manufacturers is dealing with hundreds of potential buying organizations in U.S. and Canadian markets; a paper manufacturer selling to ultimate consumers is dealing with millions of potential customers. Such market concentration, coupled with rapidly advancing marketing intelligence systems, makes it easier for the business marketer to monitor the purchasing patterns of individual organizations.

Macrolevel Bases

Table 5.1 presents selected macrolevel bases of segmentation. Recall that these are concerned with general characteristics of the buying organization, the nature of the product application, and the characteristics of the buying situation.

Macrolevel Characteristics of Buying Organizations   The marketer may find it useful to partition the market by size of potential buying organizations. Large buying organizations may possess unique requirements and respond to marketing stimuli that are different from those responded to by smaller firms. The influence of presidents, vice presidents, and owners declines with an increase in corporate size; the influence of other participants, such as purchasing managers, increases.[17] Alternatively, the marketer may recognize regional variations and adopt geographical units as the basis for differentiating marketing strategies.

Usage rate constitutes another macrolevel variable. Buyers are classified on a continuum ranging from nonuser to heavy user. Heavy users may have different needs than moderate or light users. For example, heavy users may place more value on technical or delivery support services than their counterparts. Likewise, an opportunity may exist to convert moderate users into heavy users through adjustments in the product or service mix.

---

[15] Gary McWilliams, "How Dell Fine-Tunes Its PC Pricing to Gain Edge in a Slow Market," *The Wall Street Journal*, June 8, 2001, p. A1.

[16] Wind and Cardozo, "Industrial Market Segmentation," p. 155; see also Mitchell and Wilson, "Balancing Theory and Practice," pp. 429–455.

[17] Joseph A. Bellizzi, "Organizational Size and Buying Influences," *Industrial Marketing Management* 10 (February 1981): pp. 17–21; see also Arch G. Woodside, Timo Liukko, and Risto Vuori, "Organizational Buying of Capital Equipment Involving Persons across Several Authority Levels," *Journal of Business & Industrial Marketing* 14, no. 1 (1999): pp. 30–48.

TABLE 5.1 | SELECTED MACROLEVEL BASES OF SEGMENTATION

Variables	Illustrative Breakdowns
Characteristics of Buying Organizations	
Size (the scale of operations of the organization)	Small, medium, large; based on sales or number of employees
Geographical location	New England, Middle Atlantic, South Atlantic, East North Central, etc.
Usage rate	Nonuser, light user, moderate user, heavy user
Structure of procurement	Centralized, decentralized
Product/Service Application	
SIC or NAICS category	Varies by product or service
End market served	Varies by product or service
Value in use	High, low
Characteristics of Purchasing Situation	
Type of buying situation	New task, modified rebuy, straight rebuy
Stage in purchase decision process	Early stages, late stages

The structure of the procurement function constitutes a final macrolevel characteristic of buying organizations. Firms with a centralized purchasing function behave differently than do those with decentralized procurement (see Chapter 3). The structure of the purchasing function influences the degree of buyer specialization, the criteria emphasized, and the composition of the buying center. Centralized buyers place significant weight on long-term supply availability and the development of a healthy supplier complex. Decentralized buyers emphasize short-term cost efficiency.[18] Thus, the position of procurement in the organizational hierarchy provides a base for categorizing organizations and for isolating specific needs and marketing requirements. Many business marketers develop a national accounts sales team to meet the special requirements of large centralized procurement units.

Product/Service Application   Because a specific industrial good is often used in different ways, the marketer can divide the market on the basis of specific end-use applications. The NAICS or SIC system and related information sources are especially valuable for this purpose. To illustrate, the manufacturer of a component such as springs may reach industries incorporating the product into machine tools, bicycles, surgical devices, office equipment, telephones, and missile systems. Similarly, Intel's microchips are used in household appliances, retail terminals, toys, and aircraft as well as in computers. By isolating the specialized needs of each user group, the firm is better equipped to differentiate customer requirements and to evaluate emerging opportunities.

---

[18]Timothy M. Laseter, *Balanced Sourcing: Cooperation and Competition in Supplier Relationships* (San Francisco: Jossey-Bass, 1998), pp. 59–86.

Value in Use   Strategic insights are also provided by exploring the value in use of various customer applications. Recall our discussion of value analysis in Chapter 2. **Value in use** is a product's economic value to the user relative to a specific alternative in a particular application. The economic value of an offering frequently varies by customer application. Milliken & Company, the textile manufacturer, has built one of its businesses by becoming a major supplier of towels to industrial laundries. These customers pay Milliken a 10 percent premium over equivalent towels offered by competitors.[19] Why? Milliken provides added value, such as a computerized routing program that improves the efficiency and effectiveness of the industrial laundries' pick-up and delivery function.

The segmentation strategy adopted by a manufacturer of precision motors further illuminates the value-in-use concept.[20] The firm found that its customers differed in the motor speed required in their applications and that a dominant competitor's new, low-priced machine wore out quickly in high- and medium-speed applications. The marketer concentrated on this vulnerable segment, demonstrating the superior life cycle cost advantages of the firm's products. The marketer also initiated a long-term program to develop a competitively priced product and service offering for customers in the low-speed segment.

Purchasing Situation   A final macrolevel base for segmenting the organizational market is the purchasing situation. First-time buyers have perceptions and information needs that differ from those of repeat buyers. Therefore, buying organizations are classified as being in the early or late stages of the procurement process, or alternatively, as *new-task, straight rebuy,* or *modified rebuy* organizations (see Chapter 3). The position of the firm in the procurement decision process or its location on the buying situation continuum dictates marketing strategy.

These examples illustrate those macrolevel bases of segmentation that business marketers can apply to the organizational market. Other macrolevel bases may more precisely fit a specific situation. A key benefit of segmentation is that it forces the manager to search for bases that explain similarities and differences among buying organizations.

Illustration: Macrosegmentation[21]

A business marketer with an innovative technical product sought to become the leader in a market that comprised many small- and medium-sized firms. Based on the purchase decision process, three segments were identified:

1. **First-time prospects:** Customers who see a possible need for the product and have started to evaluate alternative suppliers—but who have not yet purchased the product.

2. **Novices:** Customers who have purchased the product for the first time within the past three months.

3. **Sophisticates:** Experienced customers who have either purchased the product before and are now ready to rebuy or who have recently repurchased.

---

[19] Philip Kotler, "Marketing's New Paradigm: What's Really Happening Out There," *Planning Review* 20 (September–October 1992): pp. 50–52.

[20] Robert A. Garda, "How to Carve Niches for Growth in Industrial Markets," *Management Review* 70 (August 1981): pp. 15–22.

[21] Thomas S. Robertson and Howard Barich, "A Successful Approach to Segmenting Industrial Markets," *Planning Review* 20 (November–December 1992): pp. 4–11.

TABLE 5.2 | **WHAT BUYERS OF INDUSTRIAL PRODUCTS LOOK FOR**

First-Time Prospects	Novices	Sophisticates
Dominant theme		
"Take care of me."	"Help me make it work."	"Talk technology to me."
Benefits sought		
A sales rep who knows and understands my business	Easy-to-read manuals	Compatibility with existing systems
An honest sales rep	Technical support hot lines	Products customized to customer needs
A vendor who has been in business for some time	A high level of training	Track record of vendor
A sales rep who can communicate in understandable manner	Sales reps who are knowledgeable	Maintenance speed in fixing problems
A trial period		Post-sales support and technical support
A high level of training		
What's less important		
Sales rep's knowledge of products and services	An honest sales rep	Training
	A sales rep who knows and understands my business	Trial
		Easy-to-read manuals
		A sales rep who can communicate in an understandable manner

SOURCE: Adapted from Thomas S. Robertson and Howard Barich, "A Successful Approach to Segmenting Industrial Markets," *Planning Review* 20 (November–December 1992), p. 7.

Observe from Table 5.2 that, for this particular business market, the three segments value different benefits. For example, novices seek easy-to-read manuals and technical support hot lines, whereas sophisticates want system compatibility and products customized to their needs. The business marketer responded by developing sharply focused marketing strategies for each macrosegment.

Microlevel Bases

Having identified macrosegments, the marketer often finds it useful to divide each macrosegment into smaller microsegments on the basis of the similarities and differences between decision-making units. Often, several microsegments—each with unique requirements and unique responses to marketing stimuli—are buried in macrosegments. To isolate them effectively, the marketer must move beyond secondary sources of information by soliciting input from the sales force or by conducting a special market segmentation study. Selected microbases of segmentation appear in Table 5.3.

TABLE 5.3 | SELECTED MICROLEVEL BASES OF SEGMENTATION

Variables	Illustrative Breakdowns
Key criteria	Quality, delivery, supplier reputation
Purchasing strategies	Optimizer, satisficer
Structure of decision-making unit	Major decision participants (for example, purchasing manager and plant manager)
Importance of purchase	High importance . . . low importance
Attitude toward vendors	Favorable . . . unfavorable
Organizational innovativeness	Innovator . . . follower
Personal characteristics	
Demographics	Age, educational background
Decision style	Normative, conservative, mixed mode
Risk	Risk taker, risk avoider
Confidence	High . . . low
Job responsibility	Purchasing, production, engineering

Key Criteria For some business products, the marketer can divide the market according to which criteria are the most important in the purchase decision.[22] Criteria include product quality, prompt and reliable delivery, technical support, price, and supply continuity. The marketer also might divide the market based on supplier profiles that appear to be preferred by decision makers (for example, high quality, prompt delivery, premium price versus standard quality, less-prompt delivery, low price).

Illustration: Price versus Service[23] Signode Corporation produces and markets a line of steel strapping used for packaging a range of products, including steel and many manufactured items. Facing stiff price competition and a declining market share, management wanted to move beyond traditional macrolevel segmentation to understand how Signode's 174 national accounts viewed price versus service tradeoffs. Four segments were uncovered:

1. **Programmed buyers** (sales = $6.6 million): Customers who were not particularly price or service sensitive and who made purchases in a routine fashion—product is not central to their operation.

2. **Relationship buyers** (sales = $31 million): Knowledgeable customers who valued partnership with Signode and did not push for price or service concessions—product is moderately important to the firm's operations.

[22] David E. Schnedler, "Use Strategic Models," pp. 85–92; and Kenneth E. Mast and Jon M. Hawes, "Perceptual Differences between Buyers and Engineers," *Journal of Purchasing and Materials Management* 22 (spring 1986): pp. 2–6; Donald W. Jackson Jr., Richard K. Burdick, and Janet E. Keith, "Purchasing Agents' Perceived Importance of Marketing Mix Components in Different Industrial Purchase Situations," *Journal of Business Research* 13 (August 1985): pp. 361–373; and Donald R. Lehmann and John O'Shaughnessy, "Decision Criteria Used in Buying Different Categories of Products," *Journal of Purchasing and Materials Management* 18 (spring 1982): pp. 9–14.

[23] V. Kasturi Rangan, Rowland T. Moriarty, and Gordon S. Swartz, "Segmenting Customers in Mature Industrial Markets," *Journal of Marketing* 56 (October 1992): pp. 72–82.

B2B TOP PERFORMERS

Steering Customers to the Right Channel

Dow Corning Corporation is the world's largest and most innovative producer of silicone-based products. While being the leader in this large and diverse market, smaller, regional competitors began to take market share away from Dow Corning by selling low-priced silicone products with little or no technical support. Rather than paying for a host of high-quality services such as new-product-development assistance that Dow Corning customarily provides, these customers eagerly sought the lowest price. To meet the challenge, Dow Corning conducted a market segmentation study, isolated the characteristics of this "low-cost" buyer, and created a no-frills Web-based business model to reach this customer segment. To avoid confusion with existing customers and the firm's premium product lines, a new brand was created—Xiameter (http://www.xiameter.com).

To clarify the brand premise and the company connection, the tag line—"The new measure of value from Dow Corning"—was added. By steering price-sensitive customers to the Internet—a low-cost sales channel—the branding strategy allows Dow Corning "to compete head-on with the low-price suppliers of mature product lines, without damaging its position as a value-added leader at the premium price end of the market." Customers, from the United States to high-growth potential countries like China, have responded positively to the Xiameter brand. (See the Dow Corning ad in Figure 5.1.)

SOURCE: Bob Lamons, "Dow Targets Segment to Keep Market Share," *Marketing News*, June 15, 2005, p. 8. See also Randall S. Rozin and Liz Magnusson, "Processes and Methodologies for Creating a Global Business-to-Business Brand," *Journal of Brand Management* 10 (February 2003): pp. 185–207.

3. **Transaction buyers** (sales = $24 million): Large and very knowledgeable customers who actively considered the price versus service tradeoffs, but often placed price over service—product is very important to their operations.

4. **Bargain hunters** (sales = $23 million): Large-volume buyers who were very sensitive to any changes in price or service—product is very important to their operations.

The study enabled Signode to sharpen its strategies in this mature business market and to understand more clearly the cost of serving the various segments. Particularly troubling to management was the bargain-hunter segment. These customers demanded the lowest prices and the highest levels of service, and had the highest propensity to switch. Management decided to use price cuts only as a defense against competitors' cuts and directed attention instead at ways to add service value to this and other segments.

Value-Based Strategies   Many customers actively seek business marketing firms that can help them create new value to gain a competitive edge in their markets. Based on a comprehensive study of its customer base, Dow Corning identified three important customer segments and the value proposition that customers in each segment are seeking[24]:

Innovation-focused customers who are committed to being first to the market with new technologies and who seek new-product-development expertise and innovative solutions that will attract new customers.

---

[24]Eric W. Balinski, Philip Allen, and J. Nicholas DeBonis, *Value-Based Marketing for Bottom-Line Success* (New York: McGraw-Hill and the American Marketing Association, 2003), pp. 147–152.

FIGURE 5.1 | AN AWARD-WINNING AD BY DOW CORNING FOR ITS WEB-BASED BUSINESS MODEL

ARE YOU GETTING ENOUGH SILICONE FOR THE BUCK?

DARE TO COMPARE

If you're not using Xiameter, you're probably paying too much for your bulk silicones. With Xiameter, you get just the basics—high quality silicon-based products at the lowest-base prices available. Don't take our word for it. See for yourself, anytime at www.quote.xiameter.com.

© 2003 Dow Corning Corporation. Xiameter is a Trademark of the Dow Corning Corporation. Ad#990 AV06313

|XIAMETER|™ *The new measure of value. From Dow Corning.*

SOURCE: Reprinted by permission of XIAMETER.

Customers in fast-growing markets who are pressured by competitive battles over market growth and seek proven performance in technology, manufacturing, and supply-chain management.

Customers in highly-competitive markets who produce mature products, center on process efficiency and effectiveness in manufacturing, and seek cost-effective solutions that keep overall costs down.

The marketer can benefit by examining the criteria decision-making units in various sectors of the business market—commercial, governmental, and institutional—use. As organizations in each sector undergo restructuring efforts, the buying criteria key decision makers use also change. For example, the cost pressures and reform efforts in the health-care industry are changing how hospitals buy medical equipment and pharmaceuticals. To reduce administrative costs and enhance bargaining power, hospitals are following the lead of commercial enterprises by streamlining their operations. Also, they are forming buying groups, centralizing the purchasing function, and insisting on lower prices and better service. Reform efforts are likewise moving government buyers to search for more efficient purchasing procedures and for better value from vendors. Marketers that respond in this challenging environment are rewarded.

Purchasing Strategies   Microsegments can be classified according to buying organizations' purchasing strategy. Richard Cardozo has identified two purchasing profiles: satisficers and optimizers.[25] **Satisficers** approach a given purchasing requirement by contacting familiar suppliers and placing the order with the first supplier to satisfy product and delivery requirements. **Optimizers** consider numerous suppliers, familiar and unfamiliar, solicit bids, and examine all alternative proposals carefully before selecting a supplier.

These purchasing strategies have numerous implications. A supplier entering the market would have a higher probability of penetrating a decision-making unit made up of optimizers than of penetrating a unit consisting of satisficers who rely on familiar suppliers.

Identifying different purchasing patterns can help the marketer understand differing responses to marketing stimuli. A business marketer who serves the institutional food market, for example, encounters both satisficers and optimizers. Large universities review and test menu alternatives carefully, consult with student committees, and analyze the price-per-unit-cooked before selecting a supplier (optimizers). Restaurants and company cafeterias may follow a different pattern. The restaurant manager, consulting with the chef, selects a supplier that provides the required product quality and delivery (satisficer). Remember that satisficing and optimizing are only two of many purchasing strategies of organizational buyers.

Structure of the Decision-Making Unit   The structure of the decision-making unit, or buying center, likewise provides a way to divide the business market into subsets of customers by isolating the patterns of involvement in the purchasing process of particular decision participants (for example, engineering versus top management). For the medical equipment market, DuPont initiated a formal positioning study among

---

[25] Richard N. Cardozo, "Situational Segmentation of Industrial Markets," *European Journal of Marketing* 14, no. 5/6 (1980): pp. 264–276.

hospital administrators, radiology department administrators, and technical managers to identify the firm's relative standing and the specific needs (criteria) for each level of buying influence within each segment.[26] The growing importance of buying groups, multihospital chains, and nonhospital health-care delivery systems pointed to the need for a more refined segmentation approach.

The study indicates that the medical equipment market can be segmented on the basis of the type of institution and the responsibilities of the decision makers and decision influencers in those institutions. The structure of the decision-making unit and the decision criteria used vary across the following three segments:

- Groups that select a single supplier that all member hospitals must use, such as investor-owned hospital chains.

- Groups that select a small set of suppliers from which individual hospitals may select needed products.

- Private group practices and the nonhospital segment.

Based on the study, DuPont's salespersons can tailor their presentations to the decision-making dynamics of each segment. In turn, advertising messages can be more precisely targeted. Such an analysis enables the marketer to identify meaningful microsegments and respond with finely tuned marketing communications.

Importance of Purchase   Classifying organizational customers on the basis of the perceived importance of a product is especially appropriate when various customers apply the product in various ways. Buyer perceptions differ according to the effect of the product on the total mission of the firm. A large commercial enterprise may consider the purchase of consulting services routine; the same purchase for a small manufacturing concern is "an event."

Attitudes toward Vendors   The attitudes of decision-making units toward the vendors in a particular product class provide another means of microsegmentation. Analyzing how various clusters of buyers view alternative sources of supply often uncovers vulnerable segments that competitors are either neglecting or not fully satisfying.

Organizational Innovativeness   Some organizations are more innovative and willing to purchase new industrial products than others. A study of the adoption of new medical equipment among hospitals found that psychographic variables can improve a marketer's ability to predict the adoption of new products.[27] These include such factors as an organization's level of change resistance or desire to excel. When psychographic variables are combined with organizational demographic variables (for example, size), accuracy in predicting organizational innovativeness increases.

Because products diffuse more rapidly in some segments than in others, microsegmentation based on organizational innovativeness enables the marketer to identify segments that should be targeted first when it introduces new products. The accuracy

---

[26] Gary L. Coles and James D. Culley, "Not All Prospects Are Created Equal," *Business Marketing* 71 (May 1986): pp. 52–57.

[27] Thomas S. Robertson and Yoram Wind, "Organizational Psychographics and Innovativeness," *Journal of Consumer Research* 7 (June 1980): pp. 24–31; see also Robertson and Hubert Gatignon, "Competitive Effects on Technology Diffusion," *Journal of Marketing* 50 (July 1986): pp. 1–12.

of new product forecasting also improves when diffusion patterns are estimated segment by segment.[28]

Personal Characteristics   Some microsegmentation possibilities deal with the personal characteristics of decision makers: demographics (age, education), personality, decision style, risk preference or risk avoidance, confidence, job responsibilities, and so forth. Although some interesting studies have shown the usefulness of segmentation based on individual characteristics, further research is needed to explore its potential as a firm base for microsegmentation.

Illustration: Microsegmentation[29]

Philips Lighting Company, the North American division of Philips Electronics, found that purchasing managers emphasize two criteria in purchasing light bulbs: how much they cost and how long they last. Philips learned, however, that the price and life of bulbs did not account for the total cost of lighting. Because lamps contain environmentally toxic mercury, companies faced high disposal costs at the end of a lamp's useful life.

New Product and Segmentation Strategy   To capitalize on a perceived opportunity, Philips introduced the Alto, an environmentally friendly bulb that reduces customers' overall costs plus allows the buying organization to demonstrate environmental concern to the public. Rather than targeting purchasing managers, Philips's marketing strategists centered attention on chief financial officers (CFOs), who embraced the cost savings, and public relations executives, who saw the benefit of purchasing actions that protect the environment. By targeting different buying influentials, Philips created a new market opportunity. In fact, the Alto has already replaced more than 25 percent of traditional fluorescent lamps in U.S. stores, schools, and office buildings.

A Model for Segmenting the Organizational Market

Macrosegmentation centers on characteristics of buying *organizations* (for example, size), *product application* (for example, end market served), and the *purchasing situation* (for example, stage in the purchase decision process). Microsegmentation concentrates on characteristics of organizational decision-making *units*—for instance, choice criteria assigned the most importance in the purchase decision.

Choosing Market Segments

The model in Figure 5.2 combines these macrosegment bases and outlines the steps required for effective segmentation. This approach to organizational market segmentation

---

[28] Yoram Wind, Thomas S. Robertson, and Cynthia Fraser, "Industrial Product Diffusion by Market Segment," *Industrial Marketing Management* 11 (February 1982): pp. 1–8.

[29] W. Chan Kim and Renée Mauborgne, "Creating New Market Space," *Harvard Business Review* 77 (January–February 1999): pp. 88–89. For other segmentation studies, see Mark J. Bennion Jr., "Segmentation and Positioning in a Basic Industry," *Industrial Market Management* 16 (February 1987): pp. 9–18; Arch G. Woodside and Elizabeth J. Wilson, "Combining Macro and Micro Industrial Market Segmentation," in *Advances in Business Marketing*, ed. Arch G. Woodside (Greenwich, Conn.: JAI Press, 1986), pp. 241–257; and Peter Doyle and John Saunders, "Market Segmentation and Positioning in Specialized Industrial Markets," *Journal of Marketing* 49 (spring 1985): pp. 24–32.

FIGURE 5.2 | AN APPROACH TO SEGMENTATION OF BUSINESS MARKETS

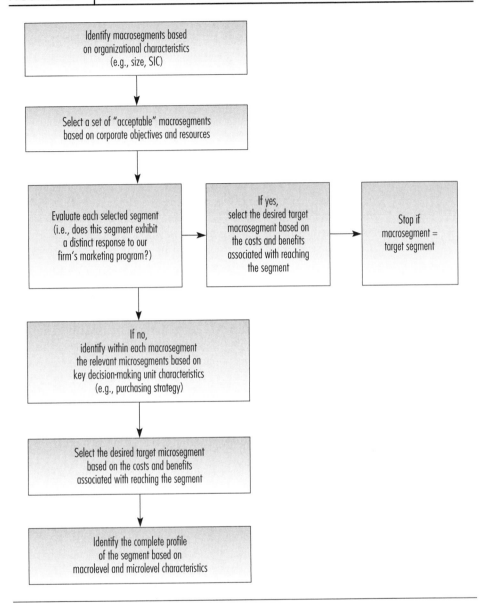

SOURCE: Adapted by permission of the publisher from Yoram Wind and Richard Cardozo, "Industrial Market Segmentation," *Industrial Marketing Management* 3 (March 1974): p. 156. Copyright 1974 by Elsevier Science Publishing Co., Inc.

begins with an analysis of key characteristics of the organization and of the buying situation (macrodimensions)[30] to identify, evaluate, and select meaningful macrosegments. Note that the segmentation task is complete at this stage if *each* of the selected macrosegments exhibits a *distinct* response to the firm's marketing stimuli. Because the

---

[30] Wind and Cardozo, "Industrial Market Segmentation," pp. 153–166; see also Art Weinstein, *Handbook of Market Segmentation: Strategic Targeting for Business and Technology Firms*, 3rd ed. (New York: Haworth Press, 2004).

information needed for macrosegmentation can often be drawn from secondary information sources, the research investment is low.

The cost of research increases, however, when microlevel segmentation is required. A marketing research study is often needed to identify characteristics of decision-making units, as the Philips Lighting case illustrated. At this level, chosen macrosegments are divided into microsegments on the basis of similarities and differences between the decision-making units to identify small groups of buying organizations that each exhibit a distinct response to the firm's marketing strategy. Observe in Figure 5.2 that the desirability of a particular target segment depends on the costs and benefits of reaching that segment. The costs stem from adjustments such as modifying the product, providing special service support, altering personal selling or advertising strategies, or entering new channels of distribution. The benefits include the short- and long-term opportunities from tapping this segment. The marketer must evaluate the potential profitability of alternative segments before investing in separate marketing strategies. As firms develop a clearer picture of the revenue and costs of serving particular segments and customers, they often find that a small group of customers subsidize a large group of marginal and, in some cases, unprofitable customers.[31]

Isolating Market Segment Profitability

To improve on traditional market segmentation, many business marketing firms categorize customers into tiers that differ in current and/or future profitability to the firm. "By knowing the characteristics of profitable customers, companies can direct their marketing efforts to specific segments that are most likely to yield profitable customers."[32] This requires a process of evaluation that makes explicit the near-term potential and the longer-term resource commitments necessary to effectively serve customers in a segment. In particular, special attention is given to the individual drivers of customer profitability, namely the cost-to-serve a particular group of customers and the revenues that result (see Chapter 4).

FedEx Corporation, for example, categorizes its business customers (for internal purposes) as the good, the bad, and the ugly—based on their profitability.[33] Rather than using the same strategy for all customers, the company assigns a priority to the good, tries to convert the bad to good, and discourages the ugly. Like many other firms, FedEx discovered that many customers are too costly to serve and demonstrate little potential to become profitable, even in the long term. By understanding the needs of customers at different tiers of profitability, service can be tailored to achieve even higher levels of profitability. For example, FedEx encourages small shippers to bring their packages to conveniently located drop-off points and offers a rapid-response pick-up service for large shippers. Once profitability tiers are identified, "highly profitable customers can be pampered appropriately, customers of average profitability can

[31] Arun Sharma, R. Krishnan, and Dhruv Grewal, "Value Creation in Markets: A Critical Area of Focus for Business-to-Business Markets," *Industrial Marketing Management* 30 (June 2001): pp. 391–402.

[32] Robert S. Kaplan and V. G. Narayanan, "Measuring and Managing Customer Profitability," *Journal of Cost Management* 15 (September–October 2001): p. 13.

[33] R. Brooks, "Alienating Customers Isn't Always a Bad Idea, Many Firms Discover," *The Wall Street Journal*, January 7, 1999, pp. A1 and A12, discussed in Valarie A. Zeithaml, Roland T. Rust, and Katherine N. Lemon, "The Customer Pyramid: Creating and Serving Profitable Customers," *California Management Review* 43 (summer 2001): p. 118.

be cultivated to yield higher profitability, and unprofitable customers can be either made more profitable or weeded out."[34]

Implementing a Segmentation Strategy

A well-developed segmentation plan will fail without careful attention to implementing the plan. Successful implementation requires attention to the following issues:

- How should the sales force be organized?

- What special technical or customer service requirements will organizations in the new segment have?

- Who will provide these services?

- Which media outlets can be used to target advertising at the new segment?

- Has a comprehensive online strategy been developed to provide continuous service support to customers in this segment?

- What adaptations will be needed to serve selected international market segments?

The astute business marketing strategist must plan, coordinate, and monitor implementation details. Frank Cespedes points out that "as a firm's offering becomes a product-service-information mix that must be customized for diverse segments, organizational interdependencies increase"[35] and marketing managers, in particular, are involved in more cross-functional tasks. Managing the critical points of contact with the customer is fundamental to the marketing manager's role.

Summary

The business market contains a complex mix of customers with diverse needs and objectives. The marketing strategist who analyzes the aggregate market and identifies neglected or inadequately served groups of buyers (segments) is ideally prepared for a market assault. Specific marketing strategy adjustments can be made to fit the unique needs of each target segment. Of course, such differentiated marketing strategies are feasible only when the target segments are measurable, accessible, compatible, responsive, and large enough to justify separate attention.

Procedurally, business market segmentation involves categorizing actual or potential buying organizations into mutually exclusive clusters (segments), each of which exhibits a relatively homogeneous response to marketing strategy variables. To accomplish this task, the business marketer can draw upon two types of segmentation bases: macrolevel and microlevel. Macrodimensions are the key characteristics of buying

---

[34]Zeithaml, Rust, and Lemon, "The Customer Pyramid," p. 141.

[35]Cespedes, *Concurrent Marketing*, p. 271.

organizations and of the purchasing situation. The SIC and NAICS, together with other secondary sources of information, are valuable in macrolevel segmentation. Microlevel bases of segmentation center on key characteristics of the decision-making unit and require a higher level of market knowledge.

This chapter outlined a systematic approach for the business marketer to apply when identifying and selecting target segments. Before a final decision is made, the marketer must weigh the costs and benefits of a segmented marketing strategy. In developing a market segmentation plan, the business marketing manager isolates the costs and revenues associated with serving particular market segments. By directing its resources to its most profitable customers and segments, the business marketer is less vulnerable to focused competitors that may seek to "cherry-pick" the firm's most valuable customers.

Discussion Questions

1. Cogent is a rapidly growing company that makes software that identifies people using biometrics—fingerprints, faces, eyeballs, and other personal characteristics. The firm is making terminals that allow customers to pay for products with their fingerprints. Assess the potential of the "pay by touch" system and suggest possible market segments that might be receptive to the new offering.

2. Automatic Data Processing, Inc. (ADP) handles payroll and tax filing processing for more than 300,000 customers. In other words, firms outsource these functions to ADP. Suggest possible segmentation bases that ADP might employ in this service market. What criteria would be important to organizational buyers in making the decision to turn payroll processing over to an outside firm?

3. AT&T, Microsoft, Google, and IBM are all involved in the information business, and all offer equipment and services that enable consumers to access information efficiently. What implications does this raise for competitive analysis and for market segmentation?

4. Firms use their information systems to track what existing customers buy, where they buy, and how they buy. A leading management expert suggests that equal attention should be given to noncustomers because they generally outnumber customers. Evaluate this position.

5. FedEx believes that its future growth will come from business-to-business e-commerce transactions where customers demand quick and reliable delivery service. Outline a segmentation plan that the firm might use to become the market leader in this rapidly expanding area.

6. Peter Drucker persuasively argues that traditional accounting systems do not capture the true benefits of automated manufacturing equipment. According to Drucker, such approaches emphasize the costs of *doing* something, whereas the main benefit of automation lies in eliminating—or at least minimizing—the cost of *not doing* something (for example, not producing defective parts that become scrap). Explain how a producer of automated equipment might use a value-in-use segmentation strategy.

7. Explain why entry into a particular market segment by an industrial firm such as DuPont often entails a greater commitment than a comparable decision made by a consumer-products company like General Foods.

8. Sara Lee Corporation derives more than $1.5 billion of sales each year from the institutional market (for example, hospitals, schools, restaurants). Explain how a firm such as Sara Lee or General Mills might apply the concept of market segmentation to the institutional market.

9. What personal selling strategy would be most appropriate when dealing with an organizational buyer who is an optimizer? A satisficer?

10. Some firms follow a single-stage segmentation approach, using macrodimensions; others use both macrodimensions and microdimensions. As a business marketing manager, what factors would you consider in making a choice between the two methods?

Internet Exercises

Xerox positions itself as "The Document Company" because the firm provides solutions to help customers manage documents—paper, electronic, online. Go to http://www.xerox.com, click on "Industry Solutions," and

1. Describe the industry sectors that the firm seems to cover in its market segmentation plan.

2. Identify the particular product and service that Xerox has developed for bank customers.

CASE

Small Businesses Represent Huge Opportunity

Large business marketing firms—like IBM, Xerox, and FedEx—can effectively use salespersons to directly serve large customer accounts such as Procter & Gamble, Target, or Bank of America. However, the millions of small businesses that, in aggregate, represent a huge business market opportunity are much more difficult to serve in a cost-efficient way. Small businesses are defined here as those with less than $25 million in annual sales. A study by Visa USA found that nonpayroll spending by small businesses exceeds $4.5 trillion annually and accounts for one-third of all expenditures by U.S. businesses. "These numbers represent how powerful small businesses are in the U.S. and what a significant opportunity the small-business market represents," observes Dave Costa, vice president of Commercial Solutions at Visa USA.[36]

Creative marketing strategies are required to define and reach this large and diverse market. Take Staples, the office supplies firm, where small businesses account for the bulk of sales through its retail, catalog, and e-commerce sales channels. Staples mails 50 million catalogs a year and features small business employees in its television, print, and radio advertising. The firm conducted extensive research on the way customers shop online and revamped the Web site's layout, look, and functionality. In turn, research demonstrates how the catalog and online channels work together. "We get many more sales online from those customers receiving catalogs," says Brian Light, executive vice president of Staples Business Delivery.[37]

Discussion Questions

1. Given the diverse array of firms that fall into the small business category, propose an approach Staples might use to segment this market.

2. Describe how marketing managers at Staples could use your segmentation plan to develop marketing strategies for each of the key market segments you have defined.

---

[36]Kate Maddox, "Marketers Pursue Small Businesses," *BtoB*, March 14, 2005, http://www.btobonline.com, accessed on July 7, 2005.

[37]"Staples Preps Easier E-Commerce Site," *BtoB*, March 14, 2005, http://www.btobonline.com, accessed on July 7, 2005.

Organizational Demand Analysis

The business marketer confronts the difficult task of predicting the market response of organizational customers. The efficiency and effectiveness of the marketing program rests on the manager's ability to isolate and measure organizational demand patterns and forecast specific sales levels. Accurate projections of market potential and future sales are among the most significant and challenging dimensions of organizational demand analysis. After reading this chapter, you will understand:

1. how the Internet provides a reservoir of business market information.

2. the importance of organizational demand analysis to business marketing management.

3. the role of market potential analysis and sales forecasting in the planning and control process.

4. specific techniques to effectively measure market potential and develop a sales forecast.

Looking back at the Internet boom, executives at telecommunications firms like Lucent Technologies and Nortel Networks Corporation now openly acknowledge that they did not see the steep drop in demand coming. Indeed, spending by phone companies on telecommunications gear nearly doubled from 1996 to 2000 to $47.5 billion; all forecasts indicated that this attractive growth path would continue.[1] During this period, telecom equipment makers were dramatically expanding production capacity and aggressively recruiting thousands of new employees. However, in 2001, the demand failed to materialize and the major telecom equipment makers reported significant financial losses. In turn, firms across the industry announced a series of massive job cuts. What happened? "Lousy" sales forecasts played an important role, according to Gregory Duncan, a telecom consultant at National Economic Research Associates.[2]

To implement business marketing strategy successfully, the business marketing manager must estimate the potential market for the firm's products. Accurate estimates of potential business enable the manager to allocate scarce resources to the customer segments, products, and territories that offer the greatest return. Estimates of market potential also provide the manager with a standard for assessing the firm's performance in the target products and markets. As one management expert suggests, "Without a forecast of total market demand, decisions on investment, marketing support, and other resource allocations will be based on hidden, unconscious assumptions about industrywide requirements, and they'll often be wrong."[3]

Likewise, sales forecasting is vital to marketing management. The sales forecast reflects management's estimate of the probable level of company sales, taking into account both potential business and the level and type of marketing effort demanded. Virtually every decision made by the marketer is based on a forecast, formal or informal.

Organizational demand analysis is composed of sales forecasting and market potential analysis, and this chapter explores its role in the planning and control process. First, attention centers on how a business marketing manager can use the Internet to capture valuable information to support decision making. Second, the nature and purpose of both the market potential estimate and the sales forecast are examined and contrasted. Once the groundwork is established, several methods of measuring market potential are described, illustrated, and evaluated. The chapter concludes by examining the salient dimensions of sales forecasting, along with selected sales forecasting techniques.

Organizational Demand Analysis

The business marketing manager must analyze organizational demand from two perspectives. First, what is the highest possible level of market demand for all producers in this industry in a particular time period? The answer constitutes the product's market potential. Market potential is influenced by the level of industry marketing effort and the assumed conditions in the external environment. Second, what level of sales can the firm reasonably expect to achieve, given a particular level and type of

---

[1] Dennis K. Berman, "'Lousy Sales Forecasts Helped Fuel the Telecom Mess," *The Wall Street Journal*, July 7, 2001, p. B1.
[2] Ibid.
[3] F. William Barnett, "Four Steps to Forecast Total Market Demand," *Harvard Business Review* 66 (July–August 1988): p. 28. See also John T. Mentzer and Mark Moon, *Sales Forecasting Management: A Demand Management Approach* (Thousand Oaks, Calif.: Sage Publications, 2005).

marketing effort and a particular set of environmental conditions? The answer constitutes the firm's sales forecast. Note that the forecast depends on the level of the firm's marketing effort. Thus, the marketing plan must be developed before the sales forecast. Much of the data used to generate estimates of organizational demand are developed through intensive market research efforts. Accurate estimates of organizational demand come from solid market research efforts; there simply is no shortcut. This section examines the significance of both components of organizational demand analysis—market potential and sales forecasts—for business marketing management. The Internet is highlighted as an effective tool for gathering data for organizational demand analysis.

Using the Internet for Business Marketing Research

Whether developed through painstaking marketing research studies or gleaned from existing publications, information exists to support business decisions. Secondary information gathered and published by government agencies, trade associations, trade publications, and independent research firms provides a valuable and often inexpensive start to building knowledge of the market. Of the many external sources of information, a principal one is secondary data about a company's competitive and external environment.

The Internet currently provides the easiest-to-locate information of almost any source for business marketing applications. There are literally thousands of searching sources on the Web, and some sites even search the search engines. Nearly every aspect of marketing intelligence is available on the Internet: competitive information, customer data, economic information, technological trends, and political and legal data. Much of the secondary information on the Internet is more current than data published in hard copy; it is inexpensive, easy to use, and quick to access. In addition to the multitude of secondary information available, the Internet can also be used to gather primary data—to do surveys via e-mail or through Web pages.

Secondary Data Available to Business Marketers on the Internet The amount of published data available to business marketers via the Internet is staggering: Up-to-date information from over 193 countries is available 24 hours a day, seven days a week, and within a matter of seconds. However, just because a wealth of data is available does not mean that the data is necessarily "good"—the decision maker must carefully scrutinize such information to assess its value and quality: how it was gathered, the size of the sample that was used, who provided the information, the purpose for which the information was collected.

The U.S. Census Bureau is a rich source of data that can be used in assessing market potential in various industries. Each month the Census Bureau publishes a variety of data, most importantly shipments and inventories in all major manufacturing segments. This data is available at its Web site (http://www.census.gov) and the data is relatively timely—some of this data may appear on the Web site within two weeks of its collection. If managers were evaluating potential target market segments for their products, the monthly census data would be useful for evaluating the size and relative health of different industry segments. Table 6.1 provides a sample of census data from May 2005. Note that the data was posted on the census Web site only one month after the data was compiled. The table shows, for example, shipments in the various industries for May and April of 2005, as well as May 2004. This allows business marketers assessing the state of a particular industry to examine changes in production in that industry on a month-to-month and year-to-year basis—all with a simple keystroke on the laptop!

TABLE 6.1 | **EXAMPLE OF THE DATA ON THE CENSUS DEPARTMENT'S WEB SITE: MONTHLY SHIPMENTS BY MANUFACTURERS**

Industry	May 2005	April 2005	May 2004
All manufacturing industries	390,838	390,960	367,073
Excluding transportation	337,020	336,575	312,075
Excluding defense	380,681	380,917	357,347
With unfilled orders	142,927	143,559	132,250
Durable goods industries	207,411	207,758	194,617
Wood products	9,163	9,293	10,087
Nonmetallic mineral products	8,451	8,328	7,586
Primary metals	14,702	14,945	13,659
Iron and steel mills	6,745	6,939	6,330
Aluminum and nonferrous metals	6,248	6,274	5,771
Ferrous metal foundries	1,709	1,732	1,558
Fabricated metal products	24,180	24,273	22,910

A wide array of Web sites exist to provide the marketing manager with data for assessing markets, evaluating market size, and understanding market structure and makeup. Table 6.2 highlights some of the Internet sites that business marketing managers use. This table provides a mere sampling of the total number of sites that might be tapped for useful market or competitive information.

Using the Internet   Table 6.2 illustrates how a manager can use the Internet to monitor almost all the economic statistics of the U.S. government, assess technological trends, analyze competitive strategies, gather data on markets and buyer behavior, evaluate global market opportunities, and investigate almost any business firm in the world. An easy, and often revealing, exercise is to browse the Web sites of major competitors. Competitive Web sites may contain useful information about product lines, channel strategy, and pricing. However, sensitive data is usually reserved for customers who are able to enter with an assigned password. Nevertheless, Web sites can contain some powerful competitive intelligence that is virtually free.

Online Business Marketing Research   Business marketers are using the Internet to gather primary data—that is, information about customer perceptions, behaviors, and desires, as well as any other information that may be unavailable from secondary sources. For example, Cisco Systems has developed a "Community of Customers" that it regularly queries for ideas, product preferences, and performance evaluations. Darren Noyce succinctly provides an effective evaluation of the pros and cons of using the Internet for business-to-business research:

> Web-based (online) surveys offer us more opportunities for success. They involve invitations to participate, sent either as e-mails, or "advertised" in pop-up windows or banner ads when visiting Web sites. Online surveys

TABLE 6.2	**EXAMPLES OF BUSINESS-TO-BUSINESS INFORMATION RESOURCES AVAILABLE ON THE INTERNET**
http://www.corporateinformation.com	A site that offers in-depth information about companies located outside the United States. Provides company profiles from 58 countries.
http://www.frost.com	This site is maintained by Frost and Sullivan, a large research firm. It provides market research reports that monitor over 300 industries.
http://www.intelliquest.com	Intelliquest specializes in providing technology companies with survey-based market research information.
http://www.census.gov	This is a huge site, which provides a wide range of data gathered and published by the U.S. Census Bureau.
http://www.stat-usa.gov	The U.S. Department of Commerce provides economic data published by the U.S. government as well as National Trade Data Bank Information for importers and exporters.
http://www.cbd.savvy.com	The Commerce Business Daily in print form provides a list of the federal government's requests for proposals. The online version includes the same material and is easily scanned.
http://www.dnb.com	Dun & Bradstreet publish business information on 11 million U.S. private and public businesses and more than 50 million businesses worldwide. D&B information can assist in determining market potentials and understanding customer operations.
http://www.liszt.com	This site helps a business marketer to build a list of potential customers.
http://www.findarticles.com	A valuable site for locating articles on particular companies, industries, or virtually any topic.
http://www.wilsonweb.com/webmarket/	Articles on Internet marketing are gathered from a wide array of sources and published on this Web site.

benefit from direct data entry, allow display of stimulus material, and can be convenient and easy to use for respondents. Indeed, the potential for conducting surveys online is enticing—it can be relatively cheap and fast, and practically anyone with a modem and some Web development software can administer them. However, the temptation to jump in without fully exploring the methodological challenges presented by the new medium has resulted in countless bad surveys—conducted not just by teenagers working out of their parents' basement, but by otherwise reputable research organizations. We should be concerned about this because badly-done Internet surveys hurt us all. They make market managers leery of commissioning the research and make the public cynical and uncooperative.[4]

---

[4]Darren Noyce, "eB2B Analysis of Business-to-Business E-Commerce and How Research Can Adapt to Meet Future Challenges," *International Journal of Market Research* 44, no. 1 (2002): p. 24.

Survey research over the Internet can be effective for gathering information easily, quickly, and at low cost. In addition, a large, diverse group of respondents can be reached instantly, data entry errors are reduced, and responses are easy to tabulate. However, the major drawback is the inability to draw a probability sample. If a questionnaire is posted on a Web site, there is no control over who responds; therefore, a manager cannot generalize the results to the broader population of customer organizations. To combat the problem, some firms have used online panels, where respondents are randomly chosen. Using Internet-generated surveys is challenging, and the business marketer must use this medium carefully. However, experts suggest that online, Internet-based research will soon replace mail surveys and telephone interviews.[5]

The Role of Market Potential in Planning and Control

Market potential is the maximum possible sales of all sellers of a given product in a defined market during a specified time period.[6] Maximum sales opportunities for an individual company's product is referred to as **sales potential,** which is the maximum share of market potential an individual company might expect for a specific product or product line.[7]

An example will clarify the nature of potentials. Assume that manufacturers of aircraft engines and parts generated shipments of $9 billion this year. What level of market potential would be expected for the industry next year? Based on commercial airline activity, total volume for the industry next year might be projected to increase by 20 percent. Thus, the aircraft-engine industry has a market potential of $10.8 billion ($9 billion $\times$ 1.20). Of this, the aircraft-engine division of General Electric in Cincinnati might expect to obtain 14 percent, based on current market share, anticipated marketing efforts, production capacity, and other factors. General Electric's sales potential is therefore $1.51 billion for next year ($10.8 billion $\times$ 0.14).

Potential for Planning Strategy   Consider a company that wishes to introduce new telecommunications services to businesses. How large is the market opportunity? A market potential (total demand) estimate provides the foundation for the planning process. Three broad groups of stakeholders require demand forecasts: engineering design and implementation teams; marketing and commercial development teams; and external entities, such as potential investors, government regulators, equipment and application suppliers, and distribution partners. In the marketing area, commercial questions that must be answered before launch of service and that depend on the estimate of demand include: Where should sales outlets be located? How many are required to cover the target market? What sales levels should be expected from each outlet? What performance targets should be established for each? Demand forecasts are needed to project the company's revenues, profits, and cash flow to assess business viability, to determine cash, equity, and borrowing requirements, and to determine appropriate pricing structures and levels.[8] In short, without knowledge of market

---

[5] Bob Lamons, "Eureka! Future of B-to-B Research Is Online," *Marketing News*, September 24, 2001, p. 9.

[6] William E. Cox Jr. and George N. Havens, "Determination of Sales Potentials and Performance for an Industrial Goods Manufacturer," *Journal of Marketing Research* 14 (November 1977): p. 574.

[7] Francis E. Humme, *Market and Sales Potentials* (New York: The Ronald Press Company, 1961), p. 8.

[8] Peter McBurney, Simon Parsons, and Jeremy Green, "Forecasting Market Demand for New Telecommunications Services: An Introduction," *Telematics and Information* 19 (2002): p. 233.

potential, marketing executives cannot develop sound strategy and make effective decisions about the allocation of resources.

Potentials: Planning and Control by Segment   The primary application of market and sales potential information is clearly in the planning and control of marketing strategy by market segment. Recall from Chapter 5 that a *segment* refers to a set of present or potential customers who share some common characteristics that help explain and predict how they will respond to marketing strategy. Once sales potential is determined for each segment, the manager can allocate expenditures on the basis of potential sales volume. Spending huge sums of money on advertising and personal selling has little benefit in segments where the market opportunity is low. Of course, expenditures would have to be based on both potential and the level of competition. Actual sales in each segment can also be compared with potential sales, taking into account the level of competition, in order to evaluate the effectiveness of the marketing program.

Consider the experience of a Cleveland manufacturer of quick-connective couplings for power transmission systems. For more than 20 years, one of its large distributors had been increasing its sales volume. In fact, this distributor was considered one of the firm's top producers. The firm then analyzed the sales potentials for each of its 31 distributors. The large distributor ranked 31st in terms of volume relative to potential, achieving only 15.4 percent of potential. A later evaluation revealed that the distributor's sales personnel did not know the most effective way to sell couplings to its large customer accounts.

Life Cycle Potential   Market potential is crucial for go/no-go decisions on new products for the business market. The "size of market" has been shown to be a significant screening factor for launching new industrial products. David Kendall and Michael French propose the concept of "life-cycle market potential" as an effective way of analyzing the market size for new industrial products.[9] They suggest that life cycle market potential is "the greatest number of product adoptions that will eventually occur in a particular market over the product life-cycle, given expected environmental conditions and expected aggregate effects of marketing actions by the industry."

The life cycle measure is useful because it provides realistic boundaries for total sales over the product's life and it is possible to make reasonable estimates of its value. Life cycle market potential is measured by estimating total annual sales of the generic product class (based on the number of customers and their usage of the product) and scaling down this estimate based on concept tests with potential customers (for example, a market share estimate is multiplied by the estimate of total product class sales). Total sales over the life cycle can then be calculated by estimating repeat purchases and length of time until saturation. This total life cycle potential then serves as a benchmark to help decide whether the new product should be introduced.

As this discussion demonstrates, market and sales potentials are pivotal in marketing planning and control. Therefore, great care must be taken to estimate markets and sales potential. The business marketing manager must thoroughly understand the various techniques for developing potentials accurately.

---

[9]David L. Kendall and Michael T. French, "Forecasting the Potential for New Industrial Products," *Industrial Marketing Management* 20, no. 3 (August 1990): p. 177. See also, W. Chan Kim and Renée Mauborgne, "Knowing a Winning Business Idea When You See One," *Harvard Business Review* 78 (September–October 2000): pp. 129–138.

FIGURE 6.1 | THE RELATIONSHIP BETWEEN POTENTIAL AND THE FORECAST

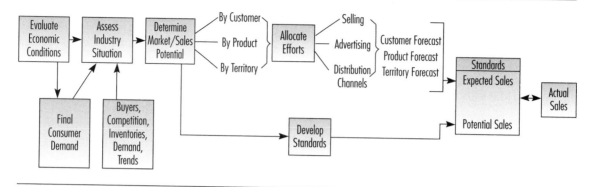

The Role of the Sales Forecast

The second component of organizational demand analysis, sales forecasting, likewise poses a significant challenge. The sales forecast answers the question: What level of sales do we expect next year, given a particular level and type of marketing effort? Once potentials have been determined, the business marketing manager can allocate resources to the various elements of the marketing mix. Only after the marketing strategy is developed can expected sales be forecasted. Many firms are tempted to use the forecast as a tool for deciding the level of marketing expenditures. One study (which sampled 900 firms) found that slightly more than 25 percent of the respondent firms set their advertising budgets after the sales forecast was developed.[10] Small companies whose budgeting and forecasting decisions were fragmented made up the majority of the firms in this group. Clearly, marketing strategy is a determinant of the level of sales and not vice versa. Figure 6.1 illustrates the position of market potential estimates and the sales forecast in the planning process.

The **sales forecast** represents the firm's best estimate of the expected sales revenue from a given marketing strategy. The forecast is usually less than sales potential. The firm may find that it is uneconomical to try to capture all available business. Strong competitors within certain segments may preclude the achievement of total potential sales. Like sales potential data, the sales forecast provides the marketing manager with a valuable gauge for allocating resources and measuring performance.

Applying Market Potential and the Sales Forecast

Market potential estimates and sales forecasts complement each other in the marketing planning process. Market potential estimates are vital to sales forecasting: They provide direction as to which opportunities the firm should pursue, and the sales forecast is generated once the level of resources to be applied to each opportunity has been determined. Market potential estimates are used to determine where the firm's attention should be focused, the total and relative levels of expenditure to apply to each opportunity, and the benchmarks for evaluating performance. The sales forecast, in

---

[10] Douglas C. West, "Advertising Budgeting and Sales Forecasting: The Timing Relationship," *International Journal of Advertising* 14, no. 1 (1995): pp. 65–77.

INSIDE BUSINESS MARKETING

Accurate Forecasts Drive Effective Collaboration between Boeing and Alcoa

Alcoa supplies raw aluminum to Boeing for constructing wings for most of Boeing's commercial airplanes. As a result of sharing accurate demand data with Alcoa, Boeing was able to achieve cost reductions and improve delivery time performance throughout the entire supply chain.

Boeing began by developing an electronic sales forecast to allow Alcoa to receive the forecast file directly into its system. Included in the forecast is all the data Alcoa needed to understand the demand for the raw aluminum to be used in constructing aircraft wings. The forecast data was provided so that it could be loaded into Alcoa's system in an efficient manner, and great emphasis was placed on forecast accuracy. Because forecast errors would totally undermine the supply process, Boeing developed a process to identify errors in demand before communicating the forecasts electronically to

Alcoa. Boeing provides Alcoa with electronic visibility into its ERP (Enterprise Resource Planning) System so that Alcoa can understand when orders will be coming and can thereby respond more effectively to Boeing's needs. In short, Boeing realized that for Alcoa to make decisions on when it should have materials in Boeing's plant, Alcoa had to be given the most accurate forecast data possible.

In working together in the supply chain, the electronic sharing of demand forecasts made it possible for Alcoa to maintain the appropriate levels of aluminum inventory to meet Boeing's requirements.

SOURCE: Adapted from Victoria A. Micheau, "How Boeing and Alcoa Implemented a Successful Vendor Managed Inventory Program," *Journal of Business Forecasting* 24 (spring 2005): pp. 17–19.

contrast, typically provides direction for making short-run, tactical decisions and for monitoring quarterly and annual performance.

Thus, estimates of actual sales over the next year guide management in planning production, estimating purchasing requirements, setting inventory levels, scheduling transportation and the warehouse workforce, estimating working capital requirements, and planning short-term expenditures on promotion and advertising. Two- to five-year projections of sales (based on market potential analysis) help guide decision making about plant and warehouse facilities, capital requirements, and channel strategy and structure. In summary, market potential provides guidelines for the general direction the firm will take (in terms of markets and product opportunities) and for budget allocations to those opportunities. The sales forecast directs the timing of short-range tactical expenditures and long-term capital spending.

Supply Chain Links   Sales forecasts are critical to the smooth operation of the entire supply chain. When timely sales forecast information is readily available to all firms in the supply chain, plans can be tightly coordinated and all parties share in the benefits.[11] Sales forecast data is used to distribute inventory in the supply chain, manage stock levels at each link, and schedule resources for all the members of a supply chain that provide materials, components, and services to a manufacturer. Accurate forecasts go hand-in-hand with good business practices and effective management

[11] John T. Mentzer and Mark A. Moon, "Understanding Demand," *Supply Chain Management Review* 8 (May–June 2004): p. 45.

policies in directing the entire supply-chain process. Specific tools are available to develop accurate estimates of market potential; the business marketer must understand the purpose of each alternative technique as well as its strengths and limitations.

Determining Market and Sales Potentials

Secondary data, whether the product is new or established, the number of potential customers, and the extent of internal company information, play a role in estimating potential. Estimating market potential requires analysis of variables that relate to, or cause, aggregate demand for the product. It is crucial to find the best measures of the underlying variables so that potential can be measured accurately. This section will examine statistical series methods and survey methods of measuring market and sales potential.

Statistical Series Methods

Statistical series methods presume a continuing close correlation between the level of product demand and some statistical set (called a statistical series), such as the number of production workers or the value added by manufacturing. Assuming the connection is logical—that is, the underlying relationship between the two items is sound—then product demand can be projected indirectly by projecting the statistical series. First, the manager must identify specific industries that either use or could use the firm's product. Second, a measure of economic activity is determined for each actual and potential consumer industry. The measure of economic activity is assumed to represent the relative sales volume of each industry.

The number of production workers is frequently used as the statistical series representing potential demand. For example, Dell could use the number of employees as a statistical series in estimating market potential for information technology (IT) products in particular market sectors like financial services. By relating annual IT expenditures by these organizations to the total number of workers employed in that sector, an estimate of "IT purchases per employee" is provided. Presumably, the larger the workforce in an industry, the greater the potential need for a given business product, whether it is a component or capital equipment. Other statistical series that business marketing managers use include value added, capital-equipment expenditures, materials consumed, total value of shipments, and total employees and payrolls.

Tapping Available Information   The rationale behind using the single series method is that many industrial products have many applications in many consuming industries. It would be impractical, if not impossible, to estimate directly all the product's potential applications as well as the total quantities involved. To make the task manageable, the analyst turns to easily available information—a statistical series. The analyst relates one of these series to the demand for the firm's product. Consider aluminum cans. Secondary data reveal that in a given year, the malt beverage industry spent $2.2 billion on aluminum cans with total shipments amounting to $12 billion. Thus, a relationship between demand for cans and total dollar shipments (the statistical series) can be established. For every dollar of malt beverage sales, 18 cents in aluminum cans is used ($2.2 billion/$12 billion = $0.18 per dollar of beverages). Potential for next year could be estimated either for a given region (by determining estimated malt beverage sales in the region for next year) or for another segment of the malt beverage industry (for example, by estimating light beer sales for next year). Past relationships between demand for a product and a statistical series provide a reasonably firm basis for evaluating market potential in various market segments and regions.

Single Series Method   The single series method calculates market potential on the basis of secondary data reflecting the relative buying power of business markets. To use this procedure, management must have adequate knowledge of the SIC or NAICS groups that are potential users of a product. Let's consider how this approach may be used to analyze absolute market potential (dollars or units).

Estimates of absolute market potential for the entire United States, various geographic areas, or specific NAICS groups can be determined with a statistical series using the following approach:

1. Select a statistical series that appears to be related to demand for the product.

2. For each target NAICS industry, determine the relationship of the series to the demand for the product whose potential is being estimated.

3. Forecast the statistical series and its relationship to demand for the desired time frame.

4. Determine market potential by relating demand to future values of the statistical series.

Selecting a Statistical Series   To determine market potential using a statistical series, the analyst must first evaluate which statistical series is best related to the demand for the product. The demand for some products may be highly correlated to the number of production workers—uniforms, hand soap, and some office products are good examples. *County Business Patterns*, updated annually by the U.S. Census Bureau, provides an excellent source for identifying the number of employees by industry (NAICS sector) at the county, state, or national level. In other cases, value added or the value of shipments is better correlated to demand. For example, because of the high level of automation in the industry, the demand for metal cans by the beverage industry is more closely related to the value of beverage shipments than to the number of industry production workers. Information on the value of shipments (sales receipts) can be found in the *Economic Census*. This valuable source is organized by NAICS industry category and offers information on the number of establishments, employment, and value of shipments for each industry on a national or local level.

Important criteria in selecting a statistical series are twofold: (1) data on the series must be available and (2) future estimates of the series should be easier to predict than product demand would be. Many of the statistical series the Department of Commerce reports in the economic census can be forecasted for one to three years with reasonable accuracy. Private research firms (such as Predicasts and Standard & Poor's), as well as some online data services, develop predictions on many of the series for various industries.

Determining the Relationship between Demand and Statistical Series

Once the series has been selected, data on the series must be collected and related to demand to develop what might be termed a "demand" or a "usage" factor—that is, the quantity of the product demanded per unit of the statistical series.

TABLE 6.3 | Usage Factor for Ball Bearings

Industry	2005 Bearing Sales to the Industry (in Millions of Dollars)	2005 Value of Using Industry Shipments (in Millions of Dollars)	Demand Factor (Bearings per Dollar of Shipments)
Motor vehicles	$1,680	$75,271	$0.022
Trucks and trailers	39	2,767	0.014

NOTE: Industry values are hypothetical.

One approach is to use the *Economic Census* to develop the database for the statistical series, and then relate this to previous levels of demand for the product—either by NAICS code or by geographic region. Assume we wish to estimate market potential for ball bearings in 2008, and that motor vehicles and truck trailers are the primary target markets. The statistical series is value of shipments (that is, the sales of these manufacturers). To determine the usage or demand factor (from, say, 2005), we relate past ball bearing demand to the value of shipments in the motor vehicle and truck trailer industry (Table 6.3).

Sales of bearings to the target industries would be gleaned from trade sources, whereas the statistical series, value of shipments, could be found in the economic census. Thus, in motor vehicles, $0.022 worth of bearings were purchased for each dollar of shipments. An estimate of market potential in 2008 would be developed by multiplying 0.022 by the projected value of shipments to be made by the motor vehicle industry in that year.

Suppose a manufacturer of plastic resins wants to analyze market potential in four industries with which the firm has never dealt. There is no published data. A short survey of firms in each industry group could be implemented to assess resin purchases and some other statistical series such as production workers. The results would be tallied for each industry group, and a usage factor of resin (pounds) per production worker calculated for each. The result could then be used to forecast market potential in each industry by estimating total production workers in the relevant year and multiplying that by the usage or demand factor. The validity of this approach depends on how well the firms in the sample represent the target industries.

Understanding Limitations   Estimating a demand or usage factor this way must take into account the limitations of the approach. The analysis is based on averages; an average consumption of a given component per dollar of output or per production worker is computed. The average may or may not hold true for a particular target industry. Product usage may vary considerably from firm to firm, even in the same industry category. Further, the demand factor is based on historical relationships that may change dramatically; that is, the industry may use more or less of the product as a result of technological change, manufacturing system reconfigurations, or changes in final consumer demand. Nevertheless, carefully derived estimates of the relationship between demand and a statistical series can be powerful tools for measuring market potential.

Forecasting the Statistical Series   Once the relationship of the demand to the series has been documented (the demand or usage factor has been determined), management estimates future values of the series in one of two ways: by independently forecasting expected values, using their own estimated growth rates; or by relying on forecasts from government, trade associations, or private research firms. The goal is to project the series forward so that future market potential can be assessed by multiplying the demand factor by the estimated future value of the series.

Future values of the usage factor must also be estimated. The demand or usage factor expresses the relationship between the demand and the series in terms such as "dollar of product per dollar of consuming industry sales" or "pounds of product per production worker." If we are estimating market potential two years into the future, we must ask whether usage of the product per unit of output in the consuming industry will change during that period. Management may want to adjust the demand or usage factor to reflect predicted changes in product usage. An analysis of production processes, technology, competitive actions, and final consumer demand may be required to adjust the usage factor properly. A good example is the plastics industry: The move to lighten automobiles to enhance gas mileage would indicate a substantial increase in the "pounds of plastic per automobile" usage factor over the next five years.

Determining Market Potential   The final step is the easiest one: The demand or usage factor is multiplied by the forecasted value of the statistical series. Once this stage has been reached, the difficult data and estimation problems have been resolved, and the calculation is routine. Strategists must be sure that potential is calculated for all relevant market segments. For planning and control purposes, market potential estimates may be required for various customer segments, industry groups, territories, and distribution channels.

In summary, the effectiveness of the single series method of estimating market potential depends on how well the demand or usage factor represents underlying demand, the quality of the data used, the ability to estimate future values of the series and usage factors, and the extent of distortion caused by using averages and gross estimates. This approach is well suited to commonly used industrial products. For new products, unique items, and rarely used components, this approach is not appropriate because the data are insufficient. Modifications to the series and considerable management judgment are required to estimate potential.

Market Research

To avoid the problems inherent in historical statistical data, firms can use market surveys to gather primary information on future buyer intentions. Market-focused businesses also use focus groups and high-touch techniques such as visiting customers to develop a thorough understanding of their environment and needs.[12]

Surveys   The survey method is particularly useful for estimating the market potential of new products. Surveys can provide information about whether specific organizations are in the market for a new product, about the extent of their needs, and about key buying influentials and the likelihood of purchase. Surveys are useful in determining the potential product use by specific industry groups, the firms in

---

[12] Stanley F. Slater and John C. Narver, "Intelligence Generation and Superior Customer Value," *Journal of the Academy of Marketing Science* 28 (winter 2000): pp. 120–127.

B2B TOP PERFORMERS

Go Deep into the Customer's Organization

A well-designed and executed business marketing research study covers multiple respondents from each customer organization sampled. A central focus, then, is on identifying individuals, particularly the most influential ones, who will participate in a buying decision. By restricting attention to a single point of contact, such as a purchasing manager or a senior executive, an incomplete or, worse yet, inaccurate picture of the customer's purchasing priorities may emerge.

To identify the full range of purchase influencers, a snowball sampling technique is often

required. To illustrate, using this approach for the health-care market, a researcher for a medical equipment firm might make initial contact with the hospital administrator. From this interview, the researcher secures the names of nurses, physicians, and purchasing specialists who are subsequently interviewed to capture the realities of the decision-making process.

SOURCE: Diane H. Schmalensee, "One Researcher's Rules of Thumb for the B-to-B Arena," *Marketing News*, November 12, 2001, pp. 17–19.

each industry that have the greatest potential, and the relative importance of each industry group to total sales. One advantage of surveys is that data can be collected on the characteristics of potential customer firms and related directly to responses on product preferences and purchase intentions. Such information enables the marketer to uncover the market segments most attracted to the product and reach them with responsive strategies.[13] Recall from Chapter 5 that a product's economic value to a user (value in use) can vary by market segment. Surveys can be profitably used to determine the value in use for various customers or market segments. Surveys have also been used to evaluate the purchase potential of individual customer firms.

A complete enumeration of the market can sometimes be made, and the potential volumes for each prospective customer can be summed to arrive at a total market potential. A complete census of the market is warranted when (1) the markets are very concentrated, (2) there is direct sales contact, (3) orders have a relatively high value, and (4) the unit volume is low.[14]

Uses and Limitations of Surveys
The survey method is appropriate in estimating the market potential for new products, especially in providing estimates based on objective facts and opinions rather than on executive judgment. In addition, the survey can target specific industries that represent the greatest market potential for new or existing products. Of course, surveys present limitations: Nonrepresentative samples and nonresponse bias can distort findings, the wrong person in the respondent companies may fill out the questionnaire, and a small sample size may make sophisticated statistical analysis impossible. A particularly difficult problem is assessing whom to contact. The researcher must invest considerable effort to find the best source of data. The marketing manager should take the lead in resolving data-collection problems and ensuring that the survey design generates valid results.

---

[13] McBurney, Parsons, and Green, "Forecasting Market Demand for New Telecommunications Services," p. 233.
[14] William E. Cox Jr., *Industrial Marketing Research* (New York: John Wiley and Sons, 1979), p. 158.

Customer Visit   Many leading firms, such as Hewlett-Packard, IBM, and 3M, include customer visits as an important component of market research. In many firms, customer visits are normally conducted early in the new-product-development process. The typical visit program might include onsite visits with 20 to 40 customer firms. Customers are chosen according to a sampling plan, and the visit program is often reinforced with additional market research.

To reap the maximum value from customer visits, the visit should be conducted by a cross-functional team and include well-defined objectives, a careful selection of customers, a discussion guide to structure the visit, and a plan for reporting the results. Customer visits provide a valuable tool for:

identifying unmet customer needs.

identifying new market opportunities.

learning about the role a product assumes within a customer's operations and strategy.

building customer relationships.

Customer visits provide fresh insights into how members of the customer organization actually use products. Ideas that originated during customer visits have spawned a stream of innovative products and services.

The Essential Dimensions of Sales Forecasting

Selection of a sales forecasting technique depends on many factors, including the period for which the forecast is desired, the purpose of the forecast, the availability of data, the company's level of technical expertise, the accuracy desired, the nature of the product, and the extent of the product line. Evaluations of each factor suggest the limits within which the firm must work in terms of forecasting methods.

The Role of Forecasting

The forecast is a major component of the decision-making process. Because all budgets in a company ultimately depend on how many units are sold, the sales forecast often determines companywide commitments for everything from raw materials and labor to capital equipment and advertising. Accurate forecasting of sales ensures better product stocking policies, improved cash management and cash flow, more efficient warehouse management, better product distribution, and finally, minimization of the company's risk in covering the market demands.[15] Moreover, accurate forecasters are ideally equipped to meet the needs of their most demanding customers.

Various types of forecasts are often required because estimates of future sales are applied to so many activities. A forecast to determine inventory commitments for the

---

[15] K. Nikolopoulos, K. Metaxiotis, V. Assimakopoulos, and E. Tararidou, "A First Approach to E-Forecasting: A Survey of Forecasting Web Services," *Information Management & Computer Security* 11 (July 2003): pp. 146–152.

next month has to be more precise than one used to set sales quotas. A five-year forecast of growth in the personal computer industry requires a very detailed and sophisticated model incorporating numerous economic variables, whereas a six-month projection of hospital supply sales may simply require the extrapolating from past sales. Some firms use *early warning systems* to alert them to changes in market demand for their products.[16] Early warning systems are designed to sample the market in advance of a selling season or period to detect major shifts in demand. The data from this early "forecast" are then used to plan operations, production, and the delivery schedule for materials and supplies.

E-Forecasting

Forecasting, like many other business activities, is migrating to the Internet. "E-forecasting" is still in the early stages of implementation, and significant research needs to be done in this emerging field. As it evolves, e-forecasting will have to deal with the classical disadvantages for all e-business applications, such as security factors, user authorization, speed of delivery, and Web programming limitations. However, as Internet technology evolves, many of these problems will be effectively solved. Experts define five categories of Web services for forecasting available to managers:

Online forecasting services.   The user (manager) can upload the firm's own data, perform forecasting, and see the forecasts online with rich visualization options.

Forecasting software packages with Web-enabled modules.

Offline forecasting services.   The user can upload data, and then the forecasting process takes place offline. The user can make forecasts at another time because the forecasting takes place offline.

Sites that provide forecasting over specific data.   The user cannot upload the firm's own data but can make forecasts over the existing data.

Sites that provide forecasts over specific data.   The user can register and purchase specific forecasts for a particular product or service.[17]

Forecasting Methods

The sales forecast may be highly mathematical or informally based on sales force estimates. Two primary approaches to sales forecasting are recognized: (1) qualitative and (2) quantitative, which includes time series and causal analysis.

Qualitative Techniques

Qualitative techniques, which are also referred to as **management judgment** or **subjective techniques,** rely on informed judgment and rating schemes. The sales force, top-level executives, or distributors may be called on to use their knowledge of the

---

[16] Paul V. Tiplitz, "Do You Need an Early Warning System?" *Journal of Business Forecasting Methods and Systems* 14 (spring 1995): pp. 8–10.

[17] Nikolopoulos, Metaxiotis, Assimakopoulos, and Tararidou, "A First Approach to E-Forecasting," p. 149.

economy, the market, and the customers to create qualitative demand estimates. Techniques for qualitative analysis include the executive judgment method, the sales force composite method, and the Delphi method.

The effectiveness of qualitative approaches depends on the close relationships between customers and suppliers that are typical in the industrial market. Qualitative techniques work well for such items as heavy capital equipment or when the nature of the forecast does not lend itself to mathematical analysis. These techniques are also suitable for new product or new technology forecasts when historical data are scarce or nonexistent.[18] An important advantage of qualitative approaches is that it brings users of the forecast into the forecasting process. The effect is usually an increased understanding of the procedure and a higher level of commitment to the resultant forecast.

Executive Judgment   According to a large sample of business firms, the **executive judgment method** enjoys a high level of usage.[19] The judgment method, which combines and averages top executives' estimates of future sales, is popular because it is easy to apply and to understand. Typically, executives from various departments, such as sales, marketing, production, finance, and purchasing, are brought together to apply their collective expertise, experience, and opinions to the forecast.

The primary limitation of the approach is that it does not systematically analyze cause-and-effect relationships. Further, because there is no established formula for deriving estimates, new executives may have difficulty making reasonable forecasts. The resulting forecasts are only as good as the executives' opinions. The accuracy of the executive judgment approach is also difficult to assess in a way that allows meaningful comparison with alternative techniques.[20]

The executives' "ballpark" estimates for the intermediate and the long-run time frames are often used in conjunction with forecasts developed quantitatively. However, when historical data are limited or unavailable, the executive judgment approach may be the only alternative. Mark Moriarty and Arthur Adams suggest that executive judgment methods produce accurate forecasts when (1) forecasts are made frequently and repetitively, (2) the environment is stable, and (3) the linkage between decision, action, and feedback is short.[21] Business marketers should examine their forecasting situation in light of these factors in order to assess the usefulness of the executive judgment technique.

Sales Force Composite   The rationale behind the **sales force composite** approach is that salespeople can effectively estimate future sales volume because they know the customers, the market, and the competition. In addition, participating in the forecasting process helps sales personnel understand how forecasts are derived and boosts their incentive to achieve the desired level of sales. The composite forecast is developed by combining the sales estimates from all salespeople. By providing the salesperson with a wealth of customer information that can be conveniently accessed and reviewed,

---

[18] A. Michael Segalo, *The IBM/PC Guide to Sales Forecasting* (Wayne, Pa.: Banbury, 1985), p. 21.

[19] Nada Sanders, "Forecasting Practices in U.S. Corporations: Survey Results," *Interfaces* 24 (March–April 1994): pp. 92–100.

[20] Spyros Makridakis and Steven Wheelwright, "Forecasting: Issues and Challenges for Marketing Management," *Journal of Marketing* 41 (October 1977): p. 31.

[21] Mark M. Moriarty and Arthur J. Adams, "Management Judgment Forecasts, Composite Forecasting Models and Conditional Efficiency," *Journal of Marketing Research* 21 (August 1984): p. 248.

customer relationship management (CRM) systems (see Chapter 4) enhance the efficiency and effectiveness of the sales force composite.[22] CRM systems also allow a salesperson to track progress in winning new business at key accounts.

Few companies rely solely on sales force estimates; rather, they usually adjust or combine the estimates with forecasts developed either by top management or by quantitative methods. The advantage of the sales force composite method is the ability to draw on sales force knowledge about markets and customers. This advantage is particularly important for a market in which buyer-seller relationships are close and enduring. The salesperson is often the best source of information about customer purchasing plans and inventory levels. The method can also be executed relatively easily at minimal cost. An added benefit is that creating a forecast forces a sales representative to carefully review these accounts in terms of future sales.[23]

The problems of sales force composites are similar to those of the executive judgment approach: They do not involve systematic analysis of cause and effect, and they rely on informed judgment and opinions. Some sales personnel may overestimate sales in order to look good or underestimate them in order to generate a lower quota. Management must carefully review all estimates. As a rule, sales force estimates are relatively accurate for short-run projections but less effective for long-term forecasts.

Delphi Method   In the **Delphi approach to forecasting,** the opinions of a panel of experts on future sales are converted into an informed consensus through a highly structured feedback mechanism.[24] As in the executive judgment technique, management officials are used as the panel, but each estimator remains anonymous. On the first round, written opinions about the likelihood of some future event are sought (for example, sales volume, competitive reaction, or technological breakthroughs). The responses to this first questionnaire are used to produce a second. The objective is to provide feedback to the group so that first-round estimates and information available to some of the experts are made available to the entire group.

After each round of questioning, the analyst who administers the process assembles, clarifies, and consolidates information for dissemination in the succeeding round. Throughout the process, panel members are asked to reevaluate their estimates based on the new information from the group. Opinions are kept anonymous, eliminating both "me too" estimates and the need to defend a position. After continued reevaluation, the goal is to achieve a consensus. The number of experts varies from six to hundreds, depending on how the process is organized and its purpose. The number of rounds of questionnaires depends on how rapidly the group reaches consensus.

Delphi Application   The Delphi technique is usually applied to long-range forecasting. The technique is particularly well suited to (1) new product forecasts, (2) estimation of future events for which historical data are limited, or (3) situations that are not suited to quantitative analysis. When the market for a new product is not well defined and the product concept is unique, the Delphi technique can produce some broad-gauged estimates.

---

[22] Robert Mirani, Deanne Moore, and John A. Weber, "Emerging Technologies for Enhancing Supplier-Reseller Partnerships," *Industrial Marketing Management* 30 (February 2001): pp. 101–114.

[23] Stewart A. Washburn, "Don't Let Sales Forecasting Spook You," *Sales and Marketing Management* 140 (September 1988): p. 118.

[24] Raymond E. Willis, *A Guide to Forecasting for Planners and Managers* (Englewood Cliffs, N.J.: Prentice-Hall, 1987), p. 343.

TABLE 6.4 | SUMMARY OF QUALITATIVE FORECASTING TECHNIQUES

Technique	Approach	Application
Executive judgment	Combining and averaging top executives' estimates of future sales	Ballpark estimates; new product sales estimates; intermediate and long-term time frames
Sales force composite	Combining and averaging individual salespersons' estimates of future sales	Effective when intimate knowledge of customer plans is important; useful for short and intermediate terms
Delphi method	Consensus of opinion on expected future sales volume is obtained by providing each panelist with the projections of all other panelists on preceding rounds. Panelists modify estimates until a consensus is achieved.	Appropriate for long-term forecasting; effective for projecting sales of new products or forecasting technological advances

The Delphi technique suffers from the same problems as any other qualitative approach, but it may be the only way to develop certain types of estimates. However, some shortcomings are specific to the approach. Assembling a panel of truly independent experts is extremely difficult. Officials in the same firm or individuals in the same profession tend to read the same literature, have similar training and background, and share the same attitudes on the phenomena under study. Some experts refuse to modify their views in light of feedback, thereby undermining the consensus-forming process.

Qualitative forecasting is important in the forecasting process. The techniques can be applied to develop ballpark estimates when the uniqueness of the product, the unavailability of data, and the nature of the situation preclude application of quantitative techniques. The accuracy of qualitative forecasts is difficult to measure because of the lack of standardization. Typically, qualitative estimates are merged with those developed quantitatively. Table 6.4 summarizes the qualitative approaches.

Quantitative Techniques

Quantitative forecasting, also referred to as systematic or objective forecasting, offers two primary methodologies: (1) time series and (2) regression or causal. **Time series** techniques use historical data ordered in time to project the trend and growth rate of sales. The rationale behind time series analysis is that the past pattern of sales will apply to the future. However, to discover the underlying pattern of sales, the analyst must first understand all of the possible patterns that may affect the sales series. Thus, a time series of sales may include trend, seasonal, cyclical, and irregular patterns. Once the effect of each has been isolated, the analyst can then project the expected future of each pattern. Time series methods are well suited to short-range forecasting because the assumption that the future will be like the past is more reasonable over the short run than over the long run.[25]

Regression or **causal** analysis, on the other hand, uses an opposite approach, identifying factors that have affected past sales and implementing them in a mathematical

[25] Spyros Makridakis, "A Survey of Time Series," *International Statistics Review* 44, no. 1 (1976): p. 63.

FIGURE 6.2 | TREND, CYCLE, AND SEASONAL COMPONENTS OF A TIME SERIES

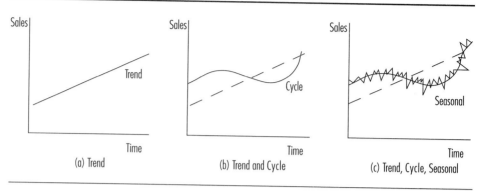

(a) Trend   (b) Trend and Cycle   (c) Trend, Cycle, Seasonal

model.[26] A sale is expressed mathematically as a function of the items that affect it. A forecast is derived by projecting values for each of the factors in the model, inserting these values into the regression equation, and solving for expected sales. Typically, causal models are more reliable for intermediate than for long-range forecasts because the magnitude of each factor affecting sales must first be estimated for some future time, which becomes difficult when estimating farther into the future.

A recent study on forecasting methods suggests choosing a methodology based on the underlying behavior of the market rather than the time horizon of the forecast.[27] This research indicates that when markets are sensitive to changes in market and environmental variables, causal methods work best, whether the forecast is short or long range; time series approaches are more effective when the market exhibits no sensitivity to market and/or environmental changes.

Time Series Analysis   A **time series** is nothing more than a set of chronologically ordered data points. Company sales reported monthly for the past five years are an example. A time series is composed of measurable patterns, and the objective of the analysis is to identify these patterns so that they may be projected. A time series has four components:

T = Trend

C = Cycle

S = Seasonal

I = Irregular

Figure 6.2 depicts the T, C, and S components of a time series.

The trend indicates the long-term general direction of the data. The trend may be a straight line of the form $y = a + bx$ (see Figure 6.2a); or a curve, $y = ab^x$; or $y = bx + cx^2$. The cycle represents the intermediate term with regular upswings and downswings of the data around the trend. For example, the industrial chemical industry in England shows a fairly regular rise and fall in demand over four- or five-year periods. Figure 6.2b

[26] Segalo, *Sales Forecasting*, p. 27.

[27] Robert J. Thomas, "Method and Situational Factors in Sales Forecast Accuracy," *Journal of Forecasting* 12 (January 1993): p. 75.

shows the cycle variations. The cycle may originate from business cycle movements in the economy as a whole, from business conditions within an industry, from consumer spending fluctuations in finished-goods markets, from inventory swings in industry, or from a succession of new product introductions. The cycle is extremely difficult to estimate because reversals need not occur at fixed intervals, and, as a result, the pattern may lack any regularity.

The **seasonal pattern** (depicted in Figure 6.2c) represents regular, recurring movements within the year. Data expressed daily, weekly, monthly, and quarterly may show seasonal patterns, which depend on such factors as seasonality of final consumption, end-of-period inventory adjustments, tax dates, business vacations, pipeline inventory adjustments, and scheduling of special promotions.

The **irregular component** in a time series reflects short-term random movements in the data that do not conform to a pattern related to the calendar. Many factors contribute to such random swings in sales patterns (for example, strikes, competitive actions). Generally, the assumption is that these short-term random effects average out over a year.

When forecasting future sales volumes, actual sales can be expressed as a combination of all four time series elements:

$$\text{Actual sales} = \text{trend} \times \text{seasonal} \times \text{cycle} \times \text{irregular}$$

To develop a forecast, the analyst must determine each pattern and then extrapolate all four into the future. This requires a significant amount of historical sales information. Once a forecast of each pattern is developed, the sales forecast is assembled by combining the estimates for each pattern.

Regression or Causal Techniques The objective of causal techniques is to determine a relationship between sales and a variable presumed to be related to sales; knowledge of the causal variable can be used to determine expected future sales volumes. The method requires a significant amount of historical data to establish a valid relationship. The model mathematically expresses the causal relationship, and the mathematical formula is usually referred to as a regression equation.

A critical aspect of regression analysis is to identify the economic variable(s) to which past sales are related. For forecasting purposes, the *Survey of Current Business* is particularly helpful because it contains monthly, quarterly, and annual figures for hundreds of economic variables. The forecaster can test an array of economic variables from the *Survey* to find the variable(s) with the best relationship to past sales.

As with the statistical series approach, two general rules should be followed in evaluating economic series. First, the economic series (variable) should be logically related to company sales.[28] Forecasters are often tempted to break this rule because they can easily "try out" any number of variables; a variable may be found to be highly correlated to past sales, but with no logical connection. Such spurious relationships are not effective for forecasting future sales because they are usually accidental and may not hold true. Second, it should be easier to forecast the economic variable than to project the sales level. The causal approach develops a sales forecast by establishing the relationship of sales to some other economic variable. Knowledge of this relationship is then used to estimate sales by determining future values of the economic variable and

---

[28]Frank H. Eby and William J. O'Neill, *The Management of Sales Forecasting* (Lexington, Mass.: Lexington Books, 1977), p. 145.

the corresponding sales level. If future projection of the variable are either not available or of questionable validity, sales may as well be estimated directly.

To create a sales forecast with causal analysis, the analyst must first determine the mathematical relationship between sales and the causal variable. This relationship is then expressed in the form of a linear equation: $y = a + bx$, where a and b are the coefficients that express the relationship and x represents the causal variable from which estimates are made. Sales are then forecast by inserting estimated future values of x into the equation.

Use of Regression Techniques   Causal models are the most sophisticated forecasting tools. A study found that only 17 percent of firms regularly use regression techniques for forecasting and that 24 percent have never tried them.[29] Regression models are useful to industrial firms in projecting final consumer demand for items of which their products become a part. For example, American Can projects motor oil sales based on a regression model that integrates auto registrations, average miles driven per car, average crankcase size, and average interval between oil changes as causal variables. Finally, an important dimension in forecasting is the ability to predict a turning point in the sales series. To the extent that turning points in causal variables can be foreseen, turns in company sales can be predicted.

Limitations   Although causal methods have measurable levels of accuracy, there are some important caveats and limitations. First, as already discussed, the fact that sales and some causal variables are correlated (associated) does not mean that the independent variable (x) caused sales. The independent variable should be logically related to sales.

Second, because both x and y have the same trend pattern, one may be, in effect, correlating only trends, whereas the other components (for example, cyclical and seasonal) are not highly correlated.[30] Thus, regression equations whose variables are highly correlated may be unsuitable for short-range projections in which cyclical and seasonal factors are important.

Third, regression methods require considerable historical data for equations to be valid and reliable, but the data may not be available. Caution must always be used in extrapolating relationships into the future. The equation relates what *has* happened; economic and industry factors may change in the future, making past relationships invalid.

The last, and probably the most crucial, limitation of causal methods is the problem of determining future values of independent or causal variables. As we have discussed, before the regression equation can be used to project future sales levels, future values of the independent variables must be determined. Thus, as Spyros Makridakis points out, "what is actually done is to shift the burden of forecasting from that of directly predicting some factor of interest (sales) to another one which attempts to estimate several independent variables before it can forecast."[31] In the final analysis, the quality of the sales forecast generated by regression models depends on the forecaster's ability to generate valid and reliable estimates of the independent variables.

---

[29] Douglas J. Dalrymple, "Sales Forecasting Methods and Accuracy," *Business Horizons* 18 (December 1975): p. 70.

[30] Paul E. Green and Donald S. Tull, *Research for Marketing Decisions*, 3d ed. (Englewood Cliffs, N.J.: Prentice-Hall, 1975), p. 669.

[31] Makridakis, "A Survey of Time Series," p. 62.

Combining Several Forecasting Techniques

Recent research on forecasting techniques indicates that forecasting accuracy can be improved by combining the results of several forecasting methods.[32] The results of combined forecasts greatly surpass most individual projections, techniques, and analyses by experts. Mark Moriarty and Arthur Adams suggest that managers should use a composite forecasting model that includes both systematic (quantitative) and judgmental (qualitative) factors.[33] In fact, they suggest that a composite forecast be created to provide a standard of comparison in evaluating the results provided by any single forecasting approach. Each forecasting approach relies on varying data to derive sales estimates. By considering a broader range of factors that affect sales, the combined approach provides a more accurate forecast. Rather than searching for the single "best" forecasting technique, business marketers should direct increased attention to the composite forecasting approach.

Summary

Estimating market potential and forecasting sales are the two most significant dimensions of organizational demand analysis. Each is fundamental to marketing planning and control. Knowledge of market potential enables the marketer to isolate market opportunity and efficiently allocate marketing resources to product and customer segments that offer the highest return. Measures of market potential also provide a standard for monitoring performance. Similarly, the sales forecast—the firm's best estimate of expected sales with a particular marketing plan—forces the manager to ask the right questions and to consider various strategies before allocating resources. To analyze market opportunities as well as the strategies of competitors, a wealth of valuable information is available to business marketers on the Internet.

The methods for developing estimates of market potential fall into two categories: (1) statistical series methods and (2) market surveys. The marketer must know the strengths and weaknesses of each and understand their appropriateness to a particular marketing environment.

The forecasting techniques available to the business marketer are (1) qualitative and (2) quantitative. Qualitative techniques rely on informed judgments of future sales and include executive judgment, the sales force composite, and the Delphi methods. By contrast, quantitative techniques have more complex data requirements and include time series and causal approaches. The time series method uses chronological historical data to project the future trend and growth rate of sales. Causal methods, on the other hand, seek to identify factors that have affected past sales and to incorporate them into a mathematical model. The computer is a valuable tool, facilitating the forecasting process for all methods.

The essence of sound forecasting is to combine effectively the forecasts provided by various methods. The process of sales forecasting is challenging and requires a good working knowledge of the available alternatives described in this chapter.

---

[32] J. Scott Armstrong, "The Forecasting Canon: Nine Generalizations to Improve Forecast Accuracy," *FORESIGHT: The International Journal of Applied Forecasting* 1, no. 1 (June 2005): pp. 29–35.

[33] Moriarty and Adams, "Management Judgment Forecasts," p. 248.

Discussion Questions

1. Explain how the use of the sales forecast differs from that of an estimate of market potential.

2. What is the underlying logic of statistical series methods used in measuring market potential?

3. What statistical series are provided by the Census Bureau? (Go to http://www.census.gov for a quick review.)

4. Distinguish between single and multiple statistical series methods for estimating market potential.

5. Why are market surveys favored over statistical series methods in measuring the market potential for new industrial products?

6. Compare and contrast the sales force composite and the Delphi methods of developing a sales forecast.

7. Although qualitative forecasting techniques are important in the sales forecasting process in many industrial firms, the marketing manager must understand the limitations of these approaches. Outline these limitations.

8. As alternative methods for sales forecasting, what is the underlying logic of (1) time series and (2) regression or causal methods?

9. What limitations must be understood before applying and interpreting the sales forecasting results generated by causal methods?

10. What role does the Internet play in facilitating the estimation of organizational demand?

11. What features of the business market support the use of qualitative forecasting approaches? What benefits does the business market analyst gain by combining these qualitative approaches with quantitative forecasting methods?

Internet Exercises

The *Economic Census* profiles the U.S. economy every five years from the national to the local level. Go to http://www.census.gov and click on "Economic Census," then for the most recent year, locate:

1. The number of manufacturing establishments (NAICS code 31-33) that are located in Denver, Colorado; and

2. The sales receipts or shipments that these establishments generated.

CASE

IBM Global Services[34]

IBM Global Services is the world's largest information technology (IT) service provider, with more than 125,000 employees operating in 160 countries. IBM Global Services, which accounts for nearly half of IBM's corporate revenue, integrates all of the firm's capabilities—services, hardware, software, and research—to help customers of all sizes in areas such as IT system design, e-business consulting, and traditional maintenance and support. The unit serves customers across all industry sectors and does a significant volume of business with government units at all levels.

Washington Mutual, a profitable and rapidly expanding bank, is among IBM's lengthy list of customers in the financial services industry. In recent years, Washington Mutual has pursued an aggressive acquisition strategy and turned to IBM Global Services for assistance in integrating the acquired businesses into its existing IT infrastructure and in launching Internet-based strategies. Consistent with a 12-year service agreement that was recently extended, IBM Global Services provides continuing services and support to Washington Mutual's data centers and branch banks.

In forecasting the market potential for the commercial banking sector, IBM might use "the number of employees" as the statistical series representing potential demand.

1. The NAICS code for commercial banking is 52211. Go to http://www.census.gov, review the subject areas, and then click on *County Business Patterns*. From this report, locate the total number of employees who work in the commercial banking sector in Illinois.

2. Concerning the "usage factor" or "information technology purchases per worker," assume that a trade association study estimates that IT expenditures per employee are $250 in the commercial banking sector. Calculate the market potential for IT products and services that might be expected from Illinois commercial banks.

---

[34]"Washington Mutual Evolves to National Presence with Help from IBM Global Services," http://www.ibm.com/services, accessed August 14, 2002.

PART

IV

FORMULATING BUSINESS MARKETING STRATEGY

Business Marketing Planning: Strategic Perspectives

To this point, you have developed an understanding of organizational buying behavior, customer relationship management, market segmentation, and a host of other tools managers use. All of this provides a fundamentally important perspective to the business marketing strategist. After reading this chapter, you will understand:

1. marketing's strategic role in corporate strategy development.

2. the multifunctional nature of business marketing decision making.

3. the components of a business model that can be converted into superior positions of advantage in the business market.

4. a valuable framework for detailing the processes and systems that drive strategy success.

Most large corporations implicitly believe that strategy is the province of senior management. This is not so at GE Capital.[1] At a recent planning session, someone suggested that each of its 28 different businesses assemble a team of lower- to mid-level managers, all under the age of 30, and give them the task of finding opportunities that their "older managers" had missed. The young teams returned with a number of fresh ideas, including several focused on how GE Capital could capitalize on the Internet. New growth strategies come from new ideas. New ideas often come from new voices. Drawing on the collective strengths of the organization is what strategy formulation is all about.

To meet the challenges brought on by growing domestic and global competition, business-to-business firms are increasingly recognizing the vital role of the marketing function in developing and implementing successful business strategies. Effective business strategies share many common characteristics, but at a minimum they are responsive to market needs, they exploit the special competencies of the organization, and they use valid assumptions about environmental trends and competitive behavior. Above all, they must offer a realistic basis for securing and sustaining a competitive advantage.[2] This chapter examines the nature and critical importance of strategy development in the business marketing firm.

First, the chapter highlights the special role of the marketing function in corporate strategy development, with a functionally integrated perspective of business marketing planning. Next, it identifies the sources of competitive advantage by exploring the key components of a business model and how they can be managed to provide superior customer benefits. Finally, a framework is offered for converting strategy goals into a tightly integrated customer strategy. This discussion provides a foundation for exploring business marketing strategy on a global scale—the theme of the next chapter.

Marketing's Strategic Role

Market-driven firms are centered on customers—they take an outside-in view of strategy and demonstrate an ability to sense market trends ahead of their competitors.[3] Many firms—like Johnson & Johnson, Motorola, and Dow Chemical—have numerous divisions, product lines, products, and brands. Policies established at the corporate level provide the framework for strategy development in each business division to ensure survival and growth of the entire enterprise. In turn, corporate and divisional policies establish the boundaries within which individual product or market managers develop strategy.

The Hierarchy of Strategies

Three major levels of strategy dominate most large multiproduct organizations: (1) corporate strategy, (2) business-level strategy, and (3) functional strategy.[4]

---

[1] Gary Hamel, "Bringing Silicon Valley Inside," *Harvard Business Review* 77 (September–October 1999): pp. 78–79. See also Gary Hamel and Gary Getz, "Funding Growth in an Age of Austerity," *Harvard Business Review* 82 (July–August 2004): pp. 76–84.

[2] Eric M. Olson, Stanley F. Slater, and G. Thomas M. Hult, "The Performance Implications of Fit among Business Strategy, Marketing Organization Structure, and Strategic Behavior," *Journal of Marketing* 69 (July 2005): pp. 49–65.

[3] For a comprehensive review, see Ahmet H. Kirca, Satish Jayachandran, and William O. Bearden, "Market Orientation: A Meta Analytic Review of Its Antecedents and Impact on Performance," *Journal of Marketing* 69 (April 2005): pp. 24–41.

[4] This discussion draws on Frederick E. Webster Jr., "The Changing Role of Marketing in the Corporation," *Journal of Marketing* 56 (October 1992): pp. 1–17. See also, Webster, "The Future Role of Marketing in the Organization," in *Reflections on the Future of Marketing*, ed. Donald Lehmann and Katherine E. Jocz (Cambridge, Mass.: Marketing Science Institute, 1997), pp. 39–66.

Corporate strategy defines the businesses in which a company competes, preferably in a manner that uses resources to convert distinctive competence into competitive advantage. Essential questions at this level include: What are our core competencies? What businesses are we in? What businesses should we be in? How should we allocate resources across these businesses to achieve our overall organizational goals and objectives? At this level of strategy, the role of marketing is to (1) assess market attractiveness and the competitive effectiveness of the firm, (2) promote a customer orientation to the various constituencies in management decision making, and (3) formulate the firm's overall value proposition (as a reflection of its distinctive competencies, in terms reflecting customer needs) and to articulate it to the market and to the organization at large. According to Frederick Webster Jr., "At the corporate level, marketing managers have a critical role to play as advocates, for the customer and for a set of values and beliefs that put the customer first in the firm's decision making."[5]

Business-level strategy centers on how a firm competes in a given industry and positions itself against its competitors. The focus of competition is not between corporations; rather, it is between their individual business units. A **strategic business unit (SBU)** is a single business or collection of businesses that has a distinct mission, a responsible manager, and its own competitors, and that is relatively independent of other business units. The 3M Corporation has defined 40 strategic business units. Each develops a plan describing how it will manage its mix of products to secure a competitive advantage consistent with the level of investment and risk that management is willing to accept. An SBU could be one or more divisions of the industrial firm, a product line within one division, or, on occasion, a single product. Strategic business units may share resources such as a sales force with other business units to achieve economies of scale. An SBU may serve one or many product-market units.

For each business unit in the corporate portfolio, the following essential questions must be answered: How can we compete most effectively for the product market the business unit serves? What distinctive skills can give the business unit a competitive advantage? Similarly, the former CEO at GE, Jack Welch, asks his operating executives to crisply answer the following questions[6]:

- Describe the global competitive environment in which you operate.

- In the last two years, what have your competitors done?

- In the same period, what have you done to them in the marketplace?

- How might they attack you in the future?

- What are your plans to leapfrog them?

The marketing function contributes to the planning process at this level by providing a detailed and complete analysis of customers and competitors and the firm's distinctive skills and resources for competing in particular market segments.

Functional strategy centers on how resources allocated to the various functional areas can be used most efficiently and effectively to support the business-level strategy. The primary focus of marketing strategy at this level is to allocate and coordinate

---

[5] Ibid., Webster, "The Changing Role of Marketing," p. 11.

[6] Noel M. Tichy and Stratford Sherman, *Control Your Destiny or Someone Else Will* (New York: Doubleday, 1993), p. 26; see also Jack Welch and John A. Byrne, *Jack: Straight from the Gut* (New York: Warner Books, 2001).

FIGURE 7.1 | **FUNCTIONAL INFLUENCES ON THE CONNECTIONS BETWEEN CENTRAL ELEMENTS OF THE FIRM**

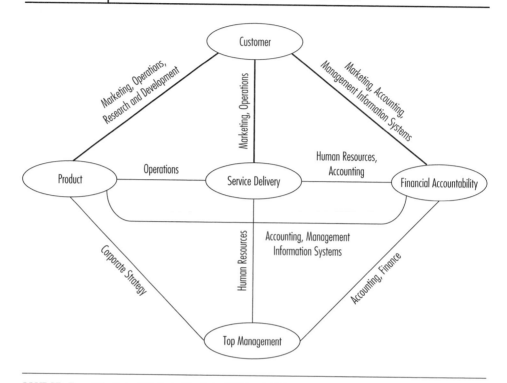

SOURCE: From "The Role of Marketing" by Roland T. Rust in JOURNAL OF MARKETING, January 1999, p. 183. Copyright © 1999. Reprinted by permission of American Marketing Association via Copyright Clearance Center.

marketing resources and activities to achieve the firm's objective within a specific product market.

Managing Three Customer Connections   Marketing is perhaps best understood as the function that manages the three primary connections between the organization and the customer[7] (see Figure 7.1).

- *The customer-product connection.* This involves linking the customer to the focal offering, particularly the knowledge and skills to discover customer needs and connect them to product design.

- *The customer-service delivery connection.* Included here are the design and delivery actions involved in providing a firm's goods and services to the customer (for example, the performance of frontline sales and customer service employees) and the activities involved in satisfying and retaining customers, particularly customer relationship management.[8]

---

[7] Christine Moorman and Roland T. Rust, "The Role of Marketing," *Journal of Marketing*, 63 (Special Issue 1999): pp. 180–197.

[8] William Boulding, Richard Staelin, Michael Ehret, and Wesley J. Johnston, "A Customer Relationship Management Roadmap: What Is Known, Potential Pitfalls, and Where to Go," *Journal of Marketing* 69 (October 2005): pp. 155–166.

- *The customer-financial accountability connection.* This refers to activities and processes that link customers to financial outcomes (for example, the link between customer satisfaction and profitability or customer retention efforts and financial outcomes). Because customers provide the primary source of earnings for a firm, marketing expenditures are now viewed as investments in customer assets that create long-term value for the firm and its shareholders.[9]

Strategy Formulation and the Hierarchy[10]

The interplay among the three levels of the strategy hierarchy can be illustrated by examining the collective action perspective of strategy formulation.[11] This approach applies to strategic decisions that (1) cut across functional areas, (2) involve issues related to the organization's long-term objectives, or (3) involve allocating resources across business units or product markets. Included here are decisions about the direction of corporate strategy, the application of a core technology, or the choice of an alliance partner.

Observe in Figure 7.2 that strategic decision processes often involve the active participation of several functional interest groups that hold markedly different beliefs about the appropriateness of particular strategies or corporate goals. Strategic decisions represent the outcome of a bargaining process among functional interest groups (including marketing), each of which may interpret the proposed strategy in an entirely different light.

Turf Issues and Thought-World Views   Two forces contribute to the conflict that often divides participants in the strategy formulation process. First, different meanings assigned to a proposed strategy are often motivated by deeper differences in what might be called "organizational subcultures." Subcultures exist when one subunit shares different values, beliefs, and goals than another subunit, resulting in different **thought-worlds.** For example, marketing managers are concerned with market opportunities and competitors, whereas R&D managers value technical sophistication and innovation. Second, functional managers are likely to resist strategic changes that threaten their turf. To the extent that the subunit defines the individual's identity and connotes prestige and power, the organizational member may be reluctant to see it altered by a strategic decision.

Negotiated Outcomes   Collective decisions emerge from negotiation and compromise among partisan participants. The differences in goals, thought-worlds, and self-interests across participants lead to conflicts about actions that should be taken. Choices must be negotiated with each interest group attempting to achieve its own ends. The ultimate outcomes of collective decisions tend to unfold incrementally and depend more on the partisan values and influence of the various interest groups than

[9] Roland T. Rust, Katherine N. Lemon, and Das Narayandas, *Customer Equity Management* (Upper Saddle River, N.J.: Prentice-Hall, 2005).

[10] Gary L. Frankwick, James C. Ward, Michael D. Hutt, and Peter H. Reingen, "Evolving Patterns of Organizational Beliefs in the Formation of Marketing Strategy," *Journal of Marketing* 58 (April 1994): pp. 96–110; see also Michael D. Hutt, Beth A. Walker, and Gary L. Frankwick, "Hurdle the Cross-Functional Barriers to Strategic Change," *Sloan Management Review* 36 (spring 1995): pp. 22–30.

[11] Orville C. Walker Jr., Robert W. Ruekert, and Kenneth J. Roering, "Picking Proper Paradigms: Alternative Perspectives on Organizational Behavior and Their Implications for Marketing Management Research," in *Review of Marketing*, ed. Michael J. Houston (Chicago: American Marketing Association, 1987), pp. 3–36.

FIGURE 7.2 | **A COLLECTIVE ACTION PERSPECTIVE OF THE STRATEGY FORMULATION PROCESS**

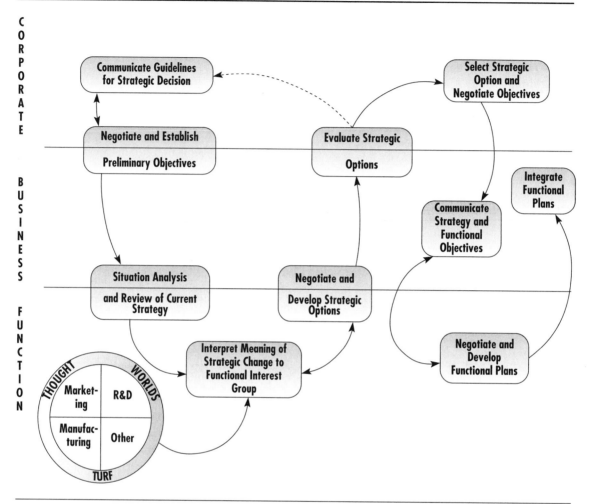

SOURCE: Gary L. Frankwick, James C. Ward, Michael D. Hutt, and Peter H. Reingen, "Evolving Patterns of Organizational Beliefs in the Formation of Strategy," *Journal of Marketing* 58 (April 1994): p. 98. Reprinted with permission by the American Marketing Association.

on rational analysis. A study of highly contested strategic decision in a *Fortune* 500 company illustrates the tension that may exist between marketing and R&D.

Two marketing executives describe how the decision was ultimately resolved.[12] According to the marketing manager:

> [Marketing] did an extremely effective job of stepping right in the middle of it and strangling it. . . . What has happened is by laying out the market unit concerns and again, refocusing on the fact that we are market-based, basically what Marketing did was force the R&D team into submission where they no longer have the autonomy they once had to go about making decisions—they

---

[12] Frankwick, Ward, Hutt, and Reingen, "Evolving Patterns of Organizational Beliefs," pp. 107–108.

INSIDE BUSINESS MARKETING

From Bullet-Point Plans to Strategic Stories at 3M

After reviewing countless business plans over several years, Gordon Shaw, executive director of planning at 3M, concluded that the firm's business plans failed to reflect deep thought or to inspire commitment and active support. He suspected that the traditional, bullet-list format of the plans was a major part of the problem. Bullet lists are too generic and fail to convey how the business will win in a particular market. To remedy the problem, he turned to strategic narratives—planning through storytelling. Like a good story, a good strategic plan "defines relationships, cause and effect, and a priority among items—*and those elements are likely to be remembered as a complex whole.*"

In using the approach, a strategist at 3M first **sets the stage** by defining the current competitive, market, and company situation in an insightful and coherent manner. Next, the planner must **introduce the dramatic conflict**—the main challenges or critical issues that provide obstacles to success. Finally, the story must **reach resolution** in a satisfying and compelling fashion. Here a logical and concise argument is provided concerning the specific actions the company can take to overcome the obstacles and win. Narrative plans create a rich picture of strategy, bring critical assumptions to the surface, and provide a central message that can motivate and mobilize employees throughout the organization.

SOURCE: Gordon Shaw, Robert Brown, and Philip Bromley, "Strategic Stories: How 3M Is Rewriting Business Planning," *Harvard Business Review* 76 (May/June 1998): pp. 41–50.

now get input. And whether it's formal or informal, they definitely get the buy-in of marketing before they move forward on what they're doing now.

According to the vice president of marketing:

> Before I felt it was technology driving the process. Now I feel that technology is partnering with the marketplace. And the reason I feel that way is because we have [marketing people] in place that are working closely with how the technology develops.

Implications for Marketing Managers In advocating a strategic course, marketing managers must be sensitive to the likely response it may arouse in other interest groups. To build pockets of commitment and trust, managers should develop and use a communication network that includes organizational members who have a major stake in the decision. Marketing managers can use these personal networks to understand the interests of other stakeholders, communicate their own interests clearly and sensitively, and thus diffuse the anxiety of others about threats to their turf.

Marketing's Cross-Functional Relationships

The creation of a boundaryless organization is an important value that underlies GE's current organizational style. To achieve this goal, senior executives at GE emphasize the importance of eliminating artificial barriers—removing the horizontal barriers that divide functional areas, the vertical barriers that come from the formal hierarchy, and the external barriers that prevent close relationships with customers, suppliers, and

TABLE 7.1	FORMULATING BUSINESS MARKETING STRATEGY: VITAL CROSS-FUNCTIONAL CONNECTIONS

Function	Contribution to Strategy	Support Required from Marketing
Manufacturing	• Determines the volume, variety, and quality of products that can be marketed • Influences the speed with which the business marketer can respond to changing market or competitive needs	• Accurate and timely sales forecast
R&D	• Provides critical technical direction in new-product-development process • Remains abreast of competitive technology	• Data on market and competitive trends • Marketing research on product features desired by target segments
Logistics	• Provides on-time accurate shipments to customers • Develops timely order tracking and status reports	• Accurate and timely sales forecasts • Delivery service requirements by customer or segment
Technical service	• Implements post-sale activities such as installation and training • Serves as troubleshooter for customer problems	• Account-specific goals and plans • Promises made to the customer during the selling process

alliance partners. For example, Beth Comstock, GE's chief marketing officer, is charged with transforming GE's culture, famously known for process and financial controls, to one that is agile, creative, and innovative.[13] Restructuring organizations, reengineering business processes, and searching for quicker, more efficient responses to changing customer needs and competitive realities are important strategic priorities in business practice. As firms adopt leaner and more agile structures and emphasize cross-functional teams, the business marketing manager assumes an important and challenging role in strategy formulation.

All business marketing decisions—product, price, promotion, or distribution—are affected, directly or indirectly, by other functional areas. In turn, marketing considerations influence business decisions in research and development and in manufacturing and procurement, as well as adjustments in the overall corporate strategy. Business marketing planning must be coordinated and synchronized with corresponding planning efforts in R&D, procurement, finance, manufacturing, and other areas.

Cross-Functional Connections

Effective business marketing managers develop close working relationships with their colleagues in manufacturing, R&D, logistics, and other functions. They understand the critical role that each function assumes in the design and execution of strategy and, in turn, what each functional area requires from marketing.

Table 7.1 explores the interrelationships between marketing and four business functions. Observe the significant role each assumes in developing and implementing marketing strategy. For example, new product development is the focus of the

---

[13] Diane Brady, "The Transformer: Beth Comstock," *Business Week Online*, August 1, 2005, http://www.businessweek.com.

B2B TOP PERFORMERS

High-Performing Cross-Functional Managers

At a *Fortune* 100 high-technology firm, detailed accounts of effective and ineffective cross-functional interactions were gathered from managers representing marketing, R&D, manufacturing, and other functions. The study provides a clear portrait of the work style and specific behaviors that distinguish high-performing cross-functional managers from their peers.

- Although many managers likely assume that their reputation in the organization is shaped by hard skills like technical proficiency or marketing savvy, the top-of-mind characteristics that colleagues emphasize in describing effective managers center on *soft* skills, like openness, initiative, or responsiveness.

- Effective managers demonstrate *perspective-taking* skills—the ability to anticipate and understand the perspectives and priorities of managers from other functional areas.

- High-performing cross-functional managers are revered by their colleagues for their *responsiveness*. Recounting effective cross-functional episodes, colleagues describe high performers as "prompt," "timely," "responsive," and willing to "take the lead."

SOURCE: Edward U. Bond III, Beth A. Walker, Michael D. Hutt, and Matthew Meuter, "Making Cross-Functional Relationships Work," working paper, Arizona State University, Tempe, Arizona, 2005.

marketing-R&D interface, from idea generation to evaluating the performance of the finished product. Reinforcing the importance of nurturing an effective marketing-R&D interface is the sizable investments R&D commands in industrial firms, particularly those that compete in the high-tech sector. Successful new product developments depend heavily on marketing research for product features target market segments desire and for how potential organizational buyers view trade-offs among product attributes. If marketing fails to provide adequate market and competitive information, R&D personnel are in the precarious position of determining the direction of new product development without the benefit of market knowledge. A successful relationship between marketing and R&D requires that each understands the strengths, weaknesses, and potential contributions of the other. For instance, a promising new product spawned by R&D may fail because the firm lacks the marketing strengths required to penetrate a particular market segment.

Once a new product is developed and manufactured, the logistics and technical services functions assume special significance in strategy implementation. Two factors assigned particular importance by customers are (1) the speed and reliability of delivery service and (2) the quality and availability of technical service after the sale (see Chapter 3). Close coordination between marketing and both of these vital service functions is required to provide the service level that organizational customers expect.

Functionally Integrated Planning: The Marketing Strategy Center[14]

Rather than operating in isolation from other functional areas, the successful business marketing manager is an integrator—one who understands the capabilities of manufacturing, R&D, and customer service and who capitalizes on their strengths in developing

---

[14]Michael D. Hutt and Thomas W. Speh, "The Marketing Strategy Center: Diagnosing the Industrial Marketer's Interdisciplinary Role," *Journal of Marketing* 48 (fall 1984): pp. 53–61; see also Jeen-Su Lim and David A. Reid, "Vital Cross-Functional Linkages with Marketing," *Industrial Marketing Management* 22 (February 1993): pp. 159–165.

TABLE 7.2 | **INTERFUNCTIONAL INVOLVEMENT IN MARKETING DECISION MAKING: AN ILLUSTRATIVE RESPONSIBILITY CHART**

Decision Area	Organizational Function						
	Marketing	Manufacturing	R&D	Logistics	Technical Service	Strategic Business Unit Manager	Corporate Level Planner
PRODUCT							
Design specifications							
Performance characteristics							
Reliability							
PRICE							
List price							
Discount structure							
TECHNICAL SERVICE SUPPORT							
Customer training							
Repair							
LOGISTICS							
Inventory level							
Customer service level							
SALES FORCE							
Training							
ADVERTISING							
Message development							
CHANNEL							
Selection							

NOTE: Decision role vocabulary: R = responsible; A = approve; C = consult; M = implement; I = inform; X = no role in decision.

marketing strategies that are responsive to customer needs. Marketing managers also assume a central role in strategy implementation.[15] **Responsibility charting** is an approach that can classify decision-making roles and highlight the multifunctional nature of business marketing decision making. Table 7.2 provides the structure of a responsibility chart. The decision areas (rows) in the matrix might, for example, relate to a planned product-line expansion. The various functional areas that may assume particular roles in this decision process head the matrix columns. The following

---

[15] Charles H. Noble and Michael P. Mokwa, "Implementing Marketing Strategies: Developing and Testing a Managerial Theory," *Journal of Marketing*, 63 (October 1999): pp. 57–73.

list defines the alternative roles that participants can assume in the decision-making process.[16]

1. *Responsible* (R): The manager takes initiative for analyzing the situation, developing alternatives, and assuring consultation with others and then makes the initial recommendation. Upon approval of decision, the role ends.

2. *Approve* (A): The manager accepts or vetoes a decision before it is implemented, or chooses from alternatives developed by the participants assuming a "responsible" role.

3. *Consult* (C): The manager is consulted or asked for substantive input before the decision is approved but does not possess veto power.

4. *Implement* (M): The manager is accountable for implementing the decision, including notifying other relevant participants about the decision.

5. *Inform* (I): Although not necessarily consulted before the decision is approved, the manager is informed of the decision once it is made.

Representatives of a particular functional area may, of course, assume more than one role in the decision-making process. The technical service manager may be consulted during the new-product-development process and may also be held accountable for implementing service-support strategy. Likewise, the marketing manager may be responsible for and approve many of the decisions related to the product-line expansion. For other actions, several decision makers may participate. To illustrate, the business unit manager, after consulting R&D, may approve (or veto) a decision for which the marketing manager is responsible.

The members of the organization involved in the business marketing decision-making process constitute the **marketing strategy center.** The composition or functional area representation of the strategy center evolves during the marketing strategy development process, varies from firm to firm, and varies from one situation to another. Likewise, the composition of the marketing strategy center is not strictly prescribed by the organizational chart. The needs of a particular strategy situation, especially the information requirements, significantly influence the composition of the strategy center. Thus, the marketing strategy center shares certain parallels with the buying center (see Chapter 3).

Managing Strategic Interdependencies A central challenge for the business marketer in the strategy center is to minimize interdepartmental conflict while fostering shared appreciation of the interdependencies with other functional units. Individual strategy center participants are motivated by both personal and organizational goals. They interpret company objectives in relation to their level in the hierarchy and the department they represent. Various functional units operate under unique reward systems and reflect unique orientations or thought-worlds. For example, marketing managers are evaluated on the basis of sales, profits, or market share; production managers on the basis of manufacturing efficiency and cost-effectiveness. In turn, R&D managers may be oriented toward long-term objectives;

[16]Joseph E. McCann and Thomas N. Gilmore, "Diagnosing Organizational Decision Making through Responsibility Charting," *Sloan Management Review* 25 (winter 1983): pp. 3–15.

FIGURE 7.3 | COMPONENTS OF A BUSINESS MODEL

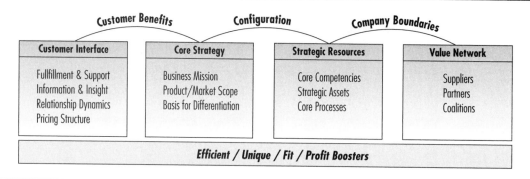

customer-service managers may emphasize more immediate ones. Strategic plans emerge out of a bargaining process among functional areas. Managing conflict, promoting cooperation, and developing coordinated strategies are all fundamental to the business marketer's interdisciplinary role. By understanding the concerns and orientations of personnel from other functional areas, the business marketing manager is better equipped to forge effective cross-unit working relationships.

The Components of a Business Model[17]

For a strategy to succeed, individuals must understand and share a common definition of a firm's existing business concept. For example, ask any employee at Dell and they will tell you about the "Dell model" that sets them apart from competitors. A **business concept** or model consists of four major components (Figure 7.3):

- Customer Interface
- Core Strategy
- Strategic Resources
- Value Network

The major components of the business concept are tied together by three important "bridge" elements: customer benefits, configuration, and company boundaries.

Customer Interface

Customer benefits provide the bridge between the core strategy and the customer interface. Customer benefits link the core strategy directly to the needs of customers. The customer interface includes four elements:

[17] Except where noted, this discussion is based on Gary Hamel, *Leading the Revolution* (Boston: Harvard Business School Press, 2000), pp. 70–94.

1. **Fulfillment and support** refers to the channels a business marketing firm uses to reach customers and the level of service support it provides.

2. **Information and insight** refers to the knowledge captured from customers and the degree to which this information is used to provide enhanced value to the customer.

3. **Relationship dynamics** refers to the nature of the interaction between the firm and its customers (for example, the proportion of relational versus transactional customers; see Chapter 4). Key question: What steps can be taken to raise the hurdle for competitors by exceeding customer expectations or strengthening the customer's sense of affiliation with the firm?

4. **Pricing structure.** A business concept may offer several pricing choices. For example, a firm can bundle products and services or price them on a menu basis. For example, when airlines buy a Boeing 777, which is equipped with jet engines produced by GE, they pay GE a fee for each flight hour in line with a fixed-priced maintenance agreement. So, rather than products, GE is selling "power by the hour."

Core Strategy

The **core strategy** determines how the firm chooses to compete. From Figure 7.3, observe that three elements are involved in setting a core strategy:

1. The **business mission** describes the overall objectives of the strategy, sets a course and direction, and defines a set of performance criteria that are used to measure progress. The business mission must be broad enough to allow for business concept innovation, and it should be distinguished from the mission of competitors in the industry. For example, by focusing its mission on copiers and copying, Xerox allowed Hewlett-Packard to build a dominant lead in the printer business.

2. **Product/market scope** defines *where* the firm competes. The product markets that constitute the domain of a business can be defined by customer benefits, technologies, customer segments, and channels of distribution.[18] Strategists might consider this question: Are particular customer segments being overlooked by competitors or customers who might welcome a new product-service solution?

3. **Basis for differentiation** captures the essence of how a firm competes differently than its rivals. George Day and Robin Wensley explain:

> A business is differentiated when some value-adding activities are performed in a way that leads to perceived superiority along dimensions that are valued by customers. For these activities to be profitable, the customer must be willing to pay a premium for the benefits and the premium must exceed the added costs of superior performance.[19]

[18] George S. Day, *Strategic Market Planning: The Pursuit of Competitive Advantage* (St. Paul, Minn.: West Publishing, 1984).

[19] George S. Day and Robin Wensley, "Assessing Advantage: A Framework for Diagnosing Competitive Superiority," *Journal of Marketing* 52 (April 1988): pp. 3–4. See also Douglas W. Vorhies and Neil A. Morgan, "Benchmarking Marketing Capabilities for Sustainable Competitive Advantage," *Journal of Marketing* 69 (January 2005): pp. 80–94.

There are many ways for a firm to differentiate products and services:

- Provide superior service or technical assistance competence through speed, responsiveness to complex orders, or ability to solve special customer problems.

- Provide superior quality that reduces customer costs or improves their performance.

- Offer innovative product features that use new technologies.

Strategic Resources

A business marketing firm gains a competitive advantage through its superior skills and resources. The firm's strategic resources include core competencies, strategic assets, and core processes.

1. **Core competencies** are the set of skills, systems, and technologies a company uses to create uniquely high value for customers.[20] For example, Dell uses its direct-distribution competencies to sell a host of new products to corporate customers, including switches, servers, storage, and a range of peripheral products.[21] Concerning core competencies, the guiding questions for the strategist are: What important benefits do our competencies provide to customers? What do we know or do especially well that is valuable to customers and is transferable to new market opportunities?

2. **Strategic assets** are the more tangible requirements for advantage that enable a firm to exercise its capabilities. Included are brands, customer data, distribution coverage, patents, and other resources that are both rare and valuable. Attention centers on this question: Can we use these strategic assets in a different way to provide new levels of value to existing or prospective customers?

3. **Core processes** are the methodologies and routines companies use to transform competencies, assets, and other inputs into value for customers. For example, drug discovery is a core process at Merck, and delivery fulfillment is a core process at FedEx. Here the strategist considers these questions: Which processes are most competitively unique and create the most customer value? Could we use our process expertise effectively to enter other markets?

From Figure 7.3, note that a configuration component links strategic resources to the core strategy. "Configuration refers to the unique way in which competencies, assets, and processes are interrelated in support of a particular strategy."[22] For example, Honda manages key activities in the new-product-development process differently than its rivals.

---

[20] James Brian Quinn, "Strategic Outsourcing: Leveraging Knowledge Capabilities," *Sloan Management Review* 40 (summer 1999): pp. 9–21.

[21] Andy Serwer, "Dell Does Domination," *Fortune*, January 21, 2002, pp. 70–75.

[22] Hamel, *Leading the Revolution*, p. 78.

The Value Network

The final component of a business concept is the **value network** that complements and further enriches the firm's research base. Included here are suppliers, strategic alliance partners, and coalitions. To illustrate, nimble competitors like Cisco and General Electric demonstrate special skills in forging relationships with suppliers and alliance partners. Concerning the value network, the guiding question for the strategist is: What market opportunities might become available to us "if we could 'borrow' the assets and competencies of other companies and marry them with our own?"[23]

Profit Potential

Gary Hamel suggests that four factors determine the profit potential of a business concept:

- The degree to which the business concept provides an *efficient* way of providing customer benefits (for example, Southwest Airlines efficiently delivers air travel to its target market).

- The extent to which the business concept is *unique* on dimensions shared by the customer.

- The degree of *fit* or internal consistency among the various components of the business concept (for example, Dell's competencies in supply-chain management and direct distribution support its core strategy).

- The extent to which the business concept can create *profit boosters* that provide the opportunity for above-average returns (for example, profit boosters are represented by high switching costs or a customer lock-in that benefits Microsoft, eBay, and Intel or the scale economies enjoyed by Wal-Mart).

By isolating and managing the components of the business concept, the strategist is ideally equipped to develop strategies that provide a competitive advantage and deliver superior value to customers.

The Balanced Scorecard[24]

As new strategies and business models are developed to achieve breakthrough results, new performance measures are needed to monitor new goals and new processes. Measurement is a central element in the strategy process. The **balanced scorecard** provides managers with a comprehensive system for converting a company's vision and strategy into a tightly connected set of performance measures. The balanced scorecard combines financial measures of *past* performance with measures of the drivers of performance. Observe in Figure 7.4 that the scorecard examines the performance of a business unit from four perspectives: (1) financial, (2) customer, (3) internal business processes, and (4) learning and growth.

---

[23] Ibid., p. 90.

[24] Except where noted, this discussion is based on Robert S. Kaplan and David P. Norton, *Strategy Maps: Converting Intangible Assets into Tangible Outcomes* (Boston: Harvard Business School Publishing Corporation, 2004). See also Robert S. Kaplan and David P. Norton, *The Balanced Scorecard: Translating Strategy into Action* (Boston: Harvard Business School Press, 1996), Chapters 1–3.

FIGURE 7.4 | THE BALANCED SCORECARD: A FRAMEWORK TO TRANSLATE A STRATEGY INTO OPERATIONAL TERMS

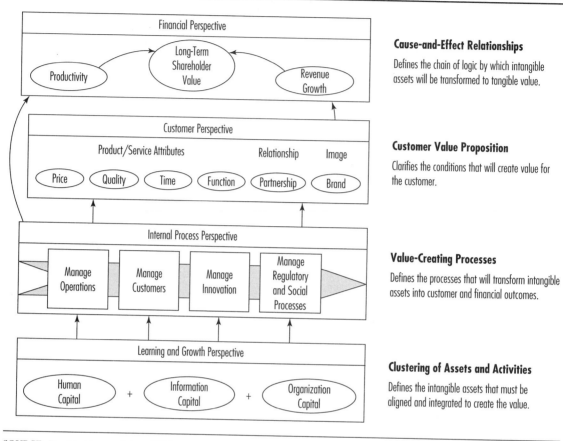

Cause-and-Effect Relationships

Defines the chain of logic by which intangible assets will be transformed to tangible value.

Customer Value Proposition

Clarifies the conditions that will create value for the customer.

Value-Creating Processes

Defines the processes that will transform intangible assets into customer and financial outcomes.

Clustering of Assets and Activities

Defines the intangible assets that must be aligned and integrated to create the value.

SOURCE: Reprinted by permission of HARVARD BUSINESS REVIEW. From "Balanced Scorecard Framework" by Robert S. Kaplan in STRATEGY MAPS, p. 31. Copyright © 2004 by Harvard Business School Publishing Corporation; all rights reserved.

The architects of the approach, Robert Kaplan and David Norton, emphasize that "the scorecard should tell the story of the strategy, starting with the long-run financial objectives, and then linking them to the sequence of actions that must be taken with financial processes, customers, and finally employees and systems to deliver the desired long-run economic performance."[25]

Financial Perspective

Financial performance measures allow business marketing managers to monitor the degree to which the firm's strategy, implementation, and execution are increasing profits. Measures such as return on investment, revenue growth, shareholder value, profitability, and cost per unit are among the performance measures that show whether the firm's strategy is succeeding or failing. Companies emphasize two basic levers in developing a financial strategy: revenue growth and productivity.[26] The revenue-growth

---

[25] Kaplan and Norton, *The Balanced Scorecard*, p. 47.

[26] Robert S. Kaplan and David P. Norton, "Having Trouble with Your Strategy? Then Map It," *Harvard Business Review* 78 (September–October 2000): pp. 167–176.

strategy centers on securing sales from new markets and new products or strengthening and expanding relationships with existing customers. The productivity strategy can also take two forms: improve the company's cost structure by reducing expenses and/or use assets more efficiently by decreasing the working and fixed capital needed to support a given level of output.

The balanced scorecard seeks to match financial objectives to a business unit's growth and life cycle stages. Three stages of a business are isolated and linked to appropriate financial objectives:

1. **Growth:** Business units that have products and services with significant growth potential and that must commit considerable resources (for example, production facilities and distribution networks) to capitalize on the market opportunity.
   Financial Objectives: Sales growth rate by segment; percentage of revenue from new product, services, and customers.

2. **Sustain:** Business units, likely representing the majority of businesses within a firm, that expect to maintain or to perhaps moderately increase market share from year to year.
   Financial Objectives: Share of target customers and accounts; customer and product-line profitability.

3. **Harvest:** Mature business units that warrant only enough investment to maintain production equipment and capabilities.
   Financial Objectives: Payback; customer and product-line profitability.

Customer Perspective

In the customer component of the balanced scorecard, the business unit identifies the market segments it will target (see Chapter 5). Those segments supply the revenue stream that support critical financial objectives. Marketing managers must also identify the value proposition—how the firm proposes to deliver competitively superior and sustainable value to the target customers and market segments. The central element of any business strategy is the value proposition that describes a company's unique product and service attributes, customer relationship management practices, and corporate reputation. Importantly, the value proposition should clearly communicate to targeted customers what the company expects to do *better* and differently than its competitors.

Key Value Propositions and Customer Strategies   Business-to-business firms typically choose among four forms of differentiation in developing a value proposition[27]:

- **Low total cost**—customers are offered attractive prices, excellent and consistent quality, ease of purchase, and responsive service (for example, Dell, Inc.).

- **Product innovation and leadership**—customers receive products that expand existing performance boundaries through new features and functions (for example, Intel and Sony).

- **Complete customer solutions**—customers feel that the company understands them and can provide customized products and services tailored to their unique requirements (for example, IBM).

---

[27] Kaplan and Norton, *Strategy Maps*, pp. 322–344.

TABLE 7.3 | THE CUSTOMER PERSPECTIVE—CORE MEASURES

Market Share	Represents the proportion of business in a given market (in terms of number of customers, dollars spent, or unit volume sold) that a business unit sells.
Customer Acquisition	Tracks, in absolute or relative terms, the rate at which a business unit attracts or wins new customers or business.
Customer Retention	Tracks, in absolute or relative terms, the rate at which a business unit retains customers
Customer Satisfaction	Matches the satisfaction level of customers on specific performance criteria such as quality, service, or on-time delivery reliability.
Customer Profitability	Assesses the net profit of a customer, or segment, after deducting the unique expenses required to support that customer or segment.

SOURCE: Adapted from Robert S. Kaplan and David P. Norton, *The Balanced Scorecard: Translating Strategy into Action* (Boston: Harvard Business School Press, 1996): p. 68.

- **Lock-in**—customers purchase a widely used proprietary product from the firm and incur high switching costs (for example, Microsoft's operating system, Cisco's infrastructure products, or eBay's dominant exchange network).

For the chosen strategy, Table 7.3 presents the core customer outcome measures used to monitor performance in each target segment. The customer perspective complements traditional market share analysis by tracking customer acquisition, customer retention, customer satisfaction, and customer profitability.

Internal Business Process Perspective

To develop the value proposition that will reach and satisfy targeted customer segments and to achieve the desired financial objectives, critical internal business processes must be developed and continually enriched. Internal business processes support two crucial elements of a company's strategy: (1) they create and deliver the value proposition for customers and (2) they improve processes and reduce costs, enriching the productivity component in the financial perspective. Among the processes vital to the creation of customer value are:

1. Operations management processes

2. Customer management processes

3. Innovation management processes

Strategic Alignment   Robert S. Kaplan and David P. Norton emphasize that "value is created through internal business processes."[28] Table 7.4 shows how key internal processes can be aligned to support the firm's customer strategy or differentiating value proposition. First, observe that the relative emphasis (see shaded areas) given to a particular process vary by strategy. For example, a firm that actively pursues a product-leadership strategy highlights innovation management processes, whereas a company adopting a low-total-cost strategy assigns priority to operations management processes.

---
[28] Ibid., p. 43.

TABLE 7.4 | ALIGNING INTERNAL BUSINESS PROCESSES TO THE CUSTOMER STRATEGY

Customer Strategy	The Focus of Internal Business Processes		
	Operations Management	Customer Relationship Management	Innovation Management
Low Total Cost Strategy	Highly Efficient Operating Processes Efficient, Timely Distribution	Ease of Access for Customers; Superb Post-Sales Service	Seek Process Innovations Gain Scale Economies
Product Leadership Strategy	Flexible Manufacturing Processes Rapid Introduction of New Products	Capture Customer Ideas for New Offering Educate Customers about Complex New Products/ Services	Disciplined, High-Performance Product Development First-to-Market
Complete Customer Solutions Strategy	Deliver Broad Product/ Service Line Create Network of Suppliers for Extended Product/ Service Capabilities	Create Customized Solutions for Customers Build Strong Customer Relationships Develop Customer Knowledge	Identify New Opportunities to Serve Customers Anticipate Future Customer Needs
Lock-in Strategies	Provide Capacity for Proprietary Product/Service Reliable Access and Ease of Use	Create Awareness Influence Switching Costs of Existing and Potential Customers	Develop and Enhance Proprietary Product Increase Breadth/Applications of Standard

SOURCE: Reprinted by permission of HARVARD BUSINESS REVIEW. From "Customer Objectives for different value propositions" by Robert S. Kaplan in STRATEGY MAPS, p. 41. Copyright © 2004 by the Harvard Business School Publishing Corporation; all rights reserved.

Second, although the level of emphasis might vary, note how the various processes work together to reinforce the value proposition. For example, a low-total-cost strategy can be reinforced by an innovation-management process that uncovers process improvements and a customer relationship management process that delivers superb postsales support.

Michael Porter argues that it is much harder for a rival to match a set of interlocked processes than it is to replicate a single process. He observes:

> Strategic fit among many activities is fundamental not only to competitive advantage but also to the sustainability of that advantage. . . . Positions built on systems of activities are far more sustainable than those built on individual activities.[29]

Learning and Growth   The fourth component of the balanced scorecard, **learning and growth,** highlights how the firm's intangible assets must be aligned to its strategy to achieve long-term goals. **Intangible assets** represent "the capabilities of

---

[29]Michael E. Porter, "What Is Strategy?" *Harvard Business Review* 74 (November–December 1996): p. 73.

the company's employees to satisfy customer needs."[30] The three principal drivers of organizational learning and growth are:

1. *Human Capital*—the availability of employees who have the skills, talent, and know-how to perform activities required by the strategy.

2. *Information Capital*—the availability of information systems, applications, and information-technology infrastructure to support the strategy.

3. *Organization Capital*—the culture (for example, values), leadership, employee incentives, and teamwork to mobilize the organization and execute the strategy.

Strategic Alignment   To create value and advance performance, the intangible assets of the firm must be aligned with the strategy. For example, consider a company that plans to invest in staff training and has two choices—a training program on total quality management (TQM) or a training initiative on customer relationship management (CRM). A company like Dell, which pursues a low-total-cost strategy, might derive higher value from TQM training, whereas IBM's consulting unit, which pursues a total customer solution strategy, would benefit more from CRM training. Unfortunately, research suggests that two-thirds of organizations fail to create strong alignment between their strategies and their human-resources and information-technology programs.[31]

Measuring Strategic Readiness   Senior management must ensure that the firm's human resources and information technology systems are aligned with the chosen strategy. To achieve desired performance goals in the other areas of the scorecard, key objectives must be achieved on measures of employee satisfaction, retention, and productivity. Likewise, front-line employees, like sales or technical service representatives, must have ready access to timely and accurate information. However, skilled employees who are supported by a carefully designed information system will not contribute to organizational goals if they are not motivated or empowered to do so. Many firms, such as FedEx and 3M, have demonstrated the vital role of motivated and empowered employees in securing a strong customer franchise.

Now that each of the components of the balanced scorecard have been defined, let's explore a clever tool that can be used to communicate the desired strategy path to all employees while detailing the processes that will be used to implement the strategy.

Strategy Map

To provide a visual representation of the cause-and-effect relationships among the components of the balanced scorecard, Kaplan and Norton developed what they call a strategy map. They say that a strategy must provide a clear portrait that reveals how a firm will achieve its desired goals and deliver on its promises to employees, customers, and shareholders. "A strategy map enables an organization to describe and illustrate, in clear and general language, its objectives, initiatives, and targets; the measures used to assess performance (such as market share and customer surveys); and the linkages that are the foundation for strategic direction."[32]

---

[30] Thomas A. Stewart, *Intellectual Capital: The New Wealth of Organizations* (New York: Doubleday, 1998), p. 67, cited in Kaplan and Norton, *Strategy Maps*, pp. 202–203.

[31] Kaplan and Norton, *Strategy Maps*, p. 13.

[32] Kaplan and Norton, "Having Trouble with Your Strategy?" p. 170.

FIGURE 7.5 | STRATEGY MAP TEMPLATE: PRODUCT LEADERSHIP

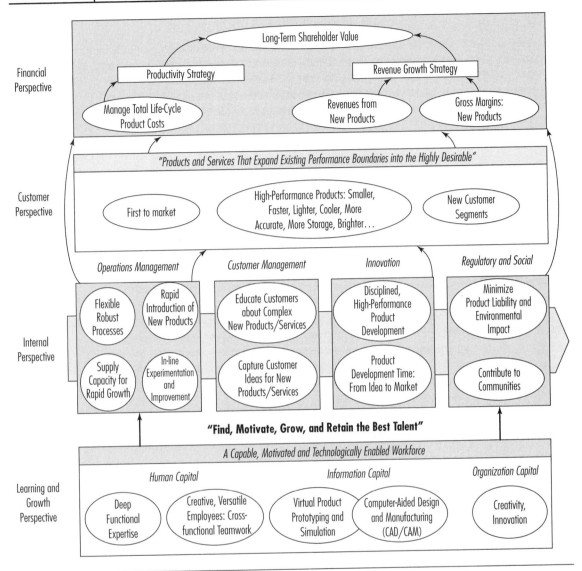

Key Strategy Principles Figure 7.5 shows the strategy map template for a firm pursuing a product leadership strategy. We can use this illustration to review and reinforce the key principles that underlie a strategy map:

- *Companies emphasize two performance levels in developing a financial strategy—a productivity strategy and a revenue growth strategy.*

- *Strategy involves choosing and developing a differentiated customer value proposition.* Note the value proposition for product leadership: "Products and services that expand existing performance boundaries into the highly desirable." Recall that the other value propositions and customer strategies include low total cost, complete customer solutions, and system lock-in.

- *Value is created through internal business processes.* The financial and customer perspectives in the balanced scorecard and strategy map describe the performance outcomes the firm seeks, such as increases in shareholder value through revenue growth and productivity improvements, as well as enhanced performance outcomes from customer acquisition, retention, loyalty, and growth.

- *Strategy involves identifying and aligning the critical few processes that are most important for creating and delivering the customer value proposition.* For a product-leadership strategy, observe how each of the internal business processes directly supports the customer value proposition—product leadership.

- *Value is enhanced when intangible assets (for example, human capital) are aligned with the customer strategy.* From Figure 7.5, note the strategic theme for learning and growth: "A capable, motivated, and technologically enabled workforce." When the three components of learning and growth—human, information, and organization capital—are aligned with the strategy, the firm is better able to mobilize action and execute that strategy.

To recap, the balanced scorecard provides a series of measures and objectives across four perspectives: financial, customer, internal business process, and learning and growth. By developing mutually reinforcing objectives across these four areas, a strategy map can be used to tell the story of a business unit's customer strategy and to highlight the internal business processes that drive performance.

Summary

Guided by a deep understanding of the needs of customers and the capabilities of competitors, market-driven organizations are committed to a set of processes, beliefs, and values that promote the achievement of superior performance by satisfying customers better than competitors do. Because many industrial firms have numerous divisions, product lines, and brands, three major levels of strategy exist in most large organizations: (1) corporate, (2) business level, and (3) functional. Moving down the strategy hierarchy, the focus shifts from strategy formulation to strategy implementation. Marketing is best viewed as the functional area that manages critical connections between the organization and customers. Business marketing planning must be coordinated and synchronized with corresponding planning efforts in other functional areas. Strategic plans emerge out of a bargaining process among functional areas. Managing conflict, promoting cooperation, and developing coordinated strategies are all fundamental to the business marketer's role.

A business model or concept consists of four major components: (1) a core strategy, (2) strategic resources, (3) the customer interface, and (4) the value network. The core strategy is the essence of how the firm competes, whereas strategic resources capture what the firm knows (core competencies), what the firm owns (strategic assets), and what employees actually do (core processes). Specifying the benefits to customers is a critical decision when designing a core strategy. The customer interface component refers to how customer-relationship-management strategies are designed and managed, whereas the value network component considers how partners and supply-chain members can complement and strengthen the resource base of the firm.

The balanced scorecard converts a strategy goal into concrete objectives, and measures are organized into four different perspectives: financial, customer, internal business process, and learning and growth. The approach involves identifying target customer segments, defining the differentiating customer value proposition, aligning the critical internal processes that deliver value to customers in these segments, and selecting the organizational capabilities necessary to achieve customer and financial objectives. Business marketers primarily emphasize one of the following value propositions or customer strategies: low total cost, product leadership, or system lock-in. A strategy map provides a visual representation of a firm's critical objectives and the cause-and-effect relationships among them that drive superior organizational performance.

Discussion Questions

1. Commenting on the decision-making process of his organization, a senior executive noted: "Sometimes the process is bloody, ugly, just like sausage meat being made. It's not pretty to watch but the end results are not too bad." Why do various functional interest groups often embrace conflicting positions during the strategic decision process? How are decisions ever made?

2. Describe how the primary focus of marketing managers at the corporate level differs from the focus marketing managers take at the business-unit or functional level.

3. A day in the life of a business marketing manager involves interactions with managers from other functions in the firm. First, identify the role of R&D, manufacturing, and logistics functions in creating and implementing marketing strategy. Next, describe some of the common sources of conflict that can emerge in cross-functional relationships.

4. Gary Hamel, a leading strategy consultant, contends that managers as well as Wall Street analysts like to talk about business models but few of them could define "what a business model or business concept really is." Describe the major components of a business model and discuss how these components are linked to the benefits a firm provides to customers.

5. Select a firm such as FedEx, Apple, IBM, Boeing, GE, or Caterpillar and assess its business model. Develop a list of particular skills and resources that are especially important to the selected firm's position of advantage. Give particular attention to those skills, resources, or characteristics that competitors would have the most difficulty in matching.

6. Critique this statement: Positions of competitive advantage tend to erode quickly in high-tech markets. Next, trace the changing fortunes of Apple, Inc., during the past decade.

7. Strategy experts argue that effective and aligned internal business processes determine how value is created in an organization. Provide an illustration to demonstrate the point.

8. Describe why a business-to-business firm that plans to enter a new market segment may have to realign its internal business processes to succeed in this segment.

9. Describe how the learning and growth objectives in a balanced scorecard might differ for a firm pursuing a low-total-cost strategy versus one that emphasizes complete customer solutions.

10. The fourth component of the balanced scorecard, learning and growth, captures the intangible assets of the firm (for example, human, information, and organization capital). Describe the role these intangible assets might assume in executing strategy at FedEx or Google.

Internet Exercises

3M is a large diversified technology company that has numerous business units and manufactures thousands of products. Go to http://www.3m.com and

1. Identify the major market or industry sectors that the firm serves.

2. Describe a new product that 3M has recently introduced for the health-care sector.

CASE

Microsoft Targets Small and Mid-Sized Businesses[33]

From 2005 to 2010, small and mid-sized businesses are expected to spend more than $185 billion on software and information-technology services. Microsoft hopes to capture at least $10 billion of that business by 2010 to offset slower growth among large enterprise customers.

This large and highly fragmented market includes small businesses with fewer than 50 employees and mid-sized firms with fewer than 500 employees. Microsoft's chairman, Bill Gates, and chief executive, Steve Ballmer, view this market sector as the most vital and fastest-growing segment of the economy. To serve small and mid-market customers, Microsoft has developed a multiyear product plan that calls for increased investment in research and development.

Challenging Intuit, Inc.

Targeting small business customers, Microsoft recently introduced Microsoft Office Small Business Accounting and Microsoft Office Small Business Management. These offerings are designed to enable small businesses to manage all their sales, marketing, and financial processes within an easy-to-use operating environment. The software is widely available through resellers and retail outlets, including Amazon.com, Best Buy, Office Depot, and Staples. Likewise, Dell offers the software preinstalled on selected Dell small-business computing systems.

By introducing a small business accounting program, Microsoft is taking direct aim at Intuit, Inc.'s widely used QuickBooks accounting software. Dan Levin, vice president of product management at Intuit, welcomed the competition, adding that the new accounting program "marks the fourth time Microsoft has attempted entry into the small business accounting software market."

Discussion Questions

1. To succeed against rivals like Intuit that specialize in small business customers, describe the differentiating value proposition that Microsoft should offer to customers.

2. Drawing on the balanced scorecard, describe how Microsoft might realign its internal business processes (for example, operations, customer, innovation management) to achieve targeted revenue and profit goals in the small and mid-sized business segment.

---

[33] "Microsoft Goes After Small Business," *CNN Money*, September 7, 2005, http://www.cnnmoney.com.

Business Marketing Strategies for Global Markets

Business marketing firms that restrict their attention to the domestic market are overlooking enormous international market opportunities and a challenging field of competitors. After reading this chapter, you will understand:

1. how to capture the sources of global advantage in rapidly developing economies such as China and India.

2. the spectrum of international market-entry options and the strategic significance of different forms of global market participation.

3. the distinctive types of international strategy.

4. the essential components of a global strategy.

A recent *Business Week* article focused on the significant increase in global competition large U.S. industrial corporations face. Huge but relatively unknown firms from emerging markets are challenging Western firms in almost every global setting.

> From India's Infosys Technologies (IT services) to Brazil's Embraer (light jets), and from Taiwan's Acer (computers) to Mexico's Cemex (building materials), a new class of formidable competitors is rising. There are 25 world-class emerging multinationals today and within 15 years, there will be at least 100 of them. The biggest challenge posed by these up-and-coming rivals will not be in Western markets, but within developing nations. That's the arena of fastest global growth—and home to 80 percent of the world's 6 billion consumers, hundreds of millions of whom have moved into the middle class . . . The rise of these new multinationals will force American business marketers to rethink strategies for Third World product development, marketing, and links with local companies.[1]

Truly, business-to-business marketing is worldwide in scope, and the very existence of many business marketing firms will hinge on their ability to act decisively, compete aggressively, and seize market opportunities in rapidly expanding global economies. Numerous business marketing firms—such as GE, IBM, Intel, Boeing, and Motorola—currently derive much of their profit from global markets. They have realigned operations and developed a host of new strategies to strengthen market positions and compete effectively against the new breed of strong global rivals.

This chapter will examine the need for, and the formulation of, global business marketing strategies. The discussion is divided into four parts. First, attention centers on rapidly developing economies, like China, and the sources of global advantage they can represent for business marketing firms. Second, international market-entry options are isolated and described. Third, the value chain concept is introduced to describe alternative types of international strategy. Fourth, the critical requirements for a successful global strategy are explored.

Capturing Global Advantage in Rapidly Developing Economies[2]

A set of rapidly developing economies (RDEs) is reshaping the playing field and forcing business marketing executives to rethink their strategies and the scope of their operations. Key RDEs include, of course, China and India, as well as Mexico, Brazil, central and eastern Europe, and Southeast Asia. Let's put the growth of these economies in perspective. Whereas the United States, western Europe, and Japan are projected to grow by roughly $3 trillion in collective gross domestic product (GDP) from 2004 to 2010, the key RDEs will grow by more than $2 trillion. Specifically, China's GDP is expected to

---

[1] Jeffrey E. Garten, "A New Threat to America, Inc.," *Business* Week, July 25, 2005, p. 114.

[2] This section is based on Arindam Bhattacharya, Thomas Bradtke, Jim Hemerling, Jean Lebreton, Xavier Mosquet, Immo Rupf, Harold L. Sirkin, and Dave Young, "Capturing Global Advantage: How Leading Industrial Companies Are Transforming Their Industries by Sourcing and Selling in China, India, and Other Low-Cost Countries," The Boston Consulting Group, Inc., April 2004, accessed at http://www.bcg.com.

increase by $750 billion, central and eastern Europe's by $450 billion, Southeast Asia's by $350 billion, India's by $300 billion, Mexico's by $250 billion, and Brazil's by $200 billion. During this period, as highly developed economies like the United States and Japan experience annual GDP growth slightly above 2 percent, China will grow four times as fast, and India, Southeast Asia, and Mexico three times as fast. This growth will translate into substantial consumption of consumer and industrial goods fueled both by businesses that invest heavily in manufacturing and service operations and infrastructure and by expanding pools of consumers who enjoy increased purchasing power.

While representing a potentially attractive market opportunity, RDEs also present a formidable competitive challenge to firms in many industries. The migration of sourcing, manufacturing, and service operations from high-cost countries (for example, the United States and western Europe) to low-cost countries (for example, China, Mexico, and India) is well under way and accelerating. In turn, imports from these rapidly developing economies are making substantial inroads into core industrial product categories that were historically thought protected from such competition. However, leading firms like GE, Motorola, and Siemens are seizing opportunities by capturing sources of global advantage. In industry after industry, firms are under enormous pressure to make the move to global operations.

Mapping Sources of Global Advantage[3]

A firm can globalize its cost structure through the migration of sourcing, manufacturing, R&D, and service operations from a high-cost country to an RDE. In creating advantaged global operations, companies might conduct R&D in the United States, manufacture some product lines in the United States and others in China and Mexico, and locate customer service in India and Ireland. "Significant portions of manufacturing are expected to remain advantaged in their current locations. Reasons for staying in higher-cost locations might include the need to safeguard intellectual property content, the importance of collocation with customers, or the requirement to use local content."[4]

Firms that quickly and intelligently seize global opportunities can secure three forms of competitive advantage: (1) a cost advantage, (2) a market access advantage, and (3) a capabilities advantage.

The Cost Advantage

The major driver for a move to RDE sourcing remains very large—and sustainable—cost advantages from two primary sources: lower operating costs and lower capital investment requirements. The savings are striking. Jim Hemerling and his colleagues at the Boston Consulting Group assert that companies that globalize their cost structures

---

[3] Unless otherwise noted, this section draws on Jim Hemerling, Dave Young, and Thomas Bradtke, "Navigating the Five Currents of Globalization: How Leading Companies Are Capturing Global Advantage," *BCG Focus* (April 2005), The Boston Consulting Group, Inc., accessed at http://www.bcg.com.

[4] Battacharya et al., "Capturing Global Advantage," p. 7.

FIGURE 8.1 | **RDEs Offer a Substantial Cost Advantage over Highly Developed Economies**

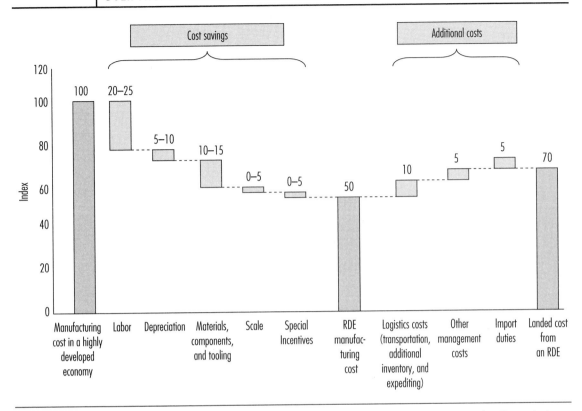

by including RDEs can realize savings of 20 to 40 percent in the landed costs of their products. The **landed cost** reflects the realized net savings after logistics costs, other management costs, and import duties involved in moving the product from the RDE (for example, China) to the market destination (for example, the United States). In addition, the capital needed to create a manufacturing facility in an RDE are 20 to 40 percent lower than in a highly developed economy.

Lower Operating Costs The difference in labor costs is a major component of the RDE cost advantage. Depending on the industry, the factory location, and the nature of employee benefits, a factory worker in the United States or Europe costs $15 to $30 or more per hour. By contrast, a factory worker in China earns $1 per hour, whereas in Mexico and in central and eastern Europe, workers earn $2 to $8 per hour. Figure 8.1 displays the realized cost savings (that is, 30 percent) for industrial products such as electric motors, transformers, and compressors that are manufactured in an RDE. Observe that companies operating in an RDE save not only directly on labor costs but also indirectly on domestic materials and components.

Business Process Outsourcing   When the focus shifts from products to highly labor-intensive sectors, such as services, the cost advantage of outsourcing to an RDE is up to 60 percent. India now represents the global market leader in offshore business-process outsourcing. Included here are not only transactional processes like call centers but also core industrial processes such as R&D and supply-chain management. A strong telecommunications infrastructure, coupled with large numbers of highly educated English-speaking managers, engineers, and workers, constitute key advantages for India. By outsourcing call centers to India, General Electric's consumer finance business saved 30 to 35 percent and American Express had savings of more than 50 percent.

Will the Cost Gap Persist?   Experts suggest that the differential in labor rates between RDEs and developed countries will remain substantial for the foreseeable future, even if they grow at dramatically different rates. Wage growth in China and India will be limited by the large number of underemployed people in both countries. Likewise, companies that operate in RDEs have been able consistently to lower purchasing costs over time, achieving cost savings that significantly exceed those that are normally found in the West.

Lower Capital Investment Requirements   Another important—and sometimes overlooked—source of the RDE cost advantage is lower capital investment requirements for plants and equipment. While lower operating costs benefit a firm's profit and loss (P&L) statement, lower capital investment requirements also represent significant savings on the balance sheet. The combination of lower product costs and lower capital investment requirements can boost the total return on investment. Figure 8.2 shows the typical cost differential for an industrial installation (for example, factory) in an RDE versus one in a highly developed economy. Observe that a factory in an RDE can be built for just 70 percent of the investment level needed in a highly developed economy. These capital savings result from the lower cost of infrastructure (15 percent savings), the lower cost of local machinery and equipment (10 percent), and the opportunity to substitute labor for costly technology (10 percent). After accounting for the higher costs (5 percent) of imported machinery, the net capital savings are 30 percent in the RDE (see Figure 8.2).

The Hidden Cost of RDE Operations   The cost advantages gained through operations in an RDE can be eroded by additional costs if companies fail to recognize them and aggressively control them. Among these hidden costs are[5]:

One-time setup costs that include the typical costs of establishing a new business, such as identifying and qualifying suppliers, creating a reliable logistics chain, and training employees.

Ongoing RDE risk management costs related to monitoring the quality of suppliers, managing inventory in a longer-than-usual logistics chain, and hedging exchange rate fluctuations.

Exit costs related to closing high-cost production or service facilities, including asset write-offs and related restructuring costs, as well as "bad will" costs (for example, damaged relations with unions) in the home country.

---

[5] Ibid., pp. 20–21.

FIGURE 8.2 | **RDEs Offer a Significant Capital Advantage over Highly Developed Economies**

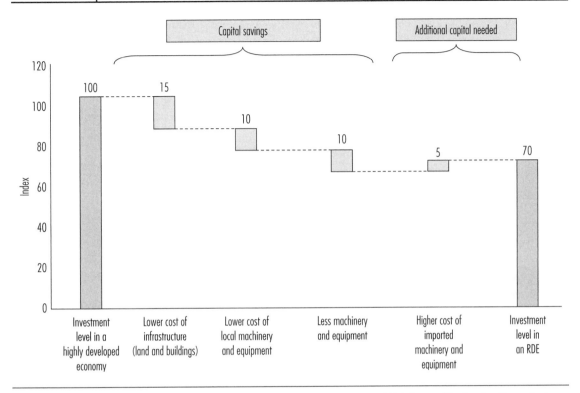

SOURCE: Jim Hemerling, Dave Young, and Thomas Bradtke, "Navigating the Five Currents of Globalization: How Leading Companies Are Capturing Global Advantage," *BCG Focus*, January 2005, The Boston Consulting Group, Inc., accessed at http://www.bcg.com. Copyright © The Boston Consulting Group, Inc. 2005. All rights reserved. Reprinted by permission.

In most cases, business-to-business firms do not exit their home country operations entirely. They prefer instead to maintain the best home-country operations while moving only the least efficient to RDEs to remain competitive and to secure market access.

The Market Access Advantage

Although companies traditionally relocated manufacturing operations to RDEs to gain cost advantages, once they are established in these countries, they are ideally positioned to serve fast-growing local markets. The striking results that GE Healthcare achieved in China illustrate the market access advantage.

GE Healthcare entered the market by transferring technology to local China R&D centers, which then developed "Chinese" versions of GE medical equipment that offered roughly 80 percent of the performance of Western systems at just 50 percent of the price. Because these products met local needs, GE Healthcare became the market leader in China. Furthermore, the China-developed products also appealed to customers in some Western countries where certain market segments found compelling value in the unique trade-off between the products' price and functionality.

China's Growing Role   For many industrial product categories, China is already the world's largest market. China is the largest market for machine tools, the second largest for power transmissions and distribution equipment, and the second largest for energy consumption. On the consumer product side, China is the world's largest market for cell phones, air conditioners, and refrigerators and represents a large and rapidly growing market for personal computers, automobiles, and consumer electronics products. Other RDEs, like India, are also growing explosively. For Cummins Inc., the diesel engine maker, China and India each represent a lucrative market today. But by 2010, Cummins projects revenues of $2 billion from India and $3 billion from China.[6]

Following Key Customers to RDEs   Many small and mid-sized companies are following their customers to RDEs. For example, Phoenix Electric Manufacturing Company, a Chicago-based producer of electric motors for power tools, kitchen appliances, and other products, added a factory in China.[7] The move enabled Phoenix Electric to retain its largest customers—GE and Emerson Electric—which have shifted most of their consumer-electronics production to the area. Similarly, Hiwasse Manufacturing, an Arkansas-based manufacturer of steel products used in the control panels of refrigerators, ovens, and other appliances, added a facility in Mexico near a GE appliance manufacturing facility.[8]

A Twofold Strategy   As major industrial sectors relocate manufacturing operations to RDEs, business-to-business firms that supply these sectors must take decisive action. Jim Hemerling and his associates at the Boston Consulting Group provide this advice:

> Most companies need to develop a twofold strategic plan: to fill market gaps at home, and to follow selected customers to their new locations. In our experience, it is rarely feasible to pursue only one or the other.[9]

For example, gaps can be filled at home by pursuing new lines of business or new product or service opportunities where the home country advantage can be defended. In turn, when moving to an RDE, suppliers must adjust their operating models to fully capture the cost advantages.

The Capabilities Advantage

To reinforce the cost advantage of operating in RDEs, top-performing global companies capture second-order benefits by tapping into the rapidly developing base of human talent in these countries. China and India each add over 350,000 science and engineering graduates to its talent pool each year. Many global companies, like GE, Microsoft, Motorola, and Siemens, have created R&D centers in both India and China. For example, Motorola employs several thousand engineers in China and operates a large R&D center in Beijing.

---

[6]Pete Engardio and Michael Arndt, "How Cummins Does It," *Business Week*, August 22–29, 2005, pp. 82–83.

[7]Dexter Roberts and Michael Arndt, "It's Getting Hotter in the East," *Business Week*, August 22–29, 2005, pp. 78–81.

[8]Louis Uchitelle, "If You Can Make It Here . . ." *New York Times*, September 4, 2005, p. B-5.

[9]Hemerling, Young, and Bradtke, "Navigating the Five Currents of Globalization," pp. 9–10.

TABLE 8.1 | **DETERMINING WHICH PRODUCTS TO OUTSOURCE TO RAPIDLY DEVELOPING ECONOMIES (RDEs) AND WHICH TO KEEP AT HOME**

Selected Criteria	Maintain Home-Based Manufacturing	Relocate to RDEs
Labor Contract	Low	High
Growth of Demand in Home Market	Low	High
Size of RDE Market	Low	High
Degree of Standardization	Low	High
Intellectual Property Content	High	Low
Logistical Requirements	High	Low

SOURCE: Adapted from Arindam Bhattacharya et al., "Capturing Global Advantage: How Leading Industrial Companies Are Transforming Their Industries by Sourcing and Selling in China, India, and Other Low-Cost Countries," The Boston Consulting Group, Inc., April 2004, accessed at http://www.bcg.com, pp. 26–30.

Leading companies can make use of this capabilities advantage to:

- *Improve research and development:* The much lower cost of engineers and skilled technicians in RDEs allows companies to increase dramatically the amount of R&D they do for a given budget level.

- *Address unmet customer needs:* The opportunity to make greater use of skilled labor in place of machines allows companies to manufacture customized products less expensively than would be feasible in a more automated setting.

- *Tailor products and services to the burgeoning local markets in RDEs:* To illustrate, Motorola's Beijing R&D center develops cell phones for the local market—the largest handset market in the world.[10]

The Outsourcing Decision[11]

The decision to relocate manufacturing, R&D, or customer service to RDEs is a strategic decision involving a host of economic, competitive, and environmental considerations. Clearly, some products and services are better candidates for outsourcing than others.

What Should Go? The criteria that favor relocation to RDEs include products or services with high labor content, high growth potential, large RDE markets, and standardized manufacturing or service delivery processes (Table 8.1). These criteria reflect each of the sources of global advantage we have explored. For services, the processes most easily relocated are those that have well-defined process maps or those that are rule-based (for example, the established protocol a customer service call center uses).

[10]Roberts and Arndt, "It's Getting Hotter in the East," pp. 78–81.
[11]Battacharya et al., "Capturing Global Advantage," pp. 26–30.

FIGURE 8.3 | SPECTRUM OF INVOLVEMENT IN INTERNATIONAL MARKETING

Low Commitment					High Commitment
Exporting	Contracting	Strategic Alliance	Joint Venture	Multidomestic Strategy	Global Strategy

Low Complexity					High Complexity

What Should Not Go?   Products and services that should remain at home include "those for which protection of intellectual property is critical, those with extreme logistical requirements, those with very high technology content or performance requirements, and those for which customers are highly sensitive to the location of production" (for example, certain military contracts).[12] Concerns about intellectual property (IP) theft is a major issue in most RDEs, particularly in China. Experts suggest that some multinational companies in China are losing the battle to protect their IP, largely because they emphasize legal tactics rather than including IP directly into their strategic and operational decisions. By carefully analyzing and selecting which products and technologies to sell in China, the best companies reduce the chance that competitors will steal their IP.

International Market-Entry Options[13]

To develop effective international marketing strategy, managers must evaluate the alternative ways that a firm can participate in international markets. The particular mode of entry should consider the level of a firm's experience overseas and the stage in the evolution of its international involvement. Figure 8.3 illustrates a spectrum of options for participating in international markets. They range from low-commitment choices, such as exporting, to highly complex levels of participation, such as global strategies. Each is examined in this section.

Exporting

An industrial firm's first encounter with an overseas market usually involves **exporting** because it requires the least commitment and risk. Goods are produced at one or two home plants, and sales are made through distributors or importing agencies in each country. Exporting is a workable entry strategy when the firm lacks the resources to make a significant commitment to the market, wants to minimize political and economic risk, or is unfamiliar with the country's market requirements and cultural norms.

---

[12] Ibid., p. 29.

[13] The following discussion is based on Franklin R. Root, *Entry Strategy for International Markets* (Lexington, Mass.: D. C. Heath, 1987); and Michael R. Czinkota and Ilka A. Ronkainen, *International Marketing*, 2d ed. (Hinsdale, Ill.: Dryden Press, 1990).

Exporting is the most popular international market entry option among small and medium-sized firms.[14]

While preserving flexibility and reducing risk, exporting also limits the future prospects for growth in the country. First, exporting involves giving up direct control of the marketing program, which makes it difficult to coordinate activities, implement strategies, and resolve conflicts with customers and channel members. George Day explains why customers may sense a lack of exporter commitment:

> In many international markets customers are loath to form long-run relationships with a company through its agents because they are unsure whether the business will continue to service the market, or will withdraw at the first sign of adversity. This problem has bedeviled U.S. firms in many countries, and only now are they living down a reputation for opportunistically participating in many countries and then withdrawing abruptly to protect short-run profits.[15]

Contracting

A somewhat more involved and complex form of international market entry is **contracting.** Included among contractual entry modes are (1) licensing and (2) management contracts.

Licensing   Under a **licensing** agreement, one firm permits another to use its intellectual property in exchange for royalties or some other form of payment. The property might include trademarks, patents, technology, know-how, or company name. In short, licensing involves exporting intangible assets.

As an entry strategy, licensing requires neither capital investment nor marketing strength in foreign markets. This lets a firm test foreign markets without a major commitment of management time or capital. Because the licensee is typically a local company that can serve as a buffer against government action, licensing also reduces the risk of exposure to government action. With increasing host country regulation, licensing may enable the business marketer to enter a foreign market that is closed to either imports or direct foreign investment.

Licensing agreements do pose some limitations. First, some companies are hesitant to enter into license agreements because the licensee may become an important competitor in the future. Second, licensing agreements typically include a time limit. Although terms may be extended once after the initial agreement, many foreign governments do not readily permit additional extensions. Third, a firm has less control over a licensee than over its own exporting or manufacturing abroad.

Management Contracts   To expand their overseas operations, many firms have turned to management contracts. In a **management contract** the industrial firm assembles a package of skills that provide an integrated service to the client. When equity participation, either full ownership or a joint venture, is not feasible or is not

---

[14]Jery Whitelock and Damd Jobber, "An Evaluation of External Factors in the Decision of UK Industrial Firms to Enter a New Non-Domestic Market: An Exploratory Study," *European Journal of Marketing* 38, no. 11/12 (2004), p. 1440.

[15]George S. Day, *Market Driven Strategy: Processes for Creating Value* (New York: The Free Press, 1990), p. 272.

permitted by a foreign government, a management contract provides a way to participate in a venture. Management contracts have been used effectively in the service sector in areas such as computer services, hotel management, and food services. Michael Czinkota and Ilka Ronkainen point out that management contracts can "provide organizational skills not available locally, expertise that is immediately available rather than built up, and management assistance in the form of support services that would be difficult and costly to replicate locally."[16]

One specialized form of a management contract is a turnkey operation. This arrangement permits a client to acquire a complete operational system, together with the skills needed to maintain and operate the system without assistance. Once the package agreement is online, the client owns, controls, and operates the system. Management contracts allow firms to commercialize their superior skills (know-how) by participating in the international market.

Other contractual modes of entry have grown in prominence in recent years. **Contract manufacturing** involves sourcing a product from a producer located in a foreign country for sale there or in other countries. Here assistance might be required to ensure that the product meets the desired quality standards. Contract manufacturing is most appropriate when the local market lacks sufficient potential to justify a direct investment, export entry is blocked, and a quality licensee is not available.

Strategic Alliances

Strategic alliances are assuming an increasingly prominent role in the global strategy of many business marketing firms. Frederick Webster Jr. defines **strategic alliances** as "collaborations among partners involving the commitment of capital and management resources with the objective of enhancing the partners' competitive positions."[17] Strategic alliances offer a number of benefits, such as access to markets or technology, economies of scale in manufacturing and marketing, and the sharing of risk among partners.

Although offering potential, global strategic alliances pose a special management challenge. Among the stumbling blocks are these:[18]

- Partners are organized quite differently for making marketing and product design decisions, creating *problems in coordination and trust.*

- Partners that combine the best set of skills in one country may be poorly equipped to support each other in other countries, leading to *problems in implementing alliances on a global scale.*

- The quick pace of technological change often guarantees that the most attractive partner today may not be the most attractive partner tomorrow, leading to *problems in maintaining alliances over time.*

---

[16] Czinkota and Ronkainen, *International Marketing*, p. 493.

[17] Frederick E. Webster Jr., "The Changing Role of Marketing in the Corporation," *Journal of Marketing* 56 (October 1992): p. 8.

[18] Thomas J. Kosnik, "Stumbling Blocks to Global Strategic Alliances," *Systems Integration Age*, October 1988, pp. 31–39. See also Eric Rule and Shawn Keon, "Competencies of High-Performing Strategic Alliances," *Strategy & Leadership*, 27 (September–October 1998): pp. 36–37.

ETHICAL BUSINESS MARKETING

The Bribery Dilemma in Global Markets

Global marketing managers often face a dilemma when home country regulations clash with foreign business practices. A good case in point is the aerospace industry. U.S. government policies about bribery by private companies have affected aircraft sales in some countries. The U.S. Foreign Corrupt Practices Act (FCPA) of 1977 prohibits payments by U.S. companies and individuals, including exporters of aircraft, to obtain or retain business and has had a major effect on how U.S. companies conduct global business. Until 1999, European laws on transnational bribery were *nonexistent*. Accordingly, some European aerospace manufacturers were widely alleged to have bribed foreign public officials to win at the expense of their U.S. competitors.

Currently, the U.S. government and the Organization for Economic Cooperation and Development (OECD) Working Group on Bribery are trying to remove the major obstacles to implementation of the OECD's antibribery convention. The U.S. government is also seeking to strengthen OECD and other multilateral and bilateral disciplines related to bribery and corruption of public officials.

Interestingly, recent press reports allege that European aerospace companies are among the business groups pressing their governments to *relax antibribery rules*. To the extent that bribery and anticorruption disciplines and enforcement in Europe remain weaker than under the U.S. Foreign Corrupt Practices Act, European aerospace companies will enjoy a competitive advantage in sales competitions to foreign governments or government-controlled airlines.

SOURCE: Joseph H. Bogosian, "Global Market Factors Affecting U.S. Jet Producers," Federal Document Clearing House Congressional Testimony, Capital Hill Hearing Testimony, House Transportation and Infrastructure, May 25, 2005.

Firms that are adept at managing global alliances choose partners carefully. They evaluate potential partners on the basis of their strengths and/or fit across five areas: resources, relationships (for example, with customers and channels), reputation, capabilities (for example, marketing and R&D), and chemistry/culture. Once alliances are established, effective relationship management skills are needed to coordinate activities, control conflict, and keep the alliance strategy centered on the ever-changing customer in the global marketplace.

Joint Ventures

In pursuing international-entry options, a corporation confronts a wide variety of ownership choices, ranging from 100 percent ownership to a minority interest. Frequently, full ownership may be a desirable, but not essential, prerequisite for success. Thus a joint venture becomes feasible. The **joint venture** involves a joint-ownership arrangement (between, for example, a U.S. firm and one in the host country) to produce and/or market goods in a foreign market. In contrast to a strategic alliance, a joint venture creates a new firm. Some joint ventures are structured so that each partner holds an equal share; in others, one partner has a majority stake. The contributions of partners can also vary widely and may include financial resources, technology, sales organizations, know-how, or plant and equipment. Representing a successful relationship is the 50-50 joint venture between Xerox Corporation and Tokyo-based Fuji Photo Film Company. Through the joint venture, Xerox gained a presence in the

Japanese market, learned valuable quality management skills that improved its products, and developed a keen understanding of important Japanese rivals such as Canon, Inc., and Ricoh Company. This joint venture has thrived for more than three decades.[19]

Advantages   Joint ventures offer a number of advantages. First, joint ventures may open up market opportunities that neither partner could pursue alone. Kenichi Ohmae explains the logic:

> If you run a pharmaceutical company with a good drug to distribute in Japan but have no sales force to do it, find someone in Japan who also has a good product but no sales force in your country. You get double the profit by putting two strong drugs through your fixed cost sales network, and so does your new ally. Why duplicate such high expenses all down the line? . . . Why not join forces to maximize contribution to each other's fixed costs?[20]

Second, joint ventures may provide for better relationships with local organizations (for example, local authorities) and with customers. By being attuned to the host country's culture and environment, the local partner may enable the joint venture to respond to changing market needs, be more aware of cultural sensitivities, and be less vulnerable to political risk.

The Downside   Problems can arise in maintaining joint-venture relationships. A study suggests that perhaps more than 50 percent of joint ventures are disbanded or fall short of expectations.[21] The reasons involve problems with disclosing sensitive information, disagreements over how profits are to be shared, clashes over management style, and differing perceptions on strategy. Some experts point to another risk that must be evaluated. What would happen in the event of a breakup? Michael R. Czinkota and Jon Woronoff warn that companies "must decide whether they really do want to tie up with a knowledgeable partner that could become a troublesome rival at a later date, or whether they would not prefer one that is just a distributor or maybe a manufacturer in a different sector."[22]

Choosing a Mode of Entry

For an initial move into the international market, the full range of entry modes, presented earlier, may be considered—from exporting, licensing, and contract manufacturing to joint ventures and wholly owned subsidiaries. In high-risk markets, firms can reduce their equity exposure by adopting low-commitment modes such as licensing, contract manufacturing, or joint ventures with a minority share. Although nonequity modes of entry—such as licensing or contract manufacturing—involve minimal risk and commitment, they may not provide the desired level of control or financial performance. Joint ventures and wholly owned subsidiaries provide a greater degree of control over operations and greater potential returns.

---

[19] David P. Hamilton, "United It Stands—Fuji Xerox Is a Rarity in World Business: A Joint Venture That Works," *The Wall Street Journal*, September 26, 1996, p. R19.

[20] Kenichi Ohmae, "The Global Logic of Strategic Alliances," *Harvard Business Review* 67 (March–April 1989): p. 147.

[21] Arvind Parkhe, "Building Trust in International Alliances," *Journal of World Business* 33 (winter 1998): pp. 417–437.

[22] Michael R. Czinkota and Jon Woronoff, *Unlocking Japan's Markets: Seizing Marketing and Distribution Opportunities in Today's Japan* (Chicago: Probus, 1991), p. 157.

The choice of a particular entry mode also depends on the size of the market and its growth potential. Susan Douglas and Samuel Craig note that

> Markets of limited size surrounded by tariff barriers may be supplied most cost effectively via licensing or contract manufacturing. Where there are potential economies of scale, exporting may, however, be preferred. Then, as local market potential builds up . . . a local production and marketing subsidiary may be established.[23]

Once operations are established in a number of foreign markets, the focus often shifts away from foreign opportunity assessment to local market development in each country. This shift might be prompted by the need to respond to local competitors or the desire to more effectively penetrate the local market. Planning and strategy assume a country-by-country focus.

Multidomestic versus Global Strategies

The most complex forms of participation in the global arena are multidomestic and global strategies. Multinational firms have traditionally managed operations outside their home country with **multidomestic strategies** that permit individual subsidiaries to compete independently in different country markets. The multinational headquarters coordinates marketing policies and financial controls and may centralize R&D and some support activities. Each subsidiary, however, resembles a strategic business unit that is expected to contribute earnings and growth to the organization. The firm can manage its international activities like a portfolio. Examples of multidomestic industries include most types of retailing, construction, metal fabrication, and many services.

In contrast, a **global strategy** seeks competitive advantage with strategic choices that are highly integrated across countries. For example, features of a global strategy might include a standardized core product that requires minimal local adaptation and that is targeted on foreign-country markets chosen on the basis of their contribution to globalization benefits. Prominent examples of global industries are automobiles, commercial aircraft, consumer electronics, and many categories of industrial machinery. Major volume and market-share advantages might be sought by directing attention to the United States, Europe, and Japan, as well as to the rapidly developing economies of China and India. The value-chain concept illuminates the chief differences between a multidomestic and a global strategy.

International Strategy and the Value Chain[24]

To diagnose the sources of competitive advantage, domestic or international, Michael Porter divides a firm's activities into distinct groups. The value chain, displayed in Figure 8.4, provides a framework for categorizing these activities. Primary activities are those involved in the physical creation of the product, the marketing and logistical

---

[23] Susan P. Douglas and C. Samuel Craig, "Evolution of Global Marketing Strategy: Scale, Scope, and Synergy," *Columbia Journal of World Business* 24 (fall 1989): p. 53.

[24] Michael E. Porter, "Changing Patterns of International Competition," *California Management Review* 28 (winter 1986): pp. 9–40; see also Porter, *Competitive Advantage: Creating and Sustaining Superior Performance* (New York: The Free Press, 1985).

FIGURE 8.4 | THE VALUE CHAIN: UPSTREAM AND DOWNSTREAM ACTIVITIES

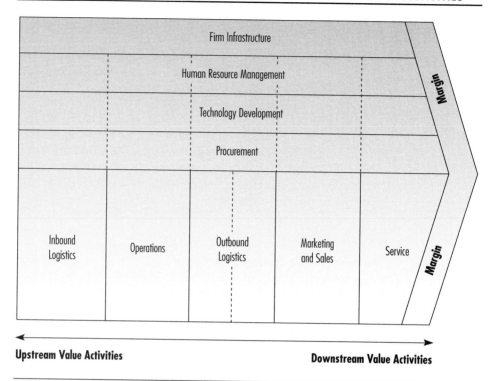

Upstream Value Activities   Downstream Value Activities

SOURCE: From "Changing Patterns of International Competition" by Michael Porter. Copyright © 1986, by The Regents of the University of California. Reprinted from the CALIFORNIA MANAGEMENT REVIEW, Vol. 28, No. 2. By permission of The Regents.

program, and service after the sale. Support activities provide the infrastructure and inputs that allow the primary activities to occur. Every activity uses purchased inputs, human resources, and a combination of technologies. Likewise, the firm's infrastructure, including such functions as general management, supports the entire value chain. Porter asserts that competitive advantage results when a firm can perform the required activities at a lower cost than rival firms or perform some activities in unique ways that create customer value and support a premium price. In short, these two types of competitive advantage result from lower relative costs or differentiation.[25] A firm that competes in the international market must decide how to spread the activities among countries. Central to this decision is the need to distinguish upstream from downstream activities (see Figure 8.4).

Downstream activities involve those primary activities that are closely tied to the buyer's location. For example, a business marketer wishing to serve the Chinese market must ensure that a local service network is in place. By contrast, upstream activities (for example, manufacturing and operations) and support activities (for example, procurement) are not tied directly to the buyer's location. Caterpillar, for example, uses a few

[25] Porter, "Changing Patterns," p. 13.

B2B TOP PERFORMERS

General Electric Aircraft Engines: Global Strategy Means Help Your Customers

General Electric's (GE's) Aircraft Engine Division must maintain a very large global presence as it markets jet engines to almost every airline in the world. Although most large airlines purchase their aircraft from either Boeing or Airbus Industrie, the individual airline makes the choice as to the jet engine manufacturer. Thus, Singapore Air can choose between Pratt & Whitney, Rolls-Royce, or GE. The stakes are high in the industry, given that a particular airline may purchase hundreds of aircraft over a relatively short period of time. The challenges are significant for the jet engine manufacturers: They must have a solid relationship with aircraft manufacturers like Boeing and Airbus, but just as important, they need to expend considerable effort to woo and then keep the airlines as customers. Making GE's job tougher are the global aspects of these relationships. First, Boeing is an American firm and Airbus is a joint venture of firms from several European Union countries. Several other airframe manufacturers are located in Brazil, Canada, and China—and these manufacturers cater to the smaller, regional airlines that fly 50- to 100-seat jets. Even more daunting is the fact that there are close to 80 airlines located all over the world, only a handful of which are U.S.-based.

A major element in GE's marketing strategy is to offer assistance to global customers in creative ways. For example, one new customer is a Chinese airframe manufacturer that had not yet built its first airplane when GE began interacting with company executives! The firm's first airplane will not roll off the assembly line until 2008, yet GE began building relationship ties with this company in 2003—in a subtle way. Because the Chinese airframe manufacturer is a brand-new company, key managers lack experience in all the key aspects of business-to-business marketing. GE's response: help educate the airframe manufacturer's sales and marketing personnel in all facets of business-to-business marketing. One element of this approach was to invite the entire marketing and sales team to GE's U.S. headquarters for a two-week seminar on B2B marketing. Follow-up would take place in China at a later date to review assignments and projects given to the participants at the first seminar. GE will also work hand-in-hand with the Chinese sales team as they begin making sales calls on the airlines that are potential buyers of their aircraft. GE's efforts illustrate the challenges of selling in rapidly growing global markets where potential customers are rather inexperienced in many facets of business. The challenges for GE are complex, as they must deal with the cultural and business process issues of their Chinese customer, as well as those of all the airlines around the world to whom the Chinese firm will sell their airplanes.

large-scale manufacturing facilities to produce components to meet worldwide demands.

A firm's strategy defines its particular configuration of value-chain activities and how they fit together. Different strategic positions can be captured by tailoring activities to produce particular products or services, by addressing the special needs of particular market segments, or by securing more efficient market access to certain types of customers. This assessment provides a foundation for valuable strategic insights. Competitive advantage created by downstream activities is largely country-specific: A firm's reputation, brand name, and service network grow out of the firm's activities in a particular country. Competitive advantage in upstream and support activities stems more from the entire network of countries in which a firm competes than from its position in any one country.

Source of Advantage: Multidomestic versus Global

When downstream activities (those tied directly to the buyer) are important to competitive advantage, a multidomestic pattern of international competition is common. In **multidomestic industries,** firms pursue separate strategies in each of their foreign markets—competition in each country is essentially independent of competition in other countries (for example, Alcoa in the aluminum industry, Honeywell in the controls industry).

Global competition is more common in industries in which upstream and support activities (such as technology development and operations) are vital to competitive advantage. A **global industry** is one in which a firm's competitive position in one country is significantly influenced by its position in other countries (for example, Intel in the semiconductor industry, Boeing in the commercial aircraft industry).

Coordination and Configuration   Further insights into international strategy can be gained by examining two dimensions of competition in the global market: configuration and coordination. **Configuration** centers on where each activity is performed, including the number of locations. Options range from concentrated (for example, one production plant serving the world) to dispersed (for example, a plant in each country—each with a complete value chain). By concentrating an activity such as production in a central location, firms can gain economies of scale or speed learning. Alternatively, dispersing activities to a number of locations may minimize transportation and storage costs, tailor activities to local market differences, or facilitate learning about market conditions in a country.

Coordination refers to how similar activities performed in various countries are coordinated or coupled with each other. If, for example, a firm has three plants—one in the United States, one in England, and one in China—how do the activities in these plants relate to one another? Numerous coordination options exist because of the many possible levels of coordination and the many ways an activity can be performed. For example, a firm operating three plants could, at one extreme, allow each plant to operate autonomously (unique production processes, unique products). At the other extreme, the three plants could be closely coordinated, utilizing a common information system and producing products with identical features. Dow Chemical, for example, uses an enterprise software system that allows it to shift purchasing, manufacturer, and distribution functions worldwide in response to changing patterns of supply and demand.[26]

Types of International Strategy

Figure 8.5 portrays some of the possible variations in international strategy. Observe that the purest global strategy concentrates as many activities as possible in one country, serves the world market from this home base, and closely coordinates activities that must be performed near the buyer (for example, service). Caterpillar, for example, views its battle with the formidable Japanese competitor Komatsu in global terms. As well as using advanced manufacturing systems that allow it to fully exploit the economies of scale from its worldwide sales volume, Caterpillar also carefully coordinates activities in its global dealer network. This integrated global strategy gives Caterpillar a competitive

---

[26]Thomas H. Davenport, "Putting the Enterprise into the Enterprise System," *Harvard Business Review,* 76 (July–August 1998): pp. 121–131.

FIGURE 8.5 | **TYPES OF INTERNATIONAL STRATEGY**

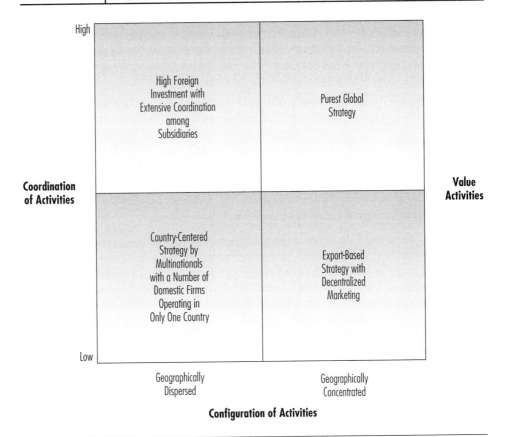

SOURCE: From "Changing Patterns of International Competition" by Michael Porter. Copyright © 1986, by The Regents of the University of California. Reprinted from the CALIFORNIA MANAGEMENT REVIEW, Vol. 28, No. 2. By permission of The Regents.

advantage in cost and effectiveness.[27] By serving the world market from its home base in the United States and by closely coordinating sales and service with customers around the world, Boeing also aptly illustrates a pure global strategy. Airbus Industrie—the European aerospace consortium—is a strong and clever rival that competes aggressively with Boeing for orders at airlines around the world.[28]

A Global Battle for the PC Market   Other interesting global face-offs involve Dell, Inc., versus Lenovo Group, Inc. Dell, the global market-share leader in personal computers, is now pursuing an integrated global strategy and challenging Lenovo, China's largest producer in its home market.[29] Meanwhile, Lenovo gained worldwide reach when it purchased IBM's PC division.

---

[27] Donald V. Fites, "Make Your Dealers Your Partners," *Harvard Business Review* 74 (March–April 1996): pp. 84–95.

[28] Alex Taylor III, "Blue Skies for Airbus," *Fortune*, August 2, 1999, pp. 102–108.

[29] Evan Ramstad and Gary McWilliams, "For Dell, Success in China Tells Tale of Maturing Market," *The Wall Street Journal*, July 5, 2005, pp. A1, A8.

Other Paths Figure 8.5 illustrates other international strategy patterns. Canon, for example, concentrates manufacturing and support activities in Japan but gives local marketing subsidiaries significant latitude in each region of the world. Thus, Canon pursues an export-based strategy. In contrast, Xerox concentrates some activities and disperses others. Coordination, however, is extremely high: The Xerox brand, marketing approach, and servicing strategy are standardized worldwide. Michael Porter notes:

> International strategy has often been characterized as a choice between worldwide standardization and local tailoring, or as the tension between the economic imperative (large-scale efficient facilities) and the political imperative (local content, local production). . . . A firm's choice of international strategy involves a search for competitive advantage from configuration/coordination throughout the value chain.[30]

A General Framework for Global Strategy[31]

The need for a global strategy is determined by the nature of international competition in a particular industry. For example, recall that many industries are *multidomestic*, and competition takes place on a country-by-country basis with few linkages across operating units (for example, construction and many service offerings). Multidomestic industries do not need a global strategy because the focus should be on developing a series of distinct domestic strategies. However, for truly global industries, a firm's position in one country significantly affects its position elsewhere, so they need a *global* strategy. Competing across countries through an integrated global strategy requires a series of choices that are highlighted in Figure 8.6.

Build on a Unique Competitive Position

A business marketing firm should globalize first in those business and product lines where it has unique advantages. To achieve international competitive success, a firm must enjoy a meaningful advantage on either cost or differentiation. To this end, the firm must be able to perform activities at a lower cost than its rivals or perform activities in a unique way that creates customer value and supports a premium price. For example, Denmark's Novo-Nordisk Group (Novo) is the world's leading exporter of insulin and industrial enzymes. By pioneering high-purity insulins and advancing insulin delivery technology, Novo achieved a level of differentiation that gave it a strong competitive position in the health-care market in the United States, Europe, and Japan.

Emphasize a Consistent Positioning Strategy

Rather than modifying the firm's product and service offerings from country to country, "a global strategy requires a patient, long-term campaign to enter every significant foreign market while maintaining and leveraging the company's unique

---

[30] Porter, "Changing Patterns," p. 25.

[31] This section is based on Michael E. Porter, "Competing across Locations: Enhancing Competitive Advantage through a Global Strategy," in Michael E. Porter, ed., *On Competition* (Boston: Harvard Business School Press, 1998), pp. 309–350. See also Shaoming Zou and S. Tamer Cavusgil, "The GMS: A Broad Conceptualization of Global Marketing Strategy and Its Effect on Firm Performance," *Journal of Marketing* 66 (October 2002): pp. 40–56.

FIGURE 8.6 | A GENERAL FRAMEWORK FOR GLOBAL STRATEGY

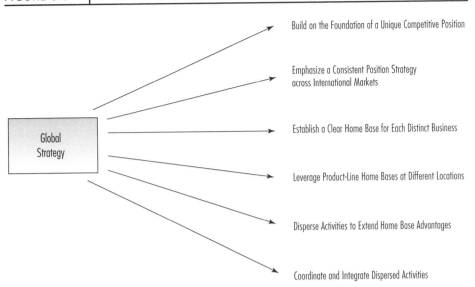

SOURCE: Adapted from Michael E. Porter, "Competing across Locations: Enhancing Competitive Advantage through a Global Strategy," in Michael E. Porter, ed., *On Competition* (Boston: Harvard Business School Press, 1998), pp. 309–350.

strategic positioning."[32] One of the greatest barriers to the success of firms in smaller countries is the perceived need to serve all customer segments and to offer an expanded product assortment to capture the limited market potential. However, by maintaining a consistent position, a firm reinforces its distinctive strategy and keeps its strategic attention focused on the much larger international opportunity.

Establish a Clear Home Base for Each Distinct Business

Although the location of corporate headquarters is less important and may reflect historical factors, a firm must develop a clear home base for competing in each of its strategically distinct businesses. "The **home base** for a business is the location where strategy is set, core product and process technology is created and maintained, and a critical mass of sophisticated production and service activities reside."[33] For example, Japan, Honda's home base for both motorcycles and automobiles, is where 95 percent of its R&D employees are located and all of its core engine research is conducted. For Hewlett-Packard (H-P), the United States hosts 77 percent of the physical space dedicated to manufacturing, R&D, and administration but only 43 percent of H-P's physical space dedicated to marketing. At H-P's home base, R&D managers with specialized expertise are designated worldwide experts; they transfer their knowledge either electronically or through periodic visits to subsidiaries around the world.

---

[32] Ibid., Porter, "Competing Across Locations," p. 331.

[33] Ibid., p. 332.

Regional subsidiaries take responsibility for some process-oriented R&D activities and for local marketing.

The home base should be located in a country or region with the most favorable access to required resources (inputs) and supporting industries (for example, specialized suppliers). Such a location provides the best environment for capturing productivity and innovation benefits. Honda, as well as H-P, each benefits from a strong supplier network that supports each of its principal businesses. The home base should also serve as the central integrating point for activities and have clear worldwide responsibility for the business unit.

Leverage Product-Line Home Bases at Different Locations

As a firm's product line broadens and diversifies, different countries may best provide the home bases for some product lines. Responsibility for leading a particular product line should be assigned to the country with the best locational advantages. Each subsidiary, then, specializes in products for which it has the most favorable advantages (for example, specialized suppliers) and serves customers worldwide. For example, H-P locates many product line home bases outside the United States, such as its line of compact inkjet printers, which is based in Singapore. In turn, Honda has begun to create a product-line home base for Accord station wagons in the United States. The model was conceived, designed, and developed through the joint efforts of Honda's California and Ohio R&D facilities.

Disperse Activities to Extend Home Base Advantages

Although the home base is where core activities are concentrated, other activities can be dispersed to extend the firm's competitive position. Potential opportunities should be examined in three areas:

- *Capturing competitive advantages in purchasing.*   Inputs that are not central to the innovation process, such as raw materials or general-purpose component parts, must be purchased from the most cost-effective location.

- *Securing or improving market access.*   By locating selected activities near the market, a firm demonstrates commitment to foreign customers, responds to actual or threatened government mandates, and may be better equipped to tailor offerings to local preferences. For example, Honda has invested more than $2 billion in facilities in the United States. Likewise, a host of firms, like Motorola, GE, and Intel, have made large investments in China and India.

- *Selectively tapping competitive advantages at other locations.*   To improve capabilities in important skills or technologies at home, global competitors can locate selected activities in centers of innovation in other countries. The goal here is to supplement, but not replace, the home base. To illustrate, Honda gains exposure to California's styling expertise and Germany's high-performance design competencies through small, local company-financed design centers that transfer knowledge back to the Japanese home base.

Coordinate and Integrate Dispersed Activities

Coordination across geographically dispersed locations raises formidable challenges, among them those of language and cultural differences and of aligning the reward systems for individual managers and subsidiaries with the goals of the global enterprise as a whole. However, successful global competitors achieve unified action by:

1. Establishing a clear global strategy that is understood by organizational members across countries.

2. Developing information and accounting systems that are consistent on a worldwide basis, thereby facilitating operational coordination.

3. Encouraging personal relationships and the transfer of learning among subsidiary managers across locations.

4. Relying on carefully designed incentive systems that weigh overall contribution to the entire enterprise in addition to subsidiary performance.

Summary

Rapidly developing economies (RDEs), like China and India, present a host of opportunities and a special set of challenges for business-to-business firms. Companies that decisively and intelligently pursue RDE strategies can secure three compelling forms of competitive advantage: significantly lower costs; direct access to the fastest-growing markets; and the capabilities for improving R&D, addressing unmet customer needs, and increasing overall business effectiveness. The migration of sourcing, manufacturing, R&D, and customer service operations from developed economies to RDEs will continue to accelerate in many industry sectors. However, some products and services are better candidates for relocation or outsourcing than others. For example, those with high labor content and large RDE markets represent solid outsourcing candidates, whereas those for which the protection of intellectual property is critical should stay at home.

Once a business marketing firm decides to sell its products in a particular country, it must select an entry strategy. The range of options includes exporting, contractual entry modes (for example, licensing), strategic alliances, and joint ventures. A more elaborate form of participation is represented by multinational firms that use multidomestic strategies. Here a separate strategy might be pursued in each country served. The most advanced level of participation in international markets is provided by firms that use a global strategy. Such firms seek competitive advantage by pursuing strategies that are highly interdependent across countries. Global competition tends to be more common in industries in which primary activities, like R&D and manufacturing, are vital to competitive advantage.

A global strategy must begin with a unique competitive position that offers a clear competitive advantage. Providing the best odds of international competitive success are businesses and product lines where companies have the most unique advantages. The home base for a business is the location where strategy is set, and the home base for some product lines may be best positioned in other countries. Although core activities are located at the home base, other activities can be dispersed to strengthen the company's competitive position. Successful global competitors demonstrate special capabilities in coordinating and integrating dispersed activities. Coordination ensures clear positioning and a well-understood concept of global strategy among subsidiary managers across countries.

Discussion Questions

1. In the business market, Motorola is the leading telecommunications supplier to India's army, police, and civil authorities. Likewise, the creation of a sub-$40 phone is aimed at expanding Motorola's foothold in India's consumer market. Could Motorola achieve these results by concentrating all of its R&D activities in the United States? Explain.

2. Many observers argue the cost advantage that rapidly developing economies enjoy will evaporate in 5 to 10 years. Agree or disagree? Explain.

3. Describe the characteristics of products and services that would represent poor candidates for outsourcing.

4. In addition to cost advantages, describe the other ways that rapidly developing economies can contribute to competitive advantage.

5. The European aerospace consortium Airbus is a strong competitor to Boeing and is climbing toward its long-stated goal of winning 50 percent of the over-100-seat airline market. What criteria would a customer like UPS or British Airways consider in choosing aircraft? What are the critical factors that shape competitive advantage in the airliner market?

6. A small Michigan-based firm that produces and sells component parts to General Motors, Ford, and DaimlerChrysler wishes to extend market coverage to Europe and Japan. What type of market entry strategy would provide the best fit?

7. Global companies must be more than just a bunch of overseas subsidiaries that execute decisions made at headquarters. Using the value-chain concept as a guide, compare a global strategy to a multidomestic strategy.

8. Downstream activities in a firm's value chain create competitive advantages that are largely country-specific. Why?

9. Why would Hewlett-Packard assign lead product line responsibility to a subsidiary located outside the United States?

10. A global strategy begins with a unique competitive position that offers a clear competitive advantage. What steps can a global competitor take to ensure that the strategy is implemented in a consistent way in countries around the world?

Internet Exercise

General Electric (GE) sells over $5 billion worth of goods and services to Chinese customers in the business market. Go to http://www.ge.com and first identify the various GE divisions, like Healthcare, that contribute to sales volume and then identify a few products from each division that likely address important needs or priorities in China.

Schwinn: Could the Story Have Been Different?[34]

At its peak, Schwinn had more than 2,000 U.S. employees, produced hundreds of thousands of bicycles in five factories, and held 20 percent of the market. Today, however, Schwinn no longer exists as an operating company. The firm, founded in 1895, declared bankruptcy in 1992 and closed its last factory one year later. The Schwinn name is now owned by a Canada-based firm and all of the bikes are manufactured in Asia.

Harold L. Sirkin, a senior vice president at the Boston Consulting Group, argues that Schwinn's story could have been different. He outlines two alternative pathways that might have provided a happier ending to the Schwinn story.

Alternative Reality One: Aim High

Under this scenario, Schwinn decided to center on midrange and premium segments of the market, leaving low-end bicycles for competitors. However, the firm determined that it could substantially reduce costs by turning to low-cost partners in rapidly developing economies for labor-intensive parts. Schwinn interviewed hundreds of potential suppliers and locked the best ones into long-term contracts. Schwinn then reconfigured its operations to perform final assembly and quality inspection in the United States. Still, the changes forced Schwinn to make some painful choices—nearly 30 percent of the workforce was laid off. However, such moves allowed Schwinn to produce bikes at half the previous cost, maintain a significant position in the midrange bicycle market, and leverage its product design capabilities to build a strong position for its brand in the high-end market. As a result, Schwinn is extremely competitive in the U.S. market and is a major exporter of premium bikes to China and Europe. Because of this growth, Schwinn now employs twice as many people in the United States as it did before outsourcing began.

Alternative Reality Two: If You Can't Beat Them, Join Them

Schwinn went on the offensive and moved as quickly as possible to open its own factory in China. By bringing its own manufacturing techniques and by training employees in China, Schwinn was able to achieve high quality and a much lower cost. However, the decision meant that 70 percent of Schwinn's U.S. workers would lose their jobs. But Schwinn kept expanding its China operations and soon started selling bicycles in the Chinese market—not only at the low end but also to the high-end, luxury segment—leveraging its brand name. Schwinn then extended its global operations and reach by adding new facilities in eastern Europe and Brazil. The company has sold over 500,000 bikes in new markets and now has more employees in the United States than it did before deciding to expand into international markets.

Discussion Question

By facing fierce competition from low-cost rivals, many business-to-business firms in the United States and Europe face a situation today similar to Schwinn's. What lessons can they draw from the Schwinn story? How can they strengthen their competitive position?

---

[34]Harold L. Sirkin, "Don't Be a Schwinn," *BCG/Perspectives*, The Boston Consulting Group, Inc., January 2005, accessed at http://www.bcg.com.

Managing Products
for Business Markets

By providing a solution for customers, the product is the central force of business marketing strategy. The firm's ability to put together a line of products and services that provide superior value to customers is the heart of business marketing management. After reading this chapter, you will understand:

1. core products—the tangible link between core competencies and end products.

2. the strategic importance of providing competitively superior value to customers.

3. the various types of industrial product lines and the value of product positioning.

4. how to build a strong high-tech brand.

5. a strategic approach for managing products across the stages of the technology adoption life cycle.

Gary Hamel asserts that "In every industry, there is a ratio that relates price to performance: X units of cash buys Y units of value. The challenge is to improve that ratio and to do so radically. . . ."[1] Smart marketing means thinking of your company and product in a fresh way and choosing the way to lead.[2] A business marketer's marketplace identity is established through the products and services it offers. Without careful product planning and control, marketers are often guilty of introducing products that are inconsistent with market needs, arbitrarily adding items that contribute little to existing product lines and maintaining weak products that could be profitably eliminated.

Product management is directly linked to market analysis and market selection. Products are developed to fit the needs of the market and are modified as those needs change. Drawing on such tools of demand analysis as business market segmentation and market potential forecasting, the marketer evaluates opportunities and selects profitable market segments, thus determining the direction of product policy. Product policy cannot be separated from market selection decisions. In evaluating potential product/market fits, a firm must evaluate new market opportunities, determine the number and aggressiveness of competitors, and gauge its own strengths and weaknesses. The marketing function assumes a lead role in transforming an organization's distinctive skills and resources into products and services that enjoy positional advantages in the market.[3]

This chapter first explores the strategic importance of core competencies—the roots of successful industrial products—and isolates the distinctive skills of leading-edge companies. Second, it examines product quality and value from the customer's perspective and directly links them to business marketing strategy. Third, because industrial products can assume several forms, the chapter describes industrial product-line options, while offering an approach for positioning and managing products in high-technology markets.

Core Competencies: The Roots of Industrial Products[4]

You can miss the strength of business market competitors by looking only at their product line, in the same way that you can underestimate the strength of a tree if you look only at its leaves. C. K. Prahalad and Gary Hamel offer this analogy: "The diversified corporation is a large tree. The trunk and major limbs are core products, the smaller branches are business units; the leaves, flowers, and fruit are end products. The root system that provides nourishment, sustenance, and stability is the core competence."[5] The success of firms such as 3M, Honda, Canon, Honeywell, Motorola, and others can be traced to a particular set of competencies that each has developed and enriched.

Core competencies are embodied in the superior skills of employees—the technologies they have mastered, the unique ways they combine these technologies, and the market

---

[1] Gary Hamel, "Strategy as Revolution," *Harvard Business Review* 74 (July–August 1996): p. 72. See also Gary Hamel and Gary Getz, "Funding Growth in an Age of Austerity," *Harvard Business Review* 82 (July–August 2004): pp. 76–84.

[2] Regis McKenna, *Relationship Marketing* (Reading, Mass.: Addison-Wesley, 1991), p. 7.

[3] Rajan Varadarajan and Satish Jayachandran, "Marketing Strategy: An Assessment of the State of the Field and Outlook," *Journal of the Academy of Marketing Science* 27 (spring 1999): pp. 120–143.

[4] This discussion is based on C. K. Prahalad and Gary Hamel, "The Core Competence of the Organization," *Harvard Business Review* 68 (May–June 1990): pp. 79–91. See also Gary Hamel, *Leading the Revolution* (Boston: Harvard Business School Press, 2000).

[5] Prahalad and Hamel, "The Core Competence," p. 82.

knowledge they accumulate.[6] Thus, core competencies constitute the collective learning of the organization. They focus on the basics of what creates value from the customer's perspective and include both technical and organizational skills. For example, a core competence of Honda is designing and developing small motors. To apply this competence to one of its products, Honda must ensure that R&D scientists, engineers, and marketers share an understanding of consumer needs and of the technological possibilities.

Identifying Core Competencies

Three tests can be applied to identify a firm's core competencies. First, a core competence provides potential access to an array of markets. Capitalizing on its core competencies in precision mechanics, fine optics, and micro-electronics, Canon is a strong competitor in markets as diverse as cameras, laser printers, fax equipment, and image scanners (Figure 9.1). Canon appeared to be merely a camera producer at the point when it was preparing to become a world leader in copiers. More recently, Canon developed display technology for flat-panel TVs and is studying a projection-type display technology for large-screen TVs.[7]

Second, a core competence should make an important contribution to the benefits customers perceive in the firm's end products. To illustrate, Honda's core competency in small engines is tied directly to important benefits customers seek: product reliability and fuel efficiency. Honda emphasizes these benefits in its marketing strategy across product lines: motorcycles, automobiles, lawn mowers, snow blowers, and lawn tools.

Third, Prahalad and Hamel point out that "a core competence should be difficult for competitors to imitate. And it will be difficult if it is a complex harmonization of individual technologies and production skills."[8] Even though rivals might acquire the same production equipment or some of the technologies that contribute to a core competence of Intel, they may encounter severe difficulty in duplicating its internal pattern of coordination and learning.

Sustaining the Lead

McKinsey consultants Kevin Coyne, Stephen Hall, and Patricia Gorman Clifford suggest that a firm should consider how quickly its best-positioned rival could imitate its competence, assuming it knew how.[9] They suggest that a firm's strategist should consider three questions:

- *How rare is our competence?*   Rareness involves comparing the competence of your firm to those of other firms across various industries. The fewer examples of similar competencies you find, the more likely it is that your firm possesses distinctive capabilities.

  Example: High-technology product development and rollout by Cisco Systems.

- *How long will it take your competitors to develop the competence?*   Even if a competitor sets out to copy a competence, your advantage will not be eroded immediately.

---

[6] George S. Day, "Marketing's Contribution to the Strategic Dialogue," *Journal of the Academy of Marketing Science* 20 (fall 1992): p. 326.

[7] "Canon Will Develop Some Display Lines in Next Two Years," *The Wall Street Journal*, September 22, 2005, p. B8.

[8] Prahalad and Hamel, "The Core Competence," p. 84.

[9] Kevin P. Coyne, Stephen J. D. Hall, and Patricia Gorman Clifford, "Is Your Core Competence a Mirage?" *The McKinsey Quarterly*, no. 1 (1997): pp. 40–54.

FIGURE 9.1 | **CORE COMPETENCIES AND SELECTED PRODUCTS AT CANON**

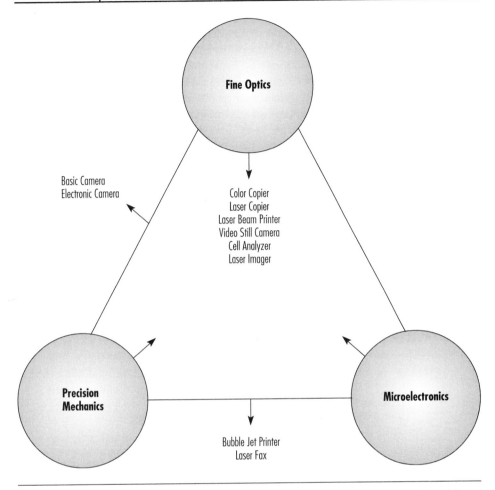

SOURCE: Adapted from C. K. Prahalad and Gary Hamel, "The Core Competence of the Corporation," *Harvard Business Review* 68 (May–June 1990): pp. 75–84.

The imitator may need months or years to train personnel, revise policies, and make the multitude of other changes necessary to create and sustain a competence. Particularly difficult and time-consuming to replicate are competencies that involve cross-functional processes and include external groups such as important suppliers and leading-edge customers.

Example: Rapid product development process at Intel.

- *Can your competitors easily understand the source of your advantage?* Often, the source of a competitor's competence is difficult to pinpoint. For example, skills may be deeply embedded in a company's culture, such as the service responsiveness in FedEx's frontline execution strategies. In general, a core competence comprising only a few elements is much easier for a competitor to understand and match than one that relies on the subtle alignment of myriad elements.

Example: The rich, informal processes and communication networks that guide strategy at 3M.

From Core Products to End Products

Core products—the tangible link between core competencies and end products—are the components or subassemblies that significantly contribute to the value of end products. Although Canon has a small share of the laser printer market (end product), the firm reputedly holds more than an 80 percent world manufacturing share in desktop laser printer "engines" (core product). Strategy experts suggest that core-product share may better predict profitability than traditional measures of end-product market share.[10] By providing core products for a variety of markets, a firm secures the resources and market knowledge to enhance and extend its chosen core competence areas. In turn, the firm can assume a leading role in shaping new applications and developing new end markets.

Exploiting Selected Core Competencies

Realizing that they cannot dominate in every activity, leading business marketers concentrate their talent and resources on selected core competencies that will be crucial in serving customers in the future. The 3M company provides a classic example.[11] The firm's growth for the past several decades has been spawned largely by its R&D skills in three critical related technologies: adhesives, abrasives, and coating/bonding. In each of these areas, 3M has developed a knowledge base and a depth of skills surpassing those of its major competitors. These historic competencies, coupled with the firm's unique innovation system and entrepreneurial values, have given 3M a continuing stream of successful products: From a producer of sandpaper in the 1920s, historic core competencies have combined to produce Post-it notes, magnetic tape, pressure-sensitive tapes, coated abrasives, photographic film, and a wealth of other products.

Business marketing strategists, then, should address these questions in planning product strategy:

- What important benefits do our core competencies allow us to deliver to customers?

- How could we combine our competencies in exciting new ways to deliver more value to existing customers or to serve new customer segments in other industries?

Experiment with Product Strategy!   Most companies would be better off if they made fewer billion-dollar bets and more $20,000 bets. In time, some of these initiatives will justify more substantial commitments.[12] Strategy requires good predictions, but the world is inherently unpredictable. So, what's a product strategist to do? McKinsey & Company studied 30 leading growth companies and found that they pursue a portfolio of strategic initiatives that includes a number of probing, experimental strategies for new markets.[13] **Strategic experimentation** occurs when a firm pursues a variety of strategy paths in parallel within a given business. Indeed, some of

---

[10] C. K. Prahalad, "Weak Signals versus Strong Paradigms," *Journal of Marketing Research* 32 (August 1995): pp. iii–vi.

[11] Andrew Hargadon, *How Breakthroughs Happen: The Surprising Truth about How Companies Innovate* (Boston: Harvard Business School Press, 2003), pp. 169–174.

[12] Gary Hamel and Liisa Välikangas, "The Quest for Resilience," *Harvard Business Review* 81 (September–October 2003): p. 59.

[13] Eric D. Beinhocker and Sarah Kaplan, "Tired of Strategic Planning?" *The McKinsey Quarterly* Special Edition: *Risk and Resilience*, no. 3 (2002): p. 55.

the tested strategies may compete directly with the firm's current strategies. However, these are not random strategy experiments—each strategy builds on the business's core competencies and is designed to test a specific hypothesis about where future market opportunities may be found.

See What Works Capital One, the highly successful financial services firm, uses experimentation. At any time, the firm is running scores of experiments with various product market strategies. The company rapidly develops new strategy ideas, tests them in the marketplace, learns "what works and what doesn't," backs the winning strategies, and cancels the losing ones. In this way, Capital One "generates more hits than its less prolific competitors, is better prepared to shift its focus when a particular product strategy starts faltering, and can afford to try things that more traditional competitors would shy away from."[14] Richard Fairbank, Capital One's chairman and chief executive officer, describes the company's strategy approach this way: "Rather than wait for the competition to obsolete our products, we do it ourselves."[15]

Product Quality

Increasing global competition and rising customer expectations make product quality and customer value important strategic priorities. On a global scale, many international companies insist that suppliers, as a prerequisite for negotiations, meet quality standards set out by the Geneva-based International Standards Organization (ISO). These quality requirements, referred to as **ISO-9000 standards,** were developed for the European Community, but have gained a global following.[16] Certification requires a supplier to thoroughly document its quality-assurance program. The certification program is becoming a seal of approval to compete for business not only overseas but also in the United States. For instance, the Department of Defense employs ISO standards in its contract guidelines. Although Japanese firms continue to set the pace in the application of sophisticated quality-control procedures in manufacturing, companies such as Kodak, AT&T, Xerox, Ford, Hewlett-Packard, Intel, GE, and others have made significant strides.

The quest for improved product quality touches the entire supply chain as these and other companies demand improved product quality from their suppliers, large and small. For example, GE has an organization-wide goal of achieving Six Sigma quality, meaning that a product would have a defect level of no more than 3.4 parts per million. Using the Six Sigma approach, GE measures every process, identifies the variables that lead to defects, and takes steps to eliminate them. GE also works directly to assist suppliers in using the approach. Overall, GE reports that Six Sigma has produced striking results—cost savings in the billions and fundamental improvements in product and service quality. Recently, GE has centered its Six Sigma efforts on functions that "teach customers," such as marketing and sales.[17]

---

[14] Eric D. Beinhocker, "Robust Adaptive Strategies," in *Strategic Thinking for the Next Economy*, ed. Michael A. Cusumano and Constantinos C. Markides (San Francisco: Jossey-Bass, 2001), pp. 131–155.

[15] Beinhocker and Kaplan, "Tired of Strategic Planning?" p. 140.

[16] Wade Ferguson, "Impact of ISO 9000 Series Standards on Industrial Marketing," *Industrial Marketing Management* 25 (July 1996): pp. 325–310.

[17] Erin White, "Rethinking the Quality-Improvement Program," *The Wall Street Journal*, September 19, 2005, p. B3.

Meaning of Quality

The quality movement has passed through several stages.[18] *Stage one* centered on conformance to standards or success in meeting specifications. But conformance quality or zero defects do not satisfy a customer if the product embodies the wrong features. *Stage two* emphasized that quality was more than a technical specialty and that pursuing it should drive the core processes of the entire business. Particular emphasis was given to total quality management and measuring customer satisfaction. However, customers choose a particular product over competing offerings because they perceive it as providing superior *value*—the product's price, performance, and service render it the most attractive alternative. *Stage three*, then, examines a firm's quality performance relative to competitors and examines customer perceptions of the value of competing products. The focus here is on market-perceived quality and value versus that of competitors. Moreover, attention shifts from zero defects in products to zero defections of customers (i.e., *customer loyalty*). Merely satisfying customers who have the freedom to make choices is not enough to keep them loyal.[19]

Meaning of Customer Value

Strategy experts Dwight Gertz and Joõa Baptista suggest that "a company's product or service is competitively superior if, at price equality with competing products, target segments always choose it. Thus, value is defined in terms of consumer choice in a competitive context."[20] In turn, the value equation includes a vital service component. For the service component, business marketing strategists must "recognize that specifications aren't just set by a manufacturer who tells the customer what to expect; instead, consumers also may participate in setting specifications." Frontline sales and service personnel add value to the product offering and the consumption experience by meeting or, indeed, exceeding the customer's service expectations.[21] **Customer value,** then, represents a "business customer's overall assessment of a relationship with a supplier based on perceptions of benefits received and sacrifices made."[22]

Benefits   Customer benefits take two forms (Figure 9.2):

1. *Core benefits*—the core requirements (for example specified product quality) for a relationship that suppliers must fully meet to be included in the customer's consideration set.

2. *Add-on benefits*—attributes that differentiate suppliers, go beyond the basic denominator provided by all qualified vendors, and create added value in a buyer-seller relationship (for example, value-added customer service).

---

[18] Bradley T. Gale, *Managing Customer Value: Creating Quality and Service That Customers Can See* (New York: The Free Press, 1994), pp. 25–30.

[19] Thomas O. Jones and W. Earl Sasser, "Why Satisfied Customers Defect," *Harvard Business Review* 73 (November–December 1995): pp. 88–99; and Richard L. Oliver, "Whence Customer Loyalty," *Journal of Marketing* 63 (Special Issue 1999): pp. 33–44.

[20] Dwight L. Gertz and João P. A. Baptista, *Grow to Be Great: Breaking the Downsizing Cycle* (New York: The Free Press, 1995), p. 128.

[21] C. K. Prahalad and M. S. Krishnan, "The New Meaning of Quality in the Information Age," *Harvard Business Review* 77 (September–October 1999): pp. 109–112. See also, C. K. Prahalad and Venkat Ramaswamy, *The Future of Competition: Co-Creating Unique Value with Customers* (Boston: Harvard Business School Press, 2004).

[22] Ajay Menon, Christian Homburg, and Nikolas Beutin, "Understanding Customer Value in Business-to-Business Relationships," *Journal of Business-to-Business Marketing* 12, no. 2 (2005): p. 5.

FIGURE 9.2 | WHAT VALUE MEANS TO BUSINESS CUSTOMERS

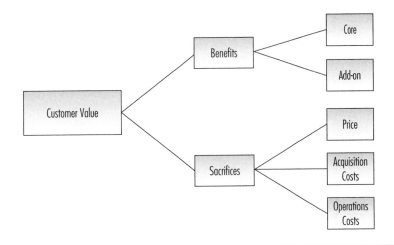

SOURCE: Adapted from Ajay Menon, Christian Homburg, and Nikolas Beutin, "Understanding Customer Value," *Journal of Business-to-Business Marketing* 12, no. 2 (2005): pp. 4–7.

Sacrifices   Consistent with the total cost perspective that business customers emphasize (Chapter 2), sacrifices include (1) the purchase price, (2) acquisition costs (for example, ordering and delivery costs), and (3) operations costs (for example, defect-free incoming shipments of component parts reduces operations costs).

What Matters Most?   Based on a large study of nearly 1,000 purchasing managers across a wide variety of product categories in the United States and Germany, Ajay Menon, Christian Homburg, and Nikolas Beutin uncovered some rich insights into customer value in business-to-business relationships.[23]

Add-on Benefits   First, the research demonstrates that add-on benefits more strongly influence customer value than do core benefits. Why? All qualified suppliers perform well on core benefits, so add-on benefits tend to be the differentiator for customer value as customers choose among competing offerings. Therefore, business marketers can use value-added services or joint working relationships that influence add-on benefits to strengthen customer relationships. For example, a leading manufacturer of tires for earthmoving equipment offers free consulting services that help customers design maintenance procedures that yield significant cost savings.[24]

Trust   Second, the study reinforces the vital role of trust in a business relationship (see Chapter 4), demonstrating, in fact, that trust has a stronger impact on core benefits than product characteristics.

Reducing Customer's Costs   Third, the results highlight the importance of marketing strategies that are designed to assist the customer in reducing operations costs. The research team observes:

> Ensuring on-time delivery of components and raw materials, getting involved in the customer firm's manufacturing and R&D strategy-making

---

[23] Ibid., pp. 1–33.

[24] Das Narayandas, "Building Loyalty in Business Markets," *Harvard Business Review* 83 (September–October 2005): p. 134.

processes, and deploying resources needed to ensure a smooth relationship with the customer will help reduce the customer's operations costs.[25]

By pursuing such initiatives, the business marketer does not have to rely solely on price to demonstrate and deliver value to the customer.

Product Support Strategy: The Service Connection

The marketing function must ensure that every part of the organization focuses on delivering superior value to customers. Business marketing programs involve a number of critical components that customers carefully evaluate: tangible products, service support, and ongoing information services both before and after the sale. To provide value and to successfully implement these programs, the business marketing firm must carefully coordinate activities among personnel in product management, sales, and service.[26] For example, to customize a product and delivery schedule for an important customer requires close coordination among product, logistics, and sales personnel. Moreover, some customer accounts might require special field-engineering, installation, or equipment support, thereby increasing the required coordination between sales and service units.

Post-purchase service is especially important to buyers in many industrial product categories ranging from computers and machine tools to custom-designed component parts. Responsibility for service support, however, is often diffused throughout various departments, such as applications engineering, customer relations, or service administration. Significant benefits accrue to the business marketer who carefully manages and coordinates product, sales, and service connections to maximize customer value.

Product Policy

Product policy involves the set of all decisions concerning the products and services that the company offers. Through product policy, a business marketing firm attempts to satisfy customer needs and to build a sustainable competitive advantage by capitalizing on its core competencies. This section explores the types of industrial product lines and the importance of anchoring product management decisions on an accurate definition of the product market. A framework is also provided for assessing product opportunities on a global scale.

Types of Product Lines Defined

Because product lines of industrial firms differ from those of consumer firms, classification is useful. Industrial product lines can be categorized into four types[27]:

1. **Proprietary or catalog products.**   These items are offered only in certain configurations and produced in anticipation of orders. Product-line decisions concern adding, deleting, or repositioning products in the line.

2. **Custom-built products.**   These items are offered as a set of basic units, with numerous accessories and options. For example, NCR offers a line of retail

---

[25] Menon, Homburg, and Beutin, "Understanding Customer Value," p. 25.

[26] Frank V. Cespedes, *Concurrent Marketing: Integrating Product, Sales, and Service* (Boston: Harvard Business School Press, 1995), pp. 58–85.

[27] Benson P. Shapiro, *Industrial Product Policy: Managing the Existing Product Line* (Cambridge, Mass.: Marketing Science Institute, 1977), pp. 37–39.

workstations used by large customers like Wal-Mart and 7-Eleven stores as well as by smaller businesses. The basic workstation can be expanded to connect to scanners, check readers, electronic payment devices, and other accessories to meet a business's particular needs. The firm's wide array of products provides retailers with an end-to-end solution, from data warehousing to the point-of-service workstation at checkout. The marketer offers the organizational buyer a set of building blocks. Product-line decisions center on offering the proper mix of options and accessories.

3. **Custom-designed products.**   These items are created to meet the needs of one or a small group of customers. Sometimes the product is a unique unit, such as a power plant or a specific machine tool. In addition, some items produced in relatively large quantities, such as an aircraft model, may fall into this category. The product line is described in terms of the company's capability, and the consumer buys that capability. Ultimately, this capability is transformed into a finished good. For example, after canvassing airlines around the world, Airbus Industrie detected enough interest in a super jumbo jet to proceed with development.[28]

4. **Industrial services.**   Rather than an actual product, the buyer is purchasing a company's capability in an area such as maintenance, technical service, or management consulting. (Special attention is given to services marketing in Chapter 11.)

All types of business marketing firms confront product policy decisions, whether they offer physical products, pure services (no physical product), or a product-service combination.[29] Each product situation presents unique problems and opportunities for the business marketer; each draws on a unique capability. Product strategy rests on the intelligent use of corporate capability.

Defining the Product Market

Accurately defining the product market is fundamental to sound product policy decisions.[30] Careful attention must be given to the alternative ways to satisfy customer needs. For example, many different products could provide competition for personal computers. Application-specific products, such as enhanced pocket pagers and smart phones that send e-mail and connect to the Web, are potential competitors. A wide array of information appliances that provide easy access to the Internet also pose a threat. In such an environment, Regis McKenna maintains, managers "must look for opportunities in—and expect competition from—every possible direction. A company with a narrow product concept will move through the market with blinders on, and it is sure to run into trouble."[31] By excluding products and technology that compete for the same end-user needs, the product strategist can quickly become out of touch with the market. Both customer needs and the ways of satisfying those needs change.

---

[28] Alex Taylor III, "Blue Skies for Airbus," *Fortune*, April 1, 1999, pp. 102–108.

[29] Albert L. Page and Michael Siemplenski, "Product-Systems Marketing," *Industrial Marketing Management* 12 (April 1983): pp. 89–99.

[30] For a related discussion on competitive analysis, see Beth A. Walker, Dimitri Kapelianis, and Michael D. Hutt, "Competitive Cognition," *MIT Sloan Management Review* 46 (summer 2005): pp. 10–12.

[31] Regis McKenna, *Relationship Marketing*, p. 184.

Product Market   A **product market** establishes the distinct arena in which the business marketer competes. Four dimensions of a market definition are strategically relevant:

1. *Customer function dimension.*   This involves the benefits that are provided to satisfy the needs of organizational buyers (for example, mobile messaging).

2. *Technological dimension.*   There are alternative ways a particular function can be performed (for example, cell phone, pager, notebook computer).

3. *Customer segment dimension.*   Customer groups have distinct needs that must be served (for example, sales representatives, physicians, international travelers).

4. *Value-added system dimension.*   Competitors serving the market can operate along a sequence of stages.[32] The value-added system for wireless communication includes equipment providers, such as Nokia and Motorola, and service providers, like Verizon and Sprint. Analysis of the value-added system may indicate potential opportunities or threats from changes in the system (for example, potential alliances between equipment and service providers).

Planning for Today and Tomorrow   Competition to satisfy the customer's need exists at the technology level as well as at the supplier or brand level. By establishing accurate product-market boundaries, the product strategist is better equipped to identify customer needs, the benefits sought by the market segment, and the turbulent nature of competition at both the technology and supplier or brand levels. Derek Abell offers these valuable strategy insights:

- Planning for today requires a clear, precise *definition* of the business—a delineation of target customer segments, customer functions, and the business approach to be taken; planning for tomorrow is concerned with how the business should be *redefined* for the future.

- Planning for today focuses on *shaping up* the business to meet the needs of today's customers with excellence. It involves identifying factors that are critical to success and smothering them with attention; planning for tomorrow can entail *reshaping* the business to compete more effectively in the future.[33]

Seeing What's Next   Strategy experts also argue provocatively that many firms are overlooking three important customer groups that may present the greatest opportunity for explosive growth[34]:

- *Nonconsumers* who may lack the specialized skills, training, or resources to purchase the product or service.

- *Undershot customers* for whom existing products are not good enough.

- *Overshot customers* for whom existing products provide more performance than they can use.

---

[32] George S. Day, *Strategic Market Planning: The Pursuit of Competitive Advantage* (St. Paul, Minn.: West, 1984), p. 73.

[33] Derek F. Abell, "Competing Today While Preparing for Tomorrow," *Sloan Management Review* 40 (spring 1999): p. 74.

[34] Clayton M. Christensen, Scott D. Anthony, and Erik A. Roth, *Seeing What's Next* (Boston: Harvard Business School Press, 2004), p. 5.

B2B TOP PERFORMERS

BASF: Using Services to Build a Strong Brand

BASF AG, headquartered in Germany, is the world's largest chemical company, with global sales over $33 billion and North American sales of $8 billion. Consistently ranked as one of *Fortune*'s most admired global companies, the firm competes in what many would describe as a commodity business. Rather than pursue a low-total-cost strategy and compete on price, BASF decided to transform itself into an innovative service-oriented company. Services, like R&D support or on-site field services, are hard for rivals to duplicate and when well executed, provide the ultimate differentiation strategy. To communicate its value proposition to customers, the firm launched its advertising campaign with the familiar tag line:

"We don't make a lot of products you buy. We make a lot of the products you buy better."

A senior executive at BASF's ad agency, Tony Graetzer, describes the rationale for this campaign, which has been recognized with numerous awards: "Companies are frequently viewed as tied on the quality of their products, but they are never viewed as tied on the quality of their services." Winning companies provide superior service. By emphasizing how it helps make its customers' products better and delivering on its promises, the BASF brand has become synonymous with customer partnerships and technology leadership.

SOURCE: Bob Lamons, *The Case for B2B Branding* (Mason, Ohio: Thomson, 2005), pp. 91–94.

Planning Industrial Product Strategy

Formulating a strategic marketing plan for an existing product line is the most vital part of a company's marketing planning efforts. Having identified a product market, attention now turns to planning product strategy. Product positioning analysis provides a useful tool for charting the strategy course.

Product Positioning

Once the product market is defined, a strong competitive position for the product must be secured. **Product positioning** represents the place that a product occupies in a particular market; it is found by measuring organizational buyers' perceptions and preferences for a product in relation to its competitors. Because organizational buyers perceive products as bundles of attributes (for example, quality, service), the product strategist should examine the attributes that assume a central role in buying decisions.

The Process[35]

Observe from Figure 9.3 that the positioning process begins by identifying the relevant set of competing products (Step 1) and defining those attributes that are **determinant** (Step 2)—attributes that customers use to differentiate among the alternatives

---

[35] This section is based on Harper W. Boyd Jr., Orville C. Walker Jr., and Jean-Claude Larréché, *Marketing Management: A Strategic Approach with a Global Orientation* (Chicago: Irwin/McGraw-Hill, 1998), pp. 190–200.

FIGURE 9.3 | STEPS IN THE PRODUCT-POSITIONING PROCESS

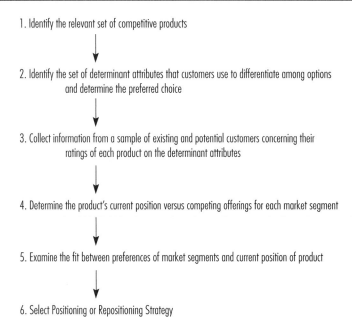

1. Identify the relevant set of competitive products

2. Identify the set of determinant attributes that customers use to differentiate among options and determine the preferred choice

3. Collect information from a sample of existing and potential customers concerning their ratings of each product on the determinant attributes

4. Determine the product's current position versus competing offerings for each market segment

5. Examine the fit between preferences of market segments and current position of product

6. Select Positioning or Repositioning Strategy

SOURCE: Adapted with modifications from Harper W. Boyd Jr., Orville C. Walker Jr., and Jean-Claude Larréché, *Marketing Management: A Strategic Approach with a Global Orientation* (Chicago: Irwin/McGraw-Hill, 1998), p. 197.

and that are important to them in determining which brand they prefer. In short, then, determinant attributes are choice criteria that are both important and differentiating. Of course, some attributes are important to organizational buyers, but they may not be differentiating. For example, safety might be an important attribute in the heavy-duty truck market, but business market customers may consider the competing products offered by Navistar, Volvo, and Mack Trucks as quite comparable on this dimension. Durability, reliability, and fuel economy might constitute the determinant attributes.

Step 3 involves collecting information from a sample of existing and potential customers concerning how they perceive the various options on each of the determinant attributes. The sample should include buyers (particularly buying influentials) from organizations that represent the full array of market segments the product strategist wishes to serve. After examining the product's current position versus competing offerings (Step 4), the analyst can isolate (1) the competitive strength of the product in different segments and (2) the opportunities for securing a differentiated position in a particular target segment (Step 5).

Isolating Strategy Opportunities

Step 6 involves the selection of the positioning or repositioning strategy. Here the product manager can evaluate particular strategy options. First, for some attributes, the product manager may wish to (1) pursue a strategy to increase the importance of an attribute to customers and (2) increase the difference between the competition's and the firm's products. For example, the importance of an attribute such as customer training might be elevated through marketing communications emphasizing how the potential buyer can increase its efficiency and employee performance through the firm's training. If successful, such efforts might move customer training from an important attribute to a determinant attribute in the eyes of customers. Second, if the firm's performance on a determinant product attribute is truly higher than that of competitors—but the market perceives that other alternatives enjoy an edge—marketing communications can be developed to bring perceptions in line with reality. Third, the competitive standing of a product can be advanced by improving the firm's level of performance on determinant attributes that organizational buyers emphasize.

Product Positioning Illustrated[36]

This product positioning approach was successfully applied to a capital equipment product at a major corporation. The product that provided the focus of the analysis is sold in three sizes to two market segments: end users and consulting engineers. Marketing research identified 15 attributes, including reliability, service support, company reputation, and ease of maintenance.

A New Strategy The research found that the firm's brand enjoyed an outstanding rating on product reliability and service support. Both attributes were generally determinant for the company against most competitors. To reinforce the importance of both attributes, management decided to offer an enhanced warranty program. Both end users and consulting engineers view warranties as important but not a point of differentiation across competing brands. Management surmised, however, that by establishing a new warranty standard for the industry, the attribute could become determinant, adding to the brand's leverage over competitors. In addition, management felt that the new warranty program might also benefit the brand's reputation on other attributes such as reliability and company reputation.

Better Targeting The study also provided some surprises. Price was not nearly as important to organizational buyers as management had initially believed. This suggested that there were opportunities to increase revenue through product differentiation and service support. Likewise, the research found that the firm's brand dominated all competitors in the large- and medium-sized products, but not in the small-sized products. This particular product had an especially weak competitive position in the consulting engineer segment. Special service support strategies were developed to strengthen the product's standing in this segment. Clearly, product positioning provides a valuable tool for designing creative strategies for business markets.

Building a Strong Brand[37]

Although consumer-packaged-goods companies like Procter & Gamble (P&G), Nabisco, and Nestlé have excelled by developing a wealth of enduring and highly profitable brands, a strong brand is also a valuable asset in business markets in general and in high-technology markets in particular. David Aaker says, "**Brand equity** is a set of brand assets

---

[36] This section is based largely on Behram J. Hansotia, Muzaffar A. Shaikh, and Jagdish N. Sheth, "The Strategic Determinancy Approach to Brand Management," *Business Marketing* 70 (fall 1985): pp. 66–69.

[37] Scott Ward, Larry Light, and Jonathan Goldstine, "What High-Tech Managers Need to Know about Brands," *Harvard Business Review* 75 (July–August 1999): pp. 85–95.

and liabilities linked to a brand, its name, and symbol that add to or subtract from the value provided by a product or service to a firm and/or to that firm's customers."[38] The assets and liabilities that impact brand equity include brand loyalty, name awareness, perceived quality, and other brand associations, and proprietary brand assets (for example, patents). Along with consumer-goods names such as Coca Cola, McDonald's, or Nike, the world's most valuable brands include high-tech representatives such as IBM, Dell, Microsoft, Intel, and Hewlett-Packard and leading-edge business-to-business firms like GE, FedEx, 3M, DuPont, and Caterpillar.

Strong Brands Promise and Deliver

Successful brand management involves developing a promise of value for customers and then ensuring that the promise is kept through the way the product is developed, produced, sold, serviced, and promoted. IBM's promise of value is built on its long tradition of superior service and customer support. One major European customer observed: "As long as IBM is in the general price range of competitors, we'll always buy IBM for the service and support. . . ."[39] A **brand,** then, is a distinctive identity that represents an enduring and credible promise of value associated with a particular product, service, or organization. Note that emphasis can be placed on the corporate level or at the subbrand level. For high-tech brands, the emphasis is generally at the corporate level (for example, Oracle or IBM).

A Means of Differentiation   According to Frederick E. Webster Jr. and Kevin Lane Keller[40]:

> The power of a brand resides in the minds of customers. . . . The brand surrounds a product or service with meaning that differentiates it from other products or services intended to satisfy the same need. . . . So, "a brand is much more than a name, and branding is a strategy problem, not a naming problem."

Building Brand Equity

To guide managers in building a strong high-tech brand, Scott Ward, Larry Light, and Jonathan Goldstine developed the brand pyramid (Figure 9.4). Level 1 represents the core product—the tangible product characteristics—whereas Level 2 centers on the "solutions" or "benefits" the brand provides. "The first two levels of the pyramid still embody the elements of product competition, not those of brand competition. Competitors can continually match and leapfrog over one another by offering better and more features and by identifying the benefits of their products for customers."[41]

By providing psychological rewards or emotional benefits to customers, a firm can truly differentiate itself from competitors at Level 3. How do customers feel about the benefits of the brand? Confident? Productive? Innovative? Brands that reside in the

---

[38] David Aaker, *Managing Brand Equity* (New York: The Free Press, 1991), p. 15. For a comprehensive review, see also John Kim, David A. Reid, Richard E. Plank, and Robert Dahlstrom, "Examining the Role of Brand Equity in Business Markets: A Model, Research Propositions, and Managerial Implications," *Journal of Business-to-Business Marketing* 5, no. 3 (1998): pp. 65–89.

[39] Ward, Light, and Goldstine, "What High-Tech Managers Need to Know," p. 89.

[40] Frederick E. Webster Jr. and Kevin Lane Keller, "A Roadmap for Branding in Industrial Markets," *Journal of Brand Management* 11 (May 2004): p. 389.

[41] Ibid., p. 91.

FIGURE 9.4 | HOW HIGH-TECH BRANDS BUILD EQUITY

To build a strong high-tech brand, managers need to answer the following questions:

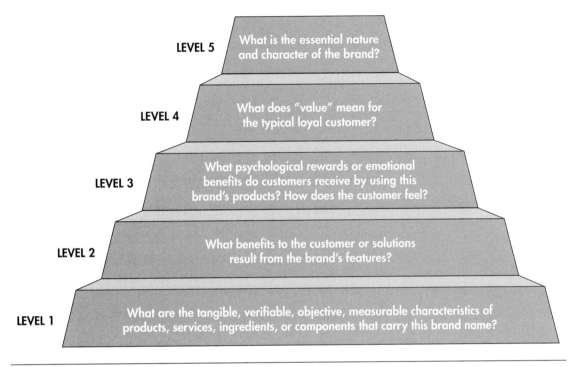

LEVEL 5 — What is the essential nature and character of the brand?

LEVEL 4 — What does "value" mean for the typical loyal customer?

LEVEL 3 — What psychological rewards or emotional benefits do customers receive by using this brand's products? How does the customer feel?

LEVEL 2 — What benefits to the customer or solutions result from the brand's features?

LEVEL 1 — What are the tangible, verifiable, objective, measurable characteristics of products, services, ingredients, or components that carry this brand name?

third level are developed and positioned to fulfill a promise of value to selected customers, not simply as technologies in search of a market. Apple Inc., particularly its iMac campaign, comes to mind.

Brand Personality   The top two levels of the pyramid suggest that a strong brand provides a promise of value that attracts and holds customers. Level 4 describes the deeper values (for example, achievement-oriented values or conservative values) the brand reflects. A strong brand reflects the values of the target customer, and this creates and reinforces brand loyalty. The top level of the pyramid captures the personality of the brand. This is how a brand would be described if it had human qualities: friendly, warm, decisive, confident, aggressive. To illustrate, the brand personality of Apple might be described as "fun"; IBM as "confident"; Sun Microsystems as "daring"; Oracle as "aggressive"; or Caterpillar as "rugged." Together, Levels 4 and 5 isolate the relevant and differentiating character of the brand.

By developing a clearly defined value proposition for customers that is understood across all business functions, strong brand management provides a powerful unifying force throughout the business-to-business firm.[42] Externally, a strong brand breeds

---

[42] Bob Lamons, *The Case for B2B Branding* (Mason, Ohio: Thomson, 2005), pp. 9–14.

loyal customers. In the face of swiftly changing technology and in times of uncertainty, buyers turn to a company that understands their needs—one they have grown to trust.[43]

Does Brand Building Pay Off?[44]

A host of high-technology companies have launched brand-building initiatives, but do such investments generate positive returns? Some recent research on the brand attitude of buyers in evaluating computer-related firms provides some answers. Brand attitude is a component and indicator of brand equity. **Brand attitude** is defined as the percentage of organizational buyers who have a positive image of a company minus those with a negative opinion. This study found that changes in brand attitude are associated with stock market performance and tend to lead accounting financial performance (that is, an increase in brand attitude will be reflected in improved financial performance three to six months later). In short, the research demonstrates that investments in building brand attitude for high-technology firms do indeed pay off and increase the firm's value.

Drivers of Brand Attitude Change   Several factors can prompt changes in brand attitude for high-technology firms:

- Dramatic and visible new products that were aggressively supported by advertising were associated with meaningful increases in brand attitude (for example, IBM ThinkPad, and Microsoft Windows).

- Increases in brand attitude were associated with the appointment of a well-recognized executive officer who introduced a new strategy (for example, Steve Jobs returned to Apple).

- Brand attitude depends on competitive actions (for example, after Canon ran a hard-hitting comparison advertising campaign about Hewlett-Packard printers, H-P's brand attitude declined).

- Product problems were associated with several declines in brand attitude (for example, Novell's operating system problems were associated with declines in brand attitude).

- Legal actions were associated with decreases in brand attitude (for example, Microsoft's brand attitude was hurt by widespread discussion of its business practices as a result of the antitrust case brought by the U.S. Department of Justice).

The Technology Adoption Life Cycle

After decades of being content with letters, telegrams, and telephones, consumers have embraced voice-mail, e-mail, Internet browsers, and a range of information appliances. In each case, the conversion of the market came slowly. Once a particular threshold of consumer acceptance was achieved, there was a stampede. Geoffrey Moore defines

---

[43] S. M. Mudambi, "Branding Importance in Business-to-Business Markets: Three Buyer Clusters," *Industrial Marketing Management* 31 (September 2002): pp. 525–533.

[44] This section is based on David A. Aaker and Robert Jacobson, "The Value Relevance of Brand Attitude in High-Technology Markets," *Journal of Marketing Research* 38 (November 2001): pp. 485–493.

| TABLE 9.1 | THE TECHNOLOGY ADOPTION LIFE CYCLE: CLASSES OF CUSTOMERS |

Customer	Profile
Technology enthusiasts (*innovators*)	Interested in exploring the latest innovation, these consumers possess significant influence over how products are perceived by others in the organization but lack control over resource commitments.
Visionaries (*early adopters*)	Desiring to exploit the innovation for a competitive advantage, these consumers are the true revolutionaries in business and government who have access to organizational resources but frequently demand special modifications to the product that are difficult for the innovator to provide.
Pragmatists (*early majority*)	Making the bulk of technology purchases in organizations, these individuals believe in technology evolution, not revolution, and seek products from a market leader with a proven track record of providing useful productivity improvements.
Conservatives (*late majority*)	Pessimistic about their ability to derive any value from technology investments, these individuals represent a sizable group of customers who are price sensitive and reluctantly purchase high-tech products to avoid being left behind.
Skeptics (*laggards*)	Rather than potential customers, these individuals are ever-present critics of the hype surrounding high-technology products.

SOURCE: Adapted from Geoffrey A. Moore, *Inside the Tornado: Marketing Strategies from Silicon Valley's Cutting Edge* (New York: HarperCollins, 1995), pp. 14–18.

discontinuous innovations as "new products or services that require the end-user and the marketplace to dramatically change their past behavior, with the promise of gaining equally-dramatic new benefits."[45] During the past quarter century, discontinuous innovations have been common in the computer-electronics industry, creating massive new spending, fierce competition, and a whole host of firms that are redrawing the boundaries of the high-technology marketplace.

A popular tool with strategists at high-technology firms is the technology adoption life cycle—a framework developed by Geoffrey Moore, a leading consultant to Sun Microsystems, Silicon Graphics, Hewlett-Packard, and others.

Types of Technology Customers

Fundamental to Moore's framework are five classes of customers who constitute the potential market for a discontinuous innovation (Table 9.1). Business marketers can benefit by putting innovative products in the hands of **technology enthusiasts.**

---

[45] Geoffrey A. Moore, *Inside the Tornado: Marketing Strategies from Silicon Valley's Cutting Edge* (New York: HarperCollins, 1995), p. 13.

INSIDE BUSINESS MARKETING

The Gorilla Advantage in High-Tech Markets

High-tech companies that can get their products designed into the very standards of the market have enormous influence over the future direction of that market. For example, all PC-based software has to be Microsoft- and Intel-compatible. All networking solutions must be compatible with Cisco Systems' standards; all printers must be Hewlett-Packard–compatible. This is the essence of gorilla power in high-tech markets that firms such as Microsoft, Intel, Cisco, and Hewlett-Packard enjoy. The gorilla advantage allows these market leaders to:

- *Attract more customers* by enjoying better press coverage and shorter sales cycles just because information technology managers expect it to be the winner.

- *Keep more customers* because the cost of switching is high for customers and the cost of entry is high for competitors.

- *Drive costs down* by shifting some costly enhancements that customers demand to suppliers while retaining control of the critical components of value creation.

- *Keep profits up* because business partners place a priority on developing complementary products and services that make the *whole product* of the market leader worth more to customers than competing products are worth.

The Internet presents an explosive area of growth in many sectors of the high-tech market as firms square off to gain a leadership position in e-procurement, wireless technologies, supply-chain integration, and Web-focused security. The gorilla games are just beginning!

SOURCE: Geoffrey A. Moore, Paul Johnson, and Tom Kippola, *The Gorilla Game: An Investor's Guide to Picking Winners in High-Technology* (New York: HarperBusiness, 1998), pp. 43–70.

They serve as a gatekeeper to the rest of the technology life cycle, and their endorsement is needed for an innovation to get a fair hearing in the organization. Whereas technology enthusiasts possess influence, they do not have ready access to the resources needed to move an organization toward a large-scale commitment to the new technology. By contrast, **visionaries** have resource control and can often be influential in publicizing an innovation's benefits and giving it a boost during the early stages of market development. However, visionaries are difficult for a marketer to serve because each demands special and unique product modifications. Their demands can quickly tax a technology firm's R&D resources and stall the market penetration of the innovation.

The Chasm   Truly innovative products often enjoy a warm welcome from early technology enthusiasts and visionaries, but then sales falter and often even plummet. Frequently, a chasm develops between visionaries who are intuitive and support revolution and the **pragmatists** who are analytical, support evolution, and provide the pathway to the mainstream market. The business marketer that can successfully guide a product across the chasm creates an opportunity to gain acceptance with the mainstream market of pragmatists and conservatives. As Table 9.1 relates, pragmatists make most technology purchases in organizations, and conservatives include a sizable group of customers who are hesitant to buy high-tech products but do so to avoid being left behind.

FIGURE 9.5 | THE LANDSCAPE OF THE TECHNOLOGY ADOPTION LIFE CYCLE

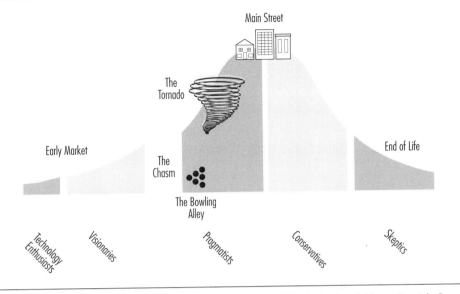

SOURCE: Figure adapted from pages 19, 25 from INSIDE THE TORNADO by Geoffrey A. Moore. Copyright © 1995 by Geoffrey A. Moore Consulting, Inc. Reprinted by permission of HarperCollins Publishers.

Strategies for the Technology Adoption Life Cycle

The fundamental strategy for crossing the chasm and moving from the early market to the mainstream market is to provide pragmatists with a 100 percent solution to their problems (Figure 9.5). Many high-technology firms err by attempting to provide something for everyone while never meeting the complete requirements of any particular market segment. Pragmatists seek the whole product—the minimum set of products and services that provide them with a compelling reason to buy. Geoffrey Moore notes that "the key to a winning strategy is to identify a simple beachhead of pragmatist customers in a mainstream market segment and to accelerate the formation of 100 percent of their whole product. The goal is to win a niche foothold in the mainstream as quickly as possible—that is what is meant by *crossing the chasm*."[46]

The Bowling Alley

In technology markets, each market segment is like a bowling pin, and the momentum from hitting one segment successfully carries over into surrounding segments. The bowling alley represents a stage in the adoption life cycle where a product gains acceptance from mainstream market segments but has yet to be adopted widely.

Consider the evolution of strategy for Lotus Notes.[47] When first introduced, Notes was offered as a new paradigm for corporatewide communication. To cross into

---

[46] Ibid., p. 22. For a related discussion, see Clayton M. Christensen and Michael E. Raynor, *The Innovator's Solution: Creating and Sustaining Successful Growth* (Boston: Harvard Business School Press, 2003), pp. 73–95.

[47] Ibid., Geoffrey A. Moore, *Inside the Tornado*, pp. 35–37.

the mainstream market, the Lotus team shifted the product's focus from an enterprisewide vision of corporate communication to specific solutions for particular business functions. The first niche served was the global account-management function of worldwide accounting and consulting firms. The solution was enhanced account activity coordination for highly visible products. This led to a second niche—global account management for sales teams, where enhanced coordination and information sharing spur productivity.

A Focused Strategy A logical next step for Lotus was movement into the customer-service function, where openly sharing information can support creative solutions to customer problems. Successful penetration of these segments created another opportunity—incorporating the customer into the Notes loop. Note the key lesson here: A customer-based, application-focused strategy provides leverage so that a victory in one market segment cascades into victories in adjacent market segments.

The Tornado

Although economic buyers who seek particular solutions are the key to success in the bowling alley, technical or infrastructure buyers in organizations can spawn a tornado (see Figure 9.5). Information technology (IT) managers are responsible for providing efficient and reliable infrastructures—the systems organizational members use to communicate and perform their jobs. They are pragmatists, and they prefer to buy from an established market leader.

IT professionals interact freely across company and industry boundaries and discuss the ramifications of the latest technology. IT managers watch each other closely—they do not want to be too early or too late. Often, they move together and create a tornado. Because a massive number of new customers are entering the market at the same time and because they all want the same product, demand dramatically outstrips supply and a large backlog of customers can appear overnight. At a critical stage, such market forces have surrounded Hewlett-Packard's laser and inkjet printers, Microsoft's Windows products, Intel's Pentium microprocessors, and Research in Motion's handheld wireless e-mail device.

Tornado Strategy The central success factors for the tornado phase of the adoption life cycle differ from those that are appropriate for the bowling alley. Rather than emphasizing market segmentation, the central goal is to gear up production to capitalize on the opportunity the broad market presents. In its printer business, Hewlett-Packard demonstrated the three critical priorities during a tornado[48]:

1. "Just ship."

2. Extend distribution channels.

3. Drive to the next lower price point.

First, Hewlett-Packard's quality improvement process allowed it to significantly increase production—first with laser printers, and later with inkjet printers—with

---

[48] Ibid., p. 81. See also Stephen Kreider Yoder, "Shaving Back: How H-P Used Tactics of the Japanese to Beat Them at Their Game," *The Wall Street Journal*, September 8, 1994, pp. A1, A6.

few interruptions. Second, to extend market coverage, H-P began to sell its laser printers through PC dealer channels and extended its distribution channels for inkjet printers to computer superstores, office superstores, mail order, and, more recently, to price clubs and other consumer outlets. Third, H-P drove down the price points for its printers—moving inkjet printers below $1,000, then below $500, and then well below that. As this example demonstrates, tornado strategy emphasizes product leadership and operational excellence in manufacturing and distribution.

Main Street

This stage of the technology adoption life cycle represents a period of aftermarket development. The frantic waves of mass-market adoption of the product begin to subside. Competitors in the industry have increased production, and supply now exceeds demand. Moore points out that "the defining characteristic of Main Street is that continued profitable market growth can no longer come from selling the basic commodity to new customers and must come instead from developing niche-specific extensions to the basic platform for existing customers."[49]

Main Street Strategy   The goal here is to develop value-based strategies targeted on particular end user segments. H-P, for example, matches its printers to the special needs of different segments of home-office users by offering:

- A compact portable printer for those users who are space-constrained.

- The OfficeJet printer-fax for those who do not yet own a fax.

- A high-performance color printer for those who create commercial flyers.

Main Street strategy emphasizes operational excellence in production and distribution as well as finely tuned market segmentation strategies. What signals the end of the technology adoption life cycle? A discontinuous innovation appears that incorporates breakthrough technology and promises new solutions for customers.

Summary

The stream of successful products introduced by leading business marketing firms can be traced to a set of unique core competencies that each has developed and continually enriched. Core competencies provide access to an array of markets, make an important contribution to the value customers perceive in a product, and are difficult for competitors to imitate. Conceptualizing a product must go beyond mere physical description to include all the benefits and services that provide value to customers. The unifying goal for the business marketer: *Provide superior market-perceived quality and value versus competitors.* To a business customer, value involves a trade-off between benefits and sacrifices. Business marketers can strengthen customer relationships by providing value-added services and helping customers reduce operations costs. A carefully coordinated product strategy recognizes the role of various functional areas in providing value to

---

[49] Geoffrey A. Moore, *Inside the Tornado*, p. 111.

business customers. Special attention should be given to synchronizing the activities among the product management, sales, and service units.

Industrial product lines can be broadly classified into (1) proprietary or catalog items, (2) custom-built items, (3) custom-designed items, and (4) industrial services. Product management can best be described as the management of capability. In monitoring product performance and in formulating marketing strategy, the business marketer can profitably use product-positioning analysis. By isolating a product's competitive standing in a market, positioning analysis provides strategy insights to the planner. A product attribute is determinant if it is both important and differentiating.

Rapidly changing high-technology markets present special opportunities and challenges for the product strategist. By developing a strong brand that organizational customers come to know and trust, the business marketing firm can gain a competitive advantage in the high-tech market. Research vividly demonstrates that investments in strengthening the image of a high-technology brand yield a positive payoff in the financial performance of the firm. The technology adoption life cycle includes five categories of customers: technology enthusiasts, visionaries, pragmatists, conservatives, and skeptics. New products gain acceptance from niches within the mainstream market, progress from segment to segment like one bowling pin knocking over another, and, if successful, experience the tornado of general, widespread adoption by pragmatists. Importantly, the technology adoption life cycle calls for different marketing strategies at different stages.

Discussion Questions

1. Dell has enjoyed rapid growth and a dominant market position in the computer industry. First, develop a list of what you believe to be the core competencies of Dell. Next, identify which of these core competencies appear to be especially hard for competitors to duplicate.

2. Research in Motion developed BlackBerry—a five-ounce two-way pager that gets e-mail messages, includes a calendar, and can fetch stock quotes, flight information, and other data from the Web. Merrill Lynch bought 1,500 of them for employees at its New York City headquarters. Which customer groups should Research in Motion target with this innovative product? Which features of the product should be emphasized in positioning the BlackBerry against competing products?

3. Regis McKenna notes that "no company in a technology-based industry is safe from unanticipated bumps in the night." In recent years, many industries have been jolted by technological change. In such an environment, what steps can a product strategist take?

4. Bradley Gale, managing director of The Strategic Planning Institute, says: "People systematically knock out income statements and balance sheets, but they often don't monitor the nonfinancial factors that ultimately drive their financial performance. These nonfinancial factors include 'relative customer-perceived quality': how customers view the marketer's offering versus how they perceive competitive offerings." Explain.

5. Distinguish between catalog items, custom-built items, custom-designed items, and services. Explain how marketing requirements vary across these classifications.

6. Evaluate this statement: A brand is much more than a name, and branding is a strategy problem, not a naming problem.

7. A particular product strategy will stimulate a response from the market and a corresponding response from competitors. Which specific features of the competitive environment should the business marketing strategist evaluate?

8. Identify two business-to-business brands that you would deem to be strong and distinctive. Next, describe the characteristics of each brand that tend to set it apart from rival brands.

9. Moving across the technology adoption life cycle, compare and contrast technology enthusiasts with pragmatists. Give special attention to the strategy guidelines that the marketing strategist should follow in reaching customers that fall into these two adoption categories.

10. Firms like Microsoft, Sony, and Intel have experienced a burst of demand for some of their products. During the "tornado" for a high-tech product, the guiding principle of operations for a market leader is "Just ship." Explain and discuss the changes in marketing strategy the firm must follow *after* the tornado.

Internet Exercise

United Technologies Corporation (UTC) provides a broad range of high-technology products and support services to the building systems and aerospace industries. Go to http://www.utc.com and identify UTC's major businesses (product lines).

CASE

NCR Self-Checkout Systems[50]

The NCR Corporation introduced the NCR FastLane, an enhanced self-checkout solution that enabled retailers to deploy self-service technology. Among the initial adopters were food retailers, such as Albertson's, and home improvement and wholesale club retailers, such as Home Depot and BJ's Wholesale Club.

In developing the product, NCR conducted focus-group interviews with consumers, retailers, and cashiers. As a result, NCR's FastLane offers a small footprint in the store and can be easily upgraded to feature small- and large-order bagging areas. The self-service checkout incorporates leading NCR technologies, including touch-screens and scanners, and can accept cash, checks, credit and debit cards, as well as coupons. NCR also recently introduced the FastLane Mini for space-constrained locations such as convenience stores.

Discussion Questions

1. Although consumers consistently rank long checkout lines as their number one shopping complaint, many retailers found that shoppers are not using the self-service checkout option to the degree that they had hoped. What steps can retailers take to spur adoption by shoppers, and how could NCR assist?

2. How might NCR use the technology adoption life cycle as a guide in developing a market strategy for FastLane?

---

[50] "NCR FastLane," Product Description accessed at http://www.ncr.com on September 25, 2005.

Managing Innovation and New Industrial Product Development

The long-term competitive position of most organizations is tied to their ability to innovate—to provide existing and new customers with a continuing stream of new products and services. Innovation is a high-risk and potentially rewarding process. After reading this chapter, you will understand:

1. the strategic processes through which product innovations take shape.

2. the characteristics of innovation winners in high-technology markets.

3. the factors that drive a firm's new product performance.

4. the determinants of new product success and timeliness.

To spur growth at General Electric, CEO Jeffrey Immelt told GE's 11 business unit managers to each take 60 days and return with five ideas for growth that would generate at least $100 million in sales within three years.[1] Of the 55 ideas proposed, 35 were funded, ranging from wind-powered energy systems to sophisticated airport security systems using medical scanning technology. To reinforce the focus on technology and innovation, Beth Comstock, GE's chief marketing officer, introduced a new integrated communications strategy—"Imagination at work"—replacing the well-known theme— "We bring good things to life." A recent global survey of senior executives conducted by the Boston Consulting Group, ranked GE among the most innovative companies in an elite group that included Apple, 3M, and Microsoft.[2]

Many firms derive much of their sales and profits from recently introduced products. But the risks of product innovation are high; significant investments are involved and the likelihood of failure is high. With shortening product life cycles and accelerating technological change, speed and agility are central to success in the innovation battle.[3]

This chapter examines product innovation in the business marketing environment. The first section provides a perspective on the firm's management of innovation. Second, product innovation is positioned within a firm's overall technological strategy. Third, key dimensions of the new-product-development process are examined. Attention centers on the forces that drive successful new product performance in the firm. The final section of the chapter explores the determinants of new product success and timeliness.

The Management of Innovation

Management practices in successful industrial firms reflect the realities of the innovation process itself. James Quinn asserts that "innovation tends to be individually motivated, opportunistic, customer responsive, tumultuous, nonlinear, and interactive in its development. Managers can plan overall directions and goals, but surprises are likely to abound."[4] Clearly, some new-product-development efforts are the outgrowth of deliberate strategies (intended strategies that become realized), whereas others result from emergent strategies (realized strategies that, at least initially, were never intended).[5] Bearing little resemblance to a rational, analytical process, many strategic decisions involving new products are rather messy, disorderly, and disjointed processes around which competing organizational factions contend. In studying successful innovative companies such as Sony, AT&T, and Hewlett-Packard, Quinn characterized the innovation process as controlled chaos:

> Many of the best concepts and solutions come from projects partly hidden or "bootlegged" by the organization. Most successful managers try to build some slack or buffers into their plans to hedge their bets. . . . They permit

[1] Bob Lamons, *The Case for B2B Branding* (Mason, Ohio: Thomson Higher Education, 2005), pp. 142–144.

[2] Jim Andrew, "Innovation 2005," *BCG Senior Management Survey* (Boston: The Boston Consulting Group, April 2005), p. 4, accessed at http://www.bcg.com.

[3] Gary Hamel and Gary Getz, "Funding Growth in an Age of Austerity," *Harvard Business Review* 82 (July–August 2004): pp. 76–84.

[4] James B. Quinn, "Managing Innovation: Controlled Chaos," *Harvard Business Review* 63 (May–June 1985): p. 83.

[5] Henry Mintzberg and James A. Walton, "Of Strategies, Deliberate and Emergent," *Strategic Management Journal* 6 (July–August 1985): pp. 257–272.

chaos and replications in early investigations, but insist on much more formal planning and controls as expensive development and scale-up proceed. But even at these later stages, these managers have learned to maintain flexibility and to avoid the tyranny of paper plans.[6]

Some new products result from a planned, deliberate process, but others follow a more circuitous and chaotic route.[7] Why? Research suggests that strategic activity within a large organization falls into two broad categories: induced and autonomous strategic behavior.[8]

Induced Strategic Behavior

Induced strategic behavior is consistent with the firm's traditional concept of strategy. It takes place in relationship to its familiar external environment (for example, its customary markets). By manipulating various administrative mechanisms, top management can influence the perceived interests of managers at the organization's middle and operational levels and keep strategic behavior in line with the current strategy course. For example, existing reward and measurement systems may direct managers' attention to some market opportunities and not to others. Examples of induced strategic behavior or deliberate strategies might emerge around product development efforts for existing markets.

Autonomous Strategic Behavior

During any period, most strategic activity in large, complex firms is likely to fit into the induced behavior category. However, large, resource-rich firms are likely to possess a pool of entrepreneurial potential at operational levels, which expresses itself in autonomous strategic initiatives. The 3M Company encourages its technical employees to devote 15 percent of their work time to developing their own ideas. Through the personal efforts of employees, new products are born. For example,

- Art Fry championed Post-it notes at 3M.

- P. D. Estridge promoted the personal computer at IBM.

- Stephanie L. Kwolek advanced the bulletproof material Kevlar at DuPont.[9]

Autonomous strategic behavior is conceptually equivalent to entrepreneurial activity and introduces new categories of opportunity into the firm's planning process. Managers at the product-market level conceive of market opportunities that depart from the current strategy course, then engage in product-championing activities to mobilize resources and create momentum for further development of the product. Emphasizing political rather than administrative channels, product champions question

---

[6]Quinn, "Managing Innovation," p. 82.

[7]This section is based on Michael D. Hutt, Peter H. Reingen, and John R. Ronchetto Jr., "Tracing Emergent Processes in Marketing Strategy Formation," *Journal of Marketing* 52 (January 1988): pp. 4–19.

[8]Robert A. Burgelman, "A Process Model of Internal Corporate Venturing in the Diversified Major Firm," *Administrative Science Quarterly* 28 (April 1983): pp. 223–244.

[9]Timothy D. Schellhardt, "David and Goliath," *The Wall Street Journal*, May 23, 1996, p. R14.

the firm's current concept of strategy and, states Robert Burgelman, "provide top management with the opportunity to rationalize, retroactively, successful autonomous strategic behavior."[10] Through these political mechanisms, successful autonomous strategic initiatives, or emergent strategies, can become integrated into the firm's concept of strategy.

Clayton M. Christensen and Michael E. Raynor observe:

> Emergent strategies result from managers' responses to problems or opportunities that were unforeseen in the analysis and planning stages of the deliberate strategy making process. When the efficacy of that strategy . . . is recognized, it is possible to formalize it, improve it, and exploit it, thus transforming an emergent strategy into a deliberate one.[11]

Product Championing and the Informal Network

Table 10.1 highlights several characteristics that may distinguish induced from autonomous strategic behavior. Autonomous strategic initiatives involve a set of actors and evoke strategic dialogue different from that found in induced initiatives. An individual manager, the product champion, assumes a central role in sensing an opportunity and in mobilizing an informal network to explore the idea's technical feasibility and market potential. A **product champion** is an organization member who creates, defines, or adopts an idea for an innovation and is willing to assume significant risk (for example, position or prestige) to successfully implement the innovation.[12] Senior managers at 3M do not commit to a project unless a champion emerges and do not abandon the effort unless the champion "gets tired." Emphasizing a rich culture of innovation embraced by all employees, senior executives at 3M also encourage product-championing behavior and calculated risk taking. Moreover, they tolerate what 3M employees call "well-intentioned" failures.[13]

Compared with induced strategic behavior, autonomous initiatives are more likely to involve a communication process that departs from the regular work flow and the hierarchical decision-making channels. The decision roles and responsibilities of managers in this informal network are poorly defined in the early phases of the strategy-formulation process but become more formalized as the process evolves. Note in Table 10.1 that autonomous strategic behavior entails a creeping commitment toward a particular strategy course. By contrast, induced strategic initiatives are more likely to involve administrative mechanisms that encourage a more formal and comprehensive assessment of strategic alternatives at various levels in the firm's planning hierarchy.

---

[10] Robert A. Burgelman, "Corporate Entrepreneurship and Strategic Management: Insights from a Process Study," *Management Science* 29 (December 1983): p. 1352.

[11] Clayton M. Christensen and Michael E. Raynor, *The Innovator's Solution: Creating and Sustaining Successful Growth* (Boston: Harvard Business School Press, 2003), pp. 215–216.

[12] Modesto A. Maidique, "Entrepreneurs, Champions, and Technological Innovations," *Sloan Management Review* 21 (spring 1980): pp. 59–70; see also Jane M. Howell, "Champions of Technological Innovation," *Administrative Science Quarterly* 35 (June 1990): pp. 317–341.

[13] George S. Day, "Managing the Market Learning Process," *Journal of Business & Industrial Marketing* 17, no. 4 (2002): p. 246.

TABLE 10.1	**INDUCED VERSUS AUTONOMOUS STRATEGIC BEHAVIOR: SELECTED CHARACTERISTICS OF THE MARKETING STRATEGY FORMULATION PROCESS**	
	Induced	**Autonomous**
Activation of the strategic decision process	An individual manager defines a market need that converges on the organization's concept of strategy.	An individual manager defines a market need that diverges from the organization's concept of strategy.
Nature of the screening process	A formal screening of technical and market merit is made using established administrative procedures.	An informal network assesses technical and market merit.
Type of innovation	Incremental (e.g., new product development for existing markets uses existing organizational resources).	Major (e.g., new product development projects require new combinations of organizational resources).
Nature of communication	Consistent with organizational work flow.	Departs from organizational work flow in early phase of decision process.
Major actors	Prescribed by the regular channel of hierarchical decision making.	An informal network emerges based on mobilization efforts of the product champion.
Decision roles	Roles and responsibilities for participants in the strategy formulation process are well defined.	Roles and responsibilities of participants are poorly defined in the initial phases but become more formalized as the strategy formulation process evolves.
Implications for strategy	Strategic alternatives are considered and commitment to a particular strategic course evolves.	Commitment to a particular strategic course emerges in the early phases through the sponsorship efforts of the product champion.

SOURCE: Adapted from Michael D. Hutt, Peter H. Reingen, and John R. Ronchetto Jr., "Tracing Emergent Processes in Marketing, Strategy Formation," *Journal of Marketing* 52 (January 1988): pp. 4–19. See also Clayton M. Christensen and Michael E. Raynor, *The Innovator's Solution: Creating and Sustaining Successful Growth* (Boston: Harvard Business School Press, 2003), pp. 213–231.

Bringing Silicon Valley Inside[14]

Although corporate leaders strive for innovative ideas and envy the success of Silicon Valley's entrepreneurs, few have considered how they might bring the passion and spirit of the valley inside—how they might ignite the entrepreneurial energy and focus of their own employees. What drives Silicon Valley are three interconnected markets: a market for ideas, a market for capital, and a market for talent. Although ideas, capital, and talent whirl through Silicon Valley at a rapid pace searching for new sources of value, the movement is stifled in most large corporations.

Market for Ideas Gary Hamel, a leading strategy consultant, observes that "the last bastion of Soviet-style central planning can be found in *Fortune* 500 companies—it's called resource allocation."[15] A crucial distinction here is that Silicon Valley is not based on resource *allocation* but, instead, on resource *attraction*. Resource allocation is perfectly suited to investments in existing businesses and managing the downside risks, whereas

---

[14]Gary Hamel, "Bringing Silicon Valley Inside," *Harvard Business Review* 77 (September–October 1999): pp. 71–84.

[15]Ibid., p. 76.

resource attraction is about pursuing fresh ideas that create new businesses and managing the upside—rule-breaking opportunities. To unleash the ideas and passion of employees, large corporations must bring new voices into the opportunity-seeking process, radically changing the conventional belief that strategy is the province of senior managers.

Here are two companies that include more voices in the innovation-management process by harvesting valuable ideas from their employees:

- Cemex, the successful cement maker, sponsors Innovation Days that center on particular themes such as improving efficiency or developing new customer solutions. In advance of the event, a senior executive personally invites hundreds of employees to submit ideas—and they respond. A recent event spawned more than 250 ideas, which were then carefully reviewed and categorized. The highest-ranked ideas are classified as stars (ideas that represent a valuable opportunity and could be implemented immediately). Ten stars (that is, big ideas) emerged from the 250 submissions![16]

- Royal Dutch/Shell, the large oil producer, created a process called GameChanger that gives a panel of employees the ability to allocate $20 million to promising new opportunities. The group meets weekly and has screened over 100 ideas annually from employees throughout the organization. An employee with a promising idea is invited to give a brief presentation to the panel. A favorable review can lead to preliminary funding ($100,000 is the average) 10 days later. Four of the five major strategic initiatives Shell recently launched emerged from the GameChanger process.

Market for Capital   Compared with corporate strategists, venture capitalists in Silicon Valley operate with a different set of expectations about success and failure in funding ideas. Out of several thousand ideas, a venture capitalist might fund 10. Out of the 10, five will fail, three will be a moderate success, one will double the investment, and one will generate 50 to 100 times the investment. Rather than ensuring that there are no losers, venture capitalists want to find a big winner.

Large corporations often miss the path-breaking idea—the big winner. Why? The typical capital budgeting process in large companies attempts to guarantee no losers. By departing from the current strategy course, creative business ideas pose a risk and seldom make it through a traditional financial screening process. To remedy this problem, a source of funding can be created that is entirely separate from the traditional capital budgeting process. That is the goal of the GameChanger process at Royal Dutch/Shell: to create an innovation-friendly market for capital inside the firm.

Market for Talent   Silicon Valley executives know that if you do not give your employees truly exhilarating work and solid incentives, those workers will jump at the chance to work on the next great thing at another company. To retain talented employees, large corporations need to create an internal market where employees can move freely, move to new jobs that capture their interests, or capitalize on their skills. In turn, firms should provide positive incentives for employees who are willing to take a risk on an unconventional initiative. At firms like Disney, Monsanto, or Royal

---

[16] Hamel and Getz, "Funding Growth in an Age of Austerity," pp. 78–79.

Dutch/Shell, employees are given the opportunity to move out of existing businesses into new businesses, or even to nominate themselves for a new venture team.

Gary Hamel notes:

> The bottom line is this: if you have highly creative and ambitious people who feel trapped in moribund businesses, they are going to leave. The only question is whether they leave to join some other company, or whether they leave to join a GameChanger kind of team in your company.[17]

Managing Technology

Eastman Kodak, Lockheed, IBM, and the management teams of other corporations failed to recognize the major technological opportunity that xerographic copying presented. These firms were among the many that turned down the chance to participate with the small and unknown Haloid Company in refining and commercializing this technology. In the end, Haloid pursued it alone and transformed this one technological opportunity into the Xerox Corporation. Among the "tales of high tech," this remains a classic.[18] Technological change, Michael Porter asserts, is "a great equalizer, eroding the competitive advantage of even well-entrenched firms and propelling others to the forefront. Many of today's great firms grew out of technological changes that they were able to exploit."[19] Clearly, the long-run competitive position of most business-to-business firms depends on their ability to manage, increase, and exploit their technology base. This section explores the nature of development projects, the disruptive innovation model, and the defining attributes of successful innovators in fast-changing high-technology markets.

Classifying Development Projects

A first step in exploring the technology portfolio of a firm is to understand the different forms that development projects can take. Some development projects center on improving the manufacturing *process*, some on improving *products*, and others on both process and product improvements. All of these represent commercial development projects. By contrast, research and development is the precursor to commercial development. A firm's portfolio can include four types of development projects.[20]

1. **Derivative projects** center on incremental product enhancements (for example, a new feature), incremental process improvements (for example, a lower-cost manufacturing process), or incremental changes on both dimensions.

   Illustration: A feature-enhanced or cost-reduced Canon fax machine.

---

[17] Hamel, "Bringing Silicon Valley Inside," p. 83.

[18] For a related discussion of Xerox's technology blunders, see Andrew Hargadon, *How Breakthroughs Happen: The Surprising Truth about How Companies Innovate* (Boston: Harvard Business School Press, 2003), pp. 168–182.

[19] Michael E. Porter, "Technology and Competitive Advantage," *Journal of Business Strategy* 6 (winter 1985): p. 60; and Tamara J. Erickson, John F. Magee, Philip A. Roussel, and Komol N. Saad, "Managing Technology as Business Strategy," *Sloan Management Review* 31 (spring 1990): pp. 73–83.

[20] This discussion is based on Steven C. Wheelwright and Kim B. Clark, "Creating Product Plans to Focus Product Development," *Harvard Business Review* 70 (March–April 1992): pp. 70–82.

2. **Platform projects** create the design and components shared by a set of products. These projects often involve a number of changes in both the product and the manufacturing process.

    Illustrations: A common motor in all Black & Decker hand tools; multiple applications of Intel's microprocessor.

3. **Breakthrough projects** establish new core products and new core processes that differ fundamentally from previous generations.

    Illustrations: Computer disks and fiber-optic cable created new product categories.

4. **Research and development** is the creation of knowledge concerning new materials and technologies that eventually leads to commercial development.[21]

    Illustration: Lucent Technologies' development of communications technology that underlies its telecommunications systems used by diverse customers like banks and hotel chains.

A Product-Family Focus

A particular technology may provide the foundation or platform for several products. For example, Honda applies its multivalve cylinder technology to power-generation equipment, cars, motorcycles, and lawn mowers.[22] Products that share a common platform but have different specific features and enhancements required for different sets of consumers constitute a **product family**.[23] Each generation of a product family has a platform that provides the foundation for specific products targeted to different or complementary markets. By expanding on technical skills, market knowledge, and manufacturing competencies, entirely new product families may be formed, thereby creating new business opportunities.

Strategists argue that a firm should move away from planning that centers on single products and focus instead on families of products that can grow from a common platform. Consider the Sony Walkman—one of the most successful products of all time. Based on how different customer segments used the product, Sony developed four basic platforms for the Walkman: playback only, playback and record, playback and tuner, and sports. Then, by applying standard design elements such as color and styling, Sony added an assortment of features and distinctive technical attributes to the basic platforms with relative ease.[24]

The move toward a product-family perspective requires close interfunctional working relationships, a long-term view of technology strategy, and a multiple-year commitment of resources. Although this approach offers significant competitive leverage, Steven Wheelwright and Kim Clark note that companies often fail to invest adequately in platforms: "The reasons vary, but the most common is that management

---

[21] Ibid., p. 74.

[22] T. Michael Nevens, Gregory L. Summe, and Bro Uttal, "Commercializing Technology: What the Best Companies Do," *Harvard Business Review* 60 (May–June 1990): pp. 154–163; see also C. K. Prahalad, "Weak Signals versus Strong Paradigms," *Journal of Marketing Research* 32 (August 1995): pp. iii–vi.

[23] Marc H. Meyer and James M. Utterback, "The Product Family and the Dynamics of Core Capability," *Sloan Management Review* 34 (spring 1993): pp. 29–47; see also Dwight L. Gertz and João P. A. Baptista, *Grow to Be Great: Breaking the Downsizing Cycle* (New York: The Free Press, 1995), pp. 92–103.

[24] Kathleen M. Eisenhardt and Shona L. Brown, "Time Pacing: Competing in Markets That Won't Stand Still," *Harvard Business Review*, 76 (March–April 1998): p. 67.

FIGURE 10.1 | **THE DISRUPTIVE INNOVATION MODEL**

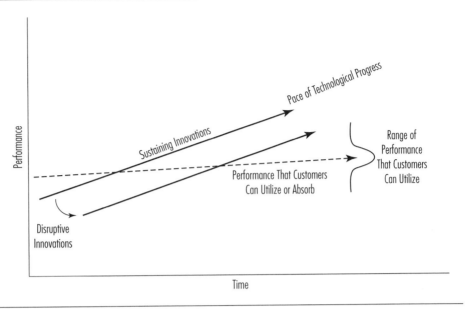

lacks an awareness of the strategic value of platforms and fails to create well-thought-out platform projects."[25]

The Disruptive Innovation Model[26]

Special insights into innovation management come from examining the rate at which products are improving and customers can use those improvements. For example, when personal computers were first introduced in the early 1980s, typists often had to pause for the Intel 286 chip to catch up. But today, only the most demanding customers can fully use the speed and performance of personal computers. For many products, from Excel spreadsheets to application-enriched handsets and information appliances, few customers absorb the performance features that innovating companies include as they introduce new and improved products.

Overshooting   Figure 10.1 shows, first, a rate of improvement in a given product or technology that customers can use, represented by the dotted line, sloping slightly upward across the chart. Second, for a given product, innovating firms offer a trajectory of improvement as they develop new and improved versions over time. The pace of technological progress usually outstrips the ability of many, if not most, customers to keep up with it (see the steeply sloping solid lines in Figure 10.1). Therefore, as

---

[25] Wheelwright and Clark, "Creating Project Plans," p. 74.

[26] This section is based on Christensen and Raynor, *The Innovator's Solution*, pp. 31–65. See also, Ashish Sood and Gerard J. Tellis, "Technological Evolution and Radical Innovation," *Journal of Marketing* 69 (July 2005): pp. 152–168.

companies strive to make better products they can sell at higher profit margins to the most demanding customers, they overshoot and provide much more performance than mainstream customers are able to use.

Sustaining versus Disruptive Innovation

Third, from Figure 10.1, a distinction is made between a sustaining innovation and a disruptive innovation. According to Clayton M. Christensen and Michael E. Raynor: "A **sustaining innovation** targets demanding, high-end customers with better performance than what was previously available (for example, incremental product improvements or breakthrough products)."[27]

A **disruptive innovation** represents a product or service that is not as good as currently available alternatives. "But disruptive technologies offer other benefits—typically, they are simpler, more convenient, and less expensive products that appeal to new or less-demanding customers."[28]

Disruptive Strategy Examples

Once a disruptive product or service gains a foothold, the improvement cycle begins and eventually it intersects with the needs of more demanding customers. For example, Xerox held a commanding position in the high-speed photocopier business until Canon's simple tabletop copier disrupted that strategy in the early 1980s. Likewise, Southwest Airlines disrupted established airlines; Amazon.com disrupted traditional bookstores; Staples disrupted small stationery stores and distributors of office supplies; and Google disrupted directories of all sorts, including Yellow Pages.

Types of Disruptive Strategies

Disruptive strategies can take two forms: low-end disruptions and new-market disruptions. Table 10.2 describes the characteristics of these strategies and contrasts them with a strategy geared to sustaining innovations. Note, for example, the targeted customers for low-end disruption are *overserved customers*, whereas new-market disruptions target *nonconsumption*—customers who historically lacked the resources to buy and use the product.

Low-End Strategy Tests

For a low-end disruptive strategy to succeed, two requirements must be met:

1. There should be customers at the low end of the market who are eager to purchase a "good enough" product if they could acquire it at a lower price.

2. The company must be able to create a business model that can yield attractive profits at the discount prices that are needed to attract customers at the low end of the market.

   Example: Southwest Airlines drew customers away from the major carriers.

New-Market Strategy Tests

For new market disruptions, at least one and generally both of these requirements must be met:

1. A large population of people can be defined who have historically lacked the money, equipment, or skill to acquire this product or service for themselves.

---

[27] Ibid., Christensen and Raynor, p. 34.
[28] Ibid., p. 34.

TABLE 10.2 | THREE APPROACHES TO CREATING NEW-GROWTH BUSINESSES

Dimensions	Sustaining Innovations	Low-End Disruptions	New-Market Disruptions
Targeted performance of the product or service	Performance improvement in *attributes most valued by the industry's most demanding customers.* These improvements may be incremental or breakthrough in character.	Performance that is good enough along the traditional metrics of performance at the low end of the mainstream market.	Lower performance in "traditional" attributes, but *improved performance in new attributes—typically simplicity and convenience.*
Targeted customers or market application	The *most attractive (i.e., profitable) customers* in the mainstream markets who are willing to pay for improved performance.	*Overserved customers* in the low end of the mainstream market.	Targets *nonconsumption:* customers who historically lacked the money or skill to buy and use the product.
Effect on the required business model (processes and cost structure)	Improves or maintains profit margins by exploiting the *existing processes and cost structure* and making better use of current competitive advantages.	Uses a new *operating or financial approach or both*— a different combination of lower gross profit margins and higher asset utilization that can earn attractive returns at the discount prices required to win business at the low end of the market.	Business model must make money at lower price per unit sold, and at unit production volumes that initially will be small. Gross margin dollars per unit sold will be significantly lower.

SOURCE: Reprinted by permission of the HARVARD BUSINESS REVIEW. From "Three Approaches to Creating New Growth Business" in THE INNOVATOR'S SOLUTION by Clayton Christensen, p. 51. Copyright © 2003 by the Harvard Business School Publishing Corporation; all rights reserved.

2. Present customers need to go to an inconvenient location to use the product or service.

Examples: Canon desktop photocopiers were a new market disruption in the 1980s because they enabled employees to make their own copies rather than taking their originals to the corporate high-speed copying center to get help from technical specialists. Also, Research in Motion, Ltd.'s BlackBerry is a new-market disruption relative to notebook computers.

A Final Litmus Test   Once an innovation passes the tests that apply to low-end or new market disruptions, a final critical test remains: The innovation must be disruptive to all the significant competitive firms in the industry. If one or more of the significant industry players is pursuing the strategy, the odds will be stacked against the new entrant.

Innovation Winners in High-Technology Markets

In rapidly changing industries with short product life cycles and quickly shifting competitive landscapes, a firm must continually innovate to keep its offerings aligned with the market. A firm's ability to cope with change in a high-velocity industry is a key to competitive success. Shona Brown and Kathleen Eisenhardt provide an intriguing comparison of successful versus less successful product innovation in the computer industry.[29] Successful innovators were firms that were on schedule, on time to the market, and on target in addressing customer needs. The study found that firms with a successful record of product innovation use different organizational structures and processes than their competitors. In particular, four distinguishing characteristics marked the innovation approach of successful firms.

1. Limited Structure   Creating successful products to meet changing customer needs requires flexibility, but successful product innovators combine this flexibility with a few rules that are never broken. First, strict priorities for new products are established and tied directly to resource allocation. This allows managers to direct attention to the most promising opportunities, avoiding the temptation to pursue too many attractive opportunities. Second, managers set deadlines for a few key milestones and always meet them. Third, responsibility for a limited number of major outcomes is set. For example, at one firm, engineering managers were responsible for product schedules while marketing managers were responsible for market definition and product profitability. Although successful firms emphasized structure for a few areas (for example, priorities or deadlines), less successful innovators imposed more control— lockstep, checkpoint procedures for every facet of new product development—or virtually no structure at all. Successful firms strike a balance by using a structure that is neither so rigid as to stiffly control the process nor so chaotic that the process falls apart.

2. Real-Time Communication and Improvisation   Successful product innovators in the computer industry emphasize real-time communication within new-product-development teams *and* across product teams. Much of the communication occurs in formal meetings, but there is also extensive informal communication throughout the organization. Clear priorities and responsibilities, coupled with extensive communications, allow product developers to improvise. "In the context of jazz improvisation, this means creating music while adjusting to the changing musical interpretations of others. In the context of product innovation, it means creating a product while simultaneously adapting to changing markets and technologies."[30]

More formally, then, **improvisation** involves the design and execution of actions that approach convergence with each other in time.[31] The shorter the elapsed time between the design and implementation of an activity, the more that activity is improvisational. Successful firms expect constant change, and new product teams have the freedom to act. One manager noted: "We fiddle right up to the end" of the new-product-development process. Real-time communications among members of the product development team, coupled with limited structure, provide the foundation for such improvisation.

3. Experimentation: Probing into the Future   Some firms make a large bet on one version of the future, whereas others fail to update future plans in light of

---

[29] This section is based on Shona L. Brown and Kathleen M. Eisenhardt, "The Art of Continuous Change: Linking Complexity Theory and Time-Paced Evolution in Relentlessly Shifting Organizations," *Administrative Science Quarterly* 42 (March 1997): pp. 1–34.

[30] Ibid., p. 15.

[31] Christine Moorman and Anne S. Miner, "The Convergence of Planning and Execution: Improvisation in New Product Development," *Journal of Marketing* 62 (July 1998): p. 3.

INSIDE BUSINESS MARKETING

Patching: The New Corporate Strategy in Dynamic Markets

Kathleen M. Eisenhardt and Shona L. Brown contend that traditional corporate planning and resource allocation approaches are not effective in volatile markets. As new technologies, novel products and services, and emerging markets create tempting opportunities, "the clear-cut partitioning of businesses into neat, equidistant rectangles on an organizational chart becomes out of date."

The new corporate-level strategic processes center on managing change and continually realigning the organization to capture market opportunities faster than the competition. Central to this newly defined approach is **patching**—the strategic process corporate executives use routinely to realign or remap businesses to changing market opportunities. Patching can take the form of adding, dividing,

transferring, exiting, or combining pieces of businesses. Hewlett-Packard used patching to launch the printer business, create businesses in related products like scanners and faxes, and develop a second printer business built around inkjet technology. Patching is less critical in stable markets but a crucial skill when markets are turbulent. Here a small agile unit of the firm can be mobilized quickly to capture fresh market opportunities.

SOURCES: Kathleen M. Eisenhardt and Shona L. Brown, "Patching: Restitching Business Portfolios in Dynamic Markets," *Harvard Business Review* 77 (May–June 1999): pp. 72–82; see also, Mark B. Houston, Beth A. Walker, Michael D. Hutt, and Peter H. Reingen, "Cross-Unit Competition for a Market Charter: The Enduring Influence of Structure," *Journal of Marketing* 65 (April 2001): pp. 19–34.

---

changing competition. Creators of successful product portfolios did not invest in any one version of the future but, instead, used a variety of low-cost probes to create options. Examples of low-cost probes include developing experimental products for new markets, entering into a strategic alliance with leading-edge customers to better understand future needs, or conducting regular planning sessions dedicated to the future. In turbulent industries, strategists cannot accurately predict which of many possible versions of the future will arrive. Probes create more possible responses for managers when the future does arrive while lowering the probability of being surprised by unanticipated futures.

4. Time Pacing   Successful product innovators carefully managed the transition between current and future projects, whereas less successful innovators let each project unfold according to its own schedule. Successful innovators, like Intel, practice **time pacing**—a strategy for competing in fast-changing markets by creating new products at predictable time intervals.[32] Organization members carefully choreograph and understand transition processes. For example, marketing managers might begin work on the definition of the next product while engineering is completing work on the current product and moving it to manufacturing. Time pacing motivates managers to anticipate change and can have a strong psychological impact across the organization. "Time pacing creates a relentless sense of urgency around meeting deadlines and concentrates individual and team energy around common goals."[33]

---

[32] Eisenhardt and Brown, "Time Pacing," pp. 59–69.

[33] Ibid., p. 60.

The New-Product-Development Process

To sustain their competitive advantage, leading-edge firms such as Canon, Microsoft, and Hewlett-Packard make new product development a top management priority. They directly involve managers and employees from across the organization to speed actions and decisions. Because new product ventures can represent a significant risk as well as an important opportunity, new product development requires systematic thought. The high expectations for new products are often not fulfilled. Worse, many new industrial products fail. Although the definitions of failure are somewhat elusive, research suggests that 40 percent of industrial products fail to meet objectives.[34] Although there may be some debate over the number of failures, there is no debate that a new product rejected by the market constitutes a substantial waste to the firm and to society.

This section explores (1) the forces that drive a firm's new product performance, (2) the sources of new product ideas, (3) cross-functional barriers to successful innovation, and (4) team-based processes used in new product development. A promising method for bringing the "voice of the consumer" directly into the development process is also explored.

What Drives a Firm's New Product Performance?

A benchmarking study sought to uncover the critical success factors that drive a firm's new product performance.[35] It identified three factors (Figure 10.2): (1) the quality of a firm's new-product-development process, (2) the resource commitments made to new product development, and (3) the new product strategy.

Process   Successful companies use a high-quality new-product-development process— they give careful attention to executing the activities and decision points that new products follow from the idea stage to launch and beyond. The benchmarking study identified the following characteristics among high-performing firms:

- The firms emphasized upfront market and technical assessments before projects moved into the development phase.

- The process featured complete descriptions of the product concept, product benefits, positioning, and target markets before development work was initiated.

- Tough project *go/kill* decision points were included in the process, and the kill option was actually used.

- The new product process was flexible—certain stages could be skipped in line with the nature and risk of a particular project.

---

[34] Robert G. Cooper, Scott J. Edgett, and Elko J. Kleinschmidt, "Benchmarking Best NPD Practices–I," *Research Technology Management* 47 (January–February 2004): pp. 31–43.

[35] Robert G. Cooper and Elko J. Kleinschmidt, "Benchmarking Firms' New Product Performance and Practices," *Engineering Management Review* 23 (fall 1995): pp. 112–120; see also, Robert G. Cooper, Scott J. Edgett, and Elko J. Kleinschmidt, "Benchmarking Best NPD Practices–II," *Research Technology Management* 47 (May–June 2004): pp. 50–59.

FIGURE 10.2 | THE MAJOR DRIVERS OF A FIRM'S NEW PRODUCT PERFORMANCE

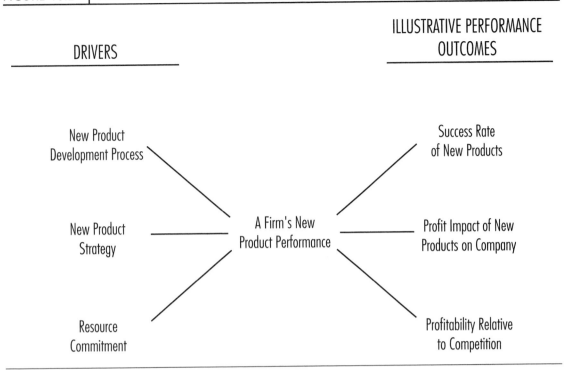

SOURCE: Adapted from Robert G. Cooper and Elko J. Kleinschmidt, "Benchmarking Firms' New Product Performance and Practices," *Engineering Management Review* 23 (fall 1995): pp. 112–120.

Detailed upfront homework on the product concept, the likely market response, and the product's technical feasibility, along with a thorough business and financial assessment, are important dimensions of the process successful product creators follow.

Resource Commitments   Adequate resources were invested in new product development in top-performing firms. Three ingredients were important here:

1. Top management committed the resources necessary to meet the firm's objectives for the total product effort.

2. R&D budgets were adequate and aligned with the stated new product objectives.

3. The necessary personnel were assigned and were relieved from other duties so that they could give full attention to new product development.

Research suggests that rather than being imposed by top management, the creative potential of new-product-development teams "is likely to be more fully realized when they are given the flexibility—within a broad strategic directive—to determine their own project controls and especially to pursue their own processes and procedures."[36]

[36] Joseph M. Bonner, Robert W. Ruekert, and Orville C. Walker Jr., "Upper Management Control of New Product Development Projects and Project Performance," *Journal of Product Innovation Management* 19 (May 2002): p. 243.

New Product Strategy   A clear and visible new product strategy was another driver of a firm's new product performance (see Figure 10.2). Successful firms like 3M set aggressive new product performance goals (for example, x percent of company sales and profit from new products) as a basic corporate goal and communicate it to all employees. In turn, Robert Cooper and Elko Kleinschmidt report that successful firms centered development efforts on clearly defined arenas—particular product, market, and technology domains—to direct the new product program:

> The new product strategy specifies "the arenas where we'll play the game," or perhaps more important, where we won't play . . . what's in bounds and out of bounds. Without arenas defined, the search for new product ideas or opportunities is unfocused. . . .[37]

Anticipating Competitive Reactions[38]

Two-thirds of new product introductions trigger reactions by competitors. Consequently, business marketers can improve the odds of new-product-launch success by implementing a strong **competitor orientation** before and during the launch. Here the new product strategist develops detailed scenarios that provide a guide for countering different competitive responses. Competitors are strongly motivated to react when (1) the new product represents a major threat to their market and (2) the market is experiencing a high rate of growth. Competitors are also more inclined to react when extensive marketing communications by the innovating firm enhance the visibility of the new product introduction.

Alternatively, if the new product introduction does not pose a direct challenge to the competitor's market, a reaction is less likely. Recent research suggests that radically new products or products that target niche markets are less likely to spawn competitive responses.

Sources of New Product Ideas

The business marketer should be alert to new product ideas and their sources, both inside and outside the company. Internally, new product ideas may flow from salespersons who are close to customer needs, from R&D specialists who are close to new technological developments, and from top management who know the company's strengths and weaknesses. Externally, ideas may come from channel members, such as distributors or customers, or from an assessment of competitive moves.

Eric von Hippel challenges the traditional view that marketers typically introduce new products to a passive market.[39] His research suggests that the customers in the

---

[37] Cooper and Kleinschmidt, "Benchmarking," p. 117; see also Jean-Marie Choffray and Gary L. Lilien, "Assessing Response to Industrial Marketing Strategy," *Journal of Marketing* 42 (April 1978): pp. 20–31; and Eunsang Yoon and Gary L. Lilien, "New Industrial Product Performance: The Effects of Market Characteristics and Strategy," *Journal of Product Innovation Management* 3 (September 1985): pp. 134–144.

[38] Marion Debruyne, Rudy Moenart, Abbie Griffin, Susan Hart, Erik Jan Hultink, and Henry Robben, "The Impact of New Product Launch Strategies on Competitive Reaction in Industrial Markets," *Journal of Product Innovation Management* 19 (March 2002): pp. 159–170. See also Beth A. Walker, Dimitri Kapelianis, and Michael D. Hutt, "Competitive Cognition," *MIT Sloan Management Review* 46 (summer 2005): pp. 10–12.

[39] Eric von Hippel, "Get New Products from Customers," *Harvard Business Review* 60 (March–April 1982): pp. 117–122; see also von Hippel, *The Sources of Innovation* (New York: Oxford University Press, 1988); see also Gerard A. Athaide and Rodney L. Stump, "A Taxonomy of Relationship Approaches during Technology Development in Technology-Based, Industrial Markets," *Journal of Product Innovation Management* 16 (September 1999): pp. 469–482.

B2B TOP PERFORMERS

Best Practices for Successful Innovation: Create a Supportive Culture

Leading companies—like 3M—create a culture for innovation by recognizing the contributions of particular product innovators each year in its annual report, celebrating the accomplishments of innovation champions on the company's Web site, and using such stories to demonstrate its continuing commitment to its mission: leading through innovation. The best-performing companies also:

- Allow scouting time and provide resources to creative, passionate employees to pursue their dream projects.
- Provide recognition and rewards to idea generators and product champions (for example, innovation rewards that can approach $100,000 are offered each year at Air Products for ideas that have been commercialized).
- Openly encourage and pursue venturesome or risky projects.
- Remove silos and encourage open communications between functions, locations, and countries.

SOURCE: Robert G. Cooper, Scott J. Edgett, and Elko J. Kleinschmidt, "Benchmarking Best NPD Processes – I," *Research Technology Management* 47 (January–February 2004): pp. 31–43.

business market often develop the idea for a new product and even select the supplier to make that product. The customer is responding to the perceived *capability* of the business marketer rather than to a specific physical product. This points up the need for involving customers in new product development and promoting corporate capability to consumers (idea generators).

Lead Users   Because many industrial product markets for high-technology and, in particular, capital equipment consist of a small number of high-volume buying firms, special attention must be given to the needs of **lead users.** These include a small number of highly influential buying organizations that are consistent early adopters of new technologies.[40] Lead users face needs that are general in the marketplace, but they confront these needs months or years before most of that marketplace encounters them. In addition, they are positioned to benefit significantly by obtaining a solution that satisfies those needs. For example, if an automobile manufacturer wanted to design an innovative braking system, marketing managers might secure insights from auto racing teams who have a strong need for better brakes. In turn, they might look to a related field like aerospace, where antilock braking systems were first developed so that military aircraft could land on short runways.[41]

The Lead User Method   Lead user projects are conducted by a cross-functional team that includes four to six managers from marketing and technical departments; one member serves as project leader. Team members typically spend 12 to 15 hours per

---

[40] von Hippel, "Get New Products," pp. 120–121.

[41] Eric von Hippel, Stefan Thomke, and Mary Sonnack, "Creating Breakthroughs at 3M," *Harvard Business Review* 77 (September–October 1999): pp. 47–57.

FIGURE 10.3 | THE LEAD USER METHOD

Phase	Central Focus	Description
Phase 1	Laying the Foundation	The team identifies target markets and secures support from internal stakeholders for the type and level of innovations desired.
Phase 2	Determining the Trends	The team talks to experts in the field who have a broad view of emerging technologies and pioneering applications in the particular area.
Phase 3	Identifying Lead Users	The team begins a networking process to identify lead users at the leading edge of the target market and to gather information that might contribute to breakthrough products.
Phase 4	Developing & Assessing Preliminary Product Ideas	The team begins to shape product ideas and to assess market potential and fit with company interests.
Phase 5	Developing the Break-throughs	To design final concepts, the team hosts a workshop bringing together lead users with other in-house managers. After further refinement, the team presents its recommendations to senior management.

SOURCE: Adapted with modifications from Eric von Hippel, Stefan Thomke, and Mary Sonnack, "Creating Breakthroughs at 3M," *Harvard Business Review* 77 (September–October 1999), p. 52.

week on the projects, which are usually completed in four to six weeks. Lead user projects proceed through five phases (Figure 10.3). 3M has now successfully used the lead user method in eight different divisions, and support among project teams and divisional managers is strong. For example, the Medical-Surgical Markets Group at 3M used the lead user method to unearth new product ideas and to identify a revolutionary approach to infection control.[42]

Staying Ahead of Customers Rather than merely asking customers what they want, some firms succeed by leading customers where they want to go before the customers actually know it themselves.[43] To illustrate, Motorola envisions a global communication environment where telephone numbers are attached to people rather than to places and where a personal communicator allows millions of business travelers to be reached anywhere, anytime. Deep insights into the needs and aspirations of today's and tomorrow's customers are needed to plan the course for innovation. In addition to providing critical customer feedback to technical personnel, procedures are needed to inform those closest to the customer (marketers) about the coming technological possibilities. Motorola succeeds by educating customers to *what is possible*.

---

[42] Ibid., p. 56.

[43] Gary Hamel and C. K. Prahalad, "Corporate Imagination and Expeditionary Marketing," *Harvard Business Review* 69 (July–August 1991): pp. 81–92.

Rather than providing precise demand forecasts, "market research acts as a catalyst for developing and enriching new ideas."[44]

Quality Function Deployment[45]

Cooperation and communication among marketing, manufacturing, engineering, and R&D are fundamental to greater new product success and more profitable products. **Quality function deployment, or QFD,** identifies critical customer attributes and establishes a specific link between customer attributes and product design attributes. Cross-functional communication is improved by linking the voice of the customer directly to engineering, manufacturing, and R&D. The approach has been adopted widely by Japanese, U.S., and European firms. The new-product-development team uses the approach to understand the voice of the consumer and translate it into the voice of the engineer.

The Voice of the Customer   The first task of QFD is to identify customer needs, which are expressions in the customers' own words of the benefits they want the product to deliver. Discussions with customers often create a lengthy list of needs. Particular attention, however, is given to the 5 to 10 top-level or primary needs that set the strategic direction for the product. Small business owners, for example, might seek these attributes in a photocopier: reliable, low cost, compact, quiet, and fast. Research suggests that interviews with 20 to 30 customers should identify 90 percent or more of the customer needs in a relatively homogeneous market segment.[46]

Because some customer attributes have more importance to some customers than others, weights are assigned to represent their relative importance from the customer's perspective. Such weighting or prioritizing enables the QFD team to balance the cost of meeting a need with the benefit sought by the customer. To guide product design, competitive data on customer perceptions of current products also constitutes a component of QFD. As Abbie Griffin and John Hauser point out, "Knowledge of which products fulfill which needs best, how well those needs are fulfilled, and whether there are any gaps between the best product and 'our' existing product provide further input into product development decisions being made by the QFD team."[47]

The Voice of the Engineer   The strength of QFD comes from translating customer needs into product design attributes. These design parameters should be measurable requirements tied to customer attributes (for example, the power of the motor in a photocopier influences the performance speed). Once the design parameters are identified, the QFD team can examine the relationship between a design parameter and a customer attribute. For example, increasing the power of the motor has a positive effect on the customer attribute "speed," but a negative effect on the customer attributes "low cost" and "quiet." An evaluation of the relationship between design parameters and customer attributes draws on information from customers, engineering experience,

---

[44]Soren M. Kaplan, "Discontinuous Innovation and the Growth Paradox," *Strategy & Leadership* 28 (March–April 1999): p. 20.

[45]This section is based on John R. Hauser, "How Puritan-Bennett Used the House of Quality," *Sloan Management Review* 34 (spring 1993): pp. 61–70.

[46]Abbie Griffin and John R. Hauser, "The Voice of the Customer," *Marketing Science* 12 (winter 1993): pp. 1–25.

[47]Ibid., p. 5.

and data from designed experiments. Design opportunities that fit customer needs might also be revealed by considering the interrelationships between design parameters.

Using Quality Function Development   QFD provides an important framework for bringing critical information on customer needs together with appropriate engineering data on fulfilling those needs. Rather than yielding design solutions, QFD provides a mechanism for exposing and tackling difficult design trade-offs that inevitably appear in the new-product-development process. The approach enables the interfunctional product team to develop a common understanding of the design issues. In a head-to-head comparison with a traditional product-development process, research indicates that QFD enhances communication among team members.[48] In some applications, QFD has reduced design time by 40 percent and design costs by 60 percent, while maintaining or enhancing design quality.[49]

Determinants of New Product Performance and Timeliness

What factors are most important in determining the success or failure of the new product? Why are some firms faster than others in moving projects through the development process? Let's review the available evidence.

The Determinants of Success

Both strategic factors and a firm's proficiency in carrying out the new-product-development process determine new product success.[50]

Strategic Factors   Research suggests that four strategic factors appear to be crucial to new product success. The level of product advantage is the most important. **Product advantage** refers to customer perceptions of product superiority with respect to quality, cost-performance ratio, or function relative to competitors. Successful products offer clear benefits, such as reduced customer costs, and are of higher quality (for example, more durable) than competitors' products. A study of more than 100 new product projects in the chemical industry illustrates the point. Here, Robert Cooper and Elko Kleinschmidt assert, "The winners are new products that offer high relative product quality, have superior price/performance characteristics, provide good value for the money to the customer, are superior to competing products in meeting customer needs, [and] have unique attributes and highly visible benefits that are easily seen by the customer."[51]

---

[48] Abbie Griffin and John R. Hauser, "Patterns of Communication among Marketing, Engineering and Manufacturing: A Comparison between Two New Product Teams," *Management Science* 38 (March 1992): pp. 360–373.

[49] John R. Hauser and Don P. Clausing, "The House of Quality," *Harvard Business Review* 66 (May–June 1988): pp. 63–73.

[50] Mitzi M. Montoya-Weiss and Roger Calantone, "Determinants of New Product Performance: A Review and Meta-Analysis," *Journal of Product Innovation Management* 11 (November 1994): pp. 397–417; see also Robert G. Cooper, Scott J. Edgett, and Elko J. Kleinschmidt, "Benchmarking Best NPD Practices–III," *Research Technology Management* 47 (November–December 2004): pp. 43–55.

[51] Robert G. Cooper and Elko J. Kleinschmidt, "Major New Products: What Distinguishes the Winners in the Chemical Industry?" *Journal of Product Innovation Management* 10 (March 1993): p. 108. See also, Tiger Li and Roger J. Calantone, "The Impact of Market Knowledge Competence on New Product Advantage: Conceptualization and Empirical Examination," *Journal of Marketing* 62 (October 1998): pp. 13–29.

Marketing synergy and technical synergy are also pivotal in new product outcomes. **Marketing synergy** is the fit between the needs of the project and the firm's resources and skills in marketing (for example, personal selling or market research). By contrast, **technical synergy** concerns the fit between the needs of the project and the firm's R&D resources and competencies. New products that match the skills of the firm are likely to succeed.

In addition to the preceding three factors, an **international orientation** also contributes to the success of product innovation.[52] New products designed and developed to meet foreign requirements and targeted at world or nearest-neighbor export markets outperform domestic products on almost every measure, including success rate, profitability, and domestic and foreign market shares. Underlying this success is a strong international focus in market research, product testing with customers, trial selling, and launch efforts.

Development Process Factors   New product success is also associated with particular characteristics of the development process. **Predevelopment proficiency** provides the foundation for a successful product. Predevelopment involves several important tasks such as initial screening, preliminary market and technical assessment, detailed market research study, and preliminary business/financial analysis. Firms that are skilled in completing these upfront tasks are likely to experience new product success.

Market knowledge and **marketing proficiency** are also pivotal in new product outcomes. As might be expected, business marketers with a solid understanding of market needs are likely to succeed. Robert Cooper describes the market planning for a successful product he examined: "Market information was very complete: there was a solid understanding of the customer's needs, wants, and preferences; of the customer's buying behavior and price sensitivity; of the size and trends of the market; and of the competitive situation. Finally, the market launch was well planned, well targeted, proficiently executed, and backed by appropriate resources."[53]

Technical knowledge and **technical proficiency** are other important dimensions of the new-product-development process. When technical developers have a strong base of knowledge about the technical aspects of a potential new product, and when they can proficiently pass through the stages of the new-product-development process (for example, product development, prototype testing, pilot production, and production start-up), these products succeed.

Determinants of Product Success for Japanese Companies

What factors separate the new product winners from the losers in Japanese companies? X. Michael Song and Mark Parry addressed this intriguing question in a study of nearly 800 new product introductions by Japanese firms.[54] They found that Japanese new product managers view the keys to new product success in much the same way as their North American counterparts. Japanese managers identified product advantage as the most important success factor. Other important success factors include technical and marketing synergy as well as predevelopment proficiency.

---

[52] Elko J. Kleinschmidt and Robert G. Cooper, "The Performance Impact of an International Orientation on Product Innovation," *European Journal of Marketing* 22, no. 9 (1988): pp. 56–71.

[53] Robert G. Cooper, *Winning at New Products: Accelerating the Process from Idea to Launch* (Reading, Mass: Addison-Wesley, 1993), p. 27.

[54] X. Michael Song and Mark E. Parry, "What Separates Japanese New Product Winners from Losers," *Journal of Product Innovation Management* 13 (September 1996): pp. 422–436.

Assessing Product Advantage   The Japanese study also provides some useful guidelines for assessing potential product advantage. In making this assessment, warn Song and Parry, "managers should consider whether the product offers potential for reducing consumer costs and expanding consumer capabilities, as well as the likelihood that the product offers improved quality, superior technical performance, and a superior benefit-to-cost ratio."[55]

Fast-Paced Product Development

Rapid product development offers a number of competitive advantages. To illustrate, speed enables a firm to respond to rapidly changing markets and technologies. Moreover, fast product development is usually more efficient because lengthy development processes tend to waste resources on peripheral activities and changes.[56] Of course, although an overemphasis on speed may create other pitfalls, it is becoming an important strategic weapon, particularly in high-technology markets.

Matching the Process to the Development Task   How can a firm accelerate product development? A major study of the global computer industry provides some important benchmarks.[57] Researchers examined 72 product development projects of leading U.S., European, and Asian computer firms. The findings suggest that multiple approaches are used to increase speed in product development. Speed comes from properly matching the approach to the product development task at hand.

Compressed Strategy for Predictable Projects   For well-known markets and technologies, a **compression strategy** speeds development. This strategy views product development as a predictable series of steps that can be compressed. Speed comes from carefully planning these steps and shortening the time it takes to complete each step. This research indicates that the compressed strategy increased the speed of product development for products that had predictable designs and that were targeted for stable and mature markets. Mainframe computers fit into this category—they rely on proprietary hardware, have more predictable designs from project to project, and compete in a mature market.

Experiential Strategy for Unpredictable Projects   For uncertain markets and technologies, an **experiential strategy** accelerates product development. The underlying assumption of this strategy, explain Kathleen Eisenhardt and Behnam Tabrizi, is that "product development is a highly uncertain path through foggy and shifting markets and technologies. The key to fast product development is, then, rapidly building intuition and flexible options in order to learn quickly about and shift with uncertain environments."[58]

Under these conditions, speed comes from multiple design iterations, extensive testing, frequent milestones, and a powerful leader who can keep the product team focused. Here real-time interactions, experimentation, and flexibility are essential.

---

[55] Ibid., p. 422.

[56] See, for example, Robert G. Cooper and Elko J. Kleinschmidt, "Determinants of Timeliness in Product Development," *Journal of Product Innovation Management* 11 (November 1994): pp. 381–417.

[57] Kathleen M. Eisenhardt and Behnam N. Tabrizi, "Accelerating Adaptive Processes: Product Innovation in the Global Computer Industry," *Administrative Science Quarterly* 40 (March 1995): pp. 84–110.

[58] Ibid., p. 91.

The research found that the experiential strategy increased the speed of product development for unpredictable projects such as personal computers—a market characterized by rapidly evolving technology and unpredictable patterns of competition.

Summary

Product innovation is a high-risk and potentially rewarding process. Sustained growth depends on innovative products that respond to existing or emerging consumer needs. Effective managers of innovation channel and control its main directions but have learned to stay flexible and expect surprises. Within the firm, marketing managers pursue strategic activity that falls into two broad categories: induced and autonomous strategic behavior.

New-product-development efforts for existing businesses or market-development projects for the firm's present products are the outgrowth of induced strategic initiatives. In contrast, autonomous strategic efforts take shape outside the firm's current concept of strategy, depart from the current course, and center on new categories of business opportunity; middle managers initiate the project, champion its development, and, if successful, see the project integrated into the firm's concept of strategy. To spawn path-breaking innovation, companies should create a vibrant market for ideas, provide a mechanism to fund nontraditional opportunities, and allow talented employees to pursue projects that capture their imagination.

The long-run competitive position of most business marketing firms depends on their ability to manage and increase their technological base. Core competencies provide the basis for products and product families. Each generation of a product family has a platform that serves as the foundation for specific products targeted at different or complementary market applications. Because companies keep working to make better products they can sell at higher profit margins to the most demanding customers, they often overshoot the needs of mainstream customers. A sustaining innovation provides demanding high-end customers with improved performance, whereas disruptive innovations target new or less-demanding customers with an easy-to-use, less expensive alternative that is "good enough." Disruptive strategies take two forms: low-end and new-market disruptions.

Firms that are successful innovators in turbulent markets combine limited structures (for example, priorities, deadlines) with extensive communication and the freedom to improvise current projects. These successful product creators also explore the future by experimenting with a variety of low-cost probes and build a relentless sense of urgency in the organization by creating new products at predictable time intervals (i.e., time pacing).

Effective new product development requires a thorough knowledge of customer needs and a clear grasp of the technological possibilities. Top-performing firms execute the new-product-development process proficiently, provide adequate resources to support new product objectives, and develop clear new product strategy. Quality function deployment provides a useful method the development team can use to link the needs of the customer directly to specific design decisions. Both strategic factors and the firm's proficiency in executing the new-product-development process are critical to the success of industrial products. Fast-paced product development can provide an important source of competitive advantage. Speed comes from adapting the process to the new-product-development task at hand.

Discussion Questions

1. Research by James Quinn suggests that few major innovations result from highly structured planning systems. What does this imply for the business marketer?

2. Compare and contrast induced and autonomous strategic behavior. Describe the role of the product champion in the new-product-development process.

3. In the Silicon Valley, if an idea has merit, it attracts funding by venture capitalists and it attracts talented employees. What steps can large organizations take to spawn promising new ideas and to better capitalize on the talents of current employees?

4. Compare and contrast a low-end versus a new-market disruptive strategy.

5. In many markets, a new entrant might consider a strategy that provides potential customers with a product or technology that is "good enough" rather than "superior" to existing options. Describe the key tests that a disruptive strategy must pass in order to stack the odds for success in its favor.

6. In fast-changing high-tech industries, some firms have a better record in developing new products than others. Describe the critical factors that drive the new product performance of firms.

7. Rather than planning for and investing in just one version of the future, some firms use low-cost probes to experiment with many possible futures. Evaluate the wisdom of this approach.

8. Describe the process you would follow in defining the customer-needs component of quality function deployment. Assume that the new product in development is an interactive notepad that, when plugged into a telephone, enables people to talk and exchange notes and diagrams.

9. New industrial products that succeed provide clear-cut advantages to customers. Define product advantage and provide an example of a recent new product introduction that fits this definition.

10. Evaluate this statement: "To increase the speed of the new product development process, a firm might follow one strategy for unpredictable projects and an entirely different one for more predictable ones."

Internet Exercise

The Media Lab at MIT has launched a new research initiative to develop a $100 laptop computer—a technology it believes will revolutionize how the world's children will be educated. The laptops will be sold directly to ministries of education or governments and then distributed to schools like textbooks. Go to http://www.laptop.media.mit.edu and (a) describe the strategies that the researchers are using to reduce production costs, thereby permitting a $100 price, and (b) assess the current status of the project.

CASE

Motorola's Disruptive Initiative: The Ultra-Cheap Cell Phone[59]

Motorola was awarded a contract to provide handsets to countries like India, Nigeria, Yemen, and Kenya at a price of $30 each. The contract was awarded by the Emerging Handset program, which is an initiative by the trade group GSM (i.e., global system for mobile communications). Ben Soppitt, a GSM director, notes: "We tend to forget that four billion people have never made a phone call."

Motorola's low-cost phone offers only the voice and text-messaging functions and lacks frills like a color screen or camera. Aided by continuing advances in chip technology that have lowered costs and allowed more functions to be included on each chip, Motorola believes that it will be able to produce the phones for less than $30.

Discussion Questions

1. Drawing on the disruptive technology model, evaluate this initiative by Motorola and discuss the tests the strategy must pass for it to succeed.

2. Will the ultra-cheap cell phone cannibalize sales from the more application-enriched handsets in Motorola's product line?

---

[59]Rebecca Buckman, "Cellphone Game Rings in New Niche: Ultracheap," *The Wall Street Journal*, August 18, 2005, p. B4.

Managing Services
for Business Markets

The important and growing market for business services poses special challenges and meaningful opportunities for the marketing manager. This chapter explores the unique aspects of business services and the special role they play in the business market environment. After reading this chapter, you will understand:

1. the central role that business services assume in customer solutions.

2. the roles that service quality, customer satisfaction, and loyalty assume in service market success.

3. significant factors to consider in formulating a service marketing strategy.

4. how firms are using the Internet to deliver a wide assortment of services.

5. the determinants of new service success and failure.

FedEx Corporation, the global package delivery service, mobilizes for trouble before it occurs: Each night, five empty FedEx jets roam over the United States.[1] Why? So the firm can respond on a moment's notice to unexpected events such as overbooking of packages in Atlanta or an equipment failure in Denver. FedEx excels by making promises to its customers and keeping them. The first major service organization to win the Malcolm Baldrige National Quality Award, FedEx makes specific promises about the timeliness and reliability of package delivery in its advertising and marketing communications. More importantly, FedEx aligns its personnel, facilities, information technology, and equipment to meet those promises. Says Scot Struminger, vice president of information technology at FedEx: "We know that customer loyalty comes from treating customers like you want to be treated."[2]

As this example demonstrates, *services* play a critical role in the marketing programs of many business-to-business firms, whether their primary focus is on a service (FedEx) or whether services provide a promising new path for growth. Indeed, high-tech brands, like IBM or Hewlett-Packard, are built on a promise of value to customers, and service excellence is part of the value package customers demand.[3] In fact, over half of IBM's massive revenue base now comes from services—not products. Clearly, many product manufacturers are now using integrated product and service solutions as a core marketing strategy for creating new growth opportunities; moreover, a vast array of "pure service" firms exist to supply organizations with everything from office cleaning to management consulting and just-in-time delivery to key customers.

This chapter examines the nature of business services, the key buying-behaviors associated with their purchase, the major strategic elements related to services marketing, and the new-service-development process.

From Products to Solutions[4]

The traditional product-centric mind-set rests on the assumption that companies win by creating superior products and continually enhancing the performance of existing products. Here services are seen as an afterthought—a way to make products more attractive. As global competition intensifies and product differentiation quickly fades, strategists at leading firms from General Electric and IBM to Staples and Home Depot are giving increased attention to services, particularly a solution-centric mind-set.

A Solution-Centered Perspective

Rather than starting with the product, a solution-centered approach begins with an analysis of a *customer problem* and ends by identifying the products and services required to solve the problem. Rather than transaction based, the focus of the exchange process is interaction based, and value is co-created by the firm in concert

---

[1] David Leonhardt, "The FedEx Economy," *New York Times*, October 8, 2005, p. B1.

[2] Don Peppers and Martha Rogers, *Return on Customer: Creating Maximum Value from Your Scarcest Resource* (New York: Currency Doubleday, 2005), p. 144.

[3] Scott Ward, Larry Light, and Jonathan Goldstine, "What High-Tech Managers Need to Know about Brands," *Harvard Business Review* 75 (July–August 1999): pp. 85–95.

[4] Except where noted, this section draws on Mohanbir Sawhney, "Going Beyond the Product: Defining, Designing, and Delivering Customer Solutions," Working Paper, Kellogg School of Management, Northwestern University, December 2004, pp. 1–10.

TABLE 11.1 | **FROM A PRODUCT TO A SOLUTIONS PERSPECTIVE**

	Product Perspective	**Solutions Perspective**
Value Proposition	Win by creating innovative products and enriching features of existing products	Win by creating and delivering superior customer solutions
Value Creation	Value is created by the firm	Value is co-created by the customer and the firm
Designing Offerings	Start with the product or service, and then target customer segments	Start with the customer problem, and then assemble required products and services to solve the problem
Company-Customer Relationship	Transaction-based	Interaction-based and centered on the co-creation of solutions
Focus on Quality	Quality of internal processes and company offerings	Quality of customer–firm interactions

SOURCE: Adapted from Mohanbir Sawhney, "Going Beyond the Product: Defining, Designing, and Delivering Customer Solutions," Working Paper, Kellogg School of Management, Northwestern University, December 2004; and C. K. Prahalad and Venkat Ramaswamy, *The Future of Competition: Co-Creating Unique Value with Customers* (Boston: Harvard Business School Press, 2004).

with the customer (Table 11.1). So, customer offerings represent an "integrated combination of products and services designed to provide customized experiences for specific customer segments."[5] Services, as a critical feature of the solution, become a valuable basis for competitive advantage and an important driver of profitability.

UPS Solutions   United Parcel Services of America began by mastering a narrow set of activities involved in the package delivery system—picking up, shipping, tracking, and delivering packages. Adopting a solution-centered focus, UPS tapped new market opportunities[6]:

- Designing transportation networks that reduced the time Ford needed to deliver vehicles from its plants to dealers by up to 40 percent.

- Managing the movement of National Semiconductor's products from its manufacturing plants to customers around the world and helping the customer reduce shipping and inventory costs by 15 percent.

- Partnering with Nike and managing all the back-office processes for direct selling from order management and delivery to customer support.

Determine Unique Capabilities   In developing solutions, business marketing firms must define their unique capabilities and determine how to use them to help customers reduce costs, increase responsiveness, or improve quality. In some cases, this

---

[5] Ibid., p. 4.

[6] Mohanbir Sawhney, Sridhar Balasubramanian, and Vish V. Krishnan, "Creating Growth with Services," *MIT Sloan Management Review* 45 (winter 2004): pp. 34–43.

may involve taking in some of the work or activities that customers now perform. To illustrate, DuPont first sold paint to Ford but now runs Ford's paint shops. "DuPont, which is paid on the basis of the number of painted vehicles, actually sells less paint than before because it has an incentive to paint cars with the least amount of waste. But the company makes more money as a result of the improved efficiency."[7] The DuPont example demonstrates a central point about solutions marketing: *Products provide the platform for the delivery of services.*[8]

Benefits of Solution Marketing

By shifting from a product to a solutions strategy, business-to-business firms gain two important benefits, namely, new avenues for growth and differentiation.

Creating Growth Opportunities   Solutions create fresh opportunities for increasing the amount of business or share-of-wallet that a company receives from its customer base. An expanded portfolio of service-intensive offerings makes this possible. Often, services represent a far larger market opportunity than the core product market. To illustrate, Deere & Company, the agricultural equipment manufacturer, found that the proportion of each dollar farmers spend on equipment has been declining for years and that the bulk of that spending now goes for services. Moreover, by centering on that profit pool, Deere is tapping into a market opportunity that is 10 times larger than the equipment market. To that end, Deere provides a range of services for its customers (for example, health insurance and banking) and is employing innovative technologies to make the farmer's life easier and more productive. For example, Deere is experimenting with global positioning systems (GPS) and biosensors on its combines. C. K. Prahalad and Venkat Ramaswamy describe the initiative:

> Imagine driverless combines and tractors with onboard sensors that can measure the oil content of grain or distinguish between weeds and crops. The benefits are enormous. Farmers can ration herbicide according to soil conditions. GPS-guided steering ensures repeatable accuracy, eliminates overtreating of crops . . . thereby reducing time, fuel, labor, and chemical costs. . . . Farmers can be more productive, minimizing the cost per acre.[9]

Sustaining Differentiation and Customer Loyalty   As farmers view more and more products as commodities, business marketers who emphasize solutions can sustain differentiation more effectively than rivals who maintain a strict focus on the core product offering. Why? According to Mohanbir Sawhney, "Solutions offer many more avenues for differentiation than products because they include a variety of services that can be customized in many unique ways for individual customers."[10] Likewise, by developing a rich network of relationships with members of the customer

---

[7] Ibid., p. 39.

[8] Stephen L. Vargo and Robert F. Lusch, "Evolving to a New Dominant Logic for Marketing," *Journal of Marketing* 68 (January 2004): pp. 1–18.

[9] C. K. Prahalad and Venkat Ramaswamy, *The Future of Competition: Co-Creating Unique Value with Customers* (Boston: Harvard Business School Press, 2004), pp. 93–94.

[10] Mohanbir Sawhney, "Going Beyond the Product," p. 6.

INSIDE BUSINESS MARKETING

To Sell Jet Engines, Teach Your Customer How to Sell Aircraft

A major segment of GE Transportation is the General Electric Aircraft Engines division. This unit is the world's largest manufacturer of jet engines, ranging from small 14,000-pound thrust engines up to the giant GE90, a 115,000-pound thrust engine that powers the Boeing 777. As important as these engines are to GE's profitability, the real profits come from the *service package* surrounding the sale of an engine. A jet engine lasts years, and what often clinches a sale and leads to long-term profits for GE is the full-service "package" that accompanies the engine over its lifespan. One GE marketing manager claims that "jet engines are almost commodities; the key differentiator is the lifetime service we offer our customers."

Interestingly, the airline that buys a new aircraft is generally the decision-making unit that chooses the engine brand to be installed—not the aircraft manufacturer, namely Boeing or Airbus Industrie. Recognizing the importance of the airline in the purchase process for jet engines, GE embarked on a creative strategy. Several new aircraft manufacturers began operations in China in the early 2000s as a result of that country's major economic growth. One manufacturer, specializing in small, regional jets (50- to 70-passenger capacity), selected GE as the engine supplier in 2004, although the

firm would not produce an airplane until at least 2008. The company was starting from scratch when it selected GE engines for its planes.

GE immediately began working with the firm to refine the plane's design and engineering, and these valuable services were one reason it selected GE as the supplier. More importantly, GE assigned one manager and a team of sales, engineering, and marketing specialists to work with the firm. One of GE's first efforts was to bring 25 sales and marketing managers from the Chinese aircraft company to the United States for two weeks of training. These managers represent the personnel who will be selling the aircraft to airline executives in China, as well as in many other parts of the world. The two-week training program centered on the basics of business-to-business marketing—something the Chinese knew little about. GE brought in experienced faculty to teach the Chinese and provided GE managers to follow up on the training at later dates. What is unique about this approach is that a supplier was actually teaching the customer how to market and sell! Of course the benefits to GE are huge: If the Chinese aircraft firm is effective at business-to-business selling to airlines, then more GE engines will be demanded in the future.

organization, co-creating solutions with the customer, and becoming directly connected to the customer's operations, they enhance customer loyalty and throw up severe barriers to competing firms when they attempt to persuade the customer to switch suppliers.

Business Service Marketing: Special Challenges

The development of marketing programs for both products and services can be approached from a common perspective; yet, the relative importance and form of various strategic elements differs between products and services. The underlying explanation for these strategic differences, asserts Henry Assael, lies in the distinctions between a product and a service:

> Services are intangible; products are tangible. Services are consumed at the time of production, but there is a time lag between the production and

FIGURE 11.1 | **BUSINESS PRODUCT-SERVICE CLASSIFICATION BASED ON TANGIBILITY**

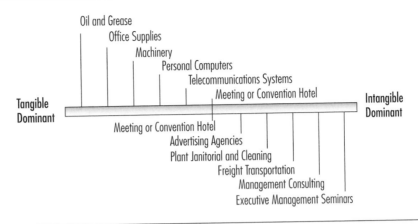

SOURCE: Adapted from G. Lynn Shostack, "Breaking Free from Product Marketing," *Journal of Marketing* 41 (April 1977): p. 77. Published by the American Marketing Association.

consumption of products. Services cannot be stored; products can. Services are highly variable; most products are highly standardized. These differences produce differences in strategic applications that often stand many product marketing principles on their head.[11]

Thus, success in the business service marketplace begins with understanding the meaning of *service*.

Services Are Different

There are inherent differences between goods and services, providing a unique set of marketing challenges for service businesses and for manufacturers that provide services as a core offering. Put simply, services are deeds, processes, and performances.[12] For example, a management consultant's core offerings are primarily deeds and actions performed for customers. The most basic, and universally recognized, difference between goods and services is *intangibility*. Services are more intangible than manufactured goods, and manufactured goods are more tangible than services. Because services are actions or performances, they cannot be seen or touched in the same way that consumers sense tangible goods.

Tangible or Intangible?

Figure 11.1 provides a useful tool for understanding the product-service definitional problem. The continuum suggests that there are very few *pure products* or *pure services*. For example, a personal computer is a physical object made up of tangible elements that facilitate the work of an individual and an organization. In addition to the computer's

---

[11] Henry Assael, *Marketing Management: Strategy and Action* (Boston.: Kent Publishing, 1985), p. 693.

[12] Valarie A. Zeithaml, Mary Jo Bitner, and Dwayne D. Gremler, *Services Marketing: Integrating Customer Focus across the Firm*, 4th ed. (Boston: McGraw-Hill Irwin, 2006), p. 2.

physical design and performance characteristics, the quality of technical service support is an important dimension of the marketing program. Thus, most market offerings comprise a combination of tangible and intangible elements.

Whether an offering is classified as a good or as a service depends on how the organizational buyer views it—whether the tangible or the intangible elements dominate. On one end of the spectrum, grease and oil are tangible-dominant; the essence of what is being bought is the physical product. Management seminars, on the other hand, are intangible-dominant because what is being bought—professional development, education, learning—has few, if any, tangible properties. A convention hotel is in the middle of the continuum because the buyer receives an array of both tangible elements (meals, beverages, notepads, and so on) and intangible benefits (courteous personnel, fast check-ins, meeting room ambiance, and so forth).

The concept of tangibility is especially useful to the business marketer because many business offerings are composed of product and service combinations. The key management task is to evaluate carefully (from the buyer's standpoint) which elements dominate. The more the market offering is characterized by intangible elements, the more difficult it is to apply the standard marketing tools that were developed for products. The business marketer must focus on specialized marketing approaches appropriate for services.

The concept of tangibility also helps the manager focus clearly on the firm's *total market offering*.[13] In addition, it helps the manager recognize that a change in one element of the market offering may completely change the offering in the customer's view. For example, a business marketer who decides to hold spare-parts inventory at a central location and use overnight delivery to meet customer requirements must refocus marketing strategy. The offering has moved toward the intangible end of the continuum because of the intangible benefits of reduced customer inventory and fast transportation. This new "service," which is less tangible, must be carefully explained, and the intangible results of lower inventory costs must be made more concrete to the buyer through an effective promotion program.

In summary, business services are market offerings that are predominantly intangible. However, few services are totally intangible—they often contain elements with tangible properties. In addition to tangibility, business services have other important distinguishing characteristics that influence how they are marketed. Table 11.2 summarizes the core characteristics that further delineate the nature of business services.

Simultaneous Production and Consumption

Because services are generally *consumed as they are produced*, a critical element in the buyer-seller relationship is the effectiveness of the individual who actually provides the service—the IBM technician, the UPS driver, the McKinsey consultant. From the service firm's perspective, the entire marketing strategy may rest on how effectively the individual service provider interacts with the customer. Here the actual service delivery takes place and the promise to the customer is kept or broken. This critical point of contact with the customer is referred to as **interactive or real-time marketing.** Recruiting, hiring, and training personnel assume special importance in business service firms.

---

[13] Arun Sharma, R. Krishnan, and Dhruv Grewal, "Value Creation in Markets: A Critical Area of Focus for Business-to-Business Markets," *Industrial Marketing Management* 30 (June 2001): pp. 391–402.

TABLE 11.2 | UNIQUE SERVICE CHARACTERISTICS

Characteristics	Examples	Marketing Implications
Simultaneous production and consumption	Telephone conference call; management seminar; equipment repair	Direct-seller interaction requires that service be done "right"; requires high-level training for personnel; requires effective screening and recruitment
Nonstandardized output	Management advice varies with the individual consultant; merchandise damages vary from shipment to shipment	Emphasizes strict quality control standards; develop systems that minimize deviation and human error; prepackage the service; look for ways to automate
Perishability: inability to store or stockpile	Unfilled airline seats; an idle computer technician; unrented warehouse space	Plan capacity around peak demand; use pricing and promotion to even out demand peaks and valleys; use overlapping shifts for personnel
Lack of ownership	Use of railroad car; use of consultant's know-how; use of mailing list	Focus promotion on the advantages of nonownership: reduced labor, overhead, and capital; emphasize flexibility

Service Variability

Observe in Table 11.2 that service is *nonstandardized*, meaning that the quality of the service output may vary each time it is provided.[14] Services vary in the amount of equipment and labor used to provide them. For example, a significant human element is involved in teaching an executive seminar compared with providing overnight air-freight service. Generally, the more labor involved in a service, the less uniform the output. In these labor-intensive cases, the user may also find it difficult to judge the quality before the service is provided. Because of uniformity problems, business service providers must focus on finely tuned quality-control programs, invest in "systems" to minimize human error, and seek approaches for automating the service.

Service Perishability

Generally, services *cannot be stored;* that is, if they are not provided at the time they are available, the lost revenue cannot be recaptured. Tied to this characteristic is the fact that demand for services is often unpredictable and widely fluctuating. The service marketer must carefully evaluate capacity—in a service business, **capacity** is a substitute for inventory. If capacity is set for peak demand, a "service inventory" must exist to supply the highest level of demand. As an example, some airlines that provide air shuttle service between New York, Washington, and Boston offer flights that leave every hour. If, on any flight, the plane is full, another plane is brought to the terminal—even for one passenger. An infinite capacity is set so that no single business traveler is dissatisfied. Obviously, setting high capacity levels is costly, and the marketer must analyze the cost versus the lost revenue and customer goodwill that might result from maintaining lower capacity.

---

[14] Valarie A. Zeithaml, A. Parasuraman, and Leonard R. Berry, "Problems and Strategies in Services Marketing," *Journal of Marketing* 49 (spring 1985): p. 34; see also Zeithaml, Berry, and Parasuraman, "Communication and Control Processes in the Delivery of Service Quality," *Journal of Marketing* 52 (April 1988): pp. 35–48.

Nonownership

The final dimension of services shown in Table 11.2 is that the service buyer uses, but *does not own*, the service purchased. Essentially, payment for a service is a payment for the use of, access to, or hire of items. Renting or leasing is "a way for customers to enjoy use of physical goods and facilities that they cannot afford to buy, cannot justify purchasing, or prefer not to retain after use."[15] The service marketer must feature the advantages of nonownership in its communications to the marketplace. The key benefits to emphasize are reductions in staff, overhead, and capital from having a third party provide the service.

Although there may be exceptions, these characteristics provide a useful framework for understanding the nature of business services and isolating special marketing strategy requirements. The framework suggests that different types of service providers should pursue different types of strategies because of the intangibility and heterogeneity of their services. In this case, providers of professional services (consulting, tax advising, accounting, and so on) should develop marketing strategies that emphasize word-of-mouth communication, provide tangible evidence, and employ value pricing to overcome the issues created by intangibility and heterogeneity.[16]

Service Quality

Quality standards are ultimately defined by the customer. Actual performance by the service provider or the provider's perception of quality are of little relevance compared with the customer's perception. "Good" service results when the service provider meets or exceeds the customer's expectations.[17] As a result, many management experts argue that service companies should carefully position themselves so that customers expect a little less than the firm can actually deliver. The strategy: underpromise and overdeliver.

Dimensions of Service Quality

Because business services are intangible and nonstandardized, buyers tend to have greater difficulty evaluating services than evaluating goods. Because they are unable to depend on consistent service performance and quality, service buyers may perceive more risk.[18] As a result, they use a variety of prepurchase information sources to reduce risk. Information from current users (word of mouth) is particularly important. In addition, the evaluation process for services tends to be more abstract, more random, and more heavily based on symbology rather than on concrete decision variables.[19]

---

[15] Christopher Lovelock and Evert Gummesson, "Whither Services Marketing? In Search of a New Paradigm and Fresh Perspectives," *Journal of Services Research* 7 (August 2004): p. 36.

[16] Michael Clemes, Diane Mollenkopf, and Darryl Burn, "An Investigation of Marketing Problems across Service Typologies," *Journal of Services Marketing* 14, no. 6–7 (2000): p. 568.

[17] "William H. Davidow and Bro Uttal, "Service Companies: Focus or Falter," *Harvard Business Review* 67 (July–August 1989): p. 84.

[18] Valarie A. Zeithaml, "How Consumer Evaluation Processes Differ between Goods and Services," in *Marketing of Services*, James H. Donnelly and William R. George, eds. (Chicago: American Marketing Association, 1981), pp. 200–204.

[19] Ibid.

TABLE 11.3 | THE DIMENSIONS OF SERVICE QUALITY

Dimension	Description	Examples
Reliability	Delivering on promises	Promised delivery date met
Responsiveness	Being willing to help	Prompt reply to customers' requests
Assurance	Inspiring trust and confidence	Professional and knowledgeable staff
Empathy	Treating customers as individuals	Adapts to special needs of customer
Tangibles	Representing the service physically	Distinctive materials: brochures, documents

SOURCE: Adapted from Valarie A. Zeithaml, Mary Jo Bitner, and Dwayne D. Gremler, *Services Marketing: Integrating Customer Focus across the Firm*, 4th ed. (Boston: McGraw-Hill Irwin, 2006), pp. 116–120.

Research provides some valuable insights into how customers evaluate service quality. From Table 11.3, note that customers focus on five dimensions in evaluating service quality: reliability, responsiveness, assurance, empathy, and tangibles. Among these dimensions, reliability—delivery on promises—is the most important to customers. High-quality service performance is also shaped by the way frontline service personnel provide it. To the customer, service quality represents a responsive employee, one who inspires confidence, and one who adapts to the customer's unique needs or preferences and delivers the service in a professional manner. In fact, the performance of employees who are in contact with the customer may compensate for temporary service quality problems (for example, a problem reoccurs in a recently repaired photocopier).[20] By promptly acknowledging the error and responding quickly to the problem, the service employee may even strengthen the firm's relationship with the customer.

Customer Satisfaction and Loyalty

Four components of a firm's offering and its customer-linking processes affect customer satisfaction:

1. The basic elements of the product or service that customers expect all competitors to provide.

2. Basic support services, such as technical assistance or training, that make the product or service more effective or easier to use.

3. A recovery process for quickly fixing product or service problems.

4. Extraordinary services that so excel in solving customers' unique problems or in meeting their needs that they make the product or service seem customized.[21]

---

[20]Christian Gronroos, "Relationship Marketing: Strategic and Tactical Implications," *Management Decision*, 34, no. 3 (1996): pp. 5–14.

[21]Thomas O. Jones and W. Earl Sasser Jr., "Why Satisfied Customers Defect," *Harvard Business Review* 73 (November–December 1995): p. 90.

Leading service firms carefully measure and monitor customer satisfaction because it is linked to customer loyalty and, in turn, to long-term profitability.[22] Xerox, for example, regularly surveys more than 400,000 customers regarding product and service satisfaction using a five-point scale from five (high) to one (low). In analyzing the data, Xerox executives made a remarkable discovery: Very satisfied customers (a five rating) were far more loyal than satisfied customers. Very satisfied customers, in fact, were *six times* more likely to repurchase Xerox products than satisfied customers.

Service Recovery

Business marketers cannot always provide flawless service. However, the way the firm responds to a client's service problems has a crucial bearing on customer retention and loyalty. **Service recovery** encompasses the procedures, policies, and processes a firm uses to resolve customer service problems promptly and effectively. For example, when IBM receives a customer complaint, a specialist, who is an expert in the relevant product or service area, is assigned as "resolution owner" of that complaint. On being assigned a customer complaint or problem, the IBM specialist must contact the customer within 48 hours (except in the case of severe problems, where the required response is made much faster). Larry Schiff, a marketing strategist at IBM, describes how the process works from there:

> They introduce themselves as owners of the customer's problem and ask: What's it going to take for you to be very satisfied with the resolution of this complaint? . . . Together with the customer, we negotiate an action plan and then execute that plan until the customer problem is resolved. The problem only gets closed when the customer says it is closed, and we measure this as well."[23] *(That is, customer satisfaction with problem resolution.)*

Service providers who satisfactorily resolve service failures often see that their customer's level of perceived service quality rises. One study in the ocean-freight-shipping industry found that clients who expressed higher satisfaction with claims handling, complaint handling, and problem resolution have a higher level of overall satisfaction with the shipping line.[24] Therefore, business marketers should develop thoughtful and highly responsive processes for dealing with service failures. Some studies have shown that customers who experienced a service failure and had it corrected to their satisfaction have greater loyalty to the supplier than those customers who did not experience a service failure!

Zero Defections

The quality of service provided to business customers has a major effect on customer "defections"—customers who do not come back. Service strategists point out that

---

[22] The Xerox illustration is based on James L. Heskett, Thomas O. Jones, Gary W. Loveman, W. Earl Sasser Jr., and Leonard A. Schlesinger, "Putting the Service-Profit Chain to Work," *Harvard Business Review* 72 (March–April 1994): pp. 164–174.

[23] Larry Schiff, "How Customer Satisfaction Improvement Works to Fuel Business Recovery at IBM," *Journal of Organizational Excellence* 20 (spring 2001): p. 12.

[24] Srinivas Durvasula, Steven Lysonski, and Subhash C. Mehta, "Business-to-Business Marketing: Service Recovery and Customer Satisfaction Issues with Ocean Shipping Lines," *European Journal of Marketing* 34, no. 3–4 (2000): p. 441.

customer defections have a powerful effect on the bottom line.[25] As a company's relationship with a customer lengthens, profits rise—and generally rise considerably. For example, one service firm found that profit from a fourth-year customer is triple that from a first-year customer. Many additional benefits accrue to service companies that retain their customers: They can charge more, the cost of doing business is reduced, and the long-standing customer provides "free" advertising. The implications are clear: Service providers should carefully track customer defections and recognize that continuous improvement in service quality is not a cost but, say Frederick Reichheld and W. Earl Sasser, "an investment in a customer who generates more profit than the margin on a one-time sale."[26]

Return on Quality

A difficult decision for the business-services marketing manager is to determine how much to spend on improving service quality. Clearly, expenditures on quality have diminishing returns—at some point, additional expenditures do not increase profits. To make good decisions on the level of expenditures on quality, managers must justify quality efforts on a financial basis, knowing where to spend on quality improvement, how much to spend, and when to reduce or stop the expenditures. Roland Rust, Anthony Zahorik, and Timothy Keiningham have developed a technique for calculating the "return on investing in quality."[27] Under this approach, service quality benefits are successively linked to customer satisfaction, customer retention, market share, and, finally, to profitability. The relationship between expenditure level and customer-satisfaction change is first measured by managerial judgment and then through market testing. When the relationship has been estimated, the return on quality can be measured statistically. The significant conclusion is that quality improvements should be treated as investments: They must pay off, and spending should not be wasted on efforts that do not produce a return.

Marketing Mix for Business Service Firms

Meeting the needs of service buyers effectively requires an integrated marketing strategy. First, target segments must be selected, and then a marketing mix must be tailored to the expectations of each segment. The business marketing manager must give special consideration to each of the key elements of the service marketing mix: development of service packages, pricing, promotion, and distribution.

In terms of the overall approach that firms develop to interact with their customers, business-to-business service firms are more likely to emphasize *relationship* strategies as opposed to *transactional* strategies.[28] Because the transactional mode

---

[25] Frederick F. Reichheld and W. Earl Sasser, "Zero Defections: Quality Comes to Services," *Harvard Business Review* 68 (September–October 1990): p. 105. See also, Frederick F. Reichheld, *Loyalty Rules! How Today's Leaders Build Lasting Relationships* (Boston: Harvard Business School Press, 2001).

[26] Reichheld and Sasser, "Zero Defections," p. 107.

[27] Roland T. Rust, Anthony J. Zahorik, and Timothy L. Keiningham, "Return on Quality (ROQ): Making Service Quality Financially Accountable," *Journal of Marketing* 59 (April 1995): pp. 58–70. See also Roland T. Rust, Katherine N. Lemon, and Valarie A. Zeithaml, "Return on Marketing: Using Customer Equity to Focus Marketing Strategy," *Journal of Marketing* 68 (January 2004): pp. 109–127.

[28] Nicole E. Coviello, Roderick J. Brodie, Peter J. Danaher, and Wesley J. Johnston, "How Firms Relate to Their Markets: An Empirical Examination of Contemporary Marketing Practices," *Journal of Marketing* 66 (summer 2002): p. 38.

involves an arm's-length relationship, success in marketing business services hinges on the business marketer's ability to develop close and long-lasting ties with customers—based on buyer-seller dependence. The emphasis in marketing business services is on managing the total buyer-seller interaction process.

Segmentation

As with any marketing situation, development of the marketing mix is contingent on the customer segment to be served. Every facet of the service, as well as the methods for promoting, pricing, and delivering it, hinges on the needs of a reasonably homogeneous group of customers. The process for segmenting business markets described in Chapter 5 applies in the services market. However, William Davidow and Bro Uttal suggest that customer service segments differ from usual market segments in significant ways.[29]

First, service segments are often narrower, often because many service customers expect services to be customized. Expectations may not be met if the service received is standardized and routine. Second, service segmentation focuses on what the business buyers expect as opposed to what they need. Assessing buyer expectations plays a major role in selecting a target market and developing the appropriate service package. This assessment is critical because so many studies have shown large differences between the ways customers and suppliers define and rank different service activities.[30]

Because service-quality expectations play such an important role in determining ultimate satisfaction with a service, they can be used to segment business-to-business markets. One study in the mainframe software industry revealed significant differences between "software specialists" (software experts) and "applications developers" (users of software) in the same firm regarding their expectations of new software. The developers (users) had higher expectations about the quality of a supplier's equipment, its employees' responsiveness, and the amount of personal attention provided.[31] The study concluded that different buying-center members may well have different perspectives and different expectations of service quality. The business marketer should carefully evaluate the possibility of using service-quality expectations as a guide for creating marketing strategy.

Finally, segmenting service markets helps the firm adjust service capacity more effectively. Segmentation usually reveals that total demand is made up of numerous smaller, yet more predictable, demand patterns. A hotel can individually forecast and adjust its capacities to the demand patterns of convention visitors, business travelers, foreign tourists, or vacationers.

Service Packages

The **service package** can be thought of as the product dimension of service, including decisions about the essential concept of the service, the range of services provided, and the quality and level of service. In addition, the service package must consider some unique factors—the personnel who perform the service, the physical product

[29] Davidow and Uttal, "Service Companies," p. 79.

[30] Ibid., p. 83.

[31] Leyland Pitt, Michael H. Morris, and Pierre Oosthuizen, "Expectations of Service Quality as an Industrial Market Segmentation Variable," *Service Industries Journal* 16 (January 1996): pp. 1–9. See also Ralph W. Jackson, Lester A. Neidell, and Dale A. Lunsford, "An Empirical Investigation of the Differences in Goods and Services as Perceived by Organizational Buyers," *Industrial Marketing Management* 24 (March 1995): pp. 99–108.

FIGURE 11.2 | **Conceptualizing the Service Product**

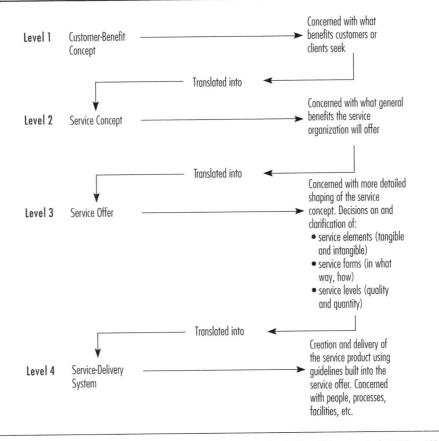

SOURCE: Adapted from Donald Cowell, *The Marketing of Services* (London: William Heinemann, Ltd., 1984), p. 100.

that accompanies the service, and the process of providing the service.[32] A useful way to conceptualize the service product is shown in Figure 11.2.

Customer-Benefit Concept   Services are purchased because of the benefits they offer, and a first step in either creating a service or evaluating an existing one is to define the **customer-benefit concept**—that is, evaluate the core benefit the customer derives from the service. Understanding the customer-benefit concept focuses the business marketer's attention on those attributes—functional, effectual, and psychological— that must be not only offered but also tightly monitored from a quality-control standpoint. For example, a sales manager selecting a resort hotel for an annual sales meeting is purchasing a core benefit that could be stated as "a successful meeting." The hotel marketer must then assess the full range of service attributes and components necessary to provide a successful meeting. Obviously, a wide variety of service elements come into play: (1) meeting-room size, layout, environment, acoustics; (2) meals; (3) comfortable and quiet sleeping rooms; (4) audiovisual equipment; and (5) staff responsiveness.

---

[32] Donald Cowell, *The Marketing of Services* (London: William Heinemann, 1984), p. 73.

As another example, Dun & Bradstreet does not provide its customers with "financial services." Its customer-benefit concept focuses on objective and accurate credit information, security, and even "peace of mind."[33]

Service Concept   Once the customer-benefit concept is understood, the next step is to articulate the **service concept,** which defines the general benefits the service company will provide through the bundle of goods and services it sells to the customer. The service concept translates the customer-benefit concept into the range of benefits the service marketer will *provide*. For a hotel, the service concept might specify the benefits that it will develop: flexibility, responsiveness, and courteousness in providing meeting rooms; a full range of audiovisual equipment; flexible meal schedules; message services; professional personnel; and climate-controlled meeting rooms.

Service Offer   Intimately linked with the service concept is the **service offer,** which spells out in more detail those services to be offered; when, where, and to whom they will be provided; and how they will be presented. The service elements that make up the total service package, including both tangibles and intangibles, must be determined. The service offer of the hotel includes a multitude of tangible elements (soundproof meeting rooms, projection equipment, video players, slide projectors, flip charts, refreshments, heating and air-conditioning, meals) and intangible elements (attitude of meeting-room setup personnel, warmth of greetings from desk clerks and bellhops, response to unique requests, meeting-room ambiance). Generally, management finds it easier to manage the tangible (equipment and physical) elements of the service than to control the intangible elements.

Service Delivery System   The final dimension of the service product is the service delivery system—how the service is provided to the customer. The delivery system includes carefully conceived jobs for people; personnel with capabilities and attitudes necessary for successful performance; equipment, facilities, and layouts for effective customer work flow; and carefully developed procedures and processes aimed at a common set of objectives.[34] Thus, the service delivery system should provide a carefully designed blueprint that describes how the service is rendered for the customer.

For physical products, manufacturing and marketing are generally separate and distinct activities; for services, these two activities are often inseparable.[35] The service performance and the delivery system both create the product and deliver it to customers. This feature of services underscores the important role of people, particularly service providers, in the marketing process. Technicians, repair personnel, and maintenance engineers are intimately involved in customer contact, and they decidedly influence the customer's perception of service quality. The business service marketer must pay close attention to both people and physical evidence (tangible elements such as uniforms) when designing the service package.

Lean Consumption   James Womack and Daniel Jones suggest that the concept of "lean consumption" provides an effective way to think about how services are used.[36]

[33] James L. Heskett, *Managing in the Service Economy* (Boston: Harvard Business School Press, 1986), p. 17.

[34] Ibid., p. 20.

[35] Cowell, *The Marketing of Services*, p. 110.

[36] James Womack and Daniel Jones, "Lean Consumption," *Harvard Business Review* 83 (March 2005): p. 60.

Lean consumption is focused on providing the full value that buyers desire from their goods and services, with the greatest efficiency and least trouble. When a business buys a computer system, for example, this is not a one-time transaction. The company has embarked on the arduous process of researching, obtaining, integrating, maintaining, upgrading, and finally, disposing of this product. For computer manufacturers (whether employees, managers, or entrepreneurs), developing lean consumption processes requires determining how to configure linked business activities, especially across firms, to meet customer needs without wasting their own—or the customer's—time, effort, and resources. These favorable results are achieved by tightly integrating and streamlining the processes of provision and consumption. This approach has been pursued effectively by Fujitsu Services, a leading global provider of outsourced customer service. Companies that contract with Fujitsu to manage their in-house information technology help desks find that the number of calls their desks receive about a recurring problem—say, malfunctioning printers—often falls to near zero. What Fujitsu does is identify and fix the source of the problem—for example, replace the flawed printers with new ones. By seeking the root cause of the problem somewhere up the value stream (often involving multiple companies), Fujitsu has pioneered a way to eliminate problems and reduce costs.[37]

Service Personnel   A first step in creating an effective service package is to ensure that all personnel know, understand, and accept the customer-benefit concept. As Donald Cowell states, "So important are people and their quality to organizations and . . . services that 'internal marketing' is considered to be an important management role to ensure that all staff are customer conscious."[38] In short, the attitudes, skills, knowledge, and behavior of service personnel have a critical effect on the customer's level of satisfaction with the service.

Pricing Business Services

Although product and service pricing policies and strategies share many common threads, the unique characteristics of services create some special pricing problems and opportunities.

Perishability and Managing Demand/Capacity   The demand for services is rarely steady or predictable enough to avoid service perishability. An extremely difficult decision for the business service marketer is to determine the capacity (inventory) of the system: Should it meet peak demand, average demand, or somewhere in between? Pricing can be used to manage the timing of demand and align it with capacity.

To manage demand, the marketer may offer off-peak pricing schemes and price incentives for service orders placed in advance. For example, resort hotels, crowded with pleasure travelers during school vacations and holidays, develop special packages for business groups during the off-season. Similarly, utilities may offer significant rate reductions for off-peak usage. It may also be possible, depending on demand elasticity and competition, to charge premium rates for services provided at peak demand periods. Interestingly, however, a recent study showed that many service firms do not reduce prices to increase business during slow periods.[39]

---

[37] Ibid., p. 61.

[38] Cowell, *The Marketing of Services*, p. 110.

[39] Zeithaml, Parasuraman, and Berry, "Problems and Strategies in Services Marketing," p. 41.

B2B Top Performers

Growing the Service Business at Siemens Building Technologies

Siemens Building Technologies, Inc., with North American headquarters in Buffalo Grove, Illinois, is one of 13 Siemens operating companies in the United States and part of the Automation and Controls group of global parent Siemens AG (Munich, Germany). Siemens Building Technologies was formed through multiple acquisitions of companies that specialized in building automation (heating, ventilation, and air-conditioning controls), life safety systems (fire detection/suppression), and security systems (access/egress systems, motion detection, and monitoring). From its inception in 1998, Siemens Building Technologies began operations in North America as four separate and independent business units (BUs), providing solutions and services in Building Automation, Fire Safety Systems, Security Systems, and Energy Solutions.

When a customer organization purchases building technologies, the decision maker for the "system solution" (that is, equipment) is often different from the decision maker for services. The general contractor decides which building automation, fire safety, and security systems are purchased, and often this decision is based more on price than on functionality. By contrast, service contracts are purchased by the building owner or building manager, whose primary concerns are occupant comfort, convenience, and safety.

Although Siemens Building Technologies service delivery and customer satisfaction ranked among the highest in the industry, market share and growth targets for the service business were not being met. Based on focus groups and customer satisfaction surveys, the leadership team initiated several actions.

First, building owners were simply tired of dealing with three or four different Siemens Building Technologies representatives to sell them service (one for building automation, one for security, etc.). This led Siemens Building Technologies to launch a business alignment initiative that would unite and consolidate field offices, putting all field service departments under individual operations managers and instituting processes and procedures to create common, sustainable service delivery processes. In other words, Siemens Building Technologies began to align itself so it could present *one face to the customer* for service. Dedicated service sales representatives were assigned and empowered to provide a single source for customers' service needs across all business units.

Second, major changes were also made to the information technology (IT) function to allow for better tracking of service performance, contract-capture rates of the installed base, sales performance, and program success. Third, to advance the unification initiative, a new department—Business Excellence—was created. This group reports directly to the president and CEO and allows for a concerted, focused, and high-level commitment to growing Siemens Building Technologies' service business. The new department also provides a platform for launching service growth initiatives across the entire enterprise.

According to Stephen Kohler, senior director of services marketing,

> the most significant impact on the growth of the Siemens Building Technology service business was the development and launch of multi-level service plans that could be configured to meet the level of criticality and price points of the customer. Previously, service contracts were approached from a one-size-fits-all methodology. The result, however, was that customers were receiving the same level of service "experience," but at different prices. The multi-level plan, or service menu, better captures the unique cost-to-serve characteristics that different customers present and provides a way for us to tailor our services to the needs of the customer.

Looking ahead, Kohler adds:

> Siemens Building Technologies will never stop looking for ways to measure customer satisfaction and, more importantly, *loyalty*. Currently this is done through telephone surveys and a series of "Voice-of-the-Customer" forums. These allow direct, face-to-face discussions of customer needs that are not being met and provide a way to uncover additional customer service opportunities that the company might address and leverage to increase growth.

SOURCE: Interview with Stephen Kohler, senior director, Services Marketing, Siemens Building Technologies, Inc., October 17, 2005.

Service Bundling Many business services include a core service as well as various peripheral services. How should the services be priced—as an entity, as a service bundle, or individually? **Bundling** is the practice of marketing two or more services in a package for a special price.[40] Bundling makes sense in the business service environment because most service businesses have a high ratio of fixed costs to variable costs and a high degree of cost sharing among their many related services. Hence, the marginal cost of providing additional services to the core service customer is generally low.

A key decision for the service provider is whether to provide pure or mixed bundling.[41] In **pure bundling,** the services are available only in bundled form—they cannot be purchased separately. In **mixed bundling,** the customer can purchase one or more services individually or purchase the bundle. For example, a public warehouse firm can provide its services—storage, product handling, and clerical activities—in a price-bundled form by charging a single rate (eight cents) for each case the warehouse receives from its manufacturer-client. Or the firm may market each service separately and provide a rate for each service individually (three cents per case for storage, four cents per case for handling, and one cent per case for clerical). Additionally, a multitude of peripheral services can be quoted on an individual basis: physical inventory count, freight company selection and routing, merchandise return and repair, and so on. In this way, the customer can choose the services desired and pay for each separately.

Attracting New Business Various bundling strategies can be used to expand sales either by **cross-selling**—selling a new service to customers who buy an existing service—or by attracting entirely new customers. In the cross-selling situation for a public warehouse, current customers (who use storage services) may be attracted to a new product-labeling service by the offer of a bundled price that results in a discount on the total cost of the two services. Bundling services to attract new customers can be efficient when the service attributes can be evaluated before purchase and the core service is demand elastic.[42] Thus, noncustomized services, where significant competition exists, would seem to be a fertile environment. Bundling insurance coverage with the rental of an automobile may be effective in attracting new business customers for a car rental firm.

In the computer service industry, manufacturers are finding that services formerly sold on an ad hoc basis can be sold more effectively if bundled together. Dell, IBM, and Hewlett-Packard test a variety of service bundles with customers to determine how customers want to buy the services. Clearly, the services, how they are combined, and how the bundle is priced have critical effects on the service firm's success.

Isolate Service Profitability In many industries, firms often supply customers with myriad services such as next-day delivery, customized handling, and specialized labeling. However, not all companies track the real costs of the many services they offer and they have no concrete data on net profit margins. As a result, the high-volume customers who receive the lion's share of these services may be far less profitable than companies think. As business marketers develop and price service offerings, they should give special attention to *cost-to-serve* particular customers and market segments[43] (see Chapter 4). By incorporating cost-to-serve data into the calculation of gross margin,

---

[40] Joseph P. Guiltinan, "The Price Bundling of Services: A Normative Framework," *Journal of Marketing* 51 (April 1987): p. 74.

[41] Ibid., p. 75.

[42] Ibid., p. 81.

[43] Remko Van Hoek and David Evans, "When Good Customers Are Bad," *Harvard Business Review* 83 (September 2005): p. 9.

business marketing strategists are better equipped to price services, identify unprofitable customers, and take action to restore profitability.

Services Promotion

The promotional strategies for services follow many of the same prescriptions as those for products. However, the unique characteristics of business services pose special challenges for the business marketer.

Developing Tangible Clues   Service marketers must concentrate either on featuring the physical evidence elements of their service or on making the intangible elements more tangible. Physical evidence plays an important role in creating the atmosphere and environment in which a service is bought or performed, and it influences the customer's perception of the service. Physical evidence is the tangible aspect of the service package that the business marketer can control. Attempts should be made to translate the image of a service's intangible attributes into something more concrete.

For business service marketers, uniforms, logos, written contracts and guarantees, building appearance, and color schemes are some of the many ways to make their services tangible. An equipment maintenance firm that provides free, written, quarterly inspections helps make its service more tangible. Xerox, IBM, and FedEx offer service guarantees for selected offerings. The credit card created by car rental companies is another example of an attempt to make a service more tangible. A key concern for the service marketer is to develop a well-defined strategy for managing physical evidence—to enhance and differentiate service evidence by creating tangible clues.

Services Distribution

Distribution decisions in the service industry are focused on how to make the service package available and accessible to the user. Direct sale may be accomplished by the user going to the provider (for example, a manufacturer using a public warehouse for storing its product) or, more often, by the provider going to the buyer (for example, photocopier repair). Services can also be delivered over the Internet or provided by channel members.

Delivering Services through the Internet   The Internet provides a powerful new channel for a host of services. For example, application service providers serve business market customers by allowing them to rent access to computer software and hardware, often providing the access over the Internet.[44] To illustrate, for Dunn and Bradstreet, IBM pulls together credit information on 63 million companies, handles customer support and electronic credit-report distribution, and identifies good customer prospects with its analytic software.[45]

Channel Members   Some manufacturers simply rely on their channel members to provide the services associated with the product. Because wholesalers and distributors are much closer to the customer, this arrangement can be a cost-effective way to deliver installation, repair, and maintenance services. IBM, although well known for its physical

---

[44] Jon G. Auerbach, "Playing the New Order: Stocks to Watch as Software Meets the Internet," *The Wall Street Journal*, November 15, 1999, p. R28.

[45] Steve Hamm, "Beyond Blue," *Business Week*, April 18, 2005, pp. 68–76.

products, transformed itself into a services firm as a way to gain competitive advantage. While using a direct sales force to sell its services to large corporate customers, IBM found it difficult to cover the vast middle market in a cost-effective way. The middle market comprises customers with fewer than 2,000 employees or less than $500 million in revenue. IBM's solution was to rely on business partners (channel members) to sell its services to these customers and to provide continuous support to partners and customers via the Internet. In this way, IBM expands its market coverage, responds to the service needs of customers, and increases the profitability and loyalty of its partners.[46]

Developing New Services

The conventional process for developing new physical products—exploration, screening, business analysis, development, testing, and commercialization—appears to apply equally well to services (see Chapter 10).[47] However, designing and introducing new service offerings have been cited as the more difficult challenges for managers in the service sector:

> New product development is inherently more difficult, messier and less successful in the service sector. If a service company perceives a new need and develops a new service, there is less confidence in the result because the service is not subject to the same rigor and predictable outcomes that new products are subject to in the R&D lab. Most service companies focus on geographic extensions of their service or on minor modifications rather than on truly innovative approaches. Innovation in the service sector is the result of trial and error. . . . Service firms have difficulty in linking innovations and imagination to execution of a new offer.[48]

A major stumbling block to creating and launching a new service is the difficulty in "tangibilizing" the service concept. Traditional approaches, such as product prototyping, do not work effectively with services because it is hard to prototype services that are often customized for individual buyers. However, the business service firm can overcome these difficulties by taking steps to improve the new-service-development process. James Heskett offers five steps a firm can take to improve the new-service-development process (Table 11.4). Consistent with the discussion of product innovation, it is important to create the proper organizational climate (for example, entrepreneurial culture, championing, taking risks).

Scenarios for Success and Failure[49]

Services depend on the skills and expertise of the people who deliver them; if a new service lies outside the knowledge base of company personnel (no synergy), the quality and delivery of the service may be deficient, resulting in a less than effective experience

---

[46]Craig Zarley, Joseph Kovar, and Edward Moltzen, "IBM Reaches," *Computer Reseller News* 26 (February 2001): p. 14.

[47]Cowell, *The Marketing of Services*, p. 133.

[48]"Service Management: The Toughest Game in Town," *Management Practice*, 7 (fall 1984): p. 8.

[49]This section is based on Ulrike de Brentani, "New Industrial Service Development: Scenarios for Success and Failure," *Journal of Business Research* 32 (February 1995): pp. 93–103.

TABLE 11.4 | STEPS FOR ENHANCING THE NEW SERVICE DEVELOPMENT PROCESS

Step	Description
1. Establish a culture for the entrepreneurship	Facilitate risk taking and new ideas by creating proper climate: providing R&D funds, doing customer-need research, allowing employees to voice contrary opinions
2. Create an organization to foster new service development	Assemble a "cast": senior sponsor, who has authority; product champion, who provides continuity and enthusiasm; integrator, who brings the functions together and coordinates them; and referee, who establishes rules for the process and then administers them
3. Test ideas in the marketplace	New ideas must weather the acid test of the marketplace because the service concept is intangible
4. Monitor results	Establish success measures and evaluate against these; track customer reaction
5. Reward risk-takers	Reward those taking good risks, even when they are not consistently successful

SOURCE: Adapted from James L. Heskett, *Managing in the Service Economy* (Boston: Harvard Business School Press, 1986), pp. 86–90.

for the customer. Therefore, when managers screen and select new service ideas, they should favor those proposals that score highest on marketing, technical, and operations synergy.

An interesting study tackled these issues: What new-service-development scenarios do managers in industrial service companies typically pursue, and what factors explain why some are likely to succeed while others fail? Observe in Table 11.5 that three scenarios describe the characteristics of successful situations, and two others characterize failed attempts at developing and launching new business services.

New Service Projects That Succeed   The three successful scenarios differ in the nature of the service initiative, the extent of service innovativeness, and the approach followed in developing and marketing the new service offering. The following profiles highlight key differences.

- **The Customized, Expert Service:** These new services are relatively straightforward and inexpensive but are customized to fit the needs and operating systems of client firms. To respond to a customer's unique requirements, expert personnel are crucial to successful strategy execution. Examples include a customized learning center offered by management consultants and a media-planning model developed by a marketing communication firm.

- **The Planned, Pioneering Venture:** These are first-to-market services that are unique, complex, and expensive. A formal and carefully planned new-service-development process is a distinguishing feature of these service projects. Special attention is given to providing potential customers with tangible evidence that illuminates the benefits of the new service offering for them. Examples of these services include a terminal device linking stockbrokers to multiple information origins developed by a telecommunications firm and a

TABLE 11.5	NEW INDUSTRIAL SERVICE DEVELOPMENT: SCENARIOS FOR SUCCESS AND FAILURE

Successes

Customized expert service—New services that fully leverage the firm's expert capabilities and resources—in particular, its expert personnel—in providing clients with a customized and high-quality service outcome. Success at new service development depends on a high-involvement and innovation-oriented corporate environment.

Planned "pioneering" venture—Pioneering new service ventures aimed at attractive, high volume markets. Key descriptive factors include companies first to market, excellent fit with customer/market segment needs—as well as with the company expertise and resources, tangible evidence used to promote the service, and a detailed and high quality execution of the stages of the new service development (NSD) process.

Improved service experience—Enhanced speed and reliability are essential features of these equipment-based new service offerings. Developers have a good understanding of client needs, they have a reputation for service quality, and they use a fairly planned approach for researching, designing, and marketing the new service product.

Failures

Peripheral, low market potential service—The service offers few real benefits and has only low market potential. It is peripheral to the firm's core line of services and appears to lack any real commitment on the part of the firm. The NSD process is haphazard, and companies misuse tangible evidence to feign service quality.

Poorly planned, "industrialized" clone—These are failed "me-too" attempts at "industrializing" complex, equipment-based services. Entering the market long after competitors, the new service projects are deficient in terms of customer orientation, service quality and innovativeness, their fit with corporate capabilities and resources, and the quality of execution of new service development activities.

SOURCE: Figure from "New Industrial Service Development: Scenarios for Success and Failure" by Ulrike de Brentani from JOURNAL OF BUSINESS RESEARCH, 32 (February 1995), p. 96. Reprinted with permission from Elsevier.

computer-based remote access system developed by a bank to simplify payroll processing by organizations.

- **The Improved Service Experience:** Represented here are equipment-based improvements made to a current service offering that increase speed and reliability. Examples include an information systems–based expert production system provided by a computer systems organization and a mutual-fund order network developed by a large financial services organization.

These scenarios share elements that appear to be crucial to the success of new service offerings—they provide a solution for the customer. Whereas industrial services can take many forms, new services are more likely to be successful if they respond to market needs; capitalize on a firm's reputation, skills, and resources; and issue from a well-managed new-service-development process.

New Service Projects That Fail What are the characteristics of new service initiatives that fail, and what can we learn from them? Table 11.5 also describes the following two common scenarios for failure.

- **The Peripheral, Low-Market-Potential Service:** These new services tend to be peripheral to the firm's core offerings, fail to provide added value to the customer, and enter a market with very limited potential. Failures of this type are common across service sectors in the business market.

- **The Poorly Planned "Industrialized" Clone:** These are complex new services that rely on "hard" technology (that is, equipment) for their production and delivery. Often, these are "me-too" services that offer no real customer benefits or improvements over those of well-entrenched competitors. Although banks and insurance firms developed many new industrial service initiatives that fit this profile, inadequate planning was the key feature distinguishing these failed services from other more successful projects.

Clearly, efforts to improve the efficiency and reliability of services by reducing customer contact and introducing equipment-intensive processes have succeeded in certain sectors of the business market. However, states Ulrike de Brentani,

> such development efforts must be accompanied by apparent customer benefits—that is, greater efficiencies and/or superior solutions to problems; a good fit with the capabilities of the developing firm; some competitive advantage in terms of service competitiveness; as well as a set of activities for researching, designing, and launching the new service offerings.[50]

Overall, then, the determinants of success for new services closely resemble those found for successful new products (see Chapter 10).

Summary

Rather than selling individual products and services, leading-edge business-to-business firms focus on what customers really want—solutions. To design a solution, the business marketing manager begins by analyzing a customer problem and then identifies the products and services required to solve that problem. Because solutions can be more readily customized for individual customers, they provide more avenues for differentiation than products can offer.

Business services are distinguished by their intangibility, linked production and consumption, lack of standardization, perishability, and use as opposed to ownership. Together, these characteristics have profound effects on how services should be marketed. Buyers of business services focus on five dimensions of service quality: reliability, responsiveness, assurance, empathy, and tangibles. Because of intangibility and lack of uniformity, service buyers have significant difficulty in comparing and selecting service vendors. Service providers must address this issue in developing their marketing mix.

The marketing mix for business services centers on the traditional elements—service package, pricing, promotion, and distribution—as well as on service personnel, service delivery system, and physical evidence. The goal of the services marketing program is to create satisfied customers. A key first step in creating strategies is to define the customer-benefit concept and the related service concept and offer. Pricing concentrates on influencing demand and capacity as well as on the bundling of service elements. Promotion emphasizes developing employee communication, enhancing

---

[50] Ibid., p. 101.

word-of-mouth promotion, providing tangible clues, and developing interpersonal skills of operating personnel. Distribution is accomplished through direct means, intermediaries, or the Internet. Firms, large and small, are using the Internet to forge closer relationships with customers and to deliver a vast array of new services.

New service marketing can improve effectiveness by creating an organizational culture that fosters risk taking and innovation. Successful new services respond to carefully defined market needs, capitalize on the strengths and reputation of the firm, and issue from a well-planned new-service-development process.

Discussion Questions

1. Local contractors who handle home remodeling and other building projects turn to Home Depot or Lowe's for many products, tools, and materials. Describe how these retailers could adopt a solutions marketing focus to serve those customers.

2. When a company buys a high-end document processor from Xerox or Canon, it is buying a physical product with a bundle of associated services. Describe some of the services that might be associated with such a product. How can buyers evaluate the quality or value of these services?

3. Explain why the growth opportunities for many firms, such as IBM or GE, are far greater in services than they are in products.

4. Leading service companies such as American Express and FedEx measure customer satisfaction on a quarterly basis across the global market. Discuss the relationship between customer satisfaction and loyalty.

5. Many firms have a recovery process in place for situations when their products or services fail to deliver what has been promised to the customer. Illustrate how such a process might work.

6. A new firm creates Web sites and electronic commerce strategies for small businesses. Describe the essential elements to be included in its service product.

7. What is the role of physical evidence in the marketing of a business service?

8. As a luxury resort hotel manager, what approaches might you utilize to manage business demand for hotel space?

9. Critique this statement: "A key dimension of success in services marketing, as opposed to products marketing, is that operating personnel in the service firm play a critical selling and marketing role."

10. What steps can a manager take to enhance the chances of success for a new business service?

Internet Exercise

Autodesk, Inc., a leading design software and digital content company, provides online collaborative services for the building industry that enables more effective management of all project information. Go to http://www.buzzsaw.com and describe the service solutions Autodesk provides for architects and engineers.

CASE

SafePlace Corporation[51]

In February 2002, a guest staying at the Hilton in Cherry Hill, New Jersey, died while attending a convention. Several other guests were sent to the hospital amid fears of an outbreak of Legionnaires' disease or an anthrax attack. Later, it was determined that the guest had died from pneumonia and a blood infection unrelated to the hotel. The alarm surrounding this incident illustrates how important safety has become to a hotel's business.

In response to this need, John C. Fannin III, a fire protection and industrial security expert, formed and is the president of the SafePlace Corporation. The firm is an independent provider of safety accreditation of lodging, health care, educational, and commercial buildings, and other occupancies where the safety of people is a concern. Like the "Good Housekeeping Seal of Approval," SafePlace® Accreditation requirements are based on the security, fire protection, and health and life safety provisions of selected nationally recognized codes, standards, and best practices.

The Hotel du Pont in Wilmington, Delaware, was the first lodging facility in the United States to receive the SafePlace seal of approval. Such an accreditation process involves a rigorous inspection of the facility and identifies the best practices the hotel should employ, such as the use of key cards (as opposed to keys), self-closing doors, smoke detectors and sprinklers in the guest rooms, throw-bolt locks on the doors, excellent water quality, and safe work and food-handling practices among the hotel staff. The Hotel du Pont, which paid a $45,000 fee for the inspection and consulting services, displays the SafePlace seal in the lobby and plans to feature the credential on all of the hotel's marketing materials.

Since launching its program, SafePlace is doing particularly well with four- and five-star luxury properties that, according to Fannin, are "quicker to respond to customer-preferences than a chain would be." In turn, Fannin feels that there is a huge opportunity in the education market, particularly with colleges and universities (for example, the accreditation of dormitories).

Discussion Questions

1. Describe the core service concept and benefits that SafePlace provides to a hotel and its guests. How would you describe these benefits in the body of an ad?

2. Assess the prospects for SafePlace in the education market and suggest a potential strategy the firm might follow to penetrate this market.

---

[51] Maureen Milford, "Hotel Safety Rises to a New Standard," *The News Journal*, May 13, 2002, p. i, accessed September 27, 2002, at http://safeplace.com, and "SafePlace Makes Hospitality Inroads," *Lodging Hospitality*, February 2005, accessed October 15, 2005, at http://safeplace.com.

Managing Business Marketing Channels

The channel of distribution is the marketing manager's bridge to the market. Channel innovation represents a source of competitive advantage that separates market winners from market losers. The business marketer must ensure that the firm's channel is properly aligned to the needs of important market segments. At the same time, the marketer must also satisfy the needs of channel members, whose support is crucial to the success of business marketing strategy. After reading this chapter, you will understand:

1. the alternative paths to business market customers.

2. the critical role of industrial distributors and manufacturers' representatives in marketing channels.

3. the central components of channel design.

4. requirements for successful channel strategy.

Go to Market Strategy, an influential book by Lawrence G. Friedman, aptly describes the central focus of a channel strategy in the business market:

> The success of every go-to-market decision you make, indeed your ability to make smart go-to-market decisions at all, depends on how well you understand your customers. . . . You must build an accurate customer fact-base that clarifies who the customers are in your target market, what they buy, how they buy it, how they want to buy it, and what would motivate them to buy more of it from you.[1]

The channel component of business marketing strategy has two important and related dimensions. First, the channel structure must be designed to accomplish marketing objectives. However, selecting the best channel to accomplish objectives is challenging because (1) the alternatives are numerous, (2) marketing goals differ, and (3) business market segments are so various that separate channels must often be used concurrently. The ever-changing business environment requires managers periodically to reevaluate the channel structure. Stiff competition, new customer requirements, and the rapid growth of the Internet are among the forces that create new opportunities and signal the need for fresh channel strategies.

Second, once the channel structure has been specified, the business marketer must manage the channel to achieve prescribed goals. To do so, the manager must develop procedures for selecting intermediaries, motivating them to achieve desired performance, resolving conflict among channel members, and evaluating performance. This chapter provides a structure for designing and administering the business marketing channel.

The Business Marketing Channel

The link between manufacturers and customers is the **channel of distribution.** The channel accomplishes all the tasks necessary to effect a sale and deliver products to the customer. These tasks include making contact with potential buyers, negotiating, contracting, transferring title, communicating, arranging financing, servicing the product, and providing local inventory, transportation, and storage. These tasks may be performed entirely by the manufacturer or entirely by intermediaries, or may be shared between them. The customer may even undertake some of these functions—for example, customers granted certain discounts might agree to accept larger inventories and the associated storage costs.

Fundamentally, channel management centers on these questions: *Which channel tasks will be performed by the firm, and which tasks, if any, will be performed by channel members?* Figure 12.1 shows various ways to structure business marketing channels. Some channels are **direct;** the manufacturer must perform all the marketing functions needed to make and deliver products. The manufacturer's direct sales force and online marketing channels are examples. Others are **indirect;** that is, some type of intermediary (such as a distributor or dealer) sells or handles the products.

A basic issue in channel management, then, is how to structure the channel so that the tasks are performed optimally. One alternative is for the manufacturer to do it all.

---

[1] Lawrence G. Friedman, *Go to Market: Advanced Techniques and Tools for Selling More Products, to More Customers, More Profitably* (Boston: Butterworth-Heinemann, 2002): p. 116.

FIGURE 12.1 | **B2B Marketing Channels**

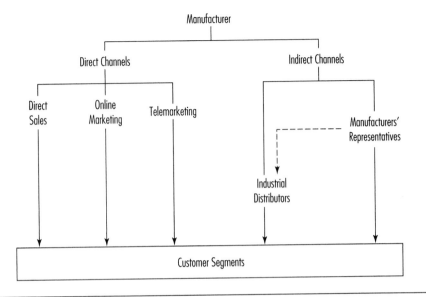

Direct Channels

Direct distribution, common in business marketing, is a channel strategy that does not use intermediaries. The manufacturer's own sales force deals directly with the customer, and the manufacturer has full responsibility for performing all the necessary channel tasks. Direct distribution is often required in business marketing because of the nature of the selling situation. The direct sales approach is feasible when (1) the customers are large and well defined, (2) the customers insist on direct sales, (3) sales involve extensive negotiations with upper management, and (4) selling has to be controlled to ensure that the total product package is properly implemented and to guarantee a quick response to market conditions.

A direct sales force is best used for the most complex sales opportunities: highly customized solutions, large customers, and complex products. Customized solutions and large customer accounts require professional account management, deep product knowledge, and a high degree of selling skill—all attributes a sales representative must possess. Also, when risk in a purchase decision is perceived as high and significant expertise is required in the sale, customers demand a high level of personal attention and relationship building from the direct sales force as a precondition for doing business. However, according to Lawrence Friedman and Timothy Furey, "in the broad middle market and small-customer market, where transactions are generally simpler, other channels can do a more cost-effective job—and can often reach more customers."[2]

Many business marketing firms, such as Xerox, Cisco, and Dell, emphasize e-commerce strategies. Surprisingly, many firms use their Web sites only for promotional purposes and not yet as a sales channel. E-channels can be used by business

---

[2] Lawrence G. Friedman and Timothy R. Furey, *The Channel Advantage* (Boston: Butterworth-Heinemann, 1999), p. 84.

INSIDE BUSINESS MARKETING

IBM Uses the Internet to Collaborate with Channel Partners and Build Customer Loyalty

The Internet provides a valuable way for business marketers to collaborate with distributors or other resellers, sharing resources and cooperating on electronic marketing initiatives. An excellent example of this channel outreach program is IBM TeamPlayers (http://www.ibm-teamplayers.com). This program uses the Web as a communications and information delivery tool to service the channel members (business partners) of IBM.

IBM TeamPlayers offers channel members customized direct-mail campaigns using mail, fax, and e-mail to reach those customers. The Web site is also an outlet for providing help to channel partners in managing their customer databases, developing Web pages, executing telemarketing campaigns, and more, with IBM acting as a clearinghouse for other needed resources.

The program strengthens IBM's relationship with its channel partners. Moreover, the initiative allows IBM to identify and reach end users through the partners and helps strengthen customer loyalty to both IBM channel members and to IBM itself.

SOURCE: Barry Silverstein, *Business-to-Business Internet Marketing: Five Proven Strategies for Increasing Profits Through Internet Direct Marketing* (Gulf Breeze, Fla.: MAXIMUM Press, 1999), p. 307.

marketing firms as (1) information platforms, (2) transaction platforms, and (3) platforms for managing customer relationships. The effect on the business increases as a firm moves from level one to level three. E-commerce strategies are fully explored in Chapter 13.

Indirect Channels

Indirect distribution uses at least one type of intermediary, if not more. Business marketing channels typically include fewer types of intermediaries than do consumer-goods channels. Indirect distribution accounts for a large share of sales in the United States. The Gartner Group reports that 60 percent of the U.S. Gross Domestic Product (GDP) is sold through indirect channels.[3] Manufacturers' representatives and industrial distributors account for most of the transactions handled in this way. Indirect distribution is generally found where (1) markets are fragmented and widely dispersed, (2) low transaction amounts prevail, and (3) buyers typically purchase a number of items, often different brands, in one transaction.[4] For example, IBM's massive sales organization concentrates on large corporate, government, and institutional customers. Industrial distributors effectively and efficiently serve literally thousands of other IBM customers—small to medium-sized organizations. These channel partners assume a vital role in IBM's strategy on a global scale.

---

[3] The Gartner Group, "Partnerware Reports, 'Top 10 Tips for Managing Indirect Sales Channels'," http://www.businesswire.com, June 18, 2002.

[4] E. Raymond Corey, Frank V. Cespedes, and V. Kasturi Rangan, *Going to Market: Distribution Systems for Industrial Products* (Boston: Harvard University Press, 1989), p. 26.

FIGURE 12.2 | TYPICAL SALES CYCLE: TASKS PERFORMED THROUGHOUT THE SALES PROCESS

Lead Generation
↓

Triggered by a sales call, a customer's response to direct mail, or by a request for information through a Web site, an initial contact with a prospect is made.

Lead Qualification
↓

Potential customer is screened: the prospect's need for the product or service, buying interest, funding, and timeframe for making the purchase.

Bid and Proposal
↓

Preparation of bid and proposal to meet customer's requirements (a complex task for large technical projects).

Negotiation and Sales Closure
↓

The negotiation of prices, terms, and conditions, followed by agreement on a binding contract.

Fulfillment
↓

For standardized product or service, delivery of offering to customer. Configuration, customization, and installation for more complex sales.

Customer Care and Support

Post-sale problem resolution, customer guidance, and ongoing contact to insure customer retention, loyalty, and growth.

SOURCE: Adapted from Lawrence G. Friedman, *Go to Market Strategy: Advanced Techniques and Tools for Selling More Products, to More Customers, More Profitably* (Boston: Butterworth-Heinemann, 2002), pp. 234–236.

Integrated Multichannel Models[5]

Leading business marketing firms use multiple sales channels to serve customers in a particular market. The goal of a multichannel model is to coordinate the activities of many channels, such as field sales representatives, channel partners, call centers, and the Web, to enhance the total customer experience and profitability. Consider a typical sales cycle that includes the following tasks: lead generation, lead qualification, negotiation and sales closure, fulfillment, and customer care and support (Figure 12.2). In a multichannel system, different channels can perform different tasks within a single sales transaction with a customer. For example, business marketing firms might use a call center and direct mail to generate leads, field sales representatives to close sales, business partners (for example, industrial distributors) to provide fulfillment (that is, deliver or install product), and a Web site to provide postsale support.

Managing Customer Contact Points Figure 12.3 shows a particular multichannel strategy that a number of leading firms like Oracle Corporation use to reach the vast middle market composed of many small and medium-sized businesses. First, the channels are arranged from top to bottom in terms of their *relative cost of sales* (that is,

[5]This section is based on Friedman, *Go to Market*, pp. 229–257.

FIGURE 12.3 | MULTICHANNEL INTEGRATION MAP: SIMPLE EXAMPLE OF HIGH-COVERAGE PARTNERING MODEL

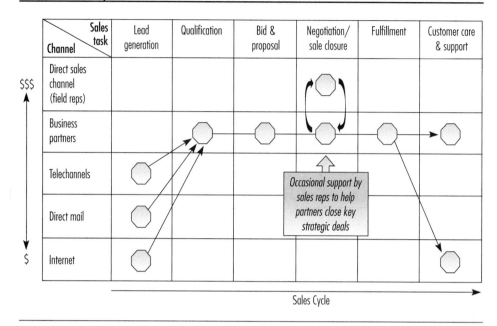

SOURCE: Lawrence G. Friedman, *Go to Market Strategy: Advanced Techniques and Tools for Selling More Products, to More Customers, More Profitably* (Boston: Butterworth-Heinemann, 2002), p. 243. Copyright 2002. Reprinted with permission from Elsevier Science.

direct sales is the most expensive, whereas the Internet is the least). By shifting any selling tasks to lower-cost channels, the business marketer can boost profit margins and reach more customers, in more markets, more efficiently.

Business Partner's Key Role   Returning to Figure 12.3, observe the central role of business partners across the stages of the sales cycle. Low-cost, direct-to-customer channels—like the Internet—are used to generate sales leads, which are then given to channel partners. These partners are then expected to complete the sales cycle but can secure assistance from Oracle's sales representatives to provide guidance and support (when needed) in closing the sale. By emphasizing the partner channel for middle-market customers, Oracle can significantly increase market coverage and penetration while enjoying higher profit margins and lower selling costs. Moreover, this allows the sales force to concentrate on large enterprise customers.

This provides just one example of how a firm can coordinate and configure sales cycle tasks across various sales channels to create an integrated strategy for a particular market. Any firm that serves a variety of markets requires distinctly different multi-channel models to serve customers in those markets. To illustrate, a company might serve key corporate accounts through sales representatives and the middle market through channel partners, call centers, and the Internet.

Customer Relationship Management (CRM) Systems   Many business marketing firms pursue very complex market coverage strategies and use *all* of the alternative paths to the market we have discussed. For example, Hewlett-Packard sells directly through a field sales organization to large enterprises; through channel partners and resellers to the government, education, and the midsize business market; and through retail stores to the small business and home market. Notes Lawrence Friedman, a leading sales strategy consultant, "Add in its customer support channels, Web presence, and H-P has an army of channels that it deploys to provide sales, service, and support to its different market segments."[6] This multichannel mix features many points of contact that H-P must manage and coordinate to ensure a "singular" customer experience across channels. CRM systems provide a valuable tool for coordinating sales channel activities and managing crucial connections and handoffs between them (see Chapter 4). Friedman notes:

> Channel coordination used to be a difficult, messy problem involving the tracking and frequent loss of hand-written memos, voice mails, paper lists of sales leads, and dog-eared customer history files. CRM has ushered in a new era of IT-driven channel coordination, enabling electronic transmission of leads and customer histories from one channel to another, with no loss of information or sales information falling through the cracks.[7]

Participants in the Business Marketing Channel

Channel members assume a central role in the marketing strategies of business-to-business firms, large and small. A channel management strategy begins with an understanding of the intermediaries that may be used. Primary attention is given to two: (1) industrial distributors and (2) manufacturers' representatives. They handle a sizable share of business-to-business sales made through intermediaries.

Distributors

Industrial distributors are the most pervasive and important single force in distribution channels. U.S. distributors number more than 10,000, with sales exceeding $50 billion. Distributors are heavily used for MRO (maintenance, repair, and operations) supplies, with many industrial buyers reporting that they buy as much as 75 percent of their MRO supplies from distributors. Generally, about 75 percent of all business marketers sell *some* products through distributors. What accounts for the unparalleled position of the distributor in the industrial market? What role do distributors play in the industrial distribution process?

Distributors are generally small, independent businesses serving narrow geographic markets. Sales average almost $2 million, although some top $3 billion. Net profits are relatively low as a percentage of sales (4 percent); return on investment averages 11 percent. The typical order is small, and the distributors sell to a multitude of customers in many industries. The typical distributor is able to spread its costs over a sizable group of vendors—it stocks goods from between 200 and 300 manufacturers.

---

[6] Ibid., p. 254.
[7] Ibid., p. 253.

TABLE 12.1 | KEY DISTRIBUTION RESPONSIBILITIES

Responsibility	Activity
Contact	Reach all customers in a defined territory through an outside sales force that calls on customers or through an inside group that receives telephone orders
Product availability	Provide a local inventory and include all supporting activities: credit, just-in-time delivery, order processing, and advice
Repair	Provide easy access to local repair facilities (unavailable from a distant manufacturer)
Assembly and light manufacturing	Purchase material in bulk, then shape, form, or assemble to user requirements

A sales force of outside and inside salespersons generates orders. *Outside salespersons* make regular calls on customers and handle normal account servicing and technical assistance. *Inside salespersons* complement these efforts, processing orders and scheduling delivery; their primary duty is to take telephone orders. Most distributors operate from a single location, but some approach the "supermarket" status with as many as 130 branches.

Compared with their smaller rivals, large distributors seem to have significant advantages. Small distributors are typically unable to achieve the operating economies larger firms enjoy.[8] Large firms can automate much of their operations, enabling them to significantly reduce their sales and general administrative expenses, often to levels approaching 10 percent of sales.

Distributor Responsibilities Table 12.1 shows industrial distributors' primary responsibilities. The products they sell—cutting tools, abrasives, electronic components, ball bearings, handling equipment, pipe, maintenance equipment, and hundreds more—are generally those that buyers need quickly to avoid production disruptions. Thus, the critical elements of the distributor's function are to have these products readily available and to serve as the manufacturer's selling arm.

Distributors are full-service intermediaries; that is, they take title to the products they sell, and they perform the full range of marketing functions. Some of the more important functions are providing credit, offering wide product assortments, delivering goods, offering technical advice, and meeting emergency requirements. Not only are distributors valuable to their manufacturer-suppliers, but their customers generally view them favorably. Some purchasing agents view the distributor as an extension of their "buying arms" because they provide service, technical advice, and product application suggestions.

A Service Focus To create more value for their customers, many large distributors have expanded their range of services. Value is delivered through various supply chain and inventory management services, including automatic replenishment, product assembly,

---

[8] Heidi Elliott, "Distributors, Make Way for the Little Guys," *Electronic Business Today* 22 (September 1996): p. 19.

in-plant stores, and design services.[9] The most popular services involve helping customers design, construct, and, in some cases, operate a supply network. Other value-adding activities include partnerships in which the distributor's field application engineers work at a customer's site to help select components for new product designs. To reap the profits associated with these important services, many distributors now charge separate fees for each unique service.

Classification of Distributors   To select the best distributor for a particular channel, the marketing manager must understand the diversity of distributor operations. Industrial distributors vary according to product lines and user markets. Firms may be ultraspecialized (for example, selling only to municipal water works), or they may carry a broad line of generalized industrial products. However, three primary distributor classifications are usually recognized.

1. **General-line distributors** cater to a broad array of industrial needs. They stock an extensive variety of products and could be likened to the supermarket in consumer-goods markets.

2. **Specialists** focus on one line or on a few related lines. Such a distributor may handle only power transmission equipment—belts, pulleys, and bearings. The most common specialty is fasteners, although specialization also occurs in cutting tools, power transmission equipment, pipes, valves, and fittings. There is a trend toward increased specialization as a result of increasing technical complexity of products and the need for higher levels of precision and quality control.

3. A **combination house** operates in two markets: industrial and consumer. Such a distributor might carry electric motors for industrial customers and hardware and automotive parts to be sold through retailers to final consumers.

Choosing a Distributor   The selection of a distributor depends on the manufacturer's requirements and the needs of target customer segments. The general-line distributor offers the advantage of one-stop purchasing. If customers do not need a high level of service and technical expertise, the general-line distributor is a good choice. The specialist, on the other hand, provides the manufacturer with a high level of technical capability and a well-developed understanding of complex customer requirements. Specialists handle fasteners, for instance, because of the strict quality-control standards that users impose. Manufacturers and their distributors are finding the Internet to be a major catalyst for stimulating collaboration. A recent poll asked distributors which business strategies would have the largest effect on them in the future, and the top two were collaboration with supply-chain partners and new information technologies.[10] E-collaboration includes sales and services, ordering and billing, technical training and engineering, Internet meetings, auctions, and exchanges. These results suggest that Internet collaboration is a critical strategic force in the business-to-business arena.

---

[9]Jim Carbone, "Distributors See Slow Growth Ahead; Expect Electronics Distributors to Offer More Supply Chain and Inventory Services, but Be Prepared to Pay for Them," *Purchasing* 130 (May 16, 2002): p. 27.

[10]Al Tuttle, "E-Collaboration: Build Trust and Success," *Industrial Distribution* 92 (June 1, 2002): p. 59.

The Distributor as a Valuable Partner   The quality of a firm's distributors is often the difference between a highly successful marketing strategy and an ineffective one. Customers prize good distributors, making it all the more necessary to strive continually to engage the best in any given market. Distributors often provide the only economically feasible way of covering the entire market.

In summary, the industrial distributor is a full-service intermediary who takes title to the products sold; maintains inventories; provides credit, delivery, wide product assortment, and technical assistance; and may even do light assembly and manufacturing. Although the distributor is primarily responsible for contacting and supplying present customers, industrial distributors also solicit new accounts and work to expand the market. They generally handle established products—typically used in manufacturing operations, repair, and maintenance—with a broad and large demand.

Industrial distributors are a powerful force in business marketing channels, and all indications point to an expanded role for them. The manufacturer's representative is an equally viable force in the business marketing channel.

Manufacturers' Representatives

For many business marketers who need a strong selling job with a technically complex product, **manufacturers' representatives,** or reps, are the only cost-effective answer. In fact, Erin Anderson and Bob Trinkle note that the one area untouched by the outsourcing boom is field selling in the business-to-business area. They contend that many companies could benefit by using outsourced sales professionals, namely manufacturers' reps, to augment or even replace the field sales force.[11] Reps are salespeople who work independently (or for a rep company), represent several companies in the same geographic area, and sell noncompeting but complementary products.

The Rep's Responsibilities   A rep neither takes title to nor holds inventory of the products handled. (Some reps do, however, keep a limited inventory of repair and maintenance parts.) The rep's forte is expert product knowledge coupled with a keen understanding of the markets and customer needs. Reps are usually limited to defined geographical areas; thus, a manufacturer seeking nationwide distribution usually works with several rep companies.

The Rep-Customer Relationship   Reps are the manufacturers' selling arm, making contact with customers, writing and following up on orders, and linking the manufacturer with the industrial end users. Although paid by the manufacturer, the rep is also important to customers. Often, the efforts of a rep during a customer emergency (for example, an equipment failure) mean the difference between continuing or stopping production. Most reps are thoroughly experienced in the industries they serve—they can offer technical advice while enhancing the customer's leverage with suppliers in securing parts, repair, and delivery. The rep also provides customers with a continuing flow of information on innovations and trends in equipment, as well as on the industry as a whole.

Commission Basis   Reps are paid a commission on sales; the commission varies by industry and by the nature of the selling job. Commissions typically range from a low

---

[11]Erin A. Anderson and Bob Trinkle, *Outsourcing the Sales Function: The Real Cost of Field Sales* (Mason, Ohio: Thomson Higher Education, 2005).

B2B TOP PERFORMERS

Why Intel Uses Reps

Intel has a strong corporate brand, an experienced corporate sales force, and long-standing relationships with broad-line distributors like Arrow Electronics. Intel also uses manufacturers' representatives. Why?

After purchasing a business unit from Digital Equipment Corporation in 1998, Intel realized that several product lines from the acquired unit provided promising market potential, particularly in networking and communications. Specifically, the product lines could spur profitable growth in embedded applications market segments, such as medical equipment and point-of-sale terminals, where the proper application function is based on microprocessors and network connections. At Intel, however, marketing managers argued that the go-to-market strategy that has proved so successful in the PC market would not be suitable for original equipment manufacturers (OEMs) in these sectors.

George Langer, Intel's worldwide representative program manager, explains:

> There was no sales organization, few customer relationships, and more than a few OEMs who questioned Intel's renewed interest in the embedded segments. Intel did not have existing capability to get these product lines in front of appropriate customers. The customer base was large and diverse. (This was not the PC OEM customer base where Intel had nurtured strong relationships over time.) And, finally, the value of the Intel brand was not clearly associated with communications, embedded, and networking market segments. Intel turned to outsourced selling [that is, manufacturers' reps].

SOURCE: Erin Anderson and Bob Trinkle, *Outsourcing the Sales Function: The Real Cost of Field Sales* (Mason, Ohio: Thomson Higher Education, 2005), pp. 74–75.

---

of 2 percent to a high of 18 percent for selected products. The average commission rate is 5.3 percent.[12] Percentage commission compensation is attractive to manufacturers because they have few fixed sales costs. Reps are paid only when they generate orders, and commissions can be adjusted based on industry conditions. Because reps are paid on commission, they are motivated to generate high levels of sales—another fact the manufacturer appreciates.

Experience Reps possess sophisticated product knowledge and typically have extensive experience in the markets they serve. Most reps develop their field experience while working as salespersons for manufacturers. They are motivated to become reps by the desire to be independent and to reap the substantial monetary rewards possible on commission.

When Reps Are Used

- *Large and Small Firms:* Small and medium-sized firms generally have the greatest need for a rep, although many large firms—for example, Dow Chemical, Motorola, and Intel—use them. The reason is primarily economic: Smaller firms cannot justify the expense of maintaining their own sales forces. The rep provides an efficient way to obtain total market coverage, with costs incurred only as sales are made. The quality of the selling job is often very good as a result of the rep's prior experience and market knowledge.

---

[12] Ibid., p. 22.

- *Limited Market Potential:* The rep also plays a vital role when the manufacturer's market potential is limited. A manufacturer may use a direct sales force in heavily concentrated business markets, where the demand is sufficient to support the expense, and use reps to cover less dense markets. Because the rep carries several lines, expenses can be allocated over a much larger sales volume.

- *Servicing Distributors:* Reps may also be employed by a firm that markets through distributors. When a manufacturer sells through hundreds of distributors across the United States, reps may sell to and service those distributors.

- *Reducing Overhead Costs:* Sometimes the commission rate paid to reps exceeds the cost of a direct sales force, yet the supplier continues to use reps. This policy is not as irrational as it appears. Assume, for example, that costs for a direct sales force approximate 8 percent of sales and that a rep's commission rate is 11 percent. Using reps in this case is often justified because of the hidden costs of a sales force. First, the manufacturer does not provide fringe benefits or a fixed salary to reps. Second, the costs of training a rep are usually limited to those required to provide product information. Thus, using reps eliminates significant overhead costs.

Channel Design

Channel design is the dynamic process of developing new channels where none existed and modifying existing channels. The business marketer usually deals with modification of existing channels, although new products and customer segments may require entirely new channels. Regardless of whether the manager is dealing with a new channel or modifying an existing one, channel design is an active rather than a passive task. Effective distribution channels do not simply evolve; they are developed by management, which takes action on the basis of a well-conceived plan that reflects overall marketing goals.

Channel design is best conceptualized as a series of stages that the business marketing manager must complete to be sure that all important channel dimensions have been evaluated (Figure 12.4). The result of the process is to specify the structure that provides the highest probability of achieving the firm's objectives. Note that the process focuses on channel structure and not on channel participants. **Channel structure** refers to the underlying framework: the number of channel levels, the number and types of intermediaries, and the linkages among channel members. Selection of individual intermediaries is indeed important—it is examined later in the chapter.

Stage 1: Channel Objectives

Business firms formulate their marketing strategies to appeal to selected market segments, to earn targeted levels of profits, to maintain or increase sales and market share growth rates, and to achieve all this within specified resource constraints. Each element of the marketing strategy has a specific purpose. Thus, whether the business marketer is designing a totally new channel or redesigning an existing one, the first phase of channel design is to comprehend fully the marketing goals and to formulate corresponding objectives.

FIGURE 12.4 | THE CHANNEL DESIGN PROCESS

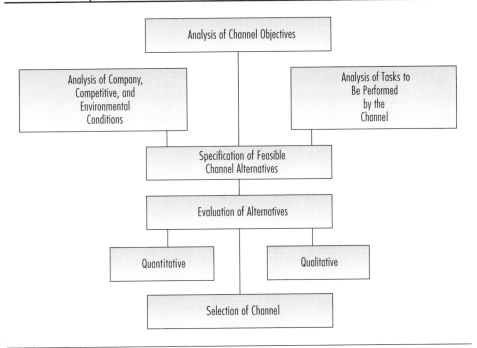

SOURCE: Michael D. Hutt and Thomas W. Speh, "Realigning Industrial Marketing Channels," *Industrial Marketing Management* 12 (July 1983): pp. 171–177.

Structure Based on Profits and Strategy Integration   Channel objectives and design must reflect profit considerations and asset utilization. For example, the cost of maintaining a salesperson in the field—including lodging, meals, and auto rental—is substantial: The total cost-per-call figure is over $200.[13] For the manufacturer, these costs are somewhat fixed in the short run. The need to commit working capital to these costs might be eliminated by switching from a direct sales force to manufacturers' reps, whose compensation, as a percentage of sales, is totally variable. Of course, many other factors, such as the quality of the selling job, must also be evaluated. Channel structure must be compatible with all marketing strategy elements.

Channel Objectives Reflect Marketing Goals   Specific distribution objectives are established on the basis of broad marketing objectives. Distribution objectives force the manager to relate channel design decisions to broader marketing goals. A manufacturer of industrial cleaning products might have a distribution objective of making the products available in every county in the Midwest with more than $5 million in market potential. The distribution objective of a supplier of air-conditioning units might be to make contact with industrial plant architects once every month and with industrial contractors once every two months.

---

[13] "The Cost of Doing Business," *Sales & Marketing Management* 151 (September 1999): p. 56.

FIGURE 12.5 | **FACTORS LIMITING CHOICE OF INDUSTRIAL CHANNEL**

1. **Availability of Good Intermediaries**
   Competitors often "lock up" the better intermediaries.
   Established intermediaries are not always receptive to new products.

2. **Traditional Channel Patterns**
   Established patterns of distribution are difficult to violate.
   Large customers may demand direct sales.

3. **Product Characteristics**
   Technical complexity dictates direct distribution.
   Extensive repair requirements may call for local distributors to service the product line.

4. **Company Financial Resources**
   Capital requirements often preclude direct distribution.

5. **Competitive Strategies**
   Direct service by competitors may force all firms to sell direct.

6. **Geographic Dispersion of Customers**
   A widely dispersed market of small customers often requires low-cost representation afforded by intermediaries.

Marketing and distribution objectives guide the channel design process and actually limit the range of feasible structures. Channel structures need to be developed to reflect both strategic goals (for example, to achieve market share) and efficiency goals (for example, to reduce administrative costs). Generally, management decision models have emphasized effectiveness criteria (strategic issues) and evaluated channel arrangements on the basis of their ability to accomplish certain functions.[14] Both efficiency and effectiveness criteria need to be evaluated when alternative channel arrangements are investigated. Before the alternative channel structures can be evaluated, the business marketing manager must examine other limitations on the choice of channel structures.

Stage 2: Channel Design Constraints

Frequently, the manager has little flexibility in the selection of channel structures because of trade, competitive, company, and environmental factors. In fact, the decision on channel design may be imposed on the manager. The variety of constraining factors is almost limitless.[15] Figure 12.5 summarizes those factors most relevant to the business marketer.

[14] Jan B. Heide, "Interorganizational Governance in Marketing Channels," *Journal of Marketing* 58 (January 1994): p. 83.

[15] For example, see Louis W. Stern and Frederick D. Sturdivant, "Customer-Driven Distribution Systems," *Harvard Business Review* 65 (July–August 1987): pp. 34–41; and Louis Stern and Adel I. El-Ansary, *Marketing Channels*, 4th ed. (Englewood Cliffs, N.J.: Prentice-Hall, 1992), pp. 202–223.

Stage 3: Pervasive Channel Tasks

Each channel structure is evaluated on its ability to perform the required channel activities effectively and efficiently. The concept of a channel as a sequence of activities rather than as a set of institutions is essential to channel design. The business marketing manager must creatively structure the tasks necessary to meet customer requirements and company goals rather than merely accepting existing channel structures or traditional distribution patterns. Increasing manufacturer power may diminish the distributor's role in the channel as the manufacturer assumes more channel activities; the distributor's share of profits and revenues could be reduced accordingly.

Manufacturers' reps typically carry no inventory of their suppliers' products. A manufacturer of semiconductors and microcircuits, after carefully analyzing required channel activities, may decide that although reps can provide the level of sales service needed, large accounts need emergency local inventories of a few selected microcircuits. In this case the solution would not be to abandon the rep as a channel but to compensate the rep for carrying a limited inventory of emergency circuits. Analysis of required tasks and a view of the channel as a sequence of activities would lead the firm to a creative solution to the inventory problem.

The backbone of channel design is the analysis of objectives, constraints, and channel activities. Once these are understood, channel alternatives can be evaluated.

Stage 4: Channel Alternatives

Specification of channel alternatives involves four primary issues:

1. The number of levels in the channel (that is, the degree of "directness").

2. The types of intermediaries to use.

3. The number of channel intermediaries at each level of the channel.

4. The number of channels to use.

The decisions made for each are predicated on the objectives, constraints, and activities previously analyzed.

Degree of Directness   The issue of directness concerns whether products are marketed directly to customers or through intermediaries. The critical aspects of this decision were presented earlier in the chapter.

Assessing Product/Market Factors   The number of channel levels depends on a host of company, product, and market variables. The length of business marketing channels is influenced by availability of capable intermediaries, market factors, and customer characteristics. Market factors include the number of customers, their geographic concentration, and the industry concentration. Customer characteristics include customer perceptions of the significance of the purchase and a customer's volume potential. Channel length increases with greater availability of effective intermediaries and with the number of customers; it decreases when the purchase becomes more significant, when customer potential increases, and when market or industry concentration increases.

There is a greater tendency in business than in consumer-goods marketing to sell directly to the customer. However, direct selling is often not feasible. For such products as tools, abrasives, fasteners, pipes, valves, materials-handling equipment, and wire rope, as much as 97 percent of the annual volume moves only through industrial distributors. This is how customers buy and how they *want* to buy. These products are typically bought frequently, repetitively (straight rebuy), and in small quantities. Instantaneous availability is fundamental; industrial distributors handle such products efficiently.

Type of Intermediary   A wide array of factors influences the choice of intermediaries, with the tasks they perform being of prime importance. These tasks were carefully detailed for both reps and distributors earlier in the chapter.

Different Market Segments   The primary reason for using more than one type of intermediary for the same product is that different market segments require different channel structures. Some firms use three distinct approaches. Large accounts are called on by the firm's own sales force, distributors handle small repeat orders, and manufacturers' reps develop the medium-sized firm market.[16]

How Customers Buy   Like size of accounts, differences in purchase behavior may also dictate using more than one type of intermediary. If a firm produces a wide line of industrial products, some may require high-caliber selling to numerous buying influences in a single buyer's firm. When this occurs, the firm's own sales force would focus on the more complex buying situations, whereas the distributors would sell standardized products from local stocks.

The Number of Intermediaries   How many intermediaries of each type are required to effectively cover a particular market? For a rep channel, the business marketer would select the single best rep organization in each of the geographic areas to be covered. However, companies that use industrial distributors may require two, three, or even more distributors in a geographic market to ensure adequate coverage.

Intensive   Generally, the more standardized the products, the more frequently they are purchased, and the smaller their unit value, the greater the number of distributors in a given market. For example, a firm that requires a number of distributors in each geographic market is following an **intensive distribution** policy.

Selective   By contrast, the policy of carefully choosing one or two channel members in a particular area is referred to as **selective distribution**. The nature of the product and the purchasing process usually dictate a selective approach. For complex products—like material-handling systems or power transmission equipment—the purchasing process is more elaborate and responsive support is of fundamental importance to the customer; the business marketer wants to be represented by a channel partner who can satisfy those requirements. Only a carefully chosen few are used in a given market.

---

[16]Daniel H. McQuiston, "A Conceptual Model for Building and Maintaining Relationships between Manufacturers' Reps and Their Principals," *Industrial Marketing Management* 30 (February 2001): pp. 165–181.

TABLE 12.2 | PROCEDURE FOR EVALUATING CHANNEL ALTERNATIVES

Process	Key Analytical Activities
Step 1: Determine customer requirements	Assess desire for sales assistance, locational convenience, one-stop buying, depth of assortment, and the whole range of possible services.
Step 2: Evaluate potential intermediaries	Assess which type of intermediaries are possible, including direct sale.
Step 3: Analyze costs	Involves three dimensions: (1) Is it feasible for the company to satisfy all customer requirements? (2) What types of supplier support are required? (3) What are the costs of the support systems for each type of channel alternative?
Step 4: Specify constraints— create the "bounded" system	Develop management input on key constraints and company long-term objectives. Specify the channel system structure based on these constraints.
Step 5: Compare options	Compare the "ideal system" specified by customers with the "feasible" system specified by constraints and objectives. If an existing channel is being reviewed, compare it with the ideal and feasible systems.
Step 6: Review constraints and assumptions	Use experts—consultants, lawyers, accountants—to evaluate assumptions.
Step 7: Evaluate gaps	If gaps exist between the existing, ideal, and feasible systems, analyze the underlying reasons.
Step 8: Implementation	Modify the ideal system according to objectives and constraints.

SOURCE: Adapted from Louis W. Stern and Frederick Sturdivant, "Customer-Driven Distribution Systems," *Harvard Business Review* 65 (July–August 1987): pp. 34–41.

The Number of Channels   More than one channel is required when various market segments are served and when the characteristics of the segment dictate a fundamentally unique approach to distribution. Recall, for example, the full complement of sales channels that Hewlett-Packard uses to reach its diverse market segments.

Stage 5: Channel Selection

Most channel design decisions are only slight modifications of the channel structure in response to changing markets, expanding geographic coverage, new customer requirements, or new products. Selection of the appropriate modification in channel structure may be fairly straightforward; in fact, the range of choices may be quite limited.

Evaluating Alternative Channels   A useful approach to evaluating channel options is provided by Louis Stern and Frederick Sturdivant.[17] The approach, depicted in Table 12.2, takes into account all the elements of channel design as well as important customer requirements. The focus of their approach is to create an "ideal" channel system that fully addresses customer needs; once this system is specified, it is compared with the "feasible" channel system created on the basis of management

[17] Stern and Sturdivant, "Customer-Driven Distribution Systems," pp. 34–41.

objectives and constraints. The critical element is to compare both systems on the basis of customer service performance, structure, and costs.

Channel selection is facilitated by looking at "gaps" that may exist between the systems—existing, ideal, and feasible. One of three conclusions could emerge:

1. *All three systems resemble each other.* In this case, the existing system is about as good as it can be. If customer satisfaction is low, the fault is not with the channel design, it is with poor management.

2. *Existing and feasible systems are similar, but differ from the ideal.* Management constraints and objectives may be causing the gap. A careful review is required as specified in step 6 of Table 12.2.

3. *All three systems are different.* If the feasible system lies between the ideal and existing system, the existing system can be changed without sacrificing management goals. Relaxing management constraints might produce even greater benefits.

Qualitative Dimensions   The channel decision maker must consider qualitative as well as quantitative factors. Given two channels with similar economic performance, the critical factor may be the degree of *control* the business marketer can exercise over the channels. Compared with a distributor channel, a rep generally gives the manager more control because the manufacturer maintains title and possession of the goods. The manufacturer may be willing to trade short-run economic benefits for long-term control over channel activities. *Adaptation* by channel members may be important in the long run. Small, undercapitalized distributors may not be able to respond effectively to new competitive challenges or to problems caused by economic downturns.

Channel Administration

Once a particular industrial channel structure is chosen, channel participants must be selected, and arrangements must be made to ensure that all obligations are assigned. Next, channel members must be motivated to perform the tasks necessary to achieve channel objectives. Third, conflict within the channel must be properly controlled. Finally, performance must be controlled and evaluated.

Selection of Channel Members

Why is the selection of channel members (specific companies, rather than *type*, which is specified in the design process) part of channel management rather than an aspect of channel design? The primary reason is that intermediary selection is an ongoing process—some intermediaries choose to leave the channel, and the supplier terminates others. Thus, selection of intermediaries is more or less continuous. Performance of individual channel members must be evaluated continually. The manufacturer should be prepared to move quickly, replacing poor performers with potentially better ones. Including the selection process in ongoing channel management puts the process in its proper perspective.

Securing Good Intermediaries   The marketer can identify prospective channel members through discussions with company salespeople and existing or potential customers, or through trade sources, such as *Industrial Distribution* magazine or the *Verified Directory of Manufacturers' Representatives*. Once the list of potential intermediaries is reduced to a few names, the manufacturer uses the selection criteria to evaluate them. For example, the McGraw-Edison Company uses an intensive checklist to compare prospective channel members; important criteria are market coverage, product lines, personnel, growth, and financial standing.

The formation of the channel is not at all a one-way street. The manufacturer must now persuade the intermediaries to become part of the channel system. Some distributors evaluate potential suppliers just as rigorously as the manufacturers rate them—using many of the same considerations. Manufacturers must often demonstrate the sales and profit potential of their product and be willing to grant the intermediaries some territorial exclusivity. Special efforts are required to convince the very best rep in a market to represent a particular manufacturer's product. Those efforts must demonstrate that the manufacturer will treat the rep organization as a partner and support it.

Motivating Channel Members

Distributors and reps are independent and profit oriented. They are oriented toward their customers and toward whatever means are necessary to satisfy customer needs for industrial products and services. Their perceptions and outlook may differ substantially from those of the manufacturers they represent. As a consequence, marketing strategies can fail when managers do not tailor their programs to the capabilities and orientations of their intermediaries. To manage the business marketing channel effectively, the marketer must understand the intermediaries' perspective and devise ways to motivate them to perform in a way that enhances the manufacturer's long-term success. The manufacturer must continually seek support from intermediaries, and the quality of that support depends on the motivational techniques used.

A Partnership   Channel member motivation begins with the understanding that the channel relationship is a *partnership*. Manufacturers and intermediaries are in business together; whatever expertise and assistance the manufacturer can provide to the intermediaries improves total channel effectiveness. One study of channel relationships suggested that manufacturers may be able to increase the level of resources directed to their products by developing a trusting relationship with their reps; by improving communication through recognition programs, product training, and consultation with the reps; and by informing the reps of plans, explicitly detailing objectives, and providing positive feedback.[18]

Another study of distributor-manufacturer working partnerships recommended similar approaches. It also suggested that manufacturers and their distributors engage in joint annual planning that focuses on specifying the cooperative efforts each firm requires of its partner to reach its objectives and that periodically reviews progress toward objectives.[19] The net result is trust and satisfaction with the partnership as the relationship leads to meeting performance goals.

---

[18]Erin Anderson, Leonard M. Lodish, and Barton A. Weitz, "Resource Allocation in Conventional Channels," *Journal of Marketing Research* 24 (February 1987): p. 95. See also McQuiston, "A Conceptual Model for Building and Maintaining Relationships between Manufacturers' Reps and Their Principals," pp. 165–181.

[19]James C. Anderson and James A. Narus, "A Model of Distribution Firm and Manufacturing Firm Working Partnerships," *Journal of Marketing* 54 (January 1990): p. 56.

Dealer Advisory Councils   One way to enhance the performance of all channel members is to facilitate the sharing of information among them. Distributors or reps may be brought together periodically with the manufacturer's management to review distribution policies, provide advice on marketing strategy, and supply industry intelligence.[20] Intermediaries can voice their opinions on policy matters and are brought directly into the decision-making process. Dayco Corporation uses a dealer council to keep abreast of distributors' changing needs.[21] One month after their meeting, council members receive a written report of suggestions they made and of the programs to be implemented as a result. Generally, Dayco enacts 75 percent of distributor proposals. For dealer councils to be effective, the input of channel members must have a meaningful effect on channel policy decisions.

Margins and Commission   In the final analysis, the primary motivating device is compensation. The surest way to lose intermediary support is compensation policies that do not meet industry and competitive standards. Reps or distributors who feel cheated on commissions or margins shift their attention to products generating a higher profit. The manufacturer must pay the prevailing compensation rates in the industry and must adjust the rates as conditions change.

Intermediaries' compensation should reflect the marketing tasks they perform. If the manufacturer seeks special attention for a new industrial product, most reps require higher commissions. As noted earlier in the chapter, many industrial distributors charge separate fees for the value-added services they provide. For this approach to work effectively, it is critical that the client understands the value it is receiving for the extra charges.

Building Trust   The very nature of a distribution channel—with each member dependent on another for success—can invite conflict. Conflict can be controlled in various ways, including channelwide committees, joint goal setting, and cooperative programs involving a number of marketing strategy elements. To compete, business marketers need to be effective at cooperating within a network of organizations—the channel. For example, an IBM executive who led the team that developed the first IBM PC in 1981 also drove the decision to sell it through dealers and later through the channel. Soon after the introduction of the PC, an executive with American Express Travel Related Services approached the IBM executive with an idea to sell the PCs directly to American Express card members. The IBM executive refused—he wanted the *channel* to get the sale. As a result, IBM secured the commitment and trust of its channel partners, setting the stage for many other strategy initiatives.[22]

Successful cooperation results from relationships in which the parties have a strong sense of communication and trust. Robert M. Morgan and Shelby D. Hunt suggest that relationship commitment and trust develop when (1) firms offer benefits and resources that are superior to what other partners could offer; (2) firms align themselves with other firms that have similar corporate values; (3) firms share valuable information on expectations, markets, and performance; and (4) firms avoid taking

[20] Doug Harper, "Councils Launch Sales Ammo," *Industrial Distribution* 80 (September 1990): pp. 27–30.

[21] James A. Narus and James C. Anderson, "Turn Your Distributors into Partners," *Harvard Business Review* 64 (March–April 1986): p. 68.

[22] Jeff O'Heir, "The Advocates: They Raised Their Voices to Legitimize the Channel," *Computer Reseller News*, June 17, 2002, p. 51.

advantage of their partners.[23] By following these prescriptions, business marketers and their channel networks can enjoy sustainable competitive advantages over their rivals and their networks.

Summary

Channel strategy is an exciting and challenging aspect of business marketing. The challenge derives from the number of alternatives available to the manufacturer in distributing business products. The excitement results from the ever-changing nature of markets, user needs, and competitors.

Channel strategy involves two primary management tasks: designing the overall structure and managing the operation of the channel. Channel design includes evaluating distribution goals, activities, and potential intermediaries. Channel structure includes the number, types, and levels of intermediaries to be used. A central challenge is determining how to create a strategy that effectively blends e-commerce with traditional channels. Business marketing firms use multiple sales channels to serve customers in a particular market segment: company salespersons, channel partners, call centers, direct mail, and the Internet. The goal of a multichannel strategy is to coordinate activities across those channels to enhance the customer's experience while advancing the firm's performance.

The primary participants in business marketing channels are distributors and reps. Distributors provide the full range of marketing services for their suppliers, although customer contact and product availability are their most essential functions. Manufacturers' representatives specialize in selling, providing their suppliers with quality representation and with extensive product and market knowledge. The rep is not involved with physical distribution, leaving that burden to the manufacturers.

Channel management is the ongoing task of administering the channel structure to achieve distribution objectives. Maintaining effective relationships through sound supply-chain management is a key ingredient for success. Selection and motivation of intermediaries are two management tasks vital to channel success. The business marketing manager may need to apply interorganizational management techniques to resolve channel conflict. Conflict can be controlled through a variety of means, including channelwide committees, joint goal setting, and cooperative programs that demonstrate trust and commitment.

Discussion Questions

1. Describe the specific tasks in the typical sales cycle and discuss how different channels (for example, business partners versus the Internet) can perform different tasks within a single sales transaction.

2. Using a multichannel integration map (see Figure 12.3), illustrate how a firm might cover small and medium-sized businesses versus large corporate customers.

3. Explain how a direct distribution channel may be the lowest-cost alternative for one business marketer and the highest-cost alternative for another in the same industry.

---

[23] Robert M. Morgan and Shelby D. Hunt, "The Commitment-Trust Theory of Relationship Marketing," *Journal of Marketing* 58 (July 1994): pp. 20–38.

4. Describe specific product, market, and competitive conditions that lend themselves to (a) a direct channel of distribution, and (b) an indirect channel of distribution.

5. Compare and contrast the functions performed by industrial distributors and manufacturers' representatives.

6. What product/market factors lend themselves to the use of manufacturers' representatives?

7. Often, the business marketer may have very little latitude in selecting the number of channel *levels*. Explain.

8. Explain how a change in segmentation policy (that is, entering new markets) may trigger the need for drastic changes in the industrial channel of distribution.

9. Both business marketers and distributors are interested in achieving profit goals. Why, then, are manufacturer-distributor relationships characterized by conflict? What steps can the marketer take to reduce conflict and thus improve channel performance?

10. For many years, critics have charged that intermediaries contribute strongly to the rising prices of goods in the American economy. Would business marketers improve the level of efficiency and effectiveness in the channel by reducing as far as possible the number of intermediate links in the channel? Support your position.

Internet Exercise

Sysco Corporation is a large distributor of food and food-related products to the food-service industry. The company provides its products and services to approximately 415,000 customers, including restaurants, health-care and educational facilities, lodging establishments, and other food-service customers. Although Cisco Systems is most visible in the business press, Sysco generates over $23 billion in sales annually and has more than 45,000 employees. Go to http://www.sysco.com and identify some of the services Sysco provides.

CASE

Direct Marketing Campaigns at IBM[24]

To reach small to medium-sized businesses, IBM uses a number of different sales channels. For example, when specialized software applications were developed for its AS/400 computer, the firm targeted the community banking market. In launching the campaign, IBM's direct marketing department sent out brochures (which contained an 800 number) to a carefully developed list of prospective banking customers. A call by a prospect to that 800 number went to IBM's call center, where the sales lead was screened and qualified. Qualified leads were then transmitted to business partners (channel members) who then closed the sale. Once the sale was made, IBM then shipped the product to the customer site. Business partners then provided on-site installation and support.

Discussion Question

Describe the benefits of this market coverage strategy to IBM. Next, consider the potential risks of this strategy to IBM and the steps the firm might take to ensure that the strategy works.

---

[24]Friedman and Furey, *The Channel Advantage*, pp. 182–183.

E-Commerce Strategies for Business Markets

Leading-edge firms are using the Internet to transform the way they do business. The Internet provides a powerful platform for conveying information, conducting transactions, delivering innovative services, and building close customer relationships. After reading this chapter, you will understand:

1. the nature of e-commerce in business markets.

2. the role of e-commerce in a firm's marketing strategy.

3. the key issues involved in designing an e-commerce strategy.

Before the Internet, customers had to call Dow Chemical and request a specification sheet for the products they were considering. The information would arrive a few days later by mail. After choosing a product, the customer could then place an order by calling Dow (during business hours, of course). Now, though, such information is available anytime at Dow.com. In turn, a host of more personalized services are available through MyAccount@Dow, which provides information tailored to the customer's requirements.[1] For example, MyAccount@Dow offers secure internal monitoring of a customer's chemical tank levels. When tanks reach a predetermined level, reordering can be automatically triggered. Similarly, Dell's large enterprise customers can use its online resources to manage the inventory of personal computers across the organization, properly configure and upgrade them for different departments, and control the purchase order process in line with the customer's own budget restrictions.[2]

Dow Chemical and Dell represent just two of thousands of business marketers who have integrated the Internet and electronic commerce into their corporate strategies. E-commerce not only speeds up and automates a company's internal processes, but just as importantly, it spreads the efficiency gains to the business systems of its suppliers and customers. E-commerce seamlessly moves data and information over open and closed networks, bringing together previously separate groups inside the organization and throughout the supply chain. By integrating suppliers and customers in this way, the Internet and e-commerce provide powerful tools that are ideally suited to the business-to-business (B2B) arena.

Data on the scope and size of business-to-business transactions on the Internet provide perspective: B2B sales transactions account for over 90 percent of e-commerce transactions.[3] Likewise, total B2B e-commerce in the United States alone will exceed $1 trillion by 2008.[4]

As the massive growth in e-commerce continues, significant opportunities and challenges emerge for all firms that market products and services in the business market. Witness the success of Google's search engine. The Internet is also becoming the main way that managers research B2B purchases.[5] For example, instead of lugging home piles of brochures from a trade show, prospects look up potential suppliers on the Web to learn more about their products and services. Suppliers must change their communication strategy and develop content for the Web first, and print second—if at all. The Web offers interaction and hypertext, and a much better way to communicate complex B2B information tailored to the customer's situation.

Firms that can enter the e-commerce marketplace by leveraging Internet capabilities with information processing, delivery capability, interorganizational collaboration, and flexibility may be able to develop important differential advantages in selected market segments. At the same time, major challenges confront organizations attempting to formulate an e-commerce strategy. These firms must craft a comprehensive e-commerce strategy, radically transform their traditional business models, and deal with rapid changes in e-commerce technology.

[1] George S. Day and Katrina J. Bems, "Capitalizing on the Internet Opportunity," *Journal of Business & Industrial Marketing* 20, no. 4–5 (2005): pp. 160–168.

[2] Don Peppers and Martha Rogers, *Return on Customer* (New York: Currency–Doubleday, 2005), p. 42.

[3] "US E-Commerce Performance Reported," *I-Ways* 28, Issue 3 (2005): pp. 129–132.

[4] "U.S. B-to-B Commerce: Internet Spending 2004–2008," *Marketing News*, July 15, 2005, p. 29.

[5] Jacob Nielsen, "B-to-B Users Want Sites with B-to-C Service, Ease," *B to B* 90 (June 2005): p. 48.

This chapter examines the nature of e-commerce, the role it can play in the organization's marketing strategy, the key elements in designing an e-commerce strategy, and the future direction and potential for e-commerce in business marketing.

Defining E-Commerce[6]

E-commerce involves "business communications and transmissions over networks and through computers, specifically the buying and selling of goods and services, and the transfer of funds through digital communications."[7] Who is going to gain an advantage in the customer-empowered, competitive markets that are being reshaped by e-commerce? A recent study suggests that firms that already excel at managing customer relationships were best equipped to capitalize on the opportunities of the Internet. According to the researchers, George S. Day and Katrina J. Bens: "Those leaders were able to anticipate earlier how to use the Internet to connect with their customers, exploited it faster, and implemented the initiative better." Such best-of-breed relationship builders like Dell, Cisco Systems, FedEx, GE Healthcare, and Johnson Controls relish the prospects presented by e-commerce.[8]

E-commerce can be viewed from several perspectives, each relevant to the business marketer:

1. From a *communications* standpoint, e-commerce is the delivery of information, products/services, or payments via telephone lines, computer networks, or any other electronic means.

2. From a *business process* perspective, e-commerce is the application of technology to the automation of business transactions and work flows.

3. From a *service* perspective, e-commerce is a tool that addresses the desire of firms, customers, and management to cut service costs while improving the quality of goods and increasing the speed of service delivery.

4. From an *online* standpoint, e-commerce provides a vehicle for the buying and selling of products and information on the Internet and for other online services.[9]

As these definitions suggest, e-commerce is multifaceted and complex. However, the rationale for e-commerce is easy to understand: In certain markets and for selected customers, e-commerce can increase sales volume, lower costs, or provide more

---

[6]Some authors and business marketing experts have suggested that the more appropriate term is "e-business," as opposed to "e-commerce." They reason that e-commerce is a broad term that deals with all transactions that are Internet-based, whereas e-business specifically refers to transactions and relationships between organizations. In reality, IBM is given credit for coining the term "e-business" in a major 1997 advertising campaign promoting the notion of *e-business*. The term was new then but has since become routinely used in the press and marketing campaigns of other companies. This chapter will use *e-commerce*.

[7]David J. Good and Roberta J. Schultz, "E-Commerce Strategies for Business-to-Business Service Firms in the Global Environment," *American Business Review* 14 (June 2002): p. 111.

[8]George S. Day and Katrina J. Bens, "Capitalizing on the Internet Opportunity," p. 164; see also Chuang Ming-Ling and Wade H. Shaw, "A Roadmap for E-Business Implementation," *Engineering Management Journal* 17 (June 2005): pp. 3–13.

[9]Ravi Kalkota and Andrew B. Whinston, *Electronic Commerce* (Reading, Mass.: Addison-Wesley, 1997), p. 3.

real-time information to customers. Ravi Kalkota and Andrew Whinston effectively describe the role of e-commerce for the typical organization:

> Depending on how it is applied, e-commerce has the potential to increase revenue by creating new markets for old products, creating new information-based products, and establishing new service delivery channels to better serve and interact with customers. The transaction management aspect of electronic commerce can also enable firms to reduce operating cost by enabling better coordination in the sales, production, and distribution processes (or better supply chain management), and to consolidate operations and reduce overhead.[10]

In short, e-commerce can be applied to almost all phases of business, with the net effect of creating new demand or making most business processes more efficient. E-commerce can be applied to procuring and purchasing products; managing the process for fulfilling customers' orders; providing real-time information on the status of orders, online marketing and advertising; creating online product catalogs and product information data sets; managing the logistics process; and processing the payment of invoices.[11] The applications are limitless, yet not all products and markets can be effectively served through the e-commerce approach. Later in the chapter we will identify situations that offer the greatest potential for effective application of e-commerce. The different applications of e-commerce are depicted in Figure 13.1. Note that e-commerce can play a pivotal role across all functional areas of the business, yet the most important application from the marketing perspective is how e-commerce facilitates interactions with customers.

Key Elements Supporting E-Commerce

The Internet and World Wide Web

E-commerce is possible as a result of the development of the Internet and the World Wide Web. The Internet is not new: Its roots lie in a collection of computers that were linked together in the 1960s as a project of the Advanced Research Projects Agency and the U.S. Department of Defense. Initially, four mainframe computers from four different universities were linked to create a network that would safely transmit data between military computers at different sites. Eventually, other government networks were hooked up to the original network and the system became the Internet. By 1995, companies were allowed to provide uncontrolled for-profit Internet access. Growth in Internet use since that time has been phenomenal, as thousands of new Web sites are being added to the World Wide Web *every hour*.[12]

---

[10] Ibid., p. 5.

[11] Ming-Ling and Shaw, "A Roadmap for E-Business," p. 5.

[12] Ravi Kalkota and Andrew B. Whinston, *Frontiers of Electronic Commerce* (Reading, Mass.: Addison-Wesley, 1996).

FIGURE 13.1 | TYPES OF E-COMMERCE

Interorganizational E-Commerce

1. *Supplier management:* helps to reduce the number of suppliers, lower procurement costs, and increase order cycle time.

2. *Inventory management:* instantaneous transmission of information allows reduction of inventory; tracking of shipments reduces errors and safety stock; out-of-stocks are reduced.

3. *Distribution management:* e-commerce facilitates the transmission of shipping documents and ensures the data is accurate.

4. *Channel management:* rapid dissemination of information to trading partners on changing market and customer conditions. Technical, product, and pricing information can now be posted to electronic bulletin boards. Production information easily shared with all channel partners.

5. *Payment management:* payments can be sent and received electronically among suppliers and distributors, reducing errors, time, and costs.

Intraorganizational E-Commerce

1. *Workgroup communications:* e-mail and electronic bulletin boards are used to facilitate internal communications.

2. *Electronic publishing:* all types of company information, including price sheets, market trends, and product specifications can be organized and disseminated instantaneously.

3. *Sales force productivity:* e-commerce facilitates information flow between production and the sales force and between the sales force and the customer. Firms gain greater access to market and competitor intelligence supplied by the sales force.

Business-to-Customer E-Commerce

1. *Product information:* information on new and existing products is readily available to customers on the firm's Web site.

2. *Sales:* certain products can be sold directly from the firm's Web site, reducing the cost of the transaction and allowing the customer to have real-time information about their order.

3. *Service:* customers can electronically communicate about order status, product applications, problems with products, and product returns.

4. *Payment:* payment can be made by the customer using electronic payment systems.

5. *Marketing research:* firms can use e-commerce, the Internet, and their own Web sites to gather significant quantities of information about customers and potential customers.

Intranets and Extranets

The Internet has become an important element in the marketing strategy of many business marketers; two other very important technological elements, however, are integrated with an Internet strategy. **Intranets** are basically company-specific, internal Internets. An intranet links documents on the organization's scattered internal networks together. A firm's intranet allows different functions and people to share databases, communicate with each other, disseminate timely bulletins, view proprietary information, be trained in various aspects of the firm's business, and share any type of information system the company uses to manage its business. For example, Boeing, the world's largest commercial aircraft manufacturer, maintains a company intranet that is available to more than 200,000 Boeing employees worldwide. One segment of its intranet contains an online course catalog for company educational programs in supervisor training and quality control. Intranets can also incorporate outside news. For example, Factiva, an information company, streams news into enterprise intranets. Much of the external information can be precisely tailored news, relevant to a particular firm.[13]

Extranets, on the other hand, are links that allow business partners such as suppliers, distributors, and customers to connect to a company's internal networks (intranets) over the Internet or through virtual private networks. An extranet is created when two organizations connect their intranets for business communications and transactions. The purpose of an extranet is to provide a communication mechanism to streamline business processes that normally take place elsewhere. Hewlett-Packard and Procter & Gamble, for example, have established extranet links to their advertising agencies to speed the review of ad campaigns. Extranets allow business partners to use the Internet by providing a unique password to access the company's intranet. Companies in the printing industry allow customers access to their internal networks to track print jobs as they move through production or to browse databases of images of other media assets.[14] Extranets allow the firm to customize information and interaction with each specific customer who is granted access to its intranet. Hewlett-Packard offers one of the largest medical sites on the Web. To secure customized information, hospital customers have special passwords (based on a profile they provide) that automatically connects them to "special pricing" negotiated through that institution's contracts with Hewlett-Packard.[15]

The Strategic Role of E-Commerce

For the business marketer, the crucial question is: What role does e-commerce assume in the firm's overall marketing strategy? One of the great dangers of e-commerce is the potential for managers to become enamored with the technology and ignore the strategic elements and the role of e-commerce in the firm's overall mission. The Internet and, more specifically, e-commerce are just instruments for accomplishing marketing goals—the need for sound marketing strategy remains. Many companies have made Internet decisions based on hype and new business models that do not fit their organization, with unfortunate and unprofitable results (Table 13.1).

---

[13] Marydee Ojola, "Adding External Knowledge to Business Web Sites," *Online* 26, no. 4 (July–August 2002): p. 3.

[14] "Extranets Enhance Customer Relations," *Graphic Arts Monthly* (January 1999): p. 89.

[15] Curt Werner, "Health Care E-Commerce, Still in Its Infancy, But Growing Fast," *Health Industry Today* 8 (September 1998): p. 9.

TABLE 13.1 | THE "HYPE" AND REALITY OF E-COMMERCE

Hype	Reality
1. E-commerce enables businesses to bypass channel partners.	1. If existing channels provide key services like shipping, support, training, credit, etc., they are still needed.
2. Businesses can use the Internet as their sole means of acquiring new customers.	2. The Internet extends the firm's reach; most firms in the B2B market have not found the Internet an effective way to get new customers. All forms of communication are usually required to acquire a new customer.
3. B2B firms with extensive Web sites are able to substantially eliminate their advertising and promotion expenditures.	3. Advertising and promotion are key elements of a Web-based strategy to inform potential prospects about the site. Advertising is still needed to play its typical role of building awareness and recognition.
4. Web sites need to provide all the information that any prospect would ever need.	4. Providing all possible information on a Web site is a great way to provide competitors with all the competitive intelligence they need on your firm.
5. A B2B Web site's success is measured by how long a visitor stays.	5. Success of a B2B Web site is measured by the successful action it has triggered, not the length of stay. The goal is to provide access to information quickly and accurately.
6. Internet marketing will replace traditional marketing media.	6. The computer cannot achieve many of the functions of traditional media or the benefits of personal iteraction with the customer. Radio didn't replace newspapers, and TV didn't replace radio.

SOURCE: Adapted from: Hank Barnes, "Getting Past the Hype: Internet Opportunities for B-to-B Marketers," *Marketing News*, February 1, 1999, pp. 11–12.

E-Commerce as a Strategic Component

The use of e-commerce and, more specifically, the Internet is just like any other element the business marketer uses to accomplish the firm's mission: It must be focused, based on carefully crafted objectives, and directed at specific target segments. For the marketer, the Internet can be viewed as:

1. a communication device to build customer relationships.

2. an alternative distribution channel.

3. a valuable medium for delivering services to customers.

4. a tool for gathering marketing research data.

5. a method for integrating supply-chain members.

In short, the Internet usually does not replace existing distribution channels; rather, it supports or supplements them. In a similar way, the Internet does not eliminate the selling function; rather, it facilitates the salesperson's efforts and enhances the effectiveness and efficiency of the sales function. Likewise, B2B e-commerce should be viewed as an end-to-end business process, involving the entire supply chain.[16]

---

[16] Judith Lamont, "Collaborative Commerce Revitalizes Supply Chain," *KM World* 14 (July–August 2005): pp. 16–18.

INSIDE BUSINESS MARKETING

UPS Delivers the Goods Using Sophisticated E-Commerce Technology

UPS (United Parcel Service Inc.) is an express carrier, package delivery company, and a global provider of specialized transportation and logistic services. Over more than 90 years, the firm has expanded from a small regional parcel delivery service into a global company. The company's primary business is the time-definite delivery of packages and documents throughout the United States and more than 200 other countries and territories. UPS is a leading adopter of e-commerce applications, offering new services like UPS online tools and many other service applications to customers through its logistics group at http://www.e-logistics.ups.com and at http://www.upslogistics.com.

As the Internet was taking shape, UPS made a financial commitment to transform its operations to meet the changing needs of the digital economy by establishing electronic connectivity with its extensive base of customers. UPS is responding to the challenge of meeting these changing needs as the e-business evolution continues to unfold. The company has a variety of business solutions that give customers productive ways to manage, grow, and even transform their businesses to stay on course in a fast-changing, competitive market.

UPS uses a carefully crafted e-commerce strategy to deliver the goods quickly, reliably, and securely. Customers can obtain accurate account and shipping information in real time. Consistently meeting or exceeding service expectations enhances customer satisfaction and loyalty. Every day, UPS links 1.8 million sellers to 7 million buyers all over the world and delivers $1.5 billion worth of packages, including more than 55 percent of all the goods ordered online. The company has formed alliances with the leading e-commerce software providers and helps customers build or improve their Web sites so they, in turn, can better serve their customers. UPS e-Logistics, a subsidiary of UPS, provides integrated, end-to-end supply-chain management services to e-commerce businesses and dot.com divisions of established companies. Whether the customers' orders come via Web site, phone, mail, or other channel, UPS e-Logistics can manage the entire fulfillment process from inventory management to shipping—providing clients with new capabilities for managing information, moving inventory, and advancing customer loyalty.

SOURCE: Nabil Alghalith, "Competing with IT: The UPS Case," *Journal of American Academy of Business* 7 (September 2005): pp. 7–15.

According to Hank Barnes, to be successful, business marketers must integrate the Internet and e-commerce into the "fabric of their traditional business operations, leveraging it as a new communications tool that can increase sales, satisfaction and service levels."[17] Essentially, e-commerce extends a firm's reach but does not change the fundamentals of how a firm acquires, responds to, and satisfies its customers. Andy Grove, a legendary Intel executive, aptly concludes, "Implementing the new e-commerce model does not mean simply selling something over the Internet, but incorporating the Net into the day-to-day functioning of the company, in particular, as a mode for B2B transactions and for building customer relationships."[18] From the perspective of the entire supply chain, a key issue is to include further use of e-commerce to automate and reduce the cost of transactions and to increase the quality of product data flows throughout the supply chain.[19]

---

[17] Hank Barnes, "Getting Past the Hype: Internet Opportunities for B-to-B Marketers," *Marketing News*, February 1, 1999, p. 11.

[18] As quoted in David Troy, "E-Commerce: Foundations of Business Strategy," Caliber Learning Systems, http://www.caliber.com.

[19] Aislinn McCormick, "Meeting Global Supply Demands," *Bookseller*, September 16, 2005, pp. 12–13.

What the Internet Can Do

Before exploring the strategic elements of e-commerce, let's explore the important benefits of an effectively developed e-commerce strategy. The Internet is a powerful tool when used properly, and the advantages are significant in terms of more effectively serving customers, communicating useful information, and lowering the cost of doing business.

The Internet: Strategy Still Matters[20]

As an important new technology, many executives, entrepreneurs, and investors assumed that the Internet would change everything and render many of the old rules about competition obsolete. Michael Porter, the noted strategist, argues persuasively that the old rules still apply and the fundamentals of strategy remain unchanged. Indeed, caught up in the excitement over Internet technology, many firms—dot-coms and established firms alike—made bad decisions. For example, some firms have shifted the basis of competition toward price and away from traditional factors like quality, features, and service. Under such conditions, all competitors in an industry struggle to turn a profit. Alternatively, other firms forfeited important proprietary advantages by rushing into misguided partnerships and outsourcing relationships.

The lesson for business marketers is that the Internet is an enabling technology—a powerful set of tools that complements, rather than replaces, traditional ways of competing. So, the key decision is not whether to use Internet technology but rather how to deploy it. Successful companies integrate Internet initiatives directly into established operations rather than setting these strategies apart in a specialized e-commerce unit. Michael Porter provides this incisive forecast:

> Basic Internet applications will become table stakes—companies will not be able to survive without them, but they will not gain any advantage from them. The more robust competitive advantages will arise from traditional strengths such as unique products, proprietary content, distinctive physical activities, superior product knowledge, and strong service and relationships. . . . Ultimately, strategies that integrate the Internet and traditional competitive advantages and ways of competing should win in many industries.[21]

Enhanced Customer Focus, Responsiveness, and Relationships   The Internet allows business marketers to align with their customers on order management and also on product configuration and design, resulting in better customer service and more satisfied customers. Because the Internet creates direct links between customers and factories, corporate buyers can tailor products to meet their exact requirements. Many business marketers now encourage customers to customize products exactly to their specifications right on the Web site.

Reduced Transaction Costs   When customers use the Internet to communicate with suppliers, the supplier is able to provide low-cost access to both order entry and

---

[20] This section is based on Michael Porter, "Strategy and the Internet," *Harvard Business Review* 79 (March 2001): pp. 63–78.
[21] Ibid., p. 78.

order tracking 24 hours a day, seven days a week. Transactions that do not require in-person services can be handled in a cost-effective manner on a Web site, and the firm can devote more staff to working with higher-margin customers requiring personal attention. In effect, e-commerce transfers operations to "self-service," allowing customers to download materials themselves and reducing costs for all involved. Some companies report that by automating transactions over the Internet, the cost of a purchasing transaction has declined from $150 to $25.[22]

Integration of the Supply Chain   The Internet allows companies to electronically link far-flung constituencies, including customers, suppliers, intermediaries, and alliance partners, in spite of organizational, geographical, and functional boundaries. All the supply-chain participants can be linked by a common database that is shared over the Internet, making the entire value-adding process seamless and more efficient. The key to effective supply-chain operations is the sharing of vital information: sales forecasts, production plans, delivery schedules, tracking of finished product shipments through the distribution network, inventory levels at various points in the supply chain, final sales versus planned sales, and the like.

QAD, Inc., is the developer of *Total eCommerce Solution*, which provides a menu of software and services that help companies more consistently integrate global partners into their back-end systems. The *Total eCommerce Solution* lets users extend supply-chain processes to partners, providing the ultimate in business integration. QAD's services include capabilities for communications, translation, application integration, business process management, and business activity management.[23]

Focus on Core Business   The Internet makes it easier for companies to focus on what they do best and spin off or contract out other operations to third parties that are tied to them through the Internet. In this way, the Internet helps companies develop a "virtual company" that contracts with other firms to perform such functions as manufacturing to warehousing. Boeing developed its latest airplane, the Boeing 777, with a portfolio of relationships among subcontractors and lead customers that were linked electronically.[24] This approach allows Boeing to devote more assets and human resources to the critical area of product design.

Access Global Markets   E-commerce provides a powerful means for B2B firms to penetrate far-flung global markets. Using the latest in IT technology, firms can exploit and expand their customer base all over the world by implementing order and procurement management systems, as well as sales, marketing, and customer support functionality.[25] By relying on an e-commerce solution, there is no need to invest in a sales force or "bricks and mortar" assets in every potential market—the Web provides the necessary coverage. The approach requires a highly effective Internet strategy and the logistics capacity to efficiently make products available to customers in a

[22] Dave Rumar, "Electronic Commerce Helps Cut Transaction Costs, Reduce Red Tape," *Computing Canada* 25, no. 32 (1999): p. 24.

[23] Renee Boucher Ferguson, "E-com Gets Integration Help," *eWeek*, September 9, 2005, pp. 25–35.

[24] N. Venkatraman and John C. Henderson, "Real Strategies for Virtual Organizing," *Sloan Management Review* 40 (winter 1999): p. 5.

[25] "E-commerce Market in Asia Still Hot after Dotcom Burst," *Xinhua*, July 31, 2002, accessed at WorldSources, Inc., Online.

timely fashion. Once markets are established through e-commerce, the sales volume in a particular geographic area may, in fact, justify the presence of a sales force, offices, and logistics operations.

Crafting an E-Commerce Strategy

Developing a B2B strategy for e-commerce is no different from developing any other type of marketing strategy. The process begins with an evaluation of the company's products, customers, competitive situation, resources, and operations to better understand how all of these elements mesh with an e-commerce strategy. Figure 13.2 provides a valuable framework that outlines important strategic and tactical questions that surround e-commerce strategies. Answering these questions helps the business marketing manager to carefully define what the firm hopes to accomplish through an e-commerce strategy and to assess several important resource issues associated with implementing the strategy.

Delineating E-Commerce Objectives

A guiding principle in formulating an Internet strategy is to understand that the Internet and the associated technology are nothing more than *tools* the business marketing strategist uses in satisfying the customer at a profit: "It is not a competitive strategy or the capability to deliver the strategy."[26] Often, there is a temptation to think that the Internet can eliminate the need for salespeople, reduce expenditures on trade advertising, or totally replace traditional distribution channels and marketing intermediaries. For most firms, the Internet *supplements* the company's traditional marketing strategy, making it more effective or less costly, or both.

In the channels area, for example, many companies find it beneficial to use the Web to support their dealers' e-business efforts by providing Web-based information to them, offering Web co-op advertising dollars, and allowing the dealers to build a front-end site onto the company's site.[27] Moreover, firms have found that a sales force remains vital in forging customer relationships once an Internet strategy is implemented. In fact, the Internet can make the sales force more productive. For example, PSS WorldMedical is a huge medical products distributor with a sales force of over 700 people. The company developed a closed Customer Link system that allows customers to order products online. The system does not replace the sales force; rather, sales reps continue to earn commissions on Customer Link sales from their accounts. The salespeople can then concentrate more fully on higher-profit capital equipment sales.

Synchronizing the Web with Strategy   Just as important as enhancing effectiveness and efficiency, the Internet is often used to reach an entirely new or different target market. Many experts consider Dell the "poster child for business-to-business e-commerce" because of its legendary success in cost-effectiveness by providing custom-designed personal computers through the Internet.[28] Yet what makes Dell a great Internet marketer is its ability to take its customer-obsessed direct-sales practices

---

[26]Day and Bens, "Capitalizing on the Internet Opportunity," p. 167.

[27]Ginger Conlon, "Direct Impact," *Sales & Marketing Management* 151 (December 1999): p. 57.

[28]Eryn Brown, "Nine Ways to Win on the Web," *Fortune*, May 17, 1999, p. 114.

FIGURE 13.2 | QUESTIONS TO GUIDE E-COMMERCE STRATEGY FORMULATION

1. Customers and Markets

What are we already doing on the Internet, and how do our activities align with customer needs?

How can we use the Internet to provide better customer service?

How can we use the Internet to make our sales channels more effective?

2. Competitive Threats

How might traditional competitors and e-business startups change market dynamics and take away market share or customers?

Will failure to act now precipitate a crisis within the next two years in any of our lines of business?

Can we ignore the Internet if our competitors are using it to gain attention and pricing advantages?

3. People and Infrastructure

Do our management teams and technical staff have the skills to run an Internet business?

What will it cost to fix weaknesses—exposed by our Internet business strategy—in our processes, infrastructure, and enterprise systems?

What are appropriate business and financial structures for managing Internet business risk?

4. Sources and Operations

Are we blinding ourselves by making assumptions based on our old way of doing business that doesn't fit with the Internet?

What are the Internet-relevant models that match ours, threaten us, or are suitable ways to conduct business?

How can we use the Internet to make supply chains more efficient?

How can we use the Internet to lower our operating costs? How long will it take?

SOURCE: "A CEO's Internet Business Strategy Checklist: The Leading Questions," *Business Technology Journal—Recent Research*, http://gartner112.gartnerweb.com (accessed April 19, 1999).

and enhance them using the Web. Says Eryn Brown in *Fortune*, "There isn't anything the company does online that it doesn't do in the physical world. Yet Dell and its customers know that nothing beats the Web for taking care of the 'annoying stuff.'"[29] Dell serves as an excellent model for any B2B marketer seeking to fully synchronize an Internet strategy with its traditional salesperson-based strategy. The key to Dell's

[29] Ibid., p. 114.

FIGURE 13.3 | **3M's Web Site Makes It Easy to Personalize Post-it Notes**

SOURCE: http://www.postitcustomnotes.com, accessed November 6, 2005, Courtesy of 3M.

success is understanding the Internet's role and its relationship to all other elements of the firm's marketing strategy.

Specific Objectives of Internet Marketing Strategies

The Internet can be effective in providing information as well as in stimulating customer action. Internet marketing objectives resemble those of any type of communication strategy in the business marketplace. The Internet can be used to focus on cognitive objectives like stimulating awareness and knowledge of the company, creating a favorable attitude toward the firm, or stimulating the buyer to purchase. Note the Web site for "Personalized Post-it Notes" displayed in Figure 13.3. In this case, 3M allows the customer to use its "Post-it Custom Notes" Web site to create the exact personalized Post-it note desired. This site also illustrates how easy it is for customers to customize the product to their requirements, place an order, and visit "distributor studios" online to create the product. By visiting http://www.postitcustomnotes.com, you can experience firsthand how easy it is to use this online service. The following are some of the most common objectives that business marketers may have for the e-commerce portion of their business[30]:

1. Target a specific market or group of customers.

2. Build recognition of the company name and brands.

3. Convey a cutting-edge image.

---

[30]Adapted from Neal J. Hannon, *The Business of the Internet* (Cambridge, Mass.: International Thompson Publishing Company, 1998): p. 210.

B2B TOP PERFORMERS

GE Healthcare: Using the Web to Create New Services

GE Healthcare discovered a way to use the Web to capture data from its medical equipment and create valuable new services for its customers. The resulting service application, called eCenter, monitors and transmits patient data from MRI machines and other GE medical equipment directly to the radiologist (the customer). In addition to enhancing a patient's care, GE can also provide valuable information that can enhance the productivity of a health-care organization. GE can analyze the data from one customer and compare it to that of other customer sites to see how productive a specific radiology department is compared with others that use the same equipment.

Building on the success of this initiative, GE has developed similar eCenter applications for other GE divisions. To illustrate, GE Power Systems customers, such as utilities, can analyze the performance of their turbines versus others in the industry. By viewing information technology as a strategic capability rather than a support function, GE is enhancing its products and co-creating new value with customers.

SOURCE: C. K. Prahalad and Venkat Ramaswamy, *The Future of Competition: Co-Creating New Value with Customers* (Boston: Harvard Business School Press, 2004), p. 223.

4. Conduct market research.

5. Interact with existing customers and cultivate new ones.

6. Provide real-time information on products, services, and company finances to customers and supply-chain partners.

7. Sell products and services.

8. Sell in a more efficient manner.

9. Advertise in a new medium.

10. Generate leads for the sales force.

11. Provide a medium for customer service.

12. Build strong relationships with customers.

The specific objectives for a firm's Internet business dictate the issues it must deal with in formulating its strategy. For example, if the objective is to create new sales volume, critical attention must be given to creating systems for handling transactions and providing logistical and service support. Internet strategies vary dramatically based on the objectives.

Internet Strategy Implementation

With the Internet objectives fully delineated, the business marketer is positi͏ ͏ ͏ develop an Internet strategy. As with any marketing process, the Internet strate͏ carefully address product, promotion, channels, and pricing. Discussion of͏ implementation begins by examining the important product-related dimensi͏

FIGURE 13.4 | W.W. GRAINGER MAKES IT EASY TO FIND PRODUCTS AND PLACE ORDERS

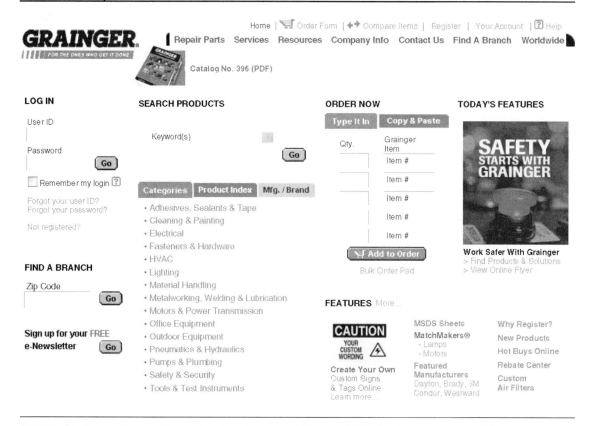

SOURCE: http://www.grainger.com/Grainger/wwg/start.shtml, accessed November 8, 2005. Reprinted by permission of Grainger.

The Internet Product

The Internet product is a complex array of physical elements, software, hardware, extranets, intranets, services, and information. The Web site is the major product element in a company's e-commerce strategy. Even though it may include other dimensions, the heart of an e-commerce strategy is the company's Web site, for here all interactions with the customer are most cost-effectively handled.

As indicated, a Web site has to be developed on the basis of a careful delineation of company objectives, and it is rare that a Web site is developed on the basis of a single objective. Thus, the design of the Web site becomes more complicated as top management articulates additional objectives. Other obvious ingredients in the planning process are the needs of the targeted Web site visitors. A focus on both dimensions assures that both the company and the customer are accommodated.

Observe from Figure 13.4 how W. W. Grainger uses its Web site to make it easy for customers to look for products and place an order. If the customer wants to browse through different product lines, that can be done with a single click. For a repetitive order, the customer simply types in the product number and quantity desired. To pick up a product immediately at a Grainger location, the customer only needs to click on "find a branch."

INSIDE BUSINESS MARKETING

Top-Rated B2B Web Sites

The best Web sites present rich and detailed information in an easy-to-understand format. They avoid clutter and preserve the company's brand identity. Rather than emphasizing a one-sided sales pitch, they engage users in two-way communication and offer case studies and success stories tailored to their industry or particular requirements. Included among leading Web sites that experts assign high marks are:

Company	Features
Hewlett-Packard	Modern design
	Excellent e-commerce function and plentiful customer service options
3Com Corporation	Extensive product information presented clearly and without clutter
	Industry-specific case studies and customer success stories
Dell	Professional and sophisticated e-commerce focus that presents content and products in a compelling fashion
	Excellent tools for product comparisons
Microsoft	Extensive site with many useful interactive tools, such as online demos, product comparison features, and software downloads segmented for various audiences
Office Depot, Inc.	Superb e-commerce focus
	Users can browse comprehensive product content or do "catalog quick shop."

SOURCE: "10 Great Web Sites," *B to B*, September 12, 2005, accessed at http://www. btobonline.com and "The 2003 NetMarketing 100: Best B-to-B Web Sites," *B to B*, November 15, 2003, accessed at http://www.btobonline.com.

Successful Web Site Design To effectively develop a Web site, the designer needs to think like a user—to anticipate how the customer will use the site and the features that will make it easy to use. To use the Internet as a marketing tool, the Web site should allow customers to easily move along the sales process, provide a quick and easy way to find the product they desire, and determine whether the products fit their needs. If the site can accomplish these goals, then the next function is to ease the financial transaction. Speed, ease of use, and security are central to completing the sales transaction and meeting the customer's service expectations.

Internet Catalogs One of the first applications of e-commerce for many business marketers that sell components, materials, and maintenance and operating resources is to develop an electronic catalog on their Web site. Rather than leafing through thousands of pages, the user can define exact requirements and easily locate the appropriate item in the catalog. Moreover, the catalog can be continuously updated.

As Chapter 3 indicated, many firms have embraced e-purchasing applications. They have found that electronic purchasing dramatically enhances the effectiveness of buyers and reduces the time and expense they spend searching for operating resources or non-production goods. Firms without Internet catalogs will probably be unable to compete in the future because of the great savings buyers can glean through e-purchasing.

Reverse Auctions   Reverse auctions, which involve one buyer and many sellers, have been embraced by purchasing managers across business market sectors, including government. Why? Many companies such as Quaker Oats, DaimlerChrysler, and GlaxoSmithKline report millions of dollars of savings with reverse auctions compared with traditional buying methods. FreeMarkets, Inc.—now a part of Ariba—organizes reverse auctions for manufacturers like United Technologies. Here suppliers bid on purchase contracts for component parts, raw materials, and commodities. Firms that sell commodity items face the greatest threat. Experts suggest that reverse auctions can damage long-standing buyer-seller relationships.

Some purchasers have realized that continuously pressing for deeper price cuts might backfire by inhibiting collaboration. If profit margins continually decline, suppliers might be forced to consolidate, thereby enhancing their power.[31]

Channel Considerations with Internet Marketing

Firms that develop an Internet strategy must consider several important distribution channel issues. An Internet marketing presence requires the manager to evaluate the following: the effect on channel efficiencies, current marketing intermediaries, and information sharing among channel members; the ability to rapidly deliver product, and the need to consider the outsourcing of some key channel functions.

Channel Efficiencies   One significant benefit of B2B Internet marketing is its positive impact on efficiency in the channels of distribution. The Internet uses low-cost communications technology to automate all kinds of business transactions. As a result, much of the back-office paperwork and tasks required in dealing with channel members that once occupied the time of several employees can now be automated. By linking information systems with channel members through the Web, a firm helps intermediaries more effectively monitor inventory and the flow of goods through their warehouses.

For example, a large tool distributor uses an e-commerce platform from *PartsWatch*.[32] The architecture enables many innovative benefits like central price updating and automatic catalog updates—without the need to send or receive disks. The primary effect on the channel is that a company has real-time information on demand at every level of distribution. Customers can use the system to direct and manage the channel and efficiently provide real-time central services for all channel partners. These types of networks allow purchase order transactions, order acknowledgments, and shipment notices to flow seamlessly between distributors and their suppliers.

Effect on Current Intermediaries   Internet strategies pose interesting questions about the structure of a firm's distribution channel. Depending on the nature of the manufacturer's Internet strategy, the role of current channel members may be expanded, unchanged, or dramatically reduced. The key variable is how much value the

---

[31] Sandy D. Jap, "An Exploratory Study of the Introduction of Online Reverse Auctions," *Journal of Marketing* 67 (July 2003): pp. 96–107.

[32] Chris Miller, "E-commerce Advances," *Aftermarket Business* 115 (September 2005): p. 14.

channel member adds to the process of marketing and physically distributing products. In some instances, the channel members may be called on to serve target markets that cannot be effectively covered through an Internet approach. Traditional channel members have often been relegated to the role of serving very small niche markets that cannot be efficiently served through direct or Internet marketing approaches. Others have been able to expand their role because of a manufacturer's new Internet strategy. Because many Internet transactions involve one or a few items, a real need exists for someone to handle the process of physically fulfilling orders, and hence a new opportunity is presented to a distributor who can perform this function effectively.

Disintermediation   Because the Internet improves connectivity among firms, it dramatically reduces the cost of communication and coordination in exchange transactions. In a networked channel, firms can bypass intermediaries who have traditionally facilitated the flow of information and goods between firms and their customers. This situation is referred to as **disintermediation,** and indications are that it is taking hold in several B2B sectors. Large travel agencies that sell airline tickets to corporate accounts are experiencing disintermediation as airlines have created their own Web sites that provide as much or more information to the corporate traveler as did the agencies. Itineraries, including hotels, rental cars, and airline tickets, can be arranged with the click of a mouse, and payment can be processed through a secure channel right on the Web site. In fact, because of the success of these Internet strategies, the airlines have reduced or eliminated travel agent commissions, forcing many to either go out of business or focus on leisure travel segments.

The Internet as a Channel Alternative

The Internet can be a very effective "channel" of distribution for reaching selected target markets. Rarely do business marketers rely solely on the Internet as their only approach for contacting customers and consummating sales. Rather, the Internet is but one channel or method for doing business with target markets. At AMP, the large manufacturer of electronic connectors, its Internet catalog complements traditional channels such as the sales force, distributors, and in-house customer-service representatives. The catalog simply gives customers another avenue for doing business with the company.[33]

In some cases, the Internet is particularly effective for "distributing" certain types of products like software and written material. The software industry pioneered the use of the Internet for product distribution. Computer software firms like Adobe Systems and Microsoft take advantage of the new Web distribution channels to sell and distribute software electronically. The advantage is that companies of any size, with very small marketing budgets, can take advantage of the Web to create and distribute new products. Anything that can be digitized can be transmitted over the Internet, which offers numerous advantages to marketers desiring to distribute printed materials. In short, the Internet broadens the reach of marketers, providing them with an efficient channel to serve customers on a global scale.

Digital Channel Advantages   By providing an effective mechanism for contacting potential buyers, the Internet offers some advantages over traditional channels of

---

[33] Jim Kesseler, "Defining the Future of Business-to-Business Electronic Commerce," *Journal of Global Information Management* 6, no. 1 (1999): p. 43.

distribution for business products. According to Judy Strauss and Raymond Frost, the Internet adds value for several reasons:[34]

1. The contact can be customized to the buyer's needs.

2. The Internet provides a wide range of referral sources such as Web pages, search engines, shopping agents, newsgroups, chat rooms, and e-mail.

3. The Internet is always open for business: Buyers can contact the site 24 hours a day, seven days a week.

Using the Internet, business marketers can create customized solutions for customers. For example, Staples (http://www.staples.com) offers customized catalogs for its corporate clients. Such a strategy would be costly to implement through traditional channels. The Internet provides Staples with unparalleled flexibility in creating just the type of catalog a particular organization desires. Other firms, like Hewlett-Packard, have developed an online store to more efficiently reach small and medium-sized businesses that are unprofitable for resellers.[35] The Internet channel, if targeted properly and integrated with traditional channel partners, can be a cost-effective approach for serving selected business market segments.

The Effect of the Internet on Pricing Strategy

By providing buyers with easier access to information about products and suppliers, the Internet bolsters the buyer's bargaining power. The major impact has been to substantially reduce the business marketer's control over price. Says Michael Porter,

> The great paradox of the Internet is that its very benefits—making information widely available; reducing the difficulty of purchasing, marketing, and distribution; allowing buyers and sellers to find and transact business with one another more easily—also makes it more difficult for companies to capture these benefits as profits.[36]

Where sellers may have enjoyed selected geographical advantages because of the lack of nearby competition, the Internet has opened up markets to many new suppliers, resulting in downward pressure on prices. The pressure on price is particularly severe for any products or services that buyers perceive as "commodities." These are precisely the types of items for which buyers are using reverse auctions. The net effect is that business marketers of raw materials, components, and supplies that can be priced and sold on the Internet must carefully rethink their pricing approach by developing a more efficient way of competing on price or by creating new service-enriched offerings that add value in the eyes of potential customers.

The Internet and Customer Communication

The Internet expands the business marketer's communication capabilities. Providing real-time, up-to-date, low-cost information is one of the salient features of an Internet strategy. Within seconds and with a few keystrokes, an entire database can be corrected,

---

[34] Judy Strauss and Raymond Frost, *Marketing on the Internet* (Upper Saddle River, N.J.: Prentice-Hall, 1997), p. 168.

[35] Deborah Gage, "HP Opens Up Online Store for Smaller Businesses," *PC Week*, June 7, 1999, p. 51.

[36] Porter, "Strategy and the Internet," p. 66.

updated, and appended, and the information can be shared with potential buyers all over the world. The scope of the communications capability of the Internet is illustrated by the different phases of electronic commerce through which companies typically move.[37] At the most basic level, a firm might offer simple *online information*, like their product catalog, facilitating access to information and enhancing product search capabilities. The limitation is the inability to help the user search for information on the basis of predefined criteria—the catalog simply exists in an electronic format. In the next phase of e-commerce, *database publishing*, the user is provided with search capabilities. Using a search engine, the customer can scan the catalog database and target particular requirements. The third phase, *customer self-service*, provides customized information for specific users. Here customers can download search-assisted catalogs and service diagnostics, along with information on price and product availability. The final, and most complex, phase of e-commerce, *transactions*, provides for full transactions, from information gathering to purchase to fulfillment to billing to secure payment, all in a single environment.

Meet the Customer's Requirements   Compared with traditional, paper-based approaches, each phase or level of e-commerce improves the way business marketers interact with their customers and potential customers. Reflecting this fact is the recent move of the venerable *Thomas Register* to online availability *only*.[38] The Thomas Publishing Company will no longer print its multivolume directories—the *Thomas Register of American Manufacturers* and *The Thomas Register Regional Buying Guides* have been staples for decades at North American industrial facilities. After 2006, Thomas—which was founded more than 100 years ago—will make these directories available exclusively online at http://www.ThomasNet.com. The move to online directories resulted from requests from customers. Increasingly, users were opting against the print format and for the online version because the online directories offer search functionality, immediate access to vendor catalogs, direct links to vendor Web sites, e-commerce capability, and a library of CAD drawings. ThomasNet.com contains information on more than 650,000 manufacturers, distributors, and service companies indexed by 67,000 product and service categories.

Of course, Internet communication often merely complements personal contact between buyers and sellers, particularly for complex, expensive products that require customer-specific engineering and customization, extensive negotiations, and long-term contractual arrangements. For example, Boeing's Web site is used more to describe the company and how it is organized, explain each of its aircraft models, describe and explain the firm's full range of services, and outline how potential buyers can work with the company in creating a product for their specific requirements. However, for many firms that market supplies, standard components, repair parts, and the like, e-commerce provides the greatest potential for reducing transaction costs while making marketing communications more efficient and effective.

To recap, the Internet is just one component of the business marketer's overall strategy: It simply extends the firm's reach, and it must be integrated into the overarching strategy the firm uses to reach and interact with its customers. Even at Dell, where the firm operates at the phase-four level of e-commerce—full transaction

---

[37] Kesseler, "Defining the Future of Business-to-Business Electronic Commerce," p. 43. See also, D. Eric Boyd and Robert Spekman, "Internet Usage Within B2B Relationships and Its Impact on Value Creation: A Conceptual Model and Research Propositions," *Journal of Business-to-Business Marketing* 11, no. 1–2 (2004): pp. 9–32.

[38] Sean B. Callahan, "Thomas Plans to Drop Print Directories," *B to B*, 90 (June 2005): p. 6.

capability—the Internet is just one approach to the marketplace. According to Chairman Michael Dell, "We work with customers face-to-face, on the telephone, or over the Internet. Depending on the customer, some or all of those techniques will be used, they're all intertwined."[39]

The Role of the Sales Force   Many firms find that the Internet simply makes sales representatives more effective because they can concentrate on solving customer problems and building customer relationships. The Internet streamlines the sales process and eliminates order-processing details for customers and salespersons alike. Although the Internet will supplant some sales that were once the province of the sales force, Internet strategies generally *support* sales force efforts. By using customer relationship management systems (CRM) (see Chapter 4), the salesperson can customize presentations, respond to specific customer idiosyncrasies, and fend off competitive challenges. Successful companies have developed approaches for integrating sales force strategies with Internet strategies and for compensating salespeople so that they support online initiatives.[40]

Promotion   To capitalize on the investment in creating and maintaining a Web site, promotions highlighting a site need to be run frequently and in a variety of media to stimulate use. An 18-month analysis of small-, medium-, and large-company B2B Web sites indicated that the number of hits is directly related to the amount of off-line advertising and sales promotion.[41] Advertising in trade publications and handouts at trade shows and conferences appear to be especially effective in stimulating the use of business Web sites. Based on the success of leading search engines like Google and Yahoo, keyword advertising has also become a central element in the promotional budgets of B2B firms—reaching potential customers at a critical point in the purchase decision process. Search engine marketing and other interactive marketing communication tools are examined in Chapter 16.

For business marketers, the Internet provides a powerful vehicle for demonstrating the value of offerings and customizing them for individual customers. Rosabeth Moss Kanter states that e-commerce pacesetters "embrace the Internet as an opportunity for questioning their existing models and experimenting with new ways technology can improve their businesses."[42]

Summary

Business marketers of all types, whether manufacturers, distributors, or service providers, are integrating the Internet and electronic communications into the core of the business marketing strategies. "E-commerce" is the broad term applied to communications, business processes, and transactions that are carried out through electronic technology—mainly the Internet. E-commerce can be applied to almost any aspect of business to make all processes more efficient. Based on Internet technologies,

[39] *Financial Times Guide to Digital Business* (autumn 1999), p. 11.

[40] Stewart Alsop, "E or Be Eaten," *Fortune*, November 8, 1999, p. 87.

[41] Carol Patten, "Marketers Promote Online Traffic through Traditional Media, with a Twist," *Business Marketing* 84 (August 1999): p. 40.

[42] Rosabeth Moss Kanter, "The Ten Deadly Mistakes of Wanna-dots," *Harvard Business Review* 79 (January 2001): p. 99.

an intranet is an internal network accessible only to company employees and other authorized users. By contrast, an extranet is a private network that uses Internet-based technology to link companies with suppliers, customers, and other partners. Extranets allow the business marketer to customize information for a particular customer and to seamlessly share information with that customer in a secure environment.

For business marketers, the Internet has been effective as a powerful communication medium, an alternative channel, a new venue for a host of services, a data-gathering tool, and a way to integrate the supply chain. To be successful, the Internet strategy must be carefully woven into the fabric of the firm's overall marketing strategy. The Internet offers important benefits, including reduced transaction costs, reduced cycle time, supply-chain integration, access to information, and closer customer relationships. Given the failure of many dot.com companies, the lesson for business marketers is that the Internet is an enabling technology—a powerful set of tools that complements, rather than replaces, traditional ways of competing.

The e-commerce strategy must be carefully crafted, beginning with a focus on objectives. Once a firm has established objectives, it can formulate an Internet strategy. Included in the strategy is a consideration of the product-related dimensions of the Internet offering, the most visible of which is the firm's Web site. Extranets, electronic catalogs, and customer information must also be integrated into the "product." Several fundamental channel-of-distribution issues must be evaluated, including the effect of the Internet on present channels and channel partners, channel efficiencies, and the Internet as a separate channel to the market. Pricing issues are also significant, particularly in light of the effect of trading communities and auction sites. Finally, marketing communication strategies consider the extent to which the firm provides transactional capabilities on the Web site and how the Internet strategy is integrated with other promotional vehicles. To an important degree, the Internet provides a powerful medium for developing a one-to-one relationship with business market customers.

Discussion Questions

1. How do the different definitions of e-commerce apply to the marketing tasks of a typical business marketer?

2. Comment on the following statement: Given the power and pervasiveness of Internet marketing strategies, many business marketers will probably become almost pure Internet marketers in the near future.

3. What advantages do Internet marketing strategies have over traditional strategies?

4. Discuss some of the possible objectives a manufacturer of business jet airplanes might have for the Internet strategy.

5. The Crespy Company makes control systems that regulate large gas turbine engines. Describe the key elements of the Internet product Crespy might develop for its customers.

6. Find a business marketing company's Web site and evaluate how easy it is for a potential customer to move through the site and eventually purchase a product.

7. What are the key challenges that electronic purchasing via electronic catalogs pose for the typical marketer of office products?

8. Evaluate this statement: The most important determinant of the profit potential of a digital marketplace is the power of buyers and sellers in the particular product arena. Agree or disagree? Explain.

9. Comment on the following: Internet marketing strategies will eventually wipe out most business-to-business intermediaries.

10. Will the Internet result in stiffer price competition in the business-to-business marketplace? Explain.

Internet Exercise

Many B2B firms use Google's AdWords product as a component of their integrated marketing communications strategy. Go to http://www.google.com and describe the benefits this product might offer to a B2B firm. Describe how Xerox Corporation might use AdWords to reach prospective customers for its new line of network color printers.

Using the Internet at W. W. Grainger

W. W. Grainger is one of the largest B2B distributors in the world. With nearly 600 branch locations throughout North America, 1,900 customer service associates, and a robust line of 500,000 products (tools, pumps, motors, safety and material handling products, and lighting, ventilation, and cleaning items), Grainger is the leading industrial distributor of products that allow organizations of all types to keep their facilities and equipment running smoothly. Grainger's objective is to grow by capturing market share in the highly fragmented North American facilities maintenance market. For the longer term, the company is focused on these goals:

Accelerate sales growth and increase market share by
- capturing a greater share of the business of existing accounts;
- targeting high-potential customer segments.

Increase operating leverage through
- accelerating sales growth;
- targeting high-potential customer segments;
- reconfiguring the logistics network to improve efficiency and customer service;
- enhancing internal processes with technology.

Improve return on invested capital by
- growing those business units that earn more than the cost of capital;
- improving the profitability of business units that earn less than the cost of capital.

Its large sales force and product line allow Grainger to meet customer needs in a highly responsive manner. From its nearly 600 branch locations, products can be delivered to customers within hours of a call. In 2005, the company's major strategic focus was on offering a multichannel approach for purchasing maintenance and operating supplies. This involved providing consistent service through its branches, service centers, and distribution centers. Investments in sales training and a revamped logistics/distribution network were at the heart of this effort. The company's goal of "zero carryovers"—meaning that all orders received by 5:00 P.M. are shipped that day—is very demanding and provides a severe challenge to regularly achieve. Grainger was recently cited by *Industrial Distribution Magazine* as "the strongest brand in the industrial distribution industry—because customers believe Grainger can get them what they need when they need it, you can find a Grainger catalog in virtually every purchasing agent's office in North America." In 2005, Grainger was ranked 375th on the *Fortune* 500 list and was included in *Fortune*'s list of "Most Admired Companies."

Discussion Questions

1. What role would the Internet play in Grainger's strategy, given the firm's past success, the nature of its product line (rather "'stodgy" basic industrial items), and the organization of the firm (a 500,000-item catalog, a 1,900-person sales force, and 600 branch locations)? Visit http://www.grainger.com to see the special services that Grainger offers on its Web site.

2. By providing a very brief description of 500,000 items, a Grainger catalog is massive—weighing several pounds. In the past, Grainger executives worried that the catalog could get too heavy for the average person to lift and, therefore, limited product descriptions to a couple of lines. Go to the firm's Web site, select a particular item, and evaluate the extensive amount of information that is now accessible for each item on the Web.

Supply Chain Management

When suppliers fail to deliver products or services as promised, buyers search for a new supplier. Organizational buyers assign great importance to supply chain processes that eliminate the uncertainty of product delivery. Supply chain management assures that product, information, service, and financial resources all flow smoothly through the entire value-creation process. Business marketers invest considerable financial and human resources in creating supply chains to service the needs and special requirements of their customers. After reading this chapter, you will understand:

1. the role of supply chain management in business marketing strategy.

2. the importance of integrating both firms and functions throughout the entire supply chain.

3. the critical role of logistics activities in achieving supply chain management goals.

4. the importance of achieving high levels of logistics service performance while simultaneously controlling the cost of logistics activities.

Johnson Controls is a major supplier to the automotive industry of a variety of components, including dashboards, seats, and consoles. For DaimlerChrysler's Jeep Liberty, for example, Johnson Controls supplies complete cockpit modules, seating systems, overhead consoles, and several electronic components. The cockpit module alone consists of 11 major components—from mechanical, electrical, and audio systems to the instrument panel trim. The company integrates parts from 35 suppliers, assembles the complete cockpit, and delivers it to DaimlerChrylser as one module—all within what is called the "204-minute broadcast window." As soon as DaimlerChrysler notifies the company that it has received an order for a Jeep Liberty, Johnson Controls has 204 minutes to build and deliver that cockpit to the DaimlerChrysler plant nine miles away with any one of 200 different color and interior combinations or options.[1] The company performs that operation 900 times a day, just for that one model.

Interestingly, this choreographed supply chain sequence takes place daily at several Johnson Controls plants around the world for a number of vehicles, such as the C-class Mercedes, the Buick Rendezvous, and the Pontiac Aztek. How does Johnson Controls make this happen? The firm applies effective *supply chain management processes* that include (1) integrated computer systems that provide production schedules and demand forecasts to all supply chain members; and (2) collaborative program-management tools that allow manufacturers and suppliers to synchronize activities and respond to events in real time. From the time a component system is engineered to when it is sold, Johnson Controls has adopted processes that tightly connect engineering, manufacturing, procurement, marketing, and sales. Because supply chain partners manufacture components of the firm's interior modules, Johnson Controls works closely with them to design the right product, at the right cost, and deliver it at the right time.

These efforts at Johnson Controls are part of an innovative approach to tightening distribution processes, bolstering links with suppliers and customers, and integrating production and marketing that is referred to as **supply chain management (SCM).** As business evolves into the 21st century, SCM is one of the predominant management approaches driving many organizations.[2] Bill Copacino, a noted supply chain consultant, puts the importance of SCM in focus:[3]

> In almost every industry, supply chain management has become a much more important strategic and competitive variable. It affects all of the shareholder value levers—cost, customer service, asset productivity, and revenue generation. Yet we are seeing a growing gap in performance between the leading and the average companies. The best are getting better faster than the average companies across almost every industry. For instance, Dell operates with 60 to 100 inventory turns, more than two or three times most of its competitors. So, clearly, the performance gap is widening, and we see this happening in almost every industry segment. The leading *supply chain* performers are applying new technology, new innovations, and new process thinking to great advantage. The average-performing companies and the laggards have a limited window of opportunity in which to catch up.

---

[1] Lorie Toupin, "Needed: Suppliers Who Can Collaborate throughout the Supply Chain," Supply Chain Automotive Supplement to *Supply Chain Management Review* 6 (July–August, 2002): p. 6.

[2] Peter C. Brewer and Thomas W. Speh, "Using the Balanced Scorecard to Measure Supply Chain Performance," *Journal of Business Logistics* (spring 2000): p. 75.

[3] Bill Copacino, "Supply Chain Challenges: Building Relationships," *Harvard Business Review* 81 (July 2003): p. 69.

This chapter describes the nature of SCM, explains its important goals, discusses the factors that lead to successful supply chain strategies, and demonstrates how logistics management is a key driver of supply chain success. Once SCM has been defined, the chapter highlights how the business marketer's logistics processes form the core of the SCM strategy. The logistical elements are described in terms of their interface within the distribution channel and how they must be integrated to create desired customer service standards. The chapter then addresses the role of logistics in purchasing decisions, the types of logistics services buyers seek, and the design of effective logistics processes.

The Concept of Supply Chain Management

A supply chain encompasses all the activities associated with moving goods from the raw materials stage through to the end user (for example, a personal computer buyer). A formal definition of SCM is:

> Supply chain management (SCM) is the integration of business processes from end user through original suppliers that provides products, services, and information that add value for customers.[4]

The supply chain includes a variety of firms, ranging from those that process raw materials to make component parts to those engaged in wholesaling. Included also are organizations engaged in transportation, warehousing, information processing, and materials handling. Supply chain functions include sourcing, procurement, product design, production scheduling, manufacturing, order processing, inventory management, materials handling, warehousing, and customer service.[5] Successful SCM coordinates and integrates these activities into a seamless process. Figure 14.1 illustrates the key elements of SCM and highlights the importance of integrating a variety of business functions across several different organizations in the supply chain.

Supply chains should be managed in an integrated manner. Integrated SCM focuses on managing relationships, information, and material flow across organizational borders to cut costs and enhance flow. When the multicompany nature of the supply chain focus is combined with a process-flow approach to business, the critical role that SCM assumes becomes clear. Rather than merely handling order fulfillment, SCM is instrumental in a full range of activities from product development and new-product-launch strategies to fulfillment and recycling. To that end, SCM must be fully integrated into business strategy and fine-tuned throughout the product's life cycle.[6] Leading supply chain–oriented firms focus intensely on monitoring actual user demand instead of forcing into markets products that may or may not sell quickly. In so doing, they minimize the flow of raw materials, finished product, and packaging materials, thereby reducing inventory costs across the entire supply chain.

---

[4] Martha C. Cooper, Douglas M. Lambert, James D. Pagh, "Supply Chain Management: More Than a New Name for Logistics," *International Journal of Logistics Management* 8, no. 1 (1997): p. 1.

[5] Francis J. Quinn, "A Supply Chain Management Overview," *Supply Chain Yearbook 2000* (January 2000): p. 15.

[6] Laura Rock Kopczak and M. Eric Johnson, "The Supply Chain Management Effect," *MIT Sloan Management Review* 44 (spring 2003): p. 28.

FIGURE 14.1 | THE SUPPLY CHAIN MODEL

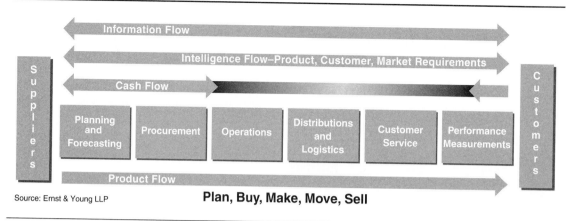

Source: Ernst & Young LLP   **Plan, Buy, Make, Move, Sell**

SOURCE: Karl B. Manrodt, Mary Collins Holcomb, and Richard H. Thompson, "What's Missing in Supply Chain Management?" *Supply Chain Management Review* (fall 1997): p. 81. Reprinted with permission of *Supply Chain Management Review*, a Cahners publication.

Partnerships: The Critical Ingredient

Thomas Stalkamp, former CEO of DaimlerChrysler, notes that many old-line U.S. industrial firms are hampered by the fact that the atmosphere between the parties in supply chains is more adversarial than it needs to be. He refers to this old-line, nonintegrated approach to business as "adversarial commerce."[7] Fueling the movement to SCM has been the recognition by many firms that adversarial commerce is costly and limits the ability of all supply chain members to compete in the global marketplace.

Integrating activities across the supply chain requires close working relationships. SCM may require that all firms in the supply chain share sensitive and proprietary information about customers, actual demand, point-of-sale transactions, and corporate strategic plans. SCM involves significant joint planning and communication; firms often create teams of personnel that cut across functional and firm boundaries to coordinate the movement of product to market. In other words, achieving the real potential of SCM requires integration not only among departments within the organization but also with external partners.

A wonderful example of the effect of integration among supply chain partners is the case of Avnet, a huge electronics distributor. Avnet developed a program to integrate its supply chain processes with those of a major manufacturer supplier and with the major component supplier to that manufacturer. By sharing demand and production information, the participants raised on-time delivery from 80 percent to 100 percent of all orders, increased inventory turnover by a factor of five, and tripled the return on materials! The collaboration of all supply chain partners is required to achieve such performance results.

Traditional, nonintegrated approaches to managing product and information flows are expensive and time-consuming. Such approaches often involve much higher transportation and handling costs; they demand considerable time from salespeople, buyers, and others in the organization. For example, material is often moved around too much—one major computer manufacturer reported that some of the components it used had traveled 250,000 miles before they reached the ultimate buyer. Furthermore, traditional transactions processes create excess inventory in the pipeline leading to the customer.

---

[7] Thomas T. Stallkamp, "Ending Adversarial Commerce," *Supply Chain Management Review* 9 (October 2005): pp. 46–52.

FIGURE 14.2 | STAGES FIRMS GO THROUGH IN ADOPTING SUPPLY CHAIN MANAGEMENT

The Supply Chain Stages

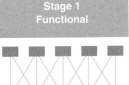

The lack of functional policies/processes and basic operations management results in unpredictable product quality and supply.

Functional orientation suboptimizes enterprise performance in asset management, cost, and customer satisfaction.

With alignment across all subprocesses and levels of management, operations management processes are integrated and display world-class performance and continuous improvement.

There is internal and external process integration, allowing each enterprise to focus on its customers and core competencies and on creating value.

SOURCE: Tom Brunell, "Managing a Multicompany Supply Chain," *Supply Chain Management Review* (spring 1999): p. 49. Reprinted with permission of *Supply Chain Management Review*, a Cahners publication.

In the pharmaceutical industry, firms that have not adopted SCM incur higher inventory-carrying costs and provide lower levels of customer service than their competitors.

SCM seeks to create an "overlap" among participants in the supply chain, where the partners share a long-term commitment and an interwoven relationship not unlike a good marriage.[8] Until some type of partnership is in place, the true benefits of supply chain integration cannot be achieved. Dell, for example, strives to maintain long-term relationships with high-reliability suppliers, such as Sony, so that items like monitors can be shipped from the supplier (Sony's factory) directly to the customer. The result is that Dell is able to fulfill customer orders in real time.[9] Many industry experts have concluded that Dell has created the best SCM model and, as a result, one of the most financially successful companies ever.[10]

Not only do effective supply chains conduct business as partners, they also openly share information. Intelligence about the customer and what the customer has ordered is transmitted upstream so that every organization in the supply chain has it and can respond accordingly. When information is made immediately available to supply chain members, Tier 1 and Tier 2 suppliers can act immediately, eliminating the delays that created inefficiencies in the past. This allows the supply chain to reduce inventories (safety stocks) and speed up cash flow. Figure 14.2 depicts the stages that companies go

---

[8] James E. Morehouse, "Extending the Enterprise: The Paradigm," *Supply Chain Management Review* 1 (fall 1997): p. 38.

[9] S. Chopra and J. A. Van Mieghan, "Which e-Business Is Right for Your Supply Chain?" *Supply Chain Management Review* 4 (July–August 2000): p. 34.

[10] Thomas A. Stewart and Louise O'Brien, "Execution Without Excuses," *Harvard Business Review* 83 (March 2005): p. 110.

through when forming intercompany networks. Note that in Stage 3, the "Extended Enterprise," companies have successfully aligned both their internal and external processes. This is the ultimate goal of SCM.

Supply Chain Management: A Tool for Competitive Advantage

The supply chain can be a powerful competitive weapon as market leaders like Dell, Grainger, and Hewlett-Packard have demonstrated. Research by Mercer Management Consulting has found that "best-practice" SCM companies typically excel in reducing operating costs, improving asset productivity, and compressing order cycle time.[11] Nucor Incorporated, operating in the mature steel industry, reinvented the traditional steel supply chain and developed a "mini-mill" strategy that is highly responsive to customer needs and has fueled an 18 percent compounded annual five-year revenue growth rate.[12] As a primary interface point with the customer, SCM can offer value in the form of competitively superior delivery and value-added services, as defined by customers. Best-in-class SCM practices provide advantages including 10 to 30 percent higher on-time delivery performance, a 40 to 65 percent (or one- to two-month) advantage in cash-to-cash cycle time, and 50 to 80 percent less standing inventory, which all translates into 3 to 6 percent of a company's revenue. For a $100 million company, earnings improvements of up to $6 million are achievable by thoroughly adopting SCM practices.[13] However, SCM, as a source of competitive advantage, is not simply a way to reduce cost but also as a way to boost revenues.[14]

Supply Chain Management Goals

SCM is both a boundary- and function-spanning endeavor. The underlying premise of SCM is that waste reduction and enhanced supply chain performance come only with both intrafirm and interfirm functional integration, sharing, and cooperation. Thus, each firm within the supply chain must tear down functional silos and foster true coordination and integration of marketing, production, procurement, sales, and logistics. Furthermore, actions, systems, and processes among *all* the supply chain participants must be integrated and coordinated. Firmwide integration is a necessary, but not sufficient, condition for achieving the full potential benefits of SCM. Integration must be taken to a higher plane, so that functions and processes are coordinated across all the organizations in the supply chain. SCM is undertaken to achieve four major goals: waste reduction, time compression, flexible response, and unit cost reduction.[15] These goals have been articulated in several contexts associated with SCM, and they speak to the importance of both interfunctional and interfirm coordination.

---

[11] Quinn, "A Supply Chain Management Overview," p. 15.

[12] Robert E. Sabath and David G. Frentzel, "Go for the Growth! Supply Chain Management's Role in Growing Revenues," *Supply Chain Management Review* 1 (summer 1997): p. 17.

[13] Bill Faherenwald, "Supply Chain: Managing Logistics for the 21st Century," *Business Week*, December 28, 1998, Special Section, p. 3.

[14] Charles Batchelor, "Moving Up the Corporate Agenda," *The Financial Times*, December 1, 1998, p. 1.

[15] Brewer and Speh, "Using the Balanced Scorecard," p. 76.

Waste Reduction   Firms that practice SCM seek to reduce waste by minimizing duplication, harmonizing operations and systems, and enhancing quality. With respect to duplication, firms at all levels in the supply chain often maintain inventories. Efficiencies can be gained for the chain as a whole if the inventories can be centralized and maintained by just a few firms at critical points in the distribution process. With a joint goal of reducing waste, supply chain partners can work together to modify policies, procedures, and data-collection practices that produce or encourage waste.[16] Typically, waste across the supply chain manifests itself in excess inventory. Effective ways to address this are through postponement and customization strategies, which push the final assembly of a completed product to the last practical point in the chain. Dell provides an excellent illustration of how to reduce waste through effective "waste" management strategies. The company's build-to-order model produces a computer only when there is an actual customer order. Dell works with its suppliers to achieve a system where inventory turns are measured in hours rather than days. Because Dell does not maintain stocks of unsold finished goods, it has no need to conduct "fire sales." The result: Waste has been eliminated both on the component side and on the finished-goods side.

Time Compression   Another critical goal of SCM is to compress order-to-delivery cycle time. When production and logistics processes are accomplished in less time, everyone in the supply chain is able to operate more efficiently, and a primary result is reduced inventories throughout the system. Time compression also enables supply chain partners to more easily observe and understand the cumulative effect of problems that occur anywhere in the chain and respond quickly. Reduced cycle time also speeds the cash-to-cash cycle for all chain members, enhancing cash flow and financial performance throughout the system. Dell Computer's well-managed supply chain excels on all of these performance dimensions. Time compression means that information and products flow smoothly and quickly, thus permitting all parties to respond to customers in a timely manner while maintaining minimal inventory.

Flexible Response   The third goal of SCM is to develop flexible response throughout the supply chain. Flexible response in order handling, including how orders are handled, product variety, order configuration, order size, and several other dimensions means that a customer's unique requirements can be met cost-effectively. To illustrate, a firm that responds flexibly can configure a shipment in almost any way (for example, different pallet patterns or different product assortments) and do it quickly without problems for the customer. Flexibility also may mean customizing products in the warehouse to correspond to a customer's need for unique packaging and unitization. The key to flexibility is to meet individual customer needs in a way that the customer views as cost effective and the supply chain views as profitable.

Unit Cost Reduction   The final goal of SCM is to operate logistics in a manner that reduces cost per unit for the end customer. Firms must determine the level of performance the customer desires and then minimize the costs of providing that service level. The business marketer should carefully assess the balance between level of cost and the degree of service provided. The goal is to provide an appropriate value equation for the customer, meaning that cost in some cases is higher for meaningful

[16] Kate Vitasek, Karl B. Manrodt, and Jeff Abbott, "What Makes a LEAN Supply Chain?" *Supply Chain Management Review* 9 (October 2005): pp. 39–45.

enhancements in service. Cost cutting is not an absolute, but the SCM approach is focused on driving costs to the lowest possible level for the level of service requested. For example, shipping product in full truckload quantities weekly is less expensive than shipping pallet quantities every day; however, when a customer like Honda wants daily deliveries to minimize inventories, the SCM goal is to offer daily shipments at the lowest possible cost. SCM principles drive down costs because they focus management attention on eliminating activities that unnecessarily add cost, such as duplicate inventories, double and triple handling of the product, unconsolidated shipments, and uncoordinated promotions such as special sales.

Hau Lee, an internationally recognized expert, points out that supply chain efficiency is necessary, but it is not enough to ensure that firms do better than their rivals. Only companies that build agile, adaptable, and aligned supply chains get ahead of the competition.[17] Efficient supply chains often become uncompetitive because they do not adapt to changes in market structures: Supply chains need to keep adapting so they can adjust to changing customer needs. In addition, low-cost supply chains are not always able to respond to sudden and unexpected changes in markets—like a shift in resource availability or the effect of a natural disaster. Finally, excellent supply chain companies align the interests of all the firms in their supply chain with their own—if any company's interests differ from those of the other organizations in the supply chain, its actions do not maximize the chain's performance.

Benefits to the Final Customer

A well-managed supply chain ultimately creates tangible benefits for customers throughout the supply chain. When the supply chain reduces waste, improves cycle time and flexible response, and minimizes costs, these benefits should flow through to ultimate customers. Thus, a key focus of the supply chain members is monitoring how much the customer is realizing these important benefits and assessing what may be preventing them from doing so.

A supply chain's customer can be viewed on several dimensions, and it is important to focus on each. A producer of electronic radio parts views the radio manufacturer as an absolutely critical customer, but the auto manufacturer that installs the radio in a car is equally important, if not more so, and ultimately the final buyer of the automobile must be satisfied. Thus, different demands, desires, and idiosyncrasies of customers all along the supply chain must be understood and managed effectively.

The Financial Benefits Perspective

When supply chain partners are achieving their goals and the benefits are flowing through to customers, supply chain members should succeed financially. The most commonly reported benefits for firms that adopt SCM are lower costs, higher profit margins, enhanced cash flow, revenue growth, and a higher rate of return on assets. Because activities are harmonized and unduplicated, the cost of transportation, order processing, order selection, warehousing, and inventory is usually reduced. A study to validate the correlation between supply chain integration and business success shows

---

[17] Hau L. Lee, "The Triple-A Supply Chain," *Harvard Business Review* 82 (October 2004): pp. 102–112.

that best-practice SCM companies have a 45 percent total supply chain cost advantage over their median supply chain competitors.[18] Cash flows are improved because the total cycle time from raw materials to finished product is reduced. The leading firms also enjoy greater cash flow—they have a cash-to-order cycle time exactly half that of the median company. On the other hand, recent evidence suggests that the stock market punishes firms that stumble in SCM. For example, one study showed that supply chain glitches can result in an 8.6 percent drop in stock price on the day the problem is announced and up to a 20 percent decline within six months.[19]

Information and Technology Drivers

Supply chains could not function at high levels of efficiency and effectiveness without powerful information systems. Many of the complex Internet supply chains maintained by companies like Dell and Cisco could not operate at high levels without sophisticated information networks and interactive software. The Internet—and Internet technology—is the major tool business marketers rely on to manage their lengthy and integrated systems. In addition, a host of software applications play a key role in helping a supply chain operate at peak efficiency.

Supply Chain Software SCM software applications provide real-time analytical systems that manage the flow of products and information through the supply chain network.[20] Of course, many supply chain functions are coordinated, including procurement, manufacturing, transportation, warehousing, order entry, forecasting, and customer service. Much of the software is focused on each one of the different functional areas (for example, inventory planning or transportation scheduling). However, the trend is to move toward software solutions that integrate several or all of these functions. The result is that firms can work with a comprehensive "supply chain suite" of software that manages flow across the supply chain while including all of the key functional areas. Several firms producing Enterprise Resource Planning (ERP) software—such as SAP or Oracle—have developed applications that attempt to integrate functional areas and bridge gaps across the supply chain.

SCM software creates the ability to transmit data in real time and helps organizations *transform* supply chain processes into competitive advantages. Equipping employees with portable bar code scanners that feed a centralized database, FedEx is a *best practices* leader at seamlessly integrating a variety of technologies to enhance all processes across an extended supply chain.[21] The company uses a real-time data transmission system (via the bar code scanners used for every package) to assist in routing, tracking, and delivering packages. The information recorded by the scanners is transmitted to a central database and is made available to *all* employees and customers. Each day FedEx's communications network processes nearly 400,000 customer service calls and tracks the

[18] Brad Ferguson, "Implementing Supply Chain Management," *Production and Inventory Management Journal* (Second Quarter 2000), p. 64.

[19] Robert J. Bowman, "Does Wall Street Really Care about the Supply Chain?" *Global Logistics and Supply Chain Strategies* (April 2001), pp. 31–35.

[20] Steven Kahl, "What's the 'Value' of Supply Chain Software?" *Supply Chain Management Review* 3 (winter 1999): p. 61.

[21] Sandor Boyson and Thomas Corsi, "The Real-Time Supply Chain," *Supply Chain Management Review* 5 (January–February 2001): p. 48.

location, pickup time, and delivery time of 2.5 million packages! FedEx is electronically linked so tightly with some customers that when the customer receives an order, FedEx's server is notified to print a shipping label, generate an internal request for pickup, and then download the label to the customer's server. The label, with all the needed customer information, is printed at the customer's warehouse and applied to the package just before FedEx picks it up. This tight electronic linkage adds significant efficiency to the customer's supply chain process and allows FedEx to deliver on its promises.[22]

Successfully Applying the Supply Chain Management Approach

The nature of the firm's supply chain efforts often depend on the nature of the demand for its products. Marshall Fisher suggests that products can be separated into two categories: "functional" items, like paper, maintenance supplies, and office furniture, for example, or "innovative" items, like Research in Motion's BlackBerry (wireless e-mail device) or other high-tech products. The importance of this distinction is that functional items require different supply chains than do innovative products.[23]

Functional products typically have predictable demand patterns, whereas innovative products do not. The goal for functional products is to design a supply chain with efficient physical distribution; that is, it minimizes logistics and inventory costs and assures low-cost manufacturing. Here, the key information sharing takes place within the supply chain so that all participants can effectively orchestrate manufacturing, ordering, and delivery to minimize production and inventory costs.

Innovative products, on the other hand, have less predictable demand, and the key concern is reacting to short life cycles, avoiding shortages or excess supplies, and taking advantage of high profits during peak demand periods. Rather than seeking to minimize inventory, supply chain decisions center on the questions of where to *position* inventory, along with production capacity, in order to hedge against uncertain demand. The critical task is to capture and distribute timely information on customer demand to the supply chain. When designing the supply chain, firms should concentrate on creating *efficient* processes for functional products and *responsive* processes for innovative products.

Successful Supply Chain Practices

Most successful supply chains have devised approaches for participants to work together in a partnering environment. Supply chains are not effective and, in reality, are *not* supply chains when the participants are adversaries. Supply chain partnerships form the foundation. Highly effective supply chains feature integrated operations across supply chain participants, timely information sharing, and delivering value-added to the customer. As testimony to the importance of supply chain partnerships, the Malcolm Baldrige National Quality Award Committee recently made "key supplier and customer partnering and communication mechanisms" a separate category it would use to

---

[22] For a related discussion, see Pierre J. Richard and Timothy M. Devinney, "Modular Strategies: B2B Technology and Architectural Knowledge," *California Management Review* 47 (summer 2005): pp. 86–113.

[23] Marshall Fisher, "What Is the Right Supply Chain for Your Product?" *Harvard Business Review* 75 (March–April 1997): p. 106.

B2B TOP PERFORMERS

Making Supplier Relationships Work

During the past decade, Toyota and Honda have struck remarkable partnerships with some of the same suppliers who describe their relationships with the Big Three U.S. automakers as adversarial. Of the 2.1 million Toyota/Lexuses and the 1.6 million Honda/Acuras sold in North America in 2003, Toyota manufactured 60 percent and Honda 80 percent in North America. Moreover, the two companies source about 70 to 80 percent of the costs of making each automobile from North American suppliers. Despite the odds, Toyota and Honda have managed to replicate in an alien Western culture the same kind of supplier webs they developed in Japan. Consequently, they enjoy the best supplier relations in the U.S. automobile industry, have the fastest product development processes, and reduce costs and improve quality year after year.

Both firms:

- understand how their suppliers work and develop deep knowledge of the degree of

efficiency and effectiveness that particular suppliers demonstrate.

- turn supplier rivalry into an opportunity by rewarding quality, innovation, and cost-reduction initiatives.

- actively supervise suppliers and help them improve their operational capabilities.

- continuously and intensively share information with suppliers.

- conduct joint improvement activities to advance mutual goals.

Rather than excelling on one dimension, Toyota and Honda win by applying all of them as a system for continuously improving supplier relationships.

SOURCE: Jeffrey K. Liker and Thomas Y. Choi, "Building Deep Supplier Relationships," *Harvard Business Review* 82 (December 2004): pp. 104–113.

recognize the best companies in the United States.[24] In considering the economic value created across the supply chain, one expert observes, "You should go for the best return on net assets for *the supply chain*, and trade off costs between income statements and balance sheets to see that *everybody* shares in that gain."[25] For the supply chain partners to work as a unit, this enlightened perspective of collaboration is mandatory.

For the supply chain partnership to succeed, the partners need to clearly define their strategic objectives, understand where their objectives converge (and perhaps diverge), and resolve any differences.[26] Because the supply chain strategy drives all the important processes in each firm as well as those that connect the firms, managers in both organizations must participate in key decisions and support the chosen course. Once key participants specify and endorse supply chain strategies, performance metrics can be established to track how well the supply chain is meeting its common goals. The metrics used to measure performance are tied to the strategy and must be linked to the performance evaluation and reward systems for employees in each of the participating firms. Without this step, individual managers would not be motivated to accomplish the broad goals of the supply chain.

---

[24]Jeffrey K. Liker and Thomas Y. Choi, "Building Deep Supplier Relationships," *Harvard Business Review* 82 (December 2004): p. 104.

[25]Richard H. Gamble, "Financing Supply Chains," *businessfinancemag.com* (June 2002): p. 35.

[26]Peter C. Brewer and Thomas W. Speh, "Adapting the Balanced Scorecard to Supply Chain Management," *Supply Chain Management Review* 5 (March–April 2001): p. 49.

Logistics as the Critical Element in Supply Chain Management

Nowhere in business marketing strategy is SCM more important than in logistics. **Logistics** is an imposing and sometimes mysterious term that originated in the military. In business usage, logistics refers to designing and managing all activities (primarily transportation, inventory, warehousing, and communications) necessary to make materials available for manufacturing and to offer finished products to customers when and in the condition they are needed. Logistics thus embodies two primary product flows:

1. Physical supply, or those flows that provide raw materials, components, and supplies to the production process.

2. Physical distribution, or those flows that deliver the completed product to customers and channel intermediaries.

The flows of physical supply and physical distribution must be coordinated to meet delivery requirements of business customers successfully. Physical supply requires a business supplier's logistical system to interact with the customer's logistics and manufacturing process. A repair part delivered a few hours late may cost a manufacturer thousands of dollars in lost production time. Although physical supply is important, this chapter concentrates on physical distribution because it is the key element of a business marketer's strategy.

Effective business marketing demands efficient, systematic delivery of finished products to channel members and customers. The importance of this ability has elevated the logistics function to a place of prominence in the marketing strategy of many business marketers.

Distinguishing between Logistics and Supply Chain Management

Logistics is the critical element in SCM. In fact, there is considerable confusion over the difference between the discipline of SCM and logistics. As our definition stated, SCM is focused on the *integration of* all *business processes* that add value for customers. Logistics, on the other hand, is focused on *moving and storing activities* as products and information wind their way through the supply chain to customers. Thus, SCM is a broader, integrative discipline that includes the coordination of several business processes, including logistics.

The 1990s witnessed the rising importance of time-based competition, rapidly improving information technology, expanding globalization, increasing attention to quality, and the changing face of interfirm relationships. These trends combined to cause companies to expand their perspective on logistics to include all the firms involved in creating a finished product and delivering it to the buyer or user on time and in perfect condition. For example, the supply chain for electric motors would include raw material suppliers, steel fabricators, component parts manufacturers, transportation companies, the electric motor manufacturer, the distributor of electric motors, the warehouse companies that store and ship components and finished products, and the motor's ultimate buyer. Figure 14.3 graphically depicts such a supply chain. The SCM concept is an integrating philosophy for coordinating the total flow of a supply channel from supplier to ultimate user. Logistics is critical, however, to

FIGURE 14.3 | SUPPLY CHAIN FOR ELECTRIC MOTORS

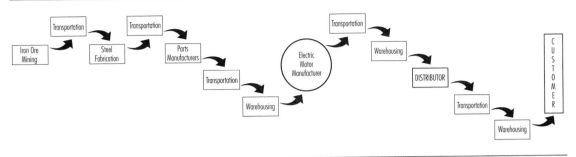

business marketers, because regardless of the orientation to the entire supply chain, the firm relies on its logistics system to deliver product in a timely, low-cost manner.

Managing Flows

The significance of the supply chain perspective in logistical management is that the business marketing manager focuses attention on the performance of *all participants* in the supply chain. The manager also coordinates their efforts to enhance the timely delivery of the finished product to the ultimate user at the lowest possible cost. Inherent in the supply chain approach is the need to form close *relationships* with the supply chain participants, including vendors, transportation suppliers, warehousing companies, and distributors. The focus of logistics in the SCM for business marketers is the *flow of product* through the supply chain, with *timely information* driving the entire process.

Product flow in the reverse direction is also important in business supply chains. Many companies, like Xerox and Canon, routinely remanufacture products that are worn out or obsolete. Effective linkages and processes must be in place to return such products to a facility in order to remanufacture or retrofit them. If the reverse supply chains are operating effectively, companies can sometimes realize higher margins on the remanufactured products than they do on new items.[27]

The Strategic Role of Logistics

In the past, logistics was viewed simply as a cost of doing business and a function whose only goal was higher productivity. Today, many companies view logistics as a critical strategic weapon because of its tremendous effect on a customer's operation. For many business marketers, logistics is their *primary* marketing tool for gaining and maintaining competitive superiority. These firms typically recognize that logistics performance is an important part of marketing strategy, and they exploit their logistics competencies. Companies that incorporate logistics planning and management into long-term business strategies can achieve significant benefits, which create real value for the company.

---

[27]James Stock, Thomas W. Speh, and Herbert Shear, "Many Happy (Product) Returns," *Harvard Business Review* 80 (July 2002): p. 14.

Nucor Steel enjoys strong customer loyalty because it can deliver steel to a construction site within a two- to four-hour window and offload the truck in the sequence in which the steel beams will be used on the job! This advantage is significant because storage space is limited at most construction sites in urban areas. This strong value-added service allows Nucor to achieve higher levels of profitability than its competitors.

Sales-Marketing-Logistics Integration

The rising value of logistics as a strategic marketing weapon has fostered the integration of the sales, marketing, and logistics functions of many business marketers. In progressive firms, unified teams of sales, production, logistics, information systems, and marketing personnel develop integrated logistics programs to offer to potential customers. Sales calls are made by teams of specialists from each area, and the teams tailor logistics solutions to customer problems. United Stationers, one of the largest U.S. office products distributors, brings operations and salespeople together to meet with the company's resellers in an effort to create customer-responsive logistics service. As a result of its efforts, United guarantees customers that orders placed by 7:00 P.M. will be received before noon on the following day. Customers can dial into United's mainframe computer and place orders electronically. The company considers all of its logistics people to be part of the sales function. Some firms have taken the integration even further. Baxter Healthcare warehouse workers team up with warehouse personnel at the hospitals that Baxter serves. During visits to the customer warehouse, the Baxter warehouser evaluates the operation, looking for ways to improve packing so shipments are easier to unload and unpack. As a result, Baxter warehousers have become salespeople.

Just-in-Time Systems

To serve a customer, business marketers must be prepared to deliver their products frequently and with precise timing. The reason is the widespread adoption by manufacturing firms, like Honda of America, of the **just-in-time (JIT)** inventory principle. Under this principle, suppliers carefully coordinate deliveries with the manufacturer's production schedule—often delivering products just hours before they are used. The objective of a JIT system is to eliminate waste of all kinds from the production process by requiring the delivery of the specified product at the precise time, and in the exact quantity needed. Importantly, the quality must be perfect—there is no opportunity to inspect products in the JIT process. Because JIT attempts to relate purchases to production requirements, the typical order size shrinks, and more frequent deliveries are required. Increased delivery frequency presents a challenge to the business marketing production and logistics system. However, business marketers will have to meet this challenge as many competitors now compete on the basis of inventory turns and speed to market.[28]

Just-in-Time Relationship A significant effect of JIT purchasing has been to drastically reduce the number of suppliers manufacturers use. Suppliers who are able to meet customers' JIT requirements find their share of business growing.[29] Meeting JIT requirements often represents a marketing edge, and may mean survival for some suppliers. The relationship between JIT suppliers and manufacturers is unique and

---

[28] Andrew Tanzer, "Warehouses That Fly," *Forbes*, October 18, 1999, p. 121.

[29] Peter Bradley, "Just-in-Time Works, but. . . ." *Purchasing* 118 (September 1995): p. 36.

TABLE 14.1 | **CONTROLLABLE ELEMENTS IN A LOGISTICS SYSTEM**

Elements	Key Aspects
Customer service	The "product" of logistics activities, *customer service* relates to the effectiveness in creating time and place utility. The level of customer service provided by the supplier has a direct impact on total cost, market share, and profitability.
Order processing	Order processing triggers the logistics process and directs activities necessary to deliver products to customers. Speed and accuracy of order processing affect costs and customer service levels.
Logistics communication	Information exchanged in the distribution process guides the activities of the system. It is the vital link between the firm's logistics system and its customers.
Transportation	The physical movement of products from source of supply through production to customers is the most significant cost area in logistics, and it involves selecting modes and specific carriers as well as routing.
Warehousing	Providing storage space serves as a buffer between production and use. Warehousing may be used to enhance service and to lower transportation costs.
Inventory control	Inventory is used to make products available to customers and to ensure the correct mix of products is at the proper location at the right time.
Packaging	The role of packaging is to provide protection to the product, to maintain product identity throughout the logistics process, and to create effective product density.
Materials handling	Materials handling increases the speed of, and reduces the cost of, picking orders in the warehouse and moving products between storage and the transportation carriers. It is a cost-generating activity that must be controlled.
Production planning	Utilized in conjunction with logistics planning, production planning ensures that products are available for inventory in the correct assortment and quantity.
Plant and warehouse location	Strategic placement of plants and warehouses increases customer service and reduces the cost of transportation.

SOURCE: Adapted from James R. Stack and Douglas M. Lambert, *Strategic Logistics Management*, 5th ed. (Homewood, Ill.: McGraw-Hill, 2000).

includes operational linkages that unite the buyer and seller. As a result, suppliers find that the relationships are longer lasting and usually formalized with a written contract that may span up to five years.

Elements of a Logistical System   Table 14.1 presents the controllable variables of a logistical system. Almost no decision on a particular logistical activity can be made without evaluating its effect on other areas. The system of warehouse facilities, inventory commitments, order-processing methods, and transportation linkages determines the supplier's ability to provide timely product availability to customers. As a result of poor supplier performance, customers may have to bear the extra cost of higher inventories, institute expensive priority-order-expediting systems, develop secondary supply sources, or, worst of all, turn to another supplier.

Total-Cost Approach

In the management of logistical activities, two performance variables must be considered: (1) total distribution costs and (2) the level of logistical service provided to customers. The logistical system must be designed and administered to achieve that combination of cost and service levels that yields maximum profits. Logistical costs vary widely for business marketers, depending on the nature of the product and on the importance of logistical service to the buyer. Logistical costs can consume 16 to 36 percent of each sales dollar at the manufacturing level, and logistical activities can consume more than 40 percent of total assets. Thus, logistics can have a significant effect on corporate profitability. How, then, can the marketer manage logistical costs?

The **total-cost** or trade-off **approach** to logistical management guarantees to minimize total logistical costs in the firm and within the channel. The assumption is that costs of individual logistical activities are interactive; that is, a decision about one logistical variable affects all or some of the others. Management is thus concerned with the efficiency of the entire system rather than with minimizing the cost of any single logistical activity. The interactions among logistical activities (that is, transportation, inventory, warehousing) are described as cost trade-offs because a cost increase in one activity is traded for a large cost decrease in another activity, the net result being an overall cost reduction.

Calculating Logistics Costs

Activity-Based Costing

The activity-based costing (ABC) technique is used to precisely measure the costs of performing specific activities, and then trace those costs to the products, customers, and channels that consumed the activities.[30] This is a powerful tool in managing the logistics operations of a supply chain. ABC provides a mechanism to trace the cost of performing logistics services to the customers that use these services, making it easier to assess the appropriate level of customer service to offer. Firms using ABC analysis can obtain more accurate information about how a particular customer or a specific product contributes to overall profitability.[31]

Total Cost of Ownership

Total cost of ownership (TCO) determines the total costs of acquiring and then using a given item from a particular supplier (see Chapter 2). The approach identifies costs—often buried in overhead or general expenses—that relate to the costs of holding inventory, poor quality, and delivery failure.[32] A buyer using TCO explicitly considers the costs that the supplier's logistics system either added to, or eliminated from, the purchase

---

[30] Bernard J. LaLonde and Terrance L. Pohlen, "Issues in Supply Chain Costing," *International Journal of Logistics Management* 7, no. 1 (1996): p. 3.

[31] Thomas A. Foster, "Time to Learn the ABCs of Logistics," *Logistics* (February 1999): p. 67.

[32] Lisa Ellram, "Activity-Based Costing and Total Cost of Ownership: A Critical Linkage," *Journal of Cost Management* 8 (winter 1995): p. 22.

price and would take a long-term perspective in evaluating cost.[33] Thus, a supplier particularly efficient at logistics might be able to reduce the buyer's inventory costs and the buyer's expenses of inspecting inbound merchandise. As a result, the total cost of ownership from that supplier would be lower than the cost from other suppliers that were not able to rapidly deliver undamaged products. Increasing acceptance of the TCO approach will cause logistics efficiency to become an even more critical element of a business marketer's strategy.

Business-to-Business Logistical Service

Many studies have shown that logistics service is often just as important as product quality as a measure of supplier performance. In many industries a quality product at a competitive price is a given, so customer service is the key differentiator among competitors. In one industry, for example, purchasing agents begin the buying process by calling suppliers with the best delivery service to see whether they are willing to negotiate prices. Because it is so important to customers, reliable logistics service can lead to higher market share and higher profits. A study by Bain and Company showed that companies with superior logistics service grow 8 percent faster, collect a 7 percent price premium, and are 12 times as profitable as firms with inferior service levels.[34] These facts, together with the extensive spread of just-in-time manufacturing, make it clear that logistical service is important to organizational buyers.

Logistical service relates to the availability and delivery of products to the customer. It comprises the series of sales-satisfying activities that begin when the customer places the order and that end when the product is delivered. Responsive logistical service satisfies customers and creates the opportunity for closer and more profitable buyer-seller relationships.[35] Logistical service includes whatever aspects of performance are important to the business customer (Table 14.2). These service elements range from delivery time to value-added services, and each of these elements can affect production processes, final product output, costs, or all three.

Logistics Service Impacts on the Customer

Supplier logistical service translates into product availability. For a manufacturer to produce or for a distributor to resell, industrial products must be available at the right time, at the right place, and in usable condition. The longer the supplier's delivery time, the less available the product; the more inconsistent the delivery time, the less available the product. For example, a reduction in the supplier's delivery time permits a buyer to hold less inventory because needs can be met rapidly. The customer reduces the risk that the production process will be interrupted. Consistent delivery enables the buyer to program more effectively—or routinize—the purchasing process, thus lowering

---

[33] Bruce Ferrin and Richard E. Plank, "Total Cost of Ownership Models: An Exploratory Study," *Journal of Supply Chain Management* 38 (summer 2002): p. 18.

[34] Mary Collins Holcomb, "Customer Service Measurement: A Methodology for Increasing Customer Value through Utilization of the Taguchi Strategy," *Journal of Business Logistics* 15, no. 1 (1994): p. 29.

[35] Arun Sharma, Dhruv Grewal, and Michael Levy, "The Customer Satisfaction/Logistics Interface," *Journal of Business Logistics* 16, no. 2 (1995): p. 1.

TABLE 14.2 | COMMON ELEMENTS OF LOGISTICS SERVICE

Elements	Description
Delivery time	The time from the creation of an order to the fulfillment and delivery of that order encompasses both order-processing time and delivery or transportation time.
Delivery reliability	The most frequently used measure of logistics service, delivery reliability focuses on the capability of having products available to meet customer demand.
Order accuracy	The degree to which items received conform to the specification of the order. The key dimension is the incidence of orders shipped complete and without error.
Information access	The firm's ability to respond to inquiries about order status and product availability.
Damage	A measure of the physical conditions of the product when received by the buyer.
Ease of doing business	A range of factors including the ease with which orders, returns, credits, billing, and adjustments are handled.
Value-added services	Such features as packaging, which facilitates customer handling, or other services such as prepricing and drop shipments.

SOURCE: Reprinted with permission from Jonathon L. S. Byrnes, William C. Copacino, and Peter Metz, "Forge Service into a Weapon with Logistics," *Transportation & Distribution, Presidential Issue* 28 (September 1987): p. 46.

buyer costs. Consistent delivery-cycle performance allows buyers to cut their level of buffer or safety stock, thereby reducing inventory cost. However, for many business products, such as those that are low in unit value and relatively standardized, the overriding concern is not inventory cost but simply having the products. A malfunctioning $0.95 bearing could shut down a whole production line.

Determining the Level of Service

Buyers often rank logistics service right behind "quality" as a criterion for selecting a vendor. However, not all products or all customers require the same level of logistical service. Many made-to-order products—such as heavy machinery—have relatively low logistical service requirements. Others, such as replacement parts, components, and subassemblies, require extremely demanding logistical performance. Similarly, customers may be more or less responsive to varying levels of logistical service.

Profitable Levels of Service   In developing a logistical service strategy, business marketing strategists should assess the profit impact of the service options that they provide to customers. In nearly all industries, firms provide numerous supply chain services such as next-day delivery, customized handling, and specialized labeling. However, few companies actually trace the true costs of specialized services and the resulting effect on customer profitability (see Chapter 4).

To combat this unhealthy situation, some companies are now using *cost-to-serve* analytics to address the problem—among them are Dow Chemical, Eastman Chemical, and Georgia-Pacific (GP). GP used total-delivered-cost analysis to improve the performance of a major customer account.[36] By incorporating cost-to-serve data into the calculation of gross margin, GP's supply chain team determined that the costs to provide this customer with expedited transportation and distribution services were significantly reducing the account's profitability. In a top-to-top meeting with the customer, GP used the data to expose the root causes of the high costs and poor service, which included last-minute, uncoordinated promotional planning and purchasing across the customer's major business units and the customer's unwillingness to share inventory levels and positioning. Customers, once confronted with the data, are often willing to collaborate on ways to improve service, reduce costs, and restore profitability.

To recap, service levels are developed by assessing customer service requirements. The sales and cost of various service levels are analyzed to find the service level generating the highest profits. The needs of various customer segments dictate various logistical system configurations. For example, when logistical service is critical, industrial distributors can provide the vital product availability, whereas customers with less rigorous service demands can be served from factory inventories.

Logistics Impacts on Other Supply Chain Participants

A supplier's logistical system directly affects a distributor's ability to control cost and service to end users. Delivery time influences not only the customer's inventory requirements but also the operations of channel members. If a supplier provides erratic delivery service to distributors, the distributor is forced to carry higher inventory in order to provide a satisfactory level of product availability to end users.

Inefficient logistics service to the distributors either increases distributor costs (larger inventories) or creates shortages of the supplier's products at the distributor level. Neither result is good. In the first instance, distributor loyalty and marketing efforts will suffer; in the second, end users will eventually change suppliers. Palm Inc., the firm that developed the Palm Pilot, created such an effective logistics system that its distributors in Latin America were able to offer the same level of after-sales service available in the United States, allowing Palm to reach sales exceeding $250 million in Latin America in a short time frame.[37] In some industries, distributors are expanding their role in the logistics process, which makes them even more valuable to their suppliers and customers. In the chemical industry, for example, the role of distributors is completely transforming as they offer logistics solutions—JIT delivery, repackaging, inventory management—to their customers.[38] The logistics expertise distributors provide enables their vendors (manufacturers) to focus on their own core competencies of production and marketing.

Business-to-Business Logistical Management

The elements of logistics strategy are part of a system, and as such, each affects every other element. The proper focus is the total-cost view. Although this section treats the decisions on facilities, transportation, and inventory separately, these areas are so intertwined that decisions in one area influence the others.

---

[36] Remko Van Hoek, "When Good Customers Are Bad," *Harvard Business Review* 83 (September 2005): p. 19.

[37] Toby Gooley, "Service Stars," *Logistics* (June 1999): p. 37.

[38] Daniel J. McConville, "More Work for Chemical Distributors," *Distribution* 95 (August 1996): p. 63.

Logistical Facilities

The strategic development of a warehouse provides the business marketer with the opportunity to increase the level of delivery service to buyers, reduce transportation costs, or both. Business firms that distribute repair, maintenance, and operating supplies often find that the only way to achieve desired levels of delivery service is to locate warehouses in key markets. The warehouse circumvents the need for premium transportation (air freight) and costly order processing by keeping products readily available in local markets.

Serving Other Supply Chain Members   The nature of the business-to-business (B2B) supply chain affects the warehousing requirements of a supplier. Manufacturers' representatives do not hold inventory, but distributors do. When manufacturers' reps are used, the supplier often requires a significant number of strategically located warehouses. On the other hand, a supply chain using distributors offsets the need for warehousing. Obviously, local warehousing by the distributor is a real service to the supplier. A few well-located supplier warehouses may be all that is required to service the distributors effectively.

Outsourcing the Warehousing Function   Operating costs, service levels, and investment requirements are essential considerations regarding the type of warehouse to use. The business firm may either operate its own warehouses or turn them over to a "third party"—a company that specializes in performing warehousing services. The advantages of third-party warehousing are flexibility, reduced assets, and professional management—the firm can increase or decrease its use of space in a given market, move into or out of any market quickly, and enjoy an operation managed by specialists. Third-party warehousing may sometimes supplement or replace distributors in a market.

Many third-party warehouses provide a variety of logistical services for their clients, including packaging, labeling, order processing, and some light assembly. APL Logistics, a third-party warehouse company based in Jacksonville, Florida, maintains warehouse facilities in a number of major markets. Clients can position inventories in all these markets while dealing with only one firm. Also, APL can link its computer with the suppliers' computers to facilitate order processing and inventory updating. The APL warehouse also repackages products to the end user's order, label, and arrange for local delivery. A business marketer can ship standard products in bulk to the APL warehouse—gaining transportation economies—and still enjoy excellent customer delivery service. The public or contract warehouse is a feasible alternative to the distributor channel when the sales function can be economically executed either with a direct sales force or with reps.

Transportation

Transportation is usually the largest single logistical expense, and with continually rising fuel costs, its importance will probably increase. Typically, the transportation decision involves evaluating and selecting both a mode of transportation and the individual carrier(s) that will ensure the best performance at the lowest cost. Mode refers to the type of carrier—rail, truck, water, air, or some combination of the four. Individual carriers are evaluated on rates and delivery performance.[39] The supply chain view

---

[39]For example, see James C. Johnson, Donald F. Wood, Danile L. Warlow, and Paul R. Murphy, *Contemporary Logistics*, 7th ed. (Upper Saddle River, N.J.: Prentice-Hall, 1998).

is important in selecting individual carriers. Carriers become an integral part of the supply chain, and close relationships are important. One study found evidence that carriers' operating performance improved when they were more involved in the relationship between buyer and seller.[40] By further integrating carriers into the supply chain, the entire supply chain can improve its competitive position. In this section we consider (1) the role of transportation in industrial supply chains, and (2) the criteria for evaluating transportation options.

Transportation and Logistical Service   A business marketer must be able to effectively move finished inventory between facilities, to channel intermediaries, and to customers. The transportation system is the link that binds the logistical network together and ultimately results in timely delivery of products. Efficient warehousing does not enhance customer service levels if transportation is inconsistent or inadequate.

Effective transportation service may be used in combination with warehouse facilities and inventory levels to generate the required customer-service level, or it may be used in place of them. Inventory maintained in a variety of market-positioned warehouses can be consigned to one centralized warehouse when rapid transportation services exist to deliver products from the central location to business customers. Xerox is one company that uses premium airfreight service to offset the need for high inventories and extensive warehouse locations. The decision on transportation modes and particular carriers depends on the cost trade-offs and service capabilities of each. It is interesting that in the age of next-day delivery and express airfreight services, barges that weave their way through a maze of rivers, lakes, and channels are thriving.[41] A barge trip that takes 17 hours would take a train 4 hours and a truck 90 minutes for a similar trip. Although very slow (averaging 15 miles per hour), the barge offers huge cost advantages compared with truck and rail. For products like limestone, coal, farm products, and petroleum, the slow and unglamorous barge is an effective logistics tool.

Transportation Performance Criteria   Cost of service is the variable cost of moving products from origin to destination, including any terminal or accessory charges. The cost of service may range from as little as $0.25 per ton-mile via water to as high as $0.50 per ton-mile via airfreight. The important aspect of selecting the transportation mode is not cost per se but cost relative to the objective to be achieved. Bulk raw materials generally do not require prepaid delivery service, so the cost of anything other than rail or water transportation could not be justified. On the other hand, although airfreight may be almost 10 times more expensive than motor freight, the cost is inconsequential to a customer who needs an emergency shipment of spare parts. The cost of premium (faster) transportation modes may be justified by the resulting inventory reductions.

Speed of service refers to the elapsed time to move products from one facility (plant or warehouse) to another facility (warehouse or customer plant). Again, speed of service often overrides cost. Rail, a relatively slow mode used for bulk shipments, requires inventory buildups at the supplier's factory and at the destination warehouse. The longer the delivery time, the more inventory customers must maintain to service their needs while the shipment is in transit. The slower modes involve lower variable

---

[40]Julie Gentry, "The Role of Carriers in Buyer-Supplier Strategic Partnerships: A Supply Chain Management Approach," *Journal of Business Logistics* 17, no. 2 (1996): p. 52.

[41]Anna Wilde Mathews, "Jet-Age Anomalies, Slowpoke Barges Do Brisk Business," *The Wall Street Journal*, May 15, 1998, p. B1.

costs for product movement, yet they result in lower service levels and higher investments in inventory. The faster modes produce just the opposite effect. Not only must a comparison be made between modes in terms of service, but various carriers within a mode must be evaluated on their "door-to-door" delivery time.

Service consistency is usually more important than average delivery time, and all modes of transportation are not equally consistent. Although air provides the lowest average delivery time, generally it has the highest variability in delivery time relative to the average. The wide variations in modal service consistency are particularly critical in business marketing planning. The choice of transportation mode must be made on the basis of cost, average transit time, and consistency if effective customer service is to be achieved.

In summary, because business buyers often place a premium on effective and consistent delivery service, the choice of transportation mode is an important one—one where cost of service is often secondary. However, the best decision on transportation carriers results from a balancing of service, variable costs, and investment requirements. The manager must also consider the transportation requirements of ordinary, versus expedited (rush order), shipments.

Inventory Management

Inventory management is the buffer in the logistical system. Inventories are needed in business channels because:

1. Production and demand are not perfectly matched.

2. Operating deficiencies in the logistical system often result in product unavailability (for example, delayed shipments, inconsistent carrier performance).

3. Business customers cannot predict their product needs with certainty (for example, because a machine may break down or there may be a sudden need to expand production).

Inventory may be viewed in the same light as warehouse facilities and transportation: It is an alternative method for providing the level of service customers require, and the level of inventory is determined on the basis of cost, investment, service required, and anticipated revenue.

Quality Focus: Eliminate Inventories   Today's prevalent total quality management techniques and just-in-time management principles emphasize the reduction or outright elimination of inventories. Current thinking suggests that inventories exist because of inefficiencies in the system: Erratic delivery, poor forecasting, and ineffective quality control systems all force companies to hold excessive stocks to protect themselves from delivery, forecasting, and product failure. Instead, improved delivery, forecasting, and manufacturing processes should prevent the need to buffer against failures and uncertainty. Information technology involving bar coding, scanner data, total quality processes, better transportation management, and more effective information flow among firms in the supply chain have made it possible to more carefully control inventories and reduce them to the lowest possible levels.

The Internet connectivity that unites the supply chain from an information standpoint has permitted substantial inventory reductions in several industries. One recent study showed that average inventory turnover for manufacturers has increased from 8

INSIDE BUSINESS MARKETING

The Profit Impact of Inventory Management

Deere & Company's core business is manufacturing equipment: agricultural, construction, commercial, and consumer equipment. For its supply chain practices, the firm enjoys an edge over its competitors in the industry, particularly in inventory management. The following illustration demonstrates the significance of this advantage.

On average, assume that Deere maintains 59 days' worth of sales in inventory and the worst firm in the industry maintains 137 days' worth of sales in inventory. Each 30 days' worth of inventory translates to a profit difference of 1.66 percent of sales in the industry. The difference between Deere and the worst competitor is 78 days' worth of inventory. To calculate the profit difference, the following calculations can be made:

Worst firm, inventories:	137 days
Deere & Company, inventories:	59 days
Difference:	78 days

Each *30 days* is worth *1.66 percent of sales* in profits. The difference between Deere and its "worst" competitor is 78/30 = *2.6 times.*

The difference in profitability is: 2.6 × 1.66% = *4.3% of sales.*

The difference between the worst firm and the best firm as a result of effectively managing inventories is equal to 4.3 percent of sales. If each firm has $1 billion in sales, the best-managed firm would have *$43 million more profits*, all other things being equal!

to more than 12 times per year.[42] Much of the credit for this improvement is attributed to more information sharing among the supply chain members, sophisticated inventory management software, and generally higher levels of supply chain coordination. Successful business marketing managers must develop quality processes that in themselves reduce or eliminate the need to carry large inventories, while coordinating and integrating a supply chain system that can function effectively with almost no inventory.

Inventory in Rapidly Changing Markets   Many companies in rapidly changing high-tech industries must look at inventory characteristics like obsolescence, devaluation, price protection, and return costs.[43] For a company like Hewlett-Packard, with products that have very fast product life cycles, all four of these factors can significantly reduce profits if inventories are not managed effectively. H-P refers to these costs as "inventory-driven costs" (IDCs). In 1995, for example, H-P found that costs related to inventory equaled their PC business's *total operating margin!* For many of their products that are held in the supply chain by various resellers, the major inventory costs to H-P are price protection costs, as they must reimburse resellers for any loss in the market value of the products kept in inventory. Because the inventories of channel partners represent the largest component of inventory costs to H-P, managers are taking steps to improve SCM practices downstream in the channel. For example, H-P has introduced new processes such as vendor-managed inventory (VMI)—where H-P assists resellers in planning inventories and works with the marketing managers of those resellers to estimate and manage demand.

---

[42] Thomas W. Speh, *Changes in Warehouse Inventory Turnover* (Chicago: Warehousing Education and Research Council, 1999).

[43] Gianpaolo Callioni, Xavier de Montgros, Regine Slagmulder, Luk N. Van Wassenhove, and Linda Wright, "Inventory-Driven Costs," *Harvard Business Review* 83 (March 2005): pp. 135–141.

Third-Party Logistics

An emerging development in performing logistics is the use of **third-party logistics firms.** These external firms perform a wide range of logistics functions traditionally performed within the organization. Most companies use some type of third-party firm, whether for transportation, warehousing, or information processing. The strategic decision to outsource logistics is often made by top management. The functions the third-party company performs can encompass the entire logistics process or selected activities within that process. Third parties can perform the warehousing; they may perform the transportation function (for example, a truck line like Schneider National); or they may perform the entire logistics process from production scheduling to delivery of finished products to the customer (for example, Ryder Dedicated Logistics). Third parties enable a manufacturer or distributor to concentrate on its core business while enjoying the expertise and specialization of a professional logistics company. The results are often lower costs, better service, improved asset utilization, increased flexibility, and access to leading-edge technology. Recently, some firms have advocated the use of "Fourth-Party Logistics"—firms that own no assets but serve to manage several third parties that are employed to perform various logistics functions.[44]

Despite the advantages of third-party logistics firms, some firms are cautious because of reduced control over the logistics process, diminished direct contact with customers, and the problems of terminating internal operations. In analyzing the most effective and efficient way to accomplish logistics cost and service objectives, the business marketing manager should carefully consider the benefits and drawbacks of outsourcing part or all logistics functions to third-party providers. In an interesting application of third-party logistics, Caterpillar (the manufacturer of earthmoving equipment) formed a logistics services company to manage the parts distribution for other manufacturers.[45] The company applies the knowledge gained from its own experiences in distributing 300 families of products that require over 530,000 spare parts. Caterpillar transfers knowledge from the company's internal operations to customers and vice versa.

Summary

Leading business marketing firms demonstrate superior capabilities in supply chain management. SCM focuses on improving the flow of products, information, and services as they move from origin to destination. A key driver to SCM is coordination and integration among all the participants in the supply chain, primarily through sophisticated information systems and management software. Reducing waste, minimizing duplication, reducing cost, and enhancing service are the major objectives of SCM. Firms successful at managing the supply chain understand the nature of their products and the type of supply chain structure required to meet the needs of their customers. In particular, effective supply chains integrate operations, share information, and above all, provide added value to customers.

---

[44]"Fourth Party Logistics: An Analysis," *Logistics Focus* 1 (Issue 3) (summer 2002): p. 16.

[45]Peter Marsh, "A Moving Story of Spare Parts," *The Financial Times*, August 29, 1997, p. 8.

Logistics is the critical function in the firm's supply chain because logistics directs the flow and storage of products and information. Successful supply chains synchronize logistics with other functions such as production, procurement, forecasting, order management, and customer service. The systems perspective in logistical management cannot be stressed enough—it is the only way to assure management that the logistical function meets prescribed goals. Not only must each logistical variable be analyzed in terms of its effect on every other variable, but the sum of the variables must be evaluated in light of the service level provided to customers. Logistics elements throughout the supply chain must be integrated to assure smooth product flow. Logistical service is critical in the buyer's evaluation of business marketing firms. Logistically service generally ranks second only to product quality as a desired supplier characteristic.

Logistics decisions must be based on cost trade-offs among the logistical variables and on comparisons of the costs and revenues associated with alternative levels of service. The optimal system produces the highest profitability relative to the capital investment required. Three major variables—facilities, transportation, and inventory—form the basis of logistical decisions B2B logistics managers face. The business marketer must monitor the effect of logistics on all supply chain members and on overall supply chain performance. Finally, the strategic role of logistics should be carefully evaluated: Logistics can often provide a strong competitive advantage.

Discussion Questions

1. What is supply chain management and what are the types of functions and firms that make up the typical supply chain?

2. Explain how an effective supply chain can create a strong competitive advantage for the firms involved in it.

3. Explain why cooperation among supply chain participants determines whether the supply chain is effective.

4. Explain the different elements of "waste" that exist in supply chains and how supply chain management focuses on eliminating the various elements of waste.

5. Describe the role the Internet plays in enhancing supply chain management operations.

6. Adopting the perspective of an organizational buyer, carefully illustrate how the most economical source of supply might be the firm that offers the highest price but also the fastest and most reliable delivery system.

7. Describe a situation in which total logistical costs might be reduced by doubling transportation costs.

8. A key goal in logistical management is to find the optimum balance of logistical cost and customer service that yields optimal profits. Explain.

9. Explain how consistent delivery performance gives the organizational buyer the opportunity to cut the level of inventory maintained.

10. An increasing number of manufacturers are adopting more sophisticated purchasing practices and inventory control systems. What are the strategic implications of these developments for business marketers wishing to serve these customers?

Internet Exercise

Yellow-Roadway Corporation is a *Fortune* 500 transportation company and one of the largest transportation firms in the world. Go to http://www.myyellowcorp.com and examine the online tools available on the Web site. Discuss how the various tools would help a B2B marketer enhance the logistics services that they provide to customers.

Managing Logistics at Trans-Pro

Logistics management is critical in determining the profitability of B2B channel members like industrial distributors. To be successful, the industrial distributor must maintain a very large inventory of its full product line and be able to deliver products promptly when a customer places an order—the major value-added service that the distributor provides to customers is product availability. By having an extensive variety of components and replacements parts available on a round-the-clock basis, the distributor's customers are able to minimize investments in inventory. In addition, customer firms can be certain that their operations will never be shut down because they cannot get a critical component. Because of the nature of the distributor's business, inventory costs often become the single largest expense and, as such, effective inventory management is a key driver of profitability.

Trans-Pro is a large industrial distributor of power transmission equipment—bearings, gears, v-belts, and the like. The company's management, cognizant of the criticality of effective inventory management, developed an incentive scheme for its 50 branch managers to minimize inventories. Each month, average inventory in the warehouse was measured and the branch managers were assessed a penalty for inventory levels that exceeded $2.5 million. For each increment of dollars above the threshold figure, the manager would be docked 1 percent of his or her monthly salary—a very strong incentive to carefully control inventory levels! In addition, Trans-Pro also demanded that customer service be absolutely outstanding. The goal was to deliver an order within 24 hours of receiving it. As might be expected, the managers did a superlative job in managing average monthly inventories. Rarely were any of the branches in excess of the mandated maximum level. Customer service levels approached 98 percent—that is, 98 percent of all orders were delivered within the 24-hour time period.

Discussion Question

Critique Trans-Pro's approach to managing logistics.

Pricing Strategy
for Business Markets

Understanding how customers define value is the essence of the pricing process. Pricing decisions complement the firm's overall marketing strategy. The diverse nature of the business market presents unique problems and opportunities for the price strategist. After reading this chapter, you will understand:

1. the role of price in the cost/benefit calculations of organizational buyers.

2. the central elements of the pricing process.

3. how effective new product prices are established and the need to periodically adjust the prices of existing products.

4. how to respond to a price attack by an aggressive competitor.

5. strategic approaches to competitive bidding.

Customer value represents the cornerstone of business-to-business (B2B) marketing in the 21st century.[1] Thus, business marketers must pursue this unifying strategic goal: Be better than your very best competitors in providing customer value.[2]

According to Richard D'Aveni:

> While the average competitor fights for niches along a common ratio of price and value ("You get what you pay for"), innovative firms can enter the market by providing better value to the customer ("You can get more than what you pay for"). These companies offer lower cost *and* higher quality. This shift in value is like lowering the stick while dancing the limbo. All the competitors have to do the same dance with tighter constraints on both cost and quality.[3]

The business marketing manager must blend the various components of the marketing mix into a value proposition that responds to the customer's requirements and provides a return consistent with the firm's objectives. Price must be carefully meshed with the firm's product, distribution, and communication strategies. Thomas Nagle points out, "If effective product development, promotion, and distribution sow the seeds of business success, effective pricing is the harvest. Although effective pricing can never compensate for poor execution of the first three elements, ineffective pricing can surely prevent these efforts from resulting in financial success. Regrettably, this is a common occurrence."[4]

This chapter is divided into five parts. The first defines the special meaning of customer value in a business marketing context. The second analyzes key determinants of the industrial pricing process and provides an operational approach to pricing decisions. The third examines pricing policies for new and existing products, emphasizing the need to actively manage a product throughout its life cycle. The fourth provides a framework to guide strategy when a competitor cuts prices. The final section examines an area of particular importance to the business marketer: competitive bidding.

The Meaning of Value in Business Markets

When members of a buying center select a product, they are buying a given level of product quality, technical service, and delivery reliability. Other elements may be important—the reputation of the supplier, a feeling of security, friendship, and other personal benefits flowing from the buyer-seller relationship. Value represents a trade-off between benefits and sacrifices. **Customer value**, then, represents a business

---

[1] Ajay Menon, Christian Homburg, and Nikolas Beutin, "Understanding Customer Value in Business-to-Business Relationships," *Journal of Business-to-Business Marketing* 12, no. 2 (2005): pp. 1–33. See also, James C. Anderson and James A. Narus, "Business Marketing: Understand What Customers Value," *Harvard Business Review* 76 (November–December 1998): p. 65.

[2] Bradley T. Gale, *Managing Customer Value: Creating Quality and Service That Customers Can See* (New York: The Free Press, 1994), pp. 73–75.

[3] Richard A. D'Aveni, *Hypercompetitive Rivalries* (New York: The Free Press, 1995), p. 27.

[4] Thomas T. Nagle, *The Strategy and Tactics of Pricing: A Guide to Profitable Decision Making* (Englewood Cliffs, N.J.: Prentice-Hall, 1987), p. 1.

FIGURE 15.1 | CUSTOMER VALUE IN BUSINESS MARKETS

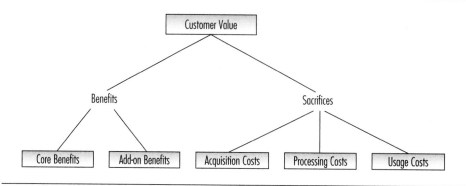

SOURCE: Adapted with modifications from Ajay Menon, Christian Homburg, and Nikolas Beutin, "Understanding Customer Value in Business-to-Business Relationships," *Journal of Business-to-Business Marketing* 12, no. 2 (2005): pp. 1–33.

customer's overall assessment of the utility of a relationship with a supplier based on benefits received and sacrifices made[5] (Figure 15.1).

Benefits

Two types of benefits can contribute to customer value in business markets: core benefits and add-on benefits (see Chapter 9).

Core Benefits   **Core benefits** are the basic requirements the business marketer must meet to be included in the customer's consideration set. Represented here would be a specific level of product quality and performance, as well as expected levels of pre- and postsales service. Likewise, by enhancing problem solving and the open sharing of ideas, a trust-based relationship adds value and the customer sees it as a core benefit.

Add-on Benefits   **Add-on benefits** are those "attributes, typically not required, that assist the customer in selecting a supplier from among a qualified set of potential suppliers."[6] These are relational characteristics or services that differentiate suppliers and focus on "attractor" attributes in buyer-seller relationships.

Examples of add-on benefits would be *joint working relationships* in product development, quality control, logistics, and delivery systems. **Supplier flexibility,** or the willingness of a business marketer to accommodate a customer's unique business needs, likewise adds customer value. The supplier's **commitment,** namely the desire to make the relationship work, can also provide an add-on benefit to the customer. Supplier commitment "takes into account the supplier's willingness to make short-term sacrifices, invest in the relationship, and be tolerant of buyer's mistakes (for example, mistakes in ordering or outlining product specifications)."[7]

---

[5] This discussion is based on Menon, Homburg, and Beutin, "Understanding Customer Value," pp. 1–33.

[6] Ibid., p. 6. See also, Das Narayandas, "Building Loyalty in Business Markets," *Harvard Business Review* 83 (September 2005): pp. 131–139.

[7] Menon, Homburg, and Beutin, "Understanding Customer Value," p. 15.

TABLE 15.1 | CUSTOMERS' COST-IN-USE COMPONENTS

Acquisition Costs	+	Possession Costs	+	Usage Costs	=	Total Cost in Use
Price		Interest cost		Installation costs		
Paperwork cost		Storage cost		Training cost		
Transportation costs		Quality control		User labor cost		
Expediting cost		Taxes and insurance		Product longevity		
Cost of mistakes in order		Shrinkage and obsolescence		Replacement costs		
Prepurchase product evaluation costs		General internal handling costs		Disposal costs		

SOURCE: Adapted from Frank V. Cespedes, "Industrial Marketing: Managing New Requirements," *Sloan Management Review* 35 (spring 1994): p. 46.

Sacrifices

A broad perspective is likewise needed in examining the sacrifices, or costs, a particular alternative may present for the buyer. When purchasing a product or service, a business customer always assumes various costs above and beyond the actual purchase price. Many businesses buy products online to reduce paperwork and lower transaction and search costs.[8] Rather than making a decision on the basis of price alone, organizational buyers emphasize the **total cost in use** of a particular product or service.[9] Observe in Table 15.1 that an organizational customer considers three different types of costs in a total cost-in-use calculation:

1. **Acquisition costs** include not only the selling price and transportation costs but also the administrative costs of evaluating suppliers, expediting orders, and correcting errors in shipments or delivery.

2. **Possession costs** include financing, storage, inspection, taxes, insurance, and other internal handling costs.

3. **Usage costs** are those associated with ongoing use of the purchased product such as installation, employee training, user labor, and field repair, as well as product replacement and disposal costs.

Value-Based Strategies

Aided by sophisticated supplier evaluation systems (see Chapter 2), buyers can measure and track the total cost/value of dealing with alternative suppliers. In turn, astute business marketers can pursue value-based strategies that provide customers with a lower cost-in-use solution. For example, the logistical expenses of health-care supplies typically account for 10 to 15 percent of a hospital's operating costs. Medical products

[8] Walter Baker, Mike Marn, and Craig Zawada, "Price Smarter on the Net," *Harvard Business Review* 79 (February 2001): pp. 122–127.
[9] Frank V. Cespedes, "Industrial Marketing: Managing New Requirements," *Sloan Management Review* 35 (spring 1994): pp. 45–60.

B2B TOP PERFORMERS

The Key to Value-Based Strategies—Understand the Customer's Economics

Rather than caving in to price pressure from their largest and most demanding customers, leading business-to-business firms are creating and capturing more value through highly collaborative relationships with key customers. The results of a survey of sales executives at *Fortune* 1000 companies found that, for the leading performers, collaborative initiatives increased revenues and profits by 20 percent, on average. To succeed with value-based strategies, top performing firms:

- Develop a deep understanding of the customer's economics and engage the appropriate customer personnel (from product developers to purchasing executives) in joint strategy sessions to define mutually beneficial opportunities.

- Assemble an appropriate internal team of sales personnel, collaboration managers, and senior executives who can deliver the required customer solutions.

- Recognize that collaborative selling is a costly business and approach it with a

hard-nosed profit focus by choosing trial customers carefully and periodically reevaluating relationships.

To illustrate the form a collaborative strategy can take, consider the solution that Sonoco, a packaging supplier, provided for Lance, the snack food maker. One improvement involved the use of flexographic printed packaging film on some of Lance's key brands. Such efforts drastically reduced Lance's packaging costs and improved the appeal of the products. Whereas other players in the packaging industry are experiencing sluggish growth or even declining revenue, Sonoco continues to enjoy solid growth in revenue and profitability—thanks in part to its value-based strategies.

SOURCE: Maryanne Q. Hancock, Roland H. John, and Philip J. Wojcik, "Better B2B Selling," *The McKinsey Quarterly*, Web exclusive, June 2005, pp. 1–8; accessed at http://www.mckinseyquarterly.com on October 21, 2005. See also, James C. Anderson and James A. Narus, "Business Marketing: Understand What Customers Value," *Harvard Business Review* 76 (November–December 1998): pp. 59–60.

firms, like Becton, Dickinson and Company, develop innovative product/service packages that respond to each component of the cost-in-use equation. Such firms can reduce a hospital's acquisition costs by offering an electronic ordering system, possession costs by emphasizing just-in-time service, and usage costs by creating an efficient system for disposing of medical supplies after use.

Benefits Provide the Edge   Value-based strategies seek to move the selling proposition from one that centers on current prices and individual transactions to a longer-term relationship built around value and lower total cost in use. Importantly, recent research suggests that benefits have a greater effect on perceived value to business customers than sacrifices (price and costs). Ajay Menon, Christian Homburg, and Nikolas Beutin note: Contrary to the general belief in a cost-driven economy, "we encourage managers to emphasize benefits accruing from a relationship and not focus solely on lowering the price and related costs when managing customer value."[10] A better way is to provide unique add-on benefits by building trust, demonstrating commitment and flexibility, and initiating joint working relationships that enhance customer value and loyalty.

---

[10]Menon, Homburg, and Beutin, "Understanding Customer Value," p. 25.

FIGURE 15.2 | KEY COMPONENTS OF THE PRICE-SETTING DECISION PROCESS

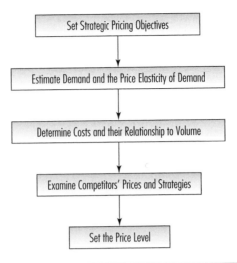

The Pricing Process in Business Markets

There is no easy formula for pricing an industrial product or service. The decision is multidimensional: The interactive variables of demand, cost, competition, profit relationships, and customer usage patterns each assumes significance as the marketer formulates the role of price in the firm's marketing strategy. Pertinent considerations, illustrated in Figure 15.2, include (1) pricing objectives, (2) demand determinants, (3) cost determinants, and (4) competition.

Price Objectives

The pricing decision must be based on objectives congruent with marketing and overall corporate objectives. The marketer starts with principal objectives and adds collateral pricing goals: (1) achieving a target return on investment, (2) achieving a market-share goal, or (3) meeting competition. Many other potential pricing objectives extend beyond profit and market-share goals, taking into account competition, channel relationships, and product-line considerations.

Because of their far-reaching effects, pricing objectives must be established with care. Each firm faces unique internal and external environmental forces. Contrasting the strategies of DuPont and Dow Chemical illustrates the importance of a unified corporate direction. Dow's strategy focuses first on pricing low-margin commodity goods *low* to build a dominant market share and then on maintaining that dominant share. DuPont's strategy, on the other hand, emphasizes higher-margin specialty products. Initially, these products are priced at a *high* level, and prices are reduced as the market expands and competition intensifies. Each firm requires explicit pricing objectives that are consistent with its corporate mission.

TABLE 15.2 | **ATTRIBUTES OF A TOTAL PRODUCT OFFERING: SOME TRADE-OFFS**

Attribute	High Level	Low Level
Quality	Impurities less than one part per million	Impurities less than ten parts per million
Delivery	Within one week	Within two weeks
System	Supply total system	Supply chemical only
Innovation	High level of R&D support	Little R&D support
Retraining	Retrain on request	Train on initial purchase
Service	Locally available	Through home office

SOURCE: Irwin Gross, "Insights from Pricing Research," in *Pricing Practices and Strategies*, Earl L. Bailey, ed. (New York: The Conference Board, 1978), p. 37. Reprinted by permission of The Conference Board.

Demand Determinants

A strong market perspective is fundamental in pricing. The business market is diverse and complex. A single industrial product can be used in many ways; each market segment may represent a unique application for the product and a separate usage level. The importance of the industrial good in the buyer's end product also varies by market segment. Therefore, potential demand, sensitivity to price, and potential profitability can vary markedly across market segments. To establish an effective pricing policy, marketers should focus first on the value a customer places on a product or service. This reverses the typical process that gives immediate attention to the product cost and the desired markup.[11]

Assessing Value[12]   How organizational buyers evaluate the cost/benefit trade-offs of the total offering determines the appropriateness of an industrial pricing strategy. Two competitors with similar products may ask different prices because buyers perceive their total offerings as unique. In the eyes of the organizational buyer, one firm may provide more value than another.

A core pricing issue concerns which of the offering's attributes contribute most to its perceived value. Table 15.2 identifies total product-offering attributes that have value to buyers and that differ among competitors. Two levels of performance are provided for each attribute. Because providing higher levels of performance on one or more of the attributes costs more, the strategist should assess the attributes' relative importance to different market segments and the strength of the firm's offering on each of the important attributes versus those of competitors.

The equation in Figure 15.3 highlights how the relative perceived values of two competing offerings are compared. Irv Gross contends that the relative perceived value

[11] Robert J. Dolan, "How Do You Know When the Price Is Right?" *Harvard Business Review* 73 (September–October 1995): pp. 174–183. See also Thomas T. Nagle and George E. Cressman Jr., "Don't Just Set Prices, Manage Them," *Marketing Management* 11 (November–December 2002): pp. 29–34.

[12] Irwin Gross, "Insights from Pricing Research," in *Pricing Practices and Strategies*, Earl L. Bailey, ed. (New York: The Conference Board, 1978), pp. 34–39. See also Valerie Kijewski and Eunsang Yoon, "Market-Based Pricing: Beyond Price-Performance Curves," *Industrial Marketing Management* 19 (February 1990): pp. 11–19; and G. Dean Kortge and Patrick A. Okonkwo, "Perceived Value Approach to Pricing," *Industrial Marketing Management* 22 (May 1993): pp. 133–140.

FIGURE 15.3 | **RELATIVE PERCEIVED VALUE OF TWO PRODUCT OFFERINGS**

SOURCE: Irwin Gross, "Insights from Pricing Research," in *Pricing Practices and Strategies*, Earl L. Bailey, ed. (New York: The Conference Board, 1978), p. 38. Reprinted by permission of The Conference Board.

of offering *A* versus offering *B* "can be thought of as the price differential at which the buyer would be indifferent between the alternatives."[13] As in Figure 15.3, the premium price differential, or perceived relative value, can be broken down into components based on each important attribute: (1) the value of the attribute to the buyer, and (2) the perception of how competing offerings perform on that attribute. By summing all of the component values, we reach an offering's total relative perceived value. Thus, *A* may have a total perceived value of $24 per unit compared with $20 per unit for *B*. The $4 premium might be derived from the value buyers assign to a high level of product quality and a responsive delivery system, and the perceived advantage of *A* over others on these attributes.

Strategy Implications of the Cost/Benefit Analysis   By isolating the important attributes and the perceptions that enter into buyers' cost/benefit calculations, the business marketer is better equipped to establish a price and shape other elements of the marketing strategy. First, if the firm's performance on a highly valued product attribute is truly higher than that of competitors, but the market perceives no differences, marketing communications can bring perceptions into line with reality. Second, marketing communications may also alter the values that organizational buyers assign to a particular attribute. The importance of an attribute such as customer training might be elevated through marketing communications emphasizing improved efficiency and safety that training provides.

Third, the perceived value of the total product offering can be changed by improving the firm's performance on attributes that organizational buyers assign special importance. Fourth, knowledge of the cost/benefit perceptions of potential customers presents market segmentation opportunities. For example, good strategy might target market segments that value the particular product attributes on which the firm has a clear competitive advantage.

Elasticity Varies by Market Segment   Price elasticity of demand measures the degree to which customers are sensitive to price changes. Specifically, **price elasticity of demand** refers to the rate of percentage change in quantity demanded attributable to a percentage change in price. Price elasticity of demand is not the same at all prices. A business marketer contemplating a change in price must understand the elasticity of demand. For example, total revenue (price times quantity) *increases* if price is decreased

---

[13] Gross, "Insights," p. 35.

and demand is price elastic, whereas revenue *falls* if the price is decreased and demand is price inelastic. Many factors influence the price elasticity of demand—the ease with which customers can compare alternatives and switch suppliers, the importance of the product in the cost structure of the customer's product, and the value that the product represents to a customer.

Satisfied Customers are Less Price Sensitive   Recent research demonstrates that highly satisfied customers are less sensitive to prices, compared with those who have a moderate level of customer satisfaction.[14] This relationship is particularly strong for purchase decisions that involve a high level of product/service complexity and a high degree of customization. Thus, reduced customer price sensitivity represents an important payoff to a business marketer for developing a customized solution for the customer.

Search Behavior and Switching Costs   The price sensitivity of buyers increases—and a firm's pricing latitude decreases—to the degree that[15]:

- Organizational buyers can easily shop around and assess the relative performance and price of alternatives; purchasing managers in many firms use information technology to track supplier prices on a global basis.

- The product is one for which it is easy to make price comparisons; for example, it is easier to compare alternative photocopiers than it is to compare specialized manufacturing equipment options.

- Buyers can switch from one supplier to another without incurring additional costs; as Chapter 4 highlights, low switching costs allow a buyer to focus on minimizing the cost of a particular transaction.

End Use   Important insights can be secured by answering this question: How important is the business marketer's product as an input into the total cost of the end product? If the business marketer's product has an insignificant effect on cost, demand is likely inelastic. Consider this example:

> A manufacturer of precision electronic components was contemplating an across-the-board price decrease to increase sales. However, an item analysis of the product line revealed that some of its low-volume components had exotic applications. A technical customer used the component in an ultrasonic testing apparatus that was sold for $8,000 a unit. This fact prompted the electronics manufacturer to raise the price of the item. Ironically, the firm then experienced a temporary surge of demand for the item as purchasing agents stocked up in anticipation of future price increases.[16]

Of course, the marketer must temper this estimate by analyzing the costs, availability, and suitability of substitutes. Generally, when the industrial product is an

---

[14] Ruth Maria Stock, "Can Customer Satisfaction Decrease Price Sensitivity in Business-to-Business Marketing?" *Journal of Business-to-Business Marketing* 12, no. 3 (2005): pp. 59–85.

[15] Dolan, "How Do You Know When the Price Is Right?" pp. 178–179.

[16] Reed Moyer and Robert J. Boewadt, "The Pricing of Industrial Goods," *Business Horizons* 14 (June 1971): pp. 27–34; see also George Rostky, "Unveiling Market Segments with Technical Focus Research," *Business Marketing* 71 (October 1986): pp. 66–69.

important but low-cost input into the end product, price is less important than quality and delivery reliability.

When, however, the product input represents a larger part of the final product's total cost, changes in price may have an important effect on the demand for both the final product and the input. When demand in the final consumer market is price elastic, a reduction in the price of the end item (for example, a personal computer) that is caused by a price reduction of a component (for example, a microprocessor) generates an increase in demand for the final product (personal computer) and, in turn, for the industrial product (microprocessor).

End Market Focus Because the demand for many industrial products is derived from the demand for the product of which they are a part, a strong end-user focus is needed. The marketer can benefit by examining the trends and changing fortunes of important final consumer markets. Different sectors of the market grow at different rates, confront different levels of competition, and face different short-run and long-run challenges. A downturn in the economy does not fall equally on all sectors. Pricing decisions demand a two-tiered market focus—on organizational customers and on final product customers. Thus, business marketers will have more success in raising prices to customers who are prospering than to customers who are hard pressed.

Value-Based Segmentation The value customers assign to a firm's offering can vary by market segment because the same industrial product may serve different purposes for different customers. This underscores the important role of market segmentation in pricing strategies. Take Sealed Air Corporation, the innovative supplier of protective packaging, including coated air bubbles.[17] The company recognized that for some applications, substitutes were readily available. But for other applications, Sealed Air had an enormous advantage—for example, its packaging materials offered superior cushioning for heavy items with long shipping cycles. By identifying those applications where the firm had a clear advantage and understanding the unique value differential in each setting, marketing managers were ideally equipped to tackle product-line expansion and pricing decisions and to ignite Sealed Air's remarkable revenue growth for nearly two decades.

Cost Determinants

Business marketers often pursue a strong internal orientation; they base prices on their own costs, reaching the selling price by calculating unit costs and adding a percentage profit. A strict cost-plus pricing philosophy overlooks customer perceptions of value, competition, and the interaction of volume and profit. Many progressive firms, such as Canon, Toyota, and Hewlett-Packard (H-P), use target costing to capture a significant competitive advantage.

Target Costing[18] **Target costing** features a design-to-cost philosophy that begins by examining market conditions: The firm identifies and targets the most attractive market segments. It then determines what level of quality and types of product

---

[17] Dolan, "How Do You Know When the Price Is Right?" pp. 176–177.

[18] This section is based on Robin Cooper and Regine Slagmulder, "Develop Profitable New Products with Target Costing," *Sloan Management Review* 40 (summer 1999): pp. 23–33.

attributes are required to succeed in each segment, given a predetermined target price and volume level. According to Robin Cooper and Regine Slagmulder, to set the target price, the business marketer has to understand the customer's perception of value: "A company can raise selling prices only if the perceived value of the new product exceeds not only that of the product's predecessor, but also that of competing products."[19]

Once the target selling price and target profit margins have been established, the firm calculates the allowable cost. The strategic cost reduction challenge isolates the profit shortfall that occurs if the product designers are unable to achieve the allowable cost. The value of distinguishing the allowable cost from the target cost lies in the pressure that this exercise exerts on the product development team and the company's suppliers. To transmit the competitive cost pressure *it* faces to its suppliers, the firm then breaks down the target price of a new product into a cascade of target costs for each component or function. For example, the major functions of an automobile include the engine, transmission, cooling system, and audio system.

A Profit-Management Tool   Toyota used target costing to reduce the price of its recently modified Camry model and did so while offering as standard equipment certain features that were expensive options on the model it replaced. Similarly, Canon used target costing to develop its breakthrough personal copier that transformed the photocopier industry.[20] Rather than a cost-control technique, Japanese managers who pioneered the approach view target costing as a profit-management tool. As Robin Cooper and W. Bruce Chew assert, "The task is to compute the costs that must not be exceeded if acceptable margins from specific products at specific price points are to be guaranteed."[21]

Classifying Costs[22]   The target costing approach stresses why the marketer must know which costs are relevant to the pricing decision and how these costs fluctuate with volume and over time; they must be considered in relation to demand, competition, and pricing objectives. Product costs are crucial in projecting the profitability of individual products as well as of the entire product line. Proper classification of costs is essential.

The goals of a cost classification system are to (1) properly classify cost data into their fixed and variable components and (2) properly link them to the activity causing them. The manager can then analyze the effects of volume and, more important, identify sources of profit. The following cost concepts are instrumental in the analysis:

1. **Direct traceable or attributable costs:** Costs, fixed or variable, are incurred by and solely for a particular product, customer, or sales territory (for example, raw materials).

2. **Indirect traceable costs:** Costs, fixed or variable, can be traced to a product, customer, or sales territory (for example, general plant overhead may be indirectly assigned to a product).

[19] Ibid., p. 26.

[20] Jean-Phillippe Deschamps and P. Ranganath Nayak, *Product Juggernauts: How Companies Mobilize to Generate a Stream of Market Winners* (Boston: Harvard Business School Press, 1995), pp. 119–149.

[21] Robin Cooper and W. Bruce Chew, "Control Tomorrow's Costs through Today's Designs," *Harvard Business Review* 74 (January–February 1996): pp. 88–97.

[22] Kent B. Monroe, *Pricing: Making Profitable Decisions* (New York: McGraw-Hill, 1979), pp. 52–57. See also Nagle, *The Strategy and Tactics of Pricing*, pp. 14–43.

3. **General costs:** Costs support a number of activities that cannot be objectively assigned to a product on the basis of a direct physical relationship (for example, the administrative costs of a sales district).

General costs rarely change because an item is added or deleted from the product line. Marketing, production, and distribution costs must all be classified. When developing a new line or when deleting or adding an item to an existing line, the marketer must grasp the cost implications:

- What proportion of the product cost is accounted for by purchases of raw materials and components from suppliers?

- How do costs vary at differing levels of production?

- Based on the forecasted level of demand, can economies of scale be expected?

- Does our firm enjoy cost advantages over competitors?

- How does the "experience effect" impact our cost projections?

Competition

Competition establishes an upper limit on price. An individual industrial firm's degree of latitude in pricing depends heavily on how organizational buyers perceive the product's level of differentiation. Price is only one component of the cost/benefit equation; the marketer can gain a differential advantage over competitors on many dimensions other than physical product characteristics—reputation, technical expertise, delivery reliability, and related factors. Regis McKenna contends, "Even if a company manufactures commodity-like products, it can differentiate the products through the service and support it offers, or by target marketing. It can leave its commodity mentality in the factory, and bring a mentality of diversity to the marketplace."[23] In addition to assessing the product's degree of differentiation in various market segments, one must ask how competitors will respond to particular pricing decisions.

Hypercompetitive Rivalries Some strategy experts emphasize that traditional patterns of competition in stable environments is being replaced by hypercompetitive rivalries in a rapidly changing environment.[24] In a stable environment, a company could create a fairly rigid strategy designed to accommodate long-term conditions. The firm's strategy focused on sustaining its own strategic advantage and establishing equilibrium where less dominant firms accepted a secondary status.

In hypercompetitive environments, successful companies pursue strategies that create temporary advantage and destroy the advantages of rivals by constantly disrupting the market's equilibrium. For example, Intel continually disrupts the equilibrium of the microprocessor industry sector, and Hewlett-Packard stirs up the computer printer business by its consistent drives to lower price points. Moreover, the Internet provides customers with real-time access to a wealth of information that drives the prices of many products lower. Leading firms in hypercompetitive environments constantly seek out new sources of advantage, further escalating competition and contributing to hypercompetition.

---

[23] Regis McKenna, *Relationship Marketing* (Reading, Mass.: Addison-Wesley, 1991), pp. 178–179.

[24] D'Aveni, *Hypercompetitive Rivalries*, pp. 149–170.

TABLE 15.3 | **SELECTED COST COMPARISON ISSUES: FOLLOWERS VERSUS THE PIONEER**

Technology/economies of scale	Followers may benefit by using more current production technology than the pioneer or by building a plant with a larger scale of operations.
Product/market knowledge	Followers may learn from the pioneer's mistakes by analyzing the competitor's product, hiring key personnel, or identifying through market research the problems and unfulfilled expectations of customers and channel members.
Shared experience	Compared with the pioneer, followers may be able to gain advantages on certain cost elements by sharing operations with other parts of the company.
Experience of suppliers	Followers, together with the pioneer, benefit from cost reductions achieved by outside suppliers of components or production equipment.

SOURCE: Adapted from George S. Day and David B. Montgomery, "Diagnosing the Experience Curve," *Journal of Marketing* 47 (spring 1983): pp. 48–49.

Consider the hypercompetitive rivalries in high-technology markets. Firms that sustain quality and that are the first to hit the next lower strategic price point enjoy a burst of volume and an expansion of market share. For example, Hewlett-Packard has ruthlessly pursued the next lower price point in its printer business, even as it cannibalized its own sales and margins.[25]

Gauging Competitive Response   To predict the response of competitors, the marketer can first benefit by examining the cost structure and strategy of both direct competitors and producers of potential substitutes. The marketer can draw on public statements and records (for example, annual reports) to form rough estimates. Competitors that have ascended the learning curve may have lower costs than those just entering the industry and beginning the climb. An estimate of the cost structure is valuable when gauging how well competitors can respond to price reductions and when projecting the pattern of prices in the future.

Under certain conditions, however, followers into a market may confront lower initial costs than did the pioneer. Why? Some of the reasons are highlighted in Table 15.3. By failing to recognize potential cost advantages of late entrants, the business marketer can dramatically overstate cost differences.

The market strategy competing sellers use is also important here. Competitors are more sensitive to price reductions that threaten those market segments they deem important. They learn of price reductions earlier when their market segments overlap. Of course, competitors may choose not to follow a price decrease, especially if their products enjoy a differentiated position. Rather than matching competitors' price cuts, one successful steel company reacts to the competitive challenge by offering customized products and technical assistance to its customers.[26] Later in the chapter, special attention is given to this question: How should you respond to price attacks by competitors?

---

[25] Geoffrey A. Moore, *Inside the Tornado: Marketing Strategies from Silicon Valley's Cutting Edge* (New York: HarperCollins, 1995), pp. 84–85

[26] Arun Sharma, R. Krishnan, and Dhruv Grewal, "Value Creation in Markets: A Critical Area of Focus for Business-to-Business Markets," *Industrial Marketing Management* 30 (June 2001): pp. 397–398.

The manager requires a grasp of objectives, demand, cost, competition, and legal factors (discussed later) to approach the multidimensional pricing decision. Price setting is not an act but an ongoing process.

Pricing across the Product Life Cycle

What price should be assigned to a distinctly new industrial product or service? When an item is added to an existing product line, how should it be priced in relation to products already in the line?

Pricing New Products

The strategic decision of pricing new products can be best understood by examining the policies at the boundaries of the continuum—from **skimming** (high initial price) to **penetration** (low initial price). Consider again the pricing strategies of DuPont and Dow Chemical. Whereas DuPont assigns an initial high price to new products to generate immediate profits or to recover R&D expenditures, Dow follows a low price strategy with the objective of gaining market share.

In evaluating the merits of skimming versus penetration, the marketer must again examine price from the buyer's perspective. This approach, asserts Joel Dean, "recognizes that the upper limit is the price that will produce the minimum acceptable rate of return on the investment of a sufficiently large number of prospects."[27] This is especially important in pricing new products because the potential profits to buyers of a new machine tool, for example, will vary by market segment, and these market segments may differ in the minimum rate of return that will induce them to invest in the machine tool.

Skimming   A skimming approach, appropriate for a distinctly new product, provides an opportunity to profitably reach market segments that are not sensitive to the high initial price. As a product ages, as competitors enter the market, and as organizational buyers become accustomed to evaluating and purchasing the product, demand becomes more price elastic. Joel Dean refers to the policy of skimming at the outset, followed by penetration pricing as the product matures, as **time segmentation**.[28] Skimming enables the marketer to capture early profits, then reduce the price to reach more price sensitive segments. It also enables the innovator to recover high developmental costs more quickly.

Robert Dolan and Abel Jeuland demonstrate that during the innovative firm's monopoly period, skimming is optimal if the demand curve is stable over time (no diffusion) and if production costs decline with accumulated volume. A penetration policy is optimal if there is a relatively high repeat purchase rate for nondurable goods or if a durable good's demand is characterized by diffusion.[29]

---

[27] Joel Dean, "Pricing Policies for New Products," *Harvard Business Review* 54 (November–December 1976): p. 151.

[28] Ibid., p. 152.

[29] Robert J. Dolan and Abel P. Jeuland, "Experience Curves and Dynamic Demand Models: Implications for Optimal Pricing Strategies," *Journal of Marketing* 45 (winter 1981): pp. 52–62. See also, Paul Ingenbleek, Marion Debruyne, Rudd T. Frambach, and Theo M. Verhallen, "Successful New Product Pricing Practices: A Contingency Approach," *Marketing Letters* 14 (December 2004): pp. 289–304.

ETHICAL BUSINESS MARKETING

On Ethics and Pricing at Raytheon

Because price negotiations present the opportunity for unfair, unethical, and even illegal behavior, most firms have established a set of business conduct guidelines. The following excerpts from Raytheon's standards of conduct for buying emphasize the importance of fairness in business relationships.

- Raytheon expects its procurement personnel to be fair, do no favors, and *accept no favors.* Accepting kickbacks is a crime—both morally and legally. It is the fastest way for procurement personnel to find the way out the door and for sellers to cease doing business with us.

- The rules apply to all Raytheon employees who influence the buying process.

- Gifts, services, or consideration other than an advertising novelty such as a paperweight,

key chain, or coffee cup will be returned to the supplier.

- Luncheons with suppliers should not be encouraged. Under some circumstances they are necessary if there is a legitimate business purpose for the get-together. But they should not be a habit. Company facilities should be used wherever possible.

- Raytheon's goal has been to establish a reputation in the marketplace that meets the highest standards of ethical conduct. We want to protect this reputation for both Raytheon and our suppliers.

SOURCE: Robert L. Janson, Linda A. Grass, Arnold J. Lovering, and Robert C. Parker, "Ethics and Responsibility," in *The Purchasing Handbook*, Harold E. Fearon, Donald W. Dobler, and Kenneth H. Killen, eds. (New York: McGraw-Hill, 1993), pp. 360–361.

Penetration   A penetration policy is appropriate when there is (1) high price elasticity of demand, (2) strong threat of imminent competition, and (3) opportunity for a substantial reduction in production costs as volume expands. Drawing on the experience effect, a firm that can quickly gain substantial market share and experience can gain a strategic advantage over competitors. The feasibility of this strategy increases with the potential size of the future market. By taking a large share of new sales, a firm can gain experience when the growth rate of the market is large. Of course, the value of additional market share differs markedly between industries and often among products, markets, and competitors in an industry.[30] Factors to be assessed in determining the value of additional market share include the investment requirements, potential benefits of experience, expected market trends, likely competitive reaction, and short- and long-term profit implications.

Product Line Considerations   The contemporary industrial firm with a long product line faces the complex problem of balancing prices in the product mix. Firms extend their product lines because the demands for various products are interdependent, because the costs of producing and marketing those items are interdependent, or both.[31]

---

[30] Robert Jacobson and David A. Aaker, "Is Market Share All that It's Cracked Up to Be?" *Journal of Marketing* 49 (fall 1985): pp. 11–22; and Yoram Wind and Vijay Mahajan, "Market Share: Concepts, Findings, and Directions for Future Research," in *Review of Marketing 1981*, Ben M. Enis and Kenneth J. Roering, eds. (Chicago: American Marketing Association, 1981), pp. 31–42.

[31] Monroe, *Pricing*, p. 143; see also Robert J. Dolan, "The Same Make, Many Models Problem: Managing the Product Line," in *A Strategic Approach to Business Marketing*, Robert E. Spekman and David T. Wilson, eds. (Chicago: American Marketing Association, 1985), pp. 151–159.

A firm may add to its product line—or even develop a new product line—to fit more precisely the needs of a particular market segment. If both the demand and the costs of individual product-line items are interrelated, production and marketing decisions about one item inevitably influence both the revenues and costs of the others.

Are specific product-line items substitutes or complements? Will changing the price of one item enhance or retard the usage rate of this or other products in key market segments? Should a new product be priced high at the outset to protect other product-line items (for example, potential substitutes) and to give the firm time to revamp other items in the line? Such decisions require knowledge of demand, costs, competition, and strategic marketing objectives.

Legal Considerations

Because the business marketer deals with various classifications of customers and intermediaries as well as various types of discounts (for example, quantity discounts), an awareness of legal considerations in price administration is vital. The **Robinson-Patman Act** holds that it is unlawful to "discriminate in price between different purchasers of commodities of like grade and quality . . . where the effect of such discrimination may be substantially to lessen competition or tend to create a monopoly, or to injure, destroy, or prevent competition. . . ." Price differentials are permitted, but they must be based on cost differences or the need to "meet competition."[32] Cost differentials are difficult to justify, and clearly defined policies and procedures are needed in price administration. Such cost-justification guidelines are useful not only when making pricing decisions but also when providing a legal defense against price discrimination charges.

Responding to Price Attacks by Competitors[33]

Rather than emphasizing the lowest price, most business marketers prefer to compete by providing superior value. However, across industries, marketing managers face constant pressure from competitors who are willing to use price concessions to gain market share or entry into a profitable market segment. When challenged by an aggressive competitor, many managers immediately want to fight back and match the price cut. However, because price wars can be quite costly, experts suggest a more systematic process that considers the long-run strategic consequences versus the short-term benefits of the pricing decision. Managers should never set the price simply to meet some immediate sales goal but, instead, to enhance long-term project goals. George E. Cressman Jr. and Thomas T. Nagle, consultants from the Strategic Pricing Group, Inc., observe: "Pricing is like playing chess; players who fail to envision a few moves ahead will almost always be beaten by those who do."[34]

---

[32] For a comprehensive discussion of the Robinson-Patman Act, see Monroe, *Pricing*, pp. 249–267; see also James J. Ritterskamp Jr. and William A. Hancock, "Legal Aspects of Purchasing," in *The Purchasing Handbook*, Harold E. Fearon, Donald W. Dobler, and Kenneth H. Killen, eds. (New York: McGraw-Hill, 1993), pp. 529–544.

[33] This section is based on George E. Cressman Jr. and Thomas T. Nagle, "How to Manage an Aggressive Competitor," *Business Horizons* 45 (March–April 2002), pp. 23–30.

[34] Ibid., p. 24.

FIGURE 15.4 | EVALUATING A COMPETITIVE THREAT

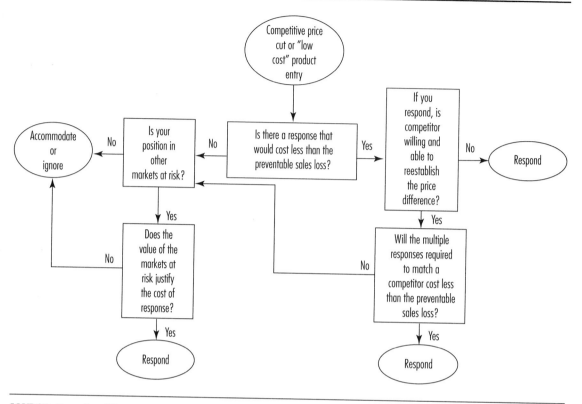

SOURCE: Figure from "How to Manage an Aggressive Competitor" by George E. Cressman, Jr. and Thomas T. Nagle from BUSINESS HORIZONS 45 (March-April 2002): p. 25. Reprinted with permission from Elsevier.

Evaluating a Competitive Threat

Figure 15.4 provides a systematic framework for developing a strategy when one or more competitors have announced price cuts or have introduced new products that offer more value to at least some of your customers. To determine whether to reduce price to meet a competitor's challenge, four important questions should be addressed.

1. *Is there a response that would cost you less than the preventable sales loss?* (See center of Figure 15.4.) Before responding to a competitor's price reduction, the marketing strategist should ask: Do the benefits justify the costs? If responding to a price change is less costly than losing sales, a price move may be the appropriate decision. On the other hand, if the competitor threatens only a small slice of expected sales, the revenue loss from ignoring the threat may be much lower than the costs of retaliation. Indeed, when the threat centers on a small segment of customers, the cost of reducing prices for *all* customers to prevent the small loss is likely to be prohibitively expensive.

    If a price response is required, the strategist should focus the firm's competitive retaliation on the most cost-effective actions. The cost of retaliating to a price threat can be reduced by incorporating one or more of the following elements into the pricing action:

- Center reactive price cuts only on those customers likely to be attracted to the competitor's offer (for example, rather than cutting the price of its flagship Pentium chip, Intel offered the lower-priced Cerrus chip for the cost-conscious market segment).

- Center reactive price cuts on a particular geographic region, distribution channel, or product line where the competitor has the most to lose from a price reduction (for example, Kodak might respond to a challenge from Fuji with price promotions in Japan where Fuji enjoys attractive margins and a larger market share).

- Capitalize on any competitive advantages to increase the value of your offer as an alternative to matching the price (for example, a firm that has better quality products can respond by offering a longer warranty period to customers).

2. *If you respond, is the competitor willing and able to merely reduce the price again to restore the price difference?* Matching a price cut will be ineffective if the competitor simply reestablishes the differential by a further price reduction. According to Cressman and Nagle, to determine the appropriate course, the strategist should attempt to understand why the competitor chose to compete on price in the first place: "If the competitor has little market share relative to the share that could be gained with a price advantage, and has no other way to attract customers, then there is little to lose from bringing the price down as low as necessary to gain sales."[35] This is especially true when competitors have made huge investments in areas such as R&D that largely represent sunk costs. Under such conditions, accommodation—market share loss—is less costly than fighting a price war.

3. *Will the multiple responses that may be required to match the competitor's price still cost less than the avoidable sales loss?* A single response is rarely enough to stop price moves by competitors that are struggling to establish a market position. Price competition is particularly likely in industries where entry requires a significant investment in fixed manufacturing capacity. Rather than idling manufacturing capacity, a competitor may be willing to aggressively pursue sales that will make at least some contribution to covering fixed costs. If competitors are likely to continue to cut prices, the best strategy for the defender is to:

- Allow the competitor to win where it is least damaging to profitability, such as in more price-sensitive, lower-margin customer segments (for example, government contracts).

- Create barriers that make it more difficult for competitors to reach less price-sensitive, more profitable customer segments (for example, build switching costs by developing unique solutions for the most valued customers).

4. *Is your position in other markets (product or geographic) at risk if the competitor increases market share? Does the value of all the markets that are at risk justify the cost of the strategy response?* Before responding with a price reduction, the business marketer

---

[35] Ibid., p. 27.

must clearly define the long-run strategic benefits as well as the risks of a particular strategy response. The benefits might include additional sales in a particular market in the future, or immediate sales gains of complementary products (such as software, peripherals, and services associated with the sale of a computer), or a lower cost of future sales resulting from increased volume.

Understanding the Rules of Competitive Strategy

Dealing effectively with an aggressive competitor requires more than a willingness to fight—it requires a competitive strategy and an understanding of when the appropriate response to a competitor's price cut is to ignore it, accommodate it, or retaliate. George E. Cressman and Thomas T. Nagle offer these guidelines for competitive strategy development:

- Never participate in a competitive engagement you cannot win. Fight those battles where you have competitive strength, and avoid those where you are clearly at a disadvantage . . .
- Always participate in competitive engagements from a position of advantage. Don't fight by competitors' rules (which they select for their advantage); use what is advantageous for you.[36]

Competitive Bidding

A significant volume of business commerce is transacted through competitive bidding. Rather than relying on a specific list price, the business marketer must develop a price, or a bid, to meet a customer's particular product or service requirements.

Government and other public agencies buy almost exclusively through competitive bidding. Competitive bidding in private industry centers on two types of purchases. One is nonstandard materials, complex fabricated products where design and manufacturing methods vary, and products made to the buyer's specifications. These types of items have no generally established market level. Competitive bids enable the purchaser to evaluate the appropriateness of the prices.[37] Second, many firms are using reverse auctions, where many sellers bid for an order from a single buyer (see Chapter 2). GE, for example, uses reverse auctions to buy both direct (for example, standard component parts) and indirect materials (for example, maintenance items, office supplies), making roughly a third of its total purchasing expenditures in this fashion. Typically, reverse auctions are best suited for product categories that buyers view as commodities.[38] Competitive bidding may be either closed or open.

---

[36] Ibid., p. 30.

[37] Stuart St. P. Slatter, "Strategic Marketing Variables under Conditions of Competitive Bidding," *Strategic Management Journal* 11 (May–June 1990): pp. 309–317; see also Arthur H. Mendel and Roger Poueymirou, "Pricing," in *The Purchasing Handbook*, Harold E. Fearon, Donald W. Dobler, and Kenneth H. Killen, eds. (New York: McGraw-Hill, 1993), pp. 201–227.

[38] See, for example, C. M. Sashi and Bay O'Leary, "The Role of Internet Auctions in the Expansion of B2B Markets," *Industrial Marketing Management* 31 (February 2002): pp. 103–110.

Closed Bidding

Closed bidding, often used by business and governmental buyers, involves a formal invitation to potential suppliers to submit written, sealed bids. All bids are opened and reviewed at the same time, and the contract is generally awarded to the lowest bidder who meets desired specifications. The low bidder is not guaranteed the contract—buyers often make awards to the lowest responsible bidder; the ability of alternative suppliers to perform remains part of the bidding process.

Online Sealed Bid Format   There is also a sealed bid format used for online auctions. The term *sealed* means that only one supplier and the buyer have access to the details of the bid. According to Sandy Jap:

> The bid process is asynchronous in the sense that the buyer and supplier take turns viewing the bid. The buyer posts the RFP (request for purchase) electronically, the supplier submits a bid, and the buyer views the submitted bid. The buyer then either makes a decision after viewing all bids or, if multiple rounds of bidding are involved, may respond to the supplier, who then resubmits a new bid.[39]

Open Bidding

Open bidding is more informal and allows suppliers to make offers (oral and written) up to a certain date. The buyer may deliberate with several suppliers throughout the bidding process. Open bidding may be particularly appropriate when specific requirements are hard to define rigidly or when the products and services of competing suppliers vary substantially.

In some buying situations, prices may be negotiated. Complex technical requirements or uncertain product specifications may lead buying organizations first to evaluate the capabilities of competing firms and then to negotiate the price and the form of the product-service offering. Negotiated pricing is appropriate for procurement in both the commercial and the governmental sectors of the business market (see Chapter 2).

Online Open Bid Format   When conducted online, open bidding takes a different form. Here suppliers are invited to bid simultaneously during a designated time period for the contract. In contrast to the sealed-bid format, all suppliers and the buyer view the bids at the same time. The goal, of course, is to push the price down. Sandy Jap, who has conducted extensive research on reverse auctions, argues that the open-bid format, when used regularly, can damage buyer-supplier relationships:

> This harm occurs because open-bid formats reveal pricing information to competition, which erodes the supplier's bargaining power. Open-bid formats also place a more explicit focus on price, a short-term variable that is usually the focus of transaction-oriented exchanges rather than relational

---

[39] Sandy D. Jap, "Online Reverse Auctions: Issues, Themes, and Prospects for the Future," *Journal of the Academy of Marketing Science* 30 (fall 2002): p. 507.

exchanges. When buyers use an open-bid format amid a context in which relational exchanges are emphasized, they send an inconsistent message to suppliers and may foster distrust.[40]

Strategies for Competitive Bidding

Because making bids is costly and time-consuming, firms should choose potential bid opportunities with care. Contracts offer differing levels of profitability according to the bidding firm's related technical expertise, past experience, and objectives. Therefore, careful screening is required to isolate contracts that offer the most promise.[41] Having isolated a project opportunity, the marketer must now estimate the probabilities of winning the contract at various prices. Assuming that the contract is awarded to the lowest bidder, the chances of the firm winning the contract decline as the bid price increases. How will competitors bid?

In many industries, business marketers confront situations in which the supplier that wins the initial contract has the advantage in securing long-term follow-up business. To illustrate, suppliers bidding on contracts to meet the worldwide information-technology service needs of American Express often submit attractive bids to form an initial relationship with the centralized purchasing unit.[42] Although they may sacrifice some immediate profit, they see the low bid as an investment that will lead to improved efficiencies and a continuing stream of profitable follow-up business.

In pursuing this type of bidding strategy, the business marketer must carefully assess how likely it is that the initial contract will lead to follow-up business opportunities. For example, the purchase of an office automation system may bond the buyer to a particular seller, thus providing the potential for future business. The costs of switching to another supplier are high because the buyer has made investments in employee training and new business procedures, as well as in the equipment itself.[43] Such investments create inertia against change. By contrast, for more standardized purchases, such bonding does not occur because the buyer's costs of switching to another supplier are quite low. In determining the initial bid strategy, the business marketer should examine the strength of the buyer-seller relationship, the probability of securing additional business, and the expected return from that business.

Summary

At the outset, the business marketer must assign pricing its role in the firm's overall marketing strategy. Giving a particular industrial product or service, an "incorrect" price can trigger a chain of events that undermines the firm's market position, channel relationships, and product and personal selling strategies. Customer value represents a business customer's overall assessment of the utility of a relationship with a supplier based on benefits received and sacrifices made. Price is but one of the costs that buyers

---

[40] Ibid., p. 514.

[41] For example, see Paul D. Boughton, "The Competitive Bidding Process: Beyond Probability Models," *Industrial Marketing Management* 16 (May 1987): pp. 87–94.

[42] Susan Avery, "American Express Charges Ahead," *Purchasing*, November 4, 2004, pp. 34–38.

[43] Barbara Bund Jackson, "Build Customer Relationships That Last," *Harvard Business Review* 63 (November–December 1985): pp. 120–128.

examine when considering the value of competing offerings. Thus, the marketer can profit by adopting a strong end-user focus that gives special attention to the way buyers trade off the costs and benefits of various products. Responsive pricing strategies can be developed by understanding the total cost in use of a product for a customer. Value-based strategies can then be designed for particular business market segments.

Price setting is a multidimensional decision. To establish a price, the manager must identify the firm's objectives and analyze the behavior of demand, costs, and competition. Hypercompetitive rivalries characterize the nature of competition in many high-technology industry sectors. Although this task is clouded with uncertainty, the industrial pricing decision must be approached actively rather than passively. For example, many business marketing firms use target costing to capture a competitive advantage. Likewise, by isolating demand, cost, or competitive patterns, the manager can gain insights into market behavior and neglected opportunities. Dealing effectively with an aggressive competitor requires more than a willingness to fight—it requires a competitive strategy and an understanding of when to ignore a price attack, when to accommodate it, and when to retaliate.

Competitive bidding, a unique feature of the business market, calls for a unique strategy. Again, carefully defined objectives are the cornerstone of strategy. These objectives, combined with a meticulous screening procedure, help the firm to identify projects that mesh with company capability.

Discussion Questions

1. Describe the core benefits and add-on benefits that FedEx provides to its business customers.

2. A Pac-10 university library recently purchased 60 personal computers from Dell. Illustrate how a purchasing specialist at the university could use a total cost-in-use approach in evaluating the value of the Dell offering in relation to the value provided by its rivals.

3. Explain why it is often necessary for the business marketer to develop a separate demand curve for various market segments. Would one total demand curve be better for making the industrial pricing decision? Explain.

4. Evaluate this statement: To move away from the commodity mentality, companies must view their products as customer solutions, and then sell the products on that basis.

5. Illustrate the process a firm would follow in using target costing while developing a fax machine for the home office user.

6. The XYZ Manufacturing Corporation has experienced a rather large decline in sales for its component parts. Mary Vantage, vice president of marketing, believes that a 10 percent price cut may get things going again. What factors should Mary consider before reducing the price of the components?

7. A business marketing manager often has great difficulty in arriving at the optimum price level for a product. First, describe the factors that complicate the pricing decision. Second, outline the approach you would follow in pricing an industrial product. Be as specific as possible.

8. Rather than time to market, Intel refers to the product development cycle for a new chip as "time to money." Andrew Grove, Intel's legendary leader, said, "Speed is the only weapon we have." What pricing advantages issue from a rapid product development process?

9. If a competitor's price cut threatens only a small portion of expected sales, the sales loss from ignoring the threat is probably much less than the cost of retaliation. Agree or disagree? Explain.

10. Identify a particular industry—like software—that you would describe as hyper-competitive. Who are the key competitors in that industry? What forces contribute to its rapid rate of change?

Internet Exercise

Hill-Rom is a leading B2B firm that dominates a niche in the health-care industry. Go to http://www.hill-rom.com and, first, describe the products and services that Hill-Rom offers to hospitals. Next, describe how Hill-Rom products or solutions might reduce the total cost-in-use for a hospital.

CASE

Meeting the Challenge of Reverse Auctions[44]

The growing use of reverse auctions (one buyer, many sellers) poses a serious challenge to marketers of a diverse array of products and services in the business market. Reverse auctions gained popularity with the advent of efficient electronic capabilities and are often only feasible electronically over the Internet. A reverse auction creates "dynamic pricing," which means that the price of the items being auctioned changes instantaneously because of the electronic format. As sellers observe the price changing (usually dropping) in real time, the assumption is that it will continue to fall until a rational market price is established.

Many companies, including GE, Quaker Oats, United Technologies, and GM, report millions of dollars of savings from using reverse auctions rather than traditional purchasing methods. Needless to say, business marketing firms that are suppliers to these organizations fear that reverse auctions will transform their products and services into commodities, drive profit margins down, and severely reduce the opportunity to develop mutually beneficial relationships.

Discussion Question

As a consultant to a business marketing firm that supplies component parts to GE, propose specific strategy guidelines or action plans the marketing manager might follow to deal with the challenges of reverse auctioning. In your response, consider the role that value-based sales tools might assume in strengthening the business marketing firm's position.

---

[44]Larry R. Smeltzer and Amelia Carr, "Reverse Auctions in Industrial Marketing and Buying," *Business Horizons* 45 (March–April 2002): pp. 47–52.

Business Marketing Communications: Advertising and Sales Promotion

Advertising supports and supplements personal selling efforts. The share of the marketing budget devoted to advertising is smaller in business than it is in consumer-goods marketing. A well-integrated business-to-business marketing communications program, however, can help make the overall marketing strategy more efficient and effective. After reading this chapter, you will understand:

1. the specific role of advertising in business marketing strategy.

2. the decisions that must be made when forming a business advertising program.

3. the business media options, including the powerful role of Internet marketing communication.

4. ways to measure business advertising effectiveness.

5. the role of trade shows in the business communications mix and how to measure trade show effectiveness.

Communication with existing and potential customers is vital to business marketing success. Experience has taught marketing managers that not even the best products sell themselves: The benefits, problem solutions, and cost efficiencies of those products must be effectively communicated to everyone who influences the purchase decision. As a result of the technical complexity of business products, the relatively small number of potential buyers, and the extensive negotiation process, the primary communication vehicle in business-to-business marketing is the salesperson. However, nonpersonal methods of communication, including advertising, catalogs, the Internet, and trade shows, have a unique and often crucial role in the communication process. To maximize the return on promotional spending, business-to-business firms are developing integrated marketing campaigns that align marketing communications strategies to strategic objectives.[1]

Consider the valuable role of marketing communications in General Electric's rebranding effort.[2] The goal of the effort is to reposition GE as a provider of more than lighting and appliances and raise awareness of GE businesses such as jet engines, water technologies, health-care technologies, wind power, security systems, and financial services. The campaign, "Imagination at Work," celebrates the magic of big ideas and highlights the leading-edge technologies GE has pioneered. Says Beth Comstock, GE's chief marketing officer and corporate vice president of marketing, "The overall objective was aligning our market position with our future and creating a truly integrated campaign. It had to be global, touch our internal and external constituencies, and use as many different types of media as possible."[3] Stretching across print ads, television spots, online ads, and other features, GE highlights the distinctive capabilities (that is, the "wow" factor) of its various businesses (Figure 16.1). Market research suggests that the campaign succeeded in changing perceptions about GE. For example, perceptions of GE as a provider of high-tech solutions have increased by 40 percent and perceptions of GE as being "innovative" increased by 35 percent.

The focus of this chapter is fourfold: (1) to provide a clear understanding of the role of advertising in business marketing strategy; (2) to present a framework for structuring advertising decisions—a framework that integrates the decisions related to objectives, budgets, messages, media, and evaluation; (3) to develop an understanding of each business-to-business advertising decision area; and (4) to evaluate the valuable role of the Internet and trade shows in the promotional mix.

The Role of Advertising

Integrated Communication Programs

Advertising and sales promotion are rarely used alone in the business-to-business setting but are intertwined with the total communications strategy—particularly personal selling. Personal and nonpersonal forms of communication interact to inform key buying influencers. The challenge for the business marketer is to create an advertising and sales promotion strategy that effectively blends with personal selling in order to meet sales and profit objectives. In addition, the advertising, online media, and sales promotion

---

[1] Don Schultz and Heidi Schultz, *IMC—The Next Generation* (New York: McGraw-Hill, 2004).

[2] Bob Lamons, *The Case for B2B Branding* (Mason, Ohio: Thomson/South-Western, 2005), pp. 141–146.

[3] Kate Maddox and Beth Snyder Bulik, "Integrated Marketing Success Stories," *B2B* 89 (July 7, 2004): p. 20.

FIGURE 16.1 | **GE's Web Site Highlights the Company's Rebranding Campaign**

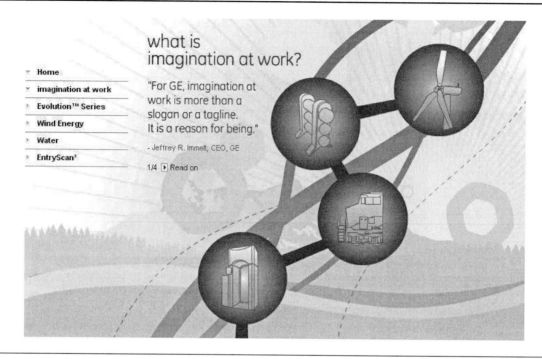

SOURCE: Reprinted by permission of General Electric.

tools must be integrated; that is, a comprehensive program of media and sales promotion methods must be coordinated to achieve the desired results.

Enhancing Sales Effectiveness

Effective advertising can make personal selling more productive. John Morrill examined nearly 100,000 interviews on 26 product lines at 30,000 buying locations in order to study the effect of business-to-business advertising on salesperson effectiveness.[4] He concluded that dollar sales per salesperson call were significantly higher when customers had been exposed to advertising. In addition to increasing company and product awareness, research indicates that buyers who had been exposed to a supplier's advertisement rated the supplier's salespeople substantially higher on product knowledge, service, and enthusiasm.[5] A primary role of business-to-business advertising is to enhance the reputation of the supplier.

Business-to-business advertising also increases sales efficiency. Increased spending on advertising lead to greater brand awareness for industrial products, which translates into larger market shares and higher profits.[6] One study used a tightly controlled

[4] John E. Morrill, "Industrial Advertising Pays Off," *Harvard Business Review* 48 (March–April 1970): pp. 4–14.

[5] Ibid., p. 6. For a comprehensive study of the relationship between brand awareness and brand preference, see Eunsang Yoon and Valerie Kijewski, "The Brand Awareness-to-Preference Link in Business Markets: A Study of the Semiconductor Manufacturing Industry," *Journal of Business-to-Business Marketing* 2, no. 4 (1995): pp. 7–36.

[6] "New Proof of Industrial Ad Values," *Marketing and Media Decisions*, February 1981, p. 64.

experimental design to measure the effect of business-to-business advertising on sales and profits. For one product, sales, gross margin, and net profit were significantly higher with advertising, compared with the pretest period with no advertising.[7] In fact, gross margins ranged from four to six times higher with advertising than with no advertising.

Increased Sales Efficiency

The effect of advertising on the marketing program's overall efficiency is evidenced in two ways. First, business suppliers frequently need to remind actual and potential buyers of their products or make them aware of new products or services. Although these objectives could be partially accomplished through personal selling, the costs of reaching a vast group of buyers would be prohibitive. Carefully targeted advertising extends beyond the salesperson's reach to unidentified buying influentials. A properly placed advertisement can reach hundreds of buying influentials for only a few cents each; the average cost of a business sales call is currently more than $200.[8] Sales call costs are determined by the salesperson's wages, travel and entertainment costs, and fringe benefits costs. If these costs total $800 per day and a salesperson can make four calls per day, then each call costs $200. Second, advertising appears to make all selling activities more effective. Advertising interacts effectively with all communication and selling activities, and it can boost efficiency for the entire marketing expenditure.

Creating Awareness

From a communications standpoint, the buying process takes potential buyers sequentially from unawareness of a product or supplier to awareness, to brand preference, to conviction that a particular purchase will fulfill their requirements, and, ultimately, to actual purchase. Business advertising often creates awareness of the supplier and the supplier's products. Sixty-one percent of the design engineers returning an inquiry card from a magazine ad indicated that they were unaware of the company that advertised before seeing the ad.[9] Business advertising may also make some contribution to creating preference for the product—all cost effectively. In addition, advertising can create a corporate identity or image. Hewlett-Packard, Dell, IBM, and others use ads in general business publications such as *Business Week* and even television advertising to trumpet the value of their brand and to develop desired perceptions in a broad audience.[10]

Interactive Marketing Communications

The Internet changes marketing communications from a one-way to a two-way process that permits the marketer and the consumer to more readily exchange information.[11] Consumers receive and provide information by navigating Web sites, specifying their

[7] "ARF/ABP Release Final Study Findings," *Business Marketing* 72 (May 1987): p. 55.

[8] "The Cost of Doing Business," *Sales & Marketing Management* 151 (September 1999): p. 56.

[9] Raymond E. Herzog, "How Design Engineering Activity Affects Supplies," *Business Marketing* 70 (November 1985): p. 143.

[10] David A. Aaker and Erich Joachimsthaler, "The Lure of Global Branding," *Harvard Business Review* 77 (November–December 1999): pp. 137–144.

[11] C. K. Prahalad and Venkat Ramaswamy, *The Future of Competition: Co-Creating Value with Customers* (Boston: Harvard Business School Press, 2004), pp. 1–17.

preferences, and communicating with business marketers.[12] Moreover, marketers can use such communications to provide consumers with better service, such as personalized e-mails and information, customized service solutions, or links to providers of complementary products and services. To illustrate, Herman Miller, the office furniture manufacturer, provides a "room planner" that Web site visitors can use to blend various combinations of new furniture options into an existing office layout. Likewise, W. W. Grainger, the large industrial distributor, strengthens customer loyalty by providing its corporate customers ready access to records that track their savings in purchasing maintenance supplies.[13] More than just an advertising medium, the Internet allows business marketers to create value by customizing their messages and offerings, helping the consumer search for specific products, and gathering information about consumer preferences to improve future products and services by creating new customer solutions.

What Business-to-Business Advertising Cannot Do

To develop an effective communications program, the business marketing manager must blend all communication tools into an integrated program, using each tool where it is most effective. Business advertising quite obviously has limitations. Advertising cannot substitute for effective personal selling—it must supplement, support, and complement that effort. In the same way, personal selling is constrained by its costs and should not be used to create awareness or to disseminate information—tasks quite capably performed by advertising.

For many purchasing decisions, advertising alone cannot create product preference—this requires demonstration, explanation, and operational testing. Similarly, conviction and actual purchase can be ensured only by personal selling. Advertising has a supporting role in creating awareness, providing information, and uncovering important leads for salespeople; that is how the marketing manager must use it to be effective.

Managing Business-to-Business Advertising

The advertising decision model in Figure 16.2 shows the structural elements involved in managing business-to-business advertising. First, advertising is only one aspect of the entire marketing strategy and must be integrated with other components to achieve strategic goals. The advertising decision process begins with formulating advertising objectives, which are derived from marketing goals. From this formulation the marketer can determine how much it has to spend to achieve those goals. Then, specific communication messages are formulated to achieve the market behavior specified by the objectives. Equally important is evaluating and selecting the media used to reach the desired audience. The result is an integrated advertising campaign aimed at eliciting a specific attitude or behavior from the target group. The final, and critical, step is to evaluate the campaign's effectiveness.

---

[12] David W. Stewart, "From Consumer Response to Active Consumer: Measuring the Effectiveness of Interactive Media," *Journal of the Academy of Marketing Science* 30 (fall 2002): pp. 376–396.

[13] David Feeny, "Making Sense of the E-Opportunity," *MIT Sloan Management Review* 42 (winter 2001): pp. 41–51.

FIGURE 16.2 | **THE DECISION STAGES FOR DEVELOPING THE BUSINESS-TO-BUSINESS ADVERTISING PROGRAM**

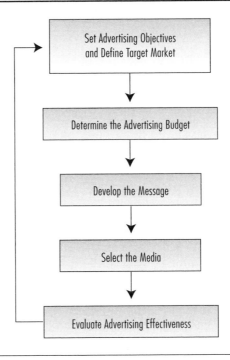

Defining Advertising Objectives

Knowing what advertising must accomplish enables the manager to determine an advertising budget more accurately and provides a yardstick for evaluating advertising. In specifying advertising goals, the marketing manager must realize that (1) the advertising mission flows directly from the overall marketing strategy; advertising must fulfill a marketing strategy objective, and its goal must reflect the general aim and purpose of the entire strategy; and (2) the advertising program's objectives must respond to the roles for which advertising is suited: creating awareness, providing information, influencing attitudes, and reminding buyers of company and product existence.

Written Objectives

An advertising objective must be measurable, realistic, and specify what is to be achieved and when. The objective must speak in unambiguous terms of a specific outcome. The purpose is to establish a single working direction for everyone involved in creating, coordinating, and evaluating the advertising program. Correctly conceived objectives set standards for evaluating the advertising effort. A specific objective might be "to increase from 15 percent (as measured in June 2006) to 30 percent (by June 2007) the proportion of general contractors associating 'energy efficiency' feature with our brand of commercial air conditioners." The objective directs the manager to create a message related to the major product benefit, using media that reaches general contractors. The objective also provides a way to measure accomplishment (awareness among 30 percent of the target audience).

Business advertising objectives frequently bear no direct relationship to specific dollar sales targets. Although dollar sales results would provide a "hard" measure of advertising accomplishment, it is often impossible to link advertising directly to sales. Personal selling, price, product performance, and competitive actions have a more direct relationship to sales levels, and it is almost impossible to sort out advertising's impact. Thus, advertising goals are typically stated in terms of *communication goals* such as brand awareness, recognition, and buyer attitudes. These goals can be measured; it is presumed that achieving them stimulates sales volume.

Target Audience   A significant task is specifying target audiences. Because a primary role of advertising is to reach buying influentials inaccessible to the salesperson, the business marketing manager must define the buying influential groups to be reached. Generally, each group of buying influentials is concerned with distinct product and service attributes and criteria, and the advertising must focus on these. Thus, the objectives must specify the intended audience and its relevant decision criteria.

Creative Strategy Statement   A final consideration is to specify the creative strategy statement. Once objectives and targets are established, the **creative strategy statement** provides guidelines for the company and advertising agency on how to position the product in the marketplace. Product position relates to how the target market perceives the product.

For example, if the commercial air conditioners cited earlier currently have an unfavorable product position with regard to energy efficiency but recent product development efforts have advanced performance, the firm might use the following creative strategy statement: "Our basic creative strategy is to reposition the product from that of a reliable air conditioner to a high-performance, energy-efficient air conditioner."

All creative efforts—copy, theme, color, and so forth—as well as media and tactics, should support the creative strategy statement. Planning an effective advertising campaign requires clearly defined objectives that provide a foundation for selecting media and measuring results.

Determining Advertising Expenditures

Collectively, business marketers spend more than $10 billion on media advertising annually. The leading advertisers are shown in Table 16.1. Note the preponderance of telecommunications and high-tech firms on the top 10 list. Typically, business marketers use a blend of intuition, judgment, experience, and, only occasionally, more advanced decision-oriented techniques to determine advertising budgets. Some of the techniques business marketers most commonly use are rules of thumb (for example, percentage of past years' sales) and the objective-task method.

Rules of Thumb   Often, because advertising is a relatively small part of the total marketing budget for business firms, the value of using sophisticated methods for advertising budgeting is not great. In these cases, managers tend to follow simple **rules of thumb** (for example, allocate 1 percent of sales to advertising or match competition spending). Unfortunately, percentage-of-sales rules are all too pervasive throughout business marketing, even where advertising is an important element.

The fundamental problem with percentage-of-sales rules is that they implicitly make advertising a consequence rather than a determinant of sales and profits and can

TABLE 16.1 | TOP BUSINESS-TO-BUSINESS ADVERTISERS

Company	Total Advertising Expenditures (millions)
Verizon Communications	$353.1
Sprint	338.5
SBC Communications	296.8
AT&T Wireless	287.9
Microsoft	253.0
Hewlett-Packard	227.1
IBM	218.8
InterActive Corp	183.3
United Parcel Service	123.6
American Express	120.9

SOURCE: "Largest U.S. B-to-B Advertising Buyers," *Marketing News,* July 15, 2005, p. 29.

easily give rise to dysfunctional policies. Percentage-of-sales rules suggest that the business advertiser reduce advertising when sales volume declines, just when increased advertising may be more appropriate. Nevertheless, simple rules of thumb continue to be applied in budget decisions because they are easy to use and familiar to management.

Objective-Task Method   The task method for budgeting advertising expenditures relates advertising costs to the objective it is to accomplish. Because the sales dollar results of advertising are almost impossible to measure, the task method focuses on the communications effects of advertising, not on the sales effects.

The **objective-task method** is applied by evaluating the tasks advertising will perform, analyzing the costs of each task, and summing up the total costs to arrive at a final budget. The process can be divided into four steps:

1. Establish specific marketing objectives for the product in terms of such factors as sales volume, market share, profit contribution, and market segments.

2. Assess the communication functions that must be performed to realize the marketing objectives and then determine the role of advertising and other elements of the communications mix in performing these functions.

3. Define specific goals for advertising in terms of the measurable communication response required to achieve marketing objectives.

4. Estimate the budget needed to accomplish the advertising goals.

The task method addresses the major problem of the rule-of-thumb methods—funds are applied to accomplish a specific goal so that advertising is a *determinant* of those results, not a consequence. Using the task approach, managers allocate all the funds necessary to accomplish a specific objective rather than allocating some arbitrary percentage of sales. The most troubling problem of the method is that management must have some instinct for the proper relationship between expenditure level and communication response. It is difficult to know what produces a certain level of awareness among business marketing buying influentials. Will 12 two-page insertions in *Purchasing* magazine over the next six months create the desired recognition level, or will 24 insertions over one year be necessary?

Budgeting for advertising must not ignore the political and behavioral aspects of the process. Nigel Piercy's research suggests that firms pay insufficient attention to budgeting technique because they operate through structures and processes that are often political in nature.[14] Piercy suggests that what actually determines advertising budgets are the power "interests" in the company and the political behavior of various parties in the budgeting process. An implication of this research is that the manager may be well served by focusing on budgeting as a political activity, and not simply as a technique-driven process.

Passing the Threshold   Several communications are often needed to capture the attention of buyers, which complicates the budgeting decision. Research suggests that a brand must surpass a threshold level of awareness in the market before meaningful additions can be made in its brand preference share. A small advertising budget may not allow the marketer to move the firm's brand beyond a threshold level of awareness and on to preference. Eunsang Yoon and Valerie Kijewski warn that "the communications manager having limited marketing resources will then be in danger of making the mistake of stopping the program prematurely, thus wasting past investment, rather than pressing on to pass the threshold awareness level."[15]

Because budgeting is so important to advertising effectiveness, managers must not blindly follow rules of thumb. Instead, they should evaluate the tasks required and their costs against industry norms. With clear objectives and proper budgetary allocations, the next step is to design effective advertising messages.

Developing the Advertising Message

Message development is a complex, critical task in industrial advertising. Highlighting a product attribute that is unimportant to a particular buying group is not only a waste of advertising dollars but also a lost opportunity. Both the appeal and the way that appeal is conveyed are vital to successful communication. Thus, creating business-to-business advertising messages involves determining advertising objectives, evaluating the buying criteria of the target audience, and analyzing the most appropriate language, format, and style for presenting the message.

Perception   For an advertising message to be successful, an individual must first be exposed to it and pay attention to it. Thus, a business advertisement must catch the decision maker's attention. Once the individual has noticed the message, he or she must interpret it as the advertiser intended. Perceptual barriers often prevent a receiver from perceiving the intended message. Even though the individual is exposed to an advertisement, nothing guarantees that he or she processes the message. In fact, the industrial buyer may read every word of the copy and find a meaning in it opposite to that the advertiser intended.

---

[14] Nigel Piercy, "Advertising Budgeting: Process and Structure as Explanatory Variables," *Journal of Advertising* 16, no. 2 (1987): p. 34.

[15] Eunsang Yoon and Valerie Kijewski, "The Brand Awareness-to-Preferences Link," p. 32.

The business advertiser must therefore contend with two important elements of perception: attention and interpretation. Buyers tend to screen out messages that are inconsistent with their own attitudes, needs, and beliefs, and they tend to interpret information in the light of those beliefs (see Chapter 3). Unless advertising messages are carefully designed and targeted, they may be disregarded or interpreted improperly. Advertisers must put themselves in the position of the receivers to evaluate how the message appears to them.

Whether an ad uses technical wording appears to have some effect on readers' perceptions of both the industrial product and the ad.[16] Technical ads were shown to create less desire in some readers to seek information because such ads suggest "more difficulty in operation." Therefore, it is important to remember that technical readers (engineers, architects, and so on) respond more favorably to the technical ads, and nontechnical readers respond more favorably to nontechnical ads. From a message-development viewpoint, the business advertiser must carefully tailor the technical aspects of promotional messages to the appropriate audience.

Focus on Benefits An industrial buyer purchases benefits—a better way to accomplish some task, a less expensive way to produce a final product, a solution to a problem, or a faster delivery time. Advertising messages need to focus on benefits the target customer seeks and to persuade the reader that the advertiser can deliver them. Messages that have direct appeals or calls to action are viewed to be "stronger" than those with diffuse or indirect appeals to action.

Robert Lamons, an advertising consultant, observes:

> A good call to action can actually start the selling process. Promise a test report; offer a product demonstration; direct them to a special section of your Web site. . . . Compare how your product stacks up to others in the field. Everyone is super-busy these days, and if you can offer something that helps them expedite or narrow their search, you're giving them something money can't buy: free time.[17]

Understanding Buyer Motivations Which product benefits are important to each group of buying influentials? The business advertiser cannot assume that a standard set of "classical buying motives" applies in every purchase situation. Many business advertisers often do not understand the buying motives of important market segments. Developing effective advertising messages often requires extensive marketing research in order to fully delineate the key buying criteria of each buying influencer in each of the firm's different target markets.

Selecting Advertising Media for Business Markets

Although the message is vital to advertising success, equally important is the medium through which it is presented. Business-to-business media are selected by target audience—the particular purchase-decision participants to be reached. Generally, the first decision is whether to use trade publications, direct mail, or both. Selection of media

---

[16] Joseph A. Bellizzi and Jacqueline J. Mohr, "Technical versus Nontechnical Wording in Industrial Print Advertising," in *AMA Educators' Proceedings*, Russell W. Belk et al., eds. (Chicago: American Marketing Association, 1984), p. 174.

[17] Robert Lamons, "Tips for Distinguishing Your Ads from Bad Ads," *Marketing News* (November 19, 2001): p. 10.

B2B TOP PERFORMERS

Search Engine Marketing at Google: The Right Message, the Right Time

To reach customers through all stages of the buying cycle, from awareness to retention, business-to-business firms are devoting a greater share of their advertising budgets to e-marketing campaigns, including keyword advertising through leading Internet search engines such as Google or Yahoo. As marketing managers face increased pressure to demonstrate the return on investment of each advertising dollar spent, keyword advertising provides compelling value—it delivers qualified leads in the form of potential customers searching on terms specifically related to your products and services. You pay only when users click on your ads. Keyword advertising provides the lowest average cost-per-lead of any direct marketing method.[1] Says Eric Grates, business service manager at Dow Chemical, "With click through rates ranging from 2.5 to 7 percent, the Google advertising program continues to be a key component of our overall marketing efforts."[2]

Russ Cohn, who leads Google's business-to-business service operations, offers some useful guidelines for successful keyword advertising:

1. Ensure that your Web site is search-crawler friendly by providing a clear hierarchy, text links, and information-rich content.

2. Understand that relevance to the user is the goal: The most successful ads connect customers to the information or solution they are seeking.

3. Create a relevant, targeted keyword list by choosing specific words that accurately reflect your Web site and advertised products.

4. Write clear and compelling ads that use the keywords and that isolate your unique value proposition.

5. Track results and measure everything.

   - Monitor click-through rates to make adjustments to the campaign.

   - Test different keywords and ad copy.

   - Use free conversion tracking tools to analyze which keywords are providing the best returns.

   - Calculate the return on investment.

---

[1]Russ Cohn, "Unlocking Keyword Advertising," *B2B Magazine*, http://www.b2bm.biz.com, accessed on November 2, 2005.

[2]"Google Named Top 5 Business-to-Business Media Property," May 5, 2003, accessed at http://www.google.com.

also involves budgetary considerations: Where are dollars best spent to generate the customer contacts desired?

Business Publications   More than 2,700 business publications carry business-to-business advertising, for a total exceeding $10 billion. For those specializing in the pharmaceutical industry, *Drug Discovery & Development*, *Pharmaceutical Executive*, and *Pharmaceutical Technology* are a few of the publications available. Business publications are either horizontal or vertical. **Horizontal publications** are directed at a specific task, technology, or function, whatever the industry. *Advertising Age*, *Purchasing*, and *Marketing News* are horizontal. **Vertical publications,** on the other hand, may be read by everyone from floor supervisor to president within a specific industry. Typical vertical publications are *Chemical Business* or *Computer Gaming World*.

If a business marketer's product has applications only within a few industries, vertical publications are a logical media choice. When many industries are potential users and well-defined functions are the principal buying influencers, a horizontal publication is effective.

Many trade publications are **requester publications,** which offer free subscriptions to selected readers. The publisher can select readers in a position to influence buying decisions and offer the free subscription in exchange for information such as title, function, and buying responsibilities. Thus, the advertiser can tell whether each publication reaches the desired audience.

Obviously, publication choice is predicated on a complete understanding of the range of purchase decision participants and of the industries where the product is used. Only then can the target audience be matched to the circulation statements of alternative business publications.

Characteristics of an Effective Print Ad   Recent research on the effectiveness of business-to-business print ads provides strong evidence that the marketing strategist should emphasize a "rational approach" and provide a clear description of the product and the benefits it offers to customers.[18] The effectiveness of ads is also enhanced by detailing product quality and performance information in a concrete and logical manner.

Advertising Cost   Circulation is an important criterion in the selection of publications, but circulation must be tempered by cost. First, the total advertising budget must be allocated among the various advertising tools such as business publications, sales promotion, direct marketing (mail and e-mail), and Internet advertising. Of course, allocations to the various media options vary with company situation and advertising mission. The allocation of the business publication budget among various journals depends on their relative effectiveness and efficiency, usually measured in cost per thousand using the following formula:

$$\text{Cost per thousand} = \frac{\text{Cost per page}}{\text{Circulation in thousands}}$$

To compare two publications by their actual page rates would be misleading, because the publication with the lower circulation is usually less expensive. The cost-per-thousand calculation should be based on circulation to the *target* audience, not the total audience. Although some publications may appear high on a cost-per-thousand basis, they may in fact be cost-effective, with little wasted circulation. Some publications also have popular Web sites that advertisers can use to create integrated marketing communications.

Frequency and Scheduling   Even the most successful business publication advertisements are seen by only a small percentage of the people who read the magazine; therefore, one-time ads are generally ineffective. Because a number of exposures are required before a message "sinks in," and because the reading audience varies from month to month, a schedule of advertising insertions is required. To build continuity and repetitive value, at least 6 insertions per year may be required in a monthly publication, and 26 to 52 insertions (with a minimum of 13) in a weekly publication.[19]

---

[18]Ritu Lohtia, Wesley J. Johnston, and Linda Rab, "Business-to-Business Advertising: What Are the Dimensions of an Effective Print Ad?" *Industrial Marketing Management* 24 (October 1995): pp. 369–378.

[19]See Stanton G. Cort, David R. Lambert, and Paula L. Garrett, "Effective Business-to-Business Frequency: New Management Perspectives from the Research Literature," *Advertising Research Foundation Literature Review* (October 1983).

Direct Marketing Tools

Direct mail and e-mail are among the direct marketing tools available to the business marketer. Direct mail delivers the advertising message firsthand to selected individuals. Possible mailing pieces range from a sales letter introducing a new product to a lengthy brochure or even a product sample. Direct mail can accomplish all of the major advertising functions, but its real contribution is in delivering the message to a precisely defined prospect. In turn, says Internet marketing consultant Barry Silverstein, direct *e-mail* can have a substantial effect on creating and qualifying customer leads, *if* some important rules are strictly followed: "always seek permission to send e-mail" and "always provide the recipient with the ability to 'opt out.'"[20] Attention first centers on direct-mail advertising.

Direct mail is commonly used for corporate image promotion, product and service promotion, sales force support, distribution channel communication, and special marketing problems. In promoting corporate image, direct mail may help to establish a firm's reputation of technological leadership. On the other hand, product advertising by direct mail can put specific product information in the hands of buying influentials. For example, as part of a successful integrated marketing campaign to change perceptions of UPS from a ground shipping company to a supply chain leader, the firm used direct mail to target decision makers—from shipping managers to front-office administrators. The direct-mail strategy had strong results, achieving a 10.5 percent response rate, with 36 percent of those responders buying services.[21]

Direct Mail: Benefits   Direct mail also supports the salespeople by providing leads from returned inquiry cards and paving the way for a first sales call. Direct mail can be used effectively to notify potential customers where to find local distributors. Deere and Company sent a series of three mailings, by name, to 20,000 farmers who had never purchased their brand in order to persuade them to simply visit a Deere dealer. More than 5,800 farmers did, and they purchased more than $35 million worth of Deere equipment over the next three months.[22] In terms of response performance, a typical direct-mail package equals approximately 10 to 50 print or broadcast exposures.[23] Finally, direct mail applies to a host of special situations such as identifying new customers and markets, meeting competitor claims, and promoting items that are not receiving enough sales support.

Direct Mail: Trade-offs   From a cost standpoint, direct mail is efficient when compared with other media. However, direct mail can be wasteful if the prospect lists are so general that it is difficult or impossible to find a common denominator among the prospects. It is a feasible advertising medium when potential buyers can be clearly identified and easily reached through the mail. It is also cost effective in making contact with buying center members. When combined with telemarketing follow-up, even "inaccessible" buying center members can be exposed to promotional efforts.[24]

[20] Barry Silverstein, *Business-to-Business Internet Marketing*, 3rd ed. (Gulf Breeze, Fla.: MAXIMUM Press, 2001), p. 171.

[21] Kate Maddox and Beth Snyder Bulik, "Integrated Marketing Success Stories," p. 23.

[22] John D. Yeck, "Direct Marketing Means Accountability," *Business Marketing* 78 (July 1993): p. A4.

[23] Shell R. Alpert, "Testing the 'TOO-Frequent' Assumption," *Business Marketing* 73 (March 1988): p. 14.

[24] Robert D. McWilliams, Earl Naumann, and Stan Scott, "Determining Buyer Center Size," *Industrial Marketing Management* 21 (February 1992): p. 48.

A direct-mail advertisement typically gains the full attention of the reader and therefore provides greater impact than a trade publication advertisement. Business buyers usually at least scan the direct-mail promotions sent to them. However, reaching top executives with direct mail may be more difficult. A survey of administrative assistants of top executives at *Fortune* 500 companies showed that the average executive receives 175 pieces of unsolicited mail each week. Less than 10 percent of this mail is passed on to the executive,[25] who then spends only five minutes a day looking at the 17 or so pieces of mail. Clearly, the direct-mail piece must have effective copy and headlines to grab the attention of both the administrative assistant and the executive.

Timing of direct-mail advertising is also flexible; a new price schedule or new service innovation can be communicated to the buyer as needed. Finally, direct mail makes it easy for the buyer to respond—usually a reply postcard is included or the name, address, and phone number of the local salesperson or distributor are provided.

Interactive Marketing   Because marketers are devoting a larger share of their advertising budgets to online marketing, IBM's customer relationship program, called *Focusing on You*, rests on a simple but powerful idea—ask customers what information they want and give it to them.[26] By giving the customer the choice, IBM learns about the customer's unique preferences and is better equipped to tailor product and service information to that customer's specific needs. The program relies on e-mail marketing, which is far less costly than direct mail. In fact, IBM found that sending customers traditional printed materials by mail was 10 times more expensive than e-mail communications. Moreover, e-mail campaigns often yield higher responses than direct-mail campaigns, and the results are generated more quickly. For example, a third of all responses to a particular IBM e-mail campaign were generated in the first 24 hours!

Let the Customer Decide   Pamela Evans, director of worldwide teleweb marketing at IBM, describes the value of interactive marketing:

> In the IBM software business, for example, we have a long sales cycle, and the Web gives us the opportunity for our prospects and customers to go online where we establish a relationship that we can then continue to nurture electronically. . . . The challenge as marketers we all face is determining how the customer wants to interact with us, and really taking advantage of the Web and the power . . . there for self-service.[27]

Firms that plan to fully integrate direct e-mail into their marketing communications strategy should make a special effort to build their own e-mail list. Often such information is already available from the firm's customer relationship management (CRM) system. From Chapter 4, recall that a goal of the CRM system is to integrate customer records from all departments, including sales, marketing, and customer service. As a result, if a customer responds to an e-mail (or direct mail) campaign, the CRM system captures that information in a centralized database for all contact employees (salespersons, call center employees, marketing managers) to retrieve.

[25] Tom Eisenhart, "Breakthrough Direct Marketing," *Business Marketing* 75 (August 1990): p. 20.

[26] Barry Silverstein, *Business-to-Business Internet Marketing*, p. 226.

[27] Carol Krol, "The Internet Continues to Reshape Direct," *BtoB*, October 10, 2005, accessed at http://www.b2bonline.com.

Other ways to create an e-mail list include offering an e-mail alert service or e-mail newsletter, asking for e-mail addresses in direct-mail campaigns, and collecting e-mail addresses at trade shows.[28] Business marketers must also realize that the response to an e-mail campaign can be immediate, so they must be prepared to acknowledge, process, and fulfill orders before the e-mail campaign is launched.

Measuring Advertising Effectiveness

The business advertiser rarely expects orders to result immediately from advertising. Advertising is designed to create awareness, stimulate loyalty to the company, or create a favorable attitude toward a product. Even though advertising may not directly precipitate a purchase decision, advertising programs must be held accountable, and marketing managers are facing increased pressure to demonstrate the actual returns on marketing expenditures.[29] Thus, the business advertiser must be able to measure the results of current advertising in order to improve future advertising and evaluate the effectiveness of advertising expenditures against expenditures on other elements of marketing strategy.

Measuring Impacts on the Purchase Decision

Measuring advertising effectiveness means assessing advertising's effect on what "intervenes" between the stimulus (advertising) and the resulting behavior (purchase decision). The theory is that advertising can affect awareness, knowledge, and other dimensions that more readily lend themselves to measurement. In essence, the advertiser attempts to gauge advertising's ability to move an individual through the purchase decision process. This approach assumes, correctly or not, that enhancement of any one phase of the process or movement from one step to the next increases the ultimate probability of purchase.

A study completed at Rockwell International Corporation suggests that business marketers should also measure the **indirect communication effects of advertising**.[30] This study revealed that advertising affects word-of-mouth communications (indirect effect), and such communications play an important role in buyer decision making. Similarly, the study showed that advertising indirectly affects buyers on the basis of its effect on overall company reputation and on the sales force's belief that advertising aids selling. The study suggested that advertising effectiveness measurement include a procedure for tracking and measuring advertising's effect on the indirect communication effects.

In summary, advertising effectiveness is evaluated against objectives formulated in terms of the elements of the buyer's decision process as well as some of the indirect communication effects. Advertising efforts are also judged, in the final analysis, on cost per level of achievement (for example, dollars spent to achieve a certain level of awareness or recognition).

---

[28] Barry Silverstein, *Internet Marketing for Information Technology Companies*, 2d ed. (Gulf Breeze, Fla.: MAXIMUM Press, 2001), p. 107.

[29] Diane Brady and David Kiley, "Making Marketing Measure Up," *Business Week*, December 13, 2004, pp. 112–113.

[30] C. Whan Park, Martin S. Roth, and Philip F. Jacques, "Evaluating the Effects of Advertising and Sales Promotion Campaigns," *Industrial Marketing Management* 17 (May 1988): p. 130.

FIGURE 16.3 | THE PRIMARY AREAS FOR ADVERTISING EVALUATION

AREA		FOCUS OF MEASUREMENT
Target Market Coverage	⟶	Degree to which advertising succeeded in reaching defined target markets
Key Buying Motives	⟶	Factors that triggered purchase decision
Effectiveness of Messages	⟶	Degree to which the message registered with key buying influentials in defined market segments
Media Effectiveness	⟶	Degree to which various media were successful in reaching defined target markets with message
Overall Results	⟶	Degree to which advertising accomplished its defined objectives

The Measurement Program

A sound measurement program entails substantial advanced planning. Figure 16.3 shows the basic areas of advertising evaluation. The advertising strategist must determine in advance what is to be measured, how, and in what sequence. A pre-evaluation phase is required to establish a benchmark for a new advertising campaign. For example, a pre-evaluation study would be conducted to capture the existing level of awareness a firm's product enjoys in a defined target market. After the advertising campaign, the evaluation study examines changes in awareness against this benchmark. Five primary areas for advertising evaluation include (1) markets, (2) motives, (3) messages, (4) media, and (5) results.

The evaluation of business-to-business advertising is demanding and complex, but absolutely essential. Budgetary constraints are generally the limiting factors. However, professional research companies can be called on to develop field research studies. When determining the effect of advertising on moving a decision participant from an awareness of the product or company to a readiness to buy, the evaluations usually measure knowledge, recognition, recall, awareness, preference, and motivation. Measuring effects on actual sales are unfortunately not often possible.

B2B TOP PERFORMERS

IBM Gold Service Customers

IBM created the Gold Service program to recognize 300 of its best corporate customers. IBM developed a special Web site customized to fit each organization's special needs. When IBM creates a site for a customer, it sends a welcome package to every executive and information technology staff member in the customer organization and encourages them to use the new site. Included in the package is a personal profile survey that helps IBM marketing managers to personalize all further communications with organizational members. Nearly all of the employees choose e-mail as the preferred method of correspondence. Response rates to e-mailed offers have exceeded expectations at IBM. The firm reports that average revenues for customer organizations enrolled in the Gold Service program are increasing by more than 30 percent per year.

SOURCE: Barry Silverstein, *Internet Marketing for Information Technology Companies* (Gulf Breeze, Fla.: MAXIMUM Press, 2001), pp. 226–227.

Managing Trade Show Strategy

Business advertising funds are designated primarily for media and direct mail, enriched by interactive marketing, but these are reinforced by other promotional activities such as exhibits and trade shows, catalogs, and trade promotion. Special attention is given here to trade shows—an important promotional vehicle for business markets.

Trade Shows: Strategy Benefits

Most industries stage an annual business show or exhibition to display new advances and technological developments in the industry. The Center for Exhibition Industry Research indicates that some 1.5 million U.S. and Canadian firms place displays at trade shows each year and that 83 percent of trade-show visitors are classified as "buying influencers."[31] Exhibiting firms spend more than $21 billion annually on floor space at North American exhibitions, and the average company participates in more than 45 trade shows per year.[32] Generally, sellers present their products and services in booths visited by interested industry members. The typical exhibitor contacts four to five potential purchasers per hour on the show floor.

A trade-show exhibit offers a unique opportunity to publicize a significant contribution to technology or to demonstrate new and old products. According to Thomas Bonoma, "For many companies, trade-show expenditures are the major—and for more than a few, the only—form of organized marketing communication activity other than efforts by sales force and distributors."[33] Through the trade show,

- An effective selling message can be delivered to a relatively large and interested audience at one time (for example, more than 30,000 people attend the annual Plant Engineering Show).

---

[31] Douglas Ducante, "The Future of the United States Exhibition Industry—Flourish or Flounder," at http://www.ceir.org, October 2002.

[32] Ruth P. Stevens, *Trade Show and Event Marketing* (Mason, Ohio: Thomson/South-Western, 2005), pp. 2–6.

[33] Thomas V. Bonoma, "Get More Out of Your Trade Shows," *Harvard Business Review* 61 (January–February 1983), p. 76.

- New products can be introduced to a mass audience.

- Customers can get hands-on experience with the product in a one-on-one selling situation.

- Potential customers can be identified, providing sales personnel with qualified leads.

- General goodwill can be enhanced.

- Free publicity is often generated for the company.

The cost of reaching a prospect at a trade show is approximately $250, much lower than the cost of making a personal sales call for many firms.[34] Furthermore, trade shows offer an excellent and cost-effective short-term method for introducing a product in new foreign markets.[35] An international trade fair enables a manufacturer to meet buyers directly, observe competition, and gather market research data. The entry time for exporting can easily be cut from six years to six months by attending foreign trade fairs.

Trade-Show Investment Returns

A recent study evaluated the effect of a trade show on the sales and profitability of a new laboratory testing device.[36] In a controlled experiment where new product sales could be traced to customers both attending and not attending the show, sales levels were higher among attendees. In turn, the proportion of customers who bought the product was higher among those who had visited the booth during the show. Importantly, there was a positive return on trade-show investment (23 percent) based on incremental profits related to the cost of the trade show. This research is one of the first studies to show that the returns from trade-show investments can indeed be measured.

Improving Sales Efficiency   Another study demonstrated the powerful way personal selling and trade shows work together in an integrated marketing communications strategy.[37] The results demonstrate that follow-up sales efforts generate higher sales productivity when customers had already been exposed to the company's products at a trade show. The return-on-sales figures are higher among show attendees than nonattendees, illuminating the positive effects of trade shows on customer purchase intentions. Although dramatically enhancing performance, trade shows can be extremely costly and must be carefully planned.

Planning Trade-Show Strategy

To develop an effective trade-show communications strategy, managers must address four questions:

1. What functions should the trade show perform in the total marketing communications program?

---

[34] Ruth P. Stevens, *Trade Show and Event Marketing*, p. 16.

[35] Brad O'Hara, Fred Palumbo, and Paul Herbig, "Industrial Trade Shows Abroad," *Industrial Marketing Management* 22 (August 1993): p. 235.

[36] Srinath Gopalakrishna, Gary L. Lilien, Jerome D. Williams, and Ian K. Sequeira, "Do Trade Shows Pay Off?" *Journal of Marketing* 59 (July 1995): pp. 75–83.

[37] Timothy M. Smith, Srinath Gopalakrishna, and Paul M. Smith, "The Complementary Effect of Trade Shows on Personal Selling," *International Journal of Research in Marketing* 21 (March 2004), pp. 61–69.

2. To whom should the marketing effort at trade shows be directed?

3. What is the appropriate show mix for the company?

4. What should the trade-show investment-audit policy be? How should audits be carried out?[38]

Answering these questions helps managers crystallize their thinking about target audiences, about expected results, and about how funds should be allocated.

Trade-Show Objectives

Functions of trade shows in generating sales include identifying decision influencers; identifying potential customers; providing product, service, and company information; learning of potential application problems; creating actual sales; and handling current customer problems. In addition to these selling-related functions, the trade show can be valuable for building corporate image, gathering competitive intelligence, and enhancing sales force morale. Specific objectives are needed to guide the development of trade-show strategy and to specify the activities of company personnel while there. Once specific objectives are formulated, however, the exhibitor must evaluate alternative trade shows in light of the target market.

Selecting the Shows

The challenge is to decide which trade shows to attend and how much of the promotional budget to expend.[39] Clearly, the firm wants to attend those shows frequented by its most important customer segments, so it begins by soliciting ideas from salespeople and customers. A wealth of information can also be found in leading trade-show directories, like the *American Tradeshow Directory* (http://www.tradeshowbiz.com) or from a Web-based trade-show searchable database like http://www.ExhibitNet.com. Here information on each show is provided and exhibitors can promote their presence at the show on the site.

Some firms use the reports published by Exhibit Surveys, Inc., a company that surveys trade-show audiences. Two of the important measures Exhibit Surveys developed are the **net buying influences** and the **total buying plans.** The first measures the percentage of the show audience that has decision authority for the types of products being exhibited; the second measures the percentage of the audience planning to buy those products within the next 12 months. These measures are very useful to the business marketing manager when selecting the most effective shows to attend.

Many firms survey their target prospects before the trade show to learn which trade shows they will attend and what they hope to gain from attending. In this way the exhibitor can prepare its trade-show strategy to fit the needs of its potential customers.

Others suggest that a firm rank order various shows based on expected profitability.[40] The expected profitability is computed by calibrating a model of "lead efficiency" using the firm's historical sales lead and lead conversion-to-sale data, gross margin information, and total attendance at past shows. **Lead efficiency** is defined as the number of sales leads obtained at the show divided by the total number of show visitors with definite plans to buy the exhibitor's product or one similar to it.

---

[38] Thomas V. Bonoma, "Get More Out of Your Trade Shows," p. 79.

[39] Ruth P. Stevens, *Trade Show and Event Marketing,* pp. 58–62.

[40] Srinath Gopalakrishna and Jerome D. Williams, "Planning and Performance Assessment of Industrial Trade Shows: An Exploratory Study," *International Journal of Research in Marketing* 9 (September 1992): pp. 207–224.

FIGURE 16.4 | REPRESENTATION OF TRAFFIC FLOW MODEL AT TRADE SHOWS AS A SEQUENCE OF STAGES

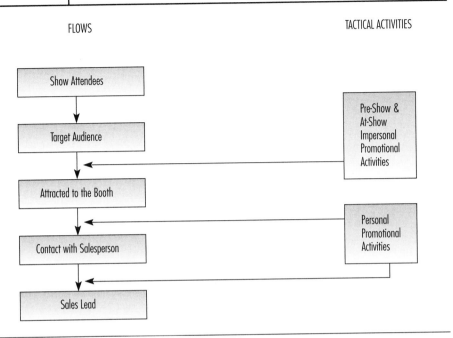

SOURCE: Srinath Gopalakrishna and Gary L. Lilien, "A Three-Stage Model of Industrial Trade Show Performance," working paper #20-1992, Institute for the Study of Business Markets, Pennsylvania State University.

Managing the Trade-Show Exhibit

To generate interest in an exhibit, business marketing firms run advertisements in business publications profiling new projects they will exhibit at the show. Trade-show strategies should also be linked to interactive marketing communications. This enables many exhibitors to schedule appointments with prospects and customers during the show.

Sales personnel must be trained to perform in the trade-show environment. The selling job differs from the typical sales call in that the salesperson may have only 5 to 10 minutes to make a presentation. On a typical sales call, salespersons usually sell themselves first, then the company, and finally the product. At the trade show, the process is reversed.

There must be a system for responding effectively to inquiries generated at the show. Some business marketers find it effective to use a laptop to transmit information to corporate headquarters electronically. Headquarters staff then generate a letter and send out the required information by mail or e-mail. When prospects return to their offices after a show, the material is immediately available.

Evaluating Trade-Show Performance

The measurement of trade-show performance is very important in assessing the success of a firm's trade-show strategy. Srinath Gopalakrishna and Gary Lilien present a useful framework to assess performance by considering traffic flow through the firm's booth as a sequence of three stages.[41] Figure 16.4 illustrates the process and three

---

[41] Srinath Gopalakrishna and Gary L. Lilien, "A Three-Stage Model of Industrial Trade Show Performance," *Marketing Science* 14 (winter 1995): pp. 22–42.

different indices of performance—attraction, contact, and conversion efficiency for the three respective stages.

An important contribution of this framework is the link between performance indices and key decision variables the firm can control. Attraction efficiency is the proportion of *interested* visitors the booth is able to attract. Notice that the firm's target audience is the pool of visitors at the show who are interested in the firm's products, which is usually smaller than the total number of attendees at the show. The booth's attraction power is a function of space (square feet), show promotion, use of attention-getting techniques, and so on. Similarly, contact and conversion efficiencies are modeled as a function of the number of booth personnel and their level of training.

For an individual firm, trade-show expenditures should be tied to concrete marketing communication goals to secure an adequate return on investment. To this end, business marketing managers must carefully evaluate each trade show and its expenses in terms of the likely effect on sales, profit, and corporate image. As with all other promotional vehicles, the planning and budgeting for trade shows must focus on specific objectives. Once these objectives have been determined, the rational approach will then identify what has to be done and how much will have to be spent.

Summary

Business-to-business marketers are developing integrated marketing communications strategies that align strategic business objectives with creative execution across a variety of media to achieve desired results. Because of the nature of the business-to-business buying process, personal selling is the primary technique for creating sales; advertising supports and supplements personal selling. Yet, advertising does perform some tasks that personal selling simply cannot perform. Advertising is able to reach buying influentials who are often inaccessible to sales personnel.

Advertising supports personal selling by making the company and product known to potential buyers. The result is greater overall selling success and firm performance. Effective advertising makes the entire marketing strategy more efficient, often lowering total marketing and selling costs. Finally, advertising can provide information and company or product awareness more efficiently than can personal selling. More than just an advertising medium, the Internet changes marketing communications from a one-way to a two-way process that permits the marketer to more readily exchange information with customers.

Managing the advertising program begins by determining advertising objectives, which must be clearly defined and directed to a specific audience. Once objectives are specified, funds are allocated to advertising efforts. Rules of thumb, though common, are not the ideal methods for specifying advertising budgets. The objective-task method is far more effective.

Advertising messages are created with the understanding that the potential buyer's perceptual process influences receptivity to the message. The most effective appeal is one that projects product benefits or the solution sought by the targeted buying influential.

Advertising media are selected on the basis of their circulation—how well their audience matches the desired audience of buying influentials. The Internet provides a powerful medium to communicate with target customers. Astute business marketers integrate the Web with other media. Interactive marketing campaigns can be readily changed, personalized, and customized, making one-to-one marketing a reality.

Finally, advertising effectiveness must be evaluated against the advertising campaign's communication objectives. Readership, recognition, awareness, attitudes, and intention to buy are typical measures of business-to-business advertising performance.

Trade-show visitors tend to be buying influentials, and the cost of reaching a prospect here is far lower than through personal selling. A carefully planned and executed strategy is needed to secure promising returns on trade-show investments. Trade shows are an effective way to reach large audiences with a single presentation, but funds must be allocated carefully.

Discussion Questions

1. Although the bulk of the promotional budget of the business marketing firm is allocated to personal selling, advertising can play an important role in business marketing strategy. Explain.

2. Evaluate this statement: "The Internet changes marketing communications from a one-way process to a two-way process that permits the marketer and the consumer to now more readily exchange information."

3. Breck Machine Tool would like you to develop a series of ads for a new industrial product. On request, Breck's marketing research department will provide you with any data they have about the new product and the market. Outline the approach you would follow in selecting media and developing messages for the campaign. Specify the types of data you would draw on to improve the quality of your decisions.

4. Outline how you would evaluate the effectiveness and efficiency of a business firm's advertising function. Focus on budgeting practices and performance results.

5. Explain how a message in a business-to-business advertisement in *The Wall Street Journal* may be favorably evaluated by the production manager, unfavorably evaluated by the purchasing manager, and fail even to trigger the attention of the quality control engineer.

6. Given the rapid rise in the cost of making personal sales calls, should the business marketer attempt to substitute direct-mail advertising or interactive marketing communications for personal selling whenever possible? Support your position.

7. Describe the role that an Internet strategy might assume in the promotional mix of the business marketer. How can the business marketer use the Web to form close relationships with customers?

8. It is argued that business advertising is not expected to precipitate sales directly. If business advertising does not persuade organizational buyers to buy brand *A* versus brand *B*, what does it do, and how can we measure its effect against expenditures on other marketing strategy elements?

Internet Exercise

Go to http://www.tsnn.com, a comprehensive source of information about trade-show events, and identify two trade shows that will be conducted in the pharmaceutical industry during the next month.

CASE

Johnson Controls, Inc.[42]

Johnson Controls, Inc., provides control and automotive systems worldwide. The Controls Division offers mechanical and electrical systems that control energy use, air conditioning, lighting, security, and fire safety for buildings. The company also provides on-site management and technical services for customers in a range of settings, including manufacturing installations, commercial buildings, government buildings, hospitals, and major sports complexes.

While serving a full range of market sectors from manufacturers to educational institutions, Johnson Controls has developed a suite of products and services for large retail chains, including department stores, discount stores, grocers, and "big box" supercenters. Most major shopping malls in North America are customers. Johnson Controls' products include a variety of control panels that manage HVAC equipment, transportation, airflow, lighting levels, energy consumption, and air quality—and even determine how many customers enter and exit a store. Behind the control systems is a Remote Operations Center for 24-hour monitoring: Many problems can be diagnosed and corrected online.

Johnson Controls has recently developed a product and service solution that targets the convenience store industry. The convenience store controller smartly manages a store's lighting, refrigeration, and HVAC, alerting store personnel of malfunctions. Building on its deep experience in working with large grocery chains, Johnson Controls can demonstrate to a convenience store chain how the system reduces energy costs, prevents food spoilage, improves occupant comfort, and lowers the cost of maintenance.

Discussion Questions

1. Outline the advertising strategy Johnson Controls might follow to promote the convenience store controller. What benefits would you emphasize in the body of an ad?

2. Develop a list of keywords you would use in promoting the product through Google's Internet search advertising program.

---

[42]"Johnson Controls, Retail Industry Solutions," accessed at http://www.johnsoncontrols.com, November 5, 2005.

Business Marketing Communications: Managing the Personal Selling Function

Business marketing communications consist of advertising, sales promotion, and personal selling. As explored in Chapter 16, advertising and related sales promotion tools supplement and reinforce personal selling. Personal selling is the most important demand-stimulating force in the business marketer's promotional mix. Through the sales force, the marketer links the firm's total product and service offering to the needs of organizational customers. After reading this chapter, you will understand:

1. the role of personal selling in business marketing strategy.

2. the skills and characteristics of high-performing account managers.

3. the nature of the sales management function.

4. selected managerial tools that can be applied to major sales force decision areas.

John Chambers, president and CEO at Cisco Systems, says that "the customer is the strategy."[1] He began his career in the 1970s as an IBM salesperson. Today, he still spends 40 percent of his time working directly with customers, and he believes that the key to Cisco's success comes through continuous customer feedback. In fact, every night, 365 days a year, he receives voice-mail updates on 10 to 15 top-tier customer accounts. By developing leading-edge technology and staying close to the customer, Cisco continues on its astonishing growth path.

In the marketing operations of the typical firm, selling has been a dominant component and a major determinant of overall company success.[2] Personal selling is dominant in business markets because, compared with consumer markets, the number of potential customers is relatively small and the dollar purchases are large. The importance of personal selling in the marketing mix depends on such factors as the nature and composition of the market, the nature of the product line, and the company's objectives and financial capabilities. Business marketers have many potential links to the market. Some rely on manufacturers' representatives and distributors; others rely exclusively on a direct sales force. Each firm must determine the relative importance of the promotional mix components—advertising versus sales promotion versus personal selling.

Across all industries, the cost of an industrial sales call is much more than $200.[3] Computer firms report much higher costs; chemical producers have much lower ones. Of course, these figures vary, depending on a host of company, product, and market conditions. They do indicate, however, that significant resources are invested in personal selling in the business market. In fact, Erin Anderson and Bob Trinkle persuasively argue that few firms have a clear understanding of the real costs of field sales.[4] To maximize effectiveness and efficiency, the personal selling function must be carefully managed and integrated into the firm's marketing mix. To enhance productivity and respond to intense competition, sales strategists are using a host of new approaches and technologies.

Regardless of how a firm implements its sales strategy, the salesperson is the initial link to the marketplace and specific customers. The task of the salesperson is both complex and challenging. To meet all their customers' expectations, salespeople must have broad knowledge that extends beyond their own products. They must be able to talk intelligently about competitors' products and about trends in the customer's industry. They must know not only their customer's business but also the business of their customer's customers. This chapter first considers the lead role of the salesperson in executing relationship marketing strategies and serving key customer accounts. Attention then turns to the characteristics of high-performing account managers and the central features of the sales management process.

---

[1] Michele Marchetti, "America's Best Sales Forces: Sales to CEO," *Sales & Marketing Management* 151 (July 1999): p. 63.

[2] James Cross, Steven W. Hartley, and William Rudelius, "Sales Force Activities and Marketing Strategies in Industrial Firms: Relationships and Implications," *Journal of Personal Selling & Sales Management* 21 (summer 2001): pp. 199–206.

[3] "The Cost of Doing Business," *Sales & Marketing Management* 151 (September 1999): p. 56.

[4] Erin Anderson and Bob Trinkle, *Outsourcing the Sales Function: The Real Costs of Field Sales* (Mason, Ohio: Thomson Higher Education, 2005).

Foundations of Personal Selling: An Organizational Customer Focus

Business marketing strategy is executed through personal selling. Once the marketer defines target market segments based on organizational characteristics (macrolevel) or the characteristics of decision-making units (microlevel), the sales force is deployed to meet the needs of these segments. The salesperson augments the total product offering and serves as a representative for both seller and buyer. The image, reputation, and the seller's ability to satisfy needs are conveyed, to an important degree, by the sales force. By helping procurement decision makers to define requirements and match the firm's product or service to them, the salesperson is offering not just a physical product but also ideas, recommendations, technical assistance, experience, confidence, and friendship. A large toy manufacturer, for example, evaluates suppliers based on product quality, delivery reliability, price, *and* the value of ideas and suggestions salespeople provide. This buying organization, in fact, openly solicits ideas and evaluates suppliers formally on the number and quality of these recommendations.

As a representative for the buyer, the salesperson often articulates a customer's specific needs to R&D or production personnel in the industrial firm. Product specifications, delivery, and technical service are often negotiated through the salesperson. The salesperson serves to absorb uncertainty, reducing conflict in the buyer-seller relationship. John Knopp, a regional sales manager at Hewlett-Packard, identifies this trait in high-performing salespersons: "They know how to get special things done for the customer inside or outside the system. When something has to be done outside of normal policies and practices, they find a way to get it done smoothly."[5]

Relationship Marketing

The trend toward close relationships, or even strategic partnerships, between manufacturers and their suppliers is accelerating in many business market sectors. Several forces highlighted throughout this textbook support the movement toward closer buyer-seller relationships and away from distant, or even adversarial, relations: rising global competition, the quest for improved quality, rapidly changing technology, and the spread of just-in-time operations.[6] Assuming a key role in the customer relationship marketing program of the firm (see Chapter 4) is the salesperson.

Selling Center   The selling organization members who initiate and maintain exchange relationships with industrial customers constitute the **organizational selling center**[7] (Figure 17.1 on page 417). The needs of a particular selling situation, especially information requirements, significantly influence the selling center's composition. Its primary

---

[5] Thayer C. Taylor, "Anatomy of a Star Salesperson," *Sales and Marketing Management* 136 (May 1986): pp. 49–51.

[6] See, for example, Adrian Payne and Pennie Frow, "A Strategic Framework for Customer Relationship Management," *Journal of Marketing* 69 (October 2005): pp. 167–176.

[7] Eli Jones, Andrea L. Dixon, Lawrence B. Chonko, and Joseph P. Cannon, "Key Accounts and Team Selling: A Review, Framework, and Research Agenda," *Journal of Personal Selling & Sales Management* 25 (spring 2005): pp. 181–198; see also Michael D. Hutt, Wesley J. Johnston, and John R. Ronchetto Jr., "Selling Centers and Buying Centers: Formulating Strategic Exchange Patterns," *Journal of Personal Selling & Sales Management* 5 (May 1985): pp. 33–40.

INSIDE BUSINESS MARKETING

Career Profile: Managing Relationships at IBM

Brad Bochart is a client executive with IBM in southern California and is responsible for 19 large customer accounts in the financial services industry (for example, banks, investment companies). He joined IBM in January 1997 after receiving a BS in marketing from Arizona State University. Brad's training at IBM involved two components: (1) six months of courses on topics such as business etiquette, territory management, business finance, and negotiation and sales skills; and (2) six months of training to learn more about his assigned industry—financial services.

As a client executive, it is my job to build market share within this industry, develop key strategic relationships with the CEOs and key managers on their staff, as well as to continuously learn about their business and industry. Ultimately, the goal is to produce long-term partnerships with each of these accounts. I am the point man for IBM for each of my clients and it is my job to understand their business strategies and the information technology (IT) tactics that they are using to support these strategies. Once this understanding is achieved, I then bring together the IBM resources that will directly support their IT and business strategies. Along with this, I must develop key internal relationships with various IBM consultants, product specialists, and business partners with the objective of using these relations to provide solutions to my customers and strengthen IBM's position across each account.

What I enjoy the most is the responsibility and authority that the job provides. I also enjoy the opportunity to call on and talk with the various CEOs who lead the organizations that I serve. To date, I have had the opportunity to golf with five different CEOs. I take great pleasure in understanding their businesses as well as how they are run. Most of all, I enjoy listening: how they think, how they run their day-to-day schedules, how they deal with critical issues, or how they balance their personal and professional lives. Lastly, I enjoy my colleagues at IBM and I enjoy representing the IBM Company.

SOURCE: Brad Bochart, interview by author (telephone and e-mail), Tempe, Arizona.

objectives are to acquire and process pertinent marketing-related information and execute selling strategies. In many industries, teamwork has emerged as a necessary prerequisite for sales success—often requiring a structured, formal selling team approach rather than the loose coalition of individuals in the selling center.[8] Some firms such as Xerox, Hewlett-Packard, and DuPont have adopted formal account management teams.

The **organizational buying center** includes individuals who participate in the purchasing decision and who share the goals and risks of that decision. The needs of a particular buying situation dictate the composition of the buying center (see Chapter 3). For example, a new complex buying situation may include several participants representing different functional areas.

Assuming visible roles in this exchange process are the salesperson (selling-center representative) and the purchasing agent (buying-center representative). The salesperson and the buyer each begin the interaction with particular plans, goals, and intentions. The salesperson provides information and assistance in solving a purchasing problem in exchange for the reward of a sale.

---

[8]Dawn R. Deeter-Schmelz and Rosemary Ramsey, "A Conceptualization of the Functions and Roles of Formalized Selling and Buying Teams," *Journal of Personal Selling & Sales Management* 15 (spring 1995): pp. 47–60.

FIGURE 17.1 | RELATIONSHIP MANAGEMENT PROCESSES IN BUSINESS MARKETING

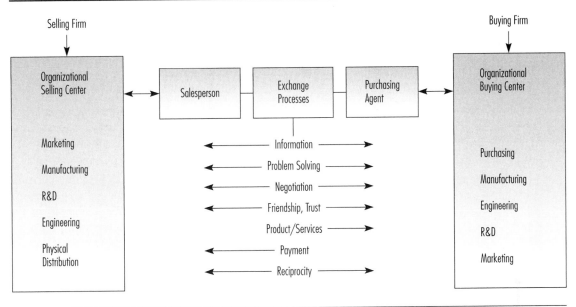

In addition to external negotiations with the buying center, the industrial sales-person, acting on behalf of the potential customer, often carries on internal negotiations with other members of the selling center, such as manufacturing or R&D, to ensure a successful exchange relationship. Internal negotiations also occur within the buying center because various members represent the interests of their functional areas in selecting suppliers. Complex flows of influence characterize buyer-seller interactions in the business market.[9] To ensure that customers are as satisfied as possible, business marketers must effectively manage the complex web of influences that intersect in buyer-seller relationships.[10]

Relationship Quality

By occupying a position close to the customer and drawing on the organization's collective strength, the industrial salesperson is often best suited to perform the role of "relationship manager." For many complex purchase decisions, organizational buyers face considerable uncertainty. From the customer's perspective, a salesperson who can reduce this uncertainty improves the quality of the relationship. **Relationship quality** comprises at least two dimensions: (1) trust in the salesperson and (2) satisfaction with

[9]Thomas V. Bonoma and Wesley J. Johnston, "The Social Psychology of Industrial Buying and Selling," *Industrial Marketing Management* 7 (July 1978): pp. 213–224; see also Nigel C. G. Campbell, John L. Graham, Alain Jolibert, and Hans Gunther Meissner, "Marketing Negotiations in France, Germany, the United Kingdom, and the United States," *Journal of Marketing* 52 (April 1988): pp. 49–62.

[10]Christian Homburg and Ruth M. Stock, "The Link between Salespeople's Job Satisfaction and Customer Satisfaction in a Business-to-Business Context: A Dyadic Analysis," *Journal of the Academy of Marketing Science* 32 (spring 2004): pp. 144–158.

the salesperson.[11] In the face of the frequent uncertainty of complex industrial exchange settings, relationship quality contributes to a lasting bond by offering assurance that the salesperson will continue to meet the customer's expectations (satisfaction) and not knowingly distort information or otherwise damage the customer's interests (trust).[12] As Lawrence Crosby, Kenneth Evans, and Deborah Cowles conclude, "The continuity of interaction that relationship quality provides then creates ongoing opportunities for the seller to identify the customer's unmet needs and propose new business."[13]

Managing the Sales Force

Effective management of the industrial sales force is fundamental to the firm's success. Sales management refers to planning, organizing, directing, and controlling personal selling efforts.[14] Sales force decisions are tempered by overall marketing objectives and must be integrated with the other elements of the marketing mix. Forecasts of the expected sales response guide the firm in determining the total selling effort required (sales force size) and in organizing and allocating the sales force (perhaps to sales territories). Techniques for estimating market potential and forecasting sales (discussed in Part III, Assessing Market Opportunities) are particularly valuable in sales planning. Sales management also involves the ongoing activities of selecting, training, deploying, supervising, and motivating sales personnel. Finally, sales operations must be monitored to identify problem areas and to assess the efficiency, effectiveness, and profitability of personal selling units.

This section considers strategic components of sales force management: (1) methods for organizing the sales force, (2) key account management, and (3) the distinctive characteristics of high-performing account managers.

Organizing the Personal Selling Effort

How should the sales force be organized? The appropriate form depends on such factors as the nature and length of the product line, the role of intermediaries in the marketing program, the diversity of the market segments served, the nature of buying behavior in each market segment, and the structure of competitive selling. The manufacturer's size and financial strength often dictate, to an important degree, the feasibility of particular organizational forms. The business marketer can organize the sales force by geography, product, or market. Large industrial enterprises that market diverse product lines may use all three.

---

[11] Lawrence A. Crosby, Kenneth R. Evans, and Deborah Cowles, "Relationship Quality in Services Selling: An Interpersonal Influence Perspective," *Journal of Marketing* 54 (July 1990): pp. 68–81. See also Jon M. Hawes, Kenneth E. Mast, and John E. Swan, "Trust Earning Perceptions of Sellers and Buyers," *Journal of Personal Selling & Sales Management* 9 (September 1989): pp. 1–8.

[12] Jon M. Hawes, James T. Strong, and Bernard S. Winick, "Do Closing Techniques Diminish Prospect Trust?" *Industrial Marketing Management* 25 (September 1996): pp. 349–360. See also Richard E. Plank, David A. Reid, and Ellen Bolman Pollins, "Perceived Trust in Business-to-Business Sales: A New Measure," *Journal of Personal Selling & Sales Management* 19 (summer 1999): pp. 61–71.

[13] Crosby, Evans, and Cowles, "Relationship Quality in Services Selling," p. 76. For a discussion of specific strategies, see James C. Anderson and James A. Narus, "Selectively Pursuing More of Your Customer's Business," *MIT Sloan Management Review* 44 (spring 2003): pp. 42–49.

[14] A comprehensive treatment of all aspects of sales management is beyond the scope of this volume. For more extensive discussion, see Mark W. Johnston and Greg W. Marshall, *Relationship Selling and Sales Management* (New York: McGraw-Hill/Irwin, 2005).

Geographical Organization   The most common form of sales organization in business marketing is geographical. Each salesperson sells all the firm's products in a defined geographical area. By reducing travel distance and time between customers, this method usually minimizes costs. Likewise, sales personnel know exactly which customers and prospects fall within their area of responsibility.

The major disadvantage of the geographical sales organization is that each salesperson must be able to perform every selling task for all of the firm's products and for all customers in the territory. If the products have diverse applications, this can be difficult. A second disadvantage is that the salesperson has substantial leeway in choosing which products and customers to emphasize. Sales personnel may emphasize products and end-use applications they know best. Of course, this problem can be remedied through training and capable first-line supervision. Because the salesperson is crucial in implementing the firm's segmentation strategy, careful coordination and control are required to align personal selling effort with marketing objectives.

Product Organization   In a product-oriented sales organization, salespersons specialize in relatively narrow components of the total product line. This is especially appropriate when the product line is large, diverse, or technically complex and when a salesperson needs a high degree of application knowledge to meet customer needs. Furthermore, various products often elicit various patterns of buying behavior. The salesperson concentrating on a particular product becomes more adept at identifying and communicating with members of buying centers.

A prime benefit of this approach is that the sales force can develop a level of product knowledge that enhances the value of the firm's total offering to customers. The product-oriented sales organization may also help identify new market segments.

One drawback is the cost of developing and deploying a specialized sales force. A product must have the potential to generate a level of sales and profit that justifies individual selling attention. Thus, a "critical mass" of demand is required to offset the costs. In turn, several salespersons may be required to meet the diverse product requirements of a single customer. To reduce selling costs and improve productivity, some firms have launched programs to convert product specialists into general-line specialists who know all the firm's products and account strategies. Often, as customers learn to use technology, they outgrow the need for product specialists and prefer working with a single salesperson for all products.

Market-Centered Organization   The business marketer may prefer to organize personal selling effort by customer type. Owens-Corning Fiberglass Corporation recently switched from a geographical sales structure to one organized by customer type. Similarly, Hewlett-Packard successfully used this structure to strengthen its market position in retailing, financial services, and oil and gas exploration.[15] Sales executives at *Fortune* 500 companies that use sales teams believe they are better able to secure customers and improve business results by adopting a more customer-focused sales structure.[16]

By learning the specific requirements of a particular industry or customer type, the salesperson is better prepared to identify and respond to buying influentials. Also, key market segments become more accessible, thus providing the opportunity

---

[15] Thayer C. Taylor, "Hewlett-Packard," *Sales and Marketing Management* 145 (January 1993): p. 59.
[16] Vincent Alonzo, "Selling Changes," *Incentive* 170 (September 1996): p. 46.

for differentiated personal selling strategies. The market segments must, of course, be sufficiently large to warrant specialized treatment.

Key Account Management[17]

Many business marketing firms find that a small proportion of customers (for example, 20 percent) often account for a major share (for example, 80 percent) of its business. These customers possess enormous purchasing power by virtue of their size, and they are searching for ways to leverage their suppliers' capabilities to enhance the value they deliver to their own customers (see Chapter 2). In turn, many of these large buying firms have centralized procurement and expect suppliers to provide coordinated and uniform service support to organizational units that are geographically dispersed on a national or global scale. In exchange for a long-term volume commitment, these customers expect the business marketing firm to provide additional value-added services (for example, new-product-development assistance) and support (for example, just-in-time delivery) that may not be available to other customers.

Key Accounts versus Regular Accounts   Given the importance of these large customers, firms are rethinking how they manage their most important customers and how they organize internal operations to meet these customers' complex needs. To that end, many firms—Hewlett-Packard, Xerox, 3M, IBM, and Dow Chemical, for example— are establishing *key account* managers and creating customer teams composed of individuals from sales, marketing, finance, logistics, and other functional groups. Key account managers are typically responsible for several important customers and report to a senior executive. For some customers, the key account manager may work directly in the customer's facilities. For example, an IBM key account team occupies offices at Boeing and works solely on that account.

A **key account** represents a customer who:

a. purchases a significant volume as a percentage of a seller's total sales.

b. involves several organizational members in the purchasing process.

c. buys for an organization with geographically dispersed units.

d. expects a carefully coordinated response and specialized services such as logistical support, inventory management, price discounts, and customized applications.[18]

Rather than as "key accounts," some companies describe such customers as strategic accounts or national accounts.

A Different Type of Relationship   Table 17.1 compares and contrasts the traditional selling paradigm with the key account selling paradigm. Key account customers purchase in very large volume, and the focus of exchange extends beyond a core product as the seller augments the offering through value-added services and support. For example, acting on behalf of Cisco Systems, FedEx coordinates the delivery of Cisco

---

[17]This section is based on Joseph P. Cannon and Narakesari Narayandas, "Relationship Marketing and Key Account Management," in Jagdish N. Sheth and Atul Parvatiyar, eds., *Handbook of Relationship Marketing* (Thousand Oaks, Calif.: Sage Publications, 2000), pp. 407–429.

[18]Frank V. Cespedes, *Concurrent Marketing: Integrating Products, Sales, and Service* (Boston: Harvard Business School Press, 1995), p. 187.

TABLE 17.1 | TRADITIONAL SELLING VERSUS KEY ACCOUNT SELLING

	Traditional Selling Focus	**Key Account Selling Focus**
Sales Volume	Varies	Large volume of purchases by the customer, often across multiple business units of the seller
Nature of Product/ Service Offering	Core product/service	Core product/service *plus* customized applications and value-added services
Time Horizon	Short-term	Long-term
Benefits to Customer	Lower prices and higher quality	Lower total costs Broader set of strategic benefits
Information Sharing	Limited: Narrow focus on price and product features	Extensive: Broader focus as firms share strategic goals
Sales Force Objectives	Maximize revenue Satisfied customers	Become preferred supplier Lower customer firm's total costs Enhance learning in the relationship
Structure of Selling Center	Individual salesperson is primary link to customer organization	Many individuals from multiple functional areas on the selling side interact with counterparts in the customer organization
Structure of Buying Center	Purchasing manager and a few other individuals are involved in buying decision	Many individuals within the customer organization interact in making decisions and evaluating the relationship

SOURCE: Adapted with modifications from Joseph P. Cannon and Narakesari Narayandas, "Relationship Marketing and Key Account Management," in *Handbook of Relationship Marketing*, Jagdish N. Sheth and Atul Parvatiyar, eds. (Thousand Oaks, Calif.: Sage Publications, 2000), p. 409; and Frank V. Cespedes, *Concurrent Marketing: Integrating Products, Sales, and Service* (Boston: Harvard Business School Press, 1995), pp. 186–202.

components from geographically dispersed facilities to ensure a seamless installation in a customer's organization. Whereas traditional sales management objectives typically emphasize maximizing revenue, key account relationships involve multiple goals. To illustrate, firms may enter into a closer, long-term relationship to lower costs to both partnering firms by reducing the seller's marketing and logistics costs and reducing the buyer's acquisition and production costs.

To effectively deliver more value to an important customer, the interpersonal connections between the buying and selling firms must extend beyond the salesperson–purchasing manager relationship. A key account relationship involves frequent interactions between a team of functional experts from both organizations. The key account manager assumes a lead role in coordinating selling center activities and facilitating these cross-firm communications among functional experts. Nurturing these interpersonal connections creates an atmosphere in which these specialized personnel can cooperatively identify new solutions that lower costs or advance performance.

Selecting Key Accounts[19]   If the business marketing firm can have close and important relationships with a rather small set of customers, each requiring a large investment,

---

[19] This section is based on Cespedes, *Concurrent Marketing*, pp. 193–198.

the choice of the key accounts is critical. Because key accounts possess buying power, demand special services, and are generally more costly to serve, the account selection process must examine the sales and profit potential as well as the long-term resource commitments the relationship demands.

Frank V. Cespedes recommends a three-phase approach in selecting key accounts. To be chosen, a potential customer must meet the screening requirements of all three phases.

Phase 1: Centers on (a) the profit potential of a customer, measured in terms of incremental sales potential, and (b) the degree to which a customer values the firm's support services and is willing to pay a premium price for them. *(For example, if the product is critical to a customer's operations, support services are more valuable.)*

Phase 2: Identifies customer accounts from Phase 1 that have unique support requirements that provide profitable organizational learning opportunities. *(For example, the goal here is to invest in support capabilities that are valued by multiple accounts.)*

Phase 3: Considers the degree to which the transactions with the potential customer complement the economics of the seller's business. *(For example, some customers purchase higher-margin products than others or provide a better match to the firm's manufacturing capabilities.)*

Says Cespedes, "When there are clear criteria for determining the profit potential, learning benefits, and cost drivers associated with customers, the firm knows when (and when not) to incur the substantial commitments required for effective key-account relationships."[20]

National Account Success

Research suggests that successful national account units enjoy senior management support; have well-defined objectives, assignments, and implementation procedures; and are staffed by experienced individuals who have a solid grasp of their entire company's resources and capabilities and how to use them to create customer solutions.[21] Do key account management programs enhance profitability? Yes. A recent comprehensive study of U.S. and German firms demonstrates the clear performance advantages that firms with active key account management programs enjoy over peers without them. In turn, the research also indicates that successful programs provide the key account manager with ready access to resources and support across functional areas.[22] Successful national account programs also adopt a strong relationship marketing perspective and consistently demonstrate their ability to meet the customer's immediate and future needs.

To this point, we have examined the central role of personal selling in business marketing strategy and alternative ways to align the sales force to customer segments. Attention now turns to key milestones in managing an engagement with a particular customer.

---

[20] Ibid., p. 197.

[21] John P. Workman, Jr., Christian Homburg, and Ove Jensen, "Intraorganizational Determinants of Key Account Management Effectiveness," *Journal of the Academy of Marketing Science* 31 (winter 2003): pp. 3–21.

[22] Christian Homburg, John P. Workman Jr., and Ove Jensen, "A Configurational Perspective of Key Account Management," *Journal of Marketing* 66 (April 2002): pp. 38–60. See also Roberta J. Schultz and Kenneth R. Evans, "Strategic Collaborative Communication by Key Account Representatives," *Journal of Personal Selling & Sales Management* 22 (winter 2002): pp. 23–32.

B2B TOP PERFORMERS

Using Customized Strategies to Outmaneuver Rivals

Competitive cognition refers to the framework a manager uses to organize and retain knowledge about competitors and to direct information acquisition and usage.[1] Research suggests that competitive cognition influences individual performance. For example, in an intriguing study in the sports literature, research demonstrates that elite athletes (for example, members of the U.S. Olympic wrestling team) use extensive competitive plans that involve customized strategies and tactics to beat individual competitors, whereas poorer performers do not develop customized plans but rely, instead, on a more generic approach to competition.[2]

Building on this line of inquiry, a study explored the role of competitive cognition in the competitive crafting that salespeople do.[3] **Competitive crafting** involves salespeople's use of information and knowledge about competitors to create a business proposition for the customer. Examples of crafting include speeding up the selling cycle to counter a slow rival or broadening the scope of the product and service offered to outmaneuver a niche rival. The results of the study indicate that each additional act of crafting increases the likelihood of the salesperson winning the customer's business by fivefold!

---

[1] Beth A. Walker, Dimitri Kapelianis, and Michael D. Hutt, "Competitive Cognition," *MIT Sloan Management Review* 46 (summer 2005): pp. 10–12.

[2] Daniel Gould, Robert C. Eklund, and Susan A. Jackson, "1988 U.S. Olympic Wrestling Excellence: I. Mental Preparation, Pre-Competitive Cognition, and Affect," *The Sports Psychologist* 6 (December 1992): pp. 358–382.

[3] Dimitri Kapelianis, Beth A. Walker, Michael D. Hutt, and Ajith Kumar, "Those Winning Ways: The Role of Competitive Crafting in Complex Sales," working paper (Tempe, Ariz.: Arizona State University 2005).

Isolating the Account Management Process[23]

To explore the work that account managers perform, our focus is on complex sales situations in business markets, which are characterized by large dollar values, protracted sales cycles, customized solutions, and the involvement of many organizational members on both the buying and selling sides. Frequently, in these sales situations an account manager is assigned to a particular set of customers and then assembles an ad hoc team as customer requirements or opportunities dictate. For example, large information-technology firms, such as IBM, reserve key account teams for a carefully chosen set of customers but rely on an assigned account manager to cover the majority of large enterprise customers.

Assuming a central role in a particular engagement is the account manager who diagnoses what the customer needs, identifies the appropriate set of internal experts, recruits them onto the ad hoc team, and then orchestrates the selling center's activities to deliver a solution that matches customer needs. Let's examine how high-performing account managers perform these activities and highlight how they differ from their peers. Recent studies that explored the characteristics of high-performing account managers at two *Fortune* 500 firms provide some valuable insights.

---

[23] This section draws on Michael D. Hutt and Beth A. Walker, "A Network Perspective of Account Manager Performance," *Journal of Business & Industrial Marketing* 21 (forthcoming 2006).

FIGURE 17.2 | THE CYCLE OF ACCOUNT MANAGEMENT SUCCESS

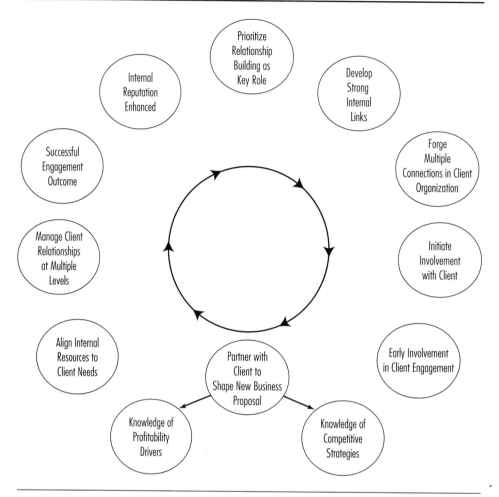

Account Management Success

For complex sales situations, account manager performance is contingent on securing access to the right people and the right information to solve novel problems for the customer. Figure 17.2 highlights the key milestones in a customer engagement and emphasizes the crucial role of relationship-building activities in the firm and in the client organization. High performers excel at relationship building. Capitalizing on these relationship connections, the account manager is better equipped to design a business proposal that aligns the firm's capabilities to customer goals. Moreover, observe that successful outcomes enhance the account manager's internal reputation, providing social capital the manager can invest in future customer engagements.

Building Internal Relationships   High-performing account managers form more cross-functional and cross-unit ties within the organization than their colleagues. A diverse social network provides a manager with access to unique skills and knowledge. Account managers with ties to a number of distinct knowledge pools in the organization can draw on a large array of skills, knowledge, and resources—thereby enhancing their customer responsiveness.

Forging Relationships within the Customer Organization   Being centrally involved in a customer organization's buying system improves an account manager's ability to understand the customer's requirements and business goals. Compared with their peers, high performers possess more cross-functional ties and a larger network of contacts within the customer organization. Because complex sales situations involve a buying center that includes participants from multiple levels of the organizational hierarchy and diverse units, an account manager's communication network must go beyond the focal purchasing unit.

Managing the Customer Engagement Process   By developing a network of relationships both within the firm and within the customer organization, an account manager is ideally equipped to manage the customer engagement process. Through these connections account managers receive vital information about emerging customer opportunities, customer requirements and solutions, and competitive challenges (see Figure 17.2). Compared with low performers, high-performing account managers are more proactive in initiating involvement with the customer and tend to be involved in client engagements earlier in the purchasing process than their peers. Capitalizing on this early involvement, high performers are also more inclined to take an active role in shaping the client's request for proposals (RFP).

Aligning and Crafting   A successful client engagement hinges on both customer knowledge and competitive intelligence. High performers know more about client goals and the drivers of client profitability than low performers. Drawing on this knowledge allows them to align the capabilities of the firm to the goals of the customer. High-performing account managers develop sound competitive intelligence and use this knowledge to outmaneuver their rivals in a particular client engagement.

Enhanced Internal Reputation   By building a strong network of relationships within both the firm and the customer organization, high-performing account managers— compared with their peers—are better able to diagnose customer requirements, mobilize internal experts, and choreograph the activities that are required to outmaneuver rivals and create the desired customer solution. Successful outcomes enhance the reputation of an account manager in the organization, thereby strengthening internal working relationships and assuring ready access to the right people and right information for future engagements.

Sales Administration

Successful sales force administration involves recruiting and selecting salespersons, then training, motivating, supervising, evaluating, and controlling them. The industrial firm should foster an organizational climate that encourages the development of a successful sales force.

Recruitment and Selection of Salespersons

The recruiting process presents numerous trade-offs for the business marketer. Should the company seek experienced salespersons, or should it hire and train inexperienced individuals? The answer depends on the specific situation; it varies with the size of the firm, the nature of the selling task, the firm's training capability, and its market experience. Smaller firms often reduce training costs by hiring experienced and more expensive salespersons. In contrast, large organizations with a more complete training function can hire less experienced personnel and support them with a carefully developed training program.

A second trade-off is quantity versus quality. Often, sales managers screen as many recruits as possible when selecting new salespersons. However, this can overload the selection process, hampering the firm's ability to identify quality candidates. Recruiting, like selling, is an exchange process between two parties. Sales managers are realizing that, for prospective salespersons, they need to demonstrate the personal development and career opportunities that a career with the firm offers. A poorly organized recruiting effort that lacks closure leaves candidates with a negative impression. A well-organized recruiting effort ensures that qualified candidates get the proper level of attention in the screening process. Thus, procedures must be established to ensure that inappropriate candidates are screened out early so that the pool of candidates is reduced to a manageable size.[24]

Responsibility for recruiting and selecting salespersons may lie with the first-line supervisor (who often receives assistance from an immediate superior), or with the human resources department, or with other executives at the headquarters level. The latter group tends to be more involved when the sales force is viewed as the training ground for marketing or general managers.

Training

To prepare new salespersons adequately, the training program must be carefully designed. Periodic training is required to sharpen the skills of experienced salespersons, especially when the firm's environment is changing rapidly. Changes in business marketing strategy (for example, new products, new market segments) require corresponding changes in personal selling styles.

The salesperson needs a wealth of knowledge about the company, the product line, customer segments, competition, organizational buying behavior, and effective communication skills.[25] All these must be part of sales training programs. Compared with their counterparts, top performing sales organizations train new salespeople in a broader range of areas: market knowledge, communication skills, listening techniques, complaint-handling skills, and industry knowledge.[26]

With the expansion in global marketing, firms need to include a sales training module that examines how to approach and respond to customers of different cultures. Such training would focus on the role of intercultural communication in developing global buyer-seller relationships.[27] Effective training builds the salesperson's confidence

[24]Wesley J. Johnston and Martha C. Cooper, "Industrial Sales Force Selection: Current Knowledge and Needed Research," *Journal of Personal Selling & Sales Management* 1 (spring/summer 1981): pp. 49–53.

[25]William L. Cron, Greg W. Marshall, Jagdip Singh, Rosann Spiro, and Harish Sujan, "Salesperson Selection, Training, and Development Trends: Implications, and Research Opportunities," *Journal of Personal Selling & Sales Management* 25 (spring 2005): pp. 123–136.

[26]Adel I. El-Ansary, "Selling and Sales Management in Action: Sales Force Effectiveness Research Reveals New Insights and Reward-Penalty Patterns in Sales Force Training," *Journal of Personal Selling & Sales Management* 13 (spring 1993): pp. 83–90.

[27]Victoria D. Bush and Thomas Ingram, "Adapting to Diverse Customers: A Training Matrix for International Marketers," *Industrial Marketing Management* 25 (September 1996): pp. 373–383.

FIGURE 17.3 | DETERMINANTS OF A SALESPERSON'S PERFORMANCE

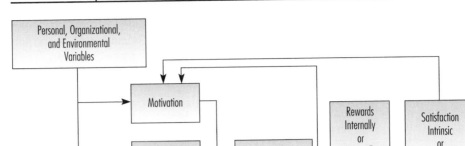

SOURCE: Orville C. Walker Jr., Gilbert A. Churchill Jr., and Neil M. Ford, "Motivation and Performance in Industrial Selling: Present Knowledge and Needed Research," *Journal of Marketing Research* 14 (May 1977): p. 158. Reprinted by permission of the American Marketing Association.

and motivation, thereby increasing the probability of success. In turn, training helps the business marketer by keeping personal selling in line with marketing program objectives. A successful training effort can reduce the costs of recruiting; many business-to-business firms have found that salesperson turnover declines as training improves. Clearly, a salesperson who is inadequately prepared to meet the demands of selling can quickly become discouraged, frustrated, and envious of friends who chose other career options. Effective training and capable first-line supervision can alleviate much of this anxiety, which is especially prevalent in the early stages of many careers.

Supervision and Motivation

The sales force must be directed in a way that is consistent with the company's policies and marketing objectives. Critical supervisory tasks are continued training, counseling, assistance (for example, time management), and activities that help sales personnel plan and execute their work. Supervision also sets sales performance standards, fulfills company policy, and integrates the sales force with higher organizational levels.

Orville Walker Jr., Gilbert Churchill Jr., and Neil Ford define **motivation** as the amount of effort the salesperson "desires to expend on each of the activities or tasks associated with his (her) job, such as calling on potential new accounts, planning sales presentations, and filling out reports."[28] The model presented in Figure 17.3 hypothesizes that a salesperson's job performance is a function of three factors: (1) level of

---

[28] Orville C. Walker Jr., Gilbert A. Churchill Jr., and Neil M. Ford, "Motivation and Performance in Industrial Selling: Present Knowledge and Needed Research," *Journal of Marketing Research* 14 (May 1977): pp. 156–168. See also Steven P. Brown, William L. Cron, and Thomas W. Leigh, "Do Feelings of Success Mediate Sales Performance–Work Attitude Relationships?" *Journal of the Academy of Marketing Science* 21 (spring 1993): pp. 91–100.

motivation, (2) aptitude or ability, and (3) perceptions about how to perform his or her role. Each is influenced by personal variables (for example, personality), organizational variables (for example, training programs), and environmental variables (for example, economic conditions). Sales managers can influence some of the personal and organizational variables through selection, training, and supervision.

Motivation is related strongly to (1) the individual's perceptions of the types and amounts of rewards from various degrees of job performance and (2) the value the salesperson places on these rewards. For a given level of performance, two types of rewards might be offered:

1. **Internally mediated rewards:** The salesperson attains rewards on a personal basis, such as feelings of accomplishment or self-worth.

2. **Externally mediated rewards:** Rewards are controlled and offered by managers or customers, such as financial incentives, pay, or recognition.

The rewards strongly influence salesperson satisfaction with the job and the work environment, which is also influenced by the individual's role perceptions. Job satisfaction declines when the salesperson's perception of the role is (1) *inaccurate* in terms of the expectations of superiors, (2) characterized by *conflicting* demands among role partners (company and customer) that the salesperson cannot possibly resolve, or (3) surrounded by *uncertainty* because of a lack of information about the expectations and evaluation criteria of superiors and customers.

Business marketers often use formal incentive programs to achieve specified customer service, sales, and profit results. Typically, an incentive program offers rewards for achieving a well-defined goal during a specified time frame. The rewards must be well conceived, based on what salespeople value, tied to achieving desired behavior, and recognize both individual and team behavior.[29] Frequently, recognition is a key ingredient in sales incentive programs and may run the gamut from Hewlett-Packard's quarterly award for a salesperson who was particularly astute in converting an objection into an order to the elaborate sales award presentations at IBM.

Organizational Climate and Job Satisfaction[30]   Churchill, Ford, and Walker, who contributed the model in Figure 17.3, also provide empirical support for some propositions that flow from the model. In examining job satisfaction in a cross section of industrial salespersons, the authors found that role ambiguity and role conflict undermine job satisfaction. Salespersons are likely to be anxious and dissatisfied when they are uncertain about the expectations of role partners or feel that role partners (for example, customers, superiors) are making incompatible and impossible demands.

An effective approach for reducing role ambiguity among new salespeople is training and socialization that offer sufficient information about role expectations and

---

[29] Katherine Morrall, "Motivating Sales Staff with Rewards," *Bank Marketing* 28 (July 1996): pp. 32–38.

[30] This section is based on Gilbert A. Churchill Jr., Neil M. Ford, and Orville C. Walker Jr., "Organizational Climate and Job Satisfaction in the Salesforce," *Journal of Marketing Research* 13 (November 1976): pp. 323–332. For related discussions, see R. Kenneth Teas and James C. McElroy, "Causal Attributions and Expectancy Estimates: A Framework for Understanding the Dynamics of Salesforce Motivation," *Journal of Marketing* 50 (January 1986): pp. 75–86; William L. Cron, Alan J. Dubinsky, and Ronald E. Michaels, "The Influence of Career Stages on Components of Salesperson Motivation," *Journal of Marketing* 52 (January 1988): pp. 78–92; and Jeffrey K. Sager, Charles M. Futrell, and Rajan Varadarajan, "Exploring Salesperson Turnover: A Causal Model," *Journal of Business Research* 18 (June 1989): pp. 303–326.

minimizes potential confusion about performance requirements. Strategies that reduce role ambiguity are likely to boost sales performance and job satisfaction.[31] Moreover, a socialization program that provides newly hired salespersons with a realistic picture of their job strengthens their commitment to the organization.[32]

Job Satisfaction Really Matters   Salespersons tend to have a higher level of job satisfaction when (1) they perceive that their first-line supervisor closely directs and monitors their activities, (2) management provides them with the assistance and support they need to solve unusual and nonroutine problems, and (3) they perceive themselves to have an active part in determining company policies and standards that affect them. Job satisfaction also appears to be related more to the substance of the contact between sales managers and salespersons than to its frequency. Also, satisfied salespersons appear to be able to accept direction from a number of departments in the organization without a significant negative effect on job satisfaction—unity of command does not appear to be a prerequisite for high morale.

Direct Link to Customer Satisfaction   A recent study by Christian Homburg and Ruth M. Stock demonstrates a positive relationship between salespeople's job satisfaction and customer satisfaction.[33] Why? First, when they are exposed to a salesperson's positive emotions, customers experience a corresponding change in their own affective state. This phenomenon, rooted in the field of social psychology, is referred to as emotional contagion and has a positive influence on customer satisfaction. Second, the higher the salesperson's job satisfaction, the higher the quality of customer interaction, reflected by the salesperson's openness, flexibility, and customer orientation. The relationship between job satisfaction and customer satisfaction is particularly strong when customer interactions are frequent, customers assume a central role in the value-creation process, or innovative products or services are involved.

Turnover   Performance and individual differences in motivation, self-esteem, and verbal intelligence may also affect job satisfaction. Richard Bagozzi notes:

> Salespeople tend to be more satisfied as they perform better, but the relationship is particularly sensitive to the level of motivation and positive self-image of the person. Although management may have no direct control over the performance achieved by salespeople, they can influence the level of motivation and self-esteem through effective incentive and sensitive supervisor-employee programs and thereby indirectly affect both performance and job satisfaction.[34]

[31] Steven P. Brown and Robert A. Peterson, "Antecedents and Consequences of Salesperson Job Satisfaction: Meta-Analysis and Assessment of Causal Effects," *Journal of Marketing Research* 30 (February 1993): pp. 63–77.

[32] Mark W. Johnston, A. Parasuraman, Charles M. Futrell, and William C. Black, "A Longitudinal Assessment of the Impact of Selected Organizational Influences on Salespeople's Organizational Commitment during Early Employment," *Journal of Marketing Research* 27 (August 1990): pp. 333–343.

[33] Homburg and Stock, "The Link between Salespeople's Job Satisfaction and Customer Satisfaction in a Business-to-Business Context: A Dyadic Analysis," pp. 144–158.

[34] Richard P. Bagozzi, "Performance and Satisfaction in an Industrial Sales Force: A Causal Modeling Approach," in *Sales Management: New Developments from Behavioral and Decision Model Research*, Richard P. Bagozzi, ed. (Cambridge, Mass.: Marketing Science Institute, 1979), pp. 70–91; see also Bagozzi, "Performance and Satisfaction in an Industrial Sales Force: An Examination of Their Antecedents and Simultaneity," *Journal of Marketing* 44 (spring 1980): pp. 65–77.

Research suggests that sales manager leadership directly and indirectly influences salespersons' job satisfaction, which in turn affects sales force turnover.[35] In addition, another study indicates that salespeople who are managed by "high-performing" sales managers exhibit less role stress and are more satisfied than their colleagues.[36] Although some factors that influence job satisfaction and performance are beyond the control of sales managers, this line of research points up the importance of responsive training, supportive supervision, and clearly defined company policies that are congruent with the needs of the sales force.

Evaluation and Control

An ongoing sales management responsibility is to monitor and control the industrial sales force at all levels—national, regional, and district—to determine whether objectives are being attained and to identify problems, recommend corrective action, and keep the sales organization in tune with changing competitive and market conditions.

Performance Measures[37]   Sales managers use both behavior-based and outcome measures of salesperson performance. When a sales force control system is more **behavior based,** the sales manager monitors and directs the activities of salespeople, uses subjective measures to evaluate performance, and emphasizes a compensation system with a large fixed component. Behavior-based selling measures include the salesperson's knowledge of product applications and the company's technology, and the clarity of the salesperson's presentations to customers. By contrast, an **outcome-based** sales force control system involves less direct field supervision of salesperson activities and uses objective measures to evaluate performance and a compensation system with a large incentive component. Sales force outcome measures include sales results, market-share gains, new-product sales, and profit contributions.

Setting Performance Standards   The standards for evaluating salespersons offer ways to compare the performance of various salespersons or sales units (for example, districts), as well as for gauging the overall productivity of the sales organization. Managerial experience and judgment are important in developing appropriate standards. Importantly, the standards must relate to overall marketing objectives, and they must take into account differences in sales territories, which can vary markedly in the number and aggressiveness of competitors, the level of market potential, and the workload.

Evidence suggests that a strict reliance on outcome measures and incentive compensation plans may not produce the desired sales or marketing performance results: "The alleged automatic supervisory power of incentive pay plans has lulled some sales executives into thinking that important sales outcomes could be reasonably accomplished without intense management reinforcement in noncompensation areas."[38] Often more effective is a more balanced approach that assigns a more prominent role to field sales managers and emphasizes behavior-based measures.[39]

[35] Eli Jones, "Leader Behavior, Work Attitudes, and Turnover of Salespeople: An Integrative Study," *Journal of Personal Selling & Sales Management* 16 (spring 1996): pp. 13–23.

[36] Frederick A. Russ, Kevin M. McNeilly, and James M. Comer, "Leadership, Decision-Making, and Performance of Sales Managers," *Journal of Personal Selling & Sales Management* 16 (summer 1996): pp. 1–15.

[37] This section is based on David W. Cravens, Thomas N. Ingram, Raymond W. LaForge, and Clifford E. Young, "Behavior-Based and Outcome-Based Salesforce Control Systems," *Journal of Marketing* 57 (October 1993): pp. 47–59.

[38] Ibid., p. 56.

[39] Richard L. Oliver, "Behavior- and Outcome-Based Sales Control Systems: Evidence and Consequences of Price-Form and Hybrid Governance," *Journal of Personal Selling & Sales Management* 15 (fall 1995): pp. 1–15.

ETHICAL BUSINESS MARKETING

Ethics in Selling

Here are some common scenarios that a salesperson confronts. Consider how you would handle each.

Scenario 1: In an attempt to negotiate the best price, sales rep Bill Smith tries to communicate to purchasing agents that plant capacity is at a very high level because of the popularity of this product. Bill does this even when plant capacity is low.

Scenario 2: Occasionally Bill Smith's customers ask which of his products he recommends for their company. Regardless of real customer need, Bill recommends one of the more expensive items in his product line.

Scenario 3: Industrial sales representative Mary Johnson needs to make a yearly quota of $500,000. During the last month of the year, Mary is $10,000 below quota. Toward the end of the month, Mary is still about $5,000 below

quota when she receives an order for $3,000. To make quota, Mary doubles the order without telling the customer. Mary turns in a $6,000 order and makes quota. Mary decides to tell the customer that the order processing department made the mistake. She figures there is a good chance the customer will accept the double order rather than go to the inconvenience of returning the goods.

Each day, salespersons encounter situations that present ethical conflicts. Consider the personal, organizational, and societal stakes that underlie each of these vignettes.

SOURCE: Joseph A. Bellizzi and Robert E. Hite, "Supervising Unethical Salesforce Behavior," *Journal of Marketing* 53 (April 1989): pp. 36–47; see also Shelby D. Hunt and Arturo Z. Vasquez-Parraga, "Organizational Consequences, Marketing Ethics, and Salesforce Supervision," *Journal of Marketing Research* 30 (February 1993): pp. 78–90.

Behavior-based measures also fit relationship selling—an important strategy in the business market. Relationship selling requires salespeople with a team orientation who can focus on activities such as sales planning and sales support, as well as on goals such as customer satisfaction.

Models for Industrial Sales Force Management

To this point, our discussion has been concerned with (1) recruiting and selection, (2) training, (3) motivating and supervising, and (4) evaluating and controlling. Poor decisions in one area can create a backlash in other areas. One critical sales management task remains: deploying the sales force. The objective is to form the most profitable sales territories, deploy salespersons to serve potential customers in those territories, and effectively allocate sales force time among those customers.

Deployment Analysis: A Strategic Approach

The size of the sales force establishes the level of selling effort that the business marketer can use. The selling effort is then organized by designating sales districts and sales territories. Allocation decisions determine how the selling effort is to be assigned to customers, prospects, and products. All these are illustrated in Table 17.2.

Proper deployment requires a multistage approach to find the most effective and efficient way to assign sales resources (for example, sales calls, number of salespersons, percentage of salesperson's time) across all of the **planning and control units (PCUs)**

TABLE 17.2 | DEPLOYMENT DECISIONS FACING SALES ORGANIZATIONS

Type of Decision	Specific Deployment Decisions
Set total level of selling effort	Determine sales force size
Organize selling effort	Design sales districts Design sales territories
Allocate selling effort	Allocate effort to trading areas Allocate sales calls to accounts Allocate sales calls to prospects Allocate sales call time to products Determine length of sales call

SOURCE: Reprinted by permission of the publisher from "Steps in Selling Effort Deployment," by Raymond LaForge and David W. Cravens, *Industrial Marketing Management* 11 (July 1982): p. 184. Copyright © 1982 by Elsevier Science Publishing Co., Inc.

TABLE 17.3 | SELECTED DETERMINANTS OF TERRITORY SALES RESPONSE

1. Environmental factors (e.g., health of economy)
2. Competition (e.g., number of competitive salespersons)
3. Company marketing strategy and tactics
4. Sales force organization, policies, and procedures
5. Field sales manager characteristics
6. Salesperson characteristics
7. Territory characteristics (e.g., potential)
8. Individual customer factors

SOURCE: Adapted from Adrian B. Ryans and Charles B. Weinberg, "Territory Sales Response," *Journal of Marketing Research* 16 (November 1979): pp. 453–465.

the firm serves (for example, prospects, customers, territories, districts, products).[40] Thus, effective deployment means understanding the factors that influence sales in a particular PCU, such as a territory.

Territory Sales Response   What influences the potential level of sales in a particular territory? Table 17.3 outlines eight classes of variables. This list shows the complexity of estimating sales response functions. Such estimates are needed, however, to make meaningful sales allocations.

Three territory traits deserve particular attention in sales response studies: potential, concentration, and dispersion.[41] **Potential** (as discussed in Chapter 6) is a measure

---

[40] David W. Cravens and Raymond W. LaForge, "Sales Force Deployment," in *Advances in Business Marketing*, vol. 1, Arch G. Woodside, ed. (Greenwich, Conn.: JAI Press, 1986), pp. 67–112; and LaForge and Cravens, "Steps in Selling Effort Deployment," *Industrial Marketing Management* 11 (July 1982): pp. 183–194.

[41] Adrian B. Ryans and Charles B. Weinberg, "Territory Sales Response," *Journal of Marketing Research* 16 (November 1979): pp. 453–465; see also Ryans and Weinberg, "Territory Sales Response Models: Stability over Time," *Journal of Marketing Research* 24 (May 1987): pp. 229–233.

of the total business opportunity for all sellers in a particular market. **Concentration** refers to how much potential lies with a few larger accounts in that territory. If potential is concentrated, the salesperson can cover with a few calls a large proportion of the potential. Finally, if the territory is geographically **dispersed,** sales are probably lower because of time wasted in travel. Past research often centered on **territory workload**—the number of accounts. However, Adrian Ryans and Charles Weinberg report that workload is of questionable value in estimating sales response: "From a managerial standpoint, the recurrent finding of an association between potential and sales results suggests that sales managers should stress territory potential when making sales force decisions."[42]

Sales Resource Opportunity Grid   Deployment analysis matches sales resources to market opportunities. Planning and control units such as sales territories or districts are part of an overall portfolio, with various units offering various levels of opportunity and requiring various levels of sales resources. A sales resource opportunity grid can be used to classify the industrial firm's portfolio of PCUs.[43] In Figure 17.4, each PCU is classified on the basis of PCU opportunity and sales organization strength.

PCU opportunity is the PCU's total potential for all sellers, whereas **sales organization strength** includes the firm's competitive advantages or distinctive competencies within the PCU. By positioning all PCUs on the grid, the sales manager can assign sales resources to those that have the greatest level of opportunity and capitalize on the particular strengths of the sales organization.

At various points in deployment decision making, the sales resource opportunity grid is important for screening the size of the sales force, the territory design, and the allocation of sales calls to customer segments. This method can isolate deployment problems or deployment opportunities worthy of sales management attention and further data analysis.

The Internet: Transforming the Selling Process

By providing ready access to a wealth of information, the Internet empowers customers and provides them with self-service capabilities that they enthusiastically embrace. They can secure extensive product and service information, compare prices, find solutions to technical problems, watch online seminars and product demonstrations, check the delivery status of orders, receive customer service support, and troubleshoot special problems. As order-processing activities move to the Web, salespersons can center more on relationship building and less on transaction details.

Sales productivity can also be increased by using the Web as an efficient and effective vehicle for communicating with customers on a global scale. For example, business marketers can hold online seminars to demonstrate new products to customers. Material can be presented in text, video, and audio forms, with questions taken by e-mail. Moving from costly in-person product demonstration seminars to online presentations can produce dramatic savings. To illustrate, Oracle Corporation traditionally relied on in-person demonstration seminars that cost $350 per attendee to stage, including special invitations, hotel space, technical support, and more.[44] These seminars were held in more than 100 countries. Today, Oracle does one online seminar for customers around the world. The cost: $1.98 per attendee!

---

[42] Ryans and Weinberg, "Territory Sales Response," p. 464.

[43] LaForge and Cravens, "Steps in Selling Effort Deployment," pp. 183–194.

[44] Matt Richtel, "The Next Waves of Electronic Commerce," *New York Times*, December 20, 1999, p. C

FIGURE 17.4 | SALES RESOURCE OPPORTUNITY GRID

<table>
<tr><td rowspan="2">PCU
Opportunity</td><td>High</td><td>**Opportunity Analysis**
PCU offers good opportunity because it has high potential and because sales organization has strong position

Sales Resource Assignment
High level of sales resources to take advantage of opportunity</td><td>**Opportunity Analysis**
PCU may offer good opportunity if sales organization can strengthen its position

Sales Resource Assignment
Either direct a high level of sales resources to improve position and take advantage of opportunity or shift resources to other PCUs</td></tr>
<tr><td>Low</td><td>**Opportunity Analysis**
PCU offers stable opportunity because sales organization has strong position

Sales Resource Assignment
Moderate level of sales resources to keep current position strength</td><td>**Opportunity Analysis**
PCU offers little opportunity

Sales Resource Assignment
Minimal level of sales resources; selectively eliminate resource coverage; possible elimination of PCU</td></tr>
<tr><td></td><td></td><td>High</td><td>Low</td></tr>
</table>

Sales Organization Strength

SOURCE: Reprinted by permission of the publisher from "Steps in Selling Effort Deployment," by Raymond LaForge and David W. Cravens, *Industrial Marketing Management* 11 (July 1982): p. 187. Copyright © 1982 by Elsevier Science Publishing Co., Inc.

Barry Silverstein, a leading Internet marketing expert, describes the effect of the Internet on the selling process:

The salesperson of the future might arrange a virtual meeting over the Web with a prospect, perhaps including live video-conferencing. The prospect, of course, could be anywhere in the world. At this virtual meeting, the salesperson makes eye contact and walks the prospect through a visual presentation on the Web, leading him or her along with live voice. The salesperson is able to stop at any point and take questions. The salesperson could show the prospect video clips of customer testimonials and success stories, or maybe the salesperson invites the prospect to view and interact with a real-time product demonstration, right then and there.[45]

[45] Barry Silverstein, *Business-to-Business Internet Marketing: Five Proven Strategies for Increasing Profits through Internet Direct Marketing* (Gulf Breeze, Fla.: MAXIMUM Press, 1999), p. 331.

If a face-to-face meeting is required, the salesperson uses a computer that has presentations and demonstrations preloaded. The salesperson might also connect to the Internet and guide the prospect through an online presentation, seminar, or demonstration on the Web.

Summary

Personal selling is a significant demand-stimulating force in the business market. Given the rapidly escalating cost of personal sales calls and the massive resources invested in personal selling, the business marketer must carefully manage this function and take full advantage of available technology to enhance sales force productivity. Business marketers are using Web-enabled strategies to streamline the sales process, deliver customized information, and develop a one-to-one relationship with customers. Recognition of both the needs of business customers and the rudiments of organizational buying behavior is fundamental to effective personal selling. Exchange processes often involve multiple parties on both the buying and selling sides—the buying center and the selling center. From the consumer's perspective, relationship quality consists of trust in and satisfaction with the salesperson.

To manage the complex web of influences that intersect in buyer-seller relationships, an account manager must initiate, develop, and sustain a network of relationships, within both the firm and the customer organization. Compared with their colleagues, high-performing account managers excel at building relationships and develop a richer base of customer and competitor knowledge that they use to create superior solutions for the customer.

Managing the sales force is a multifaceted task. First, the marketer must clearly define the role of personal selling in overall marketing strategy. Second, the sales organization must be appropriately structured—by geography, product, market, or some combination of all three. Regardless of the sales force organization, an increasing number of business-to-business firms are also establishing a key account sales force so they can profitably serve large customers with complex purchasing requirements. Third, the ongoing process of sales force administration includes recruitment and selection, training, supervision and motivation, and evaluation and control.

A particularly challenging sales management task is deploying sales effort across products, customer types, and territories. The sales resource opportunity grid is a useful organizing framework for sales deployment decisions. Likewise, the business marketer can benefit by implementing a CRM system. Such tools can help the sales manager pinpoint attractive accounts, deploy the selling effort, coordinate activities across multiple sales channels, and build customer loyalty. Sales productivity can be enhanced by using the Web as an efficient and effective vehicle for communicating with customers on a global scale and delivering a host of value-added services after a sale.

Discussion Questions

1. Relationships in the business market may involve more than the salesperson and a purchasing agent. Often, both a selling team and a buying team are involved. Describe the role that the other team members assume on the selling side.

2. When planning a sales call on a particular account in the business market, what information would you require about the buying center, the purchasing requirements, and the competition?

3. Some business marketers organize their sales force around products; others are market centered. What factors must be considered in selecting the most appropriate organizational arrangement for the sales force?

4. Christine Lojacono started as a Xerox sales rep several years ago and is now a key account manager, directing activities for five key accounts. Compare the nature of the job and the nature of the selling task for a key account manager with those of a field sales representative.

5. Explain how a successful sales training program can reduce the costs of recruiting.

6. Develop a list of skills and characteristics that distinguish high performers and average performers in a sales organization. Next, describe the steps that a firm might take to improve the skill set of the average performers.

7. To make effective and efficient sales force allocation decisions, the sales manager must analyze sales territories. Describe how the sales manager can profit by examining (a) the potential, (b) the concentration, and (c) the dispersion of territories.

8. Research suggests that the greater the salesperson's satisfaction, the greater the customer satisfaction. Given the important relationship, what steps can a business-to-business firm take to nurture and sustain job satisfaction in the sales force?

Internet Exercise

Oracle, Inc., designs, develops, markets, and supports a family of enterprise application software products for large and medium-sized organizations. For example, the company provides enterprise application software for customer relationship management (CRM). Go to http://www.oracle.com, click on "Products," then on "Customer Relationship Management" to locate case studies of customers that have purchased the Oracle CRM product. Identify one of these customers and describe the benefits that the CRM system provided.

CASE

Account Management at Yellow Roadway: Choosing Customers Wisely

Yellow Roadway Corporation is a *Fortune* 500 company that provides a full range of transportation services for customers across all U.S. industry sectors. Yellow's customers, which number more than 300,000, include industrial and consumer-goods manufacturers, large and small, as well as retailers, including those that operate on a regional or national scale. Whereas key account teams serve large corporate customers, Yellow Roadway serves the majority of its customers through a network of local sales offices.

For example, In a metropolitan area, such as Seattle, Chicago, or Boston, account managers—working out of a fully staffed sales office and directed by a sales manager and area director—are assigned a particular section of the city and given responsibility for covering all of the customers within those boundaries. Depending on the concentration of business activity in an area, the number of potential customers that fall within an account manager's assigned territory might range from 300 to more than 1,500. Of course, the transportation services each customer requires are unique—some need guaranteed, time-definite delivery service or expedited delivery, whereas others are looking for the lowest-cost route. Moreover, the products involved are equally diverse, ranging from appliances or heavy machinery to apparel, component parts, or specialty chemicals.

Given the large number of potential customers they cover, coupled with the unique shipping requirements that each can present, account managers must give special attention to the most promising prospects, reaching others only if time permits.

Discussion Question

Develop a list of criteria an account manager at Yellow Roadway could use to evaluate the relative attractiveness of 600 potential customers and isolate the "top 100" prospects. Assume that you have full access to any company information, including past purchasing behavior, revenue and profit data, customer satisfaction reports, and a complete demographic profile of each customer organization.

PART

V

Evaluating Business Marketing Strategy and Performance

Controlling Business Marketing Strategies

Two business marketing managers facing identical market conditions and with equal resources to invest in marketing strategy could generate dramatically different results. Why? One manager might carefully monitor and control the performance of marketing strategy, whereas the other might not. The astute marketer evaluates the profitability of alternative segments and examines the effectiveness and efficiency of the marketing mix components to isolate problems and opportunities and alter the strategy as market or competitive conditions dictate. After reading this chapter, you will understand:

1. a system for converting a strategic vision into a concrete set of performance measures.

2. the function and significance of marketing control in business marketing management.

3. the components of the control process.

4. specific methods for evaluating marketing strategy performance.

5. the importance of execution to the success of business marketing strategy.

Larry Bossidy and Ram Charan say, "When companies fail to deliver on their promises, the most frequent explanation is that the CEO's strategy was wrong. But the strategy by itself is not often the cause. Strategies most often fail because they aren't executed well."[1]

Managing a firm's marketing strategy is similar to coaching a football team: The excitement and challenge rest in formulating strategy. Should we focus on running or passing? What weaknesses of the opposition can we exploit? How shall we vary our standard plays? So too, the business marketer applies managerial talent creatively when developing and implementing unique marketing strategies that respond to customer needs and capitalize on competitors' weaknesses.

However, formulating effective strategy is only half of coaching or management. A truly great coach devotes significant energy to evaluating team performance during last week's game to set strategy for this week's. Did our strategy work? Why? Where did it break down? Similarly, a successful marketing strategy depends on evaluating marketing performance. The other half of strategy planning is **marketing control,** that is, checking actual against planned performance by evaluating the profitability of products, customer segments, and territories. An effective control system should measure the key drivers of success in the business environment.[2]

Information generated by the marketing control system is essential for revising current marketing strategies, formulating new ones, and allocating funds. The requirements for an effective control system are strict—data must be gathered continuously on the appropriate performance measures. Thus, an effective marketing strategy is rooted in a carefully designed and well-applied control system. Such a system must also monitor the quality of strategy implementation. Gary Hamel asserts that "implementation is often more difficult than it need be because only a handful of people have been involved in the creation of strategy and only a few key executives share a conviction about the way forward."[3]

This chapter presents the rudiments of a marketing control system, beginning with a framework that converts strategy goals into concrete performance measures. Next, it examines the components of the control process. Finally, it examines the implementation skills that ultimately shape successful business marketing strategies.

A Strategy Map: Portrait of an Integrated Plan[4]

A strategy map provides a visual representation of the cause-and-effect relationships among the components of a company's strategy. Recall that strategy maps were introduced in Chapter 7 to demonstrate how to align internal processes to support different marketing strategies. Figure 18.1 provides the strategy map for Boise Office Solutions—a $3.5 billion distributor of office and technology products, office furniture,

---

[1] Larry Bossidy and Ram Charan, *Execution: The Discipline of Getting Things Done* (New York: Crown Business, 2002), p. 15.

[2] Robert S. Kaplan and David P. Norton, "Using the Balanced Scorecard as a Strategic Management System," *Harvard Business Review* 74 (January–February 1996): pp. 75–85.

[3] Gary Hamel, "Strategy as Revolution," *Harvard Business Review* 74 (July–August 1996): p. 82. See also, Gary Hamel and Liisa Välikangas, "The Quest for Resilience," *Harvard Business Review* 81 (September 2003): pp. 52–63.

[4] This section is based on Robert S. Kaplan and David P. Norton, *Strategy Maps: Converting Intangible Assets into Tangible Outcomes* (Boston: Harvard Business School Publishing, 2004).

FIGURE 18.1 | **BOISE OFFICE SOLUTIONS STRATEGY MAP**

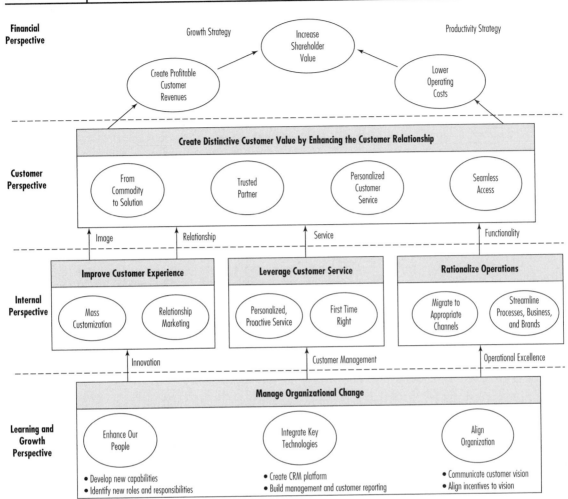

and paper products that developed a distinctive customer relationship strategy, emphasizing customer solutions and personalized service. Leading firms widely use the strategy map concept, developed by Robert S. Kaplan and David P. Norton, because it isolates the interrelationships among four perspectives of a company that the authors refer to as a balanced scorecard[5] (see Chapter 7):

1. A **financial perspective** that describes the expected outcomes of the strategy, such as revenue growth, productivity improvements, or increased shareholder value.

---

[5] Kaplan and Norton, "Using the Balanced Scorecard," pp. 75–85.

2. The **customer perspective** that defines how the firm proposes to deliver a competitively superior value proposition to targeted customers.

3. The **internal perspective** that describes the business processes that have the greatest effect on the chosen strategy, such as customer relationship management (Chapter 4), innovation management (Chapter 10), or supply-chain management (Chapter 14).

4. The **learning and growth perspective** that describes the human capital (personnel), information capital (information technology systems), and organizational capital (climate) that must be aligned to the strategy to support value-creating internal processes.

Using Boise Office Solutions as an illustrative case study, let's explore the six-step process that managers can use to build a tightly integrated strategy.[6]

Developing the Strategy: The Process

A strategy must provide a clear portrait that reveals how a firm will achieve its goals and deliver on its promises to customers, employees, and shareholders.[7] Boise Office Solutions sought a new strategy because the industry continued to consolidate and more and more of its customers viewed office products as a commodity. Without a fresh strategy, company executives believed that these challenging forces would continue to shrink profit margins and put increasing pressure on shareholder value. Likewise, in a service-driven, price-sensitive business, Boise managers were uncertain which customers might contribute the most value over time and how to allocate marketing budgets among the diverse customers that it served—from small businesses to large corporate accounts.[8]

Step 1: Define the Financial Objectives and Establish Growth and Productivity Goals   Strategy maps start with financial objectives for creating shareholder value through two paths: long-term revenue and short-term productivity. The long-term goal often establishes a stretch target that creates a value gap—the difference between a desired future state and current reality. Kaplan and Norton note that the size of the value gap must be established with care: "Executives must balance the benefits from challenging the organization to achieve dramatic improvements in shareholder value with the realities of what can possibly be achieved."[9] So, specific targets for revenue growth and productivity improvements should be established along with a corresponding time line (for example, achieve revenue growth of 15 percent by year one and 30 percent by year three).

Boise adopted a new customer strategy driven by this strategic theme: *Create Distinctive Customer Value by Enhancing the Customer Relationship* (see Figure 18.1). The financial objectives were to increase shareholder value by emphasizing market segmentation and measuring revenue, profit contribution, and cost-to-serve by individual customer segment.

---

[6] Kaplan and Norton, *Strategy Maps*, pp. 355–360.

[7] Robert S. Kaplan and David P. Norton, "Having Trouble with Your Strategy? Then Map It," *Harvard Business Review* 78 (September–October 2000), pp. 167–176.

[8] Kaplan and Norton, *Strategy Maps*, pp. 355–360.

[9] Ibid., p. 353.

Step 2: Define the Customer Value Proposition for Target Customer Segments   Achieving revenue growth goals requires explicit attention to generating revenue from new customers or increasing revenue from existing customers. Thus, the most important component of strategy is to develop and clarify the value proposition for customers in targeted segments. Recall that Chapter 7 presented four major value propositions and customer strategies: low total cost, product leadership, complete customer solutions, and system lock-in.

Boise adopted a customer solutions strategy that enhances value through one-to-one marketing, anticipates customers' needs to create customized service, and provides seamless access across sales channels (for example, sales force, Web, direct mail). A customer satisfaction survey assessed the core elements in the firm's new value proposition. The core objective, "to create distinctive value," was measured by:

- The number of customers retained in targeted segments.

- The number of new customers acquired.

- Estimates of the lifetime value of customers.

Step 3: Establish the Time Line for Results   To develop a coordinated plan, the high-level financial goals must be broken down into targets for particular functions or internal processes, like innovation management, so that organizational members unite behind the strategy and are comfortable with the overall target.

For Boise, operations management processes would reduce the costs of servicing customers, the customer management process would increase the number of relationship customers, and the innovation processes would create new offerings such as contract purchase plans. A time line for performance targets guided the efforts in each group.

Step 4: Identify the Critical Strategic Themes and Internal Processes with the Greatest Impact on the Strategy   This step identifies the key processes in delivering the customer value proposition and reaching the company's financial objectives.

Boise's internal process objectives emphasized three themes (see Figure 18.1):

- *Operational excellence:* Rationalize operations by moving more customers to an e-commerce channel to provide more convenient customer access and lower costs per customer contact.

- *Customer management:* Leverage customer service by personalizing the ordering process, making interactions easier for the customer, and meeting all the customer's needs in a single interaction.

- *Innovation management:* Redefine customer value expectations by creating new tools that customers can use to control spending on office supplies.

Once again, Boise developed measures—such as the percentage of customers in a target segment that used the e-commerce channel—for each of these themes. To illustrate, for operations, success at reaching cost reductions was measured by the percent of business in targeted segments that came through e-channels; for innovation management, success was measured by the number of customers participating in new contract purchasing plans.

Step 5: Identify the Human, Information, and Organizational Resources Required to Support the Strategy   The learning and growth objectives assess how ready the organization is to support the internal processes that drive the strategy. This stage ensures that organizational members are aligned with the strategy and get with the training, information technology, and incentives to successfully implement it.

To introduce the strategy at Boise, every employee saw a video of the CEO describing the strategy, and more than 1,000 employees attended a six-hour course on the new customer management initiative. Moreover, the firm installed a comprehensive customer relationship management (CRM) system and provided 1,500 customer service representatives and managers with 30 hours of training on it.[10] A video was likewise developed for customers to show them the benefits of the new strategy. Among the measures used were the percentage of employees trained for the new customer-centric strategy and the proportion of staff with incentives directly aligned to the strategy.

Step 6: Develop an Action Plan and Provide Required Funding for Each of the Separate Initiatives (Strategic Themes)   To reach financial targets and fulfill the strategic vision, several separate initiatives—involving different functions and processes in the company—must support the overall strategy in a coordinated fashion (see Figure 18.1). These initiatives create the performance results and form the foundation for successfully implementing the strategy. Rather than a series of stand-alone projects, these initiatives should be aligned to the overall strategy and managed as an *integrated* bundle of investments.

Strategy Results   Boise's new strategy allowed the firm to reduce costs, boost growth, and offer even their most price-sensitive customers an integrated solution that delivered greater value than lower-priced competitors. In turn, customer retention improved dramatically, and sales from the firm's most valuable customers expanded. Don Peppers and Martha Rogers describe how the strategy achieves profit targets:

> The firm now has good customer profitability data, which is yielding steady benefits on a customer-by-customer basis. For instance, relying on this data, Boise chose to discontinue working with one of its largest customers, a hospital group that apparently cost Boise money with every sale. And a senior executive visited another customer's headquarters, shared data to show that the company was one of Boise's least profitable accounts, and won a price increase over two years.[11]

Maps: A Tool for Strategy Making

Because a firm's strategy is based on developing a differentiated customer value proposition, the business marketing manager assumes a lead role in both strategy development and implementation. Fundamental to this role is the challenging job of coordinating activities across functions to create and deliver a superior solution for customers.

---

[10]Don Peppers and Martha Rogers, *Return on Customer: A Revolutionary Way to Measure and Strengthen Your Business* (New York: Currency/Doubleday, 2005), pp. 133–134.

[11]Ibid., p. 135.

Translating Objectives into Results   The strategy map, coupled with the measures and targets from the balanced scorecard, provides a valuable framework for the strategist. First, the strategy map clearly describes the strategy, detailing objectives for the critical internal processes that create value and the organizational assets (for example, information technology, employee rewards) needed to support them. Second, the balanced scorecard translates objectives into specific measures and targets that guide critical components of the strategy. Third, to achieve financial or productivity goals, a set of well-integrated action plans must be designed that are carefully aligned to the overall strategy. Attention now turns to the central role of the control process in business marketing management.

Marketing Strategy: Allocating Resources

The purpose of any marketing strategy is to yield the best possible results. Resources are allocated to marketing in general and to individual strategy elements in particular to achieve prescribed objectives. Profit contribution, market share percentage, number of new customers, cost-to-serve customers, and level of expenses and sales are typical performance criteria; but regardless of the criteria, four interrelated evaluations are required to design a marketing strategy:

1. How much should be spent on marketing in the planning period? (This is the budget for achieving marketing objectives.)

2. How are marketing dollars to be allocated? (For example, how much should be spent on advertising? On personal selling?)

3. Within each element of the marketing strategy, how should dollars be allocated to best achieve marketing objectives? (For example, which advertising media should be selected? How should sales personnel be deployed among customers and prospects?)

4. Which market segments, products, and geographic areas are most profitable? (Each market segment may require a different amount of effort because of competitive intensity or market potential.)

Guiding Strategy Formulation

Evaluation outcomes provide the foundation for integrating the market strategy formulation and the marketing control system. Results in the most recent operating period show how successful past marketing efforts were in meeting objectives. Performance below or above expectations then signals where funds should be reallocated. If the firm expected to reach 20 percent of the OEM market but reached only 12 percent, a change in strategy may be required. Performance information provided by the control system might demonstrate that sales personnel in the OEM market were reaching only 45 percent of potential buyers; additional funds could be allocated to expand either the sales force or the advertising budget.

Managing Individual Customers for Profit[12]

As explored in Chapter 4, business marketers should also focus on revenues from individual customers and isolate the cost-to-serve them. For relationship customers, attention should be given to the share-of-wallet the firm is attracting. **Share-of-wallet** represents the portion of total purchases in a product and service category (for example, information technology) that a customer makes from the firm (for example, Hewlett-Packard).

For customers with a more transactional focus, the business marketer should:

- Develop a customer database that profiles the past purchasing patterns of customers.

- Determine the cost-to-serve each customer.

- Set a revenue target and profit goal.

- Develop a customer contact plan that details the sales channel (for example, direct sales, telesales, Web-based contact) to be used.

- Monitor performance results and the relative effectiveness of different sales channels.

Marketing managers must weigh the interactions among the strategy elements and allocate resources to create effective and efficient strategies. To do so, a system for monitoring past performance is an absolute necessity. In effect, the control system enables management to keep abreast of all facets of performance.

The Marketing Control Process

Marketing control is a process management uses to generate information on marketing performance. Two major forms of control are (1) control over efficient allocation of marketing effort and (2) comparison of planned and actual performance. In the first case, the business marketer may use past profitability data as a standard for evaluating future marketing expenditures. The second form of control alerts management to any differences between planned and actual performance and may also reveal reasons for performance discrepancies.

Control at Various Levels

The control process is universal in that it can be applied to any level of marketing analysis. For example, business marketers must frequently evaluate whether their general strategies are appropriate and effective. However, it is equally important to know whether the individual elements in the strategy are effectively integrated for a given market. Further, management must evaluate resource allocation within a particular element (for example, the effectiveness of direct selling versus that of industrial distributors). The control system should work in any of these situations. The four primary levels of marketing control are delineated in Table 18.1.

---

[12]Roland T. Rust, Katherine N. Lemon, and Das Narayandas, *Customer Equity Management* (Upper Saddle River, N.J.: Prentice-Hall, 2005), pp. 426–428.

TABLE 18.1 | LEVELS OF MARKETING CONTROL

Type of Control	Primary Responsibility	Purpose of Control	Tools
Strategic control	Top management	To examine whether the company is pursuing its best opportunities with respect to markets, products, and channels	Marketing audit
Annual plan control	Top management, middle management	To examine whether the planned results are being achieved	Sales analysis; market-share analysis; expense-to-sales ratios; other ratios; attitude tracking
Efficiency and effectiveness control	Middle management	To examine how well resources have been utilized in each element of the marketing strategy to accomplish a specific goal	Expense ratios; advertising effectiveness measures; market potential; contribution margin analysis
Profitability control	Marketing controller	To examine where the company is making and losing money	Profitability by product territory, market segment, trade channel, order size

SOURCE: Adapted from Philip Kotler, *Marketing Management: The Millennium Edition* (Englewood Cliffs, N.J.: Prentice-Hall, 2000), p. 698.

Strategic Control

Strategic control is based on a comprehensive evaluation of whether the firm is headed in the right direction. Strategic control focuses on assessing whether the strategy is being implemented as planned and whether it produces the intended results.[13] Because the business marketing environment changes rapidly, existing product/market situations may lose their potential and new product/market matchups provide important opportunities. Philip Kotler suggests that the firm periodically conduct a **marketing audit**—a comprehensive, periodic, and systematic evaluation of marketing operations that specifically analyzes the market environment and the firm's internal marketing activities.[14] An analysis of the environment assesses company image, customer characteristics, competitive activities, regulatory constraints, and economic trends. Evaluating this information may uncover threats the firm can counter and future opportunities it can exploit.

An internal evaluation of the marketing system scrutinizes marketing objectives, organization, and implementation. In this way, management may be able to spot where existing products could be adapted to new markets or new products could be developed for existing markets. The regular, systematic marketing audit is a valuable technique for evaluating the direction of marketing strategies.[15]

[13] Philip Kotler, "A Three-Part Plan for Upgrading Your Marketing Department for New Challenges," *Strategy & Leadership* 32 (May 2004), pp. 4–9.

[14] Philip Kotler, *Marketing Management: The Millennium Edition* (Englewood Cliffs, N.J.: Prentice-Hall, 2000), pp. 708–709; and Michael P. Mokwa, "The Strategic Marketing Audit: An Adoption/Utilization Perspective," *Journal of Business Strategy* 7 (winter 1986), pp. 88–95.

[15] For example, see Philip Kotler, William T. Gregor, and William Rogers III, "SMR Classic Reprint: The Marketing Audit Comes of Age," *Sloan Management Review* 20 (winter 1989): pp. 49–62; and Mokwa, "The Strategic Marketing Audit," pp. 88–95.

TABLE 18.2 | **REVIEWING STRATEGIC OPTIONS: SEVEN TOUGH QUESTIONS**

1. **Suitability: Is there a sustainable advantage?**
   (For example, assess each strategy option in light of the capabilities of the business and the likely responses of key competitors.)

2. **Validity: Are the assumptions realistic?**
   (For example, are assumptions concerning sales, profits, and competition based on fact?)

3. **Flexibility: Do we have the skills, resources, and commitments?**
   (For example, is there an adequate sales force, advertising budget, and commitment of key personnel?)

4. **Consistency: Does the strategy hang together?**
   (For example, is it internally consistent across the functional areas in the firm?)

5. **Vulnerability: What are the risks and contingencies?**
   (For example, if important assumptions are wrong, what are the risks inherent in each strategy alternative?)

6. **Adaptability: Can we retain our flexibility?**
   (For example, if a major contingency occurs, could the strategy be reversed in the future?)

7. **Financial desirability: How much economic value is created?**
   (For example, relate the attractiveness of expected performance to the probable risk of each option.)

SOURCE: Adapted from George S. Day, "Tough Questions for Developing Strategies," *Journal of Business Strategy* 7 (winter 1986): pp. 60–68.

Strategic Dialogue: Ask Tough Questions To offer promise, George Day asserts, a strategic option must meet several tests. "Effective business strategies are formed in a crucible of debate and dialogue between and within many levels of management. The challenge is to encourage realism in the dialogue—so critical decisions are not distorted by wishful thinking and myopic analysis—while not suppressing creativity and risk taking."[16] Day suggests that many strategies fail because no one asks the right questions at the right time while strategy is being formulated. He offers insightful questions (Table 18.2) to guide the analysis of strategy options. These tough questions are fundamental to the strategic control process.

Annual Plan Control

In **annual plan control,** the objectives specified in the plan become the performance standards against which actual results are compared. Sales volume, profits, and market share are the typical performance standards for business marketers. **Sales analysis** is an attempt to determine why actual sales varied from planned sales. Expected sales may not be met because of price reductions, inadequate volume, or both. A sales analysis separates the effects of these variables so that corrective action can be taken.

 Market share analysis assesses how the firm is doing relative to competition. A machine-tool manufacturer's 10 percent sales increase may, on the surface, appear

---

[16]George S. Day, "Tough Questions for Developing Strategies," *Journal of Business Strategy* 7 (winter 1986), p. 68. See also George S. Day, "Aligning the Organization with the Market," *MSI Working Paper Series*, Issue Three, No. 05-003 (Cambridge, Mass.: Marketing Science Institute, 2005).

TABLE 18.3 | OPERATING RESULTS FOR A SAMPLE PRODUCT

Item	Planned	Actual	Variance
Revenues			
Sales (units)	20,000,000	22,000,000	+2,000,000
Price per unit ($)	0.50	0.4773	−0.0227
Total market (units)	40,000,000	50,000,000	−10,000,000
Share of market	50%	44%	−6%
Revenues ($)	10,000,000	10,500,000	+500,000
Variable costs ($0.30 unit) ($)	6,000,000	6,600,000	−600,000
Profit contribution ($)	4,000,000	3,900,000	−100,000

SOURCE: Adapted from James M. Hulbert and Norman E. Toy, "A Strategic Framework for Marketing Control," *Journal of Marketing* 41 (April 1977): p. 13.

favorable. However, if total machine-tool industry sales are up 25 percent, a market share analysis would show that the firm has not fared well relative to competitors.

Finally, **expense-to-sales ratios** are analyses of the efficiency of marketing operations—whether the firm is overspending or underspending. Frequently, industry standards or past company ratios provide standards of comparison. Total marketing expenses and expenses of each strategic marketing element are evaluated in relation to sales. Recall the discussion in Chapter 16 on advertising expenditures, which provided a range of advertising expense-to-sales ratios for business-to-business firms. These figures provide management with a basis for evaluating the company's performance.

A Framework for Marketing Control James Hulbert and Norman Toy suggest a comprehensive framework for integrating such measures into a marketing control system.[17] Table 18.3 describes how the framework can identify what caused actual product profitability to vary from planned profitability. The objective is to isolate the reasons for the differences between planned and actual results (the variances displayed in the last column)—specifically the profit contribution variance.

In this case, management seeks to understand why actual profit contribution was $100,000 less than planned profits. A detailed analysis of the data shows that although total sales were larger than expected (22 million versus 20 million units), the firm failed to achieve its targeted market share. In addition, the firm was unable to maintain its price policy. Management must review its forecasting, considering that it underestimated market size by 25 percent (40 million versus 50 million). To the extent that marketing strategy allocations are predicated on estimated market size, the firm may have failed to allocate sufficient effort to this market. The variances point to some real weaknesses in the forecasting process.

---

[17] James M. Hulbert and Norman E. Toy, "A Strategic Framework for Marketing Control," *Journal of Marketing* 41 (April 1977): pp. 12–19; see also Nigel F. Piercy, "The Marketing Budgeting Process: Marketing Management Implications," *Journal of Marketing* 51 (October 1987): pp. 45–59.

TABLE 18.4 | ILLUSTRATIVE MEASURES FOR EFFICIENCY AND EFFECTIVENESS CONTROL

Product

Sales by market segments
Sales relative to potential
Sales growth rates
Market share
Contribution margin
Percentage of total profits
Return on investment

Distribution

Sales, expenses, and contribution by channel type
Sales and contribution margin by intermediary type and individual intermediaries
Sales relative to market potential by channel, intermediary type, and specific intermediaries
Expense-to-sales ratio by channel, etc.
Logistics cost by logistics activity by channel

Communication

Advertising effectiveness by type of media
Actual audience/target audience ratio
Cost per contact
Number of calls, inquiries, and information requests by type of media
Dollar sales per sales call
Sales per territory relative to potential
Selling expenses to sales ratios
New accounts per time period

Pricing

Price changes relative to sales volume
Discount structure related to sales volume
Bid strategy related to new contracts
Margin structure related to marketing expenses
General price policy related to sales volume
Margins related to channel member performance

Because the firm did not share proportionately with its competitors in the market growth, the entire marketing strategy must be reevaluated. Management apparently underestimated how much it had to reduce prices to expand volume. Clearly, annual plan control provides valuable insights into where the plan faltered and suggests the type of remedial action that should be taken.

Efficiency and Effectiveness Control

Efficiency control examines how efficiently resources are being used in each element of marketing strategy (for example, sales force, advertising); **effectiveness control** evaluates whether the strategic component is accomplishing its objective. A good control system provides continuing data for evaluating the efficiency of resources used for a given element of marketing strategy to accomplish a given objective. Table 18.4 provides a representative sample of the types of data required. Performance measures and

INSIDE BUSINESS MARKETING

Digital Cockpits to Track Corporate Financial Performance

A growing number of companies have developed sophisticated control systems that allow executives to monitor key performance indicators daily or even minute by minute. The terms *digital cockpits* or *dashboards* have been coined to describe these systems. GE was one of the first companies to embrace the concept, and currently, executives within each of the firm's 11 divisions can log on to the corporate intranet and examine the division's health on several performance indicators—sales, orders and pricing, manufacturing costs, and others. If, for example, a particular measurement, like sales, goes above or below a predetermined threshold, the numbers are red. By clicking on that number, the executive sees another screen that provides the underlying data. For performance numbers that fall outside a predetermined range, the executive is alerted to the problem by e-mail. Xerox uses a similar system to analyze marketing's effect on a range of performance measures—from leads generated to cost per sale.

Larry Biagini, chief technology officer at GE, observes that digital cockpits speed decision making: "These things are all about making sure we react before things get out of hand. They're how you feel the pulse of your business."

SOURCE: Bob Tedeschi, "E-Commerce Report: Digital Cockpits Are a Faster, Much Closer Way of Tracking Performance in a Corporation's Every Corner," *New York Times*, July 29, 2002, p. C6, and Diane Brady, "Making Marketing Measure Up," *Business Week*, December 13, 2004, pp. 112–113.

standards vary by company and situation, according to the goals and objectives in the marketing plan.

Recall the extensive discussion in Chapter 6 of techniques and procedures for calculating market potential. Because potential represents the opportunity to sell, it provides an excellent benchmark for measuring performance. Analysis of performance relative to potential can be made for distribution channels, channel members, and products. The results are sometimes combined with profitability control, the last area of a comprehensive control system.

Profitability Control

The essence of **profitability control** is to describe where the firm is making or losing money in terms of the important segments of its business. A **segment** is the unit of analysis management uses for control purposes; it may be customer segments, product lines, territories, or channel structures. Suppose a business marketing firm focuses on three customer segments: health-care organizations, universities, and local government units. To allocate the marketing budget among the three segments, management must consider the profit contribution of each segment and its expected potential. Profitability control, then, provides a methodology for linking marketing costs and revenues with specific segments of the business.

Profitability by Market Segment Relating sales revenues and marketing costs to market segments improves decision making. More specifically, say Leland Beik and Stephen Buzby,

For both strategic and tactical decisions, marketing managers may profit by knowing the effect of the marketing mix on the target segment at which marketing efforts are aimed. If the programs are to be responsive to environmental change, a monitoring system is needed to locate problems and guide adjustments in marketing decisions. Tracing the profitability of segments permits improved pricing, selling, advertising, channel, and product management decisions. The success of marketing policies and programs may be appraised by a dollar-and-cents measure of profitability by segment.[18]

Profitability control, a prerequisite to strategy planning and implementation, has stringent information requirements. To be effective, the firm needs a marketing–accounting information system.

An Activity-Based Cost System   The accounting system must first be able to link costs with the various marketing activities and must then attach these "activity" costs to the important segments to be analyzed. The critical element in the process is to trace all costs to the activities (warehousing, advertising, and so on) for which the resources are used and then to the products or segments that consume them.[19] Such an **activity-based cost (ABC) system** reveals the links between performing particular activities and the demands those activities make on the organization's resources. As a result, it can give managers a clear picture of how products, brands, customers, facilities, regions, or distribution channels both generate revenues and consume resources.[20] An ABC analysis focuses attention on improving activities that have the greatest effect on profits.

Robin Cooper and Robert Kaplan capture the essence of ABC:

> ABC analysis enables managers to slice into the business many different ways—by product or group of similar products, by individual customer or client group, or by distribution channel—and gives them a close-up view of whatever slice they are considering. ABC analysis also illuminates exactly what activities are associated with that part of the business and how those activities are linked to the generation of revenues and the consumption of resources. By highlighting those relationships, ABC helps managers understand precisely where to take actions that drives profits. In contrast to traditional accounting, activity-based costing segregates the expenses of indirect and support resources by activities. It then assigns those expenses based on the drivers of the activities, rather than by some arbitrary percentage allocation.[21]

ABC System Illustrated[22]   ABC analysis highlights for managers where their actions will likely have the greatest effect on profits. The ABC system at Kanthal

[18] Leland L. Beik and Stephen L. Buzby, "Profitability Analysis by Market Segments," *Journal of Marketing* 37 (July 1973): p. 49. See also Fred A. Jacobs, Wesley Johnston, and Natalia Kotchetova, "Customer Profitability: Prospective vs. Retrospective Approaches in a Business-to-Business Setting," *Industrial Marketing Management* 30 (June 2001): pp. 353–363.

[19] Robin Cooper and Robert S. Kaplan, "Measure Costs Right: Make the Right Decisions," *Harvard Business Review* 66 (September–October 1988): p. 96. For a related discussion, see Robin Cooper and W. Bruce Chew, "Control Tomorrow's Costs through Today's Designs," *Harvard Business Review* 74 (January–February 1996): pp. 88–97.

[20] Robin Cooper and Robert S. Kaplan, "Profit Priorities from Activity-Based Costing," *Harvard Business Review* 69 (May–June 1993): p. 130. See also Robin Cooper and Robert S. Kaplan, "The Promise—and Peril—of Integrated Cost Systems," *Harvard Business Review* 76 (July–August 1998): pp. 109–118.

[21] Cooper and Kaplan, "Profit Priorities from Activity-Based Costing," p. 131. See also, Robert S. Kaplan and Steven R. Anderson, "Time-Driven Activity-Based Costing," *Harvard Business Review* 82 (November 2004): pp. 131–138.

[22] This section is based on Cooper and Kaplan, "Profit Priorities from Activity-Based Costing," p. 130 and Cooper and Kaplan, "The Promise—and Peril—of Integrated Cost Systems," pp. 109–119.

Corporation led to a review of profitability by size of customer (see Chapter 4). Kanthal, a manufacturer of heating wire, used activity-based costing to analyze its customer profitability and discovered that the well-known 80/20 rule (80 percent of sales generated by 20 percent of customers) was in need of revision. A 20/225 rule was actually operating: 20 percent of customers were generating 225 percent of profits. The middle 70 percent of customers were hovering around the break-even point, and Kanthal was losing 125 percent of its profits on 10 percent of its customers.

The Kanthal customers generating the greatest losses were among those with the largest sales volume. Initially, this finding surprised managers, but it soon began to make sense. You can't lose large amounts of money on a small customer. The large, unprofitable customers demanded lower prices, frequent deliveries of small lots, extensive sales and technical resources, and product changes. The newly revealed economics enabled management to change the way it did business with these customers—through price changes, minimum order sizes, and information technology—transforming the customers into strong profit contributors.

Using the ABC System   An ABC system requires the firm to break from traditional accounting concepts. Managers must refrain from allocating all expenses to individual units and instead separate the expenses and match them to the activity that consumes the resources.[23] Once resource expenditures are related to the activities they produce, management can explore different strategies for reducing the resource commitments. To enhance profitability, business marketing managers need to figure out how to reduce expenditures on those resources or increase the output they produce. For example, a sales manager would search for ways to reduce the number of sales calls on unprofitable customers or find ways to make the salesperson more effective with them. In summary, ABC systems enable the business marketing manager to focus on increasing profitability by understanding the sources of cost variability and developing strategies to reduce resource commitment or enhance resource productivity.

Feedforward Control

Much of the information provided by the firm's marketing control system offers feedback on what has been accomplished in both financial (profits) and nonfinancial (customer satisfaction, market share) terms. As such, the control process is remedial in its outlook. Raghu Tadepalli argues that the control system should be forward looking and preventative, and the control process should start at the same time as the planning process—the control process should check the validity of planning assumptions at each stage.[24] Such a form of control is referred to as **feedforward control.**

Feedforward control involves continuous evaluation of plans—monitoring the environment to detect changes that would support the revision of objectives and strategies. Feedforward control monitors variables other than performance—variables that may change before performance itself changes. The result is that deviations can be controlled before the firm feels their full impact. For example, a manufacturer would want to monitor events correlated to sales that provide early warnings. Thus, continuous

---

[23] Cooper and Kaplan, "Profit Priorities from Activity-Based Costing," p. 130.

[24] Raghu Tadepalli, "Marketing Control: Reconceptualization and Implementation Using the Feedforward Method," *European Journal of Marketing* 26, no. 1 (1992): pp. 24–40. See also Donald N. Sull, "Strategy as Active Waiting," *Harvard Business Review* 83 (September 2005): pp. 121–129.

evaluation of late delivery complaints by distributors would cause the firm to adjust its logistics service if the level of complaints started to increase. In this way a possible loss of sales precipitated by slow deliveries could be avoided. Feedforward control focuses on information that is prognostic: It tries to discover problems waiting to occur. Formal feedforward control processes can be incorporated into the business marketer's total control program to considerably enhance its effectiveness. A feedforward approach would help ensure that planning and control are treated as concurrent activities.

Implementation of Business Marketing Strategy

Many marketing plans fail because they are poorly implemented. Implementation is the critical link between strategy formulation and superior organizational performance.[25] **Marketing implementation** is the process that translates marketing plans into action assignments and ensures that such assignments are executed in a manner that accomplishes a plan's defined objectives.[26] Special implementation challenges emerge for the marketing manager because diverse functional areas participate in both developing and executing strategy.

The Strategy-Implementation Fit

Thomas Bonoma asserts that "marketing strategy and implementation affect each other. Although strategy obviously affects actions, execution also affects marketing strategies, especially over time."[27] Although the dividing line between strategy and execution is a bit fuzzy, it is often not difficult to diagnose implementation problems and distinguish them from strategy deficiencies. Bonoma presents the following scenario:

> A firm introduced a new portable microcomputer that incorporated a number of features that the target market valued. The new product appeared to be well positioned in a rapidly growing market, but initial sales results were miserable. Why? The 50-person sales force had little incentive to grapple with a new unfamiliar product and continued to emphasize the older models. Given the significant market potential, management had decided to set the sales incentive compensation level lower on the new machines than on the older ones. The older models had a selling cycle one-half as long as the new product and required no software knowledge or support.

In this case, poor execution damaged good strategy.[28]

Marketing strategy and implementation affect each other. When both strategy and implementation are appropriate, the firm is likely to meet its objectives. Diagnosis

---

[25] Charles H. Noble and Michael P. Mokwa, "Implementing Marketing Strategies: Developing and Testing a Managerial Theory," *Journal of Marketing* 63 (October 1999): pp. 57–73.

[26] Kotler, *Marketing Management: The Millennium Edition*, p. 695.

[27] Thomas V. Bonoma, "Making Your Marketing Strategy Work," *Harvard Business Review* 62 (March–April 1984): pp. 69–76.

[28] Ibid., p. 70.

becomes more difficult in other cases. For example, the cause of a marketing problem may be hard to detect when the strategy is on the mark but the implementation is poor. The business marketer may never become aware of the soundness of the strategy. Alternatively, excellent implementation of a poor strategy may give managers time to see the problem and correct it.

Implementation Skills

Thomas Bonoma identifies four important implementation skills for marketing managers: (1) interacting, (2) allocating, (3) monitoring, and (4) organizing.[29] Each assumes special significance in the business marketing environment.

Marketing managers are continually *interacting* with others both within and outside the corporation. Inside, a number of peers (for example, R&D personnel) over whom the marketer has little power often assume a crucial role in strategy development and implementation. Outside, the marketer deals with important customers, channel members, advertising agencies, and the like. The best implementers have good bargaining skills and the ability to understand how others feel.[30]

The implementer must also *allocate* time, assignments, people, dollars, and other resources among the marketing tasks at hand. Astute marketing managers, says Bonoma, are "tough and fair in putting people and dollars where they will be most effective. The less able ones routinely allocate too many dollars and people to mature programs and too few to richer ones."[31]

Bonoma asserts that marketing managers with good *monitoring* skills exhibit flexibility and intelligence in dealing with the firm's information and control systems: "Good implementers struggle and wrestle with their markets and businesses until they can simply and powerfully express the 'back of the envelope' ratios necessary to run the business, regardless of formal control system inadequacies."[32]

Finally, the best implementers are effective at *organizing*. Sound execution often hinges on the marketer's ability to work with both the formal and the informal organizational networks. The manager customizes an informal organization to solve problems and facilitate good execution.

The Marketing Strategy Center: An Implementation Guide[33]

Diverse functional areas participate to differing degrees in developing and implementing business marketing strategy. Research and development, manufacturing, technical service, physical distribution, and other functional areas play fundamental roles. Ronald McTavish points out that "marketing specialists understand markets, but know a good deal less about the nuts and bolts of the company's operations—its internal terrain. This is the domain of the operating specialist. We need to bring these different specialists

---

[29] Ibid.

[30] Michael D. Hutt, "Cross-Functional Working Relationships in Marketing," *Journal of the Academy of Marketing Science* 23 (fall 1995): pp. 351–357.

[31] Bonoma, "Making Your Marketing Strategy Work," p. 75.

[32] Ibid.

[33] Michael D. Hutt and Thomas W. Speh, "The Marketing Strategy Center: Diagnosing the Industrial Marketer's Interdisciplinary Role," *Journal of Marketing* 48 (fall 1984): pp. 53–61; and Michael D. Hutt, Beth A. Walker, and Gary L. Frankwick, "Hurdle the Cross-Functional Barriers to Strategic Change," *Sloan Management Review* 36 (spring 1995): pp. 22–30.

TABLE 18.5 | **INTERFUNCTIONAL INVOLVEMENT IN MARKETING STRATEGY IMPLEMENTATION: AN ILLUSTRATIVE RESPONSIBILITY CHART**

Decision Area	Marketing	Sales	Manufac-turing	R&D	Purchasing	Physical Distri-bution	Tech-nical Service	Strategic Business Unit	Corporate-Level Planner
Product/ service quality									
Technical service support									
Physical distribution service									
National accounts management									
Channel relations									
Sales support									
Product/ service innovation									

NOTE: Use the following abbreviations to indicate decision roles: R = responsible; A = approval; C = consult; M = implement; I = inform; X = no role in decision.

together in a 'synergistic pooling' of knowledge and viewpoint to achieve the best fit of the company's skills with the market and the company's approach to it."[34] This suggests a challenging and pivotal interdisciplinary role for the marketing manager in the business-to-business firm.

The marketing strategy center (discussed in Chapter 7) provides a framework for highlighting this interdisciplinary role and for exploring key implementation requirements. Table 18.5 highlights important strategic topics examined throughout this textbook. In each case, nonmarketing personnel play active implementation roles. For example, product quality is directly or indirectly affected by several departments: manufacturing, research and development, technical service, and others. In turn, successful product innovation reflects the collective efforts of individuals from several functional areas. Clearly, effective strategy implementation requires well-defined decision roles, responsibilities, timetables, and coordination mechanisms.

On a global market scale, special coordination challenges emerge when selected activities such as R&D are concentrated in one country and other strategy activities such as manufacturing are dispersed across countries. Xerox, however, has been successful in

---

[34]Ronald McTavish, "Implementing Marketing Strategy," *Industrial Marketing Management* 26 (November 5, 1988): p. 10. See also Deborah Dougherty and Edward H. Bowman, "The Effects of Organizational Downsizing on Product Innovation," *California Management Review* 37 (summer 1995): pp. 28–44.

B2B TOP PERFORMERS

Cross-Functional Relationships: Effective Managers Deliver on Promises

Ask an R&D manager to identify a colleague from marketing who is particularly effective at getting things done and he or she readily offers a name and a memorable episode to justify the selection. To explore the characteristics of high-performing cross-functional managers, detailed accounts of effective and ineffective interactions were gathered from managers at a *Fortune* 100 high-technology firm. Interestingly, the top-of-mind characteristics that colleagues emphasize when describing high performers are soft skills like openness rather than hard skills like technical proficiency or marketing savvy. Here's a profile:

- High-performing managers are revered by their colleagues for their *responsiveness*. Remembering effective cross-functional episodes, colleagues describe high performers as "timely," "prompt," and "responsive" (for example, "When I need critical information, I turn to him and he gets right back to me").

- Rather than a "functional mindset," high performers demonstrate *perspective-taking* skills—the ability to anticipate and understand the perspectives and priorities of managers from other units (for example, "He's a superb marketing strategist but he

also recognizes the special technical issues that we've been working through to get this product launched on schedule").

- When colleagues describe the *communication style* of their high-performing cross-functional counterparts, they focus on three consistent themes: openness, frequency, and quality. Interactions with high performers are described as "candid," "unencumbered," and characterized by a "free flow of thoughts and suggestions." Such high-quality interactions clarify goals and responsibilities.

By "delivering on their promises," effective managers develop a web of close relationships across functions. "He has really good personal relationships with a lot of people and he has a network—he really understands the mechanisms that you have to use to get things done."

SOURCE: Michael D. Hutt, Beth A. Walker, Edward U. Bond III, and Matthew Meuter, "Diagnosing Marketing Managers' Effective and Ineffective Cross-Functional Interactions," working paper, Tempe, Ariz.: Arizona State University, 2005. See also Edward U. Bond III, Beth A. Walker, Michael D. Hutt, and Peter H. Reingen, "Reputational Effectiveness in Cross-Functional Working Relationships," *Journal of Product Innovation Management* 21 (January 2004): pp. 44–60.

maintaining a high level of coordination across such dispersed activities. The Xerox brand, marketing approach, and servicing procedures are standardized worldwide.[35]

The Marketer's Role   To ensure maximum customer satisfaction and the desired market response, the business marketer must assume an active role in the strategy center by negotiating market-sensitive agreements and coordinating strategies with other members. While being influenced by other functional areas to varying degrees in the process, the marketer can potentially influence key areas such as the design of the logistical system, the selection of manufacturing technology, or the structure of a materials management system. Such negotiation with other functional areas is fundamental to the business marketer's strategic interdisciplinary role. Thus, the successful business marketing manager performs as an integrator by drawing on the collective strengths of the enterprise to satisfy customer needs profitably.

---

[35] Michael E. Porter, "Changing Patterns of International Competition," *California Management Review* 28 (winter 1986): pp. 9–40.

FIGURE 18.2 | **A FRAMEWORK FOR BUSINESS MARKETING MANAGEMENT**

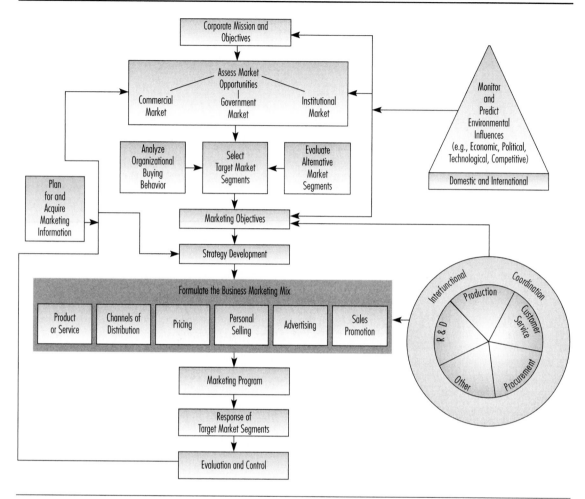

Looking Back

Figure 18.2 synthesizes the central components of business marketing management and highlights the material presented in this textbook. Part I introduced the major classes of customers that constitute the business market: commercial enterprises, governmental units, and institutions. The timely themes of organizational buying behavior and customer relationship management provided the focus of Part II. Part III discussed the tools for assessing market opportunities; it explored techniques for measuring market potential, identifying market segments, and forecasting sales. Functionally integrated marketing planning provides a framework for dealing with each component of the business marketing mix, as detailed in Part IV. Special attention was also given to the special challenges and unique opportunities that rapidly developing economies present for business-to-business firms.

Once business marketing strategy is formulated, the manager must evaluate the response of target market segments to minimize any discrepancy between planned and actual results. This chapter, which constitutes Part V, explores the critical dimensions of the marketing control process, which is the final loop in the model presented in Figure 18.2: planning for and acquiring marketing information. Such information forms the core of the firm's management information system; it is derived internally through the marketing-accounting system and externally through the marketing research function. Evaluation and control enable the marketer to reassess business market opportunities and make adjustments as needed in business marketing strategy.

Summary

Central to market strategy is the allocation of resources to each strategy element and the application of marketing efforts to segments. The marketing control system is the process by which the business marketing firm generates information to make these decisions. Moreover, the marketing control system is the means by which current performance can be evaluated and steps can be taken to correct deficiencies. Used in conjunction with the balanced scorecard, the strategy map converts a strategy vision into concrete objectives and measures, organized into four different perspectives: financial, customer, internal business process, and learning and growth. The approach involves developing a customer strategy, identifying target market segments, isolating the critical internal processes the firm must develop to deliver value to customers in these segments, and selecting the organizational capabilities needed to achieve customer and financial objectives. A strategy map provides a visual representation of a firm's critical objectives and the cause-and-effect relationships among them that drive superior organizational performance.

An effective control system has four distinct components. Strategic control, which is operationalized through the marketing audit, provides valuative information on the present and future course of the firm's basic product/market mission. Annual plan control compares annual with planned results to provide input for future planning. Efficiency and effectiveness control evaluates whether marketing strategy elements achieve their goals in a cost-effective manner. Finally, profitability control seeks to evaluate profitability by segment.

Many business marketing plans fail because they are poorly executed. Marketing implementation is the process that translates marketing plans into action assignments and ensures that such assignments are executed in a timely and effective manner. Four implementation skills are particularly important to the business marketing manager: (1) interacting, (2) allocating, (3) monitoring, and (4) organizing. Nonmarketing personnel play active roles in implementing business marketing strategy. This suggests a challenging and pivotal interdisciplinary role for the marketing manager.

Discussion Questions

1. Discuss why a firm that plans to enter a new market segment may have to develop new internal business processes to serve customers in this segment.

2. Not all customer demands can be satisfied profitably. What steps should be taken by a marketing manager who learns that particular customer accounts—including some long-standing ones—are unprofitable?

3. Describe the relationships between and among the four central perspectives represented in the balanced scorecard and included in a strategy map: financial, customer, internal business process, and learning and growth.

4. Last December, Lisa Schmitt, vice president of marketing at Bock Machine Tool, identified four market segments her firm would attempt to penetrate this year. As this year comes to an end, Lisa would like to evaluate the firm's performance in each of these segments. Of course, Lisa turns to you for assistance. First, what information would you seek from the firm's marketing information system to perform the analysis? Second, how would you know whether the firm's performance in a particular market segment was good or bad?

5. Susan Breck, president of Breck Chemical Corporation, added three new products to the firm's line two years ago to serve the needs of five SIC groups. Each of the products has a separate advertising budget, although they are sold by the same salespersons. Susan requests your assistance in determining what type of information the firm should gather to monitor and control the performance of these products. Outline your reply.

6. Assume that the information you requested in question 5 has been gathered for you. How would you determine whether advertising and personal selling funds should be shifted from one product to another?

7. Hamilton Tucker, president of Tucker Manufacturing Company, is concerned about the seat-of-the-pants approach managers use in allocating the marketing budget. He cites the Midwest and the East as examples. The firm increased its demand-stimulating expenditures (for example, advertising, personal selling) in the Midwest by 20 percent, but sales climbed only 6 percent last year. In contrast, demand-stimulating expenditures were cut by 17 percent in the East, and sales dropped by 22 percent. Hamilton would like you to assist the midwestern and eastern regional managers in allocating their funds next year. Carefully outline the approach you would follow.

8. Delineate the central components of the marketing control process. Describe the role of the control system in formal marketing planning.

9. Using the marketing strategy center concept as a guide, describe how a strategy that is entirely appropriate for a particular target market might fail because of poor implementation in the logistics and technical service areas.

10. Describe how the strategy implementation challenges for a marketing manager working at DuPont (an industrial firm) might be different from those for a marketing manager working at Pillsbury (a consumer-goods firm).

Internet Exercise

McKinsey & Company is a leading management consulting firm. The company publishes *McKinsey Quarterly,* an online journal that features the latest thinking on business strategy, finance, and management. Go to http://www.mckinsey.com, click on *McKinsey Quarterly,* and conduct a search for articles on "strategy implementation." Select a recent article on this topic and briefly outline the key insights that the article provides.

CASE

Sealed Air Corporation: Delivering Package Solutions[36]

Sealed Air Corporation is a global leader in providing business customers with performance solutions for food, protective, and specialty packaging. Best known for its Bubblewrap cushioning material, the firm has pioneered a number of packaging innovations that have sustained a remarkable pattern of sales growth for more than two decades. Sealed Air derives 40 percent of its revenue from protective packaging products that provide superior protection against shock, abrasion, and vibration, compared with other forms of packaging. Such packaging solutions are embraced by long-standing customers, like Mikasa, a company that offers delicate china, dinnerware, stemware, and decorative accessories. In addition to protective packaging, Sealed Air generates 60 percent of its sales from food and specialty packaging products. These materials are sold to food processors and food-service organizations for packaging produce, dairy products, smoked and processed meat, fish, bakery items, and related products.

Sealed Air has more than 1,200 field sales and technical support professionals worldwide, many of whom are food scientists or packaging specialists. Using a consultative selling approach, Sealed Air incorporates both packaging materials and specialized equipment to provide a complete packaging system solution. In turn, the firm supports the product development and package design activities of its customers through 35 package design and food science laboratories around the world.

Discussion Question

Sealed Air serves two distinctly different customer groups: (1) customers like Mikasa that desire protective packaging solutions, and (2) customers like Oscar Meyer or Carnation that seek food packaging solutions. Drawing on the balanced scorecard and the strategy map, how would Sealed Air's internal business processes (for example, new product development) differ for the protective packaging business versus the food packaging business? From a learning and growth perspective, are different employee competencies required to serve one customer group versus the other? Discuss.

---

[36]http://www.sealedair.com, Company Profile, accessed November 7, 2005.

Case Planning Guide

PAGE	CASE #	CASE TITLE	Relevant Chapters																	
			1	2	3	4	5	6	7	8	9	10	11	12	13	14	15	16	17	18
466	1	S.C. Johnson's Professional Division	★	★	★	★														
468	2	Westward Industries Ltd. (A)	★	★	★	★			★		★	★								
483	3	Clariant Corporation Marketing					★	★	★										★	★
498	4	RJM Enterprises, Inc.—Romancing the Vine	★	★	★	★		★								★				★
531	5	Pfizer, Inc. Animal Health Products—A: Market Segmentation and Industry Changes			★		★	★	★											
543	6	Circuit Board Corporation					★	★	★		★	★								
556	7	Beta Pharmaceuticals: Pennsylvania Distribution System													★	★				
562	8	Pivot International—Pursuing Growth					★	★	★	★			★							
583	9	Deere & Company Worldwide Logistics			★	★									★	★				
588	10	Yield Management at American Airlines															★			★
594	11	Barro Stickney, Inc.													★			★		
600	12	Advanced Elastomer Systems: Market Strategy for a New, Technical Product				★	★		★	★	★	★						★	★	★
625	13	Cyanide Destruct Systems, Inc.		★			★		★									★	★	
638	14	The Indicted CFO	★	★	★	★														
641	15	Ethical Dilemmas in Business Marketing	★	★	★	★														

S.C. Johnson's Professional Division

S.C. Johnson & Son, Inc., produces a range of well-established consumer products such as PLEDGE furniture polish, GLADE air fresheners, SHOUT laundry soil and stain remover, OFF insect repellant, RAID insecticides, and WINDEX glass cleaner. Each of these brands enjoys a strong position in the market. Through its Professional Division, the firm is also a leading producer of products and services for commercial, industrial, and institutional building maintenance and sanitation. The products include a complete line of specialty formulated cleaners, floor finishes, disinfectants, furniture polishes, and products for insect and odor control.

The Professional Division serves a diverse array of organizations in the business market such as retailers, health-care organizations, and educational institutions. Customers are served directly by the company's sales force or by a large network of distributors. Organizations follow two alternative approaches to building or store maintenance: the job is performed by its own personnel or it is "outsourced" to a building services contractor who regularly brings a trained staff on site to clean the facility.

Maintaining a sparkling and professional appearance is a desired goal in any organization but, for many, a continuing challenge. Consider the heavy store traffic that retailers such as Wal-Mart generate each day or the stream of shoppers who visit a supermarket around the clock. Some retailers spend $100,000 per store each month in cleaning, floor care, and maintenance programs. For large chains with hundreds of stores, this represents a massive expenditure. Included here are the costs of the cleaning products, labor and equipment costs, training expenses, and costs related to regulatory compliance. At a more fundamental level, retail store managers may be even more concerned about other costs—the lost sales that could arise from consumer concerns about cleanliness, food sanitation, or the unsightly appearance of a store. Moreover, there are safety concerns that worry store managers. A slippery floor that causes a shopper to slip and fall may lead to costly legal action against the retailer.

To meet the needs of organizational customers, the Professional Division at S.C. Johnson has developed an array of products and services. For a particular customer, like a supermarket chain, the salesperson will recommend a particular range of products and employee training programs to meet the unique needs of the retailer. Special dispensing systems (Solutions Centers) have been developed by S.C. Johnson to assist users in pinpointing the proper dilution level of the company's products to meet different floor-care maintenance tasks. The Professional Division also provides ongoing

This case appears in Michael D. Hutt and Thomas W. Speh, Chapter 6, "Business-to-Business Marketing," of Michael R. Czinkota et al., *Marketing, Best Practices* (Fort Worth, TX: The Dryden Press, 2000), pp. 208–209.

technical support to a customer. Each year, the unit receives over 30,000 calls from customers on issues that range from product selection for particular types of floor surfaces to environmental or safety queries.

Discussion Questions

1. In purchasing cleaning products and services, which of the following managers might be members of the buying center at a discount retailer, like Wal-Mart or Target: A purchasing executive at the headquarters level, store managers, a merchandising executive, a marketing manager, a maintenance staff supervisor, or maintenance employees? Who would be most influential in the buying decision?

2. Describe how the evaluative criteria employed by the purchasing manager might be different from those that are important to users.

3. Explore how the needs of a health-care organization might differ from the needs of a retailer in purchasing cleaning products and services. What adjustments in marketing strategy might be pursued by the Professional Division in the health-care sector?

Westward Industries Ltd. (A)

Gary A. Mischke, University of Alberta

Michael K. Mauws, University of Alberta

Frederick Starke, University of Manitoba

Bruno Dyck, University of Manitoba

Larry Mauws, the president of Westward Industries Ltd. (WIL), dropped the telephone receiver into its cradle and leaned back in his office chair. He had struggled with the design and manufacturing of the GO-4, Westward's highly successful special purpose vehicle, every day for the last 5 years, and now, this. His engine supplier, Kia Motors of Korea, was redesigning the engine he used to power the GO-4. The phone call he had just received informed him that Kia would ship the last of the engines with the current design in March 1995. The motor mounts—devices used to fasten the engine into the GO-4's frame—were being moved, and these modifications meant that he had to redesign the GO-4 yet again. Considering it was already January, there was little time.

He pursed his lips, and the air went out of him in a deep sigh. Larry was tired— tired of regulators, tired of haggling with his distributor, tired of customer complaints about parts shipments, tired of bankers, tired of board meetings, tired of the problems he couldn't solve, and tired of the critics who professed to know more about his business than he did. He longed for a company that was big enough, and successful enough, to afford a professional management team. The burden was almost too much for one person, but how could his company capitalize on its successful 3-wheeled car? What should the strategy be to take Westward Industries to the next level? What would he need to do to take it there? The questions kept coming back, only to be pushed aside by yet another daily operating crisis. He wanted to redesign the GO-4 model, and this would be a good time to do it. Moreover, his banker, not to mention his son Michael, kept telling him he needed to think about the long run. However, the fact was that most days he couldn't see beyond the day's problems, problems such as the one he'd just received over the phone. Deep in thought, he got up from his desk and wandered into the shop, where the 12 young men who were organized into fabrication and assembly crews built the GO-4.

Westward Industries Ltd.

Background

Larry Mauws, age 56, was a long-time resident of Portage la Prairie, Manitoba. He had studied agricultural engineering at the University of Manitoba but had dropped out after 2 years when he married and needed to provide for his young family. A management position with Case Power & Equipment initially brought him to Portage but, subsequent to the move, he was involved in a succession of ventures. Some of the businesses he had owned and operated included a tire and muffler business, a motorcycle/snowmobile/automobile dealership, a furniture store, and a trucking and warehousing company. Immediately prior to starting WIL, his focus had been a hotel, restaurant, bar, shopping, and recreation complex. At heart, though, he was a tireless inventor, fascinated by the mechanics of motorized vehicles.

In his early years, he built and raced stock cars. Later, he built and raced snowmobiles, winning the Canadian National Championship in 1970. For a time, he was employed as designer for Roll-o-flex, a snowmobile manufacturer located in Regina, Saskatchewan. He had also been a licensed pilot and rebuilt airplanes as a hobby. In brief, he was a creator and an inventor, and he wasn't happy unless he was working on a new mechanical challenge. Although the hospitality business provided him with a comfortable living, what he really longed to be doing was building things. For this reason, he had developed that restless itch that had plagued him earlier, that need to move onto something else. It came as no surprise, then, that when the opportunity arose to build a specialized motor vehicle for the parking patrol market, he jumped at it.

In early 1989, a group of business leaders in Portage la Prairie, Manitoba, met in the dining room of Larry Mauws' Westward Village Inn, a hotel, restaurant, bar, shopping, and recreation complex that Mauws had constructed a few years earlier. The subject of conversation was the declining business climate in this south-central Manitoba town of 13,000 people. In quick succession, the town had lost a Campbell Soup processing plant, a Philips Cable plant, and a Canadian Forces base. The town leaders were concerned that the town itself would be in jeopardy if new business development was not brought about quickly. With this in mind, the group agreed to contribute a small amount of seed money toward seeking new businesses for the community, and Larry Mauws volunteered to be their business development ambassador.

After exploring a series of opportunities suggested by investment bankers, Mauws heard of a small American firm that was looking for someone to manufacture a 3-wheeled vehicle for them. The firm, Wisconsin Lift Truck (WLT), had sold special purpose trucks to large municipalities across the United States for many years. Through its contacts, WLT became aware of a market for parking patrol vehicles in municipal police departments. The market at that time was served by Cushman Inc., an American subsidiary of the large British conglomerate Ransomes PLC. WLT determined that the police were not satisfied with the performance of the Cushman vehicles, or with their monopoly, but were resigned to using them because there were no alternative vehicles with the same level of functionality.

Encouraged by the market potential, WLT designed and produced about 40 vehicles for this market. Unfortunately, its vehicle was clumsy and had mechanical flaws. Although it had only three wheels and thus could have been classified as a motorcycle, because it weighed 500 pounds more than the 1,500-pound limit on motorcycles it was classified as an automobile by the U.S. Environmental Protection Agency (EPA). As a result of being classified an automobile, WLT was unable to get the vehicle certified by either the EPA under the tough automobile pollution standards or by the U.S. Department of Transportation (DOT). Like many of Cushman's would-be competitors in the past, WLT found itself mired in a regulatory morass. Thus, lacking both EPA and DOT certification, it decided to exit the fledgling market. Nevertheless, WLT was convinced that police departments across the United States were interested in a vehicle that could challenge the Cushman vehicle they were now using.

The champion for the parking patrol vehicle at WLT was T. J. Sommers, who was the son of the owner, Bill Sommers. The younger Sommers knew that a strong market existed for parking patrol vehicles, so he left WLT to start his own company, White Bear Sales (WBS). Having done so, he began searching for a manufacturer to correct the mechanical flaws in the vehicle WLT had designed and to manufacture additional vehicles under contract. Recognizing that design and manufacture were not his strengths, he intended to focus his energy on sales and creating a distribution network.

Larry Mauws met T. J. Sommers through an investment broker in the summer of 1989. Sommers showed Mauws the vehicle he intended to market and took Mauws to meet several of his customers. Sommers then offered Mauws a 3-year contract to manufacture his vehicle, under which he would pay Mauws $9,000 (U.S.) for each vehicle. The contract called for Mauws to manufacture 100, 300, and 500 vehicles, respectively, over 3 years. In contemplating the offer, Mauws quickly came to two conclusions. First, the market demand for a better designed parking patrol vehicle was indeed strong. Second, the vehicle Sommers proposed to market would never be a serious contender to replace the Cushman. Mauws kept this second conclusion to himself, however, and agreed to work out a manufacturing proposal within 90 days.

Three months later, Mauws invited Sommers to Portage la Prairie. Expecting to negotiate the finishing touches to a manufacturing contract, Sommers was surprised when Mauws showed him drawings of *his* GO-4 prototype. As it turned out, Mauws had not spent the 3 months prior working on a manufacturing contract but, instead, had been working on his own design for a parking patrol vehicle. The result was clearly smaller and more compact than the WLT vehicle, but the fact was that it bore virtually no resemblance to the vehicle with which Sommers was familiar. As a result, Sommers was very much caught off guard by Mauws' proposal.

Mauws told Sommers that he had no interest in manufacturing the vehicle WLT had designed, but that he was willing to make WBS the exclusive U.S. distributor of Westward Industries' GO-4 parking patrol vehicles. The agreement would require WBS to be selling 500 vehicles per year at the end of 5 years (1995). Sales were expected to be 100, 200, 300, 400, and 500 vehicles, respectively, from 1991 through 1995. Westward Industries would retain worldwide distribution rights for its vehicles, with the exception of the exclusive rights granted to WBS for the U.S. market.

Sommers agreed to consider the proposal. Privately, he was skeptical of Mauws' ability to develop a competitive vehicle and, for this reason, upon his return to Milwaukee he continued to seek another manufacturer for his company's design. Meanwhile, WBS was facing strong pressure from its municipal customers, who wanted it to either correct handling and maintenance problems on the 40 vehicles it had sold and get them certified, or replace them. The threat of lawsuits over the defective, uncertified vehicles was becoming ever more palpable.

In February 1990, Mauws invited Sommers back to Portage la Prairie to view the prototype he had built with the help of his partners, most notably his brother. Upon seeing it, Sommers was impressed with Mauws' design. Because Sommers was having little luck finding his own manufacturer, not to mention the continuing pressure to settle claims related to the 40 vehicles he had in the field, he agreed to become West- ward Industries' exclusive distributor for parking patrol vehicles in the United States. In May 1990, Sommers took a production model of the GO-4 on the road to demon- strate it to several U.S. municipalities. The response was almost universally positive and, shortly thereafter, the orders began to roll in.

The GO-4 Design

For a venerable tinkerer like Larry Mauws, designing a 3-wheeled, motorized vehicle was a labor of love. Mauws drew on his experience as a stock car racer to build a lightweight, strong, exposed tubular frame for the vehicle, similar to the roll cages he had built for his racecars. He got the idea of using a tailpipe-bending machine to bend tubular steel for the frame from his experience in the muffler business. He adapted a tailpipe fabrication bender to produce the intricate bends in the frame of the GO-4. Aluminum sheeting was used for the body parts to reduce the vehicle's weight. His snowmobile and auto-racing experience gave him an instinctive feel for weight and balance. Mauws was determined that stability and road handling were to be differentiating characteristics of the GO-4.

The engine and drive train were of critical importance in the design. The GO-4 had to have an EPA-approved engine, one already tested and in current production in an automobile. Further, by using a water-cooled automobile engine, he could provide a heated passenger compartment and a windshield defroster, which were desirable comfort and safety options for customers in northern U.S. cities. After a long search, Mauws finally arranged an engine contract with Kia Motors of Korea for the same engine that was used in the Ford Festiva, a Ford passenger vehicle sold throughout the United States. It was a rear-mounted, transverse (i.e., mounted sideways) automobile engine that would give his vehicle the high performance and stability he desired.

Customers were excited by the prospect of having an alternative to the Cushman, but they were also excited about the vehicle itself. Mauws had responded to many of their concerns and incorporated an impressive number of their suggestions. Moreover, he continued to do so on an ongoing basis as the early vehicles rolled off the production line. For example, sliding doors were made available as an option for municipalities whose weather did not lend itself to the open cabin of the standard GO-4. Options such as this, as well as many minor design changes and improvements, helped the GO-4 to quickly gain a foothold in the marketplace. Nevertheless, it would also come to haunt Westward down the road. Frequent changes meant that some modifications were never recorded in company blueprints for the GO-4. Records to show which versions of parts were installed on which vehicles were scarce. As a result of the poor records, supplying after- sale parts for repairing the GO-4 eventually became a serious service problem.

Regulatory Requirements

Mauws knew that he would have to meet tough regulations for safety and vehicle emis- sions. Although he quickly developed a rudimentary understanding of the regulations, he was quite unprepared for the unending volumes of details that plagued him from the start. As he later remarked:

> I was naive, just like White Bear Sales. You could fill this room with regu- lation manuals. It really wasn't as simple as it seemed. But when you think

you can swim and someone throws you into the pool, you don't know whether it's shorter to turn back or to swim to the other side. Like most entrepreneurs, I struck out for the far shore. I was in over my head, and it was either sink or swim, and God knows we almost sank several times. But this wasn't the first time I made that mistake, and I've been in tougher deals than this one.

In the United States, the primary regulators of motor vehicles for street and high-way use are the Department of Transportation (DOT) and the Environmental Protection Agency (EPA). The principal interest of the DOT is vehicle safety; the department prescribes a series of safety features such as seat belts and air bags that must be included in on-road vehicles. The agency also develops specifications for vehicle components such as bumpers and gas tanks. For passenger vehicles, it requires a series of front, side, and rear impact crash tests to assess the vehicle's performance in motor vehicle accidents.

The EPA's principal interest is in preserving and enhancing the quality of the natural environment. Because motor vehicles are a major source of air pollution, their emissions are highly regulated. New motor vehicles must meet strict guidelines for emissions of noxious gases and particulates that can foul the environment. Some states, particularly California, also regulate motor vehicle emissions. Moreover, California Air Resource Board (CARB) emission guidelines are often more stringent than those prescribed at the federal level.

Federal regulations for vehicle safety and environmental emissions also exist in Canada. In many cases, the regulations are similar, but minor differences exist. Further, the prescribed testing routines to demonstrate compliance or the actual controlling definitions of vehicles are in some cases different between the two countries. As a result, certification in one country does not guarantee certification in the other, and testing in one country may often need to be repeated in the other with some variations to satisfy local regulations.

In both the United States and Canada, vehicles classified as motorcycles (as opposed to passenger automobiles or trucks) were held to less stringent emissions standards and were exempted from a number of regulations related to safety features. They were also exempted from crash testing. Thus, there were considerable benefits to be had from being classified as a motorcycle as opposed to a truck or automobile. In the United States, motorcycles were defined as motorized vehicles weighing less than 1,500 pounds and having three or fewer wheels on the ground. Vehicles exceeding 1,500 pounds were considered passenger vehicles.[1] In Canada, however, a motorcycle was defined as a motorized vehicle with fewer than four wheels that is steered by handlebars and operated by a rider who sits astride the vehicle's engine. Although the GO-4 met the U.S. definition of a motorcycle, in Canada it was considered a passenger vehicle because it had a steering wheel and its operator did not straddle the engine. As a result, in Canada the GO-4 was subject to more stringent emission standards and required additional safety features and crash testing before it could be approved for use.

Mauws needed to keep his vehicle classified as a motorcycle if he wished to avoid DOT-mandated crash tests. EPA and California emission standards were also lower for motorcycles. He estimated the costs of DOT crash testing alone at $200,000 (U.S.)

---

[1] In 1998, the weight limitation was increased to 1,750 pounds.

or more. At least for the moment, such tests were out of the question because the cost of the tests was nearly equal to what he and his backers were prepared to invest in the *total* development of the vehicle.

Financing the Start-up

Six partners formed Westward Industries Ltd.: Larry Mauws, his brother, a long-time friend, his accountant, and the two Winnipeg investment brokers who found the project. The initial agreement was to capitalize the firm at $300,000.[2] Larry Mauws was credited with $100,000 for his work in the design of the vehicle. He was also obligated to contribute an additional $50,000 in cash, making him a 50 percent partner. Larry Mauws subsequently sold 25 percent of the firm (half of his initial $150,000 share) to his brother Elmer for cash and services rendered in the building of the prototype. The other four shareholders were to contribute the remaining $150,000 in cash and services. The accountant received a 5 percent share for $15,000, and Mauws' friend and the two Winnipeg investment brokers were each committed to 15 percent shares of $45,000 each. The accountant and Mauws' friend met their commitments for start-up capital with cash and services, but the two Winnipeg investors defaulted on their commitments and were subsequently required to forfeit their shares. Larry Mauws bought their 30 percent share and became a 55 percent partner in the venture.

Mauws quickly exhausted his initial capitalization in building the prototype and testing the vehicle to gain EPA and DOT certification. As a result, initial production was plagued by lack of capital and by a succession of production delays. Therefore, the first production vehicles did not begin rolling off WIL's production line until June 1991, nearly a year behind schedule. As the delays mounted, Mauws' shareholders proved unwilling and in some cases unable to make additional capital contributions to the firm, despite a shareholder agreement that required they maintain their proportional ownership. Thus, financial crises were the norm during the first 3 years of operation. At one point, WIL was forced to take on a venture capital investor to make up the shortfall.[3] Mauws personally kept the company afloat by drawing down his life savings and by heavily mortgaging the hotel, restaurant, bar, and shopping center complex he owned. His additional personal contributions were in excess of $300,000 during the start-up period (see Exhibits 1 and 2).

In addition to funding its development costs, WIL required operating capital to finance engine purchases from Kia Motors. Kia required engines to be purchased in quantities of 100, at about $5,000 each. Working-capital funding for WIL came in part from a $400,000 loan from a federal business development program called Western Economic Diversification; a $50,000 forgivable loan from the province of Manitoba; and a $75,000 loan from the local government's Community Futures Program. However, most of this money was tied up in raw materials, castings, and other parts. Thus, the bulk of the $500,000 working capital needed to buy engines was financed through an investment fund. Mauws had worked out an agreement with the investment fund manager to finance each 100-lot engine order he made. As part of the agreement, his bank agreed to credit the investment fund with $5,000 for each vehicle sold when the proceeds were received from WBS. Because engine orders sometimes overlapped due to the long lead times and

---

[2] Unless otherwise stated, all figures are in Canadian dollars (US$1=CDN$1.50).

[3] *Winnipeg Free Press*, March 4, 1994.

EXHIBIT 1 | **SALES AND OPERATING DATA ($ '000 CDN) WESTWARD INDUSTRIES LTD.[a]**

	1990	1991	1992	1993	1994
Employees (end of year)	2	5	11	14[b]	20
Number of Vehicles Sold	0	37	112	159	169
Sales	0	431.5	1,518.8	2,556.7	2,780.0
Cost of Sales	0	326.2	993.4	1,432.0	1,493.4
Net Operating Margin	0	105.3	525.4	1,124.7	1,286.5
Selling, General and Admin.	0	333.1	517.0	790.1	1,029.0
Interest on Operating Debt	0	6.0	2.3	3.0	5.9
Net Operating Profit	0	(233.8)	6.1	331.6	251.6
Other Income:					
Interest	13.9	0.3	5.7	18.9	10.7
Miscellaneous	—	—	12.4	—	14.3
Less Other Expense:					
Discounts	0	7.6	36.4	20.2	70.5
Interest on LT Debt	0	23.2	22.1	70.1	108.7
Taxes & Licenses	0	2.5	7.1	7.4	9.1
Inc. Before Extraordinary Items	13.9	(266.8)	(41.4)	252.8	88.3
Extraordinary Items	—	—	79.3	(72.0)	—
Net Income	13.9	(266.8)	37.9	180.8	88.3

[a] Prepared without audit.

[b] Seasonal demands caused peak employment to be 20 employees in the spring and summer of 1993.

the need for a letter of credit (payment in advance of the shipment), it was not uncommon for WIL to have two such loans outstanding at the same time.

The Market

Although there were other applications that the GO-4 might be suitable for (see Exhibit 3), WIL's vehicle had been specifically designed to break Cushman's stranglehold on the market for parking patrol vehicles. Thus, what was clear to WIL at the outset was that, if it was to succeed, it was going to be primarily at the expense of Cushman Inc. There were no other direct competitors for WIL in the U.S. market, and neither Cushman's vehicle nor WIL's was being used for parking patrol in Canada. It is worth noting that some municipalities were using small automobiles and jeeps for parking patrol, but this was in large part the result of frustration with the Cushman vehicle and the company's monopolistic position. Despite facing some competition from the automobile manufacturers, the most important unknown facing WIL at the outset was the response of its larger and more mature rival, Cushman Inc.

EXHIBIT 2 | **BALANCE SHEET—DEC. 31, 199x ($ '000 CDN)**
WESTWARD INDUSTRIES LTD.[a]

	1990	1991	1992	1993	1994
Current Assets					
Cash	(7.0)	35.1	1.2	292.6	26.5
Accounts Receivable	—	17.7	85.4	282.7	444.9
Income Taxes Recoverable	—	90.0	17.5	20.8	10.0
Inventory	409.9	474.5	1,048.8	325.6	782.4
Prepaid Expenses	—	—	4.1	4.1	1.1
Capital Assets	32.2	65.2	121.1	325.3	323.4
Other Assets					
Capitalized R&D	309.1	431.3	420.2	412.7	333.3
Other Organization Costs	2.0	2.0	2.0	—	—
Total Assets	746.2	1,115.9	1,700.2	1,663.8	1,921.6
Current Liabilities					
Bank Advance	85.0	160.0	—	—	—
Manitoba Capital Tax Payable	—	—	—	—	2.5
Acts Payable & Accrued Liabilities	32.3	72.5	227.3	353.8	200.0
Notes Payable	—	258.2	943.6	230.7	153.9
Current Portion LT Debt	—	150.0	45.0	217.7	401.1
Long-Term Debt					
Notes Payable	—	431.6	434.8	250.0	474.1
Shareholder Loans	614.0	153.4	121.3	502.6	492.8
Total Liabilities	731.2	1,225.6	1,772.1	1,554.8	1,724.4
Shareholders Equity					
Capital Stock	1.0	143.0	143.0	143.0	143.0
Retained Earnings	13.9	(252.8)	(214.9)	(34.0)	54.3
Total Shareholder Equity	14.9	(109.8)	(71.9)	109.0	197.3
Total Liabilities & Shareholder Equity	746.2	1,115.9	1,700.2	1,663.8	1,921.6

[a] Prepared without audit.

Cushman Inc.: The Market Leader

Introduced in the 1950s, the Cushman vehicle underwent few changes over the years through the 1980s. The Cushman parking patrol vehicle was a 3-wheeled adaptation of an old Cushman motor scooter design, with a curb weight of about 1,165 pounds.[4]

[4] *The Honolulu Advertiser*, 1994.

EXHIBIT 3 | **PRODUCT AND MARKET PROPOSALS RECEIVED BY WESTWARD INDUSTRIES**

Product	Market	Regulation and Market Considerations
Police Security Vehicles	U.S. Metro Areas	—Motorcycle weight regulations could limit necessary safety features at higher speeds. —Regulations for motorcycles could disadvantage WIL's GO-4 in competition against real motorcycles (e.g., Harleys, Hondas), because the GO-4 is a marginal motorcycle.
Mail Delivery Vehicles	Canada Post	—Canadian regulations prevent the GO-4's use in this market by virtue of the definition of motorcycles.
Special Purpose Commercial Delivery Vehicles	U.S., Canada	—U.S. applications could be sold if modifications can be made within the weight limitations. —University campus delivery vehicles were proposed. —Canadian potential for dispensation or change of regulations, as evidenced by the Dickey Dee ice cream vending vehicles.
Trash Pickup Vehicles	U.S., Canada	—Requires a dump trailer, because weight restrictions are exceeded if a dump box is incorporated into the vehicle. —Cushman has incorporated a dump box on their vehicle and is making overtures in this market.
Park Maintenance Vehicles	U.S., Canada, Federal, State, Provincial, Municipal Governments	—U.S. markets are within regulation if special purpose modifications can be made within weight limits. —Canadian markets may be available if the buyer passes exemptions from general regulations for vehicles limited to special purposes within the areas of the parks.
Recreation Vehicles	U.S., Canada	—Conceivable but unlikely markets in the United States. WIL GO-4s have safety and comfort advantages over general all-terrain vehicles (ATVs). However, high accident rates with 3-wheeled ATVs have led to regulations severely limiting their use and forcing the market toward 4-wheel designs. —Categorization as a passenger vehicle prohibits such use in Canada until safety testing is done. —The GO-4 was not designed for off-road driving. —Product liability insurance would be prohibitive. —Cushman has a sizable recreation vehicle business in golf carts. Such off-road uses may be an opportunity in Canada.
Special Purpose Vehicles	International Markets	—Regulations will need to be researched on a country-by-country basis. —Will require a significant expansion of management capacity at WIL, even if WIL is able to combine efforts with an in-country partner.

Powered by a 22-horsepower, air-cooled engine, the original canvas and plastic passenger compartment had been redesigned with fiberglass, but the plastic side windows and curtains were retained. Patrol officers complained that the windows became brown and scratched as the vehicle aged, and visibility was significantly reduced in the rain.[5] They also complained that the vehicle was unstable. For example, it was a common experience to feel a rear wheel leave the pavement when turning a corner.[6] Occasionally, the Cushman's doors would pop open when the vehicle hit a bump.

---

[5] Ibid.

[6] Ibid.

In fact, safety concerns for the Cushman allowed some police unions to negotiate a 20 percent hazard pay supplement for operating a Cushman parking patrol vehicle.[7]

The Cushman parking patrol vehicle was a machine that parking officers loved to hate. In the Cushman, the driver sat on the engine compartment, making the vehicle uncomfortably hot in the summer.[8] High maintenance costs were also a legacy of the Cushman motor scooter.[9] Despite their complaints about the vehicle, it remained the vehicle of choice for parking patrol for nearly 40 years for one simple reason: functionality. It was the only vehicle that allowed officers to lean out of either side of the vehicle and mark a parked car's tire with chalk on the end of a stick, a method of timing in nonmetered, restricted parking areas. It also allowed the officer to reach a vehicle's windshield to post a parking ticket from either side of the patrol vehicle without getting out. The vehicle's overall width of about 4 feet allowed it to maneuver easily between lines of traffic in congested city streets. These features allowed Cushman to develop a monopoly in parking patrol.

In 1958, Outboard Marine Corporation, makers of outboard boat motors, Lawnboy lawn mowers, and garden equipment, acquired Cushman Motor Works. In November 1989, Outboard Marine sold Cushman Inc. to Ransomes America, a subsidiary of Ransomes PLC of Ipswich, England, for $150 million (U.S.).[10] Ransomes PLC is a group of companies that manufacture a variety of turf maintenance equipment. Cushman's line of 3- and 4-wheeled vehicles for industrial and commercial turf maintenance, as well as recreational vehicles such as golf carts, fit well in the Ransomes family. In 1993, Cushman Inc. sales were $90 million (U.S.). The company employed 700 people.[11]

Competition between Cushman and Westward Industries

Cushman had been challenged several times in the parking patrol vehicle market, but challengers had always wilted when faced with the safety and environmental regulations and certification procedures. Few had the financial staying power to weather the regulatory processes. For this reason, Cushman ignored the early challenge from Westward Industries' GO-4, just as it had ignored the challenge of a series of other would-be competitors, relying instead on regulation to maintain a formidable entry barrier to their market. Larry comments on the effect regulations had on previous would-be competitors for Cushman:

> Every time that someone made an attempt to get into the business, they never lasted more than a couple of years, until they were gone. Everybody who went into it went with the same naïve approach, but when they got into it, it was a lot more difficult than they thought. Mostly, it was regulations.

The demand for parking patrol vehicles was stable, showing little growth over the years. Although the number of officers in parking patrol is not known, the overall growth in municipal employees and in municipal employees involved with police

---

[7] Ibid.

[8] *Sioux City Journal*, April 1994.

[9] Purchasers of the rugged GO-4 expected to save the equivalent of 15 percent to 20 percent of the GO-4's first cost in parts, compared to the Cushman, over the lives of the two vehicles, according to *The Honolulu Advertiser*, 1994.

[10] G. Hoover, et. al., editors, *Hoover's Handbook of American Business* (The Reference Press, 1993).

[11] In 1998, Ransomes' turf business, including Cushman, was sold to the American conglomerate, Textron.

EXHIBIT 4 | **EMPLOYEES IN U.S. MUNICIPAL GOVERNMENTS**[a]

	1960	1980	1990	1991	1992
Total Municipal Employees ('000)	971	2,561	2,642	2,662	2,665
Municipal Employees in Police Protection ('000)	224	365	412	418	423

[a] *Occupational Employment Patterns for 1960 and 1975, Bulletin #1599*, U.S. Department of Labor, December, 1968; U.S. Bureau of Census, Statistical Abstract of the United States: 1994 (114th edition), Exhibit 102, p. 324.

EXHIBIT 5 | **FEATURE COMPARISON**[a]

	Westward Industries GO-4	**Cushman**
Engine	1,300 cc, 4-cylinder, liquid cooled	2-cylinder, air cooled
Power	63 hp	22 hp
Fuel System	Electronic fuel injection	Carburetor
Transmission	3-speed automatic	Manual
Brakes	3-wheel disc	3-wheel drum
Tires	$155 \times 80 \times 13$	5.70×8
Cab Construction	Heavy tubular steel	Fiberglass
Crash Protection	Built-in roll cage	No roll bar
Rear Suspension	Adjustable shocks	Shocks and springs
Heater/Defroster	20,000 BTU liquid core	Warm air jacket from engine[b]

[a] *The Honolulu Advertiser*, 1994.

[b] *Seattle Times*, January 18, 1993.

protection has been low, the result of budget constraints in cash strapped municipal governments (see Exhibit 4). Suburban commercial and retail growth was usually centered on shopping malls or office complexes where parking was free or privately owned. On the other hand, street parking in the urban core, where most parking patrols worked, was a fixed quantity, defined by the geography of the city. As a result, the demand for parking patrol vehicles was largely for replacement vehicles.

Parking patrol vehicles were sold through a tender process. Selling a vehicle involved demonstrating the vehicle for various managers of municipal motor pools. One of the most important aspects of the sale was ensuring that tender specifications were favorable to the bidder's vehicle. WIL's strategy of producing a highly functional, differentiated vehicle could only succeed as the low bidder if its differentiating characteristics found their way into the tender specifications. In the case of the GO-4 versus the Cushman, any of a number of feature specification advantages could be used to disqualify a Cushman vehicle; for example, a water-cooled engine, heater BTU output, disk brakes, steel-reinforced passenger cab, and others (see Exhibit 5). This was extremely important given that WIL lacked the financial might to survive a price war with its much bigger competitor, not to mention its multinational parent.

Pricing for the two vehicles varied depending on the specific options required, the location (due to shipping costs), and bid competition in the local market. At the high end, a Honolulu Police Department analysis priced the GO-4 at $18,460 (U.S., FOB Honolulu) versus the Cushman at $18,000 (U.S.). Cushman lowered its price from $20,000 when challenged by the GO-4.[12] More typical mainland prices were $12,000 to $14,000 (U.S.) for the GO-4, versus $9,000 to $12,000 (U.S.) for the Cushman. The retail price of the Cushman was often about $4,000 (U.S.) less than the GO-4 when the two companies went head to head in tender competition.

Much of the early competition in 1991 and 1992 was played out in one- or two-vehicle contracts in municipalities across the United States. Westward Industries' big break, however, came in the battle for the New York City Police Department (NYPD) order. New York City (NYC) had over 500 parking patrol vehicles on its streets and represented the largest parking patrol fleet in the United States. Selling New York City would signal to other U.S. cities that WIL was a viable alternative to the Cushman monopoly.

The battle for the NYPD contract was intense. After an extensive sales effort by WIL and WBS in 1992, NYPD leased two vehicles to test prior to deciding on a tender for 110 new parking patrol vehicles. In response, Cushman began a letter campaign calling attention to the failed series of earlier competitors that had left NYPD and other police departments with a fleet of white elephant vehicles in their garages, vehicles that were not repairable because the companies that made them had gone out of business. The NYPD responded by giving the two leased test vehicles a punishing test on the streets of New York. As a result of jumping New York City's infamous potholes and street curbs, the suspension of one of the test vehicles was damaged. The local Cushman dealer took the damage as an opportunity to argue that the GO-4 was not roadworthy. To counter the attack on the roadworthiness of the GO-4, White Bear Sales and their local New York City distributor concentrated on the NYC parking officers' union, demonstrating the superior safety and comfort features provided by the GO-4 as compared with the Cushman. Because Mauws' tubular steel roll cage was left exposed in the vehicle design, it was obvious, even to a layperson, that the GO-4 had strength and safety characteristics that were superior to the fiberglass-molded cab of the Cushman. In the end, the union became a strong advocate for the higher priced GO-4.

Cushman parking patrol vehicles were usually sold through lawn and garden dealerships, an historical anomaly that evolved from Cushman's turf and recreational vehicle business. The anomaly extended to the WBS dealer network. Despite having no functional relationship to lawn and garden maintenance, both Cushman's and White Bear Sales' dealer networks for parking patrol vehicles were predominantly lawn and garden equipment dealers.

WIL believed that it could outmaneuver Cushman in the provision of after-sale service by being highly responsive to the needs of customers. One of the complaints that Mauws heard about Cushman was that it was unwilling or unable to modify its vehicle to fix perennial problems or add features that customers desired:

> From what I understand; Cushman is not an aggressive company. They have basically been milking the industry for years. [They] never put any money into R&D, never make any improvements on their car, never listen to their customers. They have basically been riding this thing out.

---

[12] *The Honolulu Advertiser,* 1994.

In an effort to land a long-term contract with the NYPD, Mauws made many modifications to his original vehicle, based on comments he received from the NYPD's trials of the test vehicles it had leased. WIL, WBS, and the local dealer were all highly motivated to satisfy the NYPD and land the contract. As a result, it was not always clear whether the requested modifications were the result of bona fide concerns of the NYPD or "good ideas" that had emerged from the creative minds at WIL and in the sales channel. Whatever the source, Mauws made the design changes quickly and at his own expense.

On the regulatory front, Cushman complained to the EPA that WIL vehicles violated EPA regulations. Cushman alleged that WIL vehicles exceeded the 1,500-pound limitation for motorcycles and, therefore, needed to meet the auto emission standards. In response, the EPA began to weigh GO-4s at various locations around the United States and found that the vehicles weighed from 1,485 pounds (the weight of the prototype base model) to as much as 1,700 pounds, depending on the options installed on the vehicle. As it turned out, Mauws had misunderstood the regulations. He had believed that if his base model met the weight restriction, options could be added without penalty. The correct interpretation, however, was that only after-sale, *customer-installed* options were exempt. Thus, the addition of sliding doors and the continuous stream of "improvements" to the originally certified model that flowed from Larry Mauws' creative brain had pushed many of the GO-4s over the 1,500-pound weight limit.

In the midst of contract negotiations for the New York contract in 1993, the vehicle was decertified, and the EPA ordered a halt to all sales. Cushman quickly brought the EPA action to the attention of the NYPD. However, Mauws quickly responded by redesigning the GO-4 frame to remove 20 linear feet of steel tubing to reduce the vehicle weight. The tubing had largely been cosmetic to visually signal the superior safety of the GO-4. In the end, the Portage la Prairie plant was shut down for 3 months while the modifications were made and the vehicle recertified at a lower weight, including popular options like sliding doors. It was a trying time for WIL but, despite the intense competition from Cushman, it eventually paid off when WIL finally won the 110-vehicle contract with New York City.

Other Applications for the GO-4

As the number of GO-4s in operation increased, and as WIL garnered an increasing amount of local media attention, Mauws increasingly found himself presented with alternative applications for the GO-4 vehicle (see Exhibit 3). Some of these could be dismissed out of hand, but others warranted more serious consideration in Mauws' view. One such application was using the GO-4 for the delivery of local mail. Canada Post, the federal corporation with responsibility for delivering mail in Canada, had informally approached Mauws in this regard. Canada Post had over 60,000 employees at that time, who together served more than 15,000 letter carrier routes. Most importantly, they had a fleet of more than 5,000 vehicles that logged approximately 70 million miles each year. Some of these vehicles were semitrailer trucks used for city-to-city transport, but a large number were full-sized panel vans. Thus, if the GO-4 were widely adopted within the Canada Post distribution network, it would have had a significant impact on WIL's sales. Nevertheless, Mauws was hesitant.

Mauws knew that the Canada Post application, as well as pursuing any other sales in Canada, would have to be a long-term strategy. The two options available to Mauws in pursuing such a strategy were either to carry out crash tests and get certified as a passenger vehicle or to lobby the government to have the pertinent regulations changed.

If the necessary funds were available, Mauws was fairly confident that the GO-4 could pass the crash tests. Even so, getting certified as a passenger vehicle required considerably more than this. With the move from motorcycle to passenger vehicle, many other safety regulations would apply to the GO-4. Simply learning about the regulations, let alone actually incorporating them into the design of the GO-4, would require a considerable commitment of resources. Thus, Mauws was leery of this approach. On the other hand, he was also leery of trying to get the regulations changed. Informal inquiries with politicians and bureaucrats in the past had given him little hope that changes could be easily achieved. If at all possible, it seemed it would take a well-coordinated, and most likely lengthy, lobbying effort. To Mauws, this meant a lot of time and money, both of which he perpetually lacked.

Another option for the GO-4 was as a feeder vehicle for the refuse and recycling industry. The largest firms in this industry were Waste Management Inc., with 1991 sales of $7.5 billion, and Browning-Ferris Industries, Inc., with 1991 sales of $3.1 billion. Sales in the two companies were growing at 25.7 percent and 18.1 percent *annually*, a result of industry growth and consolidation through acquisition. Sales from North American municipal solid waste collection services were 52 percent and 64 percent, respectively, of total revenues. In the 1990s, concern over filling municipal landfills and efforts to promote recycling stemmed the increases in municipal solid waste disposal. Companies like Waste Management Inc. and Browning-Ferris responded to the leveling of disposal volumes by launching recycling divisions to capitalize on those trends. Curbside recycling utilized the collector-driver as a material sorter to separate paper, glass, and metals as the materials were collected. In 1990, Americans generated 196.9 million tons of municipal solid waste or 4.3 pounds per person per day. Of this amount, about 17 percent was recycled, and 163.5 million tons were deposited in landfills. From 1960 to 1990, municipal solid waste grew at an overall rate of 2.7 percent per year. Waste generation per person grew at 1.6 percent per year during the same 30-year period. By 1995, total waste had grown to 208.0 million tons, but the rate of growth had declined to 1.1 percent. Per capita generation held constant at 4.4 pounds per person per day from 1991 to 1995. Recycling increased to 27 percent of the total tonnage, reducing deposits in landfills to 151.9 million tons. The United States EPA forecasted per capita rates to remain constant at 4.4 pounds per day and recycling to increase to 30 percent of total volume by the year 2000.

The rise in recycling forced the waste management companies to reconsider the ways in which they were gathering solid waste for disposal. It was no longer clear whether it was efficient to be sending their large trucks up and down each city street. Moreover, municipalities were beginning to wake up to the fact that, in some cases, they were spending as much money repairing the damage done to back lanes and side streets by these large trucks as they were on getting the garbage removed from city streets. As a result, they were putting pressure on waste management companies to find alternative solutions. Toward this end, one solution was to use small feeder trucks like the GO-4 to pick up the garbage from residential streets and, when they were full, to have them meet with the larger trucks at designated meeting points.

What was attractive for Mauws in this application was that he would not have to get the GO-4 certified for operation on Canadian streets. The problem with it, if there was one, was that this application was more or less at the mercy of the large waste management companies. For this reason, it would require working quite closely with these companies to bring about significant changes in the way they did their business. However, not only did Mauws lack the time and resources to work with these companies, but he was also constrained by the fact that any negotiations with these companies were really the responsibility of WIL's distributor, WBS. Although WBS was certainly interested in making additional sales, at that time it was focusing its efforts on developing the parking patrol market.

Considering the Future for Westward Industries Ltd.

Larry Mauws worked his way through the shop floor, moving from employee to employee, greeting them or stopping for short talks as they assembled the GO-4s on the short production line. He was happiest here amidst the tangible world of his vehicles, but his mind kept drifting to the future of his small company. Although demand continued to be strong and he believed he could sell all the vehicles he could produce, the current model of the GO-4 was 4 years old and was a patchwork of modifications. Perhaps he should take the opportunity created by the changes in Kia's engine design to completely redesign the vehicle. He was also thinking that he needed someone to look into after-sale customer service and parts issues. What about Cushman? The rumor was that they were finally redesigning their vehicle and were working on an electric model. What would that do to sales in the United States? Perhaps Westward should be selling the vehicle right here in Canada? The provincial and national park services had shown an interest. Canada Post had also inquired about a mail delivery model. Trash collection was also a possibility. He knew that his 3-wheeled vehicle had great potential beyond its narrow use in parking patrol in the United States, but what strategy should he pursue? What markets should he enter? They need not be large markets; large markets attract large, powerful competitors. Westward needed a market that was big enough, but one that had specialized requirements that he could design into the basic GO-4 concept. Customer responsiveness and functionality in design were the key.

Larry realized that he had been leaning against the parts bins for some time, lost in thought. Most of the crew had left for the day, and only Fred, the journeyman machinist who ran the fabrication crew, and Sid, the assembly foreman, were still on the shop floor straightening up their production areas. It was well past 6 P.M. and the foremen's wives would be waiting dinner again. Larry was lucky to have a hardworking and loyal crew. When there was a shipment to make, Sid, Fred, and anyone else who was needed pitched in to get the order filled. The workers all called it "Larry's car," but it was their car, too. They were all proud to be part of Larry's success thus far. For Larry, the question was what to do to ensure continued success.

Clariant Corporation Marketing

Bradley W. Brooks, Queens University of Charlotte
David V. Rudd, Queens University of Charlotte

> Our specialty chemicals are used in many products you encounter every day. Pigments in paint, plastic, and leather in cars and in cosmetics. Photo-resists in video game displays. De-icing fluids for airports. Agro chemicals for food production and intermediate molecules for medicines. Special visual effects in plastic packaging. Even the active ingredient insect repellants. Clariant is "All Around You."

> —Promotional video (2001)

Swiss-based Clariant International Limited, like most specialty chemical companies, organizes its six global divisions around either the products they make, the products the chemicals are used on, or the industrial customers served. TLP (Textiles, Leather, and Paper) makes process chemicals for TLP producers. P&A (Pigments and Additives) makes colorants and other functional additives for many industries, including TLP. FUN (Functional Chemical) produces a plethora of "magic molecules." LSE (Life Sciences and Electronics) serves the needs of the electronics and booming pharmaceuticals industries. MB (Masterbatches) custom-blends pigments and/or additives into various substrates for use in the production of colored plastics. CEP (Cellulose Ethers and Polymerisates) provides specialty feed-stock chemicals plastics processing.

Clariant International Limited promises "Exactly Your Chemistry" for thousands of customers in four regions (Europe, the Americas, Asia/Australia, and Africa).

In September 2000, Vincent Thompson, vice president of operations for Clariant, frowned as he reviewed sales growth and contribution margin growth for the NAFTA region arm of Clariant International, Ltd. Sales and margin growth metrics were two of the company's most critical performance trends (Table 1). The data reflected the continued volatility that plagued the NAFTA arm for several years.

Vincent Thompson ended his review of the situation with questions about how Clariant could fully develop its potential for meeting its sales and profit growth goals. Thompson felt that Clariant should pursue overall structural changes to the sales and marketing functions, but he knew that such changes could be very costly and disruptive

TABLE 1 | CLARIANT CORP. MARGIN CHANGES/SALES GROWTH BY DIVISION, 1998–2000*

Clariant North America	Margin Change (%)			Sales Growth (%)		
Division	2000	1999	1998	2000	1999	1998
Textiles, Leather, & Paper	(>100)	(68.0)	(19.6)	(7.7)	(9.1)	(6.8)
Pigments and Additives	21.4	(0.9)	51.3	(2.7)	(2.3)	(1.7)
Functional Chemicals	6.8	(7.3)	43.9	(12.0)	(3.9)	(14.1)
Life Science & Electronic	91.9	(4.2)	(78.6)	(9.8)	(5.3)	1.7
Masterbatches	26.5	370.4	26.5	(1.1)	12.9	(48.0)

*SOURCE: Internal tracking reports for Clariant Corporation.

to the company and its operations. He wanted Clariant to redesign its sales force to include cross-divisional account teams that could be assigned to the organization's most profitable customers. In doing so, Clariant would assign one account executive to serve as a single contact person for the customer and to manage the overall relationship. This account executive would then work with salespersons representing each product of interest for the specific customer (i.e., the account team). Such changes, of course, would be achieved at a great cost financially both in terms of direct expenses and disruptions in the organization's operations. It would also require a shift in the current culture within the sale force. Other Clariant executives argued that the firm should alter its training approach. Instead of an account team for certain customers, they argued that Clariant should retrain its individual sales force representatives to be capable of selling products from the company's various product divisions. They argued that this approach would be less disruptive than designing account teams. Of course, incentives for the sales representatives would also need to be modified under such an approach. Still other executives argued that actually implementing either of these changes would be too difficult and complicated. They believed that all Clariant really needed was to begin providing financial incentives to its sales representatives for referring their individual customers to other Clariant sales representatives (i.e., those representatives who sell other products that the specific customer purchases).

Thompson understood the concerns about costs and disruptions and was willing to consider each of the options. His main concern was for Clariant to position itself to be able to attack multiple growth strategies simultaneously while competing under increasing external pressures. The specialty chemical industry, however, was no easy environment in which to compete.

Chemical Industry Background

Hilfra Tandy wrote,

> Chemical processes and products affect the lives of billions of people in both developed and less developed nations.[1] Most people, especially North Americans, would be hard pressed to find an element of their daily lives not impacted by the production or use of chemicals. From the plastic that

---

[1] Tandy, Hilfra, "Core Industry Finds Cures for Old Sickness," *Financial Times Survey*, July 3, 2000, (I). London, UK.

protects their food, to the plethora of emerging medicines, to special treatments for paper, leather, and textiles, to the rainbow of colors that grace the shelves, chemicals play a major role in bringing functionality, variety, and safety into people's daily lives. This phenomenon is not limited to the industrialized nations alone.

Worldwide, according to Tandy, the chemicals industry generates sales in the neighborhood of $1.7 trillion annually. As with many established industries, the chemicals industry divided over time into two major categories: commodity chemicals and specialty chemicals.

"Commodity" chemicals (83 percent of the market) are produced and sold in high volume in standard forms and configurations. Essential to most core manufacturing industries, commodity chemicals are used in a wide range of applications but serve the same function in most cases. Their appeal is in their functionality regardless of the application. Many commodity chemicals attract so much competition that price competition has driven much of the profitability out of the business. In fact, price competition is so fierce that the sales representatives of many of the commodity chemical producers often cut prices below their company's already low list prices to attract or retain a specific customer.

In response, several companies developed marketing campaigns that would differentiate their product offerings. For example, DuPont's "Better Living through Chemistry" campaign, BASF's "We don't make a lot of the products you buy; we make a lot of the products you buy better," and CIBA's "We are all around you" attempted to differentiate commodity chemical companies through advertising-supported market positioning.

Another common response to the increasing intensity of price competition of core products has been movement of manufacturing facilities to manufacturing-friendly parts of the world. Like firms in many industries, chemical companies shopped the world for places to process and produce their products that offer lower labor costs, special considerations on capital-goods costs, less stringent environmental regulations, and favorable tax structures. At the beginning of the 21st century, this movement toward global manufacturing, a worldwide tendency toward lower tariffs, as well as transportation and communication improvements that reduced time and space barriers in general, made the chemical industry one of the most widely distributed industrial activities on the face of the earth.

Globalization also brought new, low-cost, government-supported competitors, especially from China and India. Overcapacity in many commodity chemicals made it nearly impossible for any one company to sustain acceptable growth levels through internal expansion.

These circumstances led to grave concerns within the industry. Graham Copley, an investment-banking analyst speaking at an industry conference in early 2000, stated that the chemical industry had "failed to meet growth objectives for more than 30 years" and "the underlying earnings growth is poor."[2] With narrow margins, availability issues, and standard specifications, success in all commodities rests on three factors: economies of scale, cost reduction, and constant improvement in all aspects of the business.

Two of these factors can be acquired through mergers or acquisitions among like competitors. Economies of scale can be achieved for whole corporations by combining operations and eliminating duplication and, therefore, is generally limited by the efficient sizing of individual production facilities. Table 2 shows the growth of mergers or acquisitions of $50 million or more in the chemicals industry. This pace of large-company and large-component mergers and acquisitions is expected to continue.

---

[2] Ibid.

TABLE 2 | **VALUE OF CHEMICAL INDUSTRY MERGERS AND ACQUISITIONS***

Year	1995	1997	1998	1999 (est.)
$ Billions in mergers and acquisitions	10	37	41	50

*Excluding oil and pharmaceuticals.

SOURCE: Hilfra Tandy, *Financial Times Survey of the Chemical Industry*, July 3, 2000, p. iii.

The Product Life Cycle in the Chemical Industry

A commodity chemical does not begin its product life as a low-margin, high-volume, tightly contested product. It typically begins as a specialty chemical designed to fulfill a specific customer's needs. Early in the product life cycle, a successful specialty chemical would be highly valued for improving the product or the process leading to the product. Specialty chemical companies and their direct customers are often willing to invest in research and development to find just the right combination of performance and cost to meet the immediate need. Decision makers are able to visualize a product need and to forecast demand sufficient to assure an adequate return on investment.

If the specialty chemical reaches the right target market and the end product delivers the promised performance or performance improvement, then growth follows. Because growth generated good returns, other firms would then introduce competitive products. New, competitive products can successfully enter the market through *differentiation* (providing superior performance or end-user benefits) or by *positioning* (creating the perception that one product is better than another). Successful product differentiation usually allows the maker of the superior product to charge a premium price and thus generate premium margins even as the product reached maturity.

Ultimately, however, as technology spreads and competitors gravitate toward similar best practices, pricing and customer service tend to become the deciding factors in buyer-seller-user relationships. Specialty chemicals developed to meet even a highly specialized market need usually become standardized commodity products. At the extreme, where all competitors face similar technologies and raw materials and labor costs, price becomes the principal competitive weapon. In such mature markets, customers are unwilling to pay a premium for a standardized product even with exceptional customer service support. Mature commodity markets are primarily driven by price, service, technical support, company relationships, and delivery reliability.

Markets eventually decline as the product is replaced with substitutes, as technology eliminates the need for the product, or as the end use product loses favor in the marketplace.

Thompson understood that the highest profit potential for any single product came either from exploiting pricing opportunities during the growth stage of the life cycle or from maintaining superior product differentiation or positioning throughout an extended maturity stage. Growth and profitability for a chemical firm, therefore, come from maintaining a mix of products at different stages in the product life cycle. Managing a portfolio of different product lines has become a critical part of the overall business strategy of the company.

Structure of the Specialty Chemical Industry[3]

By late 2000, specialty chemical sales were rapidly approaching $400 billion worldwide. Specialty chemicals were more application- and end-use specific than commodity chemicals. The number of distinct end-user segments was nearly 50. With the rapid expansion of technology, the dizzying pace of product innovation, and the rapid globalization of commercial competition in general, specialty chemicals companies were under tremendous pressure for growth in both sales and profits.

Not surprisingly, the specialty chemical market was highly segmented itself. The top eight end-user segments (pharmaceuticals, agrochemicals, polymers, adhesives and sealants, food additives, flavors and fragrances, electronic chemicals, and photographic chemicals) accounted for less than two-thirds of total sales. This diversity added to the challenge of growth.

The specialty chemicals segment was even more active in the area of mergers and acquisitions than the overall chemical industries. Despite accounting for only 17 percent of total sales in 1999, the specialty chemical segment accounted for 21 percent of merger-and-acquisition activity as commodity chemical companies sought specialty products to bolster their margins.

Industrial globalization brought new competition to the specialty segment, and technology-driven change demanded introduction of more and more specialty products. In the last decade of the 20th century the specialty chemical segment had evolved into three distinct tiers:

Tier-one specialty chemical producers were divisions of major chemical firms specializing in particular chemicals or user segments. Typical tier-one company sales were tens of billions of dollars annually. Their parent corporations were eager to invest in these higher-margin opportunities.

Tier-two firms were spin-off businesses, divisions of large chemical companies spun off into separate entities in order to allow them to focus on their own particular portfolio of specialty chemicals. Tier-two sales were typically in the $3–5 billion range annually.

Tier-two companies had to generate investment capital externally.

Tier-three companies typically range from $1 billion to $2 billion in annual sales and generally had a narrower range of offerings than tier-two firms. Long-term survival depended on the uniqueness of their product offering, which also had to be highly valued and protected from direct competition within their user base.

Vincent Thompson commented on Clariant's position:

We, meaning both Clariant Corporation and our parent, Clariant Limited, fall into Tier Two. Tier Two is a precarious place to be. Above us are the resource-rich divisions of large companies. Below us are narrow-line specialists who survive by doing only what they do best—meaning they build lasting relationships with the best end-users in their particular segments and

---

[3] Tandy, Hilfra, "Star Sector Struggles to Retain Status," *Financial Times Survey*, July 3, 2000. (IV). London, UK.

TABLE 3 | COST/EXPENSE PERCENT OF SALES RATIOS 2000*, CLARIANT LIMITED

	Percent of Sales
Sales	100%
—Cost of goods sold	66
Gross Profit	34
—*Sales expense*	8
—Marketing and distribution	6
—Research and development	4
—Admin & general overhead	5
Operating income	11

*This profit model is a rough approximation and is not to be used beyond the scope of this case.

they compete fiercely on price when a major account is up for grabs. One of our managers characterized our position as being caught "between a herd of elephants and a pool of sharks." We certainly understand the pressure of being in the middle.

Clariant International Limited and Clariant Corporation

Clariant International Limited was formed in 1995 when selected specialty chemical divisions of Sandoz, with sales of approximately $1.5 billion, were spun off. Selected divisions of Hoechst-Celanese were added to the mix in 1997, bringing the total annual sales to approximately $5.5 billion worldwide. (See Table 3 for a year 2000 corporate breakdown of sales and expense ratios.) The NAFTA region accounted for approximately $1.1 billion, or 20 percent of worldwide sales.

On average it appeared that the increased cost to train the sales representatives to be able sell products across other divisions would probably increase the sales activities from its current 8 percent of sales to approximately 8.5 percent for the next two to three years and then to settle in at approximately 8.2 percent thereafter. Major expenses included cross-divisional product training and building and maintaining an informational infrastructure to keep everyone up to date on product and account information. Of course, a future sales expense to sales revenue ratio that is roughly equivalent to its current level but with increased actual sales levels could represent significant actual profit increases. Thompson, however, perceived this approach to pose a high level of risk because it would certainly not be a given that the company could achieve a sales increase within only three years that would be in proportion to the required increase in expenses.

By 2000, Clariant Limited, based in Switzerland, was organized into six global business units. Two of the six divisions were organized by end user: Textiles, Leather, & Paper (TLP) and Life Science and Electronic Chemicals (LSE). Two divisions were organized by functionality: Pigments and Additives (P&A) and Masterbatches (MB). Finally, two divisions were organized by chemical class: Functional Chemicals (FUN)

TABLE 4	OPERATING EXPENSES AND OPERATING INCOME PERCENT OF SALES RATIOS BY DIVISION 2000, CLARIANT LIMITED					
	TLP	**P&A**	**FUN**	**LSE**	**MB**	**CEP***
Sales	100%	100%	100%	100%	100%	100%
Sales to other divisions	1	3	5	10	0	4
Net sales	99	97	95	90	100	96
Total Operating Expenses	82	78	82	75	87	88
Operating income	17	19	13	15	13	12

*CEP was added in summer 2000.

and Cellulose Ethers and Polymerisates (CEP). Although the exact composition of the product array in each division had varied significantly from year to year and division names had occasionally been changed, the basic alignment had persisted throughout the six-year history of Clariant Limited. In all, these six divisions contained 19 separate businesses. (See Table 4 for a breakdown of each division's costs and expenses as a percentage of sales.)

Until mid-2000, only five of the global business units had operations in Clariant Corporation's North American realm. In the summer of 2000, CEP was added to the Clariant product array as a result of the acquisition of British Tar Products (BTP) by Clariant Limited. The BTP acquisition also brought critical mass to the Life Sciences Intermediates part of the LSE unit and greatly enhanced the offerings in the TLP business unit for Clariant Corporation. Clariant Corporation was created coincident with the Sandoz spin-off to oversee Clariant's businesses in North America. Because of the size of North American markets and the level of development of the North American economies, performance in the region is especially important to the overall performance of Clariant Limited.

With a strong U.S. economy, performance expectations for Clariant Corporation were high. Going into 2000, the North American market contributed almost one-third of overall corporate sales. In the opinions of some at Clariant Limited's world headquarters, however, the specialty chemical businesses in North America should have generated more growth and profitability than it had. Overall sales figures indicated a broad general decline thought to have been caused in part by heightened competition from expanded production in China and other Far East countries. All five of Clariant Corporation's established divisions showed sales declines (see Table 1).

Contribution margin decreases in the Textiles, Leather, and Paper Division had accelerated an already precipitous decline. Extreme competitive price pressures, the growth of production capacity in Asia, and a general economic slowdown beginning in early 2000 had all contributed to the division's problems. Contribution margin had increased, however, in the other four divisions. Thompson wondered if the long, arduous, and difficult period of forming, consolidating, expanding, and integrating units that made up the global company was beginning to pay off. In light of increasing external pressures, he also wondered how Clariant could capitalize on its current margin growth strength and if there were ways to leverage the current technical, sales, and marketing capabilities to pursue growth. "Our current North American strategy," Thompson considered, "is to focus growth on fine chemicals and specialty chemicals while holding the line in price sensitive 'semi-specialties.' The nature of the industry is that sitting still for too long will probably lead to a rapid degradation in both sales and profit performance."

At Clariant Corporation headquarters in Charlotte, North Carolina, it was believed that a portion of the lower-than-expected performance could be explained by the shift of production capacity from the United States to other countries (China, India, Mexico, etc.) in key customer industries such as textile fibers, fabric, and clothing production. Additionally, logistical and other difficulties related to integrating multiple divisions, multiple product lines, and multiple business operations into a cohesive whole had provided a difficult operating environment in the late 1990s.

Clariant Corporation president David Lawrence, in speaking to the different operating units on what he called a "Town Meeting" tour in spring of 2000, had divided the brief history of Clariant Corporation in three stages:

> The consolidation stage ran from 1995 to 1997. Emphasis was on sorting out all of the pieces, reorganizing the structure, aligning the Clariant Corporation structure with the Clariant Limited structure, and eliminating excess cost brought on by duplication. The integration stage ran from 1997 to 1999. Emphasis was on discovering and capitalizing on easily obtained internal opportunities ("low hanging fruit") for cross-divisional sales or inter- intra-divisional cost reductions. The growth stage is now underway. The aim is to aggressively attack the problems of growth and profitability using the technical, marketing, and sales capacities of the many operating units.

In setting the agenda for growth, Lawrence outlined a three-pronged strategy to achieve both the sales and profit performance:

A. Sales growth through strategic acquisitions to achieve targeted growth in high-margin segments,

B. Sales growth generated by cross-divisional sales of multiple Clariant lines to key, high-potential customers, and

C. Improving margins by emphasizing sales of higher-margin specialty products over the more established "semi-specialty" products (those nearing commodity status).

In implementing these strategies, especially the cross-divisional sales strategy, Clariant had invested significant time, energy, and money into the creation of cross-divisional product understanding among the various business units. Significant training investments were already being made in the various sales forces. Technologies were being implemented, including central databases of product information, product contact information, and "center of excellence teams." All of these activities contributed to the ability of a salesperson from a particular division to probe for and identify opportunities for other divisions. Customers having potential for sales from other Clariant divisions were then to be connected with the appropriate people. Some Clariant executives argued that the company should begin offering financial incentives for such referrals, pointing out that the incentives would be paid only if the referral actually resulted in additional sales. The cost, therefore, was negligible, because it would be incurred only when Clariant makes additional revenue and because it represented a marginal amount of the increase in profit. Their argument pointed out the low initial investment and, therefore, low risk of this approach.

To capture these potential cross-divisional opportunities, which often arose from a customer's pressing needs for new approaches to product development, a fledgling national accounts system was under development and had resulted in several promising contacts with high-potential customers, including a major packaged-goods marketer, a major multiline retailer, and a major athletic sportswear and footwear manufacturer. Recognizing that the core of Clariant Limited was its strong divisional structure and worldwide presence, the national accounts effort in North America started on an ad hoc basis. This meant that each opportunity for cross-divisional cooperation had to be formed, funded, and managed as a separate task force or team. Thompson commented: "I know that this is a good thing, but I wonder how well these cross-divisional and national accounts initiatives are working and how our ad hoc approach compares to that of the competition."

Marketing and Sales in Clariant Corporation

As with most tier-two specialty chemical companies, Clariant is almost constantly involved in adjusting the mix of its businesses, with frequent acquisitions, integrations, consolidations, and dispositions. Clariant Limited, and by natural extension Clariant Corporation, is a conglomeration of the pieces that had been put together over the past five years. Unlike DuPont or BASF, no attempt has been made to create a universal Clariant brand. Most of the products are still sold under their original trade names. (See Appendix A for examples of the mix of Sandoz [Sanda, Sando, Sodye], Hoechst [Hosta], and Clariant [CAS] trade nomenclature.)

Although somewhat oversimplified, Clariant's marketing strategy consists primarily of finding the right mix of product lines and running the plants at profitable levels. Pull-oriented marketing efforts, aimed at educating customers, potential customers, and prospects to the wide range of capabilities in the Clariant portfolio of businesses are then far less important than the push-related efforts from the sales forces.

Business unit and divisional level sales forces are provided annual sales objectives that reflected the need for the company to keep its production facilities operating at profitable levels. Clariant depends on a number of separate and distinct sales organizations. Each global business unit has its own sales force. If the global business unit had distinct separations among its product lines, along user lines, along industry lines, or among geographic concentration of applications, then the business-unit sales force would be further divided. A large percentage of the sales force is composed of a legacy of salespeople from the original companies that had formed Clariant.

As with most chemical companies, most salespeople are recruited from the technical ranks of key customers and come to the sales job with extensive knowledge of how the chemicals they sell are used. With its wide range of specialty chemical applications, the Clariant sales force has very diverse backgrounds.

Through this diversity, combined with the variety of organizing schemes for the six divisions, virtually every form of sales force organizing strategy exists somewhere in Clariant Corporation. Some salespeople report to regional sales managers who report, in turn, to product-line-specific sales and marketing managers. Some salespeople report directly to national sales and marketing managers.

A summer 2000 research report on specialty chemical companies showed that virtually all of the competitive sales forces were organized by product line, by user groups or industries, or by geography. In many cases, these three methods were combined into multitiered sales organizations reflecting the same complexity that Clariant Corporation faces.[4] Most elements of DuPont, for example, were organized by industry, with coverage depending on the size of the account. BASF had 17 divisions and 100 strategic business units, most of which were organized around a formal key account structure. CIBA, committed to delivery of value through innovation, productive relationships, and operational speed and simplicity, was organized around regional business structures. PP&G tended to be organized by industry within its product divisions.

Clariant's approach to handling national accounts differs significantly from that of its major competitors. Most major competitors have permanent teams assigned to manage the relationship with high-potential and high-profit accounts. These teams generally cut across division boundaries and place the account at the center of the marketing and sales effort. In at least one case, an executive VP was assigned at company headquarters to coordinate all contacts with the account and served as a first call point for problem resolution. This executive VP had only one responsibility: to maintain and build the account relationship.

Clariant Corporation, on the other hand, occasionally assembles account teams in response to specific account opportunities. In the case of a cooperative development project with a major packaged-goods marketer, an ad hoc account team was "assembled" in response to a request from the customer's marketing and technical staff. In the case of a major retailer, an account team was "assembled" in response to a developing marketing strategy involving the Masterbatches Division and its ability to quickly match colors across multiple product categories (and therefore multiple materials and production systems). Thompson oversaw the Clariant national account work as a part of his overall responsibilities for consolidated operations. He commented:

> Part of the challenge of the national accounts approach in Clariant comes from the fact that the local business unit sales forces feel that they (personally) "own" their customers. Forming a national account team means convincing multiple divisions to allocate their limited sales, technical, and marketing resources to the national team and to allow the national team access to key customers. The divisions have been very cautious regarding this proposed approach because of the difficulty in estimating just how much of these resources would actually be required, particularly since any given division couldn't be sure that it would benefit as much as other divisions would. Furthermore, the individual account's current salesperson also tends to resist such an approach. A common concern is a fear that if other Clariant salespeople were involved with the account it could mean losing some of the customer's current level of business to the other Clariant sales members. Another common fear is that another Clariant salesperson

[4]Brooks, Bradley W., "Exploratory Research on Customer Preferences," Clariant authorized study, 2000. Unpublished.

TABLE 5 | **SALES AND MARKETING PERSONNEL AVERAGE TIME BUDGET, FALL 2000**

	Sales and Marketing Managers' Time (%)	**Salespersons' Time (%)**
Processing routine reorders	1	14
Generating new business for our product line	23	31
Identifying prospects for new business for Clariant beyond our product line	4	3
Handling customer service problems and concerns	15	17
Professional development	3	4
Administrative tasks	34	13
Other	20	18

SOURCE: Confidential survey of Clariant Corporation Sales Managers, September 2000.

might not handle the account in the same manner that he/she would handle it, particular since the new sales member would not yet "know" the customer.

Leaving the divisional sales forces as they were and adding an additional layer of sales management in the form of an account executive would add $120,000 per account per year. Thompson estimated that there were 50 major accounts that would be eligible for account executives.

Clariant Sales and Marketing Managers

When asked to describe the role of marketing in the overall sales and marketing effort, sales and marketing manager comments ranged from "none at all" to "product management and communications" and "very little" to "secondary to the sales activities." One perception of the way the company is organized to fulfill the need of high-margin or high-volume customers is that "most of the effort of the sales managers, product managers, territory reps, and customer service is focused on key customers." With regard to top customers, "We will do custom product development for them." Often, key managers are assigned to important customers along with the sales representatives. As was the case at many industrial firms, access to key customers is closely guarded by the salesperson calling on the account.

Table 5 reports statistics on time allocation from Clariant's marketing and sales managers. Thompson commented on these figures:

Clariant salespeople don't spend much of their time identifying opportunities for new business for Clariant outside of their own division. Likewise, the sales and marketing managers don't seem to focus on Clariant-wide new business development. Are those good numbers or are they lower than they should be? Does our effort reflect the size of the potential opportunity?

Since most routine orders are placed through Clariant Corporation's Customer Service Organization, the low percentage of time spent on routine order processing by salespeople and sales managers is expected. The emphasis on divisional efforts is not surprising, since the bulk of the salesperson's compensation is comprised of a base salary and a commission or bonus based on sales performance of their accounts on the products that their business unit produces.

Our incentive system doesn't exactly support the cross-divisional selling initiative. Seventy-five percent of our upper-management bonuses are tied to our North American divisional sales, earnings, return on sales, and net working capital performance. Twenty-five percent of our bonuses relate to the same performance metrics for our global division. Despite the prominence of divisional results in our incentive system, the cross-divisional selling issue has the attention of Clariant Corporation's top management. We have placed a lot of emphasis recently on the need for identifying high-potential opportunities for Clariant Corporation as a whole. We feel that success here is critical to the success of the firm as a whole. Is our initiative in its infancy or is it destined not to catch hold at all?

Customer Expectations

During the summer of 2000, Thompson had commissioned research comprised of in-depth surveys of 26 Clariant customers.[5] The results of this research are summarized in Table 6.

The customers were not informed that Clariant was the sponsor of the research, and no attempt was made to evaluate Clariant versus any of its competitors. Instead, the research delved into what the customers expected of their key specialty chemical suppliers, how they expected to get information about new products and opportunities, and what role the emerging Internet "marketplaces for chemicals" would play in their future relationships with these suppliers.

The written report that accompanied the survey results contained the following observations:

> . . . Not surprisingly, all purchasers listed quality, service (including technical support), and price as very important variables in their relationships with suppliers. Perhaps surprisingly, price came in third. It is not clear whether the Clariant sales force appropriately emphasizes the firm's quality and technical support capabilities, rather than price.
> . . . We found a willingness to pay more for "chemicals involved in a special application or where the chemical needed to be tweaked or modified." This seems consistent with the company's technical expertise and major commitment to pilot operations that routinely develops "magic molecules"

---
[5] Ibid.

| TABLE 6 | KEY FINDINGS: INTERVIEWS WITH CLARIANT CUSTOMERS |

Issue	Primary Finding	Extent of Finding
Describe the nature of your relationship with your specialty chemical suppliers	Positive, close, there are special suppliers they feel closer to.	22 of 26 described relationship as close . . . meaning regular contact, sharing important information and supplier understanding customer's business.
Length of supplier relationship	Most have maintained relationship for three or more years . . . and wish to remain with long-time suppliers.	7 of 26 are "constantly looking for information on new suppliers."
Important supplier attributes	Quality service (including technical support)	Quality is a given . . . miss quality and you lose the account.
	Price	Some willingness to pay higher price to ensure quality, service, and delivery . . . really meant pay more if chemical is special.
Who defines quality?	The customer	25 of 26 say that their customers determine what quality means.
Attitude and behavior toward companies with multiple products that you need	Majority give advantage to current suppliers when evaluating new product needs.	20 of 26 prefer to work with current suppliers.
How do you prefer to hear about new products from the supplier and about additional products from other units of the supplier's company?	Want to negotiate with just a single contact. Dislike having to work with multiple representatives from same company.	12 of 26 want single contact.

24 of 26 want new and additional product opportunities to come from supplier rep. |
	Prefer the supplier contact keep them informed of new and additional offerings.	
How will relationship with suppliers change in the future and in the face of new technology (Internet markets, etc.)?	Half would purchase commodity chemicals from an e-commerce market.	Attitude toward technology is biased by personal style in relating to suppliers. The more the purchaser values the relationship, the less technology looms as a threat to the relationship. The more distant the relationship, the more technology will threaten the interaction.
	Technology should facilitate the relationship, not replace it.	
	Purchasers need information in a more timely (read that NOW) manner than ever before.	
Other findings	Large, sophisticated clients want to integrate the supplier into the product-development process to shorten timetables and to streamline problem solving.	

for key customers. Clariant's speed of response, technical expertise, and wide range of production capabilities across all divisions give strength in this important area.

. . . Customers demand predictable, reliable, dependable delivery performance. Will increased cross-divisional customer relationships create unrealistic expectations on the various divisions' operations?

. . . We found that customers are willing to give existing suppliers more business in the interest of streamlining operations if they have multiple products that fit the customer's needs. These customers definitely want to deal with one liaison to their key suppliers and not myriad individual contacts. Furthermore, these same customers think that the suppliers bear major responsibility for informing them of new products and new opportunities. These findings seem to place a very high premium on the ability of all of the company's sales and marketing people to represent the whole of Clariant Corporation.

. . . We found that customers do not perceive the Internet to be replacing the buyer-seller relationship. According to the May 8, 2000, issue of *Business-to-Business Marketing* magazine, four of the top ten Internet based marketplaces were designed to facilitate the exchange of chemicals. Clariant's customers saw these exchanges as more appropriate for the purchase of commodity chemicals than specialty chemicals. They do, however, see technology as a boost to the process of purchasing chemicals. Affording customers a way to review the inventory availability on products of interest is seen as a boost for the relationship. Clariant's order processing and order fulfillment process involves the customer service reps taking the time to confirm availability and/or see if production schedules could be adjusted to meet the customer's needs. Customers knew that an order placed did not necessarily mean that the order could be filled. Often, a customer would probe the availability of a product and only provide a purchase order upon availability confirmation.

. . . We found that the most sophisticated customers are eager to involve suppliers in the product development process. For a specialty chemical company, if a customer's end product is designed around one of your products, the odds are very good that you will enjoy at least a short period as the preferred supplier for that product.

. . . Finally, we found that Clariant's customer's customer (i.e., the end user, the retailer, etc.) plays an important part in defining what quality really means and what is acceptable performance. Clariant's culture was heavily oriented toward the chemicals themselves, the technology and science behind the chemicals, and the use of the chemicals by its direct customers. This perspective is not unusual in primary raw material and component supplier industries. Do the Clariant sales and marketing people think past their direct customer to understand the end user's interest in Clariant's chemicals?

Pushing back from this array of reports, Thompson resolved to complete his review in time for the start of the strategic planning cycle in two weeks and develop his definitive recommendations to the president.

APPENDIX | PARTIAL LISTING OF CLARIANT CORPORATION TRADE NAMES

Algepon	Anodal	Apretan
Aquanyl	Bactosol	Carbapon
Carta . . . 16 variations	CAS . . . 290 numeric variations	Cassofix
Catolix	Ceranine	Ceridust
Colanyl	Dalamar	Deniblack
Denivat	Derma . . . 7 variations	Diaformer
Diresul	Dispersogen	Dissolvan
Drimagen Drimalan Drimarene	Duasyn	Flexonyl Flexoprint
Fluowet	Foron	Gena . . . 6 variations
Genolub Genosorb	Glyoxal Glyoxylic	Graphtol
Hosta . . . 33 variations	Humectol	Hydro
Imacol	Imerol	Lamprecide
Lana . . . 6 variations	Leuco . . . 4 variations	Lico . . . 7 variations
Lyocol Lyogen	Maroxol	Mercerol
Nipa . . . 9 variations	Novo . . . 3 variations	Nylo . . . 5 variations
Opti . . . 3 variations	Pheno . . . 3 variations	Sanda . . . or Sando . . . 44 variations
Sodye . . . 12 variations	Supronil	Tergolix
V-Brite V-Finer	Virtex Virwhite	Visco . . . 3 variations

SOURCE: Master product information directory, Clariant Corporation.

RJM Enterprises, Inc.— Romancing the Vine

Armand Gilinsky, Jr., Sonoma State University
Nancy A. Campbell, Sonoma State University

> There will still be enough good meals and good wine to last us all a few more decades; it is only that they are becoming harder to find. The rise and fall of an art takes time. The full arc is seldom manifest to a single generation. The romance of wine—it is a wonderful thing when there is chemistry.
>
> —A.J. Liebling, *Between Meals: An Appetite for Paris*, 1959, 1962

With another year's harvest well behind him, Ron McManis and his ten-year-old son, Justin, walked through well-manicured rows of grapevines while considering future plans. It was early in December of 1997, and McManis was about to meet with two North Coast wine industry consultants: Jim Ford of Fifth Resource Group, LLC, in Cotati, California, and Dave Kincaid of BDM Construction, Inc., in Santa Rosa, California. McManis hoped to decide on a direction to take his grape-growing company, RJM Enterprises, Inc. (RJM). RJM was located in Ripon, a small town in California's San Joaquin Valley (Central Valley). McManis considered how to protect RJM's outstanding reputation for quality, visionary leadership, and strong family history in the Central Valley. If McManis made the right decision, his business would grow, perhaps eventually becoming a fully integrated winery that he could pass on to his son.

Company Background

Farming had been the way of life for over four generations of the McManis family in California's lush Central Valley—an area comprising some of the world's largest wine grape growers and wineries. (See Exhibit 1 for a map of selected wine regions.) When

This case study was prepared as a basis for class discussion rather than to illustrate either effective or ineffective handling of an administrative situation. All individuals and events described are real. The case benefited from the suggestions of several anonymous reviewers of the *Case Research Journal*. The authors also wish to acknowledge the generous support of the Wine Business Program at Sonoma State University as well as the invaluable assistance of Jim Ford, Allan Hemphill, Dave Kincaid, Professor Wally Lowry, Ron McManis, Jeff Runquist, and Bill Turrentine.

EXHIBIT 1 | MAP OF SELECTED WINE REGIONS

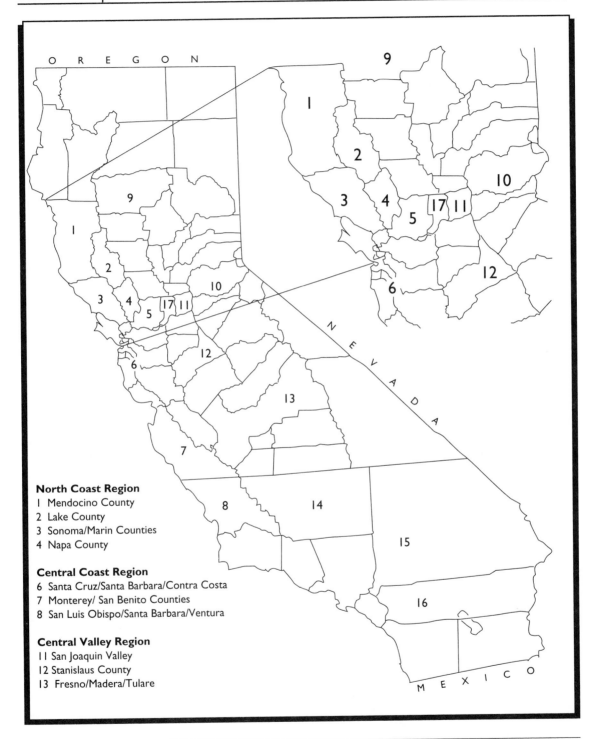

North Coast Region
1 Mendocino County
2 Lake County
3 Sonoma/Marin Counties
4 Napa County

Central Coast Region
6 Santa Cruz/Santa Barbara/Contra Costa
7 Monterey/ San Benito Counties
8 San Luis Obispo/Santa Barbara/Ventura

Central Valley Region
11 San Joaquin Valley
12 Stanislaus County
13 Fresno/Madera/Tulare

NOTE: The numbers on the map are used as a means to organize the grape-growing regions for purposes of statistical reporting only and do not rank the regions in any fashion.
SOURCE: California Agricultural Statistics Service, P.O. Box 1258, Sacramento, CA 95812.

McManis graduated from high school, he had been given the opportunity to farm the same 80-acre plot of land as his father and grandfathers before him, and he began farming grapes. During the 1980s, McManis learned the hard way how to make a living from farming. Soon, McManis considered venturing beyond his family's expertise and the life that he had known since childhood. He and his wife, Jamie (the "J" in RJM), reinvested their earnings from the vineyard operations and expanded their farm to 2,500 acres, of which 1,100 were planted in grapes.

By the time RJM Enterprises was incorporated in 1990, McManis had learned how to market his products and price his services affordably. He began to buck the Central Valley way of farming in order to improve the quality of his grapes. Central Valley grapes typically produced higher yields per acre than in the North Coast (i.e., Napa or Sonoma), but according to McManis, a prejudice existed among North Coast winemakers that high tonnage and different soil and climate conditions in the Central Valley resulted in lower quality wines. Although an average Napa Valley yield was six tons per acre, RJM's average yields were eleven tons per acre. The lower yields combined with certain farming practices in the North Coast resulted in wines with flavors of greater intensity and aging capabilities.

As early as 1995, at age 33, McManis knew he was ready for a challenge—something innovative:

> I am always on the lookout for opportunities. For example, if three farmers are selling the same apples, you have to think about what you can do differently to sell your apples. Anyone can sell in the good times. If you aren't progressive about how to market your product, you'll get hurt at the other end. Bringing wine to the wineries is the crux of the deal. Do what they need. Keep working it to make it better. I prefer new, modern systems. Now is the time to develop the learning curve. It's better to do it in the good times than when you are forced to. Keep evaluating, keep moving—you can't ever sit still.

McManis felt that he had "the right variety at the right spot," and if a winemaker started with superior grapes, quality-blending components could be added later. Nearly 60 percent of RJM's Chardonnay vineyards were planted at the convergence of the Stanislaus and San Joaquin Rivers. Bill Turrentine (of Turrentine Wine Brokerage in San Anselmo, California) advised McManis that although RJM's Chardonnay grapes would not normally be used as the main component in a $25 bottle of wine, he could capitalize on his superior Central Valley location.

McManis wanted more control over his destiny. He did not want to encounter the problems that his father and neighboring growers had faced during times of grape surpluses. During those times, buyer power among the wineries had been strong, and based on grape quality and excess supply, growers ran the risk of being paid lower prices or price penalties, or, worse yet, of having their grapes rejected. Growers had few options: sell grapes at the reduced price; drive the grapes from door to door to find an immediate buyer; crush the grapes and try to sell the juice/wine on the bulk market; or lose the load. (See the glossary for definitions of wine industry terminology.)

McManis also believed that his Chardonnay and Zinfandel grapes could bring in more than the average price per ton paid by the Valley wineries, because North Coast wineries were paying almost twice that much for North Coast grapes. The possible price enhancement from selling Central Valley grape juice versus grapes to North Coast wineries is shown in Exhibit 2.

EXHIBIT 2 | PRICES PAID FOR CALIFORNIA WINE GRAPES

Varietal Grapes	All California 1995	All California 1996	Central Valley San Joaquin 1996	North Coast Napa 1996	North Coast Sonoma 1996
Chardonnay	$893	$1,130	$773	$1,543	$1,456
Zinfandel	$521	$565	$588	$878	$1,222

SOURCE: *Final Grape Crush Report—1996 Crop*, March 10, 1997, California Department of Food and Agriculture, Sacramento, CA.

External Forces

Declining per capita consumption of wine, changing consumer tastes, regulatory constraints, and a shortage of grapes created a need for new strategies in the U.S. wine industry in the mid-1990s. Although per capita consumption of wine was decreasing, wine sales remained strong, having been fueled by an improved overall economy, positive news about the health benefits of moderate wine consumption, and increased prices due to the shortage of supply. (See Exhibit 3 and Exhibit 4.) Still, anti-alcohol groups continued to advocate stringent labeling requirements. The strong lobby of anti-alcohol groups, along with other publicity regarding the effects of alcohol on health and public safety, were considered by some industry observers to have had a negative impact on wine sales and consumption.[1]

During the mid-1990s, consumers began "trading up" from generic or jug-type wines to premium, varietal wines. Much of this change in consumer tastes was due to the fact that the largest wine-consuming group was aging baby boomers—those over 40 years old with incomes greater than $60,000. According to Jon Fredrikson, a highly respected industry analyst and publisher of the *Gomberg-Fredrikson Report*:

> While consumption of wine is barely rising in the United States . . . Americans are spending more and more money on California wine. Since 1990, Americans have doubled their spending on California table wine . . . this growth is driven by consumers' thirst for upscale wines that sell for $7 a bottle and above. The market is changing as people move upscale in a big, big way. As a result of this shift, the market for jug wines retail-priced at $3 a bottle is quickly shrinking. Sales of generic wines in U.S. supermarkets plunged 7 percent last year, while sales of the "Big Four" varietals—Chardonnay, Cabernet Sauvignon, Merlot and White Zinfandel—rose 11 percent and now generate nearly two-thirds of wine revenues.

Rising consumer demand for premium wines, most notably Chardonnay, Cabernet, and Merlot, came at a time of soft supply of grapes for these wines. California vineyards were being replanted due to the phylloxera[2] outbreak of the 1980s, and poor

---

[1] The *U.S. Wine Market*, 1997 Edition. *Impact Databank Review and Forecast*, New York. NY: M. Shanken Communications.

[2] Phylloxera, an aphid-like insect that attacks the roots of grapevines, began appearing in Napa Valley vineyards in 1983, and by 1989 a U.C. Davis phylloxera task force determined that widespread vineyard decline had been due to phylloxera. The root louse sucks the nutrients from the roots and slowly starves the vine, creating dramatic decrease in fruit production.

EXHIBIT 3 | **COMPARISONS OF PER CAPITA WINE CONSUMPTION**

Per Capita Wine Consumption in Selected Countries
1970–1995

Country	Gallons of Wine			1980–95 % Change	1970–95 % Change
	1970	1980	1995		
France	29.0	23.4	18.0	−1.73	−1.89
Italy	29.0	21.0	15.0	−2.22	−2.60
Spain	16.0	16.0	10.0	−3.08	−1.86
Australia	2.2	4.6	4.7	0.14	3.08
Chile	12.0	13.0	4.0	−7.06	−4.30
United Kingdom	1.0	8.0	3.0	−6.33	4.49
Canada	0.6	2.2	1.9	−0.97	4.72
United States	1.0	2.0	1.8	−0.70	2.38

SOURCE: *Wines & Vines*, July 1997, Statistical Issue.

EXHIBIT 4 | **PROJECTIONS FOR TOTAL WINE CONSUMPTION THROUGH YEAR 2000**

National Trends & Statistics
Projections for Total Wine Consumption
(Thousands of 9-Liter Cases)

Year		Total Cases of Wine	CAGR*%
1995		197,007	
1996	Proj. vs. 1995	200,000	1.5
1997	Proj. vs. 1995	202,300	1.3
1998	Proj. vs. 1995	204,200	1.2
1999	Proj. vs. 1995	206,000	1.1
2000	Proj. vs. 1995	207,400	1.0

*CAGR = Compound Annual Growth Rate
SOURCE: *Adams/Jobson's Wine Handbook*, 1996.

weather conditions led to decreased grape yields. In order to meet the near-term shortfalls in supply, over 90 million gallons of wine were imported to meet the increased demand for high-end wines. These steps resulted in an increase in the import market share and a decrease in the domestic market share.[3]

The wine industry was subject to extensive regulation by the Federal Bureau of Alcohol, Tobacco and Firearms, various foreign agencies, and state liquor and local authorities. These regulations and laws dictated such matters as licensing requirements,

[3] Walker, Larry. 45th Annual Statistical Issue. *Wines & Vines*, 78(7) (July 1997). San Rafael, CA: The Hiaring Company.

trade and pricing practices, channels of distribution, labeling and advertising restrictions, and relations with wholesalers and retailers. Expansion of wineries' existing facilities and development of new vineyards and wineries were limited by zoning ordinances, environmental impact restrictions, and truth-in-labeling requirements.[4] In 1983, wine-labeling laws had taken effect that included the following:

- VITICULTURAL AREA: "At least 85 percent of the grapes used to produce the wine must be from within the confines of the viticultural area stated on the label."

- VARIETAL GRAPE LABELING: "One variety—The name of a single grape may be used if not less than 75 percent of the wine is derived from grapes of that variety, the entire 75 percent of which was grown in the labeled appellation of origin."

- APPELLATION OF ORIGIN: ". . . at least 75 percent of its volume is derived from fruit or agricultural products and grown in place or region indicated . . ."[5]

Labeling regulations provided marketing opportunities to wineries, allowing them to position themselves within the premium wine categories due to the known quality and reputation of the designated regions and varietal grapes. Others, though, sought more flexibility in their sources, promoted their products in a lower-end segment, and used generic appellations such as "California" and/or nondesignated varietal claims such as "white table wine."

Winemaking

According to the *Oxford Companion to Wine* (1999), the production of wines usually entailed crushing and destemming the grape clusters or bunches on arrival at the winery (although occasionally white grapes were crushed beforehand at a field pressing station). After crushing and destemming, the sweet pomace required draining and pressing to separate the liquids from the solids (lees). Wine was then created by fermentation: the process of converting sugar to ethanol and carbon dioxide (CO_2), effected by the anaerobic metabolism of yeast. The world has relied upon fermentation since the beginning of civilization to produce bread and cheese as well as all fermented beverages such as beer, wine, and cider. First, yeast was added to grapes (H_2O and sugar and grape flavor components) to create fermentation, which produces heat and CO_2 Then, after the fermentation process was complete, the fermentable sugars were converted to alcohol, and there was a slight change in the grape flavors otherwise known as "components." The timing of the separation of juice from solids constituted the major difference between red and white winemaking; *before* fermentation for whites and *after* for reds. The differences between the red and white winemaking processes are illustrated in Exhibits 5 and 6.

[4]The Wine Institute, http://www.wineinstitute.org
[5]Title 27 Part 4 of the Code of Federal Regulations. Washington, DC: Bureau of Alcohol, Tobacco and Firearms, Regulatory Agency, United States Department of the Treasury.

EXHIBIT 5   │ THE RED WINE PRODUCTION PROCESS

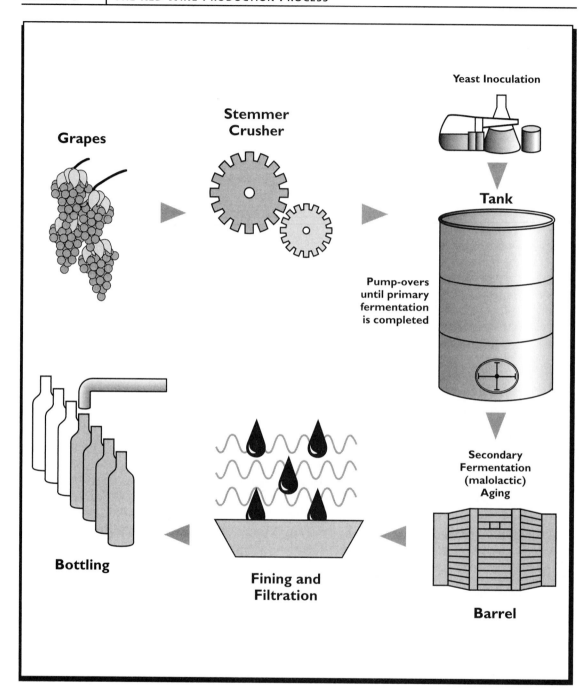

SOURCE: Adapted from the *Oxford Companion to Wine* (2nd ed.), Oxford: Oxford University Press, 1999, p. 773.

EXHIBIT 6 | **THE WHITE WINE PRODUCTION PROCESS**

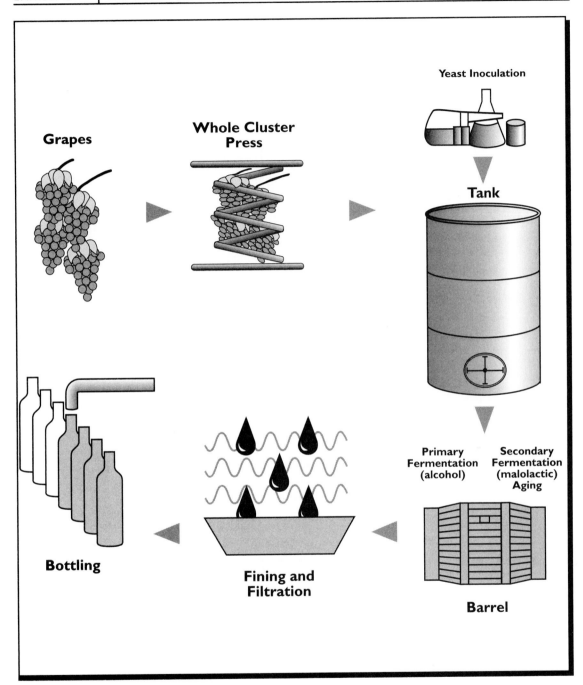

SOURCE: Adapted from the *Oxford Companion to Wine* (2nd ed.), Oxford: Oxford University Press, 1999, p. 566.

The California Wine Industry and the Market

By the early 1990s, family-owned winery dynamics were changing: According to some observers, wineries were becoming viewed as businesses rather than as an art form. Industry segmentation, consolidation, and increased competition within the United States and abroad drove many wineries to look outside the industry for business experts in the areas of marketing and finance in order to reposition themselves in preparation for a more intensely competitive future. Some, like Zelma Long of Simi Winery, sought those with bilingual capabilities and overseas experiences for a broader global and marketing perspective. Others, like Peter Mondavi, Jr., of Charles Krug Winery, sought financial and marketing professionals who already had successful track records in consumer products industries. Larger companies no longer felt the need to be vertically integrated. In the words of Allan Hemphill, president of Associated Vintage Group (AVG), "Grapes had become a commodity—to be identified with the ground was no longer important. With so many competing uses of capital, many wineries began outsourcing as a conscious strategy." Outsourcing often meant turning the entire winemaking process over to another winemaker or "custom crush" facility.

To some, "custom crush" sounded like a hug from Jesse Ventura, but it literally meant making wine in someone else's winery for a fee. A custom crush facility could handle the entire winemaking process from the time the grapes arrived at the winery door until, two or three years later, the bottled, aged, and labeled wine would head off to customers or wholesalers. For a small winemaker, the economic benefits were obvious. Outsourcing via a custom crush facility could offer a winery the opportunity of minimizing its investment risk while it tested its brand through the marketing channels. These channels included the traditional three-tier distribution system: distributor or wholesaler level, restaurant/retail trade, and consumer direct via wine clubs, mail order (within the legal states), and tasting room sales.

Back in 1994, Hemphill had said publicly that he believed that wineries would be increasingly placing future responsibilities on "co-packers." Co-packers, as defined by the food and beverage industry, provided custom processing services such as blending, packaging, storing, and shipping for major brands. In Hemphill's words,

> The future of the industry will be dominated by those who think differently. Those products that will succeed are those that taste good and are priced right. This is the first time the industry has experienced a capacity shortage. There are barriers to entry: acquisition of facilities, staff with know-how, reaching the critical mass point and the permit process. In Sonoma County, for example, it is hard to build new, and it is very tough to get use permits. Replacement costs in current dollars make it difficult to get a return. It has to be big to be done right and it requires a large investment strategy. To build a new custom crush facility would cost $1,000 per ton in Sonoma County, versus $200–$500 per ton in the San Joaquin Valley. Things are cheaper there. It takes less to support the infrastructure. The margins are lower there, too.

Industry experts like Hemphill believed that, to compete successfully on a world-class basis, wineries would need to move into higher quality or go broke. The trend was also favoring those who were able to dominate the industry through low cost and high volume. Rising grape prices were part of the cyclical nature of the wine business, and success would require a good sense of the marketplace.

Another expert, Bill Turrentine, had spent the past 20 years brokering wine between growers and wineries. Having experienced the ups and downs of the industry, he observed that those who succeeded would have to pay attention to quality as the driver and maintain their long-term focus during times of shortages (see Exhibit 7). Turrentine believed that the increased margin lay in the quality of the grapes. A commonly held projection within the industry was that premium California varietals would maintain their growth in popularity and that consumption patterns would continue to decline but at a slower rate. Consumers would be drinking less wine but would be more demanding in their search for quality and value.

Domestic Competition

The markets in which wineries operated were highly competitive. Companies with substantial financial, production, personnel, and other resources dominated the industry. The main competitors in bulk wine production and processing included E. & J. Gallo, JFJ Bronco, Delicato Winery, and Golden State Vintners, as well as a number of smaller companies. Smaller wineries included an estimated 800 commercial wineries that produced and marketed California wine and another thousand wineries that had developed capacity throughout the United States (see Exhibit 8).[6]

One new entrant, Golden State Vintners, positioned itself as a low-cost high-quality supplier of premium bulk wines and wine processing services and provided incentives to customers to outsource their grape and wine production needs. Other new entrants into the industry had been deterred due to the substantial capital investments and lengthy start-up periods involved in developing productive vineyards, building winemaking facilities, and establishing customer relationships.[7]

Foreign Competition

Numerous wine producers in Europe, South America, South Africa, and Australia also competed with domestic wineries by exporting their wine into the United States.[8] California grape and wine supply shortages in 1995, particularly in red wines, prompted some domestic national brand marketers to purchase wine from foreign sources. Although most imports were bottled wine, some wineries imported bulk wine in large tanks for bottling and sale in the United States. Because of higher production costs in the United States and the higher prices of grapes in California, wineries were able to achieve cost savings from importing crushed grapes, even after taking into account shipping costs (see Exhibit 9).

Taking into account how much the industry had been changing during the past ten years, McManis decided that he would have to look at his business differently in order to make things happen for RJM Enterprises and to set himself apart from the other Valley growers:

> In 1996 we acquired North Coast customers because they had a need for supply. Prior to that, our main customers were Gallo, Bronco, Delicato, Franzia (The Wine Group) and Canandaigua. The problem selling to them

[6]Golden State Vintners, Inc., Initial Public Offering Prospectus, July 21, 1998.
[7]Ibid.
[8]Walker, op. cit.

EXHIBIT 7 | THE MANIC-DEPRESSIVE WINE BUSINESS WHEEL OF FORTUNE

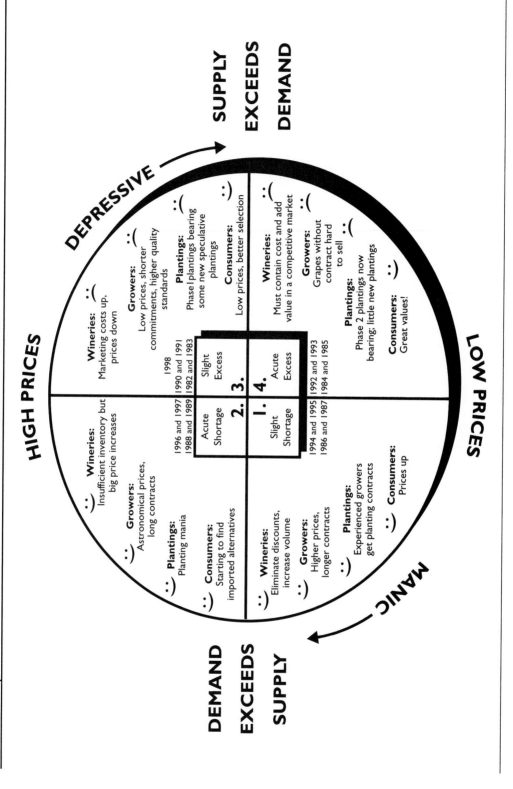

EXHIBIT 8 | TOP TEN WINE PRODUCING STATES

1997 Wine Production by State Thousands of Gallons		Percentage of U.S. Total	1997 Wine Production by State Thousands of Gallons		Percentage of U.S. Total
1. California	422,560	90.57%	6. Ohio	1,130	0.24%
2. New York	23,180	4.97%	7. Georgia	1,120	0.24%
3. Washington	5,200	1.11%	8. Texas	980	0.21%
4. Oregon	1,680	0.40%	9. New Jersey	840	0.18%
5. Vermont	1,550	0.33%	10. Kentucky	820	0.18%

SOURCE: *The New York Times*, August 1998.

EXHIBIT 9 | RECENT IMPORTS/EXPORTS OF WINE IN THE UNITED STATES

Recent Import/Export of Wine in the United States		1994 (Millions)	1995 (Millions)	1996 (Millions)
Volume of U.S. Wine Imports	Gallons	70	77	96
Value of U.S. Wine Imports	Dollars	$1,050	$1,209	$1,478
Volume of U.S. Wine Exports	Gallons	35	39	48
Value of U.S. Wine Exports	Dollars	$196	$242	$327

SOURCE: *Wines & Vines Statistical Issue*, July 1997.

was that there was no price differentiation based on grape quality. We wanted to be paid for better quality. We were profitable, but we wanted to do more. I have become a better grape grower as a result. My worst vineyards are better than my neighbors' best vineyards—thus, my value is greater than my return.

A nearby grower had held out one year and waited until the end of the growing season to sell his grapes when demand was stronger, and he had received a higher price for admittedly lesser quality.

Prior to 1995 I knew nothing about winemaking. Now I am learning what the wineries are concerned about so that we can improve the quality. We could continue to sell Chardonnay to Bronco at the going Valley rate of about $700–$800 per annual ton or sell Chardonnay to North Coast wineries for $1,000–$1,200 per (annual) ton. We have reinvested to improve our product. Our grape sales are $8–$9 million per year.

This is an opportunity to set us apart from others in the area—for us to stand out. We are serious about adding value to our long-term relationships. We believe in a handshake and I stand by my word. The grape industry is a tightly knit group—the quality of a grower's product is well known, and the buyers don't forget from year to year. The relationship between the buyer and the seller must be cultivated for the long term.

EXHIBIT 10 | TABLE WINE RETAIL SALES BY PRICE SEGMENT

Domestic Brands (750ml bottle size)		1996–1997 Retail Sales
Segment	Price	% Change
Economy	Under $3.00	–0.3%
Sub-Premium	$3.00–$6.99	7.6%
Premium	$7.00–$9.99	19.0%
Super-Premium	$10.00–$13.99	9.6%
Deluxe	$14.00 and over	2.7%

SOURCE: *The U.S. Wine Market*, 1997 Edition. *Impact Databank Review and Forecast*, a publication of M. Shanken Communications, Inc., New York, NY 10016.

McManis felt that there was a need for Central Valley product because of the economies to be gained by California's North Coast wineries. North Coast wineries were based in Sonoma, Napa, Mendocino, and Lake Counties and were segmenting the market into first and second labels according to price points (see Exhibit 10). To market his products to this group, McManis considered how he could reduce the strain placed on the North Coast wineries during harvest and crush and provide a value-added service. Many wineries did not have the added capacity of additional tank and barrel space required to expand and maintain a second label.

In the past, small North Coast wineries producing limited amounts of high-end wines traditionally had purchased some Central Valley grapes to be blended in their second label wines but had been thus far constrained due to the lack of crushing, fermenting, and storage capacity in both growing regions. Finished wine was in short supply and great demand after the 1996 and 1997 growing seasons. In those years, according to industry analyst Steve Heimoff, although new plantings of grapes had come into production, there was an increasing shortage of crushing capacity at the winery level. This shortage was due to the increased demand for premium varietal grapes and the replacement of phylloxera-infected vines.[9] In an article in the *Santa Rosa Press Democrat*, Kenwood winemaker Robert Rex observed that:

> Small wineries are getting shut out. It's always been hard, but now it has become almost impossible (to find production space). Following massive vineyard expansions across California, wineries of all sizes are planning to increase production. Many that once rented out extra space to small winemakers when grapes were scarce are now reclaiming their production equipment.

Dave Kincaid of BDM Construction Company, Inc., recalled during his first meeting with McManis in the spring of 1997 that approximately 25,000 acres of new wine grape plantings had taken place recently in the region and that the grapes would begin to produce in the fall of 1997. He indicated that all of the regional wineries were currently at maximum capacity to receive and crush grapes and that crush expansion was not a high priority in the capital budgets of the area wineries. According to McManis'

---

[9]Heimoff, Steve. "A Crush to Custom Crush," *Wine Business Monthly—Grower and Cellar News*, June 1995.

EXHIBIT 11 | TOTAL TONS CRUSHED AND GRAPE PRICE PER TON: 1990–1996

| | Total Tons Crushed | | | Grape Price Per Ton | |
Year	White Wine	Red Wine	Year	White Wine	Red Wine
1990	1,330,840	804,294	1990	$276.00	$357.00
1991	1,289,615	839,644	1991	$319.00	$383.00
1992	1,209,029	887,715	1992	$364.00	$438.00
1993	1,326,510	978,717	1993	$316.00	$430.00
1994	1,284,061	935,683	1994	$319.00	$462.00
1995	1,175,187	1,051,888	1995	$351.00	$515.00
1996	1,093,827	1,078,554	1996	$469.00	$610.00

SOURCE: State of California, *Grape Crush Reports, 1990–1996.*

informal research, both North Coast and Valley growers indicated that, by as early as 1999, the industry would see an extensive shortfall in processing equipment based on the 1996–1997 planting boom (see Exhibit 11).

The Niche for Custom Crushing

California's niche for custom crushing emerged as a resource to the wine industry during the early 1990s as North Coast wineries experienced increased production and sales, especially in the premium and super-premium sectors.[10] Growth of the red wine segment required additional barrel storage and aging; increased popularity of Chardonnay fueled the need for more fermentation capacity. Likewise, existing wineries and entrepreneurs utilized custom crush services to develop and market new brands and second labels without having to add capacity or build new facilities. Custom crushers that historically offered minimal services began to add fermentation and storage capacity to support the growing needs of the industry by supplying oak tank and barrel storage, bottling, and warehousing.[11]

Custom crush businesses offered lower cost alternatives to existing wineries, enabling them to diversify their product lines. Increased competition was forcing wineries to divert capital away from production to sales, marketing, and operations. Growers without winery contracts used the services to extend their product life cycle— the grapes could be crushed and sold on the bulk market. Speculative partnerships were formed between growers, custom crush operators, and others in the industry as a way to develop new varieties, make consignment sales, and market value-added products. According to *Wine Business Monthly*, by 1995 about 37 companies offered custom crush services to wineries in Central California and the North Coast with facilities that could crush as little as 25 tons per year to over 70,000 tons per year (see Exhibit 12).

---

[10] Heimoff, op. cit.

[11] Hinkle, Richard Paul. "Custom Crushing: Then and Now," *Wines & Vines*, 75(5) (May 1994). San Rafael, CA: The Hiaring Company.

EXHIBIT 12 | **WINE BUSINESS MONTHLY'S CUSTOM CRUSH DIRECTORY**

North Coast Facilities	Location	Annual Tons
Associated Vintage Group	Hopland, CA	10,000
Charles Krug Winery	St. Helena, CA	3,000
Chateau de Baun	Santa Rosa, CA	3,500
Louis M. Martini Corp.	St. Helena, CA	1,500
Napa Wine Company	Oakville, CA	5,400
Oakville Estate Winery	Oakville, CA	500
Rombauer Vineyards	Napa, CA	1,200
St. Supery Winery	Rutherford, CA	800
Silverado Wine Co.	Napa, CA	500
Other North Coast Facilities (<500 ton capacity)		1,535
Total		27,935

Central California Facilities	Location	Annual Tons
Arciero Winery	Paso Robles, CA	500
ASV Wines Inc.	Delano, CA	5,000
Castoro Cellars	San Miguel, CA	2,000
Central Coast Wine Whse.	Santa Maria, CA	1,000
J. Filippi Vintage Co.	Fontana, CA	300–1,000
Delicato Vineyards	Manteca, CA	70,000
Maison Deutz Winery	Arroyo Grande, CA	500
Wente Bros.	Livermore, CA	13,000
Other Central California Facilities (<500 ton capacity)		1,730
Total		94,730

SOURCE: *Wine Business Monthly*, June 1995.

Breaking New Ground

The turning point for McManis came when he met Bill Turrentine at the annual Wine Grape Symposium in Sacramento in June 1994. Turrentine had been a guest speaker at the conference and talked about the cyclical nature of the bulk wine and grape markets. Blending regulations allowed low-cost Central Valley grapes to be used in North Coast appellated[12] wines. Because federal truth-in-labeling regulations required that 75 percent of a wine's fruit be derived from the area indicated on the label in order to declare the appellation of origin, a North Coast winery could blend up to 25 percent

---

[12]Appellation of origin. In the United States, a general term for the label designations that indicate geographic origins of bottled wines that meet specific legal requirements.

Central Valley grapes into finished wine products and maintain its North Coast appellation. A North Coast winery could also use the more generic "California" appellation of origin on its second label to sell premium wine into a price-competitive market when prices were tight. A California appellation designation required that at least 75 percent of the fruit be grown within California. High grape prices and a temporary shortage of supply prevailed in the North Coast in 1994; as a result, North Coast wineries were looking for better prices for grapes from other regions to blend with their own. Turrentine told McManis that these factors represented a major opportunity.

McManis wanted more exposure in the North Coast, considered by many wine connoisseurs to be the premium wine producing spot in the United States, if not the world. He knew it would be a challenge to develop customer relationships with eight to ten North Coast wineries, but he believed it could be done. He and Turrentine arranged to meet in the Napa Valley in the winter of 1995 to present their ideas to various wineries in an attempt to break new ground. Turrentine recalled that it was at that point that he and McManis became a team:

> We were having lunch that rainy day at the Napa Valley Café and hadn't realized the severity of the storm or the fact that the roads were rapidly being closed due to the rains. When we left the restaurant, we couldn't get through to any of the roads out of town and there weren't any rooms left in town. We bought some overnight necessities in preparation, but we still wanted to try and get home. Everywhere we turned there was high water, and we saw a car that had been ditched with water up to its windows. To make matters worse, we were very low on gas. At that point, we both had to agree on and commit to a plan—whatever the consequences. Fortunately, the plan worked and I have since looked back on that experience symbolically: You might not always be able to easily get out of what you get into.

To overcome the "Central Valley" stigma and to build his reputation among North Coast wineries, Turrentine encouraged McManis to diversify by promoting the quality of his grapes to his new customers. Following Turrentine's advice, McManis made wine from his grapes and provided samples to Associated Vintage Group and Klein Family Cellars, both in Sonoma County. Due to these efforts, RJM acquired its first North Coast grape customers in late 1996.

In fall 1997, McManis sought the expertise of Dave Kincaid, project manager for BDM Construction (BDM) in Santa Rosa, California, to validate Turrentine's diversification plan on a larger scale basis. Kincaid advised McManis to take the operation past the grower level. Grape supply was by then exceeding winemaking production capacity in the North Coast: Regional wineries had not been able to expand their winemaking capacity to keep pace with increasing grape supply, as crop yields had risen from previous years. Expansion was costly for all but the largest North Coast wineries, and the permitting processes were lengthy and fraught with local opposition.

BDM had been approached by McManis because it had 18 years' experience in Sonoma County, and its first construction job had been in the wine industry. According to Kincaid:

> We grew up with the wine industry and we cater to it. We have seen five to six wine industry peaks in the history of our company. It seems that wineries are always behind and in a catch-up mode and wondering if there will be another peak and where they are in the cycle.

Recalling that first meeting in the fall of 1997, Kincaid described McManis as exuberant. Whenever McManis wanted to emphasize a point, he would slam his fist on the table—occasionally, he would slam both fists at the same time! It was in the latter manner that McManis told Kincaid, "Let's get serious about design and implementation!" To help McManis with a plan, BDM was hired to analyze throughput capability and from there design and build a process flow. BDM then brought in another Sonoma-based consultant, Jim Ford of Fifth Resource Group in Cotati. Jim Ford was given the task of evaluating McManis production capabilities and generating alternative scenarios for investments in productive capacity that could serve various levels of forward integration.

Kincaid and Ford worked with McManis to develop the possibilities for RJM. Their analysis was based on a North Coast winery survey that had been conducted by RJM's winemaker and part-time consultant, Jeff Runquist (see Exhibit 13). Following the recommendation of Bill Turrentine, Runquist was also hired as a consultant in 1997. RJM had a larger than expected 1997 crush, and McManis needed an experienced winemaker. Runquist brought two dimensions to RJM: He had earned his enology degree from the University of California at Davis and an MBA from the University of Santa Clara. McManis felt that, together with these consultants, he was now ready to choose among—and later, implement—several strategies for increasing the size of his business.

The Alternatives

Prior to the December 1997 meeting, McManis reviewed the analyses of various alternatives that had been prepared for him by consultants Ford and Kincaid that would dictate the long-term future of his business. Going into the meeting, McManis reasoned:

> As of 1995, no grapes were sold to North Coast wineries. Valley grapes were sold to the Big Five. It was unusual to sell grapes to North Coast wineries. It would require improved service and quality of fruit. We had to offer more services to justify a retail price in the $8–$10 bottle range. Napa wineries couldn't afford new infrastructure. Processing permits are cheaper here than in Napa. We could provide an added value for them: grow, harvest, process— and give product to them when they needed it. They could receive wine from storage tanks throughout the year instead of grapes within the normal 45- day crush window. We are considering bringing the North Coast processing style here, i.e., small fermenters vs. the 700-ton fermenters used by the Big Five. With the North Coast, it's a quality issue vs. the typical Valley way of doing things. We have to prove ourselves. We have to be top in quality. People will pay extra for service and accommodation.

McManis, Ford, and Kincaid examined the stages of grape and wine processing and weighed the pros and cons of the added level of commitment at each stage (see Exhibit 14 and Exhibit 15). McManis reminded the consultants that his bankers were skeptical. Few growers had done what he was attempting to do, and he would have to put up cash reserves to show his commitment. Bankers wanted to see an established customer base. Bankers also feared that McManis would be unable to break out of the "price vise" imposed by his current and prospective customers: the large Central Valley wineries on one side, and the smaller North Coast wineries on the other. McManis maintained that

EXHIBIT 13 | GRAPE PROCESSING SURVEY SUMMARY, SUMMER 1997

Questions	Napa Ridge	Monterey Vineyard	Chateau St. Jean	Hess Collection	Kendall Jackson	Vintage Group
Considered custom processing?	Yes	Yes	Yes	Yes	Yes	Yes
For what type?	Juice, wine	Juice	Juice, wine	Juice, wine	Juice, wine	Juice, wine
Preferred grape delivery?	Direct to press via gravity	Direct to press via gravity	Direct to press via gravity	Gravity or conveyor to press	Direct to press via conveyor	Gravity or conveyor to press
Preferred type must pumps?	Progressive cavity	Progressive cavity	Progressive cavity	Progressive cavity	Progressive cavity	Centrifugal
Process fruit cooler than 60°F?	Very important	Very important	Very important	Important	Very important	Very important
Process fruit near the vineyard?	Important	Machine harvest important	Very important	Very important	Very important	Doesn't matter
Process fruit quickly after harvest?	Very important	Cooling important for mech.	Very important	Very important	Very important	Very important
Acceptable time from harvest to process?	4 hours	2–3 hours mech/ 5–6 hours hand	2 hours mech/ 4–6 hours hand	2 hours	6 hours	6–8 hours
Long-distance grape transportation?	Very concerned	Somewhat concerned	Very concerned	Very concerned	Very concerned	Somewhat concerned
Preferred processing systems?	Tank press	Tank/bladder press	Tank press	Tank press	Tank press	Tank press
Preferred press manufacturer?	Bucher	None	Bucher	Diemme, Bucher	None	Diemme
Acceptable gallons per ton?	175	175	175	170	170	175
Best way to receive juice?	<2% solids @ 40°F	Chilled direct from the press	Clarified refrigerated juice	Clarified refrigerated juice	Juice directly from press	Clarified refrigerated juice
Best juice clarification systems?	Settle rack lees filter solids	Settle rack lees filter solids	Settle rack lees filter solids	Settle rack lees filter solids	Settle rack lees filter solids	Settle rack lees filter solids
Fermentation lot size?	3k to 45k gallons	20k to 40k gallons	Varies in 5000 gallon increments*	Varies	Varies	10,000–12,000 gallons
Method of grape delivery?	Deliver to winery	Deliver to winery	Vineyard and winery	Deliver to winery	Vineyard and winery	Vineyard and winery
Want to oversee press operation?	Yes	No	No	No	Yes	No
Negotiate gallon vs. tons contract?	No comments	Yes	No comments	Yes	No comments	No comments

*5500 gallons = one truck of juice.
SOURCE: Jeff Runquist, RJM Enterprises, Inc.

EXHIBIT 14 | STAGES OF GRAPE PROCESSING FOR VARIOUS ALTERNATIVES

Step	Grow Grapes	Mobile Field Crush and Press Grapes	On-Site Winery Crush/ Press Grapes
1.	Harvest grapes	Harvest grapes	Harvest grapes
2.	Load truck with grapes		Load truck with grapes
3.	Truck grapes to winery		Truck grapes to on-site winery
4.	Wait to unload grapes into crusher		Wait to unload grapes into crusher
5.	Unload grapes into crusher	Unload grapes into field crusher/presser	Unload grapes into crusher
6.	Truck return		Truck return
7a.			Winery crush
7b.		Field crush	
8a.			Winery stabilize juice
8b.		Field stabilize juice	
9.		Tank juice to client winery for fermentation	Tank juice to client winery for fermentation or pump into tanks and store on-site for future delivery

SOURCE: Prepared by Jim Ford, Fifth Resource Group, LLC, Cotati, CA, 10/26/97.

his focus would be on small lot processing. A North Coast winery like Rutherford Hill couldn't get the service they needed from a huge processor like Bronco. McManis felt that if customers wanted price, they should do business with Bronco or Delicato; if they wanted service, quality, and small lot processing, they should see him.

At the time of their meeting, new winemaking and storage equipment was in short supply and priced at a premium. The demand for fabrication and delivery schedules was stretched and if not acquired soon, McManis would have to wait another year. According to Kincaid,

> McManis struck us as a very direct individual because he shared intimate information. He had an innate sense that he probably had a good idea, that it was fiscally responsible, and an understanding that it would require an evolutionary process. He wanted us to reinforce his idea, to show him that it would be fiscally responsible and then develop what he should consider doing. Our response was that it should be a darn good idea—not just a good idea.

Five vertical integration alternatives for RJM were discussed:

1. *Remain a grape grower.* RJM's 1,100 acres produced approximately 4,000 tons of Chardonnay and 8,000 tons of Zinfandel grapes (used for white Zinfandel wine). Exhibit 16 presents the volume relationships between grapes and bulk and bottled wine.

EXHIBIT 15 | CRUSH SCENARIO FOR ON-SITE PROCESSING FACILITY

VIGORISH: Percentage of juice retained from crush that amounts to added profit for the service facility—often the result of recovery of lees wine or additional pressing of pomace above the client's yield parameters.

Potential of Vigorish	Estimated Days of Harvest	Chardonnay Grape Tons	Vigorish Tons	Zinfandel Grape Tons	Vigorish Tons	
	1			80	8.0	
Assume 10% of Harvest	2			160	16.0	
	3	76	7.6	240	24.0	
	4	196	19.6	336	33.6	
	5	272	27.2	400	40.0	
	6	320	32.0	456	45.6	
	7	360	36.0	488	48.8	
	8	384	38.4	512	51.2	
	9	392	39.2	520	52.0	
	10	392	39.2	536	53.6	
	11	384	38.4	544	54.4	
	12	360	36.0	536	53.6	
	13	320	32.0	520	52.0	
	14	272	27.2	512	51.2	
	15	196	19.6	488	48.8	
	16	76	7.6	456	45.6	
	17			400	40.0	
	18			336	33.6	
	19			240	24.0	
	20			160	16.0	
	21			80	8.0	
Total Crop		4,000	400.0	8,000	800.0	
Avoided Trucking Costs*		@$85/ton	$34,000	@$85/ton	$68,000	
Potential from Vigorish		@$1,100/ton	$440,000	@$450/ton	$360,000	Total
Added Value			$474,000		$428,000	$902,000

*Avoided Trucking Costs: It was noted by the consultants that approximately $85/ton in trucking costs would be avoided by shipping juice to the client instead of grapes. The transportation of juice is more efficient and requires fewer trips.

SOURCE: Prepared by Jim Ford, The Fifth Resource Group, LLC, Cotati, CA, 10/26/97.

According to McManis' figures, RJM was averaging around $8,000,000 annually in gross revenues from the sale of grapes (see Exhibit 17). RJM's net returns per acre placed the operation at the high end in its region (see Exhibit 18). As shown in Exhibit 19, RJM's operating costs were close to average—factors contributing to RJM's ability to generate cash flows for the diversification effort.

EXHIBIT 16 | **GRAPES TO WINE CONVERSIONS**

Conversions: Grapes to Wine (Estimated Averages)

1 acre of grapes	=	7.87 tons/acre (U.S.)
1 ton of crushed grapes	=	170 gallons of wine
1 gallon of wine	=	3.78 liters
2.38 gallons of wine	=	1 case of wine
1 case of wine	=	12 750ml bottles or 9 liters
1 ton of crushed grapes	=	72 cases of wine
1 acre of grapes	=	567 cases of wine
1 oak barrel	=	55 gallons of wine/23 cases
20,000 gallon tank	=	8,412 cases of wine

SOURCE: William Arbios, Arbios Cellars, CA.

EXHIBIT 17 | **ESTIMATED ANNUAL EARNINGS FROM VINEYARD OPERATIONS FOR RJM ENTERPRISES, INC.**

Item				
Chardonnay	4,000 tons	@	$1,100	$4,400,000
Zinfandel	8,000 tons	@	$450	3,600,000
Gross Revenues				$8,000,000
Operations				
Cost/Acre	1,100 acres	@	$2,200	2,420,000
Net Operating Income				$5,580,000
Interest on Debt				1,760,000
Earnings Before Taxes				$3,820,000

SOURCE: Jeff Runquist, Consultant/Winemaker, RJM Enterprises, Inc.

2. *Purchase equipment to do limited grape crushing "in the field" prior to shipping juice to wineries* (see Exhibit 20). This alternative considered the purchase of a mobile field belt press. Costs were presented for 4,000- and 12,000-ton crush scenarios. The equipment would be placed within McManis' vineyard site, and the grapes would be crushed and pressed immediately, eliminating the need for hauling the grapes in the hot sun to a winery—possibly two to three hours away. Instead, the juice would be immediately pumped from the mobile press into a chilled tanker and transported to the client. Runquist expressed his concerns with this alternative due to the location of the vineyard near the rivers and the occasional problems with flooding. This alternative would not provide a means to custom crush for others and retain the "vigorish." Vigorish was defined as that material remaining from grapes that had been crushed at a vineyard and that could, in turn, be resold to wineries as juice (see Exhibit 21).

EXHIBIT 18 | NET RETURNS PER ACRE ABOVE TOTAL COSTS FOR WINE GRAPES

U.C. Cooperative Extension
Lodi Appellation of Sacramento and San Joaquin Counties—1994
Net Returns per Acre Above Total Costs for Wine Grapes

Price (Dollars per Ton)	Yield (Ton/Acre)						
	5.5	6.0	6.5	7.0	7.5	8.0	8.5
400.00	−20	175	370	565	760	954	1149
450.00	255	475	695	915	1135	1354	1574
500.00	530	775	1020	1265	1510	1754	1999
550.00	805	1075	1345	1615	1885	2154	2424
600.00	1080	1375	1670	1965	2260	2554	2849
650.00	1355	1675	1995	2315	2635	2954	3274
700.00	1630	1975	2320	2665	3010	3354	3699

SOURCE: Lodi District Grape Growers Assn., 1994 Cost Study, Prepared by U.C. Cooperative Extension in Conjunction with the Lodi District Grape Growers Association.

EXHIBIT 19 | COSTS PER ACRE TO PRODUCE WINE GRAPES

U.C. Cooperative Extension
Costs per Acre to Produce Wine Grape
Local Appellation of Sacramento and San Joaquin Counties—1994

Operation	Operation Time (Hrs/A)	Cash and Labor Costs per Acre					
		Labor Cost	Fuel, Lube & Repairs	Material Cost	Custom/ Rent	Total Cost	Your Cost
Cultural:							
Prune	30.00	$185	$0	$0	$0	$185.00	
Weed Control—Disk 5X	2.10	18	12	0	0	30.00	
Disease Control—Mildew 10X	1.54	13	6	24	0	43.00	
Irrigate	2.50	15	0	24	0	39.00	
Fertilize—Nitrogen	0.00	0	0	31	0	31.00	
Green Tie (Sucker Tie & Train)	8.00	49	0	0	0	49.00	
Shoot Positioning/Thinning	16.50	102	0	0	0	102.00	
Pest Control—Leafhoppers	0.41	4	5	64	0	73.00	
Weed Control—Spot Spray 25% of Acreage	0.49	10	2	14	0	26.00	
Pickup Truck Use	0.86	7	5	0	0	12.00	
ATV Use	0.86	7	1	0	0	8.00	
TOTAL CULTURAL COSTS	63.26	$410	$31	$157	$0	$598.00	

Continued

EXHIBIT 19 | **COSTS PER ACRE TO PRODUCE WINE GRAPES**

Operation	Operation Time (Hrs/A)	Cash and Labor Costs per Acre					
		Labor Cost	Fuel, Lube & Repairs	Material Cost	Custom/ Rent	Total Cost	Your Cost
Harvest:							
Machine Harvest Fruit	0.00	$0	$0	$0	$210	$210.00	
Haul to Crusher	0.00	0	0	0	70	70.00	
TOTAL HARVEST COSTS	0.00	$0	$0	$0	$280	$280.00	
Postharvest:							
Trim Vines	0.31	$3	$2	$0	$0	$5.00	
Irrigate	0.50	3	0	6	0	9.00	
Fertilize—Nitrogen	0.00	0	0	6	0	6.00	
Weed Control—Winter Strip	0.49	4	2	9	0	15.00	
TOTAL POSTHARVEST COSTS	1.30	$10	$4	$21	$0	$35.00	
Assessment:							
Lodi-Woodbridge Wine Grape Commission	0.00	0	0	15	0	15.00	
TOTAL ASSESSMENT COSTS	0.00	$0	$0	$15	$0	$15.00	
Interest on Operating Capital @7.89%						$24.00	
TOTAL OPERATING COSTS/ACRE		$422	$36	$193	$280	$955.00	
TOTAL OPERATING COSTS/TON						$136.38	
Cash Overhead:							
Office Expense						$85.00	
Liability Insurance						3.00	
Sanitation Fees						12.00	
Manager's Salary						154.00	
Property Taxes						121.00	
Property Insurance						86.00	
Investment Repairs						8.00	
TOTAL CASH OVERHEAD COSTS						$469.00	
TOTAL CASH COSTS/ACRE						$1,424,00	
TOTAL CASH COSTS/TON						$203.41	

Continued

EXHIBIT 19 | **CONTINUED**

Operation	Operation Time (Hrs/A)	Cash and Labor Costs per Acre					
		Labor Cost	Fuel, Lube & Repairs	Material Cost	Custom/ Rent	Total Cost	Your Cost
Non-Cash Overhead	Per Producing						
Investment	Acre		Depreciation		Interest @ 3.72%		
Buildings	$195		$10		$4	$13.00	
Fuel Tanks & Pumps	66		2		1	4.00	
Shop Tools	58		3		1	5.00	
Drip Irrigation System	1,247		50		23	73.00	
Pruning Equipment	7		1		0	1.00	
Land—Lodi	8,205				305	305.00	
Vineyard Establishment	5,949		270		111	381.00	
Equipment	270		24		6	30.00	
TOTAL NON-CASH OVERHEAD COSTS	$15,997		360		$451	$812.00	
TOTAL COSTS/ACRE						$2,235.00	
TOTAL COSTS/TON						$319.35	

EXHIBIT 20 | **ADVANTAGES AND DISADVANTAGES OF FIELD PRESS**

Advantages	Disadvantages
• Customers' production limitations.	• No production of vigorish.
• Low industry capital for crush expansion.	• Eliminates storage as value added.
• Reduced transportation costs.	• New technology—requires full financing.
• Lack of production compost costs.	• New technology—unknown problems.
• Flexibility of adding additional presses.	• New technology—riskier, hard to sell.
• Good must quality via faster processing.	• Higher rate of water consumption.
• Cutting-edge technology.	• Logistics of timing and coordination.
• No use permit required.	• Delivery communication critical.
	• Client must have storage to receive juice.

SOURCE: Jim Ford, The Fifth Resource Group, Cotati, CA, December 1997.

3. *Build a state-of-the-art crushing and storage facility* (see Exhibit 22). Building such a system would provide a fixed crush, press, storage, and aging facility on RJM property. This option was prepared for 4,000- and 12,000-ton scenarios. One major advantage of this option was that McManis could incrementally phase in capacity to reach the 12,000-ton facility over a period of years (see Exhibit 23).

EXHIBIT 21 | MOBILE FIELD PRESS INVESTMENT COSTS AND PROJECTED RETURNS

4,000-TON CHARDONNAY SCENARIO

Equipment Cost Item	QTY	Unit Cost	Total Cost	Useful Life	Depr.
Wash down pad	3	$ 50,000	$ 150,000	10 yr	$ 15,000
Waste water irrigation truck	1	70,000	70,000	5 yr	14,000
Field press machine	1	556,166	556,166	10 yr	45,000
Wine lines and pumps	1	30,000	30,000	3 yr	10,000
INVESTMENT			$ 806,166		$ 84,000

Labor				
Winemaker	1	$ 11,733	$ 11,733
Assume 3 operators	3	2,304	6,912
(12/hr/d × 24 d × $8/hr)			$ 18,645

Other Operating and Overhead Costs

Interest on debt (assume $806,166 × 9%)	$ 72,555
Depreciation	84,000
Insurance/office/gas/etc.	20,000
	176,555
Total Annual Cost	(195,200)
Value Added—4,000 tons × $85/ton	340,000
ANNUAL RETURN	$ 144,800

ROI 18%

12,000-TON TOTAL HARVEST SCENARIO

Equipment Cost Item	QTY	Unit Cost	Total Cost	Useful Life	Depr.
Wash down pad	3	$ 50,000	$ 150,000	10 yr	$ 15,000
Waste water irrigation truck	2	70,000	140,000	5 yr	28,000
Field press machine	2	556,166	1,112,332	10 yr	111,232
Wine lines and pumps	2	30,000	60,000	3 yr	10,000
INVESTMENT			$1,462,332		$174,232

Labor				
Winemaker	1	$ 17,600	$ 17,600
Assume 3 operators	6	2,304	13,824
(12/hr/d × 24 d × $8/hr)			$ 31,424

Other Operating and Overhead Costs

Interest on debt (assume $1,432,333 × 9%)	$ 131,610
Depreciation	174,232
Insurance/office/gas/etc.	35,000
	340,842
Total Annual Cost	(372,267)
Value Added—12,000 tons × $85/ton	1,020,000
ANNUAL RETURN	$ 647,733

ROI 44%

(Assumes no cooperage required. 100% tanker to winery from RJM Vineyard.)

SOURCE: Prepared by Jim Ford, Fifth Resource Group, LLC, Cotati, California, 10/26/97.

EXHIBIT 22	ADVANTAGES AND DISADVANTAGES OF ON-SITE CRUSH AND STORAGE FACILITY

Advantages	Disadvantages
• Customers' production limitations.	• Removal of 40 acres of family almond orchards.
• Low industry capital for crush expansion.	• Must have customer base for financing.
• Increased planting production 1998–2000.	• Cost to transport grapes to crush facility and juice to customers.
• Cutting-edge technology available.	• Need for mechanics, press operators, cellar labor, lab technicians, additional operators.
• Can phase in own grape production.	• Facility will not provide immediate payback.
• Can reduce whole fruit sales.	
• Can add custom crush services.	
• Vigorish retained from custom work.	
• Build on-site—close to vineyards.	

SOURCE: Jim Ford, The Fifth Resource Group, Cotati, CA, December 1997.

4. *Purchase another facility to crush, ferment, and store the grapes* (see Exhibit 24). An existing site was on the market in Lodi, just north of Ripon. McManis was concerned about buying someone else's reputation—how could he economically make an older property look new, clean, and appealing (see Exhibit 25)?

5. *Become a fully integrated winery, including development of a brand label* (see Exhibit 26). According to Jim Ford, once the winery was in place as with alternatives 3 or 4, a brand label could be developed. Alternative 3 was planned for that eventual purpose with a use permit to accommodate expansion.

(See next page for Exhibit 23.)

EXHIBIT 24	ADVANTAGES AND DISADVANTAGES OF BUYING AN EXISTING FACILITY

Advantages	Disadvantages
• Existing Lodi site has 21 acres.	• Requires environmental impact studies (cost = $30,000–$50,000).
• Older technology, lower risk.	• Equipment inventory and usability studies (cost = $15,000–$20,000).
• Storage already in place: 800,000-gallon tanks.	• Design and engineering remodel (cost = $30,000–$50,000).
• Equipment already in place: scales, new crane system.	
• Buildings: 94,000 square feet, ease of conversion to be determined.	
• Infrastructure: Producing wells, process waste and site electrical.	
• Equipment on order: 8,000–15,000-gallon tanks, one Bucher press.	

SOURCE: Jim Ford, The Fifth Resource Group, Cotati, CA, December 1997.

EXHIBIT 23 | **BUILD ON-SITE FIXED PRESS FACILITY: INVESTMENT COSTS AND PROJECTED RETURNS**

4,000-TON CHARDONNAY SCENARIO

Equipment Cost Item	QTY	Unit Cost Est.	Extended Item Est.	Useful Life	Depr.	
Electrical system	1	$200,000	$ 200,000	20 yr	$ 10,000	
Waste water system	1	150,000	150,000	20 yr	7,500	
Site infrastructure/asphalt	1	150,000	150,000	20 yr	7,500	
Scale (above ground w/ramp)	1	60,000	60,000	10 yr	6,000	
Crush pit/hopper	1	200,000	200,000	10 yr	20,000	
Crane	1	5,000	5,000	10 yr	500	
Press area	4	20,000	80,000	10 yr	8,000	
Wilmes Press-Model WTP 32	4	127,501	510,004	10 yr	58,650	(1) (4)
Wilmes Press-options/parts	4	31,886	127,544	10 yr	12,754	
Rotary drum vacuum filter FTV 10	4	45,372	181,488	10 yr	20,871	(4)
Rotary drum vacuum parts	4	5,286	21,144	10 yr	2,114	
Stemmer/crusher w/infeed hopper	1	32,634	32,634	10 yr	3,753	(2) (4)
Grape and must pump	2	15,475	30,950	10 yr	3,095	
Tanks (assume all 20k/g @$5/g)	16	100,000	1,600,000	20 yr	80,000	(3)
Refrigeration	1	250,000	250,000	10 yr	25,000	
Wine lines and pumps	1	30,000	30,000	3 yr	10,000	
Air compressor	1	50,000	50,000	10 yr	5,000	
Office/maintenance/restrooms	1200 sf	45/sf	54,000	20 yr	2,700	
Pomace area	1	80,000	80,000	10 yr	8,000	
INVESTMENT			$3,812,764		$291,438	
Labor						
Winemaker	1	7,822	$ 7,822			
Assume 6 operators	3	2,400	7,200			
(12/hr/d × 30 d × $8/hr)			$ 15,022			

Other Operating and Overhead Costs

Interest on debt (assume $3.9M × 9%)	$ 352,924	
Depreciation	291,438	←
Insurance/office/gas/etc.	46,000	
	690,362	
Total Annual Cost	$ (705,384)	
Vigorish (from Chardonnay)	440,000	
Press Value Added—4,000 tons × $85/ton	340,000	ROI
ANNUAL RETURN	$ 74,616	2%

CAPACITY PLANNING NOTES:
(1) Press with 4-hour cycle and 30 ton/cycle = 120 tons/day.
(2) Stemmer @50 tons per hour (with 10 hr average production per day = 500 tons per day.
(3) SS tanks four day capacity at peak of harvest. 400 tons/day × 190 g/ton = 304,000 g of cooperage @$5/g.
(4) Assume a 15% trucking from FOB and install cost.

SOURCE: Prepared by Jim Ford, Fifth Resource Group, LLC, Cotati, CA, 10/26/97.

Continued

EXHIBIT 23 | CONTINUED

12,000-TON TOTAL HARVEST SCENARIO

Equipment Cost Item	QTY	Unit Cost Est.	Extended Item Est.	Useful Life	Depr.	
Electrical system	1	$200,000	$ 200,000	20 yr	$ 10,000	
Waste water system	1	150,000	150,000	20 yr	7,500	
Site infrastructure/asphalt	1	150,000	150,000	20 yr	7,500	
Scale (above ground w/ramp)	1	60,000	60,000	10 yr	6,000	
Crush pit/hopper	1	200,000	200,000	10 yr	20,000	
Crane	1	5,000	5,000	10 yr	500	
Press area	8	20,000	160,000	10 yr	16,000	
Wilmes Press-Model WTP 32	8	127,501	1,020,008	10 yr	117,301	(1) (4)
Wilmes Press-options/parts	8	31,886	255,088	10 yr	25,509	
Rotary drum vacuum filter FTV 10	8	45,372	362,976	10 yr	41,742	(4)
Rotary drum vacuum parts	8	5,286	42,288	10 yr	4,299	
Stemmer/crusher w/infeed hopper	2	32,634	65,268	10 yr	7,506	(2) (4)
Grape and must pump	4	15,475	61,900	10 yr	6,190	
Tanks (assume all 20k/g @$5/g)	35	100,000	3,500,000	20 yr	175,000	(3)
Refrigeration	1	250,000	250,000	10 yr	25,000	
Wine lines and pumps	1	30,000	30,000	3 yr	10,000	
Air compressor	1	50,000	50,000	10 yr	5,000	
Office/maintenance/restrooms	1200 sf	45/sf	54,000	20 yr	2,700	
Pomace area	1	80,000	80,000	10 yr	8,000	
INVESTMENT			$6,696,528		$495,677	

Labor						
Winemaker	1	17,600	$17,600			
Assume 6 operators	6	2,880	17,280			
(12/hr/d × 30 d × $8/hr)			$34,880			

Other Operating and Overhead Costs		
Interest on debt (assume $6.9M × 9%)		$622,239
Depreciation		495,677
Insurance/office/gas/etc.		46,000
		1,163,916
Total Annual Cost		$(1,198,796)

	Chard.	Zinfandel		
Vigorish	$474,000	$428,000	902,000	
Value Added	340,000	680,000	1,020,000	ROI 10%
ANNUAL RETURN			$723,204	

CAPACITY PLANNING NOTES:
(1) Press with 4-hour cycle and 30 ton/cycle = 120 tons/day.
(2) Stemmer @50 tons per hour (with 10 hr average production per day = 500 tons per day.
(3) SS tanks four day capacity at peak of harvest. 400 tons/day × 190 g/ton = 304,000 g of cooperage @$5/g.
(4) Assume a 15% trucking from FOB and install cost.

SOURCE: Prepared by Jim Ford, Fifth Resource Group, LLC, Cotati, CA, 10/26/97.

12,000-TON TOTAL HARVEST SCENARIO

Equipment Cost Item	Existing Facility	Additional Purchase	Useful Life	Depr.
Electrical system	$ 100,000	$ 100,000	20 yr	$ 5,000
Waste water system	150,000		20 yr	7,500
Site infrastructure/asphalt	100,000	50,000	20 yr	5,000
Scale (above ground w/ramp)	60,000		10 yr	6,000
Crush pit/hopper		200,000	10 yr	20,000
Crane	20,000		10 yr	2,000
Press area		160,000	10 yr	16,000
Bucher presses (2)		900,000	10 yr	90,000
Wilmes Press-Model WTP 32		127,000	10 yr	12,700
Filter and parts		57,464	10 yr	5,746
Stemmer/crusher		37,620	10 yr	3,762
Grape and must pump		15,475	10 yr	1,548
Tanks	1,303,000	139,944	20 yr	65,150
Refrigeration		250,000	10 yr	25,000
Wine lines and pumps		30,000	3 yr	10,000
Air compressor		50,000	10 yr	5,000
Office/maintenance/restrooms	40,000	14,000	20 yr	2,000
Pomace area	80,000		10 yr	8,000
Express pomace conveyor		50,000	10 yr	5,000
Land and equipment usability study		58,000	5 yr	11,600
Design and engineering remodel		40,000	5 yr	8,000
	$1,853,000	$2,279,503		$315,006
Estimated land value ($7,000/acre)	$ 147,000			
Total facility purchase price		$2,000,000		
Total additional expenditures		2,279,503		
TOTAL INVESTMENT IN FACILITY		$4,279,503		

Operating Expense Details and Assumptions

Facility operators (6)	$ 37,800	
Pomace management and handling	25,200	
Insurance and utilities	48,000	
Depreciation	315,006	←
Property taxes	$ 468,801	
Total Operating Expenses		

Incremental Revenue	Tons	Incremental Value/Ton	Incremental Revenue
Chardonnay	$4,000	$ 85	$ 340,000
White Zinfandel	8,000	85	680,000
Chardonnay Vigorish	400	1,185	474,000
White Zinfandel Vigorish	800	535	428,000
Net trucking cost avoided			46,662
TOTAL INCREMENTAL REVENUE			$1,968,662
PROJECTED PRETAX INCOME			$1,499,861

Capitalization Alternative:	100% Equity	50% Debt	80% Debt
Interest expense @ 9%		$ 192,578	$308,124
Projected pretax income	$1,499,861	$1,307,283	$1,191,737
Return on Investment Calculation:			
Net Capital Invested	$4,279,503	$2,139,752	$ 855,901
ROI (assumes interest-only pmts on debt)	35%	61%	139%

SOURCE: Prepared by Jim Ford, Fifth Resource Group, LLC, Cotati, CA, 10/26/97.

EXHIBIT 26 | **ADVANTAGES AND DISADVANTAGES OF BECOMING A FULLY INTEGRATED WINERY, INCLUDING DEVELOPMENT OF BRAND LABEL**

Advantages	Disadvantages
• Wine could be sold in bulk, bottled, or held unlabeled in storage.	• Special equipment needed.
	• Requires full-time winemaking staff.
	• San Joaquin Valley wines restricted to California or Lodi appellations.
	• Competition from Napa, Sonoma counties.

SOURCE: Jim Ford, The Fifth Resource Group, Cotati, CA, December 1997.

With respect to the last alternative, Ford strongly recommended that moving towards the fully integrated winery be done incrementally. McManis would need to prove his success at each new phase of development before attempting to market a brand.

In its *Wine Industry Update* newsletter, industry consultants Motto, Kryla & Fisher described the marketing and production aspects of building a wine brand:

Marketing: It costs more to establish a market than to maintain one. It's very expensive to set up a distributor network, organize an effective sales team, create brand awareness, get good placements and generate repeat sales.

Production: The cost of using assets inefficiently is often overlooked. Inventories must be in balance with sales. A winery must be producing near capacity to have reasonable fixed costs per case. Both of these factors affect financing costs.

Deloitte & Touche's annual review, "Winning Strategies in the Wine Industry—Benchmarking for Success," indicated that the 1996 industry average pre-tax ROE for a typical winery had risen to 16.3 percent from 14.0 percent at the end of 1995.

In weighing his decision based on the analyses prepared by the consultants, McManis trusted his gut feelings that keeping his eye on the growth target and maintaining a commitment to slow but steady progress would assure his future with North Coast winery customers. Having established a reputation as a Central Valley grape grower, however, he would be entering uncharted territory. He and his wife, Jamie, had already put aside two to three years of accumulated cash flows from the existing business for a new investment, yet he remained mindful of his assurances to her that he would not "bet the farm."

Glossary

Appellation of origin. In the United States, a general term for the label designations that indicate geographic origins of bottled wines that meet specific legal requirements. Any wine, at least 75 percent of which is made of grapes grown in the area designated on its label and that conforms to the laws and regulations relevant there, is entitled to a country, state, or county appellation.

Centrifugal pump.   Pump that has a rotor with spinning fins. This accelerates the "must" (see definition below) and forces it out of the top of the pump—not as gentle a process as the progressive cavity method.

Co-packer.   Business that provides custom processing services such as blending, packaging, storing and shipping for major brands in the food and beverage industries. A "custom crush facility" (see definition below) is an example of a co-packer for the wine industry.

Custom crush facility.   American term for a winery specializing in vinifying grapes on behalf of many different wine growers, typically those without their own winemaking equipment. The various wines are kept separate and marketed by the growers under their own labels. Such operations have played an important part in establishing new wine producers in California and in new world wine regions such as New Zealand.

Fermentation lot size.   Sizes of fermentation tanks differ based on the style and quality of wine that is being made. Different characteristics can be achieved based on the size of the fermenters being used. For example, a short, wide tank will have more skin in contact with the juice and give a more intense extraction of tannin, skin color, and flavor.

Lees filter solids.   Removing the juice from the solids by means of a special filter.

Lees.   The solids remaining at the bottom of the tank, comprised of grape debris and spent yeast.

Must.   Crushed grapes, exclusive of stems.

Pomace.   The dry or pulpy residue of material (as fruit or seeds) from which a liquid (as juice) has been pressed or extracted. Something crushed to a pulpy mass.

Processing fruit at cool temperatures.   Important because it prevents grapes from beginning fermentation, reduces oxidation and spoilage.

Processing fruit near the vineyards.   Important because it reduces crushing and compacting the grapes and exposure to daytime heat while in the truck during transportation. This reduces uncontrolled extraction of phenolics, discourages browning and wild fermentations.

Progressive cavity.   Pump with a curled rod that moves the must gently through a chamber into the tank.

Rack.   Process of pumping the clear juice off the solids that have settled to the bottom of the tank.

Second label wines.   Wines made or blended from growths or vines considered not good enough for the principal product made at an estate. The phenomenon was born in Bordeaux in the 18th century and was revived in the 1980s, when increased competition and market resegmentation forced many wineries in France and California towards even more rigorous selection of vines for their principal products or *grand vin.* A second wine made from a quality-conscious producer in a good vintage can represent good value—so long as it is not consumed along the *grand vin.*

Settle.   Period following the crush whereby solids in juice settle to the bottom of the tank by gravity. A fining agent, one of a range of special materials such as bentonite (clay) or activated charcoal, may be used to help the process along by coagulating the solids, thereby making the wine less hazy or cloudy.

Solids.   Crushed grape matter—shattered pulp and skins of berries and, occasionally, a few broken seeds.

Vigorish.   Percentage of juice retained from custom crush that amounts to added profit for the service facility—often the result of recovery of lees wine, or additional pressing of pomace above the client's yield parameters.

Bibliography

Adams/Jobson's Wine Handbook, 1996. Adams/Jobson's Publishing Corp., New York, NY 10036.

Appel, Ted. California wine business posts record year. *Santa Rosa Press Democrat*, January 21, 1999.

Appel, Ted. Feeling the squeeze. *Santa Rosa Press Democrat*, August 23, 1998.

Arbios, William L. Owner, Consultant. Arbios Cellars, Santa Rosa, California.

Deloitte & Touche LLP. *Winning Strategies in the Wine Industry: Benchmarking for Success*, 1996.

California Department of Food and Agriculture, *Final Grape Crush Report, 1996 & 1997 Crop*. California Agricultural Statistics Service, P.O. Box 942871, Sacramento, California 94271-0001.

Interviews with Jim Ford, The Fifth Resource Group, LLC., P.O. Box 30, Cotati, California 94931, November 1998 and March 1999.

Goheen, Austin C. and Pearson, Roger C. *Compendium of Grape Diseases.* © by The American Phytopathological Society.

Golden State Vintners, Inc., Initial Public Offering Prospectus, July 21, 1998.

Heimoff, Steve. A Crush to Custom Crush. *Wine Business Monthly—Grower and Cellar News*, June 1995.

Interview with Allan J. Hemphill, President, Associated Vintage Group, Graton, California, June 1998.

Hinkle, Richard Paul. Custom Crushing: Then and Now. *Wines & Vines*, May 1994, The Hiaring Co.

Interview with Dave Kincaid, BDM Construction, Inc., Santa Rosa, California, August 1998.

Lodi District Grape Growers Association and U.C. Cooperative Extension. *1994 Cost Study.* Sample costs to establish a vineyard and produce wine grapes in the Lodi Appellation.

Long, William R. Now it's grapevines climbing the Rockies. *New York Times*, August 15, 1998.

Interview with Zelma Long, Executive Vice President of Business Development, Chandon Estates, Louis Vuitton Moet-Hennessy, Healdsburg, California, Sept 1998.

Interviews with Ron McManis, President, RJM Enterprises Inc., Modesto, California, June 1998 and March 1999.

Interview with Peter Mondavi, Jr., Co-Owner, Charles Krug Winery, St. Helena, California, Sept 1998.

Motto Kryla Fisher. Wine Industry Update. September 1989.

Muscatine, Doris, Amerine, Maynard A., Thompson, Bob. *Book of California Wine*, University of California Press/Sotheby Publications, Berkeley, 1984.

Nalley, Richard. Grape Expectations. Dreaming of owning your own winery? Read this first. *Departures*, 1998.

Robinson, Jancis. (ed.), *Oxford Companion to Wine* (2nd ed.). Oxford: Oxford University Press, 1999.

Sawyer, Abby. Removal of AXR#1 continues at North Coast vineyards. Growers gaining on phylloxera. *Wine Business Monthly*, December 1998.

Title 27 Part 4 of the Code of Federal Regulations. Bureau of Alcohol, Tobacco and Firearms, Regulatory Agency, United States Department of the Treasury.

Interview with Bill Turrentine, Turrentine Wine Brokerage, San Anselmo, California, July 1998.

Simons, Bo, Wine Librarian, The Healdsburg Wine Library, Sonoma County Library.

The U.S. Wine Market, 1997 Edition. *Impact Databank Review and Forecast*, A Publication of M. Shanken Communications, Inc., New York, NY 10016.

Walker, Larry. 54th Annual Statistical Issue, *Wines & Vines* Volume 78, Number 7, July 1997, The Hiaring Co.

The Wine Institute, *http://www.wineinstitute.org*

WineKey Glossary—Wine Related Definitions. *http://www.winekey.com/defpr.htm*, September 1998.

Pfizer, Inc. Animal Health Products[1]—A: Market Segmentation and Industry Changes

Jakki Mohr, Professor of Marketing–University of Montana
Sara Streeter, MBA–University of Montana

Kipp Kreutzberg was just putting the finishing touches on his marketing plan for the coming year. As the senior marketing manager of Pfizer's Cow/Calf Division, he was responsible for a full range of animal health products Pfizer marketed to cattle ranchers, including vaccines for both newborn calves and their mothers, medications (for example, de-wormers, anti-diarrheals), and antibiotics (for pneumonia and other diseases). Pfizer positioned its products on the combination of superior science (resulting from its significant R&D efforts) and high-quality production/quality control techniques. Pfizer's pride in its sophisticated research-and-development was shown in its new and useful products for the market. The company invests more in research and development than any other animal health company.

Pfizer had historically segmented ranchers in the cow/calf business on the basis of herd size, as shown in Figure 1.

"Hobbyists" are so called because, in many cases, these ranchers run their cattle as a sideline to some other job held. For example, a schoolteacher might keep a herd of cattle simply because he grew up on a ranch and couldn't imagine not doing so. In many cases, the hobbyists' ranch income is a minor percentage of their overall income. The average age of hobbyists is 50 years old, and 15 percent hold a college degree. They have been in the cattle business for 26 years and spend 51 percent of their time with their cattle business.

"Traditionalists'" main livelihood is their cattle operation. The average traditionalist is 51 years old and 26 percent hold a college degree. They have been in the cattle business for 30 years and spend 70 percent of their time with their cattle operation.

The "Business" segment operations are headed by ranchers who average 53 years of age, 22 percent with a college degree, and 33 years in the business. They spend

---

[1] Some of the information in this case has been modified to protect the proprietary nature of firms' marketing strategies. The case is intended to be used as a basis for class discussion rather than to illustrate either effective or ineffective marketing strategies.

FIGURE 1 | PFIZER MARKET SEGMENTATION, 1998

Segment	# of Cattle	# of Operations	Percent of National Cattle Inventory
Hobbyist	<100	808,000	50%
Traditionalist	100–499	69,000	36%
Business	500+	5,900	14%

80 percent of their time with their cattle. These large ranch businesses are owned either by a family or a corporation.

Pfizer had an extensive network of field sales representatives that visited the ranchers to inform them of products, to offer seminars on herd health, and to sponsor industry activities such as stock shows and 4-H. Time spent with accounts is typically allocated on the basis of volume of product purchased. Ranchers then buy the animal health products they need from either a veterinarian or a distributor/dealer (typically, animal feed stores, and so forth). The field sales reps also call on the vets and distributors/dealers to help them manage inventory and to inform them of new products and merchandising programs.

The Problem: Industry Challenges and Change and a Need to Evaluate Segmentation Practice

As the leader of the marketing team, Kipp recognized that his customers were facing some daunting challenges that would result in significant changes in the industry, changes that would likely reverberate to Pfizer's animal health business. For example, the market share of beef products had declined from 44 percent in 1970 to 32 percent in 1997, while pork and poultry had gained share. The decline in beef consumption was due in part to well-known concerns about cholesterol and fat. In addition, preparation issues also affected the demand for beef, as they did for poultry and pork as well. For example, two-thirds of all dinner decisions are made by a consumer on the same day. Of these same-day decisions, three-quarters of the consumers still don't know what they are going to make as late as 4:30 P.M. Obviously, many beef products require cooking and preparation time, which limits consumer selection.

Of course, other types of meat products also require cooking and preparation time. One key difference, however, is that consumers were being bombarded with new products from the poultry and pork industries. For example, in 1997 Tyson Foods introduced stuffed chicken entrees, roasted chicken dinners, Southwest-style blackened fajitas, among a host of other creative products. The names "Tyson" or "Purdue" are well-recognized by the public, unlike most beef products.

Some of the changes that had occurred in the poultry and pork industries were expected to diffuse into the cattle industry. Industry analysts believed that the beef industry would need to develop products that could be more easily prepared, and to develop branded products that consumers could recognize and rely upon for quality and convenience.

In addition, industry analysts believed that the beef industry would need to improve the quality of its products (in terms of more consistent taste and tenderness). Beef quality is assessed based on U.S. production targets for tenderness, juiciness, flavoring, and marbling (fat) of the cuts of beef. The targets are based on two dimensions. The first dimension is based on taste quality (tenderness, juiciness), and specifies that 70 percent of beef production should be rated high quality (choice or prime). The second dimension is based on yield, and specifies that 70 percent of beef cattle should be rated grade 1 and 2 (implying a good amount of beef for the carcass size), with 0 percent poor yield (meaning that the carcass did not yield much meat). Currently, only 25 percent of beef cattle meet these criteria.

One way to improve the percentage meeting these criteria is participation in The Beef Quality Assurance program run through the federal government. This is a voluntary quality control program based on the education, awareness, and training of cattle producers to influence safety, quality, and wholesomeness of beef products. It specifies injection sites (neck versus rump) for shots, a seven-step quality check for cows, method and location of branding, and so forth. Forty percent of ranchers say they have participated in this program in the past two years, of which 67 percent have changed the way they manage their cattle.

In summary, consumer demand for beef products had declined over the years, resulting in a situation of over-capacity, which depressed prices. A flood of imports resulting from the NAFTA regulations further worsened the situation, as did high prices for feed. Most industry analysts were predicting a period of consolidation and alliances. Furthermore, many industry experts expected that beef quality would have to improve and be better marketed and packaged to meet consumers' changing lifestyles.

Kipp wondered how the ranchers, who were the lifeblood of his division's sales, would handle the changes. In reports from the sales representatives out in the field, he knew that the situation was dire for many ranchers. He wondered whether Pfizer's approach to marketing took account of the complicated situation. In particular, the Cow/Calf Division had been segmenting the market of ranchers on the basis of herd size for at least 15 years. In light of the significant challenges posed by industry changes, Kipp wondered whether his team's approach to the marketplace was still a useful one. He wondered whether a different approach to segmenting the market might allow his division to develop more effective marketing strategies, in light of the changes looming on the horizon.

Research Method

In order to provide some insight into the continued viability of segmenting the market on the basis of herd size, Kipp asked Joan Kuzmack, the Manager of Marketing Research for the Livestock Division, to conduct a series of depth interviews with cattle ranchers in the Rocky Mountain/Midwest Region. Depth interviews offer qualitative insights into behavioral and attitudinal differences among cow/calf ranchers. More specifically, the objectives of the research were to:

- Identify the inputs driving ranchers' success as cow/calf producers,
- Identify whether ranchers' values and beliefs about herd management differed by herd size,

TABLE 1 | SUMMARY OF TYPES OF RANCHERS INTERVIEWED

	Hobbyist*	Traditionalist*	Business*
Number of Interviews	3	6	3
Size of herd:			
<100	3		
100–250		2	
251–500		4	
501–1000			2
>1000			1
% of Time Spent With Cattle:			
<80%	2		1
81–90%			
91–99%		1	
100%	1	5	2
% of Income From Cattle:			
<80%	3	2	1
81–90%	2	1	1
91–99%		1	1
100%		1	
Type of Operation:**			
Seed-stock	2	2	
Commercial	1	4	3

*Classifications originally provided by Pfizer.

**Seed-stock operators* focus on breeding high-quality bulls for use by commercial producers. The bulls are measured by the quality of their offspring. Desirable characteristics include low birth weight, rapid growth, high carcass yield, and grading of choice or better quality meat.

Commercial producers are those who raise calves to sell to feedlots. The feedlots fatten the calves, which are then sold to the packing houses, and on to the retail distribution channel for consumers. In some cases, commercial producers might *retain ownership* of their calves, where the rancher pays the feedlot to feed out the calves, but the rancher himself still owns them. Then, the rancher sells the calves to the packing houses.

- Determine what motivates cow/calf producers in selecting products, and

- Examine ranchers' views about the future.

A stratified random sample was used to select ranchers for interviews. Rocky Mountain and Upper-Midwest ranchers in each of the three groups (Hobbyist, Traditionalist, and Business) were identified, and randomly selected from within those strata. Table 1 provides descriptive statistics on the types and numbers of ranchers interviewed.

Ranchers were asked a variety of questions using a semi-structured questionnaire. The questionnaire focused on their herd management activities, attitudes, values, and beliefs about herd management, and views of the future trends in their industry.

Research Findings

Inputs Driving Ranchers' Success as Cow/Calf Producers

The results from the interviews suggested that commercial producers across all three herd-size categories look for maximum output (weight gain, number of calves) with the minimum inputs. They attempt to improve the quality of their calves through *health and nutrition programs, genetics, and herd culling.* Activities used to manage the herd included vaccinations, nutrition, and breeding programs. Ranchers also strove for uniformity in the calves, typically based on size. These goals in managing the herd are traded off against the cost to do so. As one respondent stated:

> "We strive for the largest amount of production with the least amount of input going in. That's really the only thing we can control at this point with the economy the way it is. We can't control the price that we get for our product, so the only way we can make ends meet is to control the input cost."—Traditionalist

Some ranchers also focused on range management of their grasslands as another objective in managing their operations:

> "Basically I think of us as ranchers, we're in the business of grass managers. We grow grass, and if we don't manage our lands to grow a lot of grass, the right kind of grass, we can't run the cows properly. All the genetics in the world won't be of use without the right grass."—Traditionalist

The degree to which ranchers felt that *health management* was critical to their herds' success varied greatly. Some valued herd health as one of the most important concerns:

> "You start off with the best breeding that you think you can do through bull selection. From there, it goes on with nutrition and herd health. You're expecting more from the cows. You have to put more into them with nutrition and herd health. You can't cut corners on either one of those. Some feeds will be cheaper some years than others, but we stay with the same drugs."—Traditionalist

Others tended to put in the bare minimum on herd health, sometimes because ranchers were uncertain what results the health management programs yielded:

> "We only do the bare minimum on health care. We do more of a preventative maintenance than anything else. We don't do any more than we have to because you can vaccinate for so many things. Our philosophy has been, if you don't need it, don't do it. You can get an awful lot of money in your cows giving them shots of stuff I don't know if you need."—Traditionalist

> "I try to keep them healthy with shots and nutrition. I don't want to skimp on the health of a cow, but if I can save some money by supplementing different things in the ration or with vaccinations . . ."—Hobbyist

Seed-stock producers were seeking "best genetics," a loosely defined goal that commonly focused on breeding bulls that would maximize weight gain in commercial calves. Seed-stock producers consistently used artificial insemination on their cows and kept computer records to track information on their herd. They used software programs provided through the breed association to record animal registry and performance information.

Use of Information in Herd Management

To aid in herd management, most of the ranchers in the Hobbyist and Traditionalist categories collected information on their cows and calves. Information collected on calves included birth date, birth weight, sex, and weaning weight. Information collected on the cows included calving history, mothering ability (temperament and/or milk production), calving ease, and which cows birthed the replacement heifers. This information was typically handwritten in a book of some type. The ranchers maintained an intimate familiarity with their cattle and saw them as individuals.

> "We knew everything there was to know about our cattle. . . . We knew more about our cattle than we did about our family. We could tell you every calf a cow had, pretty much the exact minute she had it every year. I've got little books here that I wrote everything down exactly."—Traditionalist

In the Business category, ranchers collected some information on their cows and calves. This information might be collected on an exception basis, because of the number of head with which the ranchers were working. The ranchers were familiar with their cattle, but not to the same degree demonstrated by the owners of smaller herds.

Some ranchers used a very sophisticated approach to gathering information in order to refine their herd management practices. For example, one pure-bred operation sent some of its calves to a test station where all the calves from various ranches were fed and cared for similarly. This control allowed the rancher to show how well his bulls stacked up to bulls from other ranches in a controlled experiment. Another rancher stated:

> "We've performed quite a few experiments of our own over the years, and still do. I have a fair sense of what a true experiment is with controls and so forth. We get a lot of cooperation from the pharmaceutical industry. We've tested new products such as ear tags. We get a lot of things free as long as we're willing to put in some controls and report on the results. I enjoy that sort of thing. We've had some experiments going for a couple of years on range management. The opportunities are out there if you're cooperative. I think I probably have an advantage because I know how to conduct an experiment. We can get information firsthand from experiments we conduct ourselves. . . . We've changed our method of supplementing cattle in the winter. We're using more expensive supplements that don't rely on salt. We seem to distribute cattle better. I think it worked. It's cheaper in the long run because you have more grass."—Business

Changes made on the basis of the information ranchers collected varied in their sophistication. Some made changes based primarily on judgment and intuition.

> "It's done by eye and is not as scientific as it could be."—Business

> "A lot of times you know in the back of your mind what you want to do with a cow. It's sure nice to have the records, because you go back and refer to it."—Hobbyist

Many of the ranchers did attempt to get information back from the feedlot on their calves in order to assess how well they did after leaving the ranch. In some cases, they also received carcass data, which allowed them to assess weight gain, quality of the meat, and other types of information.

There were isolated, but notable, exceptions to gathering and using information about the herd. One rancher kept no information on his herd, did not attempt to gain new information on herd management practices, and relied strictly on the information "in his head" based on his cumulative years of experience. Another said:

> "It was just a matter of whatever the good Lord gives them when they come out, that's what they are. I can't change that very much."—Hobbyist

The information ranchers gathered was used primarily as a tool in culling the herd. Culling of open cows (not pregnant) or those that were "unsatisfactory producers" usually occurred in the fall. In general, it seemed that changes to herd management were highly judgment-based. Cause-and-effect links for possible problems were hard to establish. For the larger herds, information was not collected on a detailed-enough level to analyze and draw specific conclusions.

> "Where I've got a thousand head, and we've got one full-time employee, we don't track detailed information on a cow-by-cow basis. I've always got a book with me, so when we're working them, I put things down in the book. That information will be put on the computer. After a while you kind of know your cows. It's visual, when you see things you don't like."—Business

Motivations in Selecting Products

Ranchers as a whole were interested in gaining additional information on how to better manage their operations. They read industry trade publications, attended seminars, and talked to neighbors. They were most likely to view information as credible if it came from a local source that was more familiar with specific local conditions. As a whole, it was clear that the person the ranchers trusted most was their veterinarian. The ranchers also found the animal health product firm reps to be a good source of information, but not as credible as the veterinarian.

> "On a drug situation, I wouldn't necessarily trust one person over another, but I would certainly pay attention to my veterinarian. He knows my area and my situation better than the drug rep from the company does. Even though I know the drug rep from that company is going to represent the drugs he sells, I don't necessarily not trust what he says. I just like to have more information about what works in my environment."—Traditionalist

Ranchers bought their animal health products from both veterinarians and supply houses. Price was an important consideration, but not an overwhelming concern.

Ranchers' Views about the Future

The ranchers all expressed concerns about the future. The number one concern among the commercial Hobbyists and Traditionalists was the low prices on their calves. While Business producers, too, were concerned about price for their "outputs" (cattle), they were also concerned about the input side of the equation (expenses). All ranchers noted that with the low prices they were getting for their calves, they couldn't afford to maintain and replace old, dilapidated equipment they were using.

> "It takes a lot of calves to buy a new pickup, when they want about $30K or something."—Hobbyist

> "[My number one concern is] pricing, and not just the price of the product, but the price of what it costs to produce that product. Compare the price of beef with the price of machinery. Calves are bringing what they brought in the '60s, but a tractor costs three times as much."—Traditionalist

In addition, they noted the high price of land. One rancher stated, "the land around here grows houses better than cattle."

Ranchers spoke vehemently against NAFTA, and the influx of cheaper imports.

> "Well, the biggest issue we have right now is NAFTA. NAFTA is probably the worst thing they've come up with. It has lowered our cattle market so bad, it's put a lot of people out of business, driving the prices down so low. It is not fair trade from the standpoint of shipping Australian cattle into Mexico, they become Mexican cattle and come right into the U.S. They can get our top dollar (whatever we're getting here—say 60 cents), but were brought in through Mexico at 30 cents. They flooded the market. They didn't have to make as much, they don't have as much in their cattle. With this R-Calf thing, they're investigating Canada. Let's face it: They're over-running our market. It takes away the supply and demand. It's not just affecting us, it's affecting everybody—for example, the beef business, the car business, the timber business."—Traditionalist

Tightening environmental regulations (Endangered Species Act, pesticides, water quality, etc.) also made an impact on the economics of ranching operations.

Increasing market strength of the packers was viewed with fear and trepidation, and also with a sense of increasing helplessness. Ranchers sold their calves to the feed-lots, who in turn sold to the meatpackers. Packer concentration (four packers controlled 80 percent of the market) and the packers' perceived ability to set prices (the implication is "collusively") for the industry was a recurring theme. Moreover, fears of vertical integration by the packers, or packers who own their own cattle and feedlots, further worried the ranchers.

> "We have no market for our agriculture products. To back that up, when you've got packers controlling 80 percent of the cattle and they'll buy cattle for a half-hour in the middle of the week, you either take the offer or you leave it. If you turn them down, pretty soon they won't come back and look at your cattle or price your cattle. This is where we're going to have to have more players in our market or we're going to have to become one of the major players against the packer in supplying food to the consumer. We cannot compete with packers that own their own cattle and slaughter their own cattle instead of paying the market value for cattle they don't own. So that's why I say we have no market. The grain is the same way, because basically, the same companies that control the grain control the cattle, Cargill, ConAgra, ADM.

You just look through the hall of mergers. One of these days, if things don't change, we will know the true value of our food when the corporations get it and we're all working for those people. The consumer will find out what the value of it is."—Business

In general, the view among the commercial producers was one of extreme pessimism. They saw a lot of other ranchers going broke (but usually not themselves).

"I think it's all offset by the good things, but sometimes you wonder. You have to wonder about your mentality. You work and you work and you work and you work and you work and then you sell your cows at a loss, and you think 'Why am I doing this?' Either I'm really stupid, or really stubborn."
—Traditionalist

"I think the day that the old rancher who gets on his horse at daybreak and gets off his horse at sunset and never sees another human being, and everybody is knocking on his door to buy his calves—those days are through. I hate to admit it, but everywhere you turn, somebody is trying to put you out of business. If it isn't the Bambi-huggers, then it's the prices, and if it isn't that, then somebody's coming along with those brainy ideas. The small producer is really going to have to work at it to stay in business."
—Traditionalist

Solutions: Value-Added Marketing, Branded Beef, and Quality

Ranchers were asked about possible solutions to the depressed prices they were facing. Possible solutions discussed in industry publications included value-added marketing, or marketing strategies designed to increase the value and quality customers receive from beef purchases, and a branded beef model. The development of branded beef would require a tracking system from "birth-to-beef" in the supply chain. Such tracking would allow standardized health, quality, and management protocols, as well as improved feedback through the entire production model.

Branded beef production would move the industry from a cost-based (production) model to a value-added model. This change would also necessitate the producers being more closely linked to the feedlots to improve the quality of the beef. Better coordination along the supply chain would ensure an increased flow of information from the consumer to the producer. Alliances between the cow/calf producer and the feedlots would allow ranchers to better track the success of their calves (based on health and weight gain). Such data could allow the ranchers to further improve the genetics of their herd by tracking which cow/bull combinations had delivered the higher-yield calves. As part of these trends, some degree of integration or vertical coordination would occur in the beef industry. Ranchers would need to participate in order to ensure market access for their product. Ranchers would have to think beyond the boundaries of their own ranches.

Most ranchers were familiar with the concepts of value-added marketing and a branded beef model. However, most were dubious about their viability and impact on ranchers' independence.

"I don't know if any kind of marketing at this point is going to get us where we need to be without a change in the price structure of cattle."
—Traditionalist

"If there is a demand for high-quality beef, then the market should show it, and the packers will start bidding more for a piece of that quality. There may be some niches somewhere that people can fall into, but it's not going to be the salvation of many ranches. What we need is a mass market. Whatever niche there is is going to be saturated very quickly, and the price will come down. I think the solution is cutting costs. People are eating a tremendous amount of beef, but the production is enormous as well. Numbers are down, but tons are up. The amount of beef being eaten is still quite high. I just think that some people have got to quit producing beef."—Business

"We are concerned about the vertical marketing approach big companies are introducing into the system. Ranchers are very independent-minded people. We are fearful about the control that companies will be able to exert on us."—Traditionalist

Skepticism about value-added marketing is also derived from history: Other programs used in the past to provide a more consistent product to the feedlots, with supporting documentation, had not resulted in noticeable price differences. Of all the information ranchers collected on their herds, only vaccination records seemed to be valued by cattle buyers. Even ranchers with complete histories of their cattle were selling their calves at the same price as ranchers without the information. Hence, the information was not viewed as a way to command a premium for the calves.

"For many years, it seemed like having good health records on the calves didn't matter. One herd would keep excellent records and be real progressive, and the next door neighbor was the exact opposite, and it was the exact same price for both. The local cattle buyers didn't give a premium to keep the records, give the vaccines. . . . There were green tag programs in the '80s (we followed one) where the vet certified you used them (preconditioning records). But the cattle buyers didn't pay a premium for them. They as much as said 'We don't care.' Today, 10 years later, cattle buyers are starting to ask, will you precondition your calves? Will they be 'bunkbroke'? (so when they get to the feedlot, the calves will be trained to go to a feedbunk to eat). Will they be weaned? There's a stress period associated with weaning. So there's more of a focus on those questions now than there has been. But there's still no rule, it's not a given. It's still ambiguous when it comes to marketing the cattle whether the information matters or not [gets a better price for the cattle]."—Traditionalist

The feeling was that price premiums, if any, would accrue to others in the supply chain (e.g., the packers, retailers, and others). Despite that, some with more progressive views noted the need to have more of a consumer-focus in their efforts:

"We need better beef quality if we're going to increase consumption. A lot of the breed associations are concentrating on carcass quality right now. There's measurement, there's selection for marbling and yield on cattle. I think as long as there is a possibility there might be some added value, a person should start working on it a little bit, along with the other production traits. I think it's something to pay attention to."—Traditionalist

"I think in the future, all ranchers are going to have to retain ownership of their cattle more, and follow them closer to the consumer. I think that's part of our problem right now with our packer concentration. The producer's going to have to be a meat producer, and not just sell calves. I think some of our long range goals are going to have to be to get closer to the consumer with our product and know what he wants instead of listening to the packer tell us what he wants."—Business

"The money in agriculture is not in producing it. It's in processing it. This is where more ranchers and farmers have to realize that you can't produce the raw product anymore; you've got to follow it on through."—Business

Ranchers also noted that the idea of consistent quality beef was important.

"I'm expecting to see a change to where quality is more important. I think, down the road, that it's going to be mandatory that you know exactly what your cattle are doing. Those that aren't producing well at the kill floors are going to come back to haunt you."—Business

Interestingly, each of the respondents with whom we spoke felt that the quality of their beef was above-average. However, there was some doubt about whether consistent quality would be easily achieved with range cattle.

"That's going to be pretty tough with cattle. With chickens and hogs, you can throw up a confinement building. One person can control X amount of hogs and turkeys and chickens. But how do you do that with cattle? You can only have so many cattle in one spot because they're bigger and they need more feed. You're going to have to have pasture. It's going to be pretty tough to get everything uniform. There are a lot of small producers with just a few cows around."—Hobbyist

"I'm not convinced that branded products are going to magically save the beef industry. I think we're in competition on a world scale, and we're going to have to cut our costs of production. I think we could get our costs down to about 45 cents per pound of critter sold if we had to. Our total production would go down, but I think our costs would go down more."—Business

Because of the doubts about the viability of moving to a branded beef model, ranchers tended to focus more on controlling the cost of inputs, and weathering the current downturn in the production cycle. One respondent cited earlier summed this up as "striving for the largest amount of production with the least amount of input."

Ranchers' Concluding Thoughts

Despite these hardships and concerns, the ranchers were passionate about their love for their lifestyle, feeling that the benefits of living a life on the land outweighed the drawbacks.

"You get up in the morning and go out there, and everything's bright and fresh. We're fortunate in this part of the world that we don't have a lot of

noise from cars and trains. It's gratifying to see what happens when spring turns around, new things start to grow, new animals come into the world. It's pretty special, something that you can't explain to a lot of people because they don't understand what you're talking about. . . . It isn't the highest paying job in the world, but it's got a lot of happiness that money can't buy."
—Traditionalist

They expressed pride in their work, and a sense of ownership for feeding the country's people.

Back to the Segmentation Decision

As Joan perused the findings from the qualitative interviews, she wondered what she would report to Kipp about possible changes in their approach to market segmentation. Joan wondered whether their historical approach to segmenting the market based on herd size was consistent with the changes in the industry and changing needs of ranchers.

Despite the insights gathered, there was a lack of understanding of the various segments of beef consumers and their needs, how brand marketing could affect consumer demand, how alliances within the supply chain could affect the ranchers' situations. Unfortunately, the fragmented nature of the cow/calf producers, combined with their focus on production rather than marketing, meant that the beef industry was not very consumer-focused.

As she pondered how all these pieces fit together, she began to brainstorm new ways to look at the market. She wanted to work with Kipp in developing a plan to maintain Pfizer's market position in light of the changes in the industry.

Discussion Questions

1. Based on the research findings, evaluate Pfizer's Cow/Calf Team's herd-size segmentation approach.

2. If it doesn't make sense to continue segmenting on the basis of herd size, what variables can be used to segment that more accurately capture differences in the market? What would the resulting segments look like? What segments are most viable for Pfizer?

3. How does the suggested segmentation approach capitalize on changes in the cattle industry? What implications do the industry changes have for Pfizer?

4. How good is the research for drawing conclusions about market segmentation of beef producers?

5. Assuming that support is found for the recommended segmentation approach, how can it be implemented as a marketing strategy?

Circuit Board Corporation

John H. Friar, Northeastern University
Marc H. Meyer, Northeastern University

Maggie Adams sat in her office and replayed in her mind what she had just heard in the January 24, 2002, meeting of the board of directors of electronic component supplier Circuit Board Corporation (CBC). Maggie was the chairman of the board and the largest shareholder of the firm founded by her husband, Dieter. Dieter had passed away in June at the age of 67, and she had gone from being a part-time employee and secretary of the board to running the company. Maggie had been involved in the company since its founding but never had done much more than manage the insurance for the company. Dieter had been a one-man show, constantly yelling at people, running everything, and making all the decisions. He had grown the company to $30 million in sales and kept it afloat through some difficult periods. Now everyone was looking to her to make a decision, and she was getting conflicting and difficult advice.

In January 2001, the high-tech industry imploded. Most companies in the printed circuit-board industry had reported between 50 percent and 75 percent declines in quarterly revenue compared with the prior year. Excess capacity was rampant. Competitors were dropping prices and cutting their own margins just to keep their plants and equipment operating. Although many analysts had predicted a quick recovery, the unthinkable happened—terrorists crashed planes into the World Trade Towers, the Pentagon, and the Pennsylvania countryside on September 11. Forecasters began hedging their bets on any recovery, and CBC was in trouble—it had gone from making $1.2 million pretax in 2000 to losing $614,000 in 2001.

The discussion in the board meeting had caught Maggie by surprise. The company had been going through some very difficult times, but her president and CEO, Ben Cashman, had been assuring her that the market would rebound in the second quarter of 2002 and that they should invest to prepare for the turnaround. The outside board members, however, gave her three different recommendations, two of which were to get out of the business. Not only was the advice unexpected, but the fact that the outside board members even spoke up surprised her. All the outside directors were

"Circuit Board Corporation" Case by John H. Friar and Marc H. Meyer, Northeastern University. The authors thank Edward Fitzgerald for his help in developing this case. Management cooperated in the field research for this case, which was written solely for the purpose of stimulating student discussion. All events and individuals are real, but they have been disguised at the organization's request.

Reprinted by permission from the *Case Research Journal*. Copyright © by John H. Friar and Marc H. Meyer and the North American Case Research Association. All rights reserved.

EXHIBIT 1 | **OUTSIDE BOARD MEMBERS**

The board of directors consisted of Maggie Adams, Chairman, and Ben Cashman, CEO. They were also shareholders. The outside members did not own stock. They were:

Dane Lombard (Board Member): an expert in company turnarounds and asset redeployment. He was employed by Apollo Consulting.

Will Tatelman (Advisor to the Board): the company's auditor and principal at Tatelman & Associates. He attended at the request of Maggie Adams.

Don Armour (Board Member): a principal at Armour & Company. His expertise lay in mergers and acquisitions activities.

---

well-known businessmen and friends of Dieter. (See Exhibit 1 for a list.) But Dieter had never really listened to them, so they had rarely done more than rubber-stamp his decisions. Now without Dieter there, they had started to express their opinions.

Maggie wanted to do what was right but was not sure what that meant. Maggie and her children controlled 86.5 percent of the company and in 2000 had paid themselves (including Dieter) a combined total of $1.8 million in salaries. The company also employed a number of other family members and friends who could never make the same level of pay for another company. She had to think about her lifestyle and that of her family and friends. But she also had to think about the employees and the other stakeholders in the company. Maggie explained:

> Dieter and I have been through recessions in the business that felt as tough as this one, and I bet lasted longer than this one is going to last. There was a time around here in the late '80s when everything dropped by 30 percent—businesses, houses, everything—and seemed to stay there for a good three years. In addition, before that, there was the recession during the mid '70s. That one seemed to go on for five years before business picked up. Dieter always figured a way to keep our customers, keep our staff, and preserve the business.

Company History

Dieter had started Circuit Board Corporation in 1961 during the early days of the computer industry. Dieter was pursuing an undergraduate technical degree after having returned from service in the Korean War when he started the company. His first significant production contract was to design and manufacture printed circuit boards for the early minicomputer companies.

A printed circuit board (PCB) was one of the building blocks in industrial and consumer electronics. It was the platform on which a variety of electronic components, such as chips, resistors, and capacitors, were mounted. Wiring between insert points needed to be present for these mountings to function. On the printed circuit board, that wiring was "printed" by bonding copper through electrolysis in specific predefined patterns on a fiberglass board. The residual wiring on the board provided the layout both for mounting and for holding electrical components, as well as the electrical interconnections between components. In short, the PCB was the subassembly for all larger electronic systems, including computers, medical equipment, instrumentation, and controls.

Dieter became a pioneer in the electrochemical production of printed circuit boards. Before him, computer manufacturers placed electronic subassemblies onto plastic boards with wires clipped to little posts to make electrical connections. At that time, a handful of engineers, one of whom was Dieter, were using electrically charged baths to bond copper to fiberglass plates. The new process offered far greater reliability for the printed circuit boards and far higher density (chips and circuitry per square inch) for packaging components. Dieter developed his process by using his mother's kitchen oven as a curing device for his first printed circuit boards.

When Dieter launched the company, most computer and electronics manufacturers were fabricating their own boards. Independent suppliers, however, became increasingly efficient and were proving a more cost-effective solution for a broad range of printed circuit-board applications. Likewise, computer and electronics manufacturers became more comfortable using suppliers for key electronic components, including printed circuit boards. These suppliers were demonstrating reductions in time to market, engineering/prototyping costs, and manufacturing ramp-up costs to win business. In 1979, 40 percent of all rigid printed circuit-board fabrication was being outsourced to suppliers like Dieter. By 1989, that figure was about 60 percent, and by 1995, 80 percent. By 2001, 98 percent of all printed circuit-board production was going to external suppliers. Industry analysts placed total bookings for printed circuit-board production worldwide at approximately $30 billion in 2000, with the U.S. market comprising about a third of that dollar volume.

From his humble origins in his mother's kitchen, Dieter had built a thriving, profitable company doing about $30 million a year in revenue at its peak in 2000, with a 100,000-square-foot fabrication plant on Route 128 outside of Boston. He had 240 employees working two full shifts a day, and sometimes another half shift for limited production of new prototype boards.

Technology Development

As the industry grew, several basic factors increased the complexity of the boards and their production processes. The first of these was the number of "layers" on a board. The simplest printed circuit board was a single-layer, single-sided assembly. Soon, PCB manufacturers began designing and manufacturing boards with more than one "layer," that is, sheaths of fiberglass each printed with application-specific wiring that were then bonded together very much like a book. Holes were drilled at specific points in each layer and wired to provide connections between components on different layers. By the end of the 1960s, companies were regularly manufacturing four-layer PCBs. By the late 1970s, manufacturers of industrial control systems and computers were demanding ever greater functionality in the electrical interconnect capability of the boards. Six-layer PCBs became standard, and the trend continued. By the following decade, PCB manufacturers enhanced their processes to make 12-layer board assemblies in volume. The number of layers continued to increase, driven by the complexity of applications, such as medical devices and telecommunications switches.

Beginning in the late 1970s, the market divided into three distinct product segments by functionality. The functionality within each of the segments, however, changed dramatically over time. (See Exhibit 2 for a detailed breakout.) In 2001 the three product segments were:

The Low-End Segment: For simple applications requiring one- to four-layer boards; order size ranged from 50,000 to 100,000 in a given year from a customer. An example

EXHIBIT 2 | **THE EVOLUTION OF PRINTED CIRCUIT-BOARD APPLICATIONS**

	1960s	1970s	1980s	1990s	2001–
High Complexity Low Volume		Military	Instrumentation Controls	Telecom	Servers & Storage Medical Devices Telecom: Optical
		22-layer PCBs	24-layer PCBs	30-layer PCBs	30-50-layer PCBs
Medium–High Complexity Medium Volume	Defense 4-layer PCBs	Telecom Switches Repeaters	Large Computers, Fax Machines, Copiers	Servers & Storage Medical Devices, Instrumentation Controls	Military Security Medical Devices Videoconferencing
		4–8 layer PCBs	4–12 layer PCBs	8–18 layer PCBs	12–24 layer PCBs
Low Complexity High Volume	Computers	Consumer Electronics Appliances, HiFi	TVs, Radios, PCs, Games, Calculators, Typewriters	Mobile Phones	Smart Appliances
	1 or 2 layers	1 or 2 layers	1 or 2 layers	1–4 layers	1–4 layers

was PCBs for stereo equipment. In the final assembly, a dozen electronic components would be mounted on each board. The price per board as shipped to the customer could be as low as 10 cents and rarely exceeded $10 per board.

The Mid-Range Segment: For more complex applications requiring 12- to 24-layer board assemblies; the order size ranged from as few as 50 up to as many as 5,000 in a given year from a customer. An example of this type of application was a medical imaging system. Hundreds of components and processors would be mounted on these boards. The price per board as shipped to customers was in the range of $10 to $150. The supplier's design engineers might spend as much as 40 hours designing the wiring and related circuitry. Higher prices were justified because of additional costs in prototyping, production ramp, materials in the final production run, and inspection.

The High-End Segment: For the most complex applications, requiring 30- to 50-layer boards; the order quantity was between 5 and 50 boards a year. An example was a defense contractor that developed electronic-warfare jamming systems integrated into aircraft. Hundreds if not thousands of components might be "stuffed" onto these boards. A supplier might charge from several hundred dollars to thousands of dollars per board. Hundreds of hours of labor were required in designing, prototyping, and placing the PCB into limited production.

Another important factor in the development of the industry was the growth in technical services. These occurred in the front end of the fabrication process: designing the board, prototyping the design, and preproduction testing, which all focused on "quick-turns." Cycle times for developing complex electronics had shortened dramatically during the 1990s and showed no signs of slowing. For example, IBM's product-development cycles for its largest mainframes at the beginning of the 1990s were reported to be 72 months from start to commercial release. By the end of the

EXHIBIT 3 | **THE PRINTED CIRCUIT BOARD FABRICATION VALUE CHAIN**

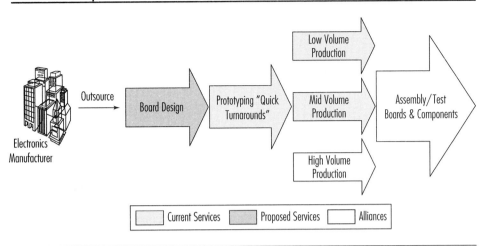

decade, its newest mainframe—packed with highly complex printed circuit boards that connected all sorts of chips and electrical components—was developed in less than 18 months. An external supplier had to work fast and effectively with such customers as IBM.

Exhibit 3 shows the spectrum of activities generally considered by industry participants as the basic elements of the PCB business. At the front-end of that spectrum was the actual design of the printed circuit board itself, complete with the printed circuitry and various electrical components. Certain competitors had developed substantial board-design capabilities largely by acquiring boutique electronic design shops starting in 1995. These competitors were able to service major accounts by locating engineers close to their customers' engineering facilities.

Dieter's Business Approach

CBC had traditionally operated in the mid-range segment, providing boards to New England–based minicomputer companies. Dieter bought state-of-the-art equipment to keep pace with the industry, but he always did it as a follower. He would wait until his competitors had all upgraded their manufacturing processes before he would upgrade his own. Dieter also had a tendency to defer maintenance on the equipment and delay tool acquisition. On several occasions, equipment had broken down so that Dieter had to call up competitors to fulfill orders for CBC.

At the beginning of the 1980s, Dieter saw that volumes in the low end were beginning to explode and decided to diversify. By 1995, only 50 percent of CBC's revenues came from its traditional mid-range customers; the other 50 percent came from low-end consumer electronics manufacturers. By 1995 his company was a $20-million-a-year business. However, this low-end strategy got the company into financial trouble and led to the hiring of Ben.

By the early 1980s, offshore manufacturers had started low-complexity, high-volume fabrication. By the end of the decade, they dominated it. In this semi-automated, high-volume process, the offshore producers were able to quote substantially lower prices because of cheap labor. By 1995, the consumer electronics manufacturers had moved virtually all their business to Asian fabricators. Because of this foray into the low end, by 1995 CBC's profits had declined 90 percent. Deiter hired Ben in 1996 to help him turn the company around. Because of the financial hardships, Dieter had increased his practice of skimping on materials and maintenance. Things had gotten so bad by the time Ben first saw the plant that his immediate reaction was, "What a pit this is!"

Ben shed the unprofitable low-end business to refocus on the mid-range, more technologically complex segment of the market. Ben had the good fortune of making these moves when the electronics industry had explosive growth. Historically, the PCB market had grown about 6 percent a year, but from 1995 to 2000 it grew at 10 percent. By 2000, he had not only gotten the company back to profitability but also increased sales to $30 million. Even though Ben had gotten the company on reasonable footing in 2000, he knew that it still had more investments to make in process technology. Laser drilling, better solder masking for finishing printed circuitry, and semi-automated systems for electrical testing of finished boards were the major improvements needed to get to industry parity.

Current Competition

The competitive landscape had three types of players: the multiproduct electronics outsourcing giants, the publicly traded focused printed circuit-board suppliers, and the smaller, independent suppliers. (See the appendix for a description of the competitors.) Well-known electronics brands had increasingly turned to third-party contract manufacturers for systems assembly. The largest contract electronics manufacturers made everything from computers to networking switches to industrial controls to consumer electronics. Often, they would take over the existing plant as well as the salaries of plant employees from a brand-name producer and use that as a foundation for manufacturing not only the current products but, over time, those of the brand's competitors as well.

The next tier of PCB suppliers comprised publicly traded manufacturers that were focused almost exclusively on PCB production. The performance of the stocks of these companies during 2001 had not been good. Some examples were: Coretec's stock dropped 67 percent, Dynamic Details dropped 60 percent, Circuit World dropped 48 percent, and TTM Technologies dropped 22 percent. Only Merix had increased in value, rising 38 percent during 2001 as investors focused on its strong balance sheet.

The third tier consisted of independent suppliers. At the end of 2001, there were approximately 500 privately held independent printed circuit-board suppliers in North America alone. The industry was highly fragmented. Only 20 suppliers had annual revenues of more than $10 million. Many of the truly small suppliers went out of business in 2001.

All printed circuit-board suppliers had suffered during 2001. Orders were 50 percent below those of the prior year. Suppliers with strong design skills and a high-tech sales focus were impacted the least in the downturn. While excess capacity hurt margins in the lower segment of the business, companies making boards with 20-plus layers were able to maintain reasonable margins. If the industry turned around—and many expected it would within 9 to 12 months—the permanent reduction in total fabrication capacity meant that the survivors might expect even greater margins.

Management Team

Maggie had married Dieter in 1957 after she had graduated high school and he was in college. She was now 62 years old. She had started college as a part-time student in the 1980s but had just completed her BA in 2001. Although she had always spent a couple of hours a day at CBC, her main task was to have lunch with Dieter. Most of her other time had been occupied in maintaining the household and raising their two children. Dieter and Maggie loved to travel and socialize—they enjoyed cooking, fine wine, and the opera. Maggie had no business experience apart from that at CBC.

Maggie's son and daughter had both worked in the company from childhood. They both had undergraduate business degrees, but neither one played an active role in the management of the company. The son, Harry, nominally was a factory worker but made $150,000 a year regardless of the number of hours he worked. The daughter, Heidi, also made $150,000, but she was an administrative assistant to the sales manager. They were both paid much more than the managers they reported to.

Ben Cashman, 46, had an MBA and had known Dieter for 30 years. He had started his own television and intercom service business before Dieter hired him as president and COO of the company. Although Dieter had controlled everything when Ben came on board, he was hoping to eventually buy the company, as he knew Dieter was in his 60s and had never developed anyone to take over when he retired. Ben was given 2.5 percent of the company when he joined.

Current Situation

To survive the market stress of 2001, Ben felt they needed to get their financial house in order, and they needed to make strategic investments to stay competitive. (See Exhibits 4 and 5 for CBC's financials.) CBC went from about $2.5 million in bookings a month in 2000 down to about $1.8 million a month in 2001. Throughout the year, Ben had taken measures to reduce costs. One was to reduce head count in the plant.

EXHIBIT 4 | INCOME STATEMENT

		2000	2001	Projected 2002
Net sales		$29,316,885	$21,877,855	$18,300,000
Cost of sales		23,790,016	19,086,179	14,587,000
Gross margin		5,526,869	2,791,676	3,713,000
Operating Expenses				
	Selling	1,035,708	988,151	846,000
	G&A	2,630,723	2,351,482	1,711,000
	Income/Loss from Operations	1,860,438	(547,957)	1,156,000
Interest Expense		708,381	659,684	564,000
	Other Income	13,096	593,743	25,000
	Income (loss) before tax	1,165,153	(613,898)	567,000

EXHIBIT 5　|　**BALANCE SHEET**

Current Assets	2001	2000	Current Liabilities	2001	2000
Cash	141,144	92,244	**Short-Term Debt**	1,222,175	993,843
A/R	2,670,771	4,672,372	**Accounts Payable**	4,020,299	3,382,278
Notes Receivable	81,400	125,650	**Accrued Expenses**	388,355	886,542
Inventory	3,382,850	3,284,724	**Total Current**	5,630,829	5,262,663
Prepaid expenses	260,280	161,485			
Deferred/prepaid income tax	162,866	3,636	**Capital leases**	421,610	637,074
			Long-Term Debt	6,336,888	7,383,814
Total Current Assets	6,699,311	8,340,111	**Deferred Income Taxes**	−92,731	578,146
			Total Liabilities	**12,296,596**	**13,861,697**
Property, Plant, Equipment	20,224,430	18,605,375	**Shareholder's Equity**	3,748,489	3,723,591
Less Accumulated Depreciation	−11,028,378	−9,743,957			
Net	9,196,052	8,861,418			
Other Assets	149,722	383,759			
Total Assets	**16,045,085**	**17,585,288**	**Total Liabilities and Equity**	**16,045,085**	**17,585,288**

He had mostly an hourly workforce operating semi-automated processes for various stages of production and quality control. While painful to do, he estimated that each head-count reduction of 10 persons saved the company about $300,000 a year in operating expense. Once having 240 full-time employees, the company now had 135, going from essentially a two-and-a-half-shift operation to a single-shift operation. He felt that the integrity of the operation at a $20 million order rate could still be maintained even with only 100 people. Ben also felt that G&A was too high, running at about 10 percent of sales. He had asked all salaried employees to take a pay reduction in keeping with the current level of sales. Ben was determined to get G&A down to 7.5 percent of sales.

Weakness in 2001 sales had drained the company's cash. By the end of 2001, the balance sheet showed $4 million in accounts payable. Suppliers had essentially financed the business for the past six months. Ben knew that this situation would not last much longer, as they were threatening to sue for collection. Half the accounts were now more than 90 days past due. He knew that he had to cut trade debt in order to keep the suppliers from abandoning the company. The company was also behind in payments to one of Dieter's early partners, who owned 11 percent of the company. He and CBC had an agreement to repurchase all his shares at a set rate and price, but CBC had stopped doing so because of the lack of cash. He was also threatening to sue.

The company had more than $3 million in inventory by the close of 2001. Ben estimated that about half of that was truly productive in the sense that it comprised unfinished goods that could be directly rolled into new orders, but he never really investigated its true worth. The utility and value of the other half was not clear, being finished goods for products that manufacturers might never make. Many suppliers had purchased materials under the reasonably positive expectations in the last half of 2000, only to be left "holding the bag" as conditions worsened and orders plummeted. Ben had cut accounts receivables by approximately half from the prior year, largely through tenacious efforts to get the company paid faster. Ben was not sure how much of the remaining accounts receivable he could collect because many of his customers were also in financial distress.

The projections on the income statement showed no marked improvement in sales for 2002. Ben saw no reason for the industry to turn around—not yet at least. However, he felt a strong rebound could again bring sales back up to the $30 million level in a single year. CBC, moreover, was adding new types of customers. Military electronics, videoconferencing systems, new generations of mobile phones, biometric systems, security devices, and security-enhanced routers and switches were potential growth opportunities for technologically advanced suppliers. It seemed that the tragic events of "9/11" were driving the business: People wanted to travel less and required security-enhanced systems of all shapes and forms. The American defense agencies and their contractors, moreover, strongly preferred that U.S. companies only make all subassemblies for them.

However, the company had fallen behind its competitors in the high-end multi-layer board business. To compete effectively in defense and other emerging high-end applications, Ben felt that the company would have to invest $2 million over the next two or three years to improve the company's fabrication technology. The manufacturing process was capital intensive. Like other PCB manufacturers, CBC had to continually invest in process technologies to meet demands for density and quality. CBC had no patents of its own. The second half of 2001 had been so difficult that the company had temporarily stopped process improvements. In addition, Ben wanted to spend another $2 million over two or three years to buy several board designer shops to execute an upstream design services.

On the revenue side, Ben thought the business was still worth pursuing. As electronics manufacturers consumed their inventories during the first half of 2002, and industry experts began forecasting a general turnaround later in the year, Ben believed that better days were ahead. A leading industry analyst projected that electronic component sales would rise by 5 percent in 2002 as electronics manufacturers were beginning to "recharge" their pipelines. In fact, during the last quarter of 2001, there had been a slight uptick in sales for both CBC and most of its competitors (Exhibit 6). Ben remained cautious, however. That uptick could just as easily reverse because consumer confidence and industrial spending remained low compared with prior years' levels. Ben hoped that the electronics industry would stabilize and that bookings for 2002 would come in at around $18 million.

Board Meeting

To start the board meeting, Ben had gone over all the moves CBC had made over the past six months to respond to the market conditions. He summarized his opinion:

> CBC is a survivor of 2001 and so is positioned to take advantage of the rebound. Needham & Co. is predicting that because others have left the industry and capacity is down, that inventory will be used up by the second

EXHIBIT 6 | **TURBULENCE IN THE MARKET**

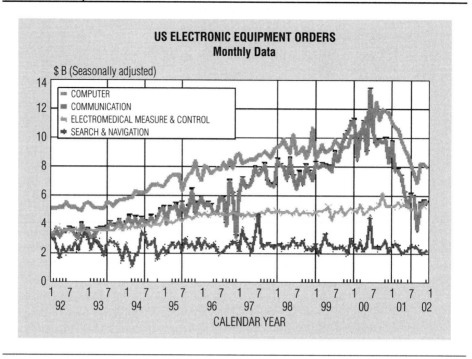

SOURCE: http://www.census.gov/indicator/www/m3/pastpressreleases/prel/2002/feb02prel.pdf

quarter. The market will then turn around, so we only have to hang in there for a couple more tough months. We can be profitable at $20 million in sales now with the cutbacks, but we can also grow back to $30 million as in 2000.

Don Armour, the mergers and acquisition specialist, was even more aggressive than Ben:

Now is the time to take advantage of the situation to not only be a survivor but to grow even larger. There are many financially struggling companies out there that we can buy up cheaply. People are willing to make deals. We should set our sights even higher! Why not look to $100 million in sales?

Dane Lombard, the turnaround specialist, was next to jump in and was heated in his response:

Don't be foolish in going after pipe dreams—get the most you can now because the market is not going to turn around. Needham has been predicting a rebound for six months and keeps pushing out the date. Henderson Ventures and DLouhy Merchant both predict there will be no recovery until 2003 at the earliest. We do not have the money needed to invest in bringing us back to industry parity, plus our balance sheet is awful. In fact, we are not worth as much as an entity as we would be if we sell off the pieces separately.

Maggie looked to Ben and asked where the money would come from to do the investments he wanted. Ben had hired consultants in turnaround financing to give guidance in restructuring CBC's debt and to help find some outside investors. Ben reported:

> The consultants have analyzed us and think that there is a possibility of finding some outside investors if the industry rebounds. I have held off on going ahead because they advise that any investors would want to put their money mainly into the company rather than into buying out the existing shareholders. The investors would also demand complete control of ownership and shed all nonproductive employees. In effect, Maggie, your ownership position would be almost worthless. Plus, you and your family will be out of the company.

Will Tatelman, the company's auditor and Maggie's personal counsel, chimed in:

> Maggie, you have to protect your own interests. You can work a deal to get ownership of the building for your shares, and then you can lease the plant back to the company. I have read two recent forecasts, one by Kaufman & Co., which said it is impossible to predict what will happen in the economy because of the risks of further terrorism and escalating military conflict, but they are saying there will be no recovery for a long time. The other by Wells Fargo is saying there would be no recession so this quarter's numbers will show we are already in recovery. So no one knows and you would be wise to protect yourself.

Ben agreed that Maggie should consider creating a sale/leaseback deal on the company's building before investors came in. The building was valued at $5 million and had a $3.5 million mortgage. The only tenant was CBC, but if CBC was successfully restructured, the rent would be a nice annuity with current rents going for $10 a square foot. The sale would take the mortgage off of CBC's books and turn the cost of the building into a rental expense. Of course, if the market did not turn around, Maggie could be stuck with a $3.5 million mortgage and a building worth much less.

Maggie had responded:

> You know, this business has provided for me and my family for 40 years. At this point in my life, I want stable income. What else can we do?

Another alternative Ben put forward was to take the company into Chapter 11 bankruptcy, which would allow it to renegotiate all its bills with its creditors. This would buy time for the company until the market turned around. The downside was that the creditors got to go over CBC's books, which would make known how much money Maggie and her family had been taking out of the business. Although reduced from the 2000 peak, they were still much overpaid for the work they did. One of the banks that had given CBC a large credit line already was putting pressure on Ben to get Maggie and her family out of the business.

The final alternative put forward, and the one Ben wanted, was to bet on the recovery and to convince the creditors that they would be paid in full if they stuck by the company for a while longer. This would not provide any of the investment needed to make the company competitive again, but it did allow Maggie and her family to maintain control of the company.

Ben recommended staying the course—he was convinced the recovery was right around the corner. The outside board members, however, suggested otherwise. Maggie was left to make the first real business decision of her life.

Appendix: Competitor Information

The competitive landscape facing Circuit Board Corporation could be divided into three tiers of companies: the multiproduct electronics outsourcing giants, the publicly traded focused printed circuit-board suppliers, and the smaller, independent focused suppliers. The major board-making contract manufacturers were:

- Flextronics: With operations throughout the world, it made both rigid and flexible circuit boards (on flexible connectors) and assembled them up to the completed product stage.

- Sanmina-SCI: Sanmina-SCI was primarily a North American operation and made only rigid boards. During the 1990s, Sanmina bought several dozen independent board suppliers. They assembled boards, including backplanes and systems. One of these was an independent focused printed-circuit board manufacturer much like Circuit Board Corporation. Altron, however, had ramped up into a $200-million-a-year business targeting complex, multilayer printed circuit-board applications. Sanmina had mothballed 9 of its 12 printed circuit-board fabrication plants during 2001. This removed $800 million of annual printed circuit-board production capacity. Much of that was a permanent removal.

The next tier of suppliers comprised publicly traded manufacturers focused almost exclusively on printed circuit-board production.

- Coretec: Roughly a $100 million Canadian company with a strategy of providing rapid turnaround to electronics manufacturers. They were setting up a multisite, time-zone spread operation to be close to the various customers. Coretec still needed to set up an operation east of the Mississippi. Its target applications were multilayer, medium-volume applications, the proclaimed strategy of Circuit Board Corporation.

- TTM Technologies: A merger of two independents, Pacific Circuits (a medium-volume producer) and Power Circuits (quick turnaround prototypes) merged together with venture money to focus on the multilayer, medium-volume market. The investors then took the company public. TTM was a direct competitor with Circuit Board Corporation. It was doing about $100 million in annual revenue.

- Dynamic Details: This was the largest firm of the group, with about $400 million in orders per year. DDI had also focused at the front end of the value chain, buying many small engineering firms and board companies. One of these was Automata, a $45 million company. DDI specialized in critical needs, extremely fast turnaround, multilayer, complex applications. It was the industry leader in the "quick turn," something to which Circuit Board Corporation aspired.

- Merix: Another $100 million company, Merix was known as the technology leader in the downstream areas of board fabrication. It had a fine-tuned process to achieve the highest layer counts and the greatest density of wiring, and it could use various exotic materials. Merix could regularly manufacture mid-20-layer boards for its telecommunications customers, and could shoot into 30–40-layer boards when required. Merix also offered upstream design services as shown in Exhibit 3. It was proceeding with plans to complete a new highly automated fabrication plant in Wood Village, Oregon. On the other hand, while Merix's sales had approached $250 million in 2000, it garnered only $25 million in sales during the third quarter of 2001. However, it had a strong balance sheet and had used these assets to invest in plant and equipment and buy other companies. This allowed it to continue adding capacity in anticipation of a turnaround in demand.

- Circuit World: strictly a medium-volume board producer with limited prototyping capability. It was about a $30 million company.

Beta Pharmaceuticals: Pennsylvania Distribution System

Jack Sexton, manager of logistics planning, walked out of his boss's office with a frown on his face. He had just learned that the top management of his company, Beta Pharmaceutical, had been taking a closer look at cost levels in the company's distribution system. In particular, high transportation costs resulting from frequent minimum-size LTL (less than truckload) shipments to customers and low-volume resupply shipments to the smaller warehouses were beginning to raise eyebrows. Total warehousing and material-handling costs had also been questioned.

When he got back to his office, Mr. Sexton sat back and thought the problem over. He recalled that the present plant, warehouse, and customer configuration had evolved during a period of high-growth years, without the systematic development of a master distribution plan. Warehouse location and customer service decisions were based mainly on marketing-centered recommendations, competitive pressures, and customer desires. Customer order frequency and shipment size had been largely in the control of the customer. Basically, Beta believed that to achieve and maintain industry leadership, it was necessary to meet customer demand 100 percent of the time. Thus the cost of customer service, inclusive of distribution, had historically been very high.

Several days later Mr. Sexton settled on a course of action. Calling in a logistics consulting firm, HLW and Associates, he asked that a pilot study be conducted to evaluate a portion of the present product logistics system for cost-service effectiveness. The state of Pennsylvania was determined to be a "typical" subsystem within the national distribution network and was designated by Mr. Sexton as the focal point for the study.[1] An outline of the study proposal is shown in Figure 1.

Background

The Company

Beta Pharmaceuticals is a multidivisional manufacturer and distributor of a diversified line of medical care products. Manufacturing, sales, and distribution facilities are located throughout the world, with major operations existing in Europe, Africa, South America, Australia, Asia, Canada, and the United States. Products include intravenous

---

[1] Pennsylvania represents a "mini model" of the total system in that it contains a three-warehouse configuration, two customer service areas, a customer service representative, and a dollar demand pattern consistent with the rest of the national system.

This case was prepared by Harvey Boatman, Paul Liguori, and Gary Wiser under the direction of Professor Alan J. Stenger, The Pennsylvania State University.

FIGURE 1 | **PROJECT DESCRIPTION**

Project: How should Beta Pharmaceuticals distribute products to customers in the state
                of Pennsylvania?

Background: Beta currently distributes products to customers from public warehouses in
                Pittsburgh, Harrisburg, and Philadelphia.

   • Cartage carriers are used in the three metropolitan areas.

   • Common carriers are used in the balance of the state.

   • Customers (hospitals) order both in patterns and randomly.

   • Shipments are made within 24 to 48 hours of order receipt.

   • Shipment sizes are small, from under 100 pounds to a few thousand pounds.

   • The full product line is stocked in Philadelphia and Pittsburgh, but only a
     partial line is stocked in Harrisburg.

   • Distribution costs are a significant element of total costs.

Objective: Determine the best method to distribute products to customers, considering
                the effects on:

   • Distribution costs (freight and handling).

   • Levels of customer service.

   • Inventory levels.

Scope: The scope of the project should be restricted to the state of Pennsylvania to
                keep it manageable.

   • Inventory policies and methods of replenishing warehouses should be
     ignored. However, the relationship between aggregate inventory levels
     and warehouse volume must be recognized.

   • Customer order patterns can be assumed to be controllable within certain
     limits, to be defined. Customer contact will not be allowed.

   • The number and location of warehouses should be determined.

   • Methods of delivery should be determined, including such alternatives as
     (1) direct shipment or (2) scheduling of customer orders for pooled delivery,
     including contact with carriers for rates and feasibility.

---

solutions, artificial organs, disposable medical devices, clinical testing and diagnostic
supplies and equipment, blood collecting and storage equipment, prescription drugs,
and industrial and medical enzymes.

Beta has twelve production or research facilities in the United States, and markets
its products through five customer-service or distribution-center regions. The company employs 13,600 persons throughout its worldwide system.

The backbone of Beta's strong marketing position in the hospital supply industry
is a well-funded R&D program. New products, as well as improvements to existing
products, are constantly being developed and exploited as a key element in market
strategy and industry leadership. As a result of this philosophy, Beta increased the 1994
expenditures for research and development by 25.7 percent over 1993 for a total dollar
investment of $46.7 million.

The aggressive competitive stance, supported by resourceful research and development, effective quality control, and customer-oriented distribution, has enabled the

company to build a sixteen-year compound growth rate in sales and earnings per share of 20 percent. Its 1994 sales were $855.9 million, which represented a 27.7 percent increase over 1993. Earnings per share for 1994 were $1.95, a 23.4 percent increase over 1993.

The Distribution System

The current distribution system used by Beta within the state of Pennsylvania makes use of three public warehouses: Philadelphia, Pittsburgh, and Harrisburg. From these three warehouses, Beta is able to serve most of its customers in forty-nine of the sixty-seven counties in Pennsylvania: this service is supplemented by shipments from nearby out-of-state warehouses or by carload shipments direct from a Beta plant. The distribution responsibilities of the three Pennsylvania warehouses include shipments to out-of-state customers as well as to the Pennsylvania customers.

Beta maintains either a company-salaried customer service representative or a warehouse employee at each warehouse to handle orders and customer inquiries. Whenever an order is received, company policy dictates that it be filled and tendered to a carrier within forty-eight hours. Orders are received either electronically or by phone, direct at the warehouse or at company headquarters in Chicago. The forty-eight-hour service goal starts at the point the order is received within the Beta system.

Once the warehouse receives the order, two possibilities exist. If the items are in stock, a bill of lading is cut and the freight is tendered to a common carrier or a cartage carrier. Of those shipments tendered to common carriers, 95 percent are delivered by the second morning. This means a maximum order filling time—including transportation—of four days 95 percent of the time. If the customer is located within the commercial zone of the city and a cartage carrier can be used, total time from order receipt by Beta to delivery to the customer is reduced to two days 95 percent of the time.

When sufficient stock is not available, the warehouse representative will contact the regional distribution center to which the warehouse is assigned. The regional distribution center will review the inventory levels of the surrounding warehouses and assign the order to one of these warehouses. Transportation cost is used as the basis for which warehouse should receive the order. If the item is not available in any of the surrounding warehouses, it will be back-ordered and expedited from a production facility. Since Beta wants to maintain high customer service levels, every attempt is made to maintain inventories high enough to avoid the need of back ordering to Chicago.

The majority of Beta's customers are hospitals. As such, they have limited storage space. They also cannot afford to wait very long after ordering items because their inventory averages approximately one week's demand. Since Beta is the major supplier of medical products in the Pennsylvania area, it falls upon them to provide hospitals with the required service. Traditional performance and marketing pressure have forced Beta into the position of maintaining inventory for its customers. However, very few of the shipments made by Beta are on a life-or-death basis for a patient.

Preliminary Findings and Plans of the Consultants

Beta's present distribution system is structured around basic customer service objectives. Competitive stress and rapid growth contributed to the piecemeal development of the present structure, wherein the customer sets the rules. This resulted in a number of marginal, close-to-the-customer warehouses. Warehouse-to-customer shipments are made without consideration of economic order quantities or potential savings to be recognized by shipping in consolidated lots. Many customers avoid assuming inventory responsibility and cost by ordering frequently, often at random intervals and in varying order quantities. Beta provides twenty-four-hour delivery to all customers within the commercial zone of each warehouse, and forty-eight-hour delivery to other customers. This situation has necessitated the establishment of safety stock of nearly 100 percent at most warehouses.

The piecemeal pattern of development has presented coordination problems at the corporate level. Many problems common to several areas are still handled on an individual basis at the local level. Rarely is the experience and information gained at one point generalized for the benefit of other areas of the system. The nearly exclusive use of public warehouses compounds this situation, particularly when quality control, damage, or liability become the question. The use of public warehouses also complicates the information-gathering process and makes the control aspects of inventory more difficult to handle.

Even though growth potential remains high for Beta, a plateau has been reached in many areas. For example, the climb to leadership in the medical products industry has been achieved; a reputation for high standards, effective quality control, and an understanding for the specialized problems experienced by hospitals has been established; an impressive record of innovation and responsible research and development has been compiled. In essence, Beta has created a "pull" situation, in the marketing sense, for the products bearing the Beta trademark.

Beta presently has good information potential. Most operations-related facts are collected in the present system, but unfortunately those items not lost due to pure volume are presented in a manner that makes their usefulness limited and suspect. Feedback and information update is slow and complicated under the present system of hand tallies, verbal order placement at each warehouse, and conflicting loyalties (due to the nearly exclusive use of public warehouses). Control at the warehouse level is shaky at best.

The Pennsylvania Subsystem

The following information is available for the Pennsylvania subsystem:

1. *Monthly demand for Pennsylvania customers.*   A computer printout for March 1995 gives demand by customers for each of Beta's major product lines. It shows how many bills of lading were cut and the number of cases per product line on each bill. Every order shipped within the state of Pennsylvania is included, with coded identification of which warehouse filled the order. There is a considerable amount of overlap in the territory served by various warehouses. Out-of-state warehouses appear throughout the printout, indicating service to cities also serviced by the Pennsylvania warehouses. The monthly demand information gives no indication of the timing throughout the month for the orders. It is easy to identify how many shipments a customer received but not when they were received. Finally, there is no indication that March 1995 was a typical month in terms of demand level. A quarterly demand schedule was requested but not provided. As a result, the assumption that March 1995 is a typical month had to be made.

2. *Quarterly transportation cost.*   This is a summary of the air and truck costs incurred by each of Beta's warehouses on an outbound basis by product line only. It does

show total pieces and weight of each product line shipped by air and truck, but it does not break total cost down past a total for air and truck. Since the total cost is a three-month figure for all shipments out of a warehouse, an average cost would not truly reflect the intrastate rate levels.

3. *March payments to carriers.*   Beta provided a list of the total billings for transportation charges paid to carriers in March 1995. The charges are broken down by product line pieces and weight. The list is not very useful because it is for bills paid in March, not for shipments made during March. Also, no information was provided concerning the number of shipments each carrier handled or the destination of these shipments.

4. *Warehouse throughput.*   Beta was able to provide estimates of the average monthly throughput in terms of total cases for the three Pennsylvania warehouses, as follows:

Philadelphia:	50,000 cases
Pittsburgh:	35,000 cases
Harrisburg:	9,000 cases

Warehouse capacity in both Philadelphia and Pittsburgh is large enough to handle the entire throughput of Harrisburg should that location be eliminated. Average monthly throughput would be useful in evaluating the methods of warehouse replenishment.

5. *Warehouse cost.*   The three Pennsylvania facilities are public warehouses. Under the contract agreements with Philadelphia and Harrisburg, a single charge is assessed for each carton that comes into the warehouse. There is no annual rental fee, no quantity discount, and no penalty for falling below a minimum level. The single rate per carton includes storage, handling, stenciling, and anything else the warehouse people might have to do to the case. The charge in Philadelphia is 44 cents per case, while the Harrisburg charge is 43 cents per case. Pittsburgh, which does not have the same type of arrangements, pays an average of 46 cents per case. There is no indication of how this figure would vary with different inventory levels. An additional 10 cents per case is assigned by Beta to each case handled through the Pittsburgh warehouse due to the presence of a Beta customer service representative in that city.

6. *Warehouse replenishment policy.*   Beta will not retain a warehouse unless it can be replenished at least once a month in carload quantity. The information provided by Beta concerning actual replenishment schedules is very sketchy. Philadelphia and Pittsburgh are replenished on a carload basis once a week. However, no information was available as to how many cars per week were used, whether they get the 40,000-pound or the 60,000-pound carload rate, or whether additional demand would also move at carload rates. If Harrisburg is eliminated, inbound freight costs to Philadelphia and Pittsburgh will change. The Harrisburg replenishment schedule was stated to be once every two to three weeks and once a month.

7. *Average inventory level.*   Both Philadelphia and Pittsburgh hold six weeks' demand in inventory, whereas Harrisburg holds eight weeks' demand in inventory. These figures were unfortunately subject to some uncertainty.

8. *Truck rates.*   Evaluating configuration changes in the current system requires a comparison of total cost for both the present and proposed systems. Costing out

a system requires a close estimate of the transportation costs generated by that system. In light of the restrictions of a linear programming algorithm in terms of homogeneous product and potential system requirement of over 2,000 rates, weighted rate per county was used. Since the three Pennsylvania warehouses service forty-nine counties in Pennsylvania, forty weighted rates were obtained. A weighted rate assumes that all freight destined to a specific county is going to the one city where the major customers' demand is located. By selecting the city having the maximum flow of freight, variation from the actual rates is minimized. The weight break to that city is computed in terms of the average weekly tonnage coming into the entire county. This requires that a maximum of four shipments per month be allowed for any county. After one rate for each commodity group was established, the four rates were combined into one weighted rate, based on the percentage of the total weekly tonnage that the product line accounted for.

Propose several ways in which the Pennsylvania distribution system might be improved.

Pivot International— Pursuing Growth

Kirk Douglass, president of Pivot International, picked up the preliminary report on the security device and systems manufacturers industry he had just received. (See Appendix A for excerpts.) Douglass had engaged an industrial marketing research firm to undertake the industry study earlier in the year. It was two weeks before the late March 1998 International Security Conference (ISC) in Las Vegas. Douglass wondered if the industry was really the appropriate one to fuel Pivot's growth or if he should look elsewhere. In his general reading and talking to contacts he had noted potential applications in other industry segments, for example, medical equipment, other sports equipment manufacturers, or perhaps training aids. However, the present work by the industrial marketing firm had taken three months and considerable expense. He wondered if a delay and additional expense was warranted to consider other industries.

Pivot International is a contract industrial design[1] and manufacturing firm located in Lenexa, a suburb of greater Kansas City. Its customers are manufacturers and assemblers in the fitness equipment industry. For these customers Pivot custom-designs and manufactures primarily LCD display and control units to customer specifications. Pivot's customers attach these customized electronic components to their fitness equipment and sell the equipment under the customer firm's brand name.

On Douglass's desk are copies of the marketing materials he intends to use at the conference. He plans to take five of his engineering staff members to the conference. One team member is a company engineer who is pursuing an advanced degree in engineering management and who had attended ISC in the summer of 1997 in New York. At the engineer's recommendation Pivot had secured a booth at the March 1998 exhibition.

To date Pivot has no customers among the manufacturing firms in the security industry. Douglass expects that more aggressive follow-up efforts with contacts identified at the 1998 conference will yield customers. If the security industry is growing as rapidly as the market research report indicates, he wonders how he should market to

---

[1] Industrial design includes design of appearance of equipment with attention to functionality and aesthetics. It can also include packaging of materials, including graphic design. Equipment design issues include ease of use for the end consumer and manufacturing process considerations.

"Pivot International" Case was prepared by Marilyn L. Taylor, University of Missouri–Kansas City, and Theresa T. Coates, Rensselaer Polytechnic Institute. It is intended to be used as a basis for class discussion. The views presented here are those of the case authors and do not necessarily reflect the views of the Society for Case Research. Authors' views are based on their own professional judgments. Copyright © 2003 by the Society for Case Research (SCR) and the authors. Permission to use granted by SCR.

this industry and what types of firms he should target in order to position Pivot as a custom-design and contract-manufacturing firm for the security device and systems manufacturers.

Pre–Pivot Company History— Applied Resources in Allegheny and PPG

Pivot began in the early 1970s as Applied Resources, Inc. (ARI), a small contract electronics design firm located in the greater Kansas City area. Douglass described the founder as "an economist who was self-taught in electronics . . . one of the brightest and most creative product designers I have ever seen . . . a great salesman [and] one of fastest thinking people on his feet that I have ever encountered." By the early 1980s ARI had developed electronic component parts for a broad range of products such as electronic components for anesthesia monitoring equipment, controllers for low-end X-ray equipment, control systems for fire suppression equipment, wireless electronic blanket controllers, and one of the first electronic monitors for fitness equipment. Patents on these products remained the property of ARI's customers, since all of ARI's contracts were on a work-for-hire basis. In the early 1980s ARI's major customer was Allegheny International.

Purchase by Allegheny International, Inc.

ARI designed for five divisions within Allegheny's Commercial and Industrial Group. The vice president of the group noted his group's reliance on ARI's capabilities. As a result, Allegheny purchased a majority interest in ARI to protect the design capacity the Kansas City firm provided. The 1984 purchase solved the perennial cash flow problems that often threatened ARI's survival. The founder stayed with the firm, but Allegheny augmented his capabilities with the background provided by Kirk Douglass. Douglass had an MBA from Carnegie-Mellon and had worked in engineering and sales for a major Kansas City firm and then moved to head a smaller firm that made quartz crystals for the electronics industry. As Douglass put it, "I joined Applied Resources as VP in late 1985 to add business strength to the organization."

Allegheny's vice president encouraged ARI to source electronic parts abroad and seek out manufacturing opportunities in the Far East. Douglass explained:

> Shortly after I came on board, we opened the Applied Resources office in Taipei, Taiwan. The purpose of the [Taiwan] office was to source parts, produce tooling, and manage subcontract manufacturing in the Far East. The price-technology issues in the low end of the market virtually dictated that we look for manufacturing opportunities in Asia. There are many subcontractors in Asia, and Taiwan is a world center for both tool-and-die operations and electronic assembly. Frankly, I am glad that Allegheny owned ARI at the time because we made many expensive mistakes as we sought to establish our overseas base!

From 1985 to 1987 the value of the New Taiwan dollar (NT$) rapidly increased. In addition, the labor market was tight, so the firm could not expand capacity to take care of sudden increases in product demand. These two factors led Applied Resources to move production from Taiwan to the Philippines. The new subcontractor was TTI, a Philippines manufacturing company wholly owned by Emilio Ching.

In 1987 Allegheny purchased Sunbeam, a well-known consumer products firm. Severe financial difficulties emerged almost immediately. Allegheny's board made the decision to retain Sunbeam and began to divest a number of its divisions and other producing assets in order to pay down the debt it had incurred in acquiring Sunbeam. One of Allegheny's units was a St. Louis–based company that manufactured the mechanical aspects of anesthesiology monitoring equipment. Allegheny purchased the remaining interest in ARI and "packaged" ARI with the St. Louis firm to form a biomedical unit, which it then sold to Pittsburgh Plate Glass (PPG).

ARI as a PPG Subsidiary

PPG's three main businesses were paint, glass, and inorganic chemicals. These were mature, slow-growth markets in which PPG had strong presence and technological leadership but limited opportunity for growth. PPG's senior executives made the decision to form a biomedical group as a vehicle for growth. The firm implemented its new strategy by acquiring divisions of other companies. One of the companies PPG purchased was Allegheny's biomedical unit. Shortly after the acquisition, ARI's founder left PPG to establish another small contract industrial design firm in the Kansas City area.

Douglass stayed on with PPG and was asked to take on the responsibility for divesting the nonmedical businesses that had come with the various acquisitions that made up the Biomedical Group. PPG's new Biomedical Group vice president was interested in having units in his area take advantage of ARI's capabilities. However, by 1988 Douglass had pointed out that while ARI had solid electronics capabilities, the other biomedical units were resistant to utilizing ARI's U.S.-based design capabilities, its Far East sourcing capabilities, and its Philippines-based manufacturing capacity. He suggested to the group vice president that the application of electronics in the fitness equipment industry was about to "blow open"[2] and recommended that PPG retain ARI and grow its capabilities with applications to fitness equipment. Douglass explained what happened:

> I was told that PPG would accept the fitness industry as the "low end" of the biomedical business and therefore within the mission of PPG Biomedical. I was made Business Unit Manager of the Health and Fitness Business Unit ("H&F"), which was a unit within PPG's Biomedical Group.

PPG ceased to use the Applied Resources name and instead referred to the business as the "Health & Fitness" unit. H&F designed and manufactured electronics components such as LCD display units and motor controllers primarily for U.S.-based fitness equipment manufacturers.

Over the next seven years (1987–1993), PPG's biomedical division as a whole lost a great deal of money. However, one unit that grew rapidly and was profitable was the Kansas City–based design and manufacturing firm. Douglass explained:

> During this time period the fitness equipment industry was growing relatively nicely, about 8 to 10 percent. However, I grew the H&F business

---

[2]For example, see Lyle H. McCarty, "Microprocessor Control Fitness Machine," *Design News* 43 (August 17, 1987), p. 102, and Stephanie J. Muraski, "Exercise Equipment Joins the Computer Age," *Machine Design* 49 (April 23, 1987), p. 28.

from $250,000 of business in 1988 to over $10 million in 1993, riding the curve of the adoption of electronics in the industry.[3] At the time the Biomedical division had sales of approximately $200 million. So, we were a very small entity indeed within the Biomedical division.

Applied Resources Becomes Pivot International, Inc.: The Buyout from PPG

In early 1993, the CEO of PPG, who had been responsible for the "fourth leg" strategy, retired. Douglass described what happened next:

> A new CEO came in from outside. The new CEO used his honeymoon period to correct a number of problems, of which Biomedical was at the top of the list. In October 1993, PPG announced the Biomedical division was for sale. Initially PPG thought they would sell H&F as part of the Biomedical Division. However, none of the buyers interested in Biomedical were interested in H&F. Therefore, I had the opportunity with Mr. Ching to negotiate a buyout of H&F.
>
> Mr. Ching had approached me and said, "Let's buy it. I will provide bridge financing until you can put a bank line in place." So he became a majority stockholder and I a minority shareholder. The sale price of $7 million was agreed to August 31, 1994, and the transaction was completed November 8, 1994. The resulting company was [named] Pivot International, Inc.

As part of the sale, Douglass became president of Pivot International. Douglass described his role in the buyout:

> The buyout process did put me in a potential conflict of interest considering my fiduciary responsibility to PPG. However, PPG was glad to sell the division profitably and relatively easily. Understand that Pivot was only a fleabite to PPG.
>
> Mr. Ching and I have gotten along very well. He comes over here and I also go to Taipei and the Philippines regularly. Mr. Ching is an investor, although he owned the Philippine manufacturing plant prior to purchasing Pivot. He owns a number of businesses and expects me to drive significant growth in Pivot. He is a self-made man. He started selling hardware to contractors. Then he became a general contractor and subsequently moved to the role of developer. He has a visceral sense about how to make money. He hit the land boom in the Philippines just right at a time when an investor could double his money very quickly. In addition, he made other investments, including a small electronics manufacturing firm (i.e., TTI).

---

[3] The sales of fitness equipment manufacturers dropped slightly from $900M to $740M from 1985 to 1987 and then grew to nearly $2 billion in 1995. (See Dave Fusaro, "Exercise Gear Market Toughens Up," *Metalworking News* 15 [July 18, 1988], p. 1, and "Fitness Retailers Lead Field," *HFN The Weekly Newspaper for the Home Furnishing Network* 70 [September 16, 1996], p. 10.)

The company was incorporated in Kansas. Pivot's wholly owned subsidiary, Applied Resources, Ltd. (ARL), was a Taiwanese corporation. Ching owned most of the Pivot International stock while Douglass had a minority position. TTI, Pivot's manufacturing partner, was a separate Philippine corporation. The Ching family owned all of the TTI stock.

In December 1994, Pivot provided contract design, tool-and-die development, and manufacturing capabilities to approximately 10 firms in the fitness manufacturers and assemblers industry. All of Pivot's customers were in the high-volume, low-cost segment of the fitness business. Douglass described the situation:

> Outside the narrow confines of the fitness [manufacturers] community Pivot was entirely unknown. We were also unknown in the Kansas City community, our own home base. We had no capability brochures or product flyers. Our work consisted of selling custom-designed LCD[4] readouts to fitness equipment manufacturers or assemblers. It was a small industry where everybody already knew us. Our competition was entirely foreign manufacturers who operated either out of Taiwan or Hong Kong. No other firms provided the breadth of services that we did, i.e., contract design, tool-and-die development, manufacturing, or combinations. For our customers we provided primarily electronic display units using custom microprocessors with embedded code.

Pivot personnel worked closely with the company's clients to develop designs and product prototypes in Lenexa. Through the Taiwan office, the company could design and develop tooling and molds for manufacturing the plastic or metal casings for the LCD readout devices. Pivot purchased most of its raw material through the Taiwan office. Products were manufactured in the Philippine plant.

Pivot International, 1994–1997

During its first full year of operation Pivot experienced significant but slower growth than it had experienced during the prior seven years. Douglass saw some signs of difficulty in the fitness equipment industry and began to make changes in strategy.

Turmoil in the Fitness Industry

Several firms among the fitness equipment manufacturers encountered significant difficulties in the mid-1990s. Primary causes of the turbulence were the entry of large-scale mass merchandisers (such as Wal-Mart, Kmart, and Target) and the effect of infomercials. Douglass explained the effect of the mass merchandisers:

> In 1995 we peaked at just under $20 million in sales. [See Tables 1 and 2 for Pivot's income statements and balance sheets.] Then the low end of the fitness industry fell apart. Two years after the buyout, 70 percent of our

---

[4]Liquid crystal display. The alternate technology is light-emitting diodes (LED), which provides a brighter image in an electronic display unit, but use more current.

TABLE 1	INCOME STATEMENTS PIVOT INTERNATIONAL, INC. 1994–1997 YEAR END DECEMBER 31 ($000)

	1997		1996		1995		1994	
	$	%	$	%	$	%	$	%
Revenues[1]	15,668	1.00	12,334	1.00	19,565	1.00	17,999	1.00
Operating expenses	15,457	0.99	12,951	1.05	18,039	0.92	16,739	0.93
Operating profit	211	0.01	(617)	(0.05)	1,526	0.08	1,260	0.07
Interest	32	0.00	79	0.01	22	0.00	9	0.00
Profit before tax	179	0.01	(696)	(0.06)	1,504	0.08	1,251	0.07
Taxes[2]	0	0	0	0	559	0.03	436	0.02
Profit after tax	179	0	(696)	(0.06)	945	0.05	815	0.05

COMPARATIVE INDUSTRY DATA

	RMA[3] SIC#3625[4]	RMA[3] SIC#8711[5]
	%	%
Net sales	1.00	1.00
		na
Gross profit	0.35	na
Operating expenses	0.28	0.96
Operating profit	0.07	0.04
All other expenses (net)	0.01	0.01
Profit Before Tax	0.04	0.04

[1]About 97 percent of all manufacturing for Pivot International was carried out by Teletech Telesystems, Inc., Passy City, Philippines, which was 100 percent owned by Edwin Ching. Revenues include manufacturing charges.

[2]Tax carry-forward from 1996.

[3]RMA refers to Robert Morris Associates, 1997 edition. RMA publishes comparative financial data on industries on a yearly basis.

[4]SIC#3625 refers to a subcategory of Manufacturing Industries—Machinery, Equipment & Components, except Computer Equipment, specifically relays and industrial controls including manufacturing relays, motor starters and controllers, control accessories, and other industrial controls. Does not include automatic temperature controls or industrial process instruments.

[5]SIC# 8711 refers to the subcategories of Services Industries-Engineering, Architectural & Surveying Services (and includes SIC codes 8712 & 8713).

TABLE 2 | **BALANCE SHEETS PIVOT INTERNATIONAL, INC. DECEMBER 31, 1996 AND 1997 ($)**

	12/31/97		12/31/96		Comparative Industry Data[2]	RMA 1997 SIC #3625	RMA 1997 SIC #8711
Assets	$	%	$	%		%	%
Cash	212,128	0.04	184,691	0.03	Cash & Equivalents	0.07	0.06
Accts. Rec.	3,285,638	0.57	4,886,056	0.70	Trade Receivables	0.31	0.56
Inventory	592,828	0.10	537,680	0.08	Inventory	0.30	0.05
Other Curr. Assets	1,095,597	0.19	938,883	0.13	All other Currents	0.02	0.07
Current Assets	5,186,191	0.91	6,547,310	0.94	Total Currents	0.69	0.74
Fixtures and Equip.	353,555	0.06	370,609	0.05	Fixed Assets	0.23	0.17
Other Assets	184,196	0.03	49,353	0.01	Intangibles & Other	0.08	0.10
Total Assets	5,723,942	1.00	6,967,272	1.00	Total Assets	1.00	1.00
Liabilities & Owners Equity							
Accounts Payable[1]	2,598,335	0.45	2,758,474	0.40	Trade Payables	0.13	0.115
Notes Payable	0	0	826,287	0.12	Notes Payable	0.09	0.142
Accruals	300,228	0.05	735,809	0.11	All Other Currents	0.18	0.197
Current Liabilities	2,898,563	0.51	4,320,570	0.62	Total Currents	0.40	0.454
Long-Term Debt and Deferred Taxes	0	0.00		0.00	Long-Term Debt	0.11	0.068
Retained Earnings	(75,097)	(0.01)	(253,774)	-0.04	All Other Non-Currents	0.06	0.073
Equity	2,900,476	0.51	2,900,476	0.42	Net Worth	0.42	0.405
Total Liab. and Owners Equity	5,723,942	1.00	6,967,272	1.00	Total Liab. and Net Worth	1.00	1.00

[1] Accounts Payable: top 10 industries accounted for about $900K, including: Wholesale electronic parts = $775K; Wholesale computer/software $1K; Nonclassifiable $20K; Wholesale electrical equipment $3K; Computer Mfg. $5K; Help Supply Service $4K, Trucking nonlocal $3K; Electric services $1K; Semiconductor mfgs $55K; Air courier service $10K.

[2] Robert Morris Associates, 1997 edition.

customers went bankrupt. Diversified Products (DP),[5] which had been 50 percent of our business, was one of the companies that failed. I talked to their CFO during this period. What happened to DP was this—DP sold a treadmill to Wal-Mart at $139. At that price DP covered its variable

[5] DP was a successful privately owned Alabama-based company with a one-million-square-foot factory. The firm did most of its manufacturing in the Alabama factory and purchased components from around the world. It was one of the leading bike-building companies. The firm launched the Airstrider home exercise equipment that sold for under $249 in 1993. A year later DP's ownership group sold operations to another leading brand, Roadmaster. Roadmaster and DP had explored a possible merger in 1991 and 1992, but then backed away from a deal. The expectation from the 1994 transaction

costs, but barely anything else. The final straw, though, was when Wal-Mart sent back 25 percent of the product. That put DP over the edge into bankruptcy. In essence, the company lost control of their operations as the mass merchandisers insisted on lower and lower costs "or else"!

Infomercials created a different difficulty, as Douglass explained:

> One of seven infomercials is a hit. When an infomercial "hits," it creates instantaneous demand. The manufacturer gears up for that level of demand. Then, all of a sudden, the market interest moves on to other products. The manufacturer cannot so readily ramp down and the company is left holding not only the higher fixed costs of expanded capacity, but probably considerable inventory as well. I've seen companies producing 5,000 units per week drop off to zero in two to three weeks. Meanwhile, the supply train of up to 26 weeks of inventory was already on its way and could not be cancelled. It is a vicious cycle. In addition to these difficulties our SKUs (store-keeping units) proliferated and complexity increased. Where once we had produced 250,000 units a year of a relatively simple product, suddenly we were asked to produce 25,000 units a year of 10 *different* units of generally greater complexity. Our engineering overhead skyrocketed.

Douglass gave three specific examples of problems encountered by companies that were among Pivot's customers:

- NordicTrack, which had negative worth as a result of the battering it took in the market.

- Health Rider, another brand name in the fitness industry, had grown from $0 to $200 million in a couple of years. The company's growth came, as Douglass put it, "solely through infomercials." After two years of tremendous success, the volume of infomercial responses suddenly declined from 15,000 units per week to very few units per week. In addition, other firms came out with riders that did not violate Health Rider's patents. The company declared bankruptcy and did not restart.

- Fitness Master supplied products to the infomercial industry. Among the company's products was the Jane Fonda Treadmill. Fitness Master's primary customer went bankrupt. The customer left Fitness Master holding $4 million of accounts receivable. Fitness Master closed.

---

was that Roadmaster would improve "DP's failing operations as a result of synergy with other Roadmaster brands." The plan was to consolidate manufacturing for Roadmaster, DP, and Vitamaster into the Alabama factory. Vitamaster was Allegheny's fitness equipment division. It had been sold to Fuqua Industries in 1987 and then to Roadmaster in 1994. Vitamaster especially was strong in mass merchant channels. Roadmaster aimed to be number one in the home fitness market. (Information from an interview with Douglass; "Roadmaster, DP Agree to Merger," *Sporting Goods Business*, September 1991, p. 7; Greg Dutter, "Roadmaster, DP Go Separate Ways [Roadmaster Industries, Inc. and Diversified Products Co., Merger Deals], *Sporting Goods Business*, May 1992; and Christopher McEvoy, "DP Get Fit after Roadmaster Merger," *Sporting Goods Business*, January 1994, p. 32.) The major company in the industry initially was a company called Weslo, which later became ICON. ICON was formed by two Mormon missionaries who spent a couple of years of their youth in Taiwan. There was a race between ICON and DP, but ICON managed the situation better than DP did. Both produced most of their merchandise under their own brand name. Basically they were squeezed by the Wal-Marts and the K-Marts. Another firm supplying Wal-Mart was Weslo/ICON, but at one point Wal-Mart said, "Here they are all back." (Source: Douglass interview.)

Changes in Strategy

Although Douglass foresaw some of the difficulties the fitness industry manufacturers encountered, it took some time for Pivot to make adjustments. He explained the situation:

> So there we were–completely unknown other than to the fitness equipment manufacturers and we were watching our market go down the drain. It sounds like a formula for [company] burial. . . . Here's what we did:
>
> - Took good care of the customers that did survive the shakeout and began moving upscale in the fitness industry (i.e., equipment retailing for $1,000 or more). That way we got a higher dollar per unit with customers that were not dependent on the mass merchandisers.
>
> - Went to a trade show in Europe and captured a significant contract with the largest manufacturer of fitness equipment in Europe. Europeans tended to buy better quality fitness equipment than had been the trend in the United States.
>
> - Recognized that we had capabilities in design and manufacturing that were applicable to businesses outside of the fitness industry and we resolved to market ourselves to those industries.

As Douglass put it, "We have a competitive advantage in product design and in the interface between product development and manufacturing abroad. We are a low-cost manufacturer and we have a reputation for good quality, which we have worked over the years at maintaining. Customers would like low price, high quality, and speed to market. But realistically they can only have two of the three."

Douglass described the change in marketing strategy:

> We developed a capabilities brochure and a mailing campaign and began to market ourselves to other companies. We have defined the new Pivot International as:
>
> - A contract product developer and manufacturing house. Our company provides turnkey product development and manufacturing services to companies interested in outsourcing some or all of these functions.
>
> - Our company provides the benefits of U.S.-based design with the economies of Far East purchasing and manufacturing.
>
> - Compare us to an engineering or industrial design company. An engineering/design firm wants to make money by charging their customer by the hour for development. If the engineering/design firm can take longer, so much the better. [In contrast,] Pivot makes money by shipping product as soon as possible and cutting time to delivery to the market. Our interests are aligned with those of our customers.
>
> - We can charge less for engineering and design services because of our manufacturing base. We try to capture the cost we incur in design and, if possible, to make a profit on design activities. However, we are generally not interested in taking on design work that does not lead to manufacturing.
>
> - We are fast. The process from design through manufacturing is carefully coordinated by one of Pivot's product managers so that things are done in parallel and the design staff provides manufacturing with a product that can in fact be made.

Pivot considered targeting several other industries, including the security device manufacturers market. For the security device manufacturers market, Pivot was particularly interested in the closed-circuit television monitoring and surveillance and the access control segments. Both segments required the component product design and manufacturing capabilities that Pivot could supply. Pivot could provide such components as LCD displays and motor controllers. Eventually the company also hoped to develop some component parts that were of a proprietary design.

Pivot's Competitors

The company had few competitors that provided the full range of design, tool and die, purchasing, and manufacturing services as one integrated package. Douglass described Pivot's competition:

> We don't appear to have many competitors. Our biggest competitor is usually internal operations of our customer. However, we have seen a few similar companies in the literature.
>
> - There was a recent *Fast Company* article that described an industrial design company in Silicon Valley that has used our strategy very successfully. That firm has expanded into engineering and has developed some sort of relationship with a Far East manufacturer so that they can provide production service. The company designed the Palm Pilot and has about $80 million in revenues.
> - There is also a Los Angeles company that is smaller and does not have production capability, but it is actively promoting outsourcing of product development.
> - There are a number of contract manufacturers in the industry—some of them quite large. Solotron is an example of a large contract manufacturing company. Solotron manufactures for companies like Hewlett-Packard.

There were other companies that focused on industrial design or still others that were contract manufacturers. However, few firms did both. As Douglass explained, "Customers that go to a firm that does one or the other have to work on coordination issues between two or more companies to get a finished component part like an LCD readout display or control unit."

Pivot Operations and Capabilities

The U.S.-Taiwan-Philippines Facilities

The company's operations included the U.S. design firm, its Taiwanese tool-and-die subsidiary (both owned by Pivot International), and the Philippine manufacturing facility (owned by TTI). The design office was located in an upscale suburb of the greater Kansas City area. Kansas City was the fifth largest engineering center in the United States thanks to two very large engineering design firms. However, most of the Kansas City firms were involved in design and building of facilities such as power plants and other commercial facilities. Pivot's Kansas City facility company personnel built electronic models and prototypes. The Kansas City facility could build a limited number of preliminary models but had very little capacity for manufacturing per se.

The Taiwan facility focused on tool-and-die development for plastic and metal parts. In addition, the Taipei office constantly searched the world, with special emphasis on Pacific Rim countries, for parts that could be used in the manufacturing process that offered customers maximized performance at minimized cost.

Pivot's manufacturing facilities were located in the Philippines. The Manila facility included 62,000 square feet.[6] Although legally a separate company, the Manila facility was operated as an integral part of Pivot. In contrast, competitors often partnered with third-party suppliers to undertake the contract manufacturing. Pivot committed to "warranty the quality and performance of every product we manufacture." Pivot had also developed considerable expertise in logistics so that it could promise "precise shipping practices that guarantee timely delivery by air or sea." The company's commitment to customers guaranteed careful attention to keeping customers fully informed with regard to design and manufacturing progress and promised meeting deadlines.

Douglass described the relationship among the three parts of the corporation as:

> We run as one operating whole. Lenexa and Taiwan are legally one company. The Philippine plant is a separate entity wholly owned by Mr. Ching; however, we operate all three as one unit. In short, we have the whole thing in one package. As a result we get to market faster and cleaner. Our designers [in Lenexa] talk to our engineers [in Taiwan] and both talk to the factory [in the Philippines]. Our project managers coordinate the entire process and are in constant communication with our customer. As a result, we offer the whole seamless process and thus considerable advantage to our customers.

The plant in the Philippines manufactured for Pivot as well as other firms and had significant additional capacity that could be utilized. Manufacturing work that Pivot arranged for was billed through Pivot. Pivot preferred to do work that included all four tasks (design, sourcing, tool and die, and manufacturing), since the coordination among these activities was where the firm excelled. Douglass explained that most design firms charged by the hour, whereas his firm generally charged for the delivered product. Thus Pivot was motivated to (1) be as expeditious in time to delivery as possible as well as to (2) design products to manufacture as efficiently as possible. Its services included project management, offshore manufacturing, product design, mechanical design, electronic design, and worldwide shipping, as well as warranty and service activities.

In its advertising material Pivot described itself as providing "the convenience of U.S.-based project management and product development, the efficiency of high-volume overseas buying power, and the economy of offshore manufacturing . . . all from one source." Employing its facilities and capabilities at three locations, Pivot could provide plastic and metal component part assemblies; engineering, quality assurance; PCB[7] assembly; through-hole technology[8]; surface-mount technology[9]; COB

---

[6] 43,560 square feet is an acre.

[7] Printed circuit board.

[8] In this technology, the printed circuit board had holes through which the wires connecting smaller component parts such as resistors, capacitors, and integrated circuits were drawn and then soldered. This technology is an older one.

[9] A newer technology than through-hole, surface-mount initially glued smaller component parts, such as resistors, capacitors, and integrated circuits, to a printed circuit board, i.e., one that had no holes. The board was then run through an oven and the solder on the resistor melted to the board to form the appropriate electrical connections.

(chip on board)[10] capabilities; MRPII;[11] prototyping and concepts; full 3-D Solids CAD[12] platform; electronic engineering; mechanical, electronic, and industrial design capabilities; and graphics and packaging. Pivot's electronic design capabilities included software development as well as LCD, circuit, and IC customer designs. Pivot had strong vendor alliances with leading microcontroller[13] manufacturers that led to shorter lead times and lower costs.

Pivot Project Managers

Pivot's project managers were primarily engineers because, as Douglass put it:

> Most of our projects have engineering aspects. The project manager has to be sensitive to the potential engineering problems and communicate them throughout the organization as early in the process as possible. There has to be a constant dialogue. We like to say that we work on projects 24 hours a day. When our people here in Lenexa go home at night, they leave an e-mail for the staff in Taipei. About the time our personnel here are leaving, our people in Taipei are arriving in our facility there—and vice versa.
>
> At the same time, someone is also talking to the factory in the Philippines about manufacturing issues. Labor costs are low in the Philippines, so we can manufacture differently there than we would in a place where labor is more expensive. Taiwan does the document package. The document package[14] transmits the project to the factory. We expedite and focus on rapid time to market. Thus we don't handle things sequentially. Because we are coordinating across the three stages, i.e., (1) design here in Lenexa, (2) tool-and-die development and parts procurement in Taiwan, and (3) manufacturing in the Philippines, we get ahead of the game in terms of parts. For example, if we know that a part takes a long time to procure, we might have already ordered it before we send the document package to the Philippines.

Customer Applications

Most of the firm's output was custom LCDs for a variety of products, especially in the higher-end physical fitness market. The new capabilities brochure depicted several projects the firm had undertaken recently. These included products that had been designed and manufactured as well as products that only had been manufactured as follows:

- An LCD readout display unit that displayed time, speed, calorie burn rate, distance, and pulse rate on one LCD display. The unit was designed for the manufacturer of the brand "Pulse."

- A unit with seven LCD displays, dedicated to time, speed, distances, calories, pulse, effort, and program. This unit was designed for NordicTrack and was described as "high design value with fast turn—18 weeks from concept to delivery. Features . . . quick assembly."

---

[10] Integrated circuit chips mounted on an integrated-circuit board. The chip was usually manufactured by Texas Instruments or Intel and contained the intelligence for the equipment.

[11] Advanced Materials Requisition Planning software system.

[12] Computer-assisted design (CAD) capabilities. 3-D modeling required additional training and higher powered computers.

[13] That is, chip manufacturers.

[14] A document package for an electronic part or product is analogous to a blueprint for a building.

- Two products that Pivot had not designed, that had no LCD display, but that had been manufactured in the Philippines:
  - A cordless telephone that was described as "Manufactured for wireless telecommunications industry."
  - An electronic handheld control device with a custom keypad[15] that was described as "Manufactured for European market and designed for high-volume production. Features . . . high reliability."

Another customer was Schwinn, a manufacturer of bicycles. Schwinn attached a LCD readout meter made by Pivot to three of its bike models. Douglass described the three stages—industrial design, engineering, and manufacturing—that Pivot undertook for Schwinn:

> Schwinn came to us and wanted us to do the following:
>
> 1. Industrial design: so we sat down and made up hand sketches. Then we made solid model here in our Kansas City facility. Basically in this stage the critical questions were: What does it have to do and what should it look like?
>
> 2. Engineering: In this stage we were thinking about how big the LCD readout display had to be in order to fit certain components inside the casing that Schwinn indicated it wanted. We designed an LCD readout display for this product, in other words, a custom LCD.

Ultimately Pivot developed the tools and dies in Taiwan and manufactured the readout meter in the Philippines. Douglass described the Schwinn LCD readout meter:

> It does readout and display of various pieces of data for the bike user. We provided it in different colors. The year after we did the original project we undertook a slight modification. The newer version does not have a control function, but we are talking to Schwinn people about that possibility.
>
> Here's the model of the original. You can see it's designed essentially in four layers including the top and bottom of the external plastic casing. The second layer has the chip and display panel. The third layer has the various connections.

The capabilities brochure described the Schwinn LCD readout as a "Family line monitor with cost-effective tooling and low-cost electronic assembly. Plastic case tooled with same inserts. High-design value with fast turn—18 weeks from concept to delivery. Features custom LCDs, keys, and COB."

Pivot Personnel

Pivot International's Kansas City–based facility employed 48 engineers and professional staff. Pivot had recently hired some very strong electronic and mechanical engineers and designers to complement the existing engineering staff. Eighteen months prior the facility had only 32 professionals. The company used AutoCAD, a well-established computer-aided design software program that had the leading market share

---

[15] Such technology could be applied, for example, to design and manufacture wireless technology products such as remote television controllers.

throughout the world for many of its applications. In recent years Pivot had moved to rely on Solidworks and ProE platforms, two other software systems that had better solid modeling capabilities. Another 30 individuals in the Taipei office worked on product integration as well as tool-and-die engineering in plastics, metal, and other materials. The Taipei group also concentrated on sourcing components in various Asian countries. The Manila manufacturing facility could undertake through-hole, surface-mount assemblies and full electronic mechanical (plastic and metal) assemblies as well as finished products including retail packaging.

J. Kirkland Douglass, president of the Lenexa division of the company, was a 1966 BSEE Yale graduate and a 1968 alumnus of the Carnegie-Mellon MBA program. Among his professors were Bill Cooper, a founding member of the Operations Research Society; Herbert Simon, an organizational theorist and later Nobel Prize winner; and Igor Ansoff, an early and highly respected theorist in the field of strategic management. Douglass talked about the challenge his professors brought to his education. As he put it,

> I have always appreciated my MBA experience. I was one of Carnegie's early MBA graduates and lucky to be exposed to minds like Dr. Ansoff. That experience was a critical part of my development. Dr. Ansoff was a major contributor to the early development of the field of strategic management and he is also considered a futurist, that is, a scholar who is very concerned about forward predictions of the state of industries, environments, technology, and the like. These aspects of my education made me want to keep my horizons sufficiently broad so that I could retain my functional specialty in finance yet never lose sight of the strategic implications. . . . It was that kind of thinking and background that led ultimately to my being able to play the role I did in the Pivot buyout and continue to have the fun I have running this firm. My wife asks frequently if I will ever slow down and then she will laugh and say that the day I do is the day I no longer exist. As long as I am having fun, and I am, I want to stay with it.

Marketing at Pivot International

Pivot had focused on relationship marketing. The firm was well known by design and manufacturing personnel in the fitness industry firms. Marketing within the industry had consisted of establishing and maintaining relationships with appropriate personnel in firms.

In preparation for more aggressive marketing among other firms where Pivot's capabilities were not known, Douglass developed a set of advertising materials. He wrote the copy and hired a copyeditor to do the wordsmithing. Douglass also hired a local artist to execute a set of thematic postcards. The seven oversized postcards could either be sent as postcards or enclosed as inserts with other materials. The set of seven postcards all had a circus theme. For example, one of them emphasizes the theme: "It's all about trust" and portrays a circus worker in close contact with a large, menacing lion. The text that is included on the back of that postcard follows:

Get Overseas Manufacturing Without Risking Your Neck
Trying your hand in overseas manufacturing can be frightening—unless you are working with Pivot International. With branches strategically located in Kansas City, Manila, and Taipei, we provide the convenience of U.S.-based project management and product development, the efficiency of high-volume

buying power, and the economy of offshore manufacturing . . . all from a single source. Don't lose your head. Call today.

The company planned to use its materials in highly directed mailings aimed at specific industries. Douglass explained his approach to marketing:

> The nature of our business is to become a backup product development and manufacturing resource for companies that want to outsource these functions. Once we develop a relationship, the total dollar volume of business with a single customer can and should become significant. This means we have a small number of customers, each of which does a large volume of business. Under these circumstances, we can only absorb a few new customers in a given year. The worst thing we could do would be to advertise on a broad scale and get several hundred responses. We would not know what to do with them. Instead, we need to develop a marketing program that is directed to a smaller group of likely prospects with the idea of generating responses from 10 or 15 of them in a year. From that group, we would hope to close two or three more customers.

As Douglass summarized his company's current position:

> We're well-positioned to help companies in several industries undertake the design, development, and manufacture of consumer, industrial, and medical products through the use of U.S.-based design and cost-effective Far East sourcing of components and manufacturing. We have full services in industrial design, mechanical engineering, electronic software and hardware design, manufacturing, and product warranty support. Now all we have to do is crack a market beyond the fitness OEMs.
>
> However, we get business in large chunks. The right customer can represent $5 million of revenue in 18 months. I want every customer's billings to be under 20 percent of our business.

As a minority shareholder, Douglass felt that that $50 million would be an appropriate revenue target. He explained:

> Then we can take the company public or some other arrangement such as an ESOP. It could remain a privately held corporation. However, at our current $20 million revenue, I don't view us as stable. We are too dependent on too few customers. That's why I would feel more comfortable at $50 million. I've got about a five-year target for getting to the $50 million.

The Opportunity in the Security Device and Systems Manufacturers Industry

In thinking about expansion and diversifying Pivot's markets, Douglass identified the security device and systems manufacturers industry as a possible target. The industry had grown steadily for a number of years. Its growth had actually exceeded forecasts in recent years and was expected to remain unabated into the early part of the 21st century.

The upcoming International Security Conference was one of several major conferences that brought the device and systems manufacturers together with the security personnel from companies and law enforcement agencies. Over 400 exhibitors were listed in the preconference materials. These included:

- Some service providers such as ADT, Guardian Monitoring, and Protection One.

- Security systems and device manufacturers such as AES, AIT Advance Information. Technologies, Cardkey Systems, Inc., Clark Security Products–Closed Circuit Television, Detex, and Identicard Systems, Inc.

- Other suppliers to the industry such as B&B Battery (USA) Inc.

Pivot had secured a booth at the conference. Douglass planned to lead a team of six people from the company who would work the conference. Douglass especially planned to circulate through the booths to make contacts for follow-up during the postconference period.

Appendix A

Excerpts from the February 1998 Industrial Marketing Research Firm's Preliminary Report to the Company Regarding the Security Device and Systems Manufacturers Industry

Below is a summary of our preliminary observations about the security device manufacturers industry; technologies and applications; potential customers for Pivot; and the interviews we conducted with executives in nearly 30 firms in the northeastern United States. Also attached is a summary of the relationships among the various segments of the Security Device and Systems Manufacturers Industry (Figure A-1) as well as a summary of the characteristics of the segments that may be of interest to Pivot (Figure A-2). The full report will follow next week.

(a) *Industry observations:*

- Overall the security industry had about $100B in revenues last year and is expected to grow at about 15% per year during the rest of the 1990s and into the next decade. Growth varies significantly in various segments.

- Both technology-based security (e.g., access control and CCTV) and "plain" "old-fashioned" guard service are experiencing continuing demand increases. Service providers are growing most slowly. Guard service is growing at about 5% and electronic security services at about 8% to 10%. Margins have been dropping, especially in the service segments.

- The industry is highly fragmented, although certain segments, such as the manufacturers and service providers, are consolidating through acquisition.

- Players evidence a considerable variety of strategies.

- Companies listed as "manufacturers" are often not manufacturers. Rather, they are system assemblers that function as system designers. These firms may also install and service the systems.

FIGURE A.1 | **INDUSTRY ACTIVITY CHAIN**

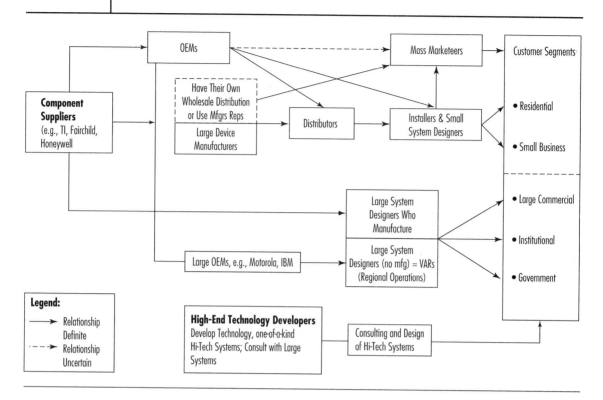

- Security systems assemblers/designers sometimes label equipment with their own brand name.

Demand overall is spurred by a number of factors including:

- Perceptions of the crime rate (e.g., some crime is actually declining, but visibility of crime is not declining; there is concern about the apparent non-selectivity of crime)
  - The aging of the population
  - Growth in upscale housing
  - The perception that public policing may be declining
  - Technology developments are spurring demand in certain segments (e.g., biometrics) and regulatory changes are responsible for increased demand in other segments (e.g., medical applications).
- Consolidation and changes in the utility industry will spur demand, as security becomes one of the components in a package of "utilities" marketed to customers along with electricity, telecommunications, and other services.

(b) *Technologies and applications* (including access control/RFID[16]/false alarms; biometrics; access and egress applications; CCTV; and system integration):

---

[16] Radio frequency identification (RFID), that is, the ability to sense a piece of identification from a distance. The identification piece could be a card that could transmit a radio frequency that the sensor would match to frequency codes that had clearance for entry.

FIGURE A.2 | **SUMMARY CHARACTERISTICS OF SELECTED SEGMENTS OF THE SECURITY DEVICE AND SYSTEMS MANUFACTURERS INDUSTRY**

#1. Mass Marketeers (General Description: Relatively new entrants selling high volume)
- Scope: Regional/national
- Customers: Primarily residential
- Offering:
  - Simple systems and devices
  - $ from service contracts
  - Low price (not quality)
  - Not so often newest technology
- Source: Buy from manufacturers
- Industry change: In 1997 Tyco acquired ADT

#2. Installers & Small System Designers (General Description: Often 20 years old, second and third generation locksmiths or fire protection migrants)
- Scope: Local or narrow regional small companies, some growing very rapidly
- Offering:
  - Access control and CCTV
  - Stress quality (customers are "family")
- Customers: Residential and small business
- Source: Prefer US-made from distributors (e.g., ADI, Alarm King)
- Examples: Ademco, Napco, Detection Systems
- Industry Observations:
  - Mass marketer effect: divided opinion
  - Forward integration into building, real estate, monitoring
  - Where population is dense, some biometrics applications
  - Customers want integration with home and office computers

#3. Large System Designers (LSDs) [General Description: Often 65 yrs old; have corporate & divisional R&D; large investment in manufacturering (some offshore) and technology]
a) Manufacture:
- Scope: Global
- Offerings: Access control; CCTV; inventory monitoring; environmental control; focus on specific applications, e.g., tag equipment; customized large systems
- Customers: Large commercial customers
- Source: Standard components, e.g., from Texas Instruments, Fairchild, Honeywell; license some technology; may develop or buy software
- Examples: Knogo and Sensormatic
- Industry Observations: Begun to merge for vertical integration backward, expand capacity, and broader product line, e.g., Knogo and Sensormatic
b) Don't manufacture (Added Value Resellers)
- Scope: Regional
- Offering: Labelled and branded equipment in fire, access, surveillance, and environmental controls; usually general system that can be modified
- Customers: Differentiated on customers and applications (differentiated and focus strategy)
- Source: Large OEMs, e.g., Motorola, Hughes, and IBM; software contracted out
- Examples: None given
- Industry Observations: Excited about biometrics as a value added to new and existing systems

#4. Device Manufacturers [General Description: Low tech (non-microprocessor based); wary of newer technologies]
a) OEMs
- Scope: National; some regional focus (sell to installers and SSDs)
- Offering: Limited product line, e.g., specialize in alarms, cameras, sensors, accessory items; lower cost with no brand recognition; may brand for VAR; some proprietary designs
- Customers: Sold into those putting in commercial installations; distributors
- Source: Standard components
- Examples: None given
- Industry Changes: Moved away from exclusive distributors; recent example of OEM acquiring a distributor
b) Large Device Manufacturers
- Scope: Global; Europe has significant potential
- Offering: Wide range of device categories (CCTV, fire alarm, access control, sensors, environmental); may have three tiers of products: low cost/simple/lower tech to high tech/quality
- Distribution: Wholesale network or manufacturers representatives
- R&D Capabilities: Vary, some with corporate and divisional. R&D labs; sometimes differentiate on tech; may license from national sources, e.g., Bell Labs;
- Customers: Residential and small business security markets
- Source: Standard components; outsource LDC and display
- Examples: Digital Security Systems, Napco, Northern Video Systems, Inc., Pittway Corp., Radionics
- Industry Observations: Had integrated backwards and were diversifying horizontally; interested in new products and segments; generally acquire rather than internal development

#5. High-End Technology Developers (General Description: Technology developers)
- Scope: International
- Customers: Large corporations; government (e.g., DOD); research and financial institutions
- Offering: Technology, design one-of-a-kind designs, or consulting/design services
- Source: Not applicable as outsource manufacturer and usually not involved in actual installation
- Industry Change: Beginning to look at commercial application of technologies and/or partnerships with manufacturers.

Access Control:

- The "old" technologies include pin numbers, magnetic-stripe cards, and Weigand wires.[17]

- An important technology for access control is RFID. RFID readers are known as proximity readers.

- RFID is the coming technology for such applications as inventory control.

[17] Weigand is a trade name for a technology used in card readers and sensors, especially those used in access control applications. The wires are a special alloy with magnetic properties that are difficulty to duplicate. The wires can contain data such as ID numbers. The wires are embedded in plastic cards. The technology was developed in the 1960s by John Weigand. See: http://www.sensorsmag.com (enter Weigand and entire site in the search capability) and http://whatis.techtarget.com/definition/0,,sid9_gci852292,00.html (accessed 8/15/03). For examples from manufacturers, see http://www.hidcorp.com, http://www.cansec.com and http://www.rs485.com/pdscard.html.

- RFID solves the problem that devices requiring insertion (e.g., cards—or, for that matter, a hand) are subject to malfunction due to dirt and grime.

- However, RFID has the drawback that the cards, tokens, and tags used to trigger access can be lost and thus wind up in non-authorized hands, thus compromising security.

- Access control is often concerned with access and also *egress* detection.

- Technologies include sound, motion, heat, and microwave detection.

- Applications include:
  - Deterrence of theft by individuals internal and external to organizations (thus monitoring the location of equipment and inventory are important applications).
  - Safety including that of older individuals (e.g., Alzheimer's patients) and newborns in hospitals.

- False alarms continue to be a problem for the industry:
  - Security systems users are less concerned about this issue than police departments because the police departments have historically had to absorb the costs of answering false alarms.
  - However, municipalities are generally tightening regulations by (i) requiring paid yearly registration of all systems, (ii) threatening non-response to alarms from non-registered systems, (iii) reducing the number of "free" responses, and (iv) increasing the fee for excessive false alarms.
  - Most false alarms appear to occur during arm/disarm procedures.
  - No one appears to have a good solution for this problem.

- A critical issue for access control overall is integration, i.e., the linking of surveillance, access, fire alarms, and climate control systems. For example, some companies link access control with employee time card systems and surveillance of employee movements.

Biometrics:

- The "hot" item in 1997 was certainly biometrics.

- However, there is considerable uncertainty on how quickly this market will become robust.

- Biometrics is a coming technology platform for access control.

- Biometric technologies are based on a number of different biometric measures including finger/thumbprint, hand scan, voice recognition, handwriting, typing/keying patterns, and eye.

- One major deterrent to adoption is cost of the readers; however, prices for some types will quickly drop to under $1,000.

- Another major deterrent to adoption is user reluctance to participate (e.g., will employees and patrons be willing to have their eye "shot" by a camera to match with the pattern of iris scan metrics in the computer?).

- There are several companies in MN and TX that are the forefront in this sector.

- Several companies appear to have promise, but most tend to be small and some are unstable.

- Our observation is that enough "ordinary" applications are coming into place that biometrics will be accepted (e.g., hand scan at the YMCA in RedWing, MN).

CCTV:

- The Oklahoma City bombing has focused attention on external surveillance of grounds, buildings, and lobbies. CCTV surveillance has had more extensive use in Europe than in the United States and Japan. However, the pattern in the United States is changing.

- Systems essentially consist of:
  - Cameras (stationary and moving; important issues include resolution and breadth of camera scan)
  - Trajectories for moving the cameras (important issues: speed of movement and turnaround; 360 degree focus capability)
  - Wire or wireless links with video and computer monitoring (either on premise or in any distant location)
  - Computer software and hardware

- Cameras: Some of the security device manufacturers manufacture their own cameras. Monitors: There is increased demand for color monitors.

- CCTV does not have much application in residential security systems primarily because of price.

- There is increasing use of CCTV in:
  - Employee surveillance (Issues included: are the employees working/did they truly have the accident as claimed or was it feigned?)
  - Public places (e.g., parks)
  - Upscale housing security systems (e.g., for intrusion detection, premise surveillance, front door security, and nanny monitoring)

- A critical issue for CCTV is integration, i.e., the linking of systems for multiple purposes. Some systems are installed that do not currently have CCTV, but have the ability to be readily upgraded for the same.

System Integration:

- As noted, integration is an important issue for both access control and CCTV. The old term was "smart" buildings. The newer words appear to be "total facilities/building/management control."

- The important issues are the software needed to control the systems; the choice of telephone versus wireless links; and the constellation of applications. For example, the swipe of an access card at the parking garage could turn on the lights in the employee's work area, adjust heating to the person's preference, alert other systems or individuals to the user's needs, and monitor the individual's movements through the parking garage and building.

- Both the technologies and the user demand for a broader array of integrated applications are one factor in the consolidation of the industry.

- Thus, integration of systems is a significant reason why companies are acquiring others to enlarge their product lines.

(c) *Potential customers for Pivot:*

- We have a source that will help identify potential companies that Pivot could target as customers.

- We have identified a number of those companies in the full report.

- Most of these companies are in the Northeast (esp. NY, NJ, and MA) or CA; there are also several companies in TX that may be of interest.

- We concentrated our efforts, as per our prior discussion, on NY but have identified companies in other states.

- One of the greatest concentrations appears to be in the Long Island area.

- Several players have applications in the medical field where issues such as newborn security are salient.

- Medical applications:
  - As suggested above, there are a number of applications in the medical field which could intersect the interests we heard Kirk express in the security industry and that your lead engineering marketing person identified in the medical field.
  - An important issue to note is that health care provider facilities (e.g., inner-city service providers and nursing homes) and hospitals are being subjected to increasing regulatory demands regarding security especially in such places as maternity/nursery, pediatrics, and emergency rooms.
  - With regard to elder care, state regulations differ with regard to the ability of facilities to control patient movement through locked doors or bracelet/anklet monitoring of movement and location.

(d) *Observations from the interviews:*

- The East Coast office has completed a number of interviews with companies located in the Northeast. These companies included systems designers/installers and device manufacturers. We did not talk to component manufacturers.

- The interviews corroborate many of the observations above, including the emphasis on access control/CCTV integration, the uncertainty about biometrics, and the variety of strategic choices among the players.

- As indicated previously, the head of our East Coast office has coordinated exhibition display booths for her company (fairly sophisticated software) and is developing several insights from the interviews that may be helpful as you prepare for the Las Vegas meeting.

Deere & Company
Worldwide Logistics

Kevin MacAuley, summer intern student at Deere & Company Worldwide Logistics, was preparing for his meeting the following week with David Panjwani, manager of logistics network design. David had asked Kevin to evaluate Deere's corporate logistics outsourcing arrangement with FedEx Logistics to identify opportunities and to make appropriate recommendations. It was now the second week of August, and Kevin had to finalize his report and recommendations before returning to school.

Worldwide Logistics Organization

Deere & Company manufactured and distributed a full line of agriculture equipment as well as a broad range of construction and forestry equipment and commercial and consumer equipment. The company had sales of $12 billion with operations in more than 160 countries.

Jay Fortenberry had been hired from Toyota as the new director of worldwide logistics at Deere the previous year, reporting to Dave Nelson, vice president of worldwide supply management. Prior to Jay's arrival, the logistics function had been decentralized, with each business unit responsible for its own logistics activities. Dave Nelson believed that logistics represented a core competency, capable of delivering competitive advantage to the organization. He asked Jay to develop a strategic plan for the worldwide logistics organization and to commit to ongoing cost reduction objectives.

The new worldwide logistics organization numbered 120 people, including the addition of 38 new positions, and Jay was given responsibility for inbound and outbound transportation, warehousing, receiving, packaging, export and customs, logistics quality, planning, and acquisition of logistics services. Jay's cost savings target was $69 million over three years.

IVEY

Richard Ivey School of Business
The University of Western Ontario

FedEx Logistics

FedEx Logistics provided services to 11 Deere facilities in North America, representing costs of approximately $10 million annually. A transportation management services contract between Deere and FedEx had been negotiated seven years prior. However, since each of the units preferred to negotiate their individual service agreements with FedEx separately, both the types of services provided and the costs tended to differ across units.[1] The FedEx logistics services contracts were all based on a cost-plus model, which ranged from 15 percent to 20 percent.

The Logistics Services Project

Kevin MacAuley started at Deere in June as a summer intern student, working in the corporate office in Moline, Illinois. He was planning to return to school in September to complete the second year of the MBA program.

Assigned to the worldwide logistics organization, Kevin had been asked by David Panjwani to evaluate Deere's corporate logistics outsourcing arrangement with FedEx. David also asked Kevin to identify opportunities and to make recommendations regarding changes to Deere's outsourced logistics service arrangement with FedEx.

Feeling that he would not be able to gather all the necessary information from his office in Moline, Kevin decided to visit the 11 facilities personally and meet with the Deere and FedEx staff. He spent one month touring the 11 Deere units, and also visited related FedEx facilities.

Kevin found that FedEx provided three logistics services for Deere: centralized transportation management, on-site transportation management, and warehousing. Centralized transportation management involved coordinating inbound less-than-truckload (LTL) and truckload (TL) shipping routes and consolidations, carrier selection, and handling freight bill audits and payments. Each unit used the FedEx centralized transportation management services.

On-site transportation services involved shipment planning and scheduling, expediting, carrier performance measurement, and handling damage claims. Kevin described FedEx's on-site transportation services as a "shopping list of potential services." The level of on-site transportation services varied substantially between units, depending on the preferences of the individual units. Exhibit 1 describes the main activities for the centralized transportation management service and the on-site transportation management service.

Finally, FedEx managed a total of eight warehouses for Deere's Dubuque (1), Horicon (1), Kernersville (2), Fuquay-Varina (2), and Welland (2) units, employing approximately 85 people. The warehouse operations handled mainly inbound materials and returnable container management.

Since payment for logistics services was handled by the individual units, Kevin also collected relevant cost information during his trips, although much of the cost data had to come directly from FedEx. A summary of the FedEx cost information is provided in Exhibit 2.

---

[1] Deere referred to its manufacturing plants as units, which were headed by business unit general managers.

EXHIBIT 1 | **TRANSPORTATION MANAGEMENT SERVICES**

1. Centralized Transportation Management Services

Service	Activities
Brokering transportation services	Inbound LTL, TL (include multistop); outbound returnable containers; domestic and Canadian transportation; small package; some outbound return and miscellaneous; third-party processors
Carrier management	Rate negotiation; contract administration; performance reporting; claims management
Freight bill audit and payment	
Mode selection and route guide development	
Shipment routing analysis	Continually analyze actual shipment data to recommend or propose generic, static, and dynamic routings
Multishipment consolidations of inbound freight	
Supplier compliance reporting	

2. On-Site Transportation Services

Service	Activities
Reports	Carrier performance; supplier compliance; CWT; cost as a percentage of material purchases; cost avoidance; tracking freight costs; Deere debts for FedEx management; quarterly analytical report updates; other metrics as defined
Route guide approval and implementation	Static route guides; consolidated run route guides; multi-unit consolidated run route guides
Analytical services	Transportation and logistical
Lead operation/unit in resolving transportation supplier compliance issues	
Carrier damage claim facilitation and resolution	
Critical shipment expediting	

Kevin summarized his major impressions from his fact-finding meetings as follows:

1. Each Deere unit negotiated with FedEx separately for logistics services. Consequently, there was a lack of standardization of logistics services provided by FedEx across the Deere units, resulting in a wide variation of services being provided across the units. At many units there had been a substantial level of "scope creep," where FedEx had taken on additional responsibilities over time.

2. Costs for similar services varied across units, ranging from cost plus 15 percent to cost plus 20 percent.

EXHIBIT 2 | **FACILITY LOGISTICS COSTS**

Facility	CTMS[1]	OSTMS[2]	OSRF[3]	FBPA[4]	EF[5]	Warehousing	Total Invoiced
Davenport, IA	$ 72,000	$ 88,080	$ 14,400	$ 21,608			$ 196,088
Harvester and Seeding, IL	114,000	192,396	40,524	48,072			394,992
Des Moines, IA	36,000	98,064	14,760	12,682			161,506
Dubuque, IA	96,000	587,391	44,040	35,574		$ 550,543	1,313,548
Ottumwa, IA	48,000			6,152	$ 196		54,348
Kernersville, NC	48,000			1,608	550	3,134,007	3,184,165
Fuquay-Varina, NC	48,000	672,039	50,000	8,363	6,162	1,296,216	2,080,780
Loundon, TN	48,000	167,220	14,760	5,100	15,700		250,780
Horicon, WI	90,000	416,786		27,375		350,000	884,161
Welland, ON, Canada[6]	48,000	1,781,689	14,760	7,710			1,852,159
Total	*$648,000*	*$4,003,665*	*$193,244*	*$174,244*	*$22,608*	*$5,330,766*	*$10,372,527*

[1]Centralized Transportation Management Service.

[2]On-Site Transportation Management Service.

[3]On-Site Recurring Fees: Include nonlabor costs, such as supplies and equipment.

[4]Freight Bill Payment and Audit: FedEx charge of $0.73 per transaction.

[5]Expedite Fees: FedEx charge of $39.25 per transaction in addition to OSTMS charges.

[6]Welland OSTMS and warehousing costs not separated; Welland costs converted into U.S. dollars.

3. Most of the Deere staff at the units were not satisfied with FedEx central management, but were generally happy with the on-site relationships.

4. There was no consensus regarding the use of third-party service providers for transportation. Some Deere managers believed that on-site transportation should be brought back in-house, while others wanted to continue to use third-party service providers. However, each of the units felt that warehousing should remain a third-party service.

5. Opportunities existed to improve communication and information sharing among sites by establishing common databases, contracts, and descriptions of services.

6. Opportunities existed to improve the level of communication between FedEx staff responsible for inbound freight with the Deere staff responsible for outbound distribution.

7. Several units were currently renegotiating contracts with FedEx. Dubuque and Horicon wanted to expand the services provided by FedEx, while Welland was considering removing FedEx completely.

Dubuque United

Kevin regarded the Dubuque unit as a typical example of the relationship between Deere and FedEx. The Dubuque unit manufactured construction equipment and employed approximately 2,000 people.

FedEx provided its standard services to Dubuque for centralized transportation management. On-site services included transportation management, warehouse services, returnable container management, processing return goods authorizations, and expediting. The unit had four expediters handling inbound components and service parts shipments, and four expediters handling production shipments. There were also 14 FedEx employees in a warehouse facility, which was also used to process returnable containers for suppliers.

Tom Schwartz, the logistics manager at Dubuque, felt satisfied with the on-site relationship with FedEx, but only after investing a lot of work to get the relationships functioning properly. Outbound logistics was handled separately by a group of Deere employees, who also reported to Tom.

Finalizing the Report

It was Thursday afternoon, and David Panjwani had asked Kevin for his report by the end of the following week. Kevin knew that David was expecting him to identify a strategy regarding how Deere should approach its relationship with FedEx. He felt that there were three different approaches that he could consider: insourcing all of the logistics services currently provided by FedEx, insourcing selected services, or maintain the existing structure. Regardless of the option selected, David wanted Kevin to identify what action could be taken to improve Deere's logistics costs and performance.

Kevin felt that, with the creation of the worldwide logistics group, there existed redundancies in services and capabilities. However, some of the Deere staff in the units that Kevin had talked to during his recent meetings indicated uncertainty regarding the role of the new worldwide logistics group and how it would affect their operations. Consequently, Kevin believed that any recommendations would have to consider the role of the units and their future relationship with the new worldwide logistics organization.

Yield Management at American Airlines

American Airlines

One of the largest passenger airlines in the world, with sales of $15 billion in 1998, American Airlines provided scheduled service to destinations throughout North America, the Caribbean, Latin America, Europe, and the Pacific. Each day the company's employees processed more than 340,000 reservation calls and operated over 2,200 flights carrying approximately 200,000 passengers.

Faced with an expanding service network, a costly fleet of aircraft, and an increasingly diverse group of customers, American Airlines began research in the 1960s on how to improve its reservation system to ensure greater capacity utilization. Natural seasonal fluctuations in demand could be partially offset by altering ticket prices. Moreover, some customer groups could plan trips well in advance, while others often booked days, or even hours, before a flight. Combined, management recognized that both supply and demand could be actively changed to alter dynamic competitive markets and to improve business performance.

American Airlines' yield management system, sometimes termed revenue management, attempted simultaneously to combine demand management, by changing fares, and supply management, by controlling availability. It took into account aircraft capacity, historical customer bookings, pricing, cancellations and no-show rates, costs of oversales, and costs of spoilage. Its purpose was to fill seats on each flight with the highest paying passengers by determining the optimal mix of fares to sell on each flight to obtain the highest possible revenue. By the late 1990s, the company, through its Sabre division, used its expertise in a variety of service industries, such as hotels and car rental agencies.

The following exercise is based on the training program used at American Airlines to introduce managers to their yield management system.

"Yield Management at American Airlines" Case by P. Fraser Johnson, Robert Klassen, and John Haywood-Farmer. The authors prepared this case to provide material for class discussion. The authors do not intend to illustrate either effective or ineffective handling of a managerial situation. The authors may have disguised certain names and other identifying information to protect confidentiality.

IVEY

Richard Ivey School of Business
The University of Western Ontario

How to Play the Exercise

In the Yield Management Exercise, your team will take on the role of a yield management analyst responsible for a single flight from Dallas–Fort Worth, Texas (DFW) to Miami, Florida (MIA). Over the course of the exercise, you will be making the actual booking decisions for the flight as customers make travel inquiries and decisions. Your objective is to maximize the flight's total revenue, taking into account penalties. Under normal circumstances, these decisions are made using American Airlines' yield management system.

The objective of the exercise is to maximize revenue on your flight (prorated fares paid, less spoilage or oversales penalties). You are scheduled to use a Super 80 jet for your flight, with a capacity of 125 seats.

Over the course of the exercise, you will be given 20 to 25 booking opportunities. To simplify this exercise, all tickets are fully refundable. Before each booking opportunity, you will have a chance to set a new *bid price*. After all groups have set their bids for the next booking, the instructor will announce the actual passenger booking price and the number of passengers (pax) for the booking.

Your bid price is used only to trigger accepting or rejecting the booking. If the passenger-requested booking price (*prorated fare*) for the DFW to MIA flight is *equal to or greater than your bid price*, you must accept the entire number of passengers at the prorated fare requested by the customer.

For example, if your bid price is $100 and you receive a request for booking for 10 passengers with a prorated fare of $110, then you must take all 10 passengers at a price of $110. If the prorated fare is less than $100, then you cannot accept the booking. Consequently, final revenue is calculated based on the prorated fare, not on your bid price.

You are responsible for setting the bid price before each bidding opportunity through whatever means you wish. Historically, fares for this flight have ranged from $170 to $750 per seat. As you might expect, there is far more demand at the lower end of the price range than the top end. As the flight starts to fill up, you normally increase your bid price to hold for more lucrative bookings. If the flight is lightly booked, you can lower your bid price to allow for more bookings. Exhibit 1 shows average historical data for the Dallas to Miami flight.

The final part of the exercise is the day of departure (*DOD*). Not every passenger who books a flight will show up on the day of departure. Historically, the no-show rate for local passengers has been 15 percent. This figure has been 20 percent for flow passengers (those with connecting flights). At the conclusion of the exercise, the instructor will identify the passengers who arrive for the flight, after which you will be asked to calculate your total revenues and penalties for this Dallas to Miami flight. If passengers fail to show up for the flight, no revenue is obtained for their booking.

Costs Involved

Two additional costs are normally incurred: spoilage and oversales. The penalty for unsold seats (spoilage) is $150 each, which is an estimate of the opportunity cost of the lost contribution on this flight as well as on connecting flights from flow passengers.

Penalties for oversales escalate as the number of disappointed passengers increases. If five or fewer passengers are oversold, the cost is $100 per passenger. Costs increase to $250 per passenger for 6 to 10 oversales, and to $500 per passenger for 11

EXHIBIT 1 | **HISTORICAL CUMULATIVE BOOKINGS: DALLAS–FORT WORTH (DFW) TO MIAMI (MIA)**

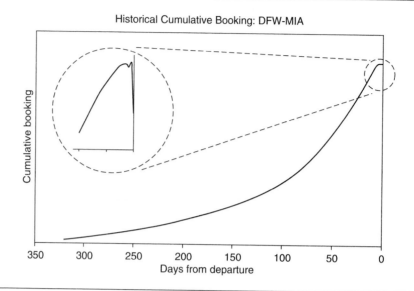

or more oversales. All oversales penalty costs are calculated on a per seat basis (e.g., for seven oversales the penalty would be $1,750). These amounts are to cover out-of-pocket costs for passengers and subsequent rebooking, as well as the inevitable "bad-will" incurred when a passenger is disappointed.

A glossary of terms that you might find useful is provided in Exhibit 2, and a list of airport codes is provided in Exhibit 3. A Yield Management Exercise Score Sheet to be used by you to keep track of your progress during the exercise is provided in Exhibit 4.

Start of Exercise

The only decision that you will be asked to make during the class is setting the bid price for each booking opportunity. In preparation for the class, you should develop a bid-price strategy for the exercise and decide on your opening bid price.

EXHIBIT 2 | GLOSSARY OF TERMS

___

Bid Price: The minimum acceptable fare for a reservation to be accommodated on a flight. The prorated fare value must equal or exceed the bid price in order for the passenger-requested booking to be accepted.

Cancellation: A passenger who makes a booking for a flight and later cancels the reservation (before departure).

Capacity: The physical number of seats on the aircraft. Coach capacity is often referred to as Y capacity (as Y is the code for the coach cabin).

DOD: Day of departure.

Fare: The price the customer pays for the flight. Typically, the fare refers to the ticket price only, and does not include taxes, departure fees, or passenger facility charges (PFCs).

Flow Passenger: A passenger traveling behind or beyond the city pair. In this example, boarding in DEN, connecting in DFW, and then deplaning in MIA. Or, boarding in DFW, connecting in MIA, and then traveling to GRU.

Itinerary: The complete trip taken by a passenger, including all flights.

Local Passenger: A passenger traveling only between the city pair. In this example, a passenger boarding in DFW and deplaning in MIA.

Market: Any given pair of cities between which a flight operates.

No Show: A passenger who does not show up for the flight in which he or she was holding a reservation.

No Show Factor: The percentage of passengers who do not show up for their flight as a percentage of total reservations at departure.

Oversales: Occur when the airline has to deny boarding to a revenue passenger because too many seats have been sold for the flight. This does not include revenue passengers booked on earlier/later flights but standing by for a different flight.

Pax: Passenger(s).

Prorated Fare: The portion of the fare for a complete itinerary that is attributed to a particular flight within the itinerary.

Spoilage: Occurs when a flight departs with empty seats and *at any point prior to departure*, the flight was closed for sale or a booking was turned away. This would indicate suboptimal yield management of the flight.

Voucher: Also known as denied boarding compensation. This is a future travel credit is some amount that is compensation for having been an oversale on a previous flight.

___

EXHIBIT 3 | AIRPORT CODES USED IN EXERCISE

ABQ	Albuquerque, New Mexico
ANU	Antigua, West Indies
AUS	Austin, Texas
DEN	Denver, Colorado
DFW	Dallas–Fort Worth, Texas
EYW	Key West, Florida
GIG	Rio de Janeiro, Brazil
GRU	Sao Paulo, Brazil
HNL	Honolulu, Hawaii
LAS	Las Vegas, Nevada
LAX	Los Angeles, California
LIM	Lima, Peru
MAD	Madrid, Spain
MCO	Orlando, Florida
MIA	Miami, Florida
MSP	Minneapolis–St. Paul, Minnesota
NAS	Nassau, Bahamas
NRT	Tokyo, Japan (Narita Airport)
PDX	Portland, Oregon
SCL	Santiago, Chile
SFO	San Francisco, California
SJO	San Jose, Costa Rica
SJU	San Juan, Puerto Rico
TUS	Tucson, Arizona
YYC	Calgary, Alberta
YYZ	Toronto

EXHIBIT 4 | **YIELD MANAGEMENT EXERCISE SCORE SHEET**

Bid Price?	Booking Code	Prorated Fare	Pax	Running Total Pax

Total Booked Passengers: _____

DOD Show-up	Revenue Value

Enter total in "Total DOD Pax" at lower left *Enter total in "Total Revenue" below*

Total DOD Pax: _____

Final Capacity: _____

Oversales? _____ x penalty _____
or
Spoilage? _____ x $150/pax _____

Total Revenue: _____

===========> _____

Total Flight _____

Barro Stickney, Inc.

Introduction

With four people and sales of $5.5 million, Barro Stickney, Inc. (BSI) had become a successful and profitable manufacturers' representative firm. It enjoyed a reputation for outstanding sales results and friendly, thorough service to both its customers and principals. In addition, BSI was considered a great place to work. The office was comfortable and the atmosphere relaxed but professional. All members of the group had come to value the close, friendly working relationships that had grown with the organization.

Success had brought with it increased profits as well as the inevitable decision regarding further growth. Recent requests from two principals, Franklin Key Electronics and R. D. Ocean, had forced BSI to focus its attention on the question of expansion. It was not to be an easy decision, for expansion offered both risk and opportunity.

Company Background

John Barro and Bill Stickney established their small manufacturers' representative agency, Barro Stickney, Inc., ten years ago. Both men were close friends who left different manufacturers' representative firms to join as partners in their own "rep" agency. The two worked very well together, and their talents complemented each other.

John Barro was energetic and gregarious. He enjoyed meeting new people and taking on new challenges. It was mainly through John's efforts that many of BSI's eight principals had signed on with BSI. Even after producing $1.75 million in sales this past year, John still made an effort to contribute much of his free time to community organizations in addition to perfecting his golf score.

Bill Stickney liked to think of himself as someone a person could count on. He was thoughtful and thorough. He liked to figure how things could get done, and how they could be better. Much of the administrative work of the agency, such as resource allocation and territory assignments, was handled by Bill. In addition to his contribution of

This case was written by Tony Langan, B. Jane Stewart, and Lawrence M. Stratton Jr., under the supervision of Professor Erin Anderson of the Wharton School, University of Pennsylvania. The writing of the case was sponsored by the Manufacturers' Representatives Educational Research Foundation. The cooperation of the Mid-Atlantic Chapter of the Electronic Representatives Association (ERA) is greatly appreciated. Copyright by Erin Anderson.

$1.5 million to total company sales, Bill also had a Boy Scout troop and was interested in gourmet cooking. In fact, he often prepared specialties to share with his fellow workers.

A few years later, as the business grew, J. Todd Smith (J.T.) joined as an additional salesperson. J.T. had worked for a nationally known corporation, and he brought his experience dealing with large customers with him. He and his family loved the Harrisburg area, and J.T. was very happy when he was asked to join BSI just as his firm was ready to transfer him to Chicago. John and Bill had worked with J.T. in connection with a hospital fund-raising project, and they were impressed with his tenacity and enthusiasm. Because he had produced sales of over $2 million this past year, J.T. was now considered eligible to buy a partnership share of BSI.

Soon after J.T. joined BSI, Elizabeth Lee, a school friend of John's older sister, was hired as office manager. She was cheerful and put as much effort into her work as she did coaching the local swim team. The three salespeople knew they could rely on her to keep track of orders and schedules, and she was very helpful when customers and principals called in with requests or problems.

Most principals in the industry assigned their reps exclusive territories, and BSI's ranged over the Pennsylvania, New Jersey, and Delaware area. The partners purchased a small house and converted it into their present office located in Camp Hill, a suburb of Harrisburg, the state capital of Pennsylvania. The converted home contributed to the familylike atmosphere and attitude that was promoted and prevalent throughout the agency.

Over the years, in addition to local interests, BSI and its people had made an effort to participate in and support the efforts of the Electronics Representative Association (ERA). A wall of the company library was covered with awards and letters of appreciation. BSI had made many friends and important contacts through the organization. Just last year BSI received a recommendation from Chuck Goodman, a Chicago manufacturers' rep who knew a principal in need of representation in the Philadelphia area. The principal's line worked well with BSI's existing portfolio, and customer response had been quite favorable. BSI planned to continue active participation in the ERA.

Each week BSI held a five o'clock meeting in the office library where all members of the company shared their experiences of the week. It was a time when new ideas were encouraged and everyone was brought up to date. For example, many customer problems were solved here, and principals' and members' suggestions were discussed. An established agenda enabled members to prepare. Most meetings took about sixty to ninety minutes, with emphasis placed on group consensus. It was during this group meeting that BSI would discuss the future of the company.

Opportunities for Expansion

R. D. Ocean was BSI's largest principal, and it accounted for 32 percent of BSI's revenues. Ocean had just promoted James Innve as new sales manager, and he felt an additional salesperson was needed in order for BSI to achieve the new sales projections. Innve expressed the opinion that BSI's large commission checks justified the additional effort, and he further commented that J.T.'s expensive new car was proof that BSI could afford it.

BSI was not sure an additional salesperson was necessary, but it did not want to lose the goodwill of R. D. Ocean or [its] business. Also, while it was customary for all principals to meet and tacitly approve new representatives, BSI wanted to be very sure that any new salesperson would fit into the close-knit BSI organization.

Franklin Key Electronics was BSI's initial principal and had remained a consistent contributor of approximately 15 percent of BSI's revenues. BSI felt its customer base was well suited to the Franklin line, and it had worked hard to establish the Franklin Key name with these customers. As a consequence, BSI now considered Franklin Key relatively easy to sell.

A few days previously, Mark Heil, Franklin's representative from Virginia, perished when his private plane crashed, leaving Franklin Key without representation in its D.C./Virginia territory. Franklin did not want to jeopardize its sales of over $800,000 and was desperate to replace Heil before its customers found other sources. Franklin offered the territory to BSI and was anxious to hear the decision within one week.

BSI was not familiar with the territory, but it did understand that there were a great number of military accounts. This meant there was a potential for sizable orders, although a different and specialized sales approach would be required. Military customers are known to have their own unique approach to purchase decisions.

Because of the distance and the size of the territory, serious consideration was needed as to whether a branch office would be necessary. A branch office would mean less interaction with and a greater independence from the main BSI office. None of the current BSI members seemed anxious to move there, but it might be possible to hire someone who was familiar with the territory. There was, of course, always the risk that any successful salesperson might leave and start his or her own rep firm.

In addition to possibilities of expanding its territory and its sales force, BSI also wanted to consider whether it should increase or maintain its number of principals. BSI's established customer base and its valued reputation put them in a strong position to approach potential principals. If, however, BSI had too many principals, it might not be able to offer them all the attention and service they might require.

Preparation for the Meeting

Each member received an agenda and supporting data for the upcoming meeting asking them to consider the issue of expansion. They would be asked whether BSI should or should not expand its territory, its sales force, and/or its number of principals. In preparation, they were each asked to take a good hard look at the current BSI portfolio and to consider all possibilities for growth, including the effect any changes would have on the company's profits, its reputation, and its work environment.

It was an ambitious agenda: one that would determine the future of the company. It would take even more time than usual to discuss everything and reach consensus. Consequently, this week's meeting was set to take place over the weekend at Bill Stickney's vacation lodge in the Poconos, starting with a gourmet dinner served at 7 P.M. sharp.

Before the meeting, Bill Stickney examined the sources of BSI's revenue and the firm's income for the previous year. He also estimated the future prospects for each of BSI's lines, considering each line's market potential and BSI's level of saturation in each market. Finally, he estimated the costs of hiring a new employee both in the current sales territory and in the Washington/Virginia area. Immediately before the meeting, Elizabeth finished compiling Bill's data into four figures (see pages 597–599).

Figure 1 evaluates the amount of sales effort (difficulty in selling) necessary to achieve a certain percentage of sales in BSI's portfolio (return). Difficulty in selling is measured by the level of marketing investment required for growth. Stickney's estimates are shown on the vertical axis. Return for this investment is measured by the

FIGURE 1 | **RETURN VERSUS DIFFICULTY IN SELLING**

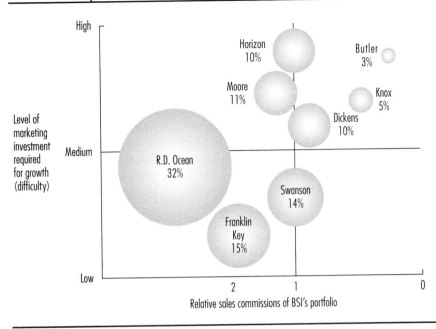

relative sales commissions as a percent of BSI's portfolio shown on the horizontal axis. If BSI's time were evenly divided among its eight principals, each would receive 12.5 percent of the agency's time. The x-axis shows each principal's time allocation as a proportion of 12.5 percent of the "par" time allocation. The area of each ellipse reflects each principal's share of BSI's commission revenue.

Bill Stickney presented the following additional comments as a result of his research:

1. Swanson's products are being replaced by the competition's computerized electronic equipment, a product category the firm has ignored. As a result, the company is losing its once prominent market position.

2. Although small amounts of effort are required to promote Ocean's product line to customers in the current sales territory, Ocean is extremely demanding of both BSI and other manufacturer's representative firms.

3. According to a seminar at the last ERA meeting, the maximum safe proportion of a rep firm's commissions from a single principal should be 25–30 percent. Also, at the meeting, one speaker indicated that if a firm commands 80 percent of a market, it should focus on another product or expand its territory rather than attempt to obtain the remainder of the market.

4. The revenue for investment for the manufacturer's representative firm comes from one or more of several sources. These sources include reduced forthcoming commission income, retained previous income, and borrowed money from a financial institution. Most successful firms expand their sales force or sales territory when they experience income growth and use the investment as a tax write-off.

FIGURE 2	**BARRO STICKNEY, INC., ESTIMATION OF COST OF ADDITIONAL SALES REPRESENTATIVE**

Compensation Costs for New Sales Representative

Depending on the new sales representative's level of experience, BSI would pay a base salary of $15,000–$25,000 with the following bonus schedule:

 0% firm's commission revenue up to $500,000 in sales
20% firm's commission revenue first $0.5 million in sales over $500,000
25% firm's commission revenue for the next $0.5 million in sales
30% firm's commission for the next $0.5 million in sales
40% firm's commission sales above $2 million

Estimate of Support Costs[1] for the New Representative[2]

Search applicant pool, psychological testing, hiring, training,[3] flying final choice to principals for approval[4]	$28,000
Automobile expenses, telephone costs, business cards, entertainment promotion	22,000
Insurance, payroll taxes (social security, unemployment compensation)	16,000
Total expenses	$66,000

Incremental Expenses for New Territory

Transportation (additional mileage from Camp Hill to Virginia)	$02,000
Office equipment and rent (same regardless of headquarter's location)	4,000
Cost of hiring office manager[5]	18,000
Total increment expenses	$24,000

[1]Rounded to the nearest thousand.   [2]In current territory.   [3]Excludes the lost revenue from selling instead of engaging in this activity (opportunity cost).   [4]Although rep agencies are not legally required to show prospective employees to principals, it is generally held to be good business practice.   [5]Discretionary.

FIGURE 3	**BARRO STICKNEY, INC., STATEMENT OF REVENUE (TOTAL SALES REVENUE 1988, $5.5 MILLION)**

Principal	Estimated Market Saturation	Product Type	Sales/ Commission Rate	Share of BSI's Portfolio	Commission Revenue
R. D. Ocean	High	Components	5.00%	32%	$96,756
Franklin Key	High	Components	5.00	15	45,354
Butler	Low	Technical/computer	12.00	3	9,070
Dickens	Low	Components	5.00	10	30,236
Horizon	Medium	Components	5.50	10	30,237
Swanson	High	Components	5.25	14	42,331
Moore	Medium	Consumer/electronics	5.25	11	33,260
Knox	Low	Technical/communications	8.50	5	15,118

FIGURE 4	**BARRO STICKNEY, INC., STATEMENT OF INCOME (FOR THE YEAR ENDING DECEMBER 31, 1988)**

Revenue		
Commission income	$302,362	
Expenses		
Salaries for sales and bonuses (includes Barro Stickney)	130,250	
Office manager's salary	20,000	
Total nonpersonnel expenses[1]	128,279	
Total expenses	$278,529	
Net income[2]	$23,833	(7.9% of revenue)

[1] Includes travel, advertising, office supplies, retirement, automobile expenses, communications, office equipment, and miscellaneous expenses.

[2] Currently held in negotiable certificates of deposit in a Harrisburg bank.

Advanced Elastomer Systems: Market Strategy for a New, Technical Product

As manager of Consumer Markets, Ms. Gayle Tomkinson was responsible for managing the firm's strategy in new markets at Advanced Elastomer Systems, L.P. (AES). Tomkinson had joined AES only one year earlier after working in a variety of technical and commercial roles in her eleven years at GE Plastics in Pittsfield, Massachusetts. While at GE Plastics, Tomkinson had worked in product development, technical support, sales, and marketing.

In early 1996, Tomkinson's supervisor (Jay Griffith, director of Global Products) assigned her the task of developing a strategy for AES's newest product—a nylon-bondable Santoprene® rubber that had been nicknamed "soft-touch" by the engineering staff. Tomkinson was well suited for the task at hand. She had earned an undergraduate degree in chemical engineering from Lafayette College and a masters degree in materials engineering from Rensselaer Polytechnical Institute. She had a thorough understanding of both the technical as well as the business advantages of this new application for both the manufacturer and the end-user. While excellence in R&D, engineering, and manufacturing was certainly critical for a technology-oriented firm such as Advanced Elastomer Systems, Tomkinson's past experience had given her a deep appreciation for the fact that a well-developed marketing strategy was a critical element in the success of a new technical product.

Tomkinson needed to evaluate the situation and then outline some of the feasible marketing plans for "soft-touch," the new nylon-bondable Santoprene® rubber. As she thought about these opportunities, she wondered what strategy would work best. She had been asked to present some potential options at their next market planning meeting, but Tomkinson also wanted to have a clear understanding in her own mind of the preferred strategy that she would like to champion to upper management. She also needed to identify the marketing tactics that would be required to support it.

By Deborah L Owens and Jon M. Hawes, University of Akron. We would like to thank Gayle Tomkinson and Scott Conway for so graciously sharing time and information with the authors in the preparation of this case. This case is intended as a basis for classroom discussion rather than to illustrate effective or ineffective handling of an administrative situation.

EXHIBIT 1 | CONSUMER GOODS, KITCHENWARE, PERSONAL CARE PRODUCTS

Creative designers and manufacturers are increasingly discovering the versatiliy of Santoprene® rubber in producing superior soft grips for consumer goods—grips that are innovative, high-performing and cost-effective. Our materials are selected for grips on consumer products found in every room of a home—pens and flashlights, umbrellas and telephones, cameras and compact CD players, toothbrushes and razors, kitchen utensils and more.

- Santoprene® rubber grips on Messer-meister gourmet kitchen knives compliment the high-performance craftsmanship.

- Santoprene® rubber grips on XACTO® knives offer exacting control and comfort for hobbyists, designers, and craftsmen.

- Even in wet and soapy environments, such as on the handles of shaving razors, Santoprene® rubber grips offer sure, non-slip control.

- Grips on BIC® pens offer non-slip control and soft touch comfort to reduce finger fatigue and resist finger oils.

- Even in simple applications, like the handy jar grippers found in most kitchens, Santoprene® rubber adds flexibility, strength, heat resistance and non-slip gripping power.

- Versatile materials from AES give designers the freedom and flexibility to be creative in designing innovative applications.

Key Benefits

- Improved appearance and colorability

- Superior design freedom and flexibility

- Resistant to heat, perspiration and cooking oil

- Soft touch, non-slip surfaces for added safety and control

- Dishwasher safe, detergent resistant

- FDA approved.

The Product's Development

The engineering design team at AES had been working over the past 16 months to develop this new grade of Santoprene® rubber that would allow it to be co-processed with nylon. This would allow the creation of applications having the feel, flexibility, and properties of rubber; however, these applications would retain the impact and strength of nylon. Exhibit 1 provides some background information on the new product and how it could be used in one of the key industry sectors. Several other industry sectors also presented attractive market opportunities.

Once the new product was ready for commercialization, Mr. Ulf Nilsson, marketing director at AES, explained to Tomkinson that this new product needed to achieve commercial success quickly in order for AES to meet its targeted growth objectives for fiscal 1997. Executives at Advanced Elastomer Systems recognized the fact that several leading competitors were in the process of developing similar products. This meant that a relatively fast commercialization was even more critical for marketing success.

Advanced Elastomer Systems was a young company. It was created in 1991 as a 50/50 joint venture between Exxon and Monsanto.[1] Growth at AES had been consistently strong,

---

[1] In 1997, Monsanto spun off the division that had originally been involved in the AES joint venture with Exxon. This new firm is now called Solutia, Incorporated.

due to the expanding use of Santoprene® rubber as a replacement material for other rubber or metal parts. During its first year of operation, AES had revenues of $100 million. For fiscal 1996, sales were projected to exceed $250 million.

To continue this strong revenue growth, management had recently refocused the firm's efforts on product research and market development. At a recent management meeting, Bill Ginter, chief operating officer, had emphasized that new products and new markets would be responsible for a larger share of company revenues over the next five years. During this meeting, Roger Sellew, president and chief executive officer, explained management's vision for the company as follows.

> AES is a capital driven company, but it is not a capital intensive one. Our growth comes from finding and developing new markets. This type of growth requires exceptional intellectual assets—our people—not just capital assets. To help our people meet these corporate objectives, we are going to place additional resources in the marketing arena. This will highlight the strategic focus of AES as an innovative company focusing on the development, application, and marketing of new thermoplastic elastomers for use in the industrial and consumer product domains.

In line with this renewed focus on new product development and marketing, Jay Griffith, Global Products director, had recently expressed to Tomkinson his confidence that this new product would be profitable. It had numerous product benefits; the firm planned to gain an early market entry advantage; and AES had an excellent reputation with current customers. Griffith had high expectations for this product in both the industrial as well as the consumer product domains. He expected success in numerous new markets, particularly in the consumer goods arena, where nylon-bondable Santoprene® could be used on products such as toothbrushes, pens, razors, and kitchen utensils to give consumers a safer, more comfortable grip that offered non-slip control. Griffith was particularly excited about this new product because it offered advantages to the manufacturer through production savings and design flexibility, as well as consumer benefits that included improved safety, control, and durability. These benefits resulted in a high degree of relative advantage for the new product.

Tomkinson also believed in the new product's potential, but she recognized the fact that its commercial success should not be taken for granted. She knew about many technically superior products that had failed to achieve their projected sales and profit goals. Her past experience, both at AES and with GE Plastics, had taught her how difficult it was to convince industrial customers to change existing buying plans in order to incorporate the use of a new product into their operations.

Indeed, Tomkinson was very familiar with the inertia that often resulted from the typical buying cycle within the plastics industry (shown in Exhibit 2), especially among large corporations that were often not adept and were certainly not predisposed to make the process and procedural changes that the purchase of a new product often required of them. Rather than embracing change, many companies resisted it and most avoided risk whenever possible. They simply found it easier to keep using the same materials, to stay with current and well-known suppliers, and to continue utilizing existing manufacturing processes—even when there were significant benefits offered by new and technologically superior alternatives.

Tomkinson wondered what could be done to facilitate the prospect's progression through the buying cycle. She knew that AES had to focus persuasive efforts on the key

EXHIBIT 2 | THE BUYING CYCLE WITHIN THE PLASTICS INDUSTRY

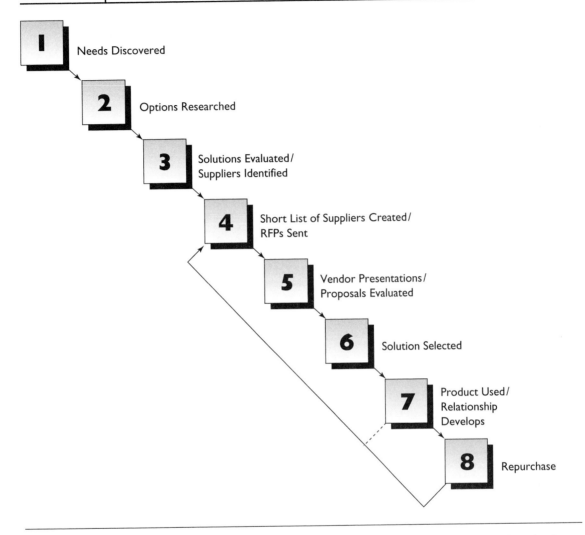

SOURCE: Adapted from the Robinson, Farris, and Wind (1967) model based on consultation with AES executives concerning unique issues within the plastics industry.

decision makers in order to have the best chance of attracting prospective users. Would it be possible to identify and reach these key decision makers? Which marketing strategies would best support the AES selling effort during each phase of the buying cycle?

Industry Background

Plastics were invented in 1860, but commercial production of plastics did not begin in earnest until the 1930s and 1940s. Since that time, the production of plastics has grown rapidly. By 1996, the plastics industry was an important sector in the global economy. In the United States alone, it accounted for over 1.3 million jobs (Probe Economics

EXHIBIT 3 | THE WORLD OF PLASTICS

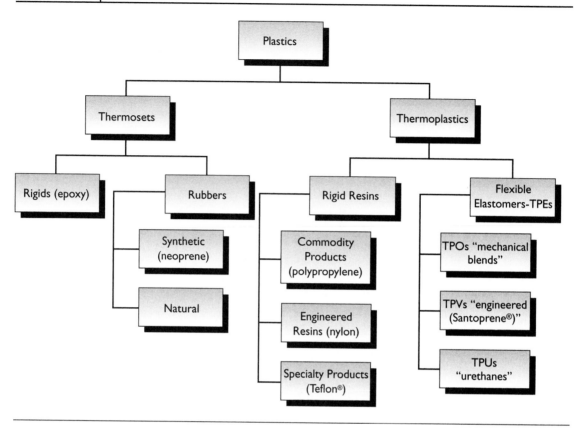

Industry Report 1997). Despite a dismal overall balance of trade for the United States in 1996, the plastics industry had a trade surplus of $5.5 billion. According to information available from an industry trade association known as the Society of the Plastics Industry (SPI), production of plastics in the United States during 1996 was valued at $274 billion, an increase of 7.1 percent over the previous year. There had been a consistent and strong upward trend over the past 20 years. In fact, production had increased from 21,196 million pounds in 1976 to 84,295 million pounds during 1996.

Some of this growth was due to changes in the component materials used by manufacturers. For example, plastics were now being used instead of alternative component materials in many industrial and automotive applications. In particular, the move to make cars more fuel efficient had increased the use of plastics by automotive manufacturers because plastics were much lighter than the steel components they replaced (Mapleston 1997).

As shown in Exhibit 3, the plastics industry was typically divided into several subcategories based on material composition, physical properties, and costs. The largest overall type was the thermoplastics category (sometimes known as "resins"). Nylon, polyethylene, polyvinyl chloride (PVC), polystyrene, and polypropylene were the dominant materials within the thermoplastic product category. This sector was further subdivided into rigid and flexible categories, each of which was further subset as depicted in Exhibit 3.

Thermoplastic Elastomers

Thermoplastic elastomers, commonly known as TPEs, were a relatively new product class. They were invented in the 1970s when companies were looking for alternative materials that could easily be molded like a plastic but retain the physical properties of rubber. In the most basic terms, thermoplastic elastomers were combinations of rubber and plastic created by mixing finely pulverized synthetic rubber with a plastic compound. This mixture was heated, and the resulting material was converted and sold in pellet form. These pellets became the raw material for manufactured parts that required the elasticity of rubber, but were more easily molded.

The thermoplastic elastomer segment of the industry grew rapidly because this plastic-like rubber had many advantages over the thermoset rubber that it often replaced. The new material could be processed faster and, unlike traditional rubber, it could be reground and reprocessed. This virtually eliminated scrap materials, and the new category was 100 percent recyclable. Furthermore, this new material could be used in the manufacturing process without costly retooling. Thermoplastic elastomers could be processed on existing plastic and rubber machinery such as injection molding or extrusion equipment.

Consequently, the growth of the TPE segment was fueled by this unique combination of physical properties and superior processing capability. Thermoplastic elastomers were extremely flexible. They also retained flexibility under both extremely low and extremely high temperature variations. This product was also resistant to detergents and oils, making it a preferred material for a broad range of industrial and consumer products. Processed like plastic, but with the physical characteristics of rubber, these new materials were in demand for use in a very diverse and growing array of applications ranging from use in various types of consumer goods to industrial applications such as bridge expansion joints (see Exhibit 4).

EXHIBIT 4 | THERMOPLASTIC ELASTOMERS BY APPLICATION AREA

Application Area	Product Examples
1. Automotive Products	
Automotive Parts	Rack and pinion boots, electrical connectors, grommets, air bag door covers, hoses
2. Industrial Products	
Electrical	Waterproof connectors, plugs, high-end wire, cable
Plumbing and Irrigation	Flexible connectors, pop-up sprinklers, seals
Medical Markets	Syringe plungers and tips, equipment grips
Construction	Bridge expansion joints, window weather seals
Other Industrial	Casters, sheet goods, conveyor components
3. Consumer Goods	
Kitchen and Cooking Utensils	Knife handles, utensil handles, appliance knobs
Cosmetics	Toothbrush grips, razor grips, cologne caps
Sporting Goods	Grips for archery, guns, bicycles
Writing Instruments	Ink pens, pencils

Competitive Situation

The plastics industry had changed dramatically in the mid-1990s as competition intensified and global sourcing became more prevalent. Acquisitions and mergers changed the structure and operations of many firms in the United States. Firms were taking more global views of the market than had been done in the past. Companies were modernizing plants and investing in new technology to lower production costs and increase profitability. International demand had grown considerably, particularly in the European and Asian markets where sales were expected to grow considerably faster than the domestic industry-wide average of 5 percent per year (Chemical Market Reporter 1997).

Success within the plastics industry had historically been heavily dependent on research and product development. There was a constant search for faster new-product applications to improve competitive position within world markets. With relatively strong financial performances at this time, Rotman (1997) reported that plastics industry executives demonstrated "cautious optimism" in their planned research and development expenditures. DuPont, for example, planned to increase its R&D budget by 2.7 percent next year. Dow Chemical projected an increase of 5 percent. On an industry-wide basis, overall spending on research and development was quite significant, with most companies dedicating between 2 to 5 percent of sales revenues for this important activity. According to Joseph Miller, senior vice president of research and development and chief technical officer at DuPont, "people have become increasingly supportive of longer term research, and there is less talk about concentrating on market focused research" (Rotman 1997, p. 24).

On a few occasions in the recent past, firms within the plastics industry had embraced the joint venture concept. For example, industry leaders DuPont and Dow aligned to form DuPont Dow Elastomers to jointly develop and market elastomers around the globe. In the nylon arena, the DSM N.V. organization, based in The Netherlands, AlliedSignal of the United States, and UBE Industries headquartered in Japan set up a promotional alliance, called the Nylon-6 Promotional Group. Its objective was to boost worldwide sales of nylon (Milmo 1995).

Nylon Producers

According to plastics industry analyst Andrew Wood (1997, p. 42), "nylon, the polymer discovered by DuPont, and still its single largest chemical business, is undergoing a big shakeup." During 1996, the domestic production and shipments of nylon hit record highs and prices rose. Approximately 2.8 million pounds of nylon fiber were produced in 1996, up from 2.7 billion pounds in 1995. Nearly 80 percent of the nylon produced was used in the carpet industry, with the remaining 20 percent split evenly between the textile and manufacturing sectors (Chapman 1997).

As shown in Exhibit 5, DuPont continued its long tradition as the industry leader in the North American nylon market, followed by the three other major nylon producers: BASF Corporation, Monsanto Corporation, and AlliedSignal (Morris 1998). In 1996, BASF sales were projected to increase 5.5 percent to a record level of $29 billion (Pfeifer 1997). At this time, the four major players in the nylon sector of the plastics industry had started focusing on performance improvement through major cost reduction programs and major capital investment programs targeted at new technology.

EXHIBIT 5 | UNITED STATES MARKET SHARE FOR NYLON

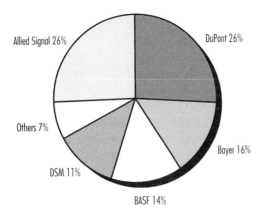

Advanced Elastomer Systems

In the early 1970s, the Monsanto Chemical Company began forecasting the potential impact of thermoplastic elastomers. In 1974, a group of Monsanto engineers assembled and began the research and development process for a new concept that combined rubber and plastic into one material. In 1976, Santoprene® thermoplastic rubber was patented and introduced as a revolutionary hybrid material offering customers multiple design options, cost reductions, and performance improvements. By 1980, their vision had become a commercial success.

During 1990, envisioning a wide range of opportunities for this unique material, Monsanto Chemical Company began a joint venture with Exxon Chemical Company. The result was the birth of Advanced Elastomer Systems, L.P. The company's mission was to bring engineered thermoplastic elastomers (TPEs) to the marketplace to replace thermoset rubber and to develop additional applications for this new technology. As shown in Exhibit 6, thermoplastic elastomers had many benefits and were used throughout the world in a wide variety of innovative applications.

Growth Strategy

Fundamental to the growth strategy at AES was the introduction of new products targeted for niche markets. This enabled the firm to develop long-term, profitable relationships with firms in industries that had not been formerly served by AES. By early 1996, the technical team at AES had been working for 16 months to develop the new nylon bondable form of Santoprene® rubber. While Santoprene® rubber and nylon had previously been used together, this had required a costly, labor-intensive step of applying an adhesive seal between the two materials. In comparison, the new form of Santoprene® rubber bonded to nylon offered many benefits to the design team, the processor, and to end-users.

These combined applications were termed "soft-touch" solutions, as they typically replaced more rigid materials. The AES team had considered a number of potential

EXHIBIT 6 | **PRODUCT BENEFITS OF SANTOPRENE® RUBBER**

1. *No Adhesive Required.* Able to bond nylon and Santoprene® without primers or adhesives, thus eliminating a costly manufacturing process.

2. *"Soft-touch" Capability.* Product designers find this attractive, particularly for consumer products that require a rigid material coupled with gripping ease.

3. *Flexibility.* Offers design freedom by providing high temperature resistance, excellent stiffness and strength, and low abrasion resistance and yet has the feel of rubber.

4. *Colorability.* Easy to add color, offering many design possibilities.

5. *Cost Savings.* Previously, the only way to bond nylon with a TPE was by mechanical interlocking, which required costly design modifications or labor-intensive manufacturing processes.

---

applications for this new Santoprene® rubber bonded to nylon. Although the designers would appreciate the colorability and improved product appearance, consumers would also welcome the added safety and control. AES foresaw applications in a number of consumer products where the consumer would benefit from a "soft-touch" grip. For example, the use of these grips on gardening tools would reduce callouses and make gardening easier. Likewise, "soft-touch" grips could be added to shaving razors, knives, and a variety of kitchen tools to assure non-slip gripping power, even in wet environments.

AES was not alone in its desire to develop this new product. Several of the large nylon manufacturers were also working to develop a TPE that would bond to nylon without adhesives or mechanical intervention. AES was concentrating resources in this area of new-product development, with the goal of being the first company to successfully create and market this new material. AES hoped that this new Santoprene® rubber product, when used in combination with nylon, would replace a number of traditional rubber/metal parts now used in a variety of manufacturing applications.

In early 1996, the breakthrough came as technologists at AES found the correct "recipe" and successfully created the new soft-touch form of Santoprene® rubber that would chemically bond directly to nylon. Mr. Ulf Nilsson, AES director of marketing, provided the following explanation.

> This new product offers many advantages including design freedom and significant cost savings in the production process. Additionally, these soft-touch applications help to reduce vibrations of hand power tools, offering greater comfort, particularly for older consumers, or those with arthritic conditions. Handle and grip applications, for example, allow product users greater control and non-slip gripping power.

Marketing Communications Strategy in the Plastics Industry

Tomkinson realized that AES needed to move quickly in order to exploit its position as the first company to successfully develop and market a thermoplastic rubber that would chemically bond with nylon. She would need to develop a strategic plan for communicating with the critical decision makers within buying organizations. As Tomkinson sat at her desk, she began to review the methods at her disposal for targeting the opinion leaders and influencers at various stages of the typical buying cycle (see Exhibit 2). With her background in industrial sales and business-to-business marketing, she had a thorough understanding of the range of marketing tools available as well as the comparative costs of each. Prior to developing her list of potential overall marketing strategy options, Gayle thought it might be helpful to review the environment as it related to the various types of marketing communications available for use within the plastics sector.

There was a big difference between the business-to-business and consumer market environments. Within the industrial sector, the physical products were typically more complex, and multiple buying influences pervaded the more lengthy buying process. James C. Reilly, an expert on business-to-business marketing, explained the situation as follows.

> The business buyer is a professional evaluator of goods and services actively pursuing a solution to a specific problem. The fundamental business-to-business promotional message is "Here is your solution. . . ." The key to success in business-to-business sales promotion is finding the right people at the right companies for which a product will make a positive difference and getting them interested in the product's solution. (Brezen Block and Robinson 1994, p. 466)

Marketing communication within the plastics industry closely resembled that found in other sectors of the business-to-business market where professional selling, trade shows, print advertising, Web sites, collateral material, and public relations served as the primary mechanisms for reaching decision makers and buyers within the plastics industry.

Professional Selling

Professional selling remained the most important promotional method within the plastics industry. The firm's sales personnel provided the means to develop a business relationship with the buyer. The salesperson also performed the important role of discovering customer needs. Sales personnel spent considerable time and effort developing programs specifically targeted at this first "needs discovered" stage of the buying cycle. Discovering an unmet need, such as the need to reduce scrap, improve design, reduce costs, or achieve greater production efficiencies, often led to significant incremental new sales that more than justified the time and expense involved. The sales representative then tailored the offering to the particular manufacturing situation or product application.

Members of the sales force were responsible for keeping existing customers informed concerning new product offerings and solutions. Sales professionals also worked to identify new prospects. When appropriate, they persuaded first-time buyers that a given offering provided a preferred solution to the problems faced. The role of the sales force was important to the success of both parties in the exchange, especially now during the current era of relationship management.

Within the plastics industry, members of the sales force often had engineering or scientific backgrounds that provided the necessary technical foundation to communicate clearly with a broad range of personnel within both the buying and selling organizations.

EXHIBIT 7	THE APPROPRIATE ROLE OF PROFESSIONAL SELLING IN THE PLASTICS INDUSTRY

Contact Point: Injection Molder or Extruder

1. Maintain good relations.

2. Provide consistent, high-quality service.

3. Communicate technical information.

4. Monitor and expedite shipments.

Contact Point: Original Equipment Manufacturer*

1. Communicate new product offerings and the solutions they provide.

2. Obtain and communicate design specifications.

3. Understand and communicate design requirements.

4. Demonstrate material benefits for design requirements and end-users.

5. Provide feedback on current materials and obtain ideas for further improvement and new materials.

*Contact was typically with a staff member in the Design, Marketing, Manufacturing, or Engineering Department.

Members of the sales force interacted with production personnel, chemists, process engineers, R&D scientists, and others to build business relationships over time. This was done by providing valuable advice and service to the buying organization and by providing important market information and assistance to the selling firm.

In a firm such as AES, salespeople needed to call on component materials processors (such as injection molders and extruders) as well as original equipment manufacturers (OEMs). Sales personnel helped both the component materials processors and OEMs by uncovering unmet needs that could potentially be solved by utilizing one of the firm's products. The appropriate selling role was different, however, depending upon the salesperson's contact point, that is, whether the client was a processor or an OEM (see Exhibit 7).

Members of the sales force had to maintain positive working relations with the design and engineering staff of the OEM because they usually determined and specified the exact materials required for inclusion in their products. It was equally important for members of the sales force to develop and support good relations with the component materials processors selected by the OEM. The processor was AES's direct customer. In addition, the processor also influenced the selection of materials by the OEM. The sales staff also had to meet the needs of the processor with respect to on-time delivery, technical support, and timely response to the problems and concerns of the processor.

Sales force organization within the plastics industry is typically based on geographic region. Sales personnel are usually responsible for all of the company's product offerings within a well-defined and usually protected geographical area. As shown in Exhibit 8, AES followed this pattern.

Within the plastics industry, salespeople typically called on a minimum of one and a maximum of four accounts per day. According to a Dartnell study, the average number of sales calls per day within the "rubber/plastics" industry was 3.1, and on

EXHIBIT 8
ORGANIZATION CHART FOR SALES AND MARKETING AT ADVANCED ELASTOMER SYSTEMS

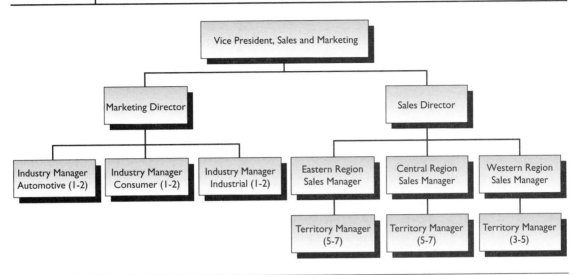

NOTE: Marketing and sales interact on a matrix basis, whereas field sales functions are divided by geography. The goals of both marketing and sales are aligned by the vice president of sales and marketing.

average it took about four calls over a period of time on a particular account to close a sale (Heide 1996). In this highly technical area, the average cost per sales call typically ranged from $300 to $500, including travel and all other personnel expense. The compensation range for sales representatives within the plastics industry was typically between $50,000 to $100,000 depending on experience and performance.

A firm similar in size to AES within this industry would typically have from 20 to 30 salespeople geographically deployed across the United States. Occasionally, a salesperson might be dedicated to a particular client type, such as automotive customers, but sales personnel were typically deployed along geographic lines and served all customers within that area.

Trade Shows

According to William Downing, president and CEO of Downing Exhibits in Copley, Ohio, "Trade shows continued to play an integral role in the promotional mix of global corporations, serving as the platform of choice for new product introductions." Trade shows provided an ideal opportunity for displaying products, reaching key markets, and networking with key individuals in the plastics industry. Trade shows provided a distinct advantage over other contact methods because the participants attended voluntarily and thus had a genuine interest in what was being offered. Many of the executives attending a trade show came to view new or existing products. Often, the people attending a national trade show had not been called on by the selling firm within the past year. Trade shows provided an excellent opportunity for firms in the plastics industry to reinforce existing customer relationships and to establish new ones.

The second major reason that trade shows were so important as a communication tool in the plastics industry was that they enabled the sales force to use selling time more efficiently. At a trade show, the potential customer came to the salesperson, allowing members of the sales force to make many more contacts with interested prospects in a short period of time. When all of the associated and relevant costs were included, the cost to make a field sales call in this sector of the plastics industry averaged from $300 to $500. In comparison, the cost for a viable sales call made during a trade show was only a small fraction of this amount.

In addition to being cost effective, trade shows were increasingly popular in the plastics industry because they allowed for a much more vivid presentation of the product. Trade shows also offered a face-to-face meeting among participants in a less threatening, neutral environment, where products were both seen and touched. Demonstrations of product usage were provided on a cost-effective per-contact basis because of the large number of prospects attending the show.

The two largest international plastics industry trade shows were sponsored by the National Plastics Exhibition (NPE), held in Chicago every third year, and by The Society of Plastic Industries (SPI), which was an annual event. At NPE, for example, more than 1,500 companies from more than 100 countries presented their products and services. To learn more about this, visit the NPE trade show Web site at http://www.fnpe.org and click on the trade show area. Some interesting facts recently reported by the NPE organizers include the following.

> NPE was the fastest growing plastics show in the world, more than doubling its exhibit space between 1985 and 2000, nearly tripling the number of exhibiting companies, and increasing visitor attendance by more than 50 percent. The chief driving force for this expansion was globalization. Situated at the hub of North America's marketplace and at the crossroads of trade with Latin America, Europe, and Asia, NPE provided access to technologies, market opportunities, and decision makers from all of the world's industrial regions. In terms of exhibiting companies that supply goods and services to plastics processors, NPE 2000 was expected to be one of the largest plastics expositions ever conducted.
>
> NPE 2000 was scheduled for June 19–23, 2000, at McCormick Place exhibition center in Chicago. A triennial event sponsored by The Society of the Plastics Industry, Inc. (SPI), this was the 23rd NPE since 1946. More than 2,000 exhibiting companies were expected to occupy 1.1 million square feet of net exhibit space. At least 25 percent of these companies were based outside the United States. More than 85,000 visitors were expected from over 100 different countries.

Though trade shows represent an effective marketing tool, they also require a substantial investment of time and money to make them effective. Beverly P. Bailey, senior account executive with Ohio Displays Inc., located in Cleveland, provided the following advice.

> Trade shows offer a unique opportunity to showcase corporate capabilities and products, to project a clearly defined message, to build and maintain existing client relationships, and to identify new sales prospects. A company must consider the direct costs of booth design, manufacture, construction, and transportation as well as other costs such as travel, entertainment, and

promotional along with collateral materials. A trade show booth for a major player in the plastics industry will be anywhere from 3,500 to 8,000 square feet in size. It will need to include very creative displays of products in order to portray the necessary corporate image in this very sophisticated and increasingly competitive industry.

Trade show costs vary widely depending on the complexity of the project and the size of the booth. An example of budget for a trade show booth of 5,000 square feet at a major show such as the National Plastics Exhibition (NPE) is shown in Exhibit 9.

EXHIBIT 9 | **SAMPLE TRADE SHOW BUDGET: 5,000 SQUARE FEET/5-DAY SHOW AT NPE**

Type of Expense	Explanation	Average Cost*
I. Booth Expense		
a. Creative team	Creative design, artwork, photography, graphic design	$8,000
b. Design	Sketches and layout of booth	$8,000
c. Construction	Material and construction expense	$50,000 to $60,000
d. Shipping	Akron, Ohio, to Chicago and return	$1,500
e. Drayage	Transporting from place of origin, storing crated booth display material, transporting to show site	$1,000 (higher for fragile equipment)
f. Set-up	Installation and dismantling of booth	$6,500
g. Space lease	Cost to lease space at NPE	$80,000 members $160,000 nonmembers
h. Electrical and cleaning	Electrical hook-up and clean-up after show	$2,500
i. Furniture and plant rental	Chairs, tables, natural plants, and fresh flowers	$1,500
II. Supporting Activities		
a. Planning activities	Meeting with vendors to explain company goals and to provide technical and product information	30 hours $1,500
b. Travel costs (10 people)	Air travel, meals, lodging	$20,000
c. Entertainment expense	Entertaining clients and networking	$7,000
d. Promotional material	Examples include golf balls/golf hats	$600 to $2,500
e. Collateral material	Product brochures/specification sheets	$1,500 to $3,000
d. Indirect costs (10 people)	Opportunity cost for time at show	One week per person

*SOURCE: *Ohio Displays Inc.* Estimates based on a conservative custom booth, although wide variations exist based on the complexity of the project, goals of the organization, and budgetary constraints provided by the client.

Print Advertising

In the plastics industry, there were four major trade publications representing the most important forums for print advertising: *Plastic News, Design News, Modern Plastics,* and *Rubber World.* Corporate image campaigns represented an important use for print advertising. These programs were designed to keep the company name in front of decision makers and to increase awareness among targeted industry influencers. Print advertisements were also used to promote new technologies, new products, differentiate products from competitors, and provide company contact information. Often the firm provided a toll-free phone number, FAX, and Web address, as well as the traditional mailing address to which requests for proposals (RFPs) could be sent.

The readership of these trade publications includes a broad spectrum of the key participants in the global plastics industry. That audience includes many of the key influencers and decision makers throughout the complex buying cycle for this type of an industrial product. In addition to these primary trade publications, there are also some smaller magazines targeted at niche segments of the plastics industry, including *Automotive & Transportation Interiors* (http://www.autointeriors.com), targeted at the automotive industry, and *Fenestration,* which is targeted at the window and door segment of the plastics industry.

Although advertising costs within these trade magazines vary depending on the publication, its circulation, and the buying power of its readership, rates are quoted on a cost-per-insertion basis and are generally based on the size, number of colors, and the number of times that the advertisement will run in the magazine. Sample rates for *Modern Plastics,* a publication of McGraw-Hill, are provided in Exhibit 10. For information on more current advertising rates and to examine the rates for specialized publications and inserts, please refer to the *Modern Plastics* Web site: http://www.modplas.com.

Collateral Materials

In the plastics industry, firms utilized collateral material in the form of direct mail, product brochures, and technical specification sheets to promote their materials to potential buyers. Sales literature, such as product brochures, were routinely used by members of the plastics industry sales force as a reason to visit a customer or as a tool during a sales presentation. If a product line was extensive or complex, a brochure effectively served to facilitate communication. Because collateral materials (sometimes called "leave-behinds") stayed with the customer, access at a later time was facilitated. In addition, the collateral materials provided a source of reference for current customers and prospects.

Web Sites

Though firms in the plastics industry were not among the first to embrace the concept of Web sites, they had recently increased their use of the World Wide Web as a method for communicating with existing customers and potential new customers. USA Chicago, Inc., (1997) examined the use of this technology during 1997 by firms within the industry.

> Despite the plastics industry's signal role in changing the way a broad range of products are conceived and manufactured—a role that has revolutionized

EXHIBIT 10 | **PRINT ADVERTISING EXPENSE ESTIMATES FOR *MODERN PLASTICS****

Ad Specifications	Number of Placements**		
	One	Three	Six
Full Page/4 Color	$10,720	$10,430	$10,150
Full Page/2Color	8,970	8,710	8,440
Full Page/Black & White	7,730	7,500	7,250
⅔ Page/4 Color	9,230	9,000	8,770
⅔ Page/2 Color	7,500	7,280	7,060
⅔ Page/Black & White	6,270	6,060	5,860
Left Side ½ Page/4 Color	8,470	8,270	8,130
Left Side ½ Page/2 Color	6,750	6,570	6,430
Left Side ½ Page/B&W	5,540	5,370	5,230

*Price per insertion as of July 1, 1999.

**Additional discounts available for more frequent insertions, or smaller ads. Additional charges for color matching and logo production.

product development and manufacturing—the industry has not kept pace in exploiting the potential benefits of the Internet. . . . The fact is that the [plastics] industry as a whole has not been aggressive in adopting the Internet.

The study reported that in 1997 only 42 percent of plastics companies had Web sites compared to more than 80 percent of the Fortune 500 firms. That research also concluded that the driving force for increased use of the Internet was customers, not suppliers, in the plastics industry.

Some of the larger companies, however, had established Internet sites that provided immediate access to marketing information. Typical information provided through these company Web sites included company news items such as press releases and trade articles, new-product information, company personnel, contact information, corporate highlights, and even investor information.

Important marketing advantages of these sites included low cost and immediate access to company-provided information. Any interested person (including competitors!) with access to the Web could easily and efficiently obtain technical specification information and new-product information without the potentially time-consuming task of contacting the company, waiting for a return telephone call from a sales representative, or waiting to receive information through the mail. Because of customization needs within the business-to-business sector, supplemental follow-up work by a sales representative was usually still needed in order to ultimately close a sale. The Web information was typically too general to meet all needs, but the Web greatly increased the productivity of both the buying as well as the selling personnel.

EXHIBIT 11 | SOME INTERNET ADDRESSES FOR FIRMS IN THE PLASTICS INDUSTRY

Company	Internet Address
Advanced Elastomer Systems (AES)	http://www.aestpe.com
GE Plastics	http://www.ge.com/plastics/
AlliedSignal Plastics	http://www.asplastics.com
BASF Corporation	http://www.basf.com/index.html
Bayer Corporation: Polymers Division	http://www.polymers-usa.bayer.com
DSM Engineering Plastics, Inc.	http://www.dsma.com/engplas.html
Dupont	http://www.dupont.com/engpolymers

Most companies in the plastics industry arrange their Web sites according to both the markets and products, and include technical product specifications as well as information on new applications. Exhibit 11 shows a sample of key Web sites within the plastics industry.

Public Relations

Public relations was a marketing communication method that supplemented the firm's other promotional activities. Coverage by members of the media was dependent upon their judgment that something "newsworthy" had occurred. This was most likely to occur when an exciting new product was introduced or for another event such as a key acquisition, merger, corporate relocation of facilities, or major personnel changes within the executive ranks at a firm. Press releases were often used to notify trade publications and the business press of such events. Not only was publication of such information by the trade press a very credible form of communication, but it was also done without the out-of-pocket expense associated with advertising. To get significant media coverage of a firm's activities, executives had to provide the trade journal with press releases that describe truly newsworthy events. This had to be done frequently and systematically in order to get the magazine to publish the information.

Promotional Articles

Promotional articles appearing in the trade press were also an important aspect of public relations strategy for firms within the plastics industry. Typically, these articles were written by people (often scientists) employed by firms within the plastics industry in conjunction with trade or professional writers who worked with the corporation's employees to tell an interesting story about a new product, to tell how a challenging customer problem was solved, or to provide insights into industry trends. These articles were important means for gaining credibility among key decision influencers and a useful way to expand awareness for the firm within the plastics industry. Sources within the field have reported that it is easier to achieve placement of promotional articles in trade magazines when the company also places advertisements in that publication. Trade magazines are very interested in maintaining the loyalty of their advertising base and are consequently more likely to use a promotional article from a company that has advertised in their magazine.

Market Strategy Options for the New Soft-Touch Product

As Tomkinson considered the marketing communications available to her, she prepared a grid summarizing the key attributes of each of these forms (see Exhibit 12). There were indeed trade-offs between the potential efficacy of the contact and the cost. It would be important to keep these attributes in mind as she considered the options available to her to launch AES's new soft-touch nylon bondable Santoprene® rubber. Gayle outlined the following options as feasible strategies for marketing the product.

Option I—Market to the Current End-User Customer Base

Tomkinson thought that marketing the product to the existing base of AES customers would be the simplest strategy to pursue in the shortest amount of time. Tomkinson's staff could quickly develop collateral materials, including sales brochures and technical specifications sheets, for the new nylon bondable product. With these promotional materials in hand, members of the sales force could visit firms already established as AES customers who were using Santoprene® rubber.

EXHIBIT 12   **A COMPARISON OF VARIOUS TYPES OF MARKETING COMMUNICATION IN THE PLASTICS INDUSTRY**

	Professional Selling	Trade Shows	Print Advertising	Collateral Materials	Web Sites	Promotional Articles
Cost per contact	$100 to $1,000	$25 to $100	15¢ to $8	$1 to $10	1¢ to 25¢	Minimal
Ability to vary presentation for each customer	High	High	Low	Moderate	Moderate	Low
Ability to make changes quickly	High	Moderate	Low	Low	Moderate	Low
Ability to demonstrate product	High	Highest	Low	Moderate	High	Low
Ability to gain customer's interest	High	Moderate	Low	Low	Moderate	Low
Ability to hold customer's interest	High	Moderate	Low	Moderate	Moderate	Low

Advanced Elastomer Systems had a very strong market presence with some large firms, such as Black and Decker, General Housewares Corporation, and GE Appliances. AES was well respected among these firms and had forged strong exchange relationships. The AES sales force had an excellent reputation for working with design, manufacturing, and purchasing personnel at these companies. AES would be able to move very quickly to begin selling the unique and valuable benefits of the new nylon-bondable Santoprene® rubber to these major customers because the key business relationships were already in place.

On the other hand, Tomkinson recognized some of the drawbacks to this option. Many of the current customers did not have the experience or the necessary equipment for the soft-touch product because it would require molding nylon. Ideally, firms using AES's new product should already have the equipment in-house to perform the two-shot injection molding. Many of the large manufacturing firms that AES currently sold to did not have this equipment.

In addition, Tomkinson was concerned that the selection of this option would overlook a large number of potential new customers. There were a lot of firms that AES did not currently serve that used nylon components and would therefore be quite interested in the benefits of the new AES product. Unfortunately, AES salespeople would have to spend a lot of time trying to identify these firms and determining which ones were the most promising prospects. Tomkinson also realized that this would require that AES develop collateral materials and provide other marketing support to adequately communicate information about this new product. Furthermore, AES would in some way have to assist the present sales staff because they had limited time now to divide between new and existing customers. Adding this responsibility would force them to make some unfortunate choices in time allocation. Tomkinson believed that in order for this new product to be successful, it would most likely require AES to reach beyond their current base of customers. Although the use of trade shows could facilitate this process, selecting this option would still take significant resources and a lot of time to develop relationships with those firms that were presently using nylon but not buying materials from AES.

Option 2—Market Directly to Nylon Producers

Tomkinson felt that another potential alternative was to market the product to the other supplier in this process, the nylon producers. The nylon producer served as another intermediary in the supply chain in much the same role as that performed by AES. The new Santoprene® rubber product had to be used in conjunction with nylon. Consequently, AES could market the new product directly to those firms that produced and/or distributed nylon.

This was feasible for AES because the nylon industry was highly concentrated. As shown in Exhibit 5, only a small number of firms supplied most of the nylon sold throughout the world. This short list of nylon producers included AlliedSignal, BASF, Bayer, DSM, DuPont Chemical, and Solutia (formerly Monsanto).

Tomkinson felt that most of the nylon suppliers would be receptive to the idea. As a very mature product, nylon had become a commodity, and the market was very price competitive. Nylon prices were at relatively low levels and expected to stay low because of an increase in planned domestic manufacturing capacity as well as an increase in supply by various foreign manufacturers of nylon.

Tomkinson reasoned that AES's new product would help the nylon producers by providing a point of competitive differentiation. This new material would also give the marketing staff an additional design alternative to present to their customers. This should result in additional sales of nylon. Selling through the nylon producers would guarantee that the end-users had the necessary manufacturing capability and would provide access to those most logically interested in this new product. In addition, it would give AES the widest possible exposure because the nylon producers knew their customer base well and they already had the necessary relationships with original equipment manufacturers.

Despite these apparent advantages, Tomkinson had several concerns associated with this option. Tomkinson knew that several of these nylon companies had independently been pursuing the development of a nylon bondable thermoplastic material very similar to that developed by Advanced Elastomer Systems. Given the competitive situation, perhaps they would not be receptive to working with AES. In addition, some of these nylon companies considered other AES products to be competition for some of their own elastomer products. At least to some extent, sales of the new AES product would represent reduced sales for the nylon companies. She questioned how motivated the nylon companies would be to sell the new AES product along with, or instead of, their existing products. For all of these reasons, Tomkinson wondered if AES could market sufficient quantities of the new product by selling it through the nylon companies.

Another concern for Tomkinson was in the technical arena. She wondered if the sales professionals working for these nylon companies would have sufficient technical knowledge to address end-user concerns and answer manufacturing questions related to the specific requirements for processing this new and technically sophisticated compound.

Could AES successfully market this new product to companies that competed with them in other areas? Should Gayle endorse Option 2 or was it too risky? Perhaps AES should retain more control over the sale of this new and potentially very profitable product.

Option 3—Market Directly to Original Equipment Manufacturers

Tomkinson next considered the feasibility of selling the new product directly to an expanded group of original equipment manufacturers, which were outside AES's current customer base. AES could target these ultimate decision makers, the design personnel at original equipment manufacturers. It was, in fact, these individuals who typically made the decision regarding the component materials chosen for the end product. If AES could get access to make presentations to these key people, Tomkinson was confident that the superior design, functionality, and performance attributes would result in the AES soft-touch product being the selected solution. Identifying the list of OEM prospects and acquiring the technical knowledge needed to adequately communicate to this diverse group would require significant sales staff resources. In addition, lead time was needed to prepare for these selling efforts.

Tomkinson had successfully used this strategy on several past occasions with the original Santoprene® product. For example, Tomkinson had recently developed a new market for the original Santoprene® through contact with the design personnel for stereo speakers. Tomkinson had asked her marketing research staff to locate and develop a list of companies and the associated company decision makers within the stereo housing industry. Tomkinson's staff had then contacted the dozen or so stereo speaker companies and had suggested using Santoprene® as a replacement material for the foamed polyurethane surrounds that were used in stereo speakers.

Working with these design personnel, AES had been able to enter a lucrative new market niche. Although time consuming and expensive, perhaps this would be the best strategy for developing profitable markets for this new nylon-bondable Santoprene® material as well.

Marketing the material directly to OEMs would give AES more control, provide direct technical support to users, and lead to greater margin per unit sold. This option would also eliminate the need to work directly with the nylon producers, as it would be left up to the OEMs to determine the nylon supplier they would be using in conjunction with the new AES material.

Although this alternative appeared promising, it had drawbacks as well. This option was very time consuming and required extensive resources for marketing research to determine the potential target industries. Tomkinson estimated that she would need to make contact initially with nearly 100 different companies in a wide variety of industries ranging from toothbrush producers to razor manufacturers such as Gillette. Once the marketing staff made the initial contact and conducted a needs analysis, this list of 100 companies could be narrowed down to determine the twenty or so companies representing attractive prospects. These accounts had to be large enough to warrant the development of specific product and marketing support. They would also require technical and time-consuming guidance from AES sales personnel. Tomkinson's staff would then need to prepare individualized sales presentations to address the specific needs and concerns of each industry. Finally, AES sales personnel would need to contact these targeted companies and invest adequate time to develop relationships with the identified decision makers within each firm.

The OEM strategy would therefore require extensive time on the part of both marketing staff members and the sales force. This approach would involve a large number of diverse industries and extensive internal resources. Tomkinson also was concerned about the lead time required. She knew that if AES lost its first-to-market advantage, the potential for commercial success of the new product could be greatly diminished.

Less obvious, but also of concern, was the time and effort required to develop business relationships in these new industries. The firms that already have business relationships with customers in a given industry better understand the buying processes, and they can interface more effectively. It would require substantial effort and time by AES marketing personnel to first identify and then for the sales staff to develop business relationships with key influencers in these industries where AES had not previously done business. This option presented the largest overall sales potential, but its implementation would likely require AES to hire several additional salespeople.

Option 4—Develop a Co-Marketing Alliance with a Nylon Producer

Tomkinson considered her fourth option to be a co-marketing alliance with one of the major, nylon producers. Although AES had never before embarked on a co-marketing alliance, Tomkinson had recently read about some companies that had found this strategy beneficial. For example, Tomkinson was familiar with the previously mentioned Nylon-6 Promotional Group. According to some of the articles she had read (see the appendix and the reference list at the end of the case), co-marketing alliances had been successfully used to gain competitive advantage. To the best of her knowledge, however, none had been created in the plastics industry other than the Nylon-6 Promotional Group.

According to the articles, co-marketing alliances could lead to greater profits than if each of the firms had worked separately. Nevertheless, the co-marketing alliance also posed risks. For example, when the firms had different goals from the venture or when their corporate cultures conflicted, the co-marketing alliance would be more difficult to manage. There were also security concerns that a high-technology firm had to evaluate prior to entering into a co-marketing alliance. This was especially true when the collaborator was (1) a competitor, (2) a firm with a history of security lapses, or (3) an organization having a reputation for expediency rather than integrity.

Tomkinson did not clearly understand all the risks and benefits of a co-marketing alliance, yet she was intrigued by the notion. Tomkinson did consider one primary benefit of such an alliance to be the partner's knowledge of the existing market and customer base. This would definitely shorten the lead time for sales personnel because AES would have direct access to the distribution channel and the customer lists of a nylon producer. As a relatively new employee at AES, Gayle was not sure she should champion such an innovative and unorthodox option.

In addition to knowledge of the market, she felt another potential advantage would be direct access to the technical knowledge of a nylon producer. Marketing this new material would be somewhat complicated because it required an understanding of the processing of both Santoprene® rubber and nylon. A co-marketing alliance would allow the technical experts of both firms to combine their previous experiences to develop customized solutions for a broader range of customer needs. In addition, this option would provide the potential for sharing some of the marketing costs, including perhaps trade show costs, print advertisements, and the preparation, design, and distribution of collateral materials. Although the option provided these important advantages, Gayle still needed to conduct an analysis of the disadvantages associated with this strategic choice in order to assess the risks-to-rewards ratio.

Regardless of its merits, Tomkinson also wondered how receptive her superiors would be to such an arrangement. Although a co-marketing alliance strategy looked interesting on paper, Tomkinson was concerned about the practicality of putting one together in a short amount of time. It would require assistance from people in many different departments at AES. Gaining and managing such cooperation could be a major source of difficulty.

Tomkinson also wondered if any nylon company would be interested in developing a co-marketing alliance with AES. Would it even be possible for two companies to be competitors in some areas and yet collaborate on this project? If Tomkinson was to pursue the co-marketing option, which nylon company should she target? The choice of partner was crucial to any co-marketing alliance, but time was at a premium.

In order to be successful in the market for soft-touch products, AES would need to sell in large volumes. Selecting one firm for a co-marketing alliance would possibly deter other nylon firms from working with AES. Tomkinson was very concerned about alienating the firms not chosen, thus making even a nonexclusive co-marketing alliance a risky alternative. For example, what if DuPont was not selected? Would this cause trouble for AES? Because this new product relied on nylon as a secondary material, AES could not afford to alienate a key material component supplier. AES was counting on nylon-bondable Santoprene® to be an important source of revenue and profit.

Tomkinson knew that the nylon industry was highly concentrated, with only four firms producing most of the world's nylon and each of these firms was considerably larger than AES. Only two of these, DuPont and AlliedSignal, were headquartered in the United States. Although AlliedSignal's Plastics Division had a larger sales force than AES (she estimated it at upwards of 30), it was still smaller than the sales staff of DuPont, which Gayle had estimated at 40 to 50. DuPont was the original producer of nylon and had a very well-known name among customers. Although it had a smaller sales force than DuPont, AlliedSignal Plastics had a corporate culture more similar to that of AES. Tomkinson was concerned about these differences in size as well as in corporate culture across the firms. DuPont and AlliedSignal were the industry leaders in the production of nylon. Both companies were very large, diverse, and global in scope. It would not be easy to work with such a large firm. Perhaps this was not the right time to try a new, high-risk approach such as a co-marketing alliance. Even if she selected this strategic alternative, what criteria should be used for selecting the co-marketing partner? Should she select one of the two industry leaders that were based in the United States, or should she consider one of the smaller nylon producers, such as DSM, BASF, or Bayer that had a presence within the United States but were headquartered abroad? Were there international and cultural differences that would further complicate a marketing alliance with one of the firms in the latter group?

It's Decision Time

Gayle Tomkinson stared out her window overlooking downtown Akron, Ohio, and focused momentarily on the beauty of the remnants of the historic Ohio-Erie Canal. It was quite a paradox that AES, a young firm in the high-technology manufacturing sector, had its new state-of-the-art corporate headquarters within what had formerly been a manufacturing plant for The B.F. Goodrich Company. The modern artwork and contemporary metal sculptures lining the walls within AES were representative of the progressive culture within, but were in sharp contrast to the historic canal outside her office.

The plastics industry was changing rapidly. She needed to make sure that her strategy was consistent with the paradigm shifts taking place. Tomkinson knew that selecting an option would be a difficult decision. To help evaluate the options, she thought it might be helpful to first identify some appropriate criteria on which to rate the potential of each option. She knew that risk, speed of implementation, cost of implementation, and sales potential would be useful evaluative criteria, but she wondered what else she should consider in making this important strategic choice. Although there were certainly other alternatives, she had been able to identify four major options: (1) market to current end-user customers, (2) market to all nylon producers, (3) market to new end-user customers, or (4) develop a co-marketing alliance with one nylon producer.

The tough questions facing Ms. Tomkinson this Monday morning in early 1996 were (1) which marketing strategy option should she choose, (2) how should it be implemented, and (3) what forms of marketing communications would be needed to support the chosen strategy? In addition, Tomkinson would need to sell her plan to upper management and convince them to allocate the necessary resources to support it.

The new nylon-bondable Santoprene® rubber product could have an important impact on the firm's overall success during the next several years. Tomkinson straightened up her desk by placing her notes neatly in stacks. She knew management was counting on her recommendations, but she was still unsure which strategy to support.

Appendix

Advanced Elastomer Systems Appendix—Co-Marketing Alliances: A New Opportunity for Competitive Advantage?

Strategic marketing alliances can be broadly defined as "relatively enduring interfirm cooperative arrangements, involving flows and linkages that utilize resources or governance structures from autonomous organizations, for the joint accomplishment of individual goals linked to the corporate mission of each sponsoring firm" (Parkhe 1991, p. 795). There are two primary forms of strategic marketing alliances: vertical supply alliances and co-marketing alliances.

Vertical supply alliances are established to support a smooth and efficient flow of raw materials from suppliers to manufacturers. These alliances may also involve supplier support in product design, tool development, or production planning (Heide and John 1992).

In contrast, co-marketing alliances are "lateral relationships between firms at the same level in the value-added chain that leverage a firm's unique skills with the specialized resources of its partners to create a more potent force in the marketplace. They involve coordination among the partners in one or more aspect of marketing and may extend into research, product development, and even production.... The partners often compete with each other in other product lines and on occasion in those directly covered by the co-marketing agreement" (Bucklin and Sengupta 1993, pp. 32–33).

Strategic marketing alliances are an opportunity for firms to develop competitive and marketplace advantages. Marketing alliances offer an innovative and proactive method for firms to enter new markets or increase market share in existing markets (Mitchell and Singh 1996). Marketing alliances may take many forms, including co-branding, co-marketing, joint marketing, cross distribution, and vertical supply alliances (Young, Gilbert, and Mcintyre 1996).

With more liberal interpretation of antitrust violations, marketing managers can more easily forge cooperative relationships with competitive firms (Jorde and Teece 1989). Therefore, the traditional view of the "lone wolf" organization competing independently against other firms in the marketplace is being significantly altered (Cravens and Shipp 1993, p. 55). Research on co-marketing alliances has provided the following conclusions.

a. Businesses that use co-marketing alliances to commercialize complex goods and services are more likely to survive over time than those businesses in the same industry that take independent commercialization approaches. In a study of 973 such alliances (exclusive of joint ventures), Mitchell and Singh (1996) found a survival rate of 57 percent for firms that collaborated compared to only 39 percent for those that did not.

b. Management satisfaction with co-marketing alliances is a function of three dimensions: competence, commitment, and compatibility (Shamdasani and Sheth 1995). The authors noted that marketing alliances are similar in nature to research and development alliances, where judgments are based on satisfaction to date and expectations of continuity of cooperation.

c. A motivation for co-marketing alliances is the ability to react more quickly and in a more flexible fashion (Webster 1992).

d. For co-marketing alliances to be effective there must be a balance of both benefits and risk for each firm (Young, Gilbert, and McIntyre 1996).

e. Despite their potential benefits, their less than formal governance mechanisms may lead to instability and the potential for conflict (Bucklin and Sengupta 1993; Parkhe 1993). Co-marketing alliances may be hard to manage due to differences in organizational culture or management philosophy (James and Weidenbaum 1993).

Reference List

Brezen Block, Tamara, and William A. Robinson, editors (1994), *Dartnell's Sales Promotion Handbook*, Eighth Edition, Chicago: Dartnell Corporation.

Bucklin, Louis P., and Sanjit Sengupta (1993), "Organizing Successful Co-Marketing Alliances," *Journal of Marketing*, 57 (April), 32–46.

Chapman, Peter (1997), "Nylon Producers Completing Year of Record Output," *Chemical Market Reporter*, 251 (January 6), 1.

Chemical Market Reporter (1997), "AlliedSignal Fibers Starts Up On Lines in China and France," 252 (October 27), 27.

Cravens, David W., Shannon H. Ship, and Karen S. Cravens (1993), "Analyses of Cooperative Interorganizational Relationships, Strategic Alliances Formation, and Strategic Alliances Effectiveness, *Journal of Strategic Marketing*, 1 (Issue 1), 55–70.

Heide, Christen P. (1996), *Dartnell's 29th Sales Force Compensation Survey: 1996–1997*, Chicago: The Dartnell Press.

Heide, Jan B., and George John (1992), "Do Norms Matter in Marketing Relationships?" *Journal of Marketing*, 56 (April), 32–44.

James, Harvey S., Jr., and Murray Weidenbaum (1993), *When Businesses Cross International Borders: Strategic Alliances and Their Alternatives*, Westport, CT: Praeger Publishing.

Jorde, Thomas M., and David J. Teece (1989), "Competition and Cooperation: Striking the Right Balance," *California Management Review*, 31 (Spring), 25–37.

Mapleston, Peter (1997), "Growth is Dependent on Fortunes of Auto Sector," *Modern Plastics*, 74 (January), 66.

Milmo, Sean (1995), "Nylon 6 Makers Launch Promotion," *Chemical Market Reporter*, 247 (January 16), 9.

Mitchell, Will, and Kulwant Singh (1996), "Survival of Businesses Using Collaborative Relationships to Commercialize Complex Goods," *Strategic Management Journal*, 17 (March), 169–195.

Morris, Gregory D. L. (1998), "DuPont Canada Brings on Nylon 6/6 Expansion," *Chemical Week*, 160 (April 29), 19.

Parkhe, Arvind (1991), "Strategic Alliance Structuring: A Game Theoretic and Transaction Cost Examination of Interfirm Cooperation," *Academy of Management Journal*, 36 (August). 794–829.

Pfeifer, Sylvia (1997), "Record 1996 Results Put BASF in Buoyant Mood," *Chemical Week*, 159 (April 9), 17.

Probe Economics Industry Report (1997), "Contribution of Plastics to the U.S. Economy," Milwood, NY: Probe Corporation.

Robinson, Patrick J., Charles W. Farris, and Yoram Wind (1967), *Industrial Buying and Creative Marketing*, Boston: Allyn and Bacon.

Rotman, David (1997), "R&D Survey: Spending for Innovation," *Chemical Week*, 159 (February 26), 23–25.

Shamdasani, Prem N., and Jagdish Sheth (1995), "An Experimental Approach to Investigating Satisfaction and Continuity in Marketing Alliances," *European Journal of Marketing*, 29 (Number 4), 6–23.

USA Chicago, Inc. (1997), "Internet Use in the Plastics Industry," a White Paper Report

Webster, Frederick E., Jr. (1992), "The Changing Role of Marketing in the Corporation," *Journal of Marketing*, 56 (October), 1–17.

Wood, Andrew (1997), "DuPont Wants to Hitch Up Nylon's Performance," *Chemical Week*, 159 (October 29), 42

Young, Joyce A., Faye W. Gilbert, and Faye S. Mcintyre (1996), "An Investigation of Relationalism Across a Range of Marketing Relationships and Alliances," *Journal of Business Research*, 35 (February), 139–151.

Cyanide Destruct Systems Inc.

It was September 2003, and Herb Robey, the founder and managing director of Cyanide Destruct Systems (CDS), put the phone down and leaned back in his chair, staring dejectedly at the ceiling. Robey had just received news that the proposed Metals Products and Machinery (MP&M) regulations in the United States, which had been slated to come into effect on January 1, 2004, were to be abandoned. The MP&M regulations would have forced much more rigorous standards for waste disposal on American metal finishing job shops. CDS would have been able to treat cyanide-contaminated waste to the levels required by the proposed legislation—but it was doubtful that competing treatment technologies could. The MP&M regulations had held the promise of increased sales and new customers. Robey had founded this profitable niche business treating cyanide-contaminated waste 17 years earlier, but during the past two years, sales had dwindled to a negligible level. Robey had been confident that the new MP&M regulations would provide new sales opportunities. It was a sunny day, but Robey darkly pondered his next steps.

Cyanide Usage

Cyanide and cyanide compounds are harmful when ingested in sufficient quantities because they combine with oxygen in the bloodstream and prevent the blood from carrying oxygen to the vital organs. The potential lethality of cyanide is both well known and well publicized. For example, in 1982, Tylenol capsules laced with cyanide by a deranged person resulted in seven deaths in the Chicago, Illinois, area, forcing the manufacturer to pull the product from shelves across North America. In 2003, a cyanide poisoning threat was used in an attempted blackmail threat against a South African supermarket chain. Certain states that practice capital punishment in the United States use cyanide as the lethal agent.

"Cyanide Destruct Systems" Case by Steve Marley. Steve Marley prepared this case under the supervision of Professor Kenneth G. Hardy solely to provide material for class discussion. The authors do not intend to illustrate either effective or ineffective handling of a managerial situation. The authors may have disguised certain names and other identifying information to protect confidentiality.

Ivey Management Services prohibits any form of reproduction, storage, or transmittal without its written permission. This material is not covered under authorization from CanCopy or any reproduction rights organization. To order copies or request permission to reproduce materials, contact Ivey Publishing, Ivey Management Services, c/o Richard Ivey School of Business, The University of Western Ontario, London, Ontario, Canada, N6A 3K7; phone (519) 661-3208; fax (519) 661-3882; e-mail cases@ivey.uwo.ca. Copyright © Ivey Management Service. One-time permission to reproduce granted by Ivey Publishing on January 12, 2006.

Richard Ivey School of Business
The University of Western Ontario

Despite the health risks, cyanide and cyanide compounds have unique and valuable properties, such as the propensity to bond readily with free metal ions, which make it invaluable in certain industrial applications. Cyanide is common in electroplating shops, circuit board printing, mining operations, and pharmaceutical operations.

Electroplaters use cyanide in plating baths because the cyanide bonds with impurities in the bath, thus allowing the surface plating to be applied free from contamination. For example, if cyanide (CN) is mixed in a liquid bath that contains iron (Fe) atoms, the iron bonds with the cyanide to form ferrocyanide (FeCN). Although the cyanide effectively draws the impurities out of a solution, the process results in cyanide-contaminated waste, and companies are required to safely treat or dispose of this cyanide-bearing waste.

In the gold mining industry, raw ore is finely crushed and then a dilute solution of sodium cyanide (NaCN) is added. The sodium cyanide bonds with the gold and draws, or leeches, the precious metal from the ore. This process, know as cyanide leeching, is used on an estimated 90 percent of the 2,500 tonnes of gold mined each year. The addition of zinc dust causes the gold to precipitate from the sodium cyanide, leaving a spent cyanide solution.

In some case, cyanide solutions are used for many years with only the occasional addition of cyanide required over time. However, when combined with water, cyanide does break down over time, although a carbonate residue remains. In electroplating operations, for example, these carbonates must be removed to maintain solution and plating quality.

The public awareness of the potential dangers of cyanide combined with the high usage levels of cyanide in industrial applications resulted in a love-hate relationship between cyanide and its industrial users. Although cyanide usage was invaluable, problems with disposal were always a concern.

Cyanide Destruct Systems

Herb Robey's Background

Herb Robey had graduated with a bachelor of engineering in water resources and had begun his working career with the Ontario Research Foundation. At that time, the Ontario Research Foundation was a not-for-profit organization that performed independent chemical testing, analysis, and research for a variety of clients. The American Electroplaters Society (AES) had approached the Ontario Research Foundation with the intent of testing the viability of large-scale, thermal cyanide hydrolysis. Robey worked on the project and co-authored a paper extolling the efficacy of a thermal hydrolysis system for treating cyanide waste. A detailed description of the chemical processes involved with thermal hydrolysis is detailed in Exhibit 1. With funding from the AES, a fully operational and successful treatment system was constructed and installed in a plating shop in 1982.

Economic conditions worsened during the early 1980s and, despite the potential of the new treatment method, the AES withdrew funding support for the project. Believing in the commercial viability of the technology, Robey pushed the Ontario Research Foundation to continue ongoing development. The board of directors, however, was hesitant to follow this path, citing possible conflicts of interest between advocating this

EXHIBIT 1 | THERMAL HYDROLYSIS PROCESS DESCRIPTION

Hydrolysis is a chemical process of decomposition that involves a splitting of a bond in a water molecule. CDS took advantage of a naturally occurring hydrolysis reaction between cyanide and water. The chemical decomposition formula is represented as follows:

$$CN + 2\ H_2O \rightarrow CHOO + NH_3$$

One cyanide (CN) molecule reacts with two water molecules to form a solid particulate formate (CHOO), known as a carbonate, and ammonia (NH_3). Thus, if 50,000 cyanide compounds were combined with one million water molecules, the mixture would eventually reduce to 900,000 water molecules, 50,000 formate elements, and 50,000 ammonia compounds. In natural conditions with high cyanide levels, this decomposition could take months or years. The CDS thermal hydrolysis systems allowed this reaction to be completed within hours, thus matching the timeframe of the treatment process with that of the cyanide usage requirements.

Initially, CDS was faced with two major design obstacles: first, how to create a commercially viable large-scale treatment process that would take advantage of this naturally occurring chemical reaction, and, second, how to deal with particulate remnants that remain after the destruction of the cyanide molecule.

The commercial viability of thermal hydrolysis was dependent on creating a system that could treat cyanide waste at a rate greater than or equal to the rate at which waste was generated. To combat this first problem, Robey developed large-scale reactor vessels that could treat the cyanide waste solution under high pressure and high temperature. Reactor vessels and heating systems were unique to each customer and were based on both the type and amount of waste to be treated.

The second problem involved the by-products of the treatment process. The CHOO formate was a carbonate salt and the ammonia was easily dissolved in water or scrubbed off harmlessly through ventilation systems. As a binding agent, however, cyanide would often be found in combination with other atoms or molecules. Ferrocyanide, FeCN, for example, was created when ferrous (iron) atoms bonded with the cyanide molecules. These types of inorganic cyanide compounds were problematic, as once the cyanide broke down in the water, the remaining solid particles would be free within the solution. The chemical decomposition for a ferrocyanide, for example, would be:

$$FeCN + 2\ H_2O \rightarrow CHOO + Fe + NH_3$$

Such solid particles, if left unchecked, could either damage the system or hinder the treatment process.

SOURCE: Company files.

new technology and the position of the Ontario Research Foundation as an independent testing lab. Although Robey accepted this decision and ultimately believed it to be in the best interest of the organization, he continued to work independently on thermal hydrolysis systems for cyanide waste treatment. In 1986, Robey founded CDS with the intent of pursuing commercial applications of this new treatment process. One of Robey's primary reasons for starting the business was ideological. He believed companies had an environmental responsibility, and his product would help achieve this goal.

Robey initially worked on the CDS venture while continuing at the Ontario Research Foundation in a consultative capacity. As the business began to grow, Robey dedicated himself fully to CDS. While much effort was expended in pursuit of new customers during the initial phase of the company, by 1997, business had grown to

EXHIBIT 2 | TYPES OF **CDS** SYSTEMS

Batch Systems

A batch system was used for slurries and high-concentration cyanide wastes of up to 100,000 milligrams per litre. Slurries were viscous solutions or solutions with a high proportion of solid particles. In a batch system, a specific volume of cyanide-bearing waste was pumped into a reactor vessel. Reactor volumes varied; existing systems as of 2003 ranged from 20 gallons (80 litres) to 1,200 gallons (4,500 litres). Depending on the size of the batch and waste characteristics, cycle times ranged from 6 to 12 hours. A complete cycle involved filling the vessel, heating the solution to a predetermined temperature, holding the solution for the treatment period, cooling the solution, and draining the vessel.

Continuous Flow Systems

A continuous flow system was designed for 24-hour constant flow operation with lower concentration cyanide wastes of up to about 2,000 milligrams per litre. Continuous flow systems were well suited to treat contaminated groundwater. In these types of systems, the cyanide-bearing waste was pumped through a heat exchanger before entering the reactor vessel. Cyanide complexes were destroyed in the reactor vessel, and the treated waste was then passed back through the heat exchanger to pre-heat the incoming solution. Reactor volumes and flow rates varied from 400 gallons per day (1,500 litres/day) to over 28,000 gallons per day (100,000 litres per day). Several continuous flow systems could be run in parallel to increase total capacity. Unlike batch systems, continuous flow systems were not well suited to cyanide complexes with high solid content.

SOURCE: Company files.

such an extent that Robey hired a project manager to oversee the construction of systems while he focused on sales and marketing. Robey adopted a cost-minimization approach that he continued into 2003. This strategy, which was in part dictated by the varying levels of sales revenues, involved expenditures on only basic office space and amenities and a reliance on subcontracted manufacturing labor. However, Robey would not cut corners on the quality of components or workmanship.

Design and Manufacturing

In 1993, Robey divided CDS into two separate business entities: the Design and Manufacturing function, in which CDS manufactured and sold complete cyanide treatment systems; and the Environmental Services division, which processed cyanide waste for nonowners of waste-processing equipment. The type of system actually purchased by a customer was dependant on several factors, including the type of cyanide waste, the cyanide concentration, and the amount of waste to be treated. Systems could vary in size, complexity, and level of automation, but each included state-of-the-art electronic monitoring equipment and safety features. Industrial users referred to cyanide usage on a basis of weight per volume (milligrams per litre) or cyanide concentration in parts per million. CDS provided a guarantee that its system would treat the waste solution to below specific cyanide concentration levels—often to less than 0.1 milligram per litre.

CDS offered both batch and continuous flow systems. Exhibit 2 describes the differences between the two system types. In both cases, although CDS designed and manufactured original equipment (OEM) treatment systems for customers, the customer would be responsible for installing the completed system. CDS would typically provide on-site installation assistance as well as training on proper system operation and maintenance.

CDS Design and Manufacturing also provided a rental or lease option on a single, small-scale continuous flow system. Customers could use this rental system to verify the effectiveness of the treatment process before issuing a purchase order. Given that each customer had specific waste characteristics, which in turn directly affected the system design, it was not possible to create large-scale, generic units for rental or leasing purposes.

Environmental Services

CDS Environmental Services operated a cyanide waste destruction and precious metal recovery processing facility that was located separately from the Design and Manufacturing business. At this facility, CDS Environmental Services treated and disposed of concentrated cyanide solids and liquids, reclaimed gold and silver from electroplating solutions, and reclaimed gold from electronic and other plated scrap.

After renting operational space for six years in Markham, Ontario, CDS Environmental Services constructed a new state-of-the-art treatment plant in Barrie, Ontario. This facility was regulated by the Ontario Ministry of the Environment and was generally used by customers who either had smaller waste volumes or did not wish to pay the upfront capital expenditures required to purchase and install a system. CDS Environmental Services was operated independently and at arm's length from CDS Design and Manufacturing. Although cannibalization of sales between the two entities was possible, Robey did not consider this to be a significant or frequent occurrence.

Marketing Strategies

Given the highly specific nature of the cyanide waste treatment industry, CDS used targeted advertising to create awareness for the Design and Manufacturing Division. Small ads, which occupied one-quarter to one-third of a page, with text and graphics, were published in plating trade journals and magazines such as *Chemical Engineering* and *Pollution Engineering*. The circulation levels for the various magazines ranged from 20,000 for *Plating & Surfacing Finishing* to 270,000 for *Chemical Engineering* (see Exhibit 3). Robey estimated that advertising costs for such magazines were $5,000 per year. This did not include the initial fees Robey paid to advertising consultants in order to design these ads.

Robey also attended various trade shows where companies known to use cyanide in their processes would be in attendance. A modular booth was designed to educate potential clients of the benefits of thermal hydrolysis as a means of safely treating cyanide waste. Such shows were also beneficial in that they allowed Robey to network with personnel from a variety of industries. He typically attended two trade shows per year. Attending a trade show, including registration, travel, and set-up, cost between $3,000 and $5,000. Different industries each held trade shows, resulting in an enormous number of potential events. After 2001, CDS sales fell and Robey reduced his participation to only one trade show, the SurFin. The American Electroplating & Surface Finishers Society sponsored the SurFin event, and Robey believed the attendees at this show represented the highest potential for future sales based on historical sales levels.

An important source for leads was word-of-mouth recommendations from existing customers. Companies that used cyanide would discuss common problems through

EXHIBIT 3 | **EXAMPLE OF CDS MAGAZINE AD**

SOURCE: Company files.

either existing networks or trade show contacts. Robey estimated that 50 percent of the Design and Manufacturing sales were at some point in the selling cycle influenced by word-of-mouth recommendations. Robey also used his networking contacts to identify other organizations that could benefit from the CDS product. Robey dedicated several hours per week cold- or warm-calling these prospective customers.

In late 2000, CDS went online with a Web site to promote its product and services. The Web site was intended to provide information and to increase name awareness. Because each system was designed and built to specific customer requirements, it was not possible to provide generic cost figures on the Web site. For specific requests, customers were provided with an e-mail link and a phone number and were asked to contact a CDS representative directly. Robey had attempted to assess the effectiveness of the Web compared to traditional published sources on potential sales, but the results were inconclusive.

Robey had attempted to establish a commissioned sales representative located in St. Louis in the United States. This attempt was predicated on Robey's belief that U.S.

customers would be more comfortable conducting business with a U.S.-based representative. Given the technical nature of the product, Robey hired an engineer with 20 years' experience in the electroplating industry to perform this function. Although Robey provided support and training, there was no noticeable increase in sales, and after one year, Robey discontinued the trial. Robey also had attempted to establish a joint venture opportunity in the European market. His strategy was to establish a partnership wherein the European partner would sell the systems for a commission. CDS began talks with a German distributor to achieve this goal. Although CDS wanted to design, build, and ship the systems to Europe, the potential partner wanted to build the systems in Europe and pay CDS a "royalty" for the design. The partner offered less than a 5 percent royalty to CDS. As the design of the systems provided the fundamental intellectual capital of the business, Robey did not pursue the venture.

Competitive Environment

Published data showed that almost two billion pounds of a cyanide precursor (hydrogen cyanide or HCN) were produced in the United States in 2003. Production demand was expected to continue to grow at 2.7 per cent, greater than the expected GDP growth rate. Given that most companies were not forthcoming regarding cyanide usage for fear of negative publicity, Robey was left to estimate potential market sizes. Robey estimated potential sales by assuming an average continuous flow system capable of treating 20 litres per minute of cyanide waste with a concentration of 2,000 milligrams per litre. This would represent 20,000 milligrams or 20 grams of cyanide treated per minute. Assuming continuous flow operation for 24 hours a day over 300 days would enable such a system to treat 17,640 kilograms of cyanide. Based on the published cyanide production levels, Robey therefore estimated the total potential market size to be over 52,000 systems. Capturing that market was difficult because many alternative treatment methods were available at lower costs. CDS sales often came when government or company regulations required post-treatment cyanide levels to reach a level that competing treatment technologies could not achieve.

To Robey's knowledge, there was no other firm in North America or Europe selling thermal hydrolysis treatment systems similar to those sold by CDS, and the main competitors were different generic approaches to treatment. Different industries used different methods of treating cyanide-contaminated waste. The most common techniques were chemical treatment such as alkaline chlorination or hydrogen peroxide addition, deep-well injecting, ultraviolet (UV) radiation, and natural hydrolysis.

Alkaline chlorination is a technique used to treat cyanide through the addition of chlorine. The chlorine reacts with and oxidizes any inorganic materials, including cyanide. Batches of waste material were collected in large tanks to which chlorine was then added. This was a simple and cost-effective technique. The cost was based on the amount of cyanide in the waste rather than the volume of waste contaminated. The type of cyanide would also influence the cost because some cyanide compounds were more difficult to treat and required more chlorine. As a result of the different amounts of chlorine required, chlorination costs could range between $9 and $15 per kilogram of cyanide to be treated.

Chlorination did have two drawbacks. First, it required the purchase, storage, and handling of chlorine, itself a corrosive and potentially dangerous chemical. Second, certain types of cyanide waste, such as ferrocyanide, could not be treated using chlorination.

Deep-well injecting involves injection of the cyanide solution into a deep, geological formation. In Texas alone, almost two million pounds of cyanide compounds were disposed of in this way in 1997. Deep-well injecting was inexpensive, and the waste did not require pretreatment if the company could demonstrate that there was no danger of the waste migrating from the injection area. A large cyanide user in the United States once shrugged off a CDS sales call by stating flatly that, "Deep-well injecting is how we have disposed of our cyanide for the past 50 years, and this is how we will dispose of it for the next 50 years."

Cyanide hydrolysis is a treatment method that takes advantage of a naturally occurring reaction between cyanide and water. One cyanide molecule in combination with two water molecules degrades into a formate salt and one ammonia molecule. This naturally occurring hydrolysis, however, can take a long period of time. Ultraviolet (UV) light helps hasten this process somewhat.

Natural or ultraviolet hydrolysis was used extensively in gold mining operations. Mining companies would construct an artificial pond with a thin liner into which the cyanide waste solution would be dumped. After the addition of water, the cyanide would slowly decompose. Environmental damage had resulted from this type of disposal technique; outdoor pond liners could crack or leak and the ponds themselves were prone to overflowing during periods of heavy rainfall. As a commodity industry, gold mining operations were cognizant of costs, and the low cost and ease of natural hydrolysis made this the preferred method of disposal. After the pond was constructed, this was a zero-cost alternative. Robey had tried but had been unable to break into the gold mining industry. In the absence of more stringent cyanide disposal regulations, leeching ponds remained the favorite choice of the mining companies.

The Selling Process

A typical selling process for CDS began when contact was initiated with an interested client. Early communication typically involved a series of questions from the potential client regarding how a CDS system operated, the effectiveness, and the cost. As thermal hydrolysis was a relatively unknown method of treating cyanide, a large amount of time was often spent in early consultation with the prospective client. Robey personally handled the sales functions, from the initial contact to the commencement of the manufacturing process. His extensive knowledge and industry experience enabled him to answer questions quickly and accurately.

If a prospective buyer was interested in a system, information was gathered concerning waste characteristics and volumes. With this information, Robey would set the preliminary design parameters and provide a quotation to the customer. During this phase of the selling cycle, CDS requested a sample of waste from the customer. This waste sample was sent to an independent lab where a bench hydrolysis test would be performed using parameters provided by Robey. Upon completion of the test, the lab provided a report to both CDS and the prospective client showing the cyanide degradation over time. Robey used these lab test results, combined with a performance guarantee and recommendations from previous customers, to provide peace of mind to potential buyers.

The internal selling process for perspective clients was more complicated, and it was at this stage in the selling process that delays were often experienced. One of the primary reasons for delay was that the initial contact person within an organization was rarely the person with the final authorization to purchase a system. Robey generally attempted to get the primary contact—the engineer or operator—to buy into concept of a CDS system so that this person could then approach management with a level of excitement. Thus, after CDS would "sell" the system to an engineer or operator, this person would then have to sell the idea within their own organization on operating and financial levels. If requested by the primary contact, Robey would talk with senior management. Long delays were often experienced during this stage of the client's internal selling process.

The length of the selling cycle was highly variable and could range between a few months and several years. Given the niche market and long selling cycle, the number of units sold per year had historically ranged from three to seven. CDS sales peaked in 1998–1999, reaching almost $3 million on sales of seven systems. To minimize fixed costs, CDS performed no in-house manufacturing. Parts and materials were purchased and delivered to subcontractors for construction and assembly. Although subcontracting labor was more expensive than in-house labor on a per unit basis, subcontracting based on the low production volumes allowed CDS to operate with little overhead and minimal labor costs.

After a customer elected to proceed with an order, the project entered the final design and manufacturing stage. Manufacturing lead times for systems were 12 to 16 weeks. Given the high ratio of design and selling time required relative to manufacturing time, a dedicated workforce was not used because it would have often been sitting idle. Subcontracted labor also allowed CDS to increase capacity quickly whenever multiple orders were issued concurrently.

When a system was delivered to a customer, CDS would provide after-sales support, including on-site installation assistance. CDS could also provide spare parts if requested by customers. While some customers would purchase parts directly from CDS, other companies purchased spare parts directly from local retailers or distributors, thus eliminating the need for CDS to serve as a middleman. CDS charged margins of 10 percent to 15 percent on spare parts. However, because of the inherent health and safety concerns present when cyanide was involved, CDS designed its systems for reliability and simplicity. This included a concerted effort to minimize parts. Breakdowns were infrequent, and CDS did not actively participate in the repair and replacement parts market.

Sales

CDS revenues varied greatly from year to year. Income statement and balance sheet information for 2001 and 2002 are shown in Exhibit 4. Sales were dependent not only on the number of units sold but also on the type and complexity of the systems. A small batch system requiring manual operation would have a base price around $80,000. Increasing the system capacity and increasing the level of automation would increase the price, but batch systems rarely exceeded $150,000. Continuous flow systems were more variable in price but were typically more expensive than batch systems. This was a by-product of the need for an in-line heat exchanger, additional valves, piping, and a dedicated pumping system. Given the complexity of the continuous flow systems, customers often elected to automate these systems. Reactor, pump, and heat exchanger size were dependent on the required flow rates. Certain corrosive fluids could also necessitate construction employing exotic and expensive materials. Prices for continuous flow systems ranged from $100,000 to $500,000, but an

EXHIBIT 4	CDS DESIGN AND MANUFACTURING DIVISION INCOME STATEMENT (AS AT JULY 31, 2003)	

	2002	2001
Revenue		
Total sales—manufacturing	$237,000	$450,000
Other revenue	66,000	66,000
Interest income	2,700	4,000
Total revenue	$305,700	$520,000
Expense		
Cost of sales—manufacturing		
Materials	$ 98,000	$181,000
Sub contracts	60,000	87,000
Total employee benefits	8,000	8,000
Laboratory and testing	5,500	4,000
Total cost of sales—manufacturing	171,500	280,000
Administrative expenses—manufacturing		
Accounting and legal	4,500	4,300
Advertising and promotion	4,000	11,000
Automobile expenses	10,000	9,000
Bank charges and interest	600	600
Total insurance	12,000	9,000
Management salaries	100,000	100,000
Office supplies and expenses	3,000	4,000
Rent	14,000	14,000
Telephone	4,200	4,000
Amortization	3,000	3,000
Total administrative expense—manufacturing	$155,300	$158,900
Total cost of sales	$326,800	$438,900
Net income	$ (21,100)	$ 81,100

SOURCE: Company files.

Continued

"average" system with a flow rate of four gallons per minute would most likely be priced around $200,000.

Although CDS had sold systems to companies in South Africa, Ireland, Israel, and Canada, almost 90 percent of sales were made to companies located in the United States. Cost of goods sold (materials and direct labor) for both system types were typically in the neighbourhood of 5 percent to 12 per cent, although Robey used the strong (30 percent to 40 percent premium) U.S. dollar relative to the Canadian dollar during the late 1990s to achieve higher margins.

EXHIBIT 4	CONTINUED		
		2002	**2001**
ASSETS			
Current assets			
Total cash		$145,000	$165,000
Receivables		73,000	96,000
Inventory—work in process		9,600	10,800
Total prepaids		18,000	23,400
Total current assets		**245,600**	**295,200**
Fixed assets			
Net automotive equipment		2,500	7,900
Net-office equipment		5,000	6,500
Total fixed assets		**7,500**	**14,400**
Other assets			
Deferred research and development		757	1,052
Total other assets		**757**	**1,052**
TOTAL ASSETS		**253,857**	**310,652**
LIABILITIES			
Current liabilities			
Total accounts payable		61,000	89,360
Total current liabilities		**61,000**	**89,360**
Long-term liabilities			
Deferred income taxes		14,315	24,350
Total long-term liabilities		**14,315**	**24,350**
Total liabilities		**75,315**	**113,710**
EQUITY			
Share capital			
Common shares		2	2
Total share capital		**2**	**2**
Retained earnings			
Retained earnings—previous year		196,940	115,840
Current earnings		(18,400)	81,100
Total retained earnings		**178,540**	**196,940**
TOTAL EQUITY		**178,542**	**196,942**
LIABILITIES AND EQUITY		**$253,857**	**$310,652**

The cost to the customer of installing a CDS treatment system could be substantially higher than the direct purchase price of the equipment. Ancillary costs included pretreatment storage tanks, posttreatment storage tanks, transportation lines to and from the CDS system, and actual installation costs. The total cost to the customer could be anywhere from two to five times the actual cost of the CDS unit. As with the initial purchase price, batch systems were less expensive to install than continuous flow systems.

One of CDS's primary customers was a manufacturer of electronic and computer equipment, and CDS had benefited greatly from the technology boom in the United States during the '90s. As a parallel and unfortunate consequence, however, Robey thought the bursting of the tech bubble in early 2000 and the subsequent economic slowdown in the United States adversely affected CDS sales. The economic slowdown could negatively affect the sales forecasts of potential customers, and if sales were expected to fall, so too would expected cyanide usage. Thus, the necessity of purchasing a system outright would be postponed.

During his years in the industry, Robey had operated the business through several economic downturns. He thought that the economic difficulties in North America at the start of the new millennium were detrimental to sales of CDS equipment. When sales prospects began to improve, the terrorist attacks of 2001 in the United States further compounded the problems facing the company as corporate capital expenditures either evaporated or were put on hold.

Robey saw the MP&M legislation that was slated to come into effect on January 1, 2004, as a potential boon for business. Regardless of whether companies wanted to spend money on treatment systems, the stringent new environmental requirements would leave CDS in an enviable position. CDS was the only treatment process that could consistently treat every type of cyanide waste to better than both current and proposed government regulatory cyanide discharge levels.

The Dilemma

With the cancellation of the MP&M legislation, Robey was left to ponder his next steps. Although this most recent North American recession from 2000 to mid-2003 had been difficult, the low overhead and cost structure had allowed CDS to weather the storm, and signs of economic recovery were beginning to appear. Based on past experience, however, Robey believed that recovery in the cyanide treatment business would trail any general economic recovery. Robey believed the political situation in the United States, by far the biggest importer of CDS systems, would continue to be detrimental to business. The current U.S. government had reduced or eliminated many environmental restrictions in an attempt to increase the international cost competitiveness of U.S. companies. Although the market was showing signs of improvement, Robey was concerned that the competitive landscape had changed and that the wait-and-see approach of the past would no longer be acceptable.

Robey wondered whether he should more aggressively pursue the gold mining companies. He believed that the gold mining industry represented the single largest group of cyanide users. In the past, gaining acceptance from these clients had proved impossible. Given the cost-sensitivity of the mining companies, Robey was unsure how to proceed down this path. Although some of the larger CDS customers had achieved cost savings after installing a CDS system, alternative disposal techniques (such as natural hydrolysis in leeching ponds) were less expensive.

The plating and metal finishing customers were stable and reliable. If Robey decided to refocus greater efforts on this particular industry, he wondered if the loss of the MP&M regulations would require a change in marketing strategy. Robey estimated that roughly 150 small to medium electroplating shops in the United States used cyanide in their processes. These customers tended to be more price sensitive than large organizations. Although large organizations provided more profitable business opportunities for CDS, they were much less receptive to cold calls, often denying cyanide usage outright.

Although Robey had wanted to capture a piece of the international market, his overseas efforts in the past had been extremely frustrating. Robey had commissioned a European marketing study by a company in Switzerland. The report found that an opportunity existed to enter the European market and that the scope of end-users seemed "almost endless" with around 400 electroplating firms in Germany and Switzerland. The study also expressed concern based on the fact that the system was not patented in the European market. Based on the findings in this report, Robey had attempted to sign the aforementioned agency agreement with the partner in Germany. Because manufacturing in China typically was less expensive than in the United States, Robey believed that many plating jobs typically produced in the United States would eventually be lost to shops in China. He wondered if he should reconsider international sales and, if so, how to best approach these new markets.

His eyes fell from the ceiling to his desk. Whatever choices he made, Robey knew that he needed to increase sales. The future of the Design and Manufacturing business at CDS was at stake.

The Indicted CFO

Jerry Rogers felt he was between the proverbial rock and a hard place. Laws Printing, the printing business he managed for his wife's family, had been experiencing financial difficulties. On the advice of the firm's outside accountant he had hired Frank Beaner as chief financial officer (CFO). Frank had done an excellent job of improving cost controls and getting the company in a position where significant improvements in its financial position were almost certain. However, a little over six months after coming to work for Jerry, Frank was indicted for embezzling from his previous employer. Jerry was concerned about the potential damage Frank's indictment and subsequent trial could have on the credibility of Laws Printing. On the other hand, he was concerned that terminating Frank would result in failure to implement Frank's plans and would likely bring about closure of the printing business.

History of Laws Printing

Brent Johnson, Jerry's father-in-law, had been a successful consultant and venture capitalist. He owned several successful small businesses. In a plan to reduce estate and inheritance taxes, Brent had given one of the businesses to his children. The business, Laws Printing, had operated successfully for many years. Originally purchased in the early 1970s, the company had been very profitable under the leadership of one of Brent's partners. Not only was the company profitable, but it also generated significant amounts of cash for distribution to its owners.

Brent's partner died unexpectedly in 1992. It was at this point that Brent gave the business to the children. They agreed to promote Mike Jefferson, the firm's second in command, to take over the company's leadership. Mike continued the successful management of the firm for nearly four years. In 1996, Mike left the company without notice and went to work at a higher salary for a competitor. He took with him several major accounts and key employees. It was necessary to find a replacement very quickly. Since most of the top-level managers left with Mike, it was necessary to look outside the business for a new manager.

Jerry Rogers was selected to run the business. He was a member of the family with several years of business experience. He was married to Brent's daughter, Susan. Jerry

"The Indicted CFO" Case was prepared by Joe Thomas and Ralph Williams, both of Middle Tennessee State University. It is intended to be used as a basis for class discussion. The views presented here are those of the case authors and do not necessarily reflect the views of the Society for Case Research. The authors' views are based on their own professional judgments. Copyright © 2003 by the Society for Case Research (SCR) and the authors. Permission to use granted by SCR.

knew little about the printing business. He had worked in machine-tool sales in the Midwest. The initial plan was for Jerry to commute from his home in a suburb of Chicago to Laws Printing each week. All of the other businesses owned by the Johnson family were located in the Chicago area. This had allowed the family to live in close proximity and maintain strong emotional ties. After struggling with learning the new business and spending hours commuting back and forth from Chicago, Jerry and Susan decided it would be best to move to Washington, Alabama, the site of Laws Printing.

The first two years managing Laws were not easy for Jerry. The loss of key employees and major accounts had transformed the company from a highly profitable, smoothly operating business to one struggling with losses. Jerry had to both regain market share and rebuild the management team while learning the business. Two years after taking charge of the business, it still had not generated a profit. Some of the family members were not accustomed to owning businesses that were losing money and were starting to question whether the problem was the business or Jerry.

Jerry proposed that Laws acquire two complementary businesses. One was a screen-printing business, the other a bindery. Jerry argued these were related businesses and would have a synergistic effect by improving Laws product mix and market share. With Brent's support, the family approved the plan. Six months after the acquisition, the company was experiencing significant revenue growth. However, the company's accounting was proving to be a nightmare. Controlling costs was a problem as there were difficulties with the transfer pricing system and the allocation of costs to jobs. Without a clear grasp of actual costs, Laws was having difficulty pricing its jobs so that they generated profits.

Hiring a Chief Financial Officer to Implement a Turnaround

Jerry and Brent discussed the situation with Laws Printing's outside accountant. The accountant recommended that the company hire Frank Beaner to serve as CFO. Beaner had a strong background in managerial/cost control. His education and experience were well suited to the problems at Laws. He was hired and soon started cleaning up what had been an accounting mess. Frank demonstrated a tremendous work ethic and was solving many of the problems Laws faced.

Six months after Frank was hired, and one year after the screen-printing and bindery acquisitions, the board of directors for Laws Printing met. The board consisted of Jerry, Brent, and one outside director. Brent served as chairman of the board. The outside director was not associated with the family but was included on the board because of his industry experience.

Although revenues were significantly improved, the year-end financial statements presented at the meeting were disturbing. Not only had the losses continued, they had grown. Jerry reported that the erosion in net worth had put the company in a position of being in violation of its covenants with the bank holding its long-term debt. The debt and the company's line of credit were up for renewal, and there was concern that the bank would not renew the loans unless Laws could show considerable progress toward a turnaround.

The outlook was not completely bleak. The marketing plan was working. Revenues had grown, and several new accounts had been added. Frank Beaner had implemented a plan to improve the collection of accounts receivable. Hopefully, this would buy the company time to start making a profit. Frank's work on the transfer pricing system and cost allocation plan was on the verge of paying off in the form of a pricing strategy that would have a positive impact on profits. Under Frank's leadership, the bookkeeping staff was providing more accurate and relevant information on a timelier basis. This information was a great asset for management's cost control efforts. Continuing the progress Frank made was vital to the short-term survival of Laws Printing.

The board meeting ended with the hope that efforts now under way would cause the company to soon turn the corner and return to profitability. Brent and Jerry agreed to provide one more infusion of capital if required by the bank. As Frank left the room, Brent thanked him for his contributions and congratulated him on a job well done. Jerry asked the two directors to remain after the meeting to discuss another issue.

The Newspaper Announcement

After Frank left the room, Jerry presented the board members with another problem. He had a copy of an article from the local newspaper that had appeared a week earlier. The article, actually a report of grand jury actions, reported that Frank Beaner had been indicted for embezzling from his previous employer. The article in the paper was the first knowledge Jerry had of the indictment.

Jerry reported that he had discussed the indictment with Frank and that Frank did not deny the allegation. Jerry also shared that several employees had seen the article. He was concerned that the situation was detrimental to employee morale. The outside director questioned the possible reaction of key customers. Brent's primary concern was the bank. Would the bank lose faith in Laws Printing and call the note because of Frank's indictment, or would they react more negatively if Frank were terminated and his plans to restore the firm's profitability were not implemented?

A great deal of discussion between Jerry, Brent, and the outside director followed. It was agreed the most pressing issues were cash and profits. Frank's recent efforts were positioning the company to turn the corner. He was to play a vital role in the company in the next 60 days. Frank had shared with Jerry that there were mitigating circumstances that he could not share for legal reasons. Jerry also felt certain that Frank had not embezzled from Laws Printing. Frank was not in a position to handle receipts, cash, or invoices, so, Jerry reasoned, the threat of him stealing from the company was minimal. One board member questioned how serious the potential public relations and employee relations were and whether or not they were more pressing than the short-term accounting needs of the company.

Since the official board meeting was over, the directors simply discussed the pros and cons of the various options and left the final decision to Jerry. What should Jerry do? How does he justify his actions?

Ethical Dilemmas in Business Marketing

Individuals in marketing and sales positions are frequently confronted by ethical problems and dilemmas. The scenarios presented below were real situations faced by individuals during their first year on the job after graduation from college. After reading each scenario you should decide what action you would have taken.

1. I presently sell a line of industrial compressors to customers and the standard sales pitch indicates that they are the best for the money available in the market. Unfortunately, I also know that this isn't true. However, they make up 40 percent of my line and I cannot successfully make my quota without selling at least $85,000 worth per month. It's probably okay, because all salespersons say theirs are the best.

    Would you take the same selling approach?

2. My field sales manager drinks excessively and has accompanied me on sales calls hung over and smelling of alcohol. This behavior does not enhance my professional reputation with my customers or the company. I have decided not to say anything, as the field sales manager writes my review and can dramatically influence my success or failure in this, my first selling assignment.

    Would you report the sales manager to upper level management?

3. I am working for a large company that is heavily involved in defense contracts. I have recently been transferred to a new division that builds nuclear weapons. These are weapons of which the public is not aware and of which I do not personally approve. However, our work is entirely legal and classified top secret. I have decided to stay with the company because I find my work challenging and I am not directly involved with any phase of the actual nuclear component of the project.

    If you had similar attitudes, would you stay with the company?

4. I recently had the opportunity to buy a new . . . computer, printer, and software for $1,000 from our MIS Director. He apparently received these items "free" with a large computer order for the company. I would be doing mostly work for the company at home on the computer. I decided to accept his offer and paid him $1,000 cash.

    What action would you have taken?

These scenarios were developed by Professor John B. Gifford and Jan Willem Bol, Miami University. They were part of a study of the ethical problems recent business school graduates faced on their first job. Copyright by John B. Gifford.

5. After a business dinner with an important client in California, he implied that he wanted to go out and "do the town" plus. . . . Although I wasn't sure what the "plus" might involve, there was a 50/50 chance he wanted an affair on the side. I said I was tired, and retired alone for the evening. I also lost the account which had been a 90 percent sure thing.

    What action would you have taken?

6. By coincidence, your salesperson and your distributor are both pitching your product to the same prospect. The distributor, however, does not know this yet. You know that when he finds out he will offer a competitor's product that will most certainly undercut your price. Your salesperson is totally dependent on commission.

    Should you ask your salesperson to back off?

7. A buyer for a large government institution (a good prospect with potentially high volume) offers you information about the sealed bids of competitors. You know the practice is questionable, but he is a good friend and no one is likely to find out. Besides, you are below quota, and need the commission badly.

    Will you accept his offer?

8. An industrial customer has indicated that our lubricants were priced about 5 percent higher than those being offered by our competition. He indicated that if I would drop my price 7½ percent, he would cancel his order with our competition and buy from me. This will mean a $1,400 commission for me personally. I agreed.

    What action would you have taken?

9. As an industrial salesperson, you are in the office of a prospect to provide a verbal price on a project. You and your sales manager have determined that a specific price is the right price for your organization and you believe you will win the contract. However, as the prospect walks out of his office you see a copy of your competitor's proposal on his desk with a substantially lower price. You will need to give him your price now, as he walks back into the room.

    Will you change your price?

10. I have a set quota of goods that I must sell every month. Sometimes it becomes necessary to overstock my customers in order to meet my quota. Most of the customers are not very sophisticated, and don't even know how much inventory they should carry.

    Is this an appropriate sales tactic?

SUBJECT INDEX